Family Research

Family Research

A Sixty-Year Review, 1930–1990

Volume 1

Edited by

Stephen J. Bahr

LEXINGTON BOOKS
An Imprint of Macmillan, Inc.
Maxwell Macmillan Canada
TORONTO
Maxwell Macmillan International
NEW YORK OXFORD SINGAPORE SYDNEY

Library of Congress Cataloging-in-Publication Data

Family research : a sixty-year review, 1930–1990 / edited by Stephen J. Bahr.
p. cm.
Includes bibliographical references and index.
ISBN 0-669-21927-4 (v. 1)
1. Family research literature. I. Bahr, Stephen J.
HQ518.F3428 1991
306.85'072—dc20 90-28145
CIP

Lexington Books
An Imprint of Macmillan, Inc.
866 Third Avenue, New York, N. Y. 10022

Maxwell Macmillan Canada, Inc.
1200 Eglinton Avenue East
Suite 200
Don Mills, Ontario M3C 3N1

Macmillan, Inc. is part of the Maxwell Communication Group of Companies.

Printed in the United States of America

printing number
1 2 3 4 5 6 7 8 9 10

Contents

Preface

The *Journal of Marriage and the Family*, the leading family journal, celebrated its fiftieth anniversary in 1988, an occasion that prompted many to assess the family field. The *Journal* asked four senior scholars to write essays in which they reviewed some of the trends and accomplishments they had seen over the fifty-year period (Adams, 1988; Broderick, 1988; Glick, 1988; Nye, 1988).

F. Ivan Nye was an active participant in family research over many years, and his academic career covered most of the *Journal*'s first fifty years. He is a former editor of the *Journal* and former president of the National Council on Family Relations. Occasionally he saw scholars conduct studies without being aware of previous work in that area. As he looked at the state of family research, he saw a need for an extensive review and evaluation of previous family research.

Ivan Nye and I discussed this need and decided to undertake a comprehensive review of family research from 1900 to 1990. He spent the 1988–1989 academic year at Brigham Young University, and we organized a research team to accomplish this task. The team spent more than two years reviewing the literature and organizing the material into chapters. The first ten chapters are the content of this volume; a second volume will consist of about twelve additional chapters.

There is a vast array of topics that have been studied by family scholars, and deciding which topics to review was difficult. Our team listed and discussed a large number of areas that could have been included, but our available resources caused us to limit our scope. Our final decision to review a topic was based on three criteria: (1) there was a substantial body of empirical research on the topic, (2) research on that topic had been sustained over several decades or more, and (3) we felt that the topic was important.

The first chapter is a general review of family research from 1900 to 1930. Each of the other chapters takes a major substantive area of family research and reviews the research from 1930 to 1990. For each topic, the author(s) attempted to locate all available research published between 1930 and 1990.

All the authors searched six major sources: (1) *Social Science Index* (called the *International Index to Periodicals* prior to 1966 and the *Social Science and Humanities Index* from 1966 to 1974); (2) *Inventory of Marriage and Family Literature* (the *International Bibliography of Research in Marriage and the Family* from 1900 to 1964 and *Research in Marriage and the Family* from 1965 to 1972); (3) *Journal of Marriage and the Family* (previously titled *Marriage and Family Living*); (4) *Psychological Abstracts;* (5) *Dissertation Abstracts* (the *Dissertation Index* from 1912 to 1986); and (6) card catalog in the university library closest to them. Where available, computerized searches were used. In addition, the authors examined the bibliography of each article they located and checked a number of other journals, particularly any specialty journals published in their topical area.

Each chapter is organized by decade and by subtopic. For each decade, the authors review some of the noteworthy studies, discuss theoretical and methodological trends, and identify some of the key studies and findings. The tables in each chapter list all research articles identified.

This book is designed as a reference work for researchers, graduate students, teachers, policymakers, and practitioners. Anyone doing research or teaching in one of the examined areas in this book will find this review to be a valuable resource.

References

Adams, Bert N. 1988. Fifty years of family research: What does it mean? *Journal of Marriage and the Family* 50:5–17.

Broderick, Carlfred B. 1988. To arrive where we started: The field of family studies in the 1930s. *Journal of Marriage and the Family* 50:569–584.

Glick, Paul C. 1988. Fifty years of family demography: A record of social change. *Journal of Marriage and the Family* 50:861–873.

Nye, F. Ivan. 1988. Fifty years of family research, 1937–1987. *Journal of Marriage and the Family* 50:305–316.

Acknowledgments

I gratefully acknowledge the contribution of F. Ivan Nye to the completion of this book. He has been involved in family research for many years, and without his ideas, work, and encouragement, this book would never have been completed. The idea for this book came from him, and he helped organize it and reviewed early drafts of several chapters. Norene Petersen gave invaluable help in manuscript preparation. The encouragement of Bruce Chadwick, Darwin Thomas, and Howard Bahr was beneficial. The Center for Studies of the Family and the College of Family, Home, and Social Sciences of Brigham Young University provided necessary institutional support.

Family Research

1
Early Family Research

Stephen J. Bahr
Gabe Wang
Jie Zhang

Christensen (1964) observed that scholarly study of the family began during the last half of the nineteenth century. He called this period "social Darwinism" because many scholars viewed the family as an evolving organism that was progressing. The general approach among early family scholars was to analyze how the family as an institution changed over time and varied across cultures. Most scholars reviewed existing literature rather than conducting original field research.

Christensen referred to the first half of the twentieth century as the period of "Emerging Science"—a time when social Darwinism faded, along with the emphasis on evolution and progress, and was replaced by a scientific perspective that emphasized objectivity, rigorous methodology, and survey techniques.

The other chapters in this book begin their reviews with the year 1930. This chapter reviews family research conducted between 1900 and 1930 and assesses the state of family research during the beginning of the "Emerging Science" period.

The early part of the twentieth century is often viewed as a time in which there was little scientific research on the family. However, Broderick (1988) reported that by 1938 there were over 800 scholarly articles on the family published in English. Although many of them were essays, there was clearly a considerable body of empirical research conducted prior to 1930.

In an attempt to locate all empirical research on the family published prior to 1930, we searched the following sources: (1) the Contents of every issue of *Annals of American Academy of Political and Social Sciences* (1895–1929), *American Journal of Sociology* (1895–1929), *Family* (1920–1929), *Journal of Applied Sociology* (*Sociology and Social Research*) (1916–1929), and *Social Forces* (1922–1929); (2) *International Index to Periodical Literature* (1907–1929); (3) *International Bibliography of Research in Marriage and the Family, 1900–1964* (1900–1929); (4) *Dissertation Index* (1912–1929); (5) lists of doctoral dissertations and masters' theses published in the *American Journal of Sociology* (1895–1929); and (6) the card catalog at the library of Brigham Young University. We looked for any title that may have relevance to the family, defined broadly. The key words in the appendix to this chapter were used as a guide in identifying literature on the family. We have included only articles that reported original, empirical research.

Research Findings

We discovered 120 empirical studies on the family published between 1900 and 1930. The two most commonly studied topics were fertility and child socialization; social change and economic problems also received considerable attention. (A complete listing of the studies is shown in table 1-1.) In this section we review only a selected number of the more important studies.

The Family and Social Change

One of the concerns during the early twentieth century was the effects of social change on the family. A classic study of this period was *The Polish Peasant in Europe and America* by Thomas and Znaniecki (1918). The authors' objective was to study how social change and migration affected family solidarity. They used a wide variety of data sources—letters, documents, newspaper articles, immigration applications, parish histories, and case records from courts and social agencies—and found that economic change and migration weakened family and community solidarity and decreased the influence of group norms on people. Individuals tended to develop hedonistic attitudes, which were in opposition to familistic values. The result was a breakdown of the conjugal relationship and increases in economic problems, juvenile delinquency, and crime.

Another classic study of family change was *Middletown* by Robert Lynd and Helen Lynd (1929). They studied Middletown extensively from January 1924 to June 1925 and compared that period with data from 1890. Their data came from a variety of sources: records (census data, city and county records, court files, and school records), histories, participant observation, interviews of 124 working-class and 40 business-class families, and questionnaires.

The Lynds found that the family in 1924 was more democratic than the 1890 family. In child rearing, there was more emphasis on "frankness and independence" and less emphasis on "strict obedience." There was less parental control over adolescents and a somewhat more tolerant attitude toward premarital sex. The automobile had changed leisure considerably, and movies and the automobile often became points of conflict between parent and child. Mothers continued to be primarily responsible for raising the children.

In 1924 there were fewer religious marriages than in 1890 (63 percent compared to 85 percent, respectively). The size of Middletown families decreased from 4.6 in 1890 to 3.8 in 1920. Compared to business-class families, working-class families were somewhat larger and less companionate. There was a rather large increase in the divorce rate between 1890, when there were 9 divorces for every 100 marriage license issued, and 1924, when there were 42 divorces per 100 marriage licenses.

Table 1-1
Family Research, 1900-1930

Year	*Author*	*Theory*	*Method*	*Sample*
		Social Change		
1909	Lichtenberger	None	Census	N.A.
1909	Byington	None	Case	90
1910	Byington	None	Case	90
1918	Thomas and Znaniecki	Disorganization	Case	N.A.
1927	Monroe	None	Census	N.A.
1928	Groves	None	Census	N.A.
1928	Groves and Ogburn	None	Census	N.A.
1928	Joy	None	Questionnaire	927
1929	Lynd and Lynd	None	Interview	164
		Marriage		
1908	Arner	None	Records	723
1917a	Anonymous	None	Records	3,654
1917b	Anonymous	None	Records	1,000
1922	Hunt	None	Questionnaire	555
1923	Mudgett	None	Records	1,047
1927	Bolin and Holmes	None	Records	2,074
1928	Hartson	None	Records	N.A.
1929	Engelman	None	Census	N.A.
1929	Brunner	None	Records	44,643
		Sexuality		
1923	Davis	None	Questionnaire	1,000
1929	Davis	None	Questionnaire	2,200
		Fertility		
1901	Kuczynski	None	Census	N.A.
1918	Eastman	None	Census	N.A.
1920	Stevenson	None	Census	N.A.
1923	Halverson	None	Interview	100
1923	Hewes	None	Questionnaire	2,010
1924	Holmes	None	Questionnaire	4,038
1925	Thompson	None	Questionnaire	9,018
1926	Carter	None	Questionnaire	N.A.
1926	Holmes	None	Questionnaire	4,181
1926	Rice and Willey	None	Questionnaire	130
1927	Pearl	None	Census	N.A.
1927	White	None	Census	N.A.
1928	Butt and Nelson	None	Questionnaire	5,000
1928	Griffing	None	Records	445
1928	Harper	None	Questionnaire	900
1928	Jones and Hsiao	None	Questionnaire	2,200
1928	Thompson	None	Questionnaire	9,018
1929	Edin	None	Census	N.A.
1929	Ogburn and Tibbitts	None	Census	N.A.
1929	Rice	None	Questionnaire	213
1929	Rollins	None	Records	431
1929	Sutherland	None	Questionnaire	3,096
		Family Economics		
1913	Bruère	None	Records	N.A.
1913	More	None	Questionnaire	200
1921	Lundberg	None	Records	9,194
1923	Watson	None	Records	629
1924	Frederick	None	Records	N.A.

Table 1–1 continued

Year	*Author*	*Theory*	*Method*	*Sample*
		Family Economics *(Continued)*		
1925	Billikopf	None	Census	402,946
1926	Houghteling	None	Interview	467
1927	Phelps	None	Records	405
1928	McCluer	None	Interview	3,207
1929	Eaves	None	Case	1,000
		Women's Employment		
1919	Brown	None	Census	N.A.
1923	Byrnes	None	Interview	776
1923	Winslow	None	Interview	500
1925	Hughs	None	Interview	728
1928	Cope	None	Records	1,000
		Child Socialization		
1913	Chapman and Abbott	None	Questionnaire	2,415
1920	Conklin	None	Questionnaire	921
1923	Kellogg	None	Case	600
1923	Peters and McGraw	None	Questionnaire	1,000
1927	Foster	None	Case	50
1927	Goodenough and Leahy	None	Case	322
1928	Hoffeditz	None	Questionnaire	100
1928	Nimkoff	None	Questionnaire	2,672
1928	Sayles	None	Case	200
1928	Witty	None	Records	258
1929	Duncan	None	Case	600
1929a	Nimkoff	None	Case	N.A.
1929b	Nimkoff	None	Case	N.A.
1929	Tilson	None	Case	225
		Educational Achievement		
1925	Williams	None	Questionnaire	591
1926	Griffitts	None	Records	657
1927	Flemming and Rutledge	None	Questionnaire	254
1928	Goodenough	None	Questionnaire	380
1928	Stroud	None	Questionnaire	1,357
1928	White	None	Questionnaire	451
1929	Chauncey	None	Questionnaire	243
		Juvenile Delinquency		
1917	Dunham	None	Interview	237
1917	Lickley	None	Records	1,554
1918	Shideler	None	Records	7,598
1919	Watson	None	Interview	50
1922	Buchan	None	Records	184
1926	Bushong	None	Records	1,000
1929	Crosby	None	Records	314
		Separation and Divorce		
1906	Coulter	None	Census	N.A.
1916	Eubank	None	Case	200
1924a	Mowrer	None	Census	N.A.
1924b	Mowrer	None	Records	1,000
1925	Sorokin	None	Census	N.A.
1926	Flinn	None	Case	200
1929	Lublinsky	None	Census	N.A.

Table 1–1 continued

Year	*Author*	*Theory*	*Method*	*Sample*
		Black Families		
1913	Park	None	Observation	N.A.
1921	Mossell	None	Interview	100
1926	Reed	None	Records	500
1929	Graham	None	Census	N.A.
1930	Graham	None	Census	N.A.
1932	Frazier	None	Records	N.A.
		Rural Families		
1909	Butterfield	None	Observation	N.A.
1929	Foster	None	Interview	59
1930	Sanderson and Foster	None	Interview	55
		Ethnographic Studies		
1900	Beauchamp	None	Observation	N.A.
1902	Furness	None	Observation	N.A.
1908	Mathews	None	Observation	N.A.
1912	Daniels	None	Observation	N.A.
1916	Thurnwald	None	Observation	N.A.
1922	Barnes	None	Observation	N.A.
1922	Chattopadhyay	Kinship	Observation	N.A.
1925	Fallaize	None	Observation	N.A.
1927	Young	None	Observation	N.A.
1929	Chatterjee	None	Observation	N.A.
		Historical Studies		
1913	Todd	None	Records	N.A.
1922	Westermarck	None	Records	N.A.
1917	Calhoun	None	Records	N.A.
1918	Calhoun	None	Records	N.A.
1919	Calhoun	None	Records	N.A.
1922	Chih Fu	None	Records	N.A.
1926	Goodsell	None	Records	N.A.
1927	Cross	None	Records	N.A.
1928	Chen	None	Records	N.A.

Byington (1909, 1910) studied the households of ninety families in a small community where a steel mill had been built in an effort to describe family life in the community and how it was influenced by the mill. She studied the families for a year through informal observations and detailed budget records kept by families. The mill provided work for men, but wages were low and hours long. A common attitude in the community was that the man was the provider, and the woman's job was to manage the income, home, and children. Byington concluded that the mill was detrimental to families because the long hours and difficult work restricted family interaction and recreation. Her study provided a case example of how industrialization weakens family solidarity.

In addition to these empirical studies, a number of scholars wrote essays on trends in American family life (Mackenzie, 1908; Bek, 1908; Sumner, 1909; Frank, 1923; Allen, 1928; Cole, 1929; Groves, 1929). They reviewed existing literature and/or discussed perceived changes in the family brought about by industrialization.

Marriage

Several studies examined marriage rates among college students, particularly women. College men had higher marriage rates than college women (Anonymous, 1917b): about three-fourths of college men married but only 50 to 70 percent of the women, depending on the college (Anonymous, 1917a; Hartson, 1928). There was no association between grades and probability of marriage (Bolin and Homes, 1927).

Hunt (1922) surveyed 555 college students to determine their attitudes toward marriage. Ninety-eight percent of men and women desired to marry, and both men and women agreed on the ideal family size of four children (two sons and two daughters). The women said that the three most important qualities in a prospective husband were sexual purity, honesty, and a good disposition. Among men the three most important qualities in a mate were moral character, health, and a good disposition. Good looks and wealth were far down the list of qualities mentioned by the respondents.

A few scholars examined intermarriage among various ethnic groups. Brunner (1929) did a study of intermarriage among rural immigrants in Nebraska, Wisconsin, and New York. The sample was 44,643 rural marriages from 1908 to 1912 and 1921 to 1925. Intermarriage was twice as frequent in the later period as in the earlier period.

Engleman (1929), using census data from 1870 through 1920 to study intermarriage among Jews in Switzerland, found a growing tendency for Jews to marry non-Jews over the period studied. Intermarriage among Jews increased more rapidly than it did among the general population, and it occurred in both urban and rural areas as well as among men and women.

Sexuality

The study of sexual attitudes and behavior was rare early in this century. We discovered only one empirical study published prior to 1930. Davis (1923, 1929) mailed an eight-page questionnaire to 10,000 women and received responses from 2,200. She found a positive correlation between having received sex instructions before marriage and marital satisfaction. Those who had sexual intercourse before marriage tended to be somewhat less satisfied in their marriages than those who did not. Marital satisfaction had a positive association with sexual pleasure in marriage. Davis noted that the cause-effect relation between these two variables could not be determined from her survey data; an unsatisfactory sexual relationship may hurt the quality of a marriage, but a poor-quality marriage may also detract from the pleasure of the sexual relationship. Sexual intensity and satisfaction were greater for men than for women. Only 3 percent of the women reported that their sexual desire was greater than their husband's. This percentage was considerably higher among the unhappy than happy women—12.5 percent to 2.7 percent, respectively. There was little difference between unhappily and happily married couples in the frequency of sexual intercourse during the early years of marriage. No relationship was found between the use of contraceptives and marital happiness.

Fertility

Fertility was the most frequently studied topic between 1900 and 1930. Several scholars observed a negative association between fertility and social class. Using census data, Pearl (1927) found that laborers (men in manufacturing, agriculture, and mining) had more children than did men in professional or trade occupations. Ogburn and Tibbitts (1929) replicated Pearl's findings and discovered a strong negative correlation between an intelligence test and fertility.

Using census data from England and Sweden, Stevenson (1920) and Edin (1929) reported higher fertility among the lower classes. Stevenson (1920) also noted that women who were employed had lower fertility than women who were not employed. Edin (1929) documented more childlessness among the lower than the upper classes, and Halverson (1923) observed that families in poverty had nearly twice as many children as families not in poverty.

Several scholars studied the impact of education on fertility. Hewes (1923), who obtained data from 670 students and 1,340 parents of students, found that women with a college education had fewer children than women without a college degree, but their children had a greater chance of survival.

Holmes (1924) analyzed data from 4,038 families and found a trend toward smaller families, substantially lower fertility when both parents had a college education, and more children by Catholics than Protestants. Several other scholars reported similar findings (Rice and Willey, 1926; Thompson, 1928; Rollins, 1929).

In a study of desired family size, Rice (1929) gave an anonymous, voluntary questionnaire to 213 college students. The average number of children wanted by women and men was 2.0 and 1.7, respectively.

Family Economics

As cities grew during the late 1800s and early 1900s, interest in the economic problems of urban families increased. Most of the research was descriptive; its purpose was to document how families earned and spent their money and the extent and nature of economic problems.

A number of scholars conducted studies of family incomes and expenditures (Le Play, 1935; Bruère 1913; More, 1913; Frederick, 1924; Billikopf, 1925; Phelps, 1927). An example of this type of research was More's (1913) extensive study of incomes and expenditures of 200 families in New York City. About 43 percent of their income was spent on food, and basic necessities took 80 percent of the average family's income.

Houghteling (1926) studied the standard of living of 467 Chicago families in which the husband was an unskilled laborer and there was at least one dependent child. In 23 percent of the families, both the mother and father were employed; in 20 percent of the families, the father and children were employed but not the mother. In two-thirds of the families, the earnings of the primary wage earner were not sufficient to meet the basic necessities of life. When incomes from all family members were combined, about 50 percent of the families earned enough to meet basic necessities.

McCluer (1928) studied the living conditions of 3,207 Chicago families. One-fourth of the families had moved within the past year, and poorer families tended to move more often. More than one-third of the families could not meet the basic necessities of life if they relied on only the husband's income. The husband's wages comprised 64 percent of the family income.

Eaves (1929) attempted to discover some of the reasons that families faced economic crises. She studied 1,000 case histories from three relief agencies in Boston. One of every four cases of dependency (poverty) was due to sickness. Thirty percent of the problems were due to unemployment, and 10 percent were due to marital problems. Chronic disease was the largest single cause of loss of earning capacity. Eighty percent of the applicants for welfare had dependent children, and 22 percent of all children were in homes broken because of desertion, divorce, or death. At the time of the study, more than one-third of the children of these families were sick.

Because of the high rate of poverty among unmarried mothers, Watson (1923) attempted to discover the facts surrounding illegitimacy in Philadelphia. She obtained information from thirty-four social agencies on 629 mothers with illegitimate children. She estimated that each year in Philadelphia about 1,100 children were born out of wedlock. About half of the children came to the attention of some social agency by the time they were two years old. Many of the mothers came from broken homes, had left their homes at an early age, and had quit school at an early age.

Employment of Women

Brown (1919) reported that from 1850 to 1905, there was an increase in the rate of women employed in manufacturing industries. Although the wages of the women were from one-fifth to one-half as much as the wages of men in similar occupations, the standard of living among these women and their families improved substantially because of the women's employment.

Using census data, Winslow (1923) found that in 1890, less than 5 percent of women were employed, compared to 9 percent in 1920. Increases were greater among married women than among women in general. Most women worked to provide necessities for their families. In an examination of 500 employed women, she found that 20 percent worked at night. In addition to working outside the home and caring for their children, most of the women cooked, cleaned, and washed for their families. The gains from her employment were money and an improved standard of living—but at the costs of long hours, overwork, and less adequate supervision of children.

Cope (1928), who conducted a study of 1,000 women in *Who's Who in America* for 1926–1927, observed that women had made achievements in almost every field but particularly in literature, art, and social service. Cope found that eminent women tended to be attracted to men of superior ability, tended to marry somewhat later than other women, and had fewer children.

Child Socialization

A major concern in the early twentieth century was the effect of the family environment on children. Kellogg (1923) examined the relationship between parental inadequacy and problems among fifty adolescent girls attending school in Los Angeles. She observed that most of the girls came from maladjusted homes characterized by chronic poverty, ineffective parents, and an absence of guidance and supervision. Oldest children usually suffered the most because they were required to miss school to work or watch younger children.

Tilson (1929) studied 225 preschool children who were referred to seven clinics because of enuresis, temper tantrums, negativism, and emotional dependence on adults. Parental disagreement on discipline, parental conflict, nagging the child, comparing the child unfavorably with other children, and lax and inconsistent discipline were the major parental characteristics that seemed to contribute to the problems in the children.

Nimkoff (1928), one of the pioneers in the study of parent-child relationships among normal families, developed and administered a questionnaire to 2,672 males and females. Compared to fathers, mothers had more frequent companionship with their children, secured more compliance, and were more likely to have their children confide in them. Compared to sons, daughters were more obedient and companionable with their fathers, but sons were more likely than daughters to confide in their fathers.

Nimkoff (1929a, 1929b) used several case studies to explore parental characteristics related to parent-child conflict. He observed that parental conflict was more frequent if parents were either neglectful or very dominant. He also noted that husband-wife conflict and lack of affection between husband and wife were associated with higher levels of parent-child conflict. When children felt that their parents favored another child over them, feelings of jealousy and inferiority resulted and precipitated parent-child conflict.

Sayles (1928) reviewed extensive clinical records of 200 children to identify common problems in parent-child relationships and discover parental behaviors that contributed to those problems. The major problems among the children were being belligerent, not being able to talk, temper tantrums, lying, and stealing. Parental behaviors that contributed to the problems were overattention and indulgence, inconsistent discipline, parental disagreements over discipline, parental domination, favoring one child over another, and achieving vicariously through the child.

Educational Achievement

The association between socioeconomic status and school achievement was studied by several researchers. Goodenough (1928) gave the Binet intelligence test to 380 children between the ages of 18 and 54 months. He found the intelligence of children was significantly higher in the upper than the lower classes, with the differences evident by 2 and 3 years of age.

Stroud (1928) gave achievement tests to 1,357 elementary school children in Georgia. He found a moderate, positive correlation between family economic status and achievement scores. Several other scholars observed that children from poor homes did not achieve as well as children from middle- or upper-class homes (Chauncey, 1929; Flemming and Rutledge, 1927; White, 1928; Williams, 1925).

Two researchers reported a negative correlation between family size and intelligence in children. Griffitts (1926) examined the school records of 657 children in the Ann Arbor, Michigan, public schools and found that the school performance of children from small families was superior to that of children from large families. White (1928) examined 451 children from 203 families involved with a New York charity organization. There was a tendency for IQ scores to be lower among children in large families.

Juvenile Delinquency

A number of scholars studied the relationship of family environment to juvenile delinquency. Shideler (1918) obtained information on the home environment of 7,598 delinquents in thirty-one states. Fifty-one percent of the delinquents came from homes broken by separation, divorce, death, insanity, or imprisonment. In the total population, the proportion of children living in broken families was only 25 percent. One of every three delinquents had lost either their mother or father by death, compared to only 16 percent of the general population. Among the delinquent boys, 14 percent of their families had been broken by divorce, separation, or desertion, compared to only 4 percent among the general population. Shideler concluded that the broken home was a major contributor to juvenile delinquency in boys.

In a similar study, Bushong (1926) used 1,000 delinquents to explore the relationship between divorce and delinquency. He observed that 28 percent of the homes were producing more than half of the delinquents. The rate of delinquents from broken homes was three times the rate of those from normal homes.

Crosby (1929) studied 314 delinquent boys from Alameda County, California. She found that the rate of broken homes was twice as high among delinquents as among nondelinquents. In most cases, the homes were broken by the absence of the father. Delinquent boys from two-parent homes tended to commit property offenses; the boys from broken homes were more likely to be involved in truancy and rape and judged incorrigible.

Buchan (1922) studied social characteristics associated with the delinquency of 184 delinquent girls. She reported a "high" correlation between "broken homes" and female delinquency. She also observed that economic stresses such as unemployment were associated with delinquency. The families of delinquents moved at least once a year, and this instability did not allow the girls to become integrated into an area.

Separation and Divorce

An important social issue during this period was the dissolution of families by desertion and divorce. Using census data, Groves (1928, Groves and Ogburn, 1928) observed that divorce was increasing and projected that one in five of all married persons would divorce sometime in their lives. Divorce was higher in urban than rural areas and higher among blacks than whites.

Using census data and 1,000 divorce cases in Chicago, Mowrer (1924a, 1924b) observed an increase in rates of desertion and divorce. He found that divorce was considerably higher in certain geographical areas and among those who were more transient, poorer, and socially disorganized.

Eubank (1916) conducted a study of 200 deserters known to the Chicago Court of Domestic Relations. He found that men were much more likely to be deserters than women and that desertion was more common in the city than in rural areas and in the lower class than in the middle and upper classes. Eubank reported that one-tenth of the poverty in the city was directly traceable to desertion.

Sorokin (1925) explored how divorce rates changed during time of war by comparing seven countries using data from 1912 to 1922. The results showed that divorces increased prior to World War I, decreased during the war, and increased substantially after the war.

A number of scholars conducted descriptive studies of the amount of divorce in a particular state or country (Coulter, 1906; Lublinsky, 1929). More common than research studies, however, were essays discussing the nature of the problem of marital dissolution and possible solutions (Tyson, 1918; Howard, 1921; Liebman, 1920; Hoffman, 1929; Mowrer, 1929a, 1929b).

Black Families

Among the scholars who studied the families of blacks, Park (1913) found that the living standards of black families had improved, that the number of black landowners was increasing, and that blacks in the North were better off economically than those in the South. The most popular profession among blacks was teaching. Park described the home life of blacks as happy and wholesome, especially among educated blacks who had to work together to maintain their standard of living and educate their children.

Mossell (1921) studied the budgets of 100 black families in Philadelphia. The most common occupations were laborers and domestic workers. One-fourth were underfed, and most lived in crowded homes. In only 41 percent of the families was the father's income sufficient to meet basic necessities. Most who earned adequate incomes were able to manage their money well. Mossell concluded that there were three major impediments to the economic well-being of black families: the large number of children, unwise spending, and prejudice.

Using the records of New York social agencies, Reed (1926) studied 500 cases of illegitimacy among black women. The unwed mothers tended to be foreign born, young (25 percent were under 19), and uneducated (80 percent had never attended school). Twenty percent of the women had more than one illegitimate child. The problems in adjusting to family and occupational life were the same for these black women as unwed mothers in other ethnic groups.

Graham (1929) used census data to describe the economic problems of black families in Chicago. Almost all of the husbands were employed and more than half of the wives. Three-fourths of the women without husbands were employed. One-half of the women had children under age 14, and one-fourth of the children were left without care while their mothers were at work. The standard of living was not satisfactory for at least half of the families.

Perhaps the classic study of the black family was Frazier's (1932) *The Negro Family in Chicago*. Data were obtained from a variety of sources, including interviews, census records, personal histories, and records from the Institute for Juvenile Research. Frazier observed trends among black families that were similar to those among the general population, including decreasing fertility rates and increasing divorce rates. The family life and sexual standards of middle- and upper-class blacks were found to be essentially the same as those of middle- and upper-class whites. However, Frazier observed that the migration of blacks from the rural South to the city tended to make families less stable. It resulted in loss of friends and associations, the breakdown of customary forms of social control, and the development of unrealistic hopes that often led to disillusionment. Although there was some progress among blacks in the accumulation of wealth and overcoming illiteracy, there was widespread family disorganization. In the poorer areas where blacks tended to settle, there were high rates of dependency, desertion, illegitimacy, and juvenile delinquency.

Ethnographic Studies

During this period, many scholars conducted ethnographic studies of family life among other cultures, mostly among primitive tribes. Most researchers did not describe their methods of data collection other than mention that they had lived for a period among the people. They described their impressions of the customs and life-styles of the group they observed. For example, Furness (1902) conducted a participant observation study by living among the Borneo Head-Hunters for one year. He described the living conditions, customs, and family life of the tribe he lived with. Another example was Thurnwald's (1916) expedition to New Guinea in 1912 to study the organization and kinship of a tribe. He described their customs regarding mate selection and marriage and compared them to the Western culture.

Historical Studies

A number of scholars made historical studies of family life, using documents to describe the purpose of the family and how it had evolved. For example, Todd (1913) used ethnographic materials to examine family change across various cultures and the role of the family in education.

Two of the classic historical studies of the family are *A Social History of the American Family* by Calhoun (1917, 1918, 1919) and *The History of Human Marriage* by Westermarck (1922). Calhoun attempted to understand the evolution of the American family from colonial times up to about 1910. Westermarck compared marriage customs in different cultures and tried to understand why the differences occurred.

Goodsell (1926) described the family in a variety of different historical periods and cultures, including the primitive family, the Hebrew family, the Greek family, and the Roman family. Later in his book, he described the family in the American colonies and how the industrial revolution had affected families.

Theory and Methodology

Although many of the early researchers studying the family may have had an implicit theory to guide their work, rarely did they explicitly discuss or use theory in any systematic way.

A listing of the primary methods of data collection is shown in table 1–2. The most common method was the use of records from an agency, followed by questionnaires and census data. If questionnaires and interviews are combined, they were the most common data collection method. The case study was used more during that period than it is today.

Sample sizes varied widely. The smallest was 50; the largest, from census data, was 402,946. Twenty-eight of the studies had sample sizes of 1,000 or more. Many researchers did not describe their methods or specify their sample, particularly when some type of observation was used as the primary method of data collection. Forty-one percent of the studies (49 of 120) did not specify the sample size.

Table 1-2
Methods Used in Family Research, 1900-1930

	Number of Studies	*Percentage*
Records	34	28
Questionnaire	28	23
Census data	20	17
Case study	14	12
Interview	12	10
Observation	12	10
Total	120	100

Note: A study that used more than one method of data collection was categorized according to the primary method used.

Key Studies

Several studies conducted during this period stand out as exceptional pieces of scholarship. *The Polish Peasant in Europe and America* by Thomas and Znaniecki (1918) became one of the classic works in sociology. The authors used a vast array of documents to study how migration and social change weakened community and family solidarity.

Another classic was *Middletown* by Robert Lynd and Helen Lynd (1929), which became a best-seller. Lynd and Lynd used observation, interviews, questionnaires, and documents to study Muncie, Indiana, intensively. They returned in 1935 for a follow-up study, *Middletown in Transition: A Study in Cultural Conflicts* (1937), and Caplow and associates (1982) did another study of Muncie forty years later. Together the three studies provide an examination of social and family change over a fifty-year period.

Davis's *Factors in the Sex Life of Twenty-two Hundred Women* (1929) was one of the first surveys of marital sexuality. The author obtained valuable information on marital satisfaction and sexuality.

A landmark in the study of black families was *The Negro Family in Chicago* by Franklin Frazier (1932), who used personal histories and census data to describe family patterns among blacks.

A number of other early studies were important in the development of family research. Groves and Ogburn (1928) compiled extensive data on marriage, divorce, and family change in the United States. Important historical studies were conducted by Calhoun (1917, 1918, 1919), Westermarck (1922), and Goodsell (1926).

Major Findings

Over the thirty years covered in this review, a large number of empirical findings were reported. In this section we list some of the major findings reported during the period 1900-1930:

Social Change

1. Economic changes weakened family solidarity and community influence.
2. Migration tended to make families less stable because of a loss of family and community social control.
3. Economic changes and migration were associated with increased rates of divorce, juvenile delinquency, and crime.
4. Industrialization was associated with decreases in fertility and parental control over children and increases in premarital sex, intermarriage and divorce.

Poverty

5. Poverty among families was caused by sickness, father's unemployment, father's death, desertion or divorce, and unmarried mothers.
6. Poor families moved more than families not in poverty.
7. Married persons had less poverty than single persons.

Fertility

8. There was a negative relationship between social class and fertility.
9. There was a negative relationship between IQ and fertility.
10. Women with a college education had fewer children than women without a college education.
11. Women who were employed had fewer children than women who were not employed.
12. Fewer infants of college-educated mothers died than infants of mothers without a college education.
13. Eminent women tended to marry later and have fewer children than other women.
14. Catholics had more children than Protestants.
15. Children from smaller families tended to have higher IQs than children from larger families.

Employment of Women

16. There was an increase in the employment of women in industry.
17. The increase in the employment of women was greater among married than unmarried women.
18. Employment of women increased the standard of living of families.
19. The wages of women were from one-fifth to one-half of the wages of men.

Sexuality

20. Sex instruction before marriage was positively associated with marital satisfaction.

21. Those who had sexual intercourse before marriage tended to have lower marital satisfaction than those who did not have sex before marriage.
22. There was a positive correlation between marital satisfaction and sexual pleasure in marriage.
23. Sexual pleasure in marriage was greater for men than women.
24. There was no difference between satisfied and unsatisfied couples in the frequency of sexual intercourse.

Child Socialization

25. Behavioral problems among children tended to be due to poverty, high parental conflict, inconsistent discipline, low husband-wife affection, high parent-child conflict, dominance of father, and parents trying to achieve vicariously through their children.
26. There was a positive association between social class and academic achievement in children.
27. The larger the family size was, the lower was the academic achievement of children in the family.
28. Two major influences on juvenile delinquency were the broken home (separation/divorce or death of parent) and poverty.

Separation and Divorce

29. Separation and divorce were higher in urban than in rural areas.
30. Areas characterized by poverty, migration, and transience tended to have higher rates of separation and divorce.
31. Divorce rates tended to increase after a war.
32. Separation and divorce were higher in the lower class than in the middle class.

Black Families

33. Blacks separated and divorced more than whites.
34. Although the family situations of blacks had improved, many remained underfed and living in poverty.
35. Black unmarried women tended to be uneducated, young, and poor.
36. The three major impediments to black families were large family size, lack of money management skills, and racial discrimination.
37. The trends among black families were similar to those occurring among families from other ethnic groups.

From 1900 to 1930, the scientific study of the family was just beginning. The research tended to focus on social change and problems associated with it. Samples were not representative, theory was absent, analytical techniques tended to be simple, and many conclusions were based on subjective impressions. Nevertheless, a number of scholars conducted empirical research on families, and some of it was of high quality. We identified 120 empirical studies, many of which used large samples and gathered data using several different techniques. Some of the topics studied are still being researched by scholars today. Although some of the findings have not been supported by more recent research, many have been replicated and refined in subsequent research. In a few cases, recent research does not appear to have added much to the findings reported early in this century. During a time when there were no computers or sophisticated statistical models, these pioneers of family research did remarkably well in laying a foundation for the scientific study of the family.

Appendix 1-A: Key Words Used in Search of Family Research, 1900–1930

- Adoption
- Counseling
- Death
  - Bereavement
  - Widowhood
- Decision making
  - Power
  - Communication
- Divorce
  - Separation
  - Marital dissolution
- Dual-career families
- Education and family
- Employment and family
- Ethnic, race
- Family
- Family and alcoholism
- Family development
- Family disorganization
- Family in other cultures
- Family life course
- Family life cycle
- Family planning
- Family problems
- Family roles
- Family and social change
- Family stress (coping)
- Father-child
- Fertility
  - Childlessness
- Foster care
- Gender
- Illegitimacy
  - Unmarried mothers
- Intermarriage
- Juvenile delinquency
- Kinship, extended family
- Marital success
  - Satisfaction
  - Happiness
  - Failure
- Marital customs
- Marriage
- Marriage rates
- Mate selection
  - Dating
  - Courtship
  - Cohabitation
- Mother-child
- Parent-child
- Parenthood
- Sex
  - Attitudes, behavior
  - Incest, rape
  - Premarital sex
  - Sex therapy
  - Sex education
  - Teenage pregnancy
- Single-parent families
- Socialization
  - Child care
  - Childrearing
  - Parental
  - Training
- Therapy
- Unemployment and family

References

Allen, F.E. 1928. Significant factors in home life as revealed through the courts. *Journal of Home Economics* 20:853–861.

Anonymous. 1917a. Coeducation and marriage. *Journal of Heredity* 8:43–45.

———. 1917b. Stanford's marriage rate. *Journal of Heredity* 8:170–173.

Arner, George, B.L. 1908. *Consanguineous Marriages in the American Population.* New York: Columbia University Press.

Barnes, H. 1922. Marriage of cousins in Nyasaland. *Man* (October):147–149.

Beauchamp, W.M. 1900. Iroquois women. *Journal of American Folk-Lore* 13:81–91.

Bek, W.G. 1908. Survivals of old marriage-customs among the low Germans of West Missouri. *Journal of American Folklore* 21:60–67.

Billikopf, J. 1925. Every-child in Philadelphia—What he has to live on. *Annals* 121: 110–119.

Bolin, J.S., and Holmes, S.J. 1927. Marriage selection and scholarship among the alumnae of the University of California. *Journal of Heredity* 18:253–255.

Broderick, C.B. 1988. To arrive where we started: The field of family studies in the 1930s. *Journal of Marriage and the Family* 50:569–584.

Brown, M.L.R. 1919. Women in war work. Master's thesis, University of Missouri.

Bruère, M.B. 1913. Utilization of the family income. *Annals* 48:117–120.

Brunner, E.D. 1929. *Immigrant Farmers and Their Children.* Garden City, N.Y.: Doubleday, Doran.

Buchan, E. 1922. The delinquency of girls. Master's thesis, University of Chicago.

Bushong, E.M. 1926. Family estrangement and juvenile delinquency. *Social Forces* 5: 79–83.

Butt, N.I., and Nelson, L. 1928. Education and size of family. *Journal of Heredity* 19: 327–330.

Butterfield, K.L. 1909. Rural life and the family. *American Sociological Society Publication* 3:106–114.

Byington, M.F. 1909. The family in a typical mill town. *American Journal of Sociology* 14 (5):648–659.

Byington, M.F. 1910. *Homestead: The Households of a Mill Town.* Philadelphia: Russell Sage Foundation; Press of Wm. F. Fell Co.

Byrnes, A.M.H. 1923. *Industrial Home Work in Pennsylvania.* Bryn Mawr, Pa.: Bryn Mawr College.

Calhoun, A.W. 1917. *A Social History of the American Family from Colonial Times to the Present: Colonial Period.* Cleveland: Arthur H. Clark Company.

———. 1918. *A Social History of the American Family from Colonial Times to the Present: From Independence through the Civil War.* Cleveland: Arthur H. Clark Company.

———. 1919. *A Social History of the American Family from Colonial Times to the Present: Since the Civil War.* Cleveland: Arthur H. Clark Company.

Caplow, T.; Bahr, H.M.; Chadwick, B.A.; Hill, R.; and Williamson, M.H. 1982. *Middletown Families: Fifty Years of Change and Continuity.* University of Minnesota Press.

Carter, W.P. 1926. A social-psychological study of the only child in the family. Ph.D. dissertation, University of Chicago.

Chapman, S.J., and Abbott, W. 1913. The tendency of children to enter their fathers' trades. *Journal of the Royal Statistics Society* (May):599–604.

Chatterjee, B.K. 1929. The marriage ceremonies of the Bathuria of Mayurbhanj State. *Man in India* 9:157–163.

Chattopadhyay, K.P. 1922. Levirate and kinship in India. *Man* 22:36–41.

Chauncey, M.R. 1929. The relation of the home factor to achievement and intelligence test scores. *Journal of Educational Research* 20:88–90.

Chen, J. 1928. Reconstruction of the Chinese family. *China Critic* (July 12):130–134.

Chih Fu, D. 1922. Ancestral worship and social control. Master's dissertation, University of Chicago.

Christensen, H.T. 1964. Development of the family field of study. in H.T. Christensen (ed.), *Handbook of Marriage and the Family,* pp. 3–32. Chicago: Rand McNally.

Cole, S.G. 1929. The changing family pattern in America. *Religious Education* 24:63–70.

Conklin, E.S. 1920. The foster-child fantasy. *American Journal of Psychology* 31:59–76.

Cope, P.M. 1928. The women of "Who's who": A statistical study. *Social Forces* 7: 212–223.

Coulter, J.L. 1906. Marriage and divorce in North Dakota. *American Journal of Sociology* 12:398–416.

Crosby, S.B. 1929. A study of Alameda County delinquent boys, with special emphasis upon the group coming from broken homes. *Journal of Juvenile Research* 13: 220–230.

Cross, E.B. 1927. *The Hebrew Family: A Study in Historical Sociology.* Chicago: University of Chicago Press.

Daniels, H.K. 1912. *Home Life in Norway.* 2d ed. New York: Macmillan.

Davis, K.B. 1923. A study of the sex life of the normal married woman. *Journal of Social Hygiene* 9:129–146.

———. 1929. *Factors in the Sex Life of Twenty-two Hundred Women.* New York: Harper and Brothers.

Duncan, W.L. 1929. Parent-child isolations. *Family* 10:115–118.

Dunham, I.D. 1917. Causes of truancy among girls. *Social Science Research* 1:3–14.

Eastman, P.R. 1918. *A Comparison of the Birth Rates of Native and Foreign-born White Women in the State of New York during 1916.* Albany: Division of Public Health Education, New York State Department of Health.

Eaves, L. 1929. Studies of breakdowns in family income. *Family* 10:227–236.

Edin, K.A. 1929. The birth rate changes. *Eugenics Review* 20:258–266.

Engelman, U.Z. 1929. Intermarriage among Jews in Switzerland, *American Journal of Sociology* 34:516–523.

Estabrooks, G.H. 1928. Some results of a pre-school clinic. *Pedagogical Seminary and Journal of Genetic Psychology* 28:139–143.

Eubank, E.E. 1916. A study of family desertion. Ph.D. dissertation, University of Chicago.

Fallaize, E.N. 1925. The study of primitive races with special reference to forms of marriage. *Eugenics Review* 17:77–87.

Flemming, C.W., and Rutledge, S.A. 1927. The importance of the social and economic quality of the home for pupil guidance. *Teachers College Record* 29:202–215.

Flinn, H. 1926. One hundred domestic-relations problems. *Mental Hygiene* 10:732–742.

Foster, R.G. 1929. Types of farm families and effects of 4-H Club work on family relations. Ph.D. dissertation, Cornell University.

Foster, S. 1927. A study of the personality make-up and social setting of fifty jealous children. *Mental Hygiene* 11:53–77.

Frank, R.W. 1923. The trend in American family life: A survey of the past decade. *Religious Education* 18:330–345.

Frazier, F.E. 1932. *The Negro Family in Chicago.* Chicago: University of Chicago Press.

Frederick, C. 1924. New wealth, new standards of living and changed family budgets. *Annals* 115:74–82.

Furness, W.H. 1902. *The Home-Life of Borneo Head-Hunters: Its Festivals and Folk-Lore.* Philadelphia: J.B. Lippincott.

Goodenough, F.L. 1928. The relation of the intelligence of pre-school children to the occupation of their fathers. *American Journal of Psychology* 40:284–294.

Goodenough, F.L., and Leahy, A.M. 1927. The effect of certain family relationships upon the development of personality. *Pedagogical Seminar* 34:45–71.

Goodsell, W. 1926. *A History of the Family as a Social and Educational Institution.* New York: Macmillan.

Graham, I.J. 1929. Family support and dependency among Chicago Negroes: A study of unpublished census data. *Social Service Review* 3:541–562.

Graham, I. 1930. The Negro family in a northern city. *Opportunity* (February):48–51.

Griffing, J.B. 1928. Size of the family in China. *Sociology and Social Research* 13: 63–72.

Griffitts, C.H. 1926. Educational research and statistics: The influence of family on school marks. *School and Society* 24:713–716.

Groves, E.R. 1928. The family. *American Journal of Sociology* 34:150–156.

———. 1929. The family. *American Journal of Sociology* 35:1017–1026.

Groves, E.R., and Ogburn, W.F. 1928. *American Marriage and Family Relationships.* New York: Henry Holt and Company.

Halverson, J. 1923. The prolificacy of dependent families. *American Journal of Sociology* 29:338–344.

Harper, R.M. 1928. Religion and family size. *Journal of Heredity* 19:169–173.

Hartson, L.D. 1928. Marriage statistics for Oberlin alumnae. *Journal of Heredity* 19: 225–228.

Hewes, A. 1923. Note on the racial and educational factors in the declining birth-rate. *American Journal of Sociology* 29:178–187.

Hoffeditz, E.L. 1928. Family resemblances in personality traits. *Journal of Social Psychology* 5:214–227.

Hoffman, F.L. 1929. Marriage and divorce. *Journal of Social Hygiene* 15 (3): 129–151.

Holmes, S.J. 1924. The size of college families. *Journal of Heredity* 15:407–415.

———. 1926. The fertility of the stocks which supply college students. *Journal of Heredity* 17:235–239.

Houghteling, L. 1926. A study of the income and standard of living of unskilled laborers in Chicago. Ph.D. dissertation, University of Chicago.

Howard, G.E. 1921. Bad marriage and quick divorce. *Journal of Applied Sociology* 6 (2): 1–10.

Hughes, G.S. 1925. *Mothers in Industry: Wage-earning by Mothers in Philadelphia.* New York: New Republic.

Hunt, H.R. 1922. Matrimonial views of university students. *Journal of Heredity* 13:14–21.

Jones, H.E., and Hsiao, H.H. 1928. A preliminary study of intelligence as a function of birth order. *Journal of Genetic Psychology* 35:428–432.

Joy, A. 1928. Note on the changes of residence of families of American business and professional men. *American Journal of Sociology* 33:614–621.

Kellogg, M.B. 1923. A study of parental inadequacy. *Journal of Applied Sociology* 7 (4): 192–200.

Kuczynski, R.R. 1901. The fecundity of the native and foreign born population in Massachusetts. *Quarterly Journal of Economics* (November):1-36.

Le Play, P.G.F. 1935. Working-class families in Europe. In Carle L. Zimmerman and Merle E. Frampton (eds.), *Family and Society: A Study of the Sociology of Reconstruction.* New York: Van Nostrum. [Original work, Paris, 1855.]

Lichtenberger, J.P. 1909. The instability of the family. *Annals of the American Academy of Psychology and Social Science* 34:97–105.

Lickley, E.J. 1917. Causes of truancy among boys based on a study of 1554 cases. *Social Science Research* 2:1–12.

Liebman, W.H. 1920. Some general aspects of family desertion. *Social Hygiene* 6:197–212.

Lublinsky, P. 1929. Marriage and divorce in Soviet Russia. *Family* 10:26–31.

Lundberg, E.O. 1921. Aid to mothers with dependent children. *Annals* 98:97–105.

Lynd, R.S., and Lynd, H.M. 1929. *Middletown: A Study in American Culture.* New York: Harcourt, Brace and World.

———. 1937. *Middletown in Transition: A Study in Cultural Conflicts.* New York: Harcourt Brace Jovanovich.

McCluer, F.L. 1928. Living conditions among wage earning families in forty-one blocks in Chicago. Ph.D. dissertation, University of Chicago.

Mackenzie, W.L. 1908. The family and the city: Their functional relations. *Sociological Review* 1:118–138.

Mathews, R.H. 1908. Marriage and descent in the Arranda Tribe, Central Australia. *American Anthropologist* 10:88–102.

Monroe, D. 1927. The family in Chicago: A study of selected census data. *Journal of Home Economics* (November):617–622.

More, L.B. 1913. The cost of living for a wage-earner's family in New York City. *Annals* 48:104–111.

Mossell, S.T. 1921. The standard of living among one hundred Negro migrant families in Philadelphia. *Annals* 98:173–218.

Mowrer, E.R. 1924a. Family disorganization. Ph.D. dissertation, University of Chicago.

———. 1924b. The variance between legal and natural causes for divorce. *Journal of Social Forces* 2:388–392.

———. 1929a. A sociological analysis of the contents of 2000 case records with special reference to the treatment of family discord. *Social Forces* 7:503–509.

———. 1929b. Effect of domestic discord upon conduct of children. *Religious Eductcion* 24:442–444.

Mudgett, M.D. 1923. Marriages of unmarried mothers. *Journal of Social Hygiene* 9: 193–199.

Nimkoff, M.F. 1928. Parent-child intimacy: An introductory study. *Social Forces* 7: 244–249.

———. 1929a. Parent-child conflict. *Sociology and Social Research* 13:446–458.

———. 1929b. Parent-child conflict II. *Sociology and Social Research* 14:135–150.

Ogburn, W.F., and Tibbitts, C. 1929. Birth rates and social classes. *Social Forces* 8:1–10.

Park, R.E. 1913. Negro home life and standards of living. *Annals of the American Academy* 49:147–163.

Pearl, R. 1927. Differential fertility. *Quarterly Review of Biology* 2:102–118.

Peters, C.C., and McGraw, M.B. 1923. Contribution of the home to the aesthetic education of children. *Journal of Applied Sociology* 8 (2):67–83.

Phelps, H.A. 1927. Problems of insured, unadjusted families. *Social Forces* 5:613–620.

Reed, R. 1926. *Negro Illegitimacy in New York City.* New York: Columbia University Press.

Rice, S.A. 1929. Undergraduate attitudes toward marriage and children. *Mental Hygiene* 13:788–793.

Rice, S.A., and Willey, M.M. 1926. College men and the birth rate. *Journal of Heredity* 17:11–12.

Rollins, W.A. 1929. The fertility of college graduates. *Journal of Heredity* 20:535–539.

Sanderson, D., and Foster, R.G. 1930. A sociological case study of farm families. *Family* 11:107–114.

Sayles, M.B. 1928. *The Problem Child at Home.* New York: Commonwealth Fund.

Shideler, E.H. 1918. Family disintegration and the delinquent boy in the United States. *Journal of Criminal Law* 8:709–732.

Sorokin, P. 1925. Influence of the world war upon divorces. *Journal of Applied Sociology* 10:131–134.

Stevenson, T.H.C. 1920. The fertility of various social classes in England and Wales from the middle of the nineteenth century to 1911. *Journal of Royal Statistical Society* 83:401–444.

Stroud, J.B. 1928. A study of the relation of intelligence test scores of public school children to the economic status of their parents. *Pedagogical Seminary and Journal of Genetic Psychology* 28:105–111.

Sumner, W.G. 1909. The family and social change. *American Journal of Sociology* 14: 577–586.

Sutherland, H.E.G. 1929. The relationship between IQ and size of family. *Journal of Educational Psychology* 20:81–90.

Thomas, W.I., and Znaniecki, F. 1918–1920. *The Polish Peasant in Europe and America.* 5 vols. The first two volumes were published by the University of Chicago Press in 1918, the last three by Badger Press of Boston in 1919 and 1920.

Thompson, W.S. 1925. Size of families from which college students come. *Journal of American Statistical Association* 20:481–495.

———. 1928. The family as a unit of survival. *Social Forces* 7:141–144.

Thurnwald, R. 1916. Social organization and kinship system of a tribe in the interior of New Guinea. *Memoirs of the American Anthropological Association* 3 (4):253–391.

Tilson, M.A. 1929. *Problems of Preschool Children: A Basis for Parental Education.* New York: Teachers College, Columbia University, Bureau of Publications.

Todd, A.J. 1913. *The Primitive Family as an Educational Agency.* New York: G.P. Putnam's Sons, Knickerbocker Press.

Tyson, H.G. 1918. The fatherless family. *Social Work with Families* 77:79–90.

Watson, A.E. 1923. Illegitimacy as a child-welfare problem, part III: Methods of care in select urban and rural communities. Ph.D. dissertation, Bryn Mawr College.

Watson, H.K. 1919. Causes of delinquency among fifty Negro boys. *Social Science Research* 4:1–12.

Westermarck, E. 1922. *The History of Human Marriage.* 3 vols. New York: Allerton Book Company.

White, R.C. 1927. The human pairing season in America. *American Journal of Sociology* 32:800–813.

White, R.C. 1928. The intelligence of children in dependent families. *Social Forces* 7: 61–68.

Williams, L.A. 1925. The intellectual status of children in cotton mill villages. *Social Forces* 4:183–186.

Winslow, M.N. 1923. Married women in industry. *Journal of Social Hygiene* 9:385–395.

Witty, P.A. 1928. Some results of a pre-school clinic. *Journal of Genetic Psychology* 28:139–141.

Young, P.V. 1927. The family organization of the Molokans. *Sociology and Social Research* 12:54–60.

2
Adolescent Sexuality

Patricia H. Dyk
Cynthia R. Christopherson
Brent C. Miller

This chapter provides a historical, comprehensive understanding of adolescent sexuality from the 1930s to the present through a summary of the available research.[1] It is appropriate to include adolescent sexuality in this book on family research because of the implications for the adolescent's family of origin, individual development, and early childbearing and family formation. Adolescence is the period of the life cycle during which sexual maturation becomes evident (puberty) and a young person becomes capable of reproduction. "This fact marks him or her as no longer being a child and as being launched on the way to adulthood" (Chilman, 1983). A decrease in the age of onset of puberty and an increase in the age of marriage has resulted in a longer period of time for adolescents to express their sexual attitudes and feelings prior to marriage (Hofferth and Hayes, 1987).

Adolescent sexuality is often described as including the physical characteristics and capacities for sex behaviors, together with psychological knowledge, values, and attitudes regarding these behaviors. As Miller and Fox (1987) have pointed out, throughout the decades, there have been two overarching and contrasting paradigms for understanding human sexuality: that it is inner driven and that it is socially shaped. One paradigm sees adolescents responding to instinctual, biologically based sexual hormones (particularly testosterone) that motivate sexual behavior. The other views adolescent sexuality as socially shaped and learned behavior. Probably the most important influence in early development is the family of origin. There are many aspects of the family that can affect sexual attitudes and behavior: parental characteristics (education, occupation, income, family background, age at marriage and first birth), family configuration (number of parents, children, extended family members), family experiences (communication, divorce, remarriage), and attitudes, values, and norms of family members.

Cultural or societal norms and values also define "appropriate" sexual attitudes and behaviors; however, these norms and values change over time and differ by social contexts, making it difficult for adolescents to define clearly appropriate sexual attitudes and behaviors. Moreover, adolescent sexuality research has also been reflective of society's norms and values, with discussion and assessment of sexuality increasing across the decades.

Prior to the 1930s, little research was conducted on adolescent sexuality. Ellis (1896) provided an overview of sexuality, but his discussion of adolescent sexuality was limited to descriptions of physical growth. In a subsequent work, Ellis (1936) described puberty as a time of physical growth and sexual desire. However, adolescent sexual activity during this time was considered promiscuous, immoral, and deviant.

During the 1930s, 1940s, and the beginning of the 1950s, adolescent sexuality research was primarily theoretical or descriptive, evaluating adolescent sexuality as an immoral, deviant behavior that needed to be controlled. The research during this period was greatly limited in methodology and empirical findings.

Beginning in the late 1950s, society became more open about sexuality, and research became more explanatory, detailed, and systematic. The sexual revolution of the 1960s increased public awareness and concerns, and researchers responded by providing empirically based information to help with the education, intervention, and prevention of early adolescent sexual behaviors. The increase of adolescent premarital intercourse, teenage pregnancies, and sexually transmitted diseases has heightened social awareness to further our understanding of the antecedents and correlates of adolescent sexuality.

The Decade 1930–1939

The 1930s were a primitive, secretive, and descriptive period regarding adolescent sexuality. The sources, methods, and findings were very limited, and the articles were primarily based on moralistic opinions rather than valid and reliable explanations for adolescent sexual attitudes and behaviors.

Research Findings

In "Sex Problems of Youth" (1930a), Wile pointed out that adolescent sexual behaviors have been a dilemma as long as history itself. Over time, society changes its viewpoints, and youth reflects that social image.

Wile's "Sex Education in Relation to Mental and Social Hygiene" (1930b) stressed that mental hygiene is concerned not only with the individual but is directly related to social stability. He explained that the greatest factor involved is the sexual desires and urges of individuals, and intellectual ideas and moral training are necessary during the adolescent maturing period in order to control sexual urges.

Wile's data consisted of records of the NeuroPsychiatric Division of the U.S. Army. From these statistics, he attempted to show how sex education and moral training could prevent venereal diseases. Of 13,567 white patients, 22.2

percent admitted having a venereal disease. Of the 4,856 black patients, 57.8 percent admitted having a venereal disease, implying that whites were better educated than blacks. Wile suggested that the incidence of venereal disease could be reduced by sex education. He stated that the purpose of sex education is education, not sex (Wile, 1929).

An article by Ernest Groves (1929), Freudian in nature, described teenage sex as the beginning of conflict between impulse and social inhibition. He specified parental discipline as a factor in controlling the adolescent's drives. In conclusion, he implied the need for further insight and for information to be gathered from experiences in order to develop a program for these problems.

In a 1934 article, Groves discussed sexuality during courtship in a subtle way, explaining sexual drive as a strong human impulse whose satisfaction is expected to be accomplished within marriage. Sexual drive is the body's preparation for mating and is distinctly physical. He stated that if boys and girls experiencing puberty throw themselves into "adult sex experience" (p. 30), allowing no time for romance, they will be unable to have a high-quality modern marriage. This article expressed a moralistic view of adolescent sexuality that reflected the widely held norm of premarital sexual abstinence.

The Decade in Review

Theory and Methodology. In order to understand the articles written about adolescent sexuality during the 1930s, it is essential to comprehend the values and norms of American society at this time. The majority of this work was moralistic, giving very little factual data but representing the prevailing norms about sexual abstinence during adolescence.

Key Studies and General findings. There was little, if any, research as we think of it today. Wile (1930) provided some statistical evidence concerning the social implications of venereal disease and the need for sex education, and Groves (1929) asked for further insight in explaining social pressure and the adolescent.

The Decade 1940–1949

The 1940s were similar to the 1930s in that morality was still a primary issue in the research and discussion of adolescent sexuality. Because those who worked in this area were thought to be evil, corrupting the innocent young minds of society, few studies were conducted in this decade. Moreover, because of the global crisis of world war, the country's focus was not on social-behavioral research but on providing food, safety, and peace.

Research Findings

Shortly after the war, Porterfield and Salley (1946) published an article about trends in sexual behavior. The sample consisted of 285 men and 328 women, many of them ministerial students. The respondents were given anonymous questionnaires that asked about their premarital practices. The results indicated that it was becoming more difficult to define sexual delinquency and that the older sex mores were breaking down.

A well-known researcher in the 1940s was Alfred C. Kinsey, described as deserving the "lion's share of the credit for belatedly placing studies of human sexuality on a firm quantitative foundation" (Breacher, 1969, p. 104). His research introduced quantitative methodology, including counting and physical measurements (Breacher, 1969).

In 1948, Kinsey, Pomeroy, and Martin published *Sexual Behavior in the Human Male,* in which adolescent sexuality was covered in great detail. The purpose of their study was to explain who does what, when, and with whom. They defined the onset of male adolescence as the date of the first ejaculation, which they found to be 13 years, 7 months on the average. The methodology consisted of analysis of groups that were homogeneous for sex, race, marital status, education level, and age of onset of adolescence. The data were obtained from thousands of histories gathered through personal interviews.

Kinsey and his colleagues reported that males who had their first ejaculation at earlier ages were more likely to experience sexual activity of some sort, including greater frequency, which continued throughout their life. These sources of outlet were masturbation, premarital intercourse, and homosexuality.

Kinsey and his associates demonstrated that it was possible to do research in an objective manner using statistical analysis in order to provide valid and reliable information. Their book stimulated other research and greatly affected the field, becoming a landmark in the history of sexual research.

Many believed that the Kinsey Report would harm the moral character of American youth, and many believed that his reports were misleading, being used as tools to convince teenagers that everyone was violating the moral code. Crepsi and Stanley (1948) thought it would be helpful to inquire how college youth felt about Kinsey's work, and "Youth Looks at the Kinsey Report" was their response. Their methodology consisted of a sample of 475 students at Princeton University who were given a questionnaire designed so that information could be obtained regarding the impact of Kinsey's study. The respondents were asked to read a substantial part of the book and respond to questions about it. The study found that the criticisms toward the Kinsey Report were unjustified. The majority of the students felt that the knowledge gained from the study would be beneficial, affecting their attitudes toward sexuality for the positive, not their behavior for the negative.

The Decade in Review

Theory and Methodology. The 1940s marked a decade of change, giving the field of adolescent research a new beginning. Although much criticism was voiced because of this move from moral thought to empirical data, it provided a starting point toward the explanations of adolescent sexuality.

Key Studies and General Findings. Kinsey's (1948) study of the sexual behaviors of men was a major step toward the study of adolescent sexual behavior and led to several other research projects. Later studies debated the validity and reliability of Kinsey's work and then conducted research to extend our knowledge of adolescent sexuality.

The Decade 1950–1959

During the 1950s, more scientific studies were conducted to explain the emergence of adolescent sexual behavior. Antecedents of teenage sexual activity, such as religion, social class, race, education, social and peer influences, and parental authority, were examined. Research was beginning to produce empirical evidence rather than moral judgments.

Research Findings

Kinsey and associates' (1953) second major report, *Sexual Behavior in the Human Female,* provided the first major data about adolescent females. This report consisted of information recorded from over 5,000 females, basically through interviews and some questionnaires. Much of the research dealt with the age at which females experience orgasm. More than 50 percent of the sample reported achieving orgasm before the age of 20. Kinsey and associates also found that 64 percent of females achieve orgasm premaritally through masturbation, petting, or coitus. This book, which showed the extent of adolescent sexual behaviors at this time, was a great eye opener to the public, and much controversy and criticism surfaced again, influencing future research (Kinsey et al., 1953).

Deadman (1959) examined whether religious persons have negative attitudes toward, and a lower incidence of, premarital sexual intercourse. Data were obtained from questionnaires administered to students at a southern coeducational university. Eighty-five percent of the students came from Protestant families that attended church every week, and most of the students were from middle-upper to upper-class families. A significant relationship was found between religiosity and premarital sexual relations, yet when social status was held constant, the relationship disappeared. Guilt seemed to be a powerful motivator among Christian adolescents, contributing to sexual attitudes and behaviors. Deadman reported findings similar to the Kinsey's.

Ehrmann's (1955) study examining the influence of partners' social class on premarital heterosexual behavior used a sample of 841 college students. An exploratory study was conducted consisting of 30 students to investigate the comparison of social class and its influence on premarital coitus. The findings showed males' crossing social class lines to obtain dating partners to a higher degree than females, and males secured companions from a lower social class about twice as often as the females did. The comparative social class position of the companion had a profound influence on premarital sexual behavior. Although the sample was relatively small, many interesting ideas emerged concerning social class and sexual behaviors.

Reiss (1956) investigated the double standard in premarital sexual intercourse, a major issue at this time. He defined the double standard in this way: "Premarital sexual intercourse is wrong for all women; women that indulge are therefore bad women. Premarital sexual intercourse is excusable (if not right) for all men and thus men that indulge are not thereby bad men" (Reiss, 1956, p. 224). Reiss referred to Kinsey's studies and data and stated six hypotheses in an attempt to show that the neglect of the double standard of premarital sexual intercourse was a serious deficiency in the field of adolescent research.

The Decade in Review

Research in the 1950s appeared to be moving away from the moral opinions of the 1930s and 1940s and toward a more explanatory, objective scholarship. Kinsey and associates (1953) began this move toward objectivity and quantification, fully realizing that their work would be criticized. Deadman (1959) and Ehrmann (1955) looked at religiosity and social status in an attempt to explain adolescent sexual attitudes and behaviors. Reiss (1956) highlighted the double standard, an important issue that would lead to further research.

Theory and Methodology. Within the four articles discussed, the sample size varied from 5,000 in Kinsey's study to 841 in Ehrmann's exploratory study. The sources of data gathering included interviews, questionnaires, personal recordings, and the use of previous research data, showing that research was beginning to provide explanations, understanding, and progress toward objectivity in the field of adolescent sexuality studies.

Key Studies and General Findings. Kinsey's research about female sexuality shocked the general public by suggesting a level of premarital sexual arousal that was much greater than had been thought. In general, Kinsey's studies highlighted a discrepancy between restrictive social norms and more permissive sexual behavior. Table 2–1 summarizes the major research studies published before 1960.

Table 2–1
Overview of Research on Adolescent Sexuality, 1929–1959

Year	*Author*	*Topic*	*Theory*	*Method*	*Sample*[a]	*Strengths*[b]
1929	Groves	Social pressure	None			
1930	Wile	Sex problems	None			
1930	Wile	Sex education	None	Existing records	18,423–S	S
1934	Groves	Courtship	None			
1936	Ellis	Physical growth	None			
1946	Porterfield and Salley	Sexual behavior	None	Questionnaire	613–P	S,I
1948	Kinsey	Sexual behavior	None	Interview/Questionnaire	5000+–P	S,I
1948	Crepsi and Stanley	Kinsey report	None	Questionnaire	475–P	
1953	Kinsey	Sexual behavior	None	Interview, Questionnaire	5000+–P	S,I
1955	Ehrmann	Sexual behavior	None	Interview	841–P	S,I
1956	Reiss	Double standard	Mini	Existing data	S	T,I
1959	Dedman	Religion/sex	None	Questionnaire	P	

[a]P = primary data; S = secondary data.
[b]S = sample; T = theory; I = importance.

The Decade 1960–1969

Research concerning adolescent sexuality began to show a rapid increase in the 1960s. The general public was more aware of sexual information and was not shocked by the research results. The issues of the 1960s were no longer moral philosophy and religion but rather a search for facts and solutions, covering almost every aspect of sex. "Birth control, abortion, sexual techniques, sexual rights of women, free love, sexual restraint, romance, promiscuity, frigidity, impotency, morals, religion, and advice to the lovelorn" (Ehrmann, 1964, p. 194) were issues of importance.

Research Findings

Sociocultural Factors. In order to explain whether certain premarital behaviors were related, Kanin (1960) emphasized the analysis of social class. The methodology consisted of 177 married women, of whom 77 indicated they had had premarital coitus with their spouse. Some of the findings indicated that the lowest incidence of premarital coitus occurred in the upper class, the next highest incidence was found among the middle class, and the highest incidence was found in the lower class. Other studies were conducted demonstrating the significance of socioeconomic status (SES) for understanding sexual behavior and its impact on future sexual behavior.

Broderick (1963) compared patterns of social heterosexuality of blacks and whites during adolescence. The methodology consisted of questionnaire data collected from 341 blacks and 921 whites between the ages of 10 and 17. An index of heterosexuality was developed to allow interracial comparisons by sex and by age. Differences between the races occurred during the pubescent ages 10–13. White adolescents were very traditional in their patterns; girls were more romantic than boys, yet both genders' actual heterosexual behavior was about the same. Black male adolescents showed a high level of preadolescent heterosexual interest and involvement but a disenchantment with marriage. Broderick suggested that only a broad outline of developmental patterns of the two races had been indicated and that longitudinal data and in-depth interviews were needed.

Parent and Family Influences. Bell and Buerkle (1961) compared mother and daughter attitudes toward virginity and sexual intercourse through questionnaires answered by 217 university students and their mothers. The theory implied that for many adolescent girls, premarital coitus is acceptable but only under specific conditions. The attitudes of daughters concerning premarital virginity were similar to their mothers' attitudes until they had spent some time in college, indicating that premarital sexual behavior is one of the greatest potential areas of mother-daughter conflict. The attitudes of college women indicate patterns of thinking different from traditional norms.

Calderwood (1963) evaluated differences in the questions adolescent boys and girls ask about sex. The study involved ninth-grade boys and girls enrolled with their parents in family life education courses. The questions, anonymously written on paper and read exactly as written, indicated the importance of discussing sex at the adolescent's level. The stereotype in which boys are expected to be well-informed initiators and girls are innocent and submissive appeared to be the overall consensus. The desire to avoid building up these stereotypes was also unanimous. Both the parents and children indicated they were able to communicate much more effectively and in a more relaxed manner than before discussing the questions.

Lewis (1963) attempted to explain how parents and peers affect adolescents' sexual behavior. The respondents were 1,969 students at a small midwestern, church-related college and a southeastern university. Males were more likely than females to have had premarital coitus and to have been promiscuous, and they were younger at initial intercourse. When parents were the major source of sex education, children were more traditional in their own values and believed in chastity. Having peers as the major source of sex education was associated with more permissive sexual behavior.

Sexual Patterns and Attitudes. Reiss (1964) developed Guttman measures of premarital sexual permissiveness. Previous research had focused a great deal on a moralistic view rather than the characteristics of a sexual relationship. The sample consisted of 1,028 students from five schools. No systematic bias appeared to be operating. All questions were dichotomized into agree or disagree. The findings suggested that significant relations may exist between sexual standards and some sociocultural factors. Also, such scales seemed to have a reliability and validity that had not been shown in the past. Research was continuing to show reliability that would help somewhat toward increased understanding of premarital sexual permissiveness.

Hall (1966) gave an overview of contemporary adolescent sexual behavior in the 1960s. The theory was that the 1960s was a time of sexual revolution; the methodology was a group of referrals and adolescent self-report data; the finding was that three patterns of sexual behavior were emerging: impulse disorders, when sex is just another fast ride; identity confusion, showing no control and disjunction concerning sexual behavior; and the new search, in which adolescents consciously used sex as a means to explore their own feelings. Hall did not go into much methodological depth; rather she described and explained the patterns she had found but stated the need for further in-depth research.

Reiss's *The Social Context of Premarital Sexual Permissiveness* (1967) was based on the first probability sample in the area of premarital sexual attitudes. The sample consisted of high school and college students plus adults. Reiss reviewed and analyzed the significant empirical findings of previous researchers, which he summarized into several propositions, and he used several new research tools, including two twelve-item Guttman scales—one for attitudes toward males and one for attitudes toward females. In reviewing previous research, developing a Guttman scale, and performing his own research, Reiss was able to develop several propositions and concluded that "sexual permissiveness is learned in a social setting in much the same formal and informal ways that other attitudes are learned. . . . The young person gains his basic set of values from his parents, his friends, and from the basic type of social groupings he is exposed to as he matures" (pp. 164–165). This study was a landmark of research on adolescent sexuality.

In response to the significant rise in the rate of illegitimacy in the United States, Furstenberg, Gordis, and Markowitz (1969) approached the sexual patterns, reactions to pregnancy, and birth control experience, knowledge, and attitudes of adolescent girls expecting their first illegitimate child. The sample consisted of 169 unmarried expectant adolescents from northwest Baltimore registered for prenatal services. Each girl was given a structured interview, and later their mothers were given the same interview at home. The girls were interviewed fifteen months after delivery to evaluate the effectiveness of the program. The findings indicated that the majority of these expecting teenagers would use birth control if it was made accessible and if they knew the methods were effective and safe. Furstenberg, Gordis, and Markowitz pointed out that the findings cannot necessarily be generalized to all adolescents, but to institute a birth control program for adolescents in this sample, many misconceptions and anxieties must be overcome.

Peer Influences. Mirande (1968) supported Reiss's (1967) finding that the reference group concept is useful for explaining and understanding premarital sexual behaviors among adolescents. The reference group concept had been influential for quite some time, yet few systematic, empirical studies regarding adolescent sexuality had been conducted. Mirande's sample consisted of ninety-three single adolescent students attending sociology classes at a midwestern university. The subjects completed a questionnaire dealing with background questions and sexual behavior. First, the students were asked to explain their crowd's or close associates' opinions on sexual behaviors. Second, a question was asked to determine how the students perceived their peers as encouraging or disencouraging premarital coitus. Information on the sexual behavior of associates was also obtained.

The findings showed that males were much more sexually active than females and that 62 percent of the women with sexual experience associated with groups approving of premarital intercourse. The overall consistency of the conclusions lead one to believe that the orientation of associates toward sex is an important determinant of adolescent sexual behavior. Although the findings showed the influence of peers, it is also important to understand that individuals seek out groups that reinforce their psychological beliefs and attitudes. Up to this point, little research had been completed concerning reference groups other than descriptors, showing the need for future research focusing on explanations.

The Decade in Review

Theory and Methodology. Both quality and quantity of progress occurred in the 1960s. New topics of interest and concern were beginning to unfold, providing a better understanding of adolescent sexuality. Many samples continued to be inadequate, however, and measurements were crude.

Key Studies and General Findings. Many of the studies conducted in the 1960s indicated why adolescents become involved sexually, showing a move toward permissiveness, leaving many traditional values behind. Social class, parental attitudes, adolescent concerns, race, the sexual revolution, peer group, and birth control knowledge were some of the factors that were discussed. Two data-gathering techniques were predominant: questionnaires and interviews. Sample sizes varied from 93 individuals in Mirande's study to 1,028 in Reiss's study; the larger samples were generally more representative of the total population, providing more generalizable results.

The diversity of research during this decade shows a desire among researchers to improve the understanding of adolescent sexuality. Table 2–2 summarizes the major studies published from 1960–1969.

The Decade 1970–1979

During the 1970s, relationships between adolescents became more egalitarian, with formal dating patterns being replaced by groups of teenagers just "hanging around" together. The double standard of sex behavior narrowed, and premarital intercourse increased for both male and female adolescents. Federal funding for family planning services for single teenagers became available in the early 1970s, and abortions were legalized by the U.S. Supreme Court in 1973. Attitudes toward unmarried parenthood became more accepting during this decade. In response to the increase in adolescent premarital intercourse and pregnancy, Congress passed the Adolescent Health Services and Pregnancy Prevention and Care Act of 1978, the first federally funded legislation to focus solely on the problems of early sexuality and pregnancy.

Research on adolescent sexuality in the 1970s primarily focused on the changing behaviors of adolescents and antecedents of this behavior. Seventeen empirical studies with adolescent samples are reported in table 2–3. Two review articles, one evaluating the research and clinical literature regarding male masturbation (Dranoff, 1974) and another considering the familial factors influencing adolescent sexual behavior (Fox, 1979), were published during this decade. Three influential books appeared: Sorenson's (1973) study of American youth's attitudes and behaviors, the Jessors' (1975) report of their four-year longitudinal study of the transition from virginity to nonvirginity, and Chilman's (1978) review of adolescent sexuality.

Table 2–2
Overview of Research on Adolescent Sexuality, 1960–1969

Year	*Author*	*Topic*	*Theory*	*Method*	*Sample*[a]	*Strengths*[b]
1960	Kanin	Social class	None	Questionnaire	177–P	I
1961	Bell and Buerkle	Sexual attitudes	None	Questionnaire	434–P	S,St,I
1963	Calderwood	Sex questions	None	Questionnaire	P	
1963	Lewis	Social agents	None	Questionnaire	1,969–P	S,St
1964	Reiss	Sexual behavior	None	Questionnaire	1,028–P	S,M,St,T,I
1966	Hall	Sexual behavior	None	Self-report	P	
1967	Reiss	Sexual attitudes	Mini	Questionnaire	2,734–P	S,M,St,T,I
1968	Mirande	Reference group	Mini	Questionnaire	93–P	M,St,T,I
1969	Furstenberg et al.	Sexual patterns	None	Interview	338 P	S,M,St,I

[a] P = primary data; s = secondary data.
[b] S = sample; M = measurement of variables; St = statistical analysis; T = theory, I = importance.

Table 2–3
Empirical Studies of Adolescent Sexuality in the 1970s

Year	*Author*	*Topic*[a]	*Theory*	*Method*[b]	*Sample*[c]
1971	Brunswick	Health, sex, and fertility (1–4)	None	Interview-P	463 MF (12–17)
1971	Offer	Sexual behavior during the 1960s (1–5)	None	Questionnaire-P	73 M (14–21)
1972	Vener, Stewart, and Hager	Sexual behavior (2–4)	None	Questionnaire-P	4,220 MF (13–18)
1972	Kantner and Zelnik	Sexual experience (4)	None	Interview-P	4,240 F (15–19)
1973	Sorenson	Adolescent sexuality (2–5)	None	Interview/ Questionnaire-P	393 MF (13–19)
1973	Miller	Sexuality (4)	Model developed	Questionnaire-P	334 MF (16–18)

1973	Wagner, Byron, and Pion	Sexual behavior knowledge (1–4)	None	Questionnaire-P	171 M, 163F
1974	Jessor and Jessor	Maternal ideology and problem behavior (3,4)	Social learning	Interview/ Questionnaire-P	184 (junior and senior high school and mother)
1974	Miller and Simon	Sexual behavior (1–4)	None	Questionnaire-P	2,064 MF (14–17)
1974	Vener and Stewart	Sexual behavior (2–4)	None	Questionnaire-P	940 MF (13–18)
1975	Finkel and Finkel	Sexual knowledge, attitudes, and behavior of male adolescents (4)	None	Questionnaire-S	421 M (12–19)
1975	Jessor and Jessor	Transition from virginity to nonvirginity (4)	Problem behavior	Questionnaire-P	432 MF (16–18)
1975	Udry, Bauman, and Morris	Coital experience (4)	None	Interview-P	3,200 F (15–44)
1976	Cvetkovich and Stanley	Psychological factors	None	Interview/ Questionnaire-P	694 MF (16–17)
1977	Goldfarb et al.	Pregnancy susceptibility	Mini	Interview-P	758 F (12–18)
1977	Roebuck and McGee	Premarital sex attitudes and behavior of black high school girls (4)	None	Questionnaire-P	242 FD (15–21)
1977	Spanier	Sources of sex information and premarital sex behavior (1–4)	None	Interview Retrospective-S	1,177 (college)
1977	Zelnick and Kantner	Sexual experience (4)	None	Questionnaire-P	2,930 (15–19)
1978	Cvetkovich et al.	Sex role development and fertility-related behavior (4)	Developmental	Interview-P	369 F (16–18)
1978	Presser	Age at menarche, sociosexual behavior (1,5)	None	Interview Retrospective-P	541 F (15–29)
1978	Thornburg	Sources of sex information (1–6)	None	Questionnaire-P	451 MF (college)

[a] 1 = dating; 2 = kissing; 3 = petting; 4 = coitus; 5 = masturbation.

[b] P = primary data; S = secondary data.

[c] M = males; F = females.

Research Findings

Trends in Sexual Behavior. The major study of this decade was conducted by Zelnik and Kantner and their associates (Zelnik and Kantner, 1981), who implemented the first national probability sample of adolescents. In 1971, 4,240 (2,389 white and 1,401 black) never-married young women aged 15 to 19 were interviewed about their sexual behavior (Kantner and Zelnik, 1972). The study was replicated in 1976 (Zelnik and Kantner, 1977) with a national probability sample of 1,886 (1,232 white and 654 black) 15- to 19-year-old females and again in 1979 (Zelnik, Kantner, and Ford, 1981) with a sample of 1,620 (938 females 15 to 19 years and 682 males 17 to 21 years). Findings indicated that the proportion of U.S. metropolitan-area females 15 to 19 years who said they had ever had intercourse before marriage rose by two-thirds between 1971 and 1979 (from 30 percent to 50 percent). The increase was greater for whites—from 26 percent (1971) to 38 percent (1976) to 47 percent (1979)—than for blacks. The proportion of black adolescents who were sexually active increased from 54 percent (1971) to 66 percent (1976), with no increase from 1976 to 1979. Although this was only a 23 percent increase, it must be noted that young black women began and ended with a higher level of sexual activity than whites.

Vener and Stewart (1974) studied the sexual behavior of middle American youth in three school systems over the three-year period 1970–1973. In 1970 they (Vener, Stewart, and Hager, 1972) surveyed 4,220 eight- to twelfth-grade students to assess behavior that ranged from holding hands, to kissing, to petting, to coitus. Their findings indicated that although the developmental progression of girls' sexual behavior was similar to that of boys, there was no evidence of a major revolution in adolescent sexual behavior. In 1973, the school system with the widest range of socioeconomic status was resurveyed ($n = 940$), and the findings indicated a significant increase in coitus for 14- and 15-year-olds of both genders. At age 15, heavy petting and coitus with two or more partners showed a significant increase.

Jessor and Jessor (1975), as part of their longitudinal research project on the socialization of problem youth (1969–1972), examined trends in sexual behavior of 432 adolescents (186 boys and 242 girls from seventh through ninth grades in 1969) from a small city in the Rocky Mountain region. The theoretical framework of this research was the social psychology of problem behavior with roots in social learning theory. Subjects completed an extensive questionnaire (approximately fifty pages) assessing a variety of personality, social, behavioral, and demographic variables. Prevalence of nonvirginity increased with grade in school, from 21 percent to 33 percent for males and from 26 percent to 55 percent for females. The substantially higher incidence of female nonvirginity, particularly among eleventh- and twelfth-grade females, was attributed to the large college male population in the vicinity.

In another study of trends in sexual behavior, Udry, Bauman, and Morris

(1975) used interview data from 3,200 females aged 15 to 44 to compare various cohorts of women on their coital experience. Their findings indicated that although there were gradual increases in coital experience over the century, the largest increase occurred between individuals born in the 1940s and those born in the 1950s, that is, the cohort who entered their teens in the late 1960s and early 1970s.

Biological Factors. Presser (1978) interviewed 541 15- to 29-year-old females who recently had their first child and obtained retrospective data regarding the subjects' age of menarche and sociosexual behavior. In assessing the relationship between the age of menarche and initiation of dating, Presser found that age at menarche has some influence on the timing of dating but only for black females. It serves as an indicator of timing of sexual maturity that may influence the timing of sociosexual behavior such as dating and intercourse. Not surprisingly, age of first date was related to age at first sexual intercourse.

Psychosocial Factors. Several psychosocial factors were found to be associated with premarital intercourse experience. Cvetkovich and Grote (1976), in their interviews of 694 16- to 17-year-old adolescents, identified nonvirgin females as being more passive in relation to males, having lower ego strength than virgin females and a risk-taking attitude. Nonvirgin males were more skilled and manipulative in interpersonal relationships, were risk takers, and were somewhat irresponsible. In a later study of 369 16- to 18-year-old adolescent females (Cvetkovich et al., 1978), the researchers noted that virgins who were not ready for intercourse but thought they might be prior to marriage held relatively nonstereotyped sex roles. Virgins who denied they would experience premarital intercourse held the most stereotyped sex roles.

Miller and Simon (1974) surveyed 2,064 14- to 17-year-old adolescents and found that a high value on academic achievement, especially for females, was strongly associated with virginity. Jessor and Jessor (1975) and Udry, Bauman, and Morris (1975) reported similar findings in their samples. Goldfarb and her colleagues (1977) interviewed 758 12- to 18-year-old indigent girls to identify the academic and psychosocial indicators of girls who engage in intercourse at a young age. Using an inferential strategy based on concepts from Bayesian inference theory, they found that girls with poor academic performance were more susceptible to pregnancy risk.

Culture. Roebuck and McGee (1977) surveyed 242 15- to 21-year-old black females to determine their premarital sex attitudes and behavior. They found that social class appeared to influence the sexual attitudes of black female teenagers, but sexual behaviors were similar across social classes. In the Vener and Stewart study (1972), girls from the professional managerial community (in comparison to the blue collar and rural) had lower rates of premarital coitus.

Family. Few studies during this decade assessed familial characteristics in relation to sexual behavior. However, Kantner and Zelnik (1972) reported that black females with college-educated fathers had lower rates of premarital coitus than other black females.

Several studies during the 1970s looked at the family's role in imparting sexual information to adolescents. Thornburg (1978) asked 451 college students from four states to report how, where, and when they received their first information about twelve topics: abortion, contraception, ejaculation, homosexuality, intercourse, masturbation, menstruation, origin of babies, petting, prostitution, seminal emissions, and venereal disease. He found that the parents' role in imparting sexual information to their children was quite limited (15.3 percent) with the exception of "origin of babies" and "menstruation," which accounted for 58 percent of the total information given by mothers. Peers tended to be the primary source of information.

In her review of the family's influence on adolescent sexual behavior, Fox (1979) noted that what little communication regarding sexuality there is in the home appears to be due to the efforts of the mother. The mother-daughter dyad is the only familial relationship of much significance in the transmission of sex education, and the content of the communication is associated with forestalling or postponing sexual activity.

Several studies found a high correlation between having experienced intercourse and poor parent-child relations. Sorenson (1973), in his national survey of 393 13- to 19-year-old adolescents, found that nonvirgin females having many sex partners were high on peer involvement and low on parent involvement (Miller and Simon, 1974; Sorenson, 1973). Jessor and Jessor (1975) selected a subsample of their longitudinal data set to assess the relationship between traditional ideology of mothers and adolescent sexual behavior. They interviewed 184 mothers of junior and senior high school students regarding their beliefs about society and morality and their child rearing practices. Their children responded separately to questionnaires. The findings identified virgins as being more likely to have mothers with conventional ideology, firm discipline, and affectionate behavior. The more consistent the parent-youth values were, the closer the ties were to home, and there was less likelihood of the child's becoming sexually experienced.

Peers. Several studies looked at peer influence in relation to sexual education. Finkel and Finkel (1975) administered a forty-six-item questionnaire to 421 male high school students in a northeastern city. The students were asked to indicate two people from whom they had learned about sexual intercourse and human reproduction. Male friends were the most frequent source (37 percent), followed by professionals (23 percent) and female friends (18 percent). Less than 11 percent indicated they learned about these topics from any family members. Similarly, in his analysis of a national probability sample of 1,177 college students, Spanier (1977) found that friends were identified as the major socialization agents. Females who were socialized by male friends were more sexually active, and males who received their information from both male and female friends also were more sexually active.

The Decade in Review

Theory and Methodology. Before the 1970s, adolescent coital behavior was considered deviant behavior. In contrast, most of the literature of the 1970s rejected the deviance thesis and began viewing adolescent sexual activity as a normal part of the maturational process (Maddock, 1973) and in the broader context of human sexuality.

The 1970s saw the development of several mini theories attempting to explain premarital sexuality by identifying the correlates and causes of permissiveness. (Clayton and Bokemeier, 1980, provide an extensive review.) Theories attempting to explain sexual permissiveness included Reiss and Miller's (1979) autonomy theory of heterosexual permissiveness, Davidson and Leslie's (1977) axiomatic theory of sexual permissiveness, and Kelley's (1978) reinforcement theory of sexuality. Somewhat broader theories used during this decade to explain sexual behavior were Jessor and Jessor's (1977) social psychological theory of problem behavior developed from social learning theory, Gagnon and Simon's (1973) gender-specific theory of the psychosocial development of sexuality, Clayton's (1972) attitude-behavior consistency theory, and the Schulz, Bohrnstedt, Borgatta, and Evans (1977) version of differential opportunity theory. However, most of these theories were developed using college student and adult samples; few of the studies on adolescents were based on a theoretical framework (see table 2–3). The lack of empirical studies based on the theories cited could be attributed to the theories' being developed late in the decade.

Methodological progress was made in the 1970s with the movement beyond descriptive studies to employment of multivariate techniques (Cvetkovich et al., 1978; Goldfarb et al., 1977), the use of national probability samples (Kantner and Zelnik, 1972; Zelnik and Kanter, 1977), and the use of longitudinal panel designs (Jessor and Jessor, 1975; Vener and Stewart, 1974). However, much of the research on adolescent sexuality was limited because of methodological problems.

Diepold and Young (1979), in their critical review of twenty empirical studies of adolescent sexual behavior, pointed out several of the shortcomings of this area of research. Many of the studies of adolescent sexuality were retrospective, asking adults to recall their adolescent sexual experiences. Even if these reports were reliable and valid, it cannot be assumed that they can be generalized to subsequent cohorts of adolescents. Also, the statistical treatment of most data, even through the 1970s, was at a relatively rudimentary level. Few studies reported standard deviations so as to get an accurate picture of the distribution, and the cross-sectional nature of the data generally precluded any conclusions regarding causality.

One of the greatest methodological problems has been obtaining adequate probability samples (Chilman, 1978). In most cases, adolescents cannot be questioned about their sexuality without parental permission. Some parents are concerned that if researchers ask their children about sexual attitudes or behavior, sexual activity will be stimulated in their children. Since conservative or sexually anxious parents hesitate to give their consent and some adolescents fail to return questionnaires, sample bias tends to result. An example of sample attrition is found in Sorenson's (1973) study of adolescent sexuality. Only 61 percent of the parents granted permission for their child to be interviewed, and of the 508 adolescents for whom parental consent was obtained, only 393 were interviewed. This represented 47 percent of the adolescents enumerated in the systematically randomly selected households. It is possible to generalize findings to all American youth only to the extent that the sample is representative of the larger population.

Personal interviews and questionnaires were the two main procedures for gathering data on sexual experience. Hence, there are issues of interview bias and adolescent understanding of written questions that may affect the results. Although *virginity* and *sexual intercourse* may be clearly understandable terms to adult researchers, these words may have entirely different meanings for some adolescents. Vener and Stewart (1974) reported that some young people in their pilot study indicated they had engaged in "sexual intercourse," but it was later discovered that these subjects thought sexual intercourse was the same as "socializing with the opposite sex" (p. 729).

Key Studies and General Findings. With the focus of this decade being the understanding of the incidence of premarital sexual intercourse, three studies stand out as contributing to our understanding of adolescent sexuality in the 1970s.

The work of Zelnik and Kantner (1947; Kantner and Zelnik, 1972) is basic to our understanding of the sexual behavior of American youth. These were the first studies using a national probability sample of adolescent females (ages 15–19) and males (ages 17–21; added in 1979) to assess the incidence of intercourse in this population. These researchers reported a large increase in sexual activity for white males and females, but the levels were higher among black youth. Also, the average age at first intercourse declined through the decade, indicating a greater number of younger adolescents at risk for pregnancy.

Vener and Stewart (1974) employed cross-sectional surveys of Michigan youth over a three-year period to assess the lifetime prevalence of eight levels of sexual behavior, which ranged from holding hands to coitus with multiple partners. They reported an increase of coital experience for females from 16 to 22 percent and for males from 28 to 33 percent.

Jessor and Jessor (1977), using a cohort-sequential design, studied the incidence and prevalence of sexual intercourse of 188 male and 244 female high school age adolescents in Colorado and used their data as evidence of the narrowing of the gap in the double standard. These researchers reported a higher incidence of coital experience for females than males and attributed this unusual finding to the large college male population in the vicinity of the high school girls.

These studies served to document the growing numbers of adolescents engaging in sexual intercourse and set the stage for the next decade of research, which focused on the antecedents and correlates of this reported behavior.

The Decade 1980–1989

The early 1980s saw the emerging political activism of conservative fundamental religions, such as the Moral Majority, that advocated a return to traditional sex roles and opposed abortion, sex education in the schools, and the availability of contraceptives for adolescents without parental knowledge and consent. The national campaign "Just Say No" to drug use also was applied to sexual intercourse. Liberals as well as conservatives reassessed their personal and family values. Many found that the new liberties to engage in recreational (as opposed to procreational) sex in uncommitted relationships tended to result in loneliness and feelings of depression. Yet the climate of the 1980s still remained open to and supportive of sexual freedoms.

Research on adolescent sexuality greatly increased in this decade. The fact that adolescents were sexually active and were engaging in this activity at younger ages had been well documented in the 1970s. As a result, there was a growing concern of parents and health professionals regarding the negative consequences of teenage sex, particularly pregnancy and sexually transmitted diseases. This concern led researchers to focus on the factors contributing to the early onset of intercourse. This concern, coupled with the availability to federal research funds from the Adolescent Family Life Act of 1981, encouraged research on adolescent sexuality. Fifty-three empirical studies published during this decade are summarized in table 2–4.[2]

Numerous reviews and monographs were published during this decade. Fox (1981) thoroughly reviewed the research available at the beginning of the decade regarding the family's influence on adolescent sexuality. Zelnik, Kantner, and Ford (1981) published a summary of their 1970–1979 findings regarding the sexual behavior of 15- to 19-year-old women. Chilman (1983) again provided a thorough review of adolescent sexuality. In 1987, a study panel of the National Research Council published its review of adolescent sexuality research and recommendations for future policy formulation, program design, research, and evaluation (Hayes, 1987). Another recent work (Moore, Simms, and Betsey, 1986) has reviewed racial differences in adolescent sexuality and fertility.

Table 2–4
Empirical Research on Adolescent Sexuality in the 1980s

Year	*Author*	*Topic*[a]	*Theory*	*Method*[b]	*Sample*
1980	Fox and Inazu	Mother-daughter communication on sex (4)	Mini	Interview-P	449 F (14–15) and mothers
1980	Morris and Udry	Instrument to assess pubertal development	None	Questionnaire-P/ physical Exam	95 MF (12–16)
1980	Zelnik and Kantner	Sexual activity	None	Questionnaire-P	1,717 (15–19)
1981	Dornbusch et al.	Sexual development, age, and dating (1)	None	Questionnaire-S	6,710 MF (12–17), parents, doctors
1981	Shah and Zelnik	Parent and peer influence on sexual behavior	None	Questionnaire-P	2,193 (15–19)
1982	Darling and Hicks	Parental influence on sexuality (1–4)	Mini	Interview-P	696 (college, living at home)
1982	Zelnik and Kim	Sex education and sexual activity (4)	None	Questionnaire-P	1,620 MF (15–21)
1983	Hepburn	Parent-daughter communication on sexuality topics	None	Interview-P	48 F (ninth–twelfth grades) and parents
1983	Jessor et al.	Time of first intercourse (4)	Problem behavior	Questionnaire-P	403 (young adults)
1983	Newcomer, Udry, and Cameron	Sex behavior and popularity (1–4)	None	Interview-P	1,405 MF (11–17)
1983	Rogers	Family configuration and sexual behavior	Mini	Questionnaire-P	504 MF (11–16)
1983	Zelnik and Shah	First intercourse (4)	None	Questionnaire-P	1,620 MF (15–21)
1984	Bennet	Family environment for sex learning	None	Questionnaire-P	182 MF (18–20)
1984	Billy, Rogers, and Udry	Sexual behavior and friendship choice (4)	None	Questionnaire-P	408 MF (12–17) and friends
1984	Fox and Colombo	Parental division of labor in sexual socialization	None	Interview-P	51 families
1984	Newcomer and Udry	Mother's influence on sexual behavior (1–4)	Mini	Interview-P	495 MF and mothers
1984	Westney et al.	Sexual development and behavior in preadolescents (1–4)	Mini	Questionnaire-P physical Exam	101 MF (8–11)

1984	Zabin et al.	Sexual attitudes and behavior (4)	None	Questionnaire-P	3,534 MF (eighth–twelfth grades)
1985	Billy and Udry	Friendship and sex behavior (4)	Mini	Questionnaire-P	1,153 MF (13–19)
1985	Coles and Stokes	Sex (1–5)	None	Interview/ Questionnaire-P	1,067 MF (13–18)
1985	Fisher	Parent-child communication on sex, sexual attitudes	None	Questionnaire-P	141 MF (12–20)
1985	Furstenberg et al.	Sex education and sexual experience	None	Questionnaire-S	500 MF (15–16)
1985	Hogan and Kitagawa	Factors affecting black adolescents' fertility (4)	Mini	Interview-S	1,078 F (13–19)
1985	Newcomer and Udry	Parent-child communication and sexual behavior (4)	Mini	Interview-P	1,405 MF (12–16) and parents
1985	Smith and Udry	Coital-noncoital behavior (1–4)	None	Questionnaire-P	1,368 MF (12–15)
1985	Smith, Udry, and Morris	Pubertal development and friends (1–4)	Biosocial	Questionnaire-P	433 MF (14–17)
1985	Udry et al.	Hormones and sex behavior (4)	Biosocial	Questionnaire/ blood test	102 M (13–16)
1986	Dawson	Sex education effects on behavior	None	Interview-S	1,888 F (15–17)
1986	Fisher	Parent-child communication and sexual attitudes and knowledge	None	Questionnaire-P	22 MF (12–14) and parent
1986	Fox and Medlin	Mothers' perception of daughters' sexual activity (1–4)	None	Interview-P	23 F (14–17) and mothers
1986	Gilbert, Bauman, and Udry	Subjective expected utility for sex behavior (4)	Utility	Questionnaire-P	225 (junior high)
1986	Harris and Associates	Sex behavior (4)	None	Interview-P	1,000 MF (12–17)
1986	Miller et al.	Parental discipline and control and parents' sexual attitudes and behavior (4)	Mini	Questionnaire-P	2,423 MF (15–18)
1986	Miller, Olson and McCoy	Dating age and stage correlates of sexual attitudes and behavior	None	Questionnaire-P	836 MF (14–19)
1986	Moore, Peterson, and Furstenberg	Parental attitudes and early sexual activity	Mini	Interview-P	461 MF (15–16)
1986	Newcomb, Huba, and Bentler	Determinants of sexual and dating behaviors (1,4)	Domain	Questionnaire-P	376 MF (12–18)
1986	Udry, Talbert, and Morris	Biosocial factors	Biosocial	Questionnaire/ blood test	99 F (13–16)

Table 2–4 continued

Year	Author	Topic[a]	Theory	Method[b]	Sample
1986	Zabin et al.	Physical maturation and first intercourse in black teenagers	None	Questionnaire-P	1,134 MF (14–18)
1987	Furstenberg et al.	Race differences in timing of intercourse	None	Questionnaire-S	468 MF (15–16)
1987	Hofferth	Premarital sexual activity (4)	None	Questionnaire-S	6,715 MF (15–44)
1987	Miller, Christensen, and Olson	Self-esteem and sexual attitudes and behaviors (4)	Mini	Questionnaire-P	2,423 MF (14–19)
1987	Miller et al.	Family configuration and sexual attitudes and behavior	None	Questionnaire–P	836 MF (14–19)
1987	Papini and Sebby	Pubertal status and affective family relationships	Mini	Questionnaire–P	51 MF (13–14) and parents
1987	Thornton and Camburn	Family influence on premenstrual syndrome attitudes and behavior (4)	Mini	Interview–P	916 MF (18) and mothers
1987	Udry and Billy	Initiation of coitus in early adolescence (1–4)	Biosocial	Interview/ Questionnaire-P	1,153 MF (11–17) and mothers
1988	Baker, Thalberg, and Morrison	Parents behavioral norms and sexual activity (1–5)	Mini	Interview-P	329 MF (14–17), 470 parents
1988	Forste and Heaton	Initiation of sexual activity (4)	None	Questionnaire-S	7,969 F (15–44)
1988	Leigh, Weddle, and Loewen	Timing of transition to intercourse/black females (4)	Life span	Questionnaire-S	1,266 (15–19)
1988	Miller and Sneesby	Education and sexual activity (4)	None	Questionnaire-P	810 MF (14–19)
1988	Miller and Olson	Sexual attitudes and behavior and contexual factors (4)	None	Questionnaire-P	2,423 MF (14–19)
1988	Papini et al.	Sexual self-disclosure	None	Questionnaire-P	169 (14–18)
1988	Udry	Biological predisposition, social control, sex behavior (4)	Biosocial	Questionnaire-P Blood samples	200 (eighth–tenth grade)
1989	Miller and Bingham	Family configuration and sex (4)	None	Questionnaire-S	1,571 F (15–19)

[a] 1 = dating; 2 = kissing; 3 = petting; 4 = coitus; 5 = masturbation.
[b] P = primary data; S = secondary data.
[c] M = males; F =females. Ages in parentheses.

Research Findings

Trends in Sexual Behavior. The results of the national studies of adolescent behavior in 1987 and 1988 are not yet available, so we cannot report trends in sexual behavior for the entire decade. However, estimates of adolescent sexual experience from Cycle III of the National Survey of Family Growth (NSFG) (N = 6,716) suggest that the sexual activity of white teenagers leveled off between 1979 and 1982 and declined for black teenagers (Hofferth, Kahn, and Baldwin, 1987). Yet it appears that sexual intercourse experience may have risen in the mid-1980s. In a recent Harris Poll (1986), 1,000 adolescents between the ages of 12 and 17 years were interviewed, and results showed that 30 percent had experienced sexual intercourse. The proportion of sexually experienced youth increased rapidly with age—rising from 4 percent at age 12 to 57 percent at 17. Results of the poll indicated that teenagers whose parents were not college graduates, who had below-average school grades, or who were black were more likely to have had sexual intercourse.

In the 1980s, researchers became more interested in the ecology of the first intercourse experience, although very little was known about the circumstances and relationship between partners. Zelnik and Shah (1983) reported that for most adolescents, the initiation of sex seems to have been a spur-of-the-moment decision. Only 17 percent of the young women and 25 percent of the young men had planned their first act of intercourse. The average age at which young women had their first sexual experience was 16.2 compared with 15.7 for the men; women tended to have their first intercourse with a partner nearly three years older, whereas men had their first intercourse with a partner less than one year older. Blacks generally experienced first coitus at an age two to three years younger than whites.

Dating is often viewed as a precursor to more intimate sexual activity. Leigh, Weddle, and Loewen (1988), using a life course perspective, designed a study to identify the relationship between significant life events and other influences on the timing of the transition to intercourse for black adolescent females between the ages of 15 and 19 years. Using a subsample of the NSFG, Cycle III consisting of 1,266 females and implementing a discrete-time logistic regression analysis to identify the relationship of independent variables with age of first coitus, these researchers found that life events such as dating were important influences on the timing of transition to sexual intercourse. Using a sample of 836 14- to 19-year-old adolescents, Miller, Olson, and McCoy (1986) also concluded that early dating, especially early steady dating, is related to permissive attitudes and to premarital sexual experience for both males and females.

A substantial amount of males' sexual intercourse occurs outside the dating relationship, however. Zelnik and Shah (1983) reported that about half of males ages 17 to 21 indicated that their first intercourse experience was with a friend or a casual acquaintance outside what they perceived to be a dating relationship. In a study of 3,534 low-income black high school students in Baltimore, Zabin and colleagues (1984) found that 61 percent of males reported having intercourse before puberty, an intriguing finding. Yet Smith and Udry (1985) have observed that for blacks in contrast to whites who generally follow a progression of sexual behaviors from less to more intimacy, sexual intercourse more often occurs prior to behaviors such as petting.

Biological Factors. There appears to be strong evidence that early pubertal development (age at menarche for girls, level of pubertal development for boys) is associated with early initiation of sexual activity. This finding appears to hold net of other factors and also using various measures of sexual activity, from masturbation to intercourse, including the frequency of such activity (Billy and Udry, 1985; Westney et al., 1984; Zabin et al., 1986; Zelnik and Kantner, 1980).

Several researchers have sought to answer the question of whether heterosexual interaction is governed by an individual's level of sexual maturation or chronological age. Dornbusch et al. (1981), in their secondary analysis of Cycle III of the National Health Examination Survey consisting of a sample of 6,710 youth, found that individual levels of sexual maturation added little to explained variance in dating after age is taken into account. Thus, they concluded that social pressures—based on behavior considered appropriate at various ages—and not maturation determined the onset of dating in adolescence. Research by Zabin and colleagues (1986) of a sample of 1,134 14- to 18-year-olds revealed that age of puberty exerted an influence separate from that of normative patterns, and when puberty occurred at a young age, this lowered the age of sexual onset. As age of puberty increases, the cultural influence of social norms, as opposed to the individual developmental timetable, becomes stronger.

Udry and co-workers (1985) obtained information on pubertal development, sexual motivation, and sexual behavior in questionnaires obtained from 102 ninth- and tenth-grade white boys. In addition, they obtained and analyzed serum samples for a variety of serum androgenic hormones. In a model of sexual intercourse and masturbation that included age, pubertal development (Tanner Scale), and hormonal levels, only the hormonal influence (especially testosterone) retained their effects. This study provided strong evidence for the hormonal basis of sexual motivation and behavior in adolescent males.

In a comparable study on ninety-nine eighth- to tenth-grade females (Udry, Talbert, and Morris, 1986), it was found that hormonal levels had weak effects on sexual behavior but stronger effects on motivation. In a model including age, pubertal development, and hormonal levels, only the hormonal influences retained their effects on certain aspects of sexual behavior and motivation. These researchers concluded that since sexual motivation is not reflected in females' behavior to the extent that it is among males, sexual behavior is influenced to a greater extent by social controls among females than males.

Further research by Udry (1988) utilizing cross-sectional survey data and blood samples from approximately 200 eighth- to tenth-grade white students revealed an interaction between hormonal and sociological variables. However, pubertal development remains the only strong predictor of the timing of the transition to coitus (Udry and Billy, 1987).

Psychosocial Factors. A study of Jessor and associates (1983) is one of the few to gather longitudinal data before and after first intercourse. This study was a ten-year follow-up to the work of the previous decade studying 403 (94 percent of earlier sample) 23- to 25-year-olds at the time of the 1979 follow-up. Several personality measures were associated with early onset of sexual intercourse. In particular, adolescents who placed a higher value on and expectation for independence and a lower value on and expectation for academic achievement, who were more socially critical, more tolerant of deviance, and less religious, experienced intercourse earlier than their peers.

Zabin and colleagues (1984) reported that the majority of adolescents had values and attitudes consistent with responsible sexual conduct, but not all were able to translate these attitudes into personal behavior. Eighty-three percent of the sexually experienced teenagers cited a best age for first intercourse older than the age at which they initiated coitus.

Gilbert, Bauman, and Udry (1986) examined adolescents' subjective expected utility (SEU, the extent to which more good or bad outcomes are expected) for intercourse in a sample of 225 junior high school students over a three-year period. They found that SEU had a significant relationship to subsequent sexual behavior in each of three one-year intervals. However, intercourse was significantly related to subsequent SEU in only the first interval.

Miller, Christensen, and Olson (1987), employing a sample of 2,423 high school students from Utah, New Mexico, and California, found that the relationship between self-esteem and permissive sexual attitudes and behaviors was mediated by personal attitudinal permissiveness. Self-esteem was positively related to sexual intercourse experience among adolescents who believed that premarital sex was usually or always right and negatively related to sexual intercourse among those who believed it was wrong.

Culture. Research has indicated that one of the most important factors differentiating early from later initiators of sexual activity is race. There are large black-white differences in levels of sexual activity in the raw data, and these differences do not disappear when controls for other factors, including poverty status, are introduced (Zelnik, Kanter, and Ford, 1981; Zelnik and Kanter, 1980). There is evidence for some important differences in attitudes between blacks and whites. In their book on the racial differences in adolescent sexuality and fertility, Moore, Simms, and Betsey (1986) indicate that blacks appear to be more sexually permissive than whites (they have a greater tolerance for sexual activity outside a marital relationship), rate marriage as less important than whites do, and perceive a greater tolerance in their neighborhood for an out-of-wedlock birth. Furstenberg and his associates (1987) tested three hypotheses regarding racial differences in the prevalence and timing of sexual behavior. Using a national sample of 468 15- and 16-year-old adolescents, they found limited support for a demographic composition argument and stronger support for a contextual subgroup argument. Blacks in a predominantly black classroom were much more likely to report ever having intercourse than blacks in racially integrated schools.

Religion has been found to be an important differentiator of early versus later initiators of sexual intercourse. Both religious affiliation and religious attendance affect adolescent sexual participation. The highest level of premarital intercourse occurs among those with no religious affiliation (Zelnik, Kantner, and Ford, 1981). Young women ages 15–19 who said religion was important to them and who attended church more frequently were less likely to have reported having had sexual intercourse (see also Forste and Heaton, 1988). In their longitudinal study of sexual activity among 916 teenagers born in 1961 in the Detroit area, Thornton and Camburn (1987) found that adherents of fundamentalist Protestant denominations were significantly less likely to report having had sexual intercourse, compared to those affiliated with other denominations.

The research findings show few regional differences in the probability of sexual activity. There do, however, appear to be rural-urban factors. Teenagers living in urban centers have indicated more permissive attitudes toward sex than those living in either the suburbs or rural areas (Coles and Stokes, 1985). Hogan and Kitagawa (1985) also cite the importance of neighborhood on sexual activity. They reported that black females ages 15–19 living in a poverty-stricken area of Chicago had a much higher rate of initial sexual intercourse than peers not living in a poverty-stricken area.

Family. One consistently reported finding during this decade was that adolescents—daughters in particular—from single-parent families are more likely to begin sexual intercourse at younger ages than their peers from two-parent families (see Hayes, 1987; Forste and Heaton, 1988; Newcomer and Udry, 1983) and adolescents whose mothers remarry have more permissive sexual attitudes and experience (Thornton and Camburn, 1987). Rogers (1983) in a sample of southern eighth- to tenth-graders reported that, in addition to living with a single parent, having an older brother was related to early adolescent sexual intercourse experience. Miller, Higginson, McCoy, and Olson (1987), in a study of western high school students, failed to replicate the older-brother effect but did replicate the effect of parents' marital status. Miller and Bingham (1989), using the 1979 Zelnik and Kantner nationally representative sample of 1,571 15- to 19-year-old females, found that young women who were raised by a single parent were more likely to have nonmarital sexual intercourse than young women from families with intact marriages. Miller and associates (1986), utilizing a sample of 2,423 high school students and their parents, found a curvilinear relationship between adolescents' perceptions of parental strictness and rules and the adolescents' sexual attitudes and behaviors. Sexual activity and permissiveness were highest among adolescents whose parents were least strict, lowest among those who said that their parents were moderately strict, and intermediate among those who perceived their parents as being very strict. Home environments that were very liberal or very conservative were associated with a higher incidence of adolescent sexual experience. In a recent study of 329 males and females aged 14 to 17 and 470 of their parents, Baker, Thalberg, and Morison (1988) found that parental behavior norms accounted for 5 percent of the variance in whether adolescents had experienced intercourse. Fathers' approval of their child's sexual activity was the variable that accounted for the greatest amount of the variance.

Several other family characteristics have been shown to be related to adolescent sexual behavior. Hogan and Kitagawa (1985), in a study of 1,078 black female respondents of the 1979 Young Chicagoans Survey, found that family size was a related variable. When other factors such as socioeconomic status were controlled, daughters in very large families (more than five children) were more likely that those in smaller families to initiate sexual activity early. Parents' education is another related variable. The more years of education completed by the parents, the less likely are their teenage children to be sexually active (Zelnik, Kantner, and Ford, 1981; Forste and Heaton, 1988).

Another family variable found to be associated with adolescents' sexual behavior is the mother's adolescent sexual experience. Using a sample of 495 junior high students and their mothers, Newcomer and Udry (1984) found a strong relationship between the mother's sexual experience as a teenager and the daughter's sexual behavior as a teenager. These researchers suggested that this association is due to a biological relationship between the sexual maturation of mother and daughter versus social factors.

A number of studies focused on the sexual socialization process within the family and sought to understand the relationship between familial communication regarding sex and adolescent sexual attitudes and behaviors. Findings indicate a somewhat ambiguous relationship between these variables, which may be attributable to the difficulty of adequately tapping the family processes and the time order of the variables of interest.

In a study (Fox and Inazu, 1980) of mother-daughter communication utilizing 449 mother-daughter dyads (daughters 14 to 15 years) from Detroit, it was reported that although the mothers and daughters discussed sex-related topics, they differed in terms of how comfortable they felt with each other, the roles each played in initiating discussions, and whether they desired more frequent discussions in the future. Higher frequencies of current communication were associated with more responsible patterns of daughters' sexual behavior. Furstenberg, Moore, and Peterson (1985), using a sample of 500 adolescents from the 1981 National Survey of Children, reported that the ability to discuss sex with parents was associated with a lower prevalence of sexual intercourse. Similarly, in their study of 169 14- to 18-year-olds, Papini and associates (1988) asked subjects to complete questionnaires designed to tap their sexual self-disclosure, quality of family functioning, and individual psychosocial and cognitive characteristics. Using analysis of variance and regression models to estimate the additive effects of familial and individual developmental characteristics of sexual disclosure, they found that adolescent sexual disclosure to parents was strongly associated with adolescent perception of the openness and adaptiveness of the family context.

On the other hand, Newcomer and Udry (1984), studying seventh through ninth graders longitudinally, reported that prior communication with mothers was not related to subsequent sexual behavior. Kahn, Smith, and Roberts (1984) reported that parent-teenager communication had an effect on the sexual activity of sons but not daughters. Boys who discussed a larger number of sexual topics with their fathers were more likely to engage in premarital sexual behaviors, but increased communication with mothers yielded opposite results; discussions between mothers and sons were associated with a lower incidence of intercourse among sons. The sexual activity of teenagers appeared to be unaffected by whether parents discouraged premarital sex, conveyed a more lenient attitude, or said nothing.

One explanation of these divergent findings is a possible interaction effect of parents' attitudes or values on the relationship between their communication and adolescent sexuality. For example, Moore, Peterson, and Furstenberg (1986) found little support in their national sample of 461 15- to 16-year-olds for the hypothesis that parent-teenager communication discourages adolescent sexual behavior. However, when their sample was partitioned based on the parents' traditional versus moderate-to-liberal values, daughters of traditional parents who had communicated about sex were found to be less likely to have had sexual intercourse.

Fisher (1985) also examined the relationship between parent-child communication about sexuality and similarity of attitudes between 141 adolescents and their parents. She found that the correlation between parents' and children's attitudes was high for early adolescents (12 to 14 years) and low for middle adolescents (15 to 17 years). Only among the late adolescents (18 to 20 years) was there a significant difference in the correlations between the sexual attitudes of parents and their children as a function of family communication level, with the attitudes of adolescents and parents in the high communication group being highly correlated and the attitudes of adolescents and parents in the low communication group not being significantly correlated. Middle adolescents had significantly more permissive sexual attitudes than early and late adolescents.

Other researchers (Fox, 1981; Hepburn, 1983) note that various forms of communication are operating within the family and that many parents indirectly teach sexual attitudes and values through discussions of and comments on the behavior of other people.

Peers. Peer influence is often blamed for the increase in sexual activity, but there appears to be little documentation for this. Peers may have been heavily overrated as a source of increased sexual activity among teenagers, particularly among blacks and among white males (Chilman, 1983; Billy and Udry, 1985). However, in the recent Harris Poll (1986), adolescents indicated that social pressure was the chief reason that so many of their peers did not wait to have sexual intercourse until they were older. Both boys and girls cited social pressure more than other factors for initiating sexual activities, but girls mentioned it (73 percent) more than boys (50 percent) did.

Recent research has attempted to test the peer influence hypothesis more adequately through longitudinal studies in selected schools. In these schools, students who filled out questionnaires identified friends by a code. Since all adolescents in these schools participated in the study, matches were made between responses, and comparisons were made. Since the data were collected at several time points, peer influences could be examined over time. Using this technique in a panel study of 1,153 seventh to ninth graders, Billy and Udry (1985) found evidence that the sexual behavior of white girls was influenced by the behavior of their best male and female friends; that is, those who were virgins at the first time point were more likely to experience intercourse between waves of the survey if they had sexually experienced friends at the first wave than if they did not. In contrast, white males appeared to pick their friends on the basis of sexual activity rather than be influenced by friends' behavior. Blacks appeared neither to be influenced by friends' sexual behavior nor to pick their friends on that basis (Billy and Udry, 1985, Billy, Rogers, and Udry, 1984). Thus, there appears to be evidence for the peer influence hypothesis, especially among middle adolescents.

The Decade in Review

Theory and Methodology. The majority of the empirical articles during the 1980s were theoretically barren. Most researchers developed an organizational framework of prior research as a basis for their study. Several efforts were directed at utilizing theoretical frameworks to study adolescent sexual behavior. Gilbert, Bauman, and Udry (1986) applied utility theory to assess the subjective expected utility of adolescent behavior. Thornton and Camburn (1987) developed a model of intergenerational transmission of sexual attitudes and behaviors between mothers and their children. Leigh, Weddle, and Loewen (1988) based their study of the timing of transition to intercourse on a life-span perspective framework that emphasizes the study of development in terms of life events, sequences, patterns, and trajectories as they occur. This perspective encompasses the variety of developmental events (biological, psychological, social and historical) that occur in an individual's life and shows promise for further research using panel data.

Newcomb, Huba, and Bentler (1986) used domain theory and chose six domains to account for adolescent sexual and dating behaviors: Behavioral Styles, Psychological Status, Intimate Support System, Self-perceived Behavioral Pressure, Socioeconomic Resources, and Environmental Stress. Operationalizing these domains with respect to adolescent sexuality, these researchers developed a model of eight latent constructs where Dating and Sexual Involvement was directly affected by Importance of Dating and indirectly by Self-Acceptance, Stressful Change Events, and Lack of Heterosexual Competence. Because of the cross-sectional nature of the data in this study, it is impossible to say that the model represents true causal associations. However, this may be another promising theoretical framework for understanding adolescent sexual development because of its theoretical hypotheses; longitudinal data should be used to test the hypotheses.

The most notable theoretical line of research of the decade was the development and refinements of the biosocial model (Smith, Udry, and Morris, 1985) that considered pubertal development, hormones, and friends' behavior to explain adolescent sexuality. By implementing self and peer reports in a panel design, Udry and Billy (1987) developed a model for transition to coitus by examining motivation, social controls, and attractiveness. Then, by considering the influence of age, hormones, pubertal development, and social controls on sexuality, Udry (1988) refined the biosocial model. He indicates that although sociological models explain some of the variance in sexuality, combining the sociological and biological models can uncover not only additive but interactive contributions.

Several of the methodological problems of the 1970s continued to plague this decade's research. Attrition and sample bias continued to be problems. Also, most studies continued to examine sex behavior and correlates concurrently. It is difficult to determine if particular factors were present prior to the initiation of coitus and therefore contributed to the behavior or if behaviors encourage the presence of such factors. Only a few studies (e.g., Jessor et al., 1983; Udry and Billy, 1987) have examined the same youth both before and after first intercourse to understand the sequencing and causal relationships between the variables. It is only by the implementation of panel designs that researchers will be able to determine the effect of attitudes on behavior. Other measurement issues, such as confusion with behavioral terms and lying associated wtih self-reports of sexual behaviors, continued to cloud the reliability and validity of results (Miller, 1988).

On the more positive side, several researchers evaluated the comparability of findings of national surveys (Kahn, Kalsbeek, and Hofferth, 1988) and documented the consistency of estimates of sexual activity and its determinants. Several studies included other reports (parents, peers) as confirmations and correlates of adolescents' behavior. Also, more sophisticated methods of obtaining measures of pubertal maturation (hormones) by means of radioimmunoassay techniques added insight into the effect of biological factors during adolescent development. Additionally, there was an increase in statistical sophistication during the decade; most researchers implemented multivariate techniques to analyze their data. Instead of a majority of correlational studies, the 1980s saw an increase in the number of studies employing multiple regression, multiple classification analyses, logistic regression, discriminant function analysis, path analysis, and LISREL techniques.

General Findings. The sexual behavior of major interest during this decade was intercourse. Results from national probability samples measuring the incidence of sexual activity during the first half of the decade indicate a leveling and slight increase in the number of adolescents who have experienced intercourse, but the age of initiation appears to be declining—a concern for parents and health professionals who are aware of the increased risk for pregnancy and sexually transmitted diseases.

There was a growing interest in considering the biological and familial factors associated with adolescent sexuality. The availability of federal funds to finance the expense of obtaining blood serum samples from adolescents has opened the door to exploring the relationship between biological and social factors. The finding of strong evidence for the hormonal basis of sexual motivation and behavior in adolescent males (Udry et al., 1985) though not for females (Udry, Talbert, and Morris, 1986) is important and points to the need to develop differential models of sexual behavior for males and females.

Much of the work in this decade focused on sexual socialization in the family context. Parental concerns regarding the appropriate timing and content of communication about sexual development, sexual behaviors, health risks, and birth control remained an issue at the end of the 1980s. Many parents, especially fathers, were still unable or unwilling to communicate with their children about these issues. In most cases, sex education in the home, particularly where parents and adolescents have similar attitudes and values, is associated with delayed initiation of intercourse, but the lack of longitudinal data hinders our understanding of the socialization process within the family.

Conclusion

The 1930s was a time of broad theorizing and moralization about the deviance of adolescent sexuality or premarital sexual activity. A major step toward scientific research occurred with Kinsey's Report (1948), moving from issues of morality to factual statistical findings. The public was shocked and much criticism arose, but the need for objectivity in understanding sexual behavior became apparent.

The 1950s continued to move toward methodological rigor and objectivity. Kinsey (1953) was again an influence during this period, writing his report, *Sexual Behavior in the Human Female.* Other researchers began to look at issues

Kinsey had raised, such as religiosity and social status and their effects on adolescent premarital sexual behavior.

Research during the 1960s began to examine more closely the antecedents of adolescent sexual behavior, among them social class, parental attitudes, race, peer group, and birth control and their influences on adolescent sexuality. Reiss (1967) made a major contribution by being the first to examine objectively the attitudes or standards of adolescents and adults concerning premarital sexuality.

A vast improvement in methodological rigor and conceptual clarity occurred during the 1970s. The work of Zelnik and Kantner (1977; Kantner and Zelnik, 1972; Zelnik, Kantner, and Ford, 1981) is the foundation of our understanding of the sexual behavior of American youth. Vener and Stewart (1974) and Jessor and Jessor (1975) also conducted major studies during this decade documenting the increasing proportions of adolescents' engaging in sexual intercourse.

Research on the antecedents of adolescent sexuality greatly increased during the 1980s. The sexual behavior of major interest during this decade was intercourse. Many of the articles focused on sexual socialization in the family context. Udry's focus on the biopsychosocial model of adolescent sexuality (Udry et al., 1985; Udry, Talbert, and Morris, 1986; Udry and Billy, 1987; Udry, 1988) was a major contribution. Parental concerns regarding the appropriate timing and content of communication about sexual development, sexual behaviors, health risks, and birth control remained an issue.

The future brings both great hope and discouragement. With the increase in adolescent sexual activity over the decades, a higher incidence of casual, less committed sexual activity has occurred. Adolescent sexual behavior previously considered deviant is accepted as part of normal development, and the emphasis is on preventing or minimizing negative outcomes. Moral reasons for abstinence are being replaced by pragmatic health-related reasons that frequent sexual activity with multiple partners increases the risk of pregnancy and/or contracting a sexually transmitted disease.

Because of the potential negative outcomes of adolescent sexual intercourse, much interest remains in understanding the factors that precede and are associated with the initiation of coitus. There does not appear to be any one theory that can explain adolescent heterosexual behavior.

It is essential to continue descriptive, objective, statistically valid research. Future research and theoretical efforts should be directed not only at understanding the antecedents of adolescent sexual behavior, but these significant findings should be put to use to educate, prevent, and intervene in cases of early adolescent sexual activity.

Notes

1. This chapter is based on a systematic review of research in the social-behavioral sciences as indexed in the *Inventory of Marriage and the Family, Psychological Abstracts,*

and *Social Science Citation Indexes.* Cynthia R. Christopherson was the primary reviewer and author for the period 1930–1969, and Patricia H. Dyk was the primary reviewer and author for the period from 1970 to the present. Brent C. Miller assisted with the review of research and revising chapter drafts.

2. Many other studies were conducted during this decade focusing on adolescent contraception, pregnancy, parenting, and marriage. A review of all such articles is beyond the scope of this chapter.

References

Baker, S.A.; Thalberg, S.P.; and Morrison, D.M. 1988. Parents' behavioral norms as predictors of sexual activity and contraceptive use. *Adolescence* 23 (90):265–282.

Bayer, A. 1977. Sexual permissiveness and correlates as determined through interaction analyses. *Journal of Marriage and the Family* 39 (1):29–40.

Bell, R.R., and Buerkle, J.V. 1961. Mother-daughter attitudes to premarital sexual behavior. *Marriage and Family Living* 23:390–392.

Bennet, S.M. 1984. Family environment for sexual learning as a function of fathers' involvement in family work and discipline. *Adolescence* 19 (75):609–627.

Billy, J.O.G.; Rodgers, J.L.; and Udry, R. 1984. Adolescent sexual behavior and friendship choice. *Social Forces* 62:653–678.

Billy, J.O.G., and Udry, J.R. 1985. Patterns of adolescent friendship and effects on sexual behavior. *Social Psychology Quarterly* 48:27–41.

Bloch, D. 1972. Sex education practices of mothers. *Journal of Sex Education and Therapy* 7 (1):7–12.

Brecher, E.M. 1969. *The Sex Researchers.* Boston: Little, Brown & Co.

Broderick, C.B. 1963. Social heterosexual development among urban negroes and whites. *Journal of Marriage and the Family* 27:200–203.

Brunswick, A. 1971. Adolescent health, sex and fertility. *American Journal of Public Health* 61 (4):711–729.

Calderwood, D. 1963. Differences in sex questions of adolescent boys and girls. *Marriage and Family living* 25:492–495.

Chilman, C.S. 1978. *Adolescent Sexuality in a Changing American Society: Social and Psychological Perspectives.* Washington, D.C.: Government Printing Office.

———. 1983. *Adolescent Sexuality in a Changing American Society: Perspectives for the Human Services Professions.* New York: Wiley.

Clayton, R.R. 1972. Premarital sexual intercourse: A substantive test of the contingent consistency model. *Journal of Marriage and the Family* 34 (May):273–281.

Clayton, R.R., and Bokemeier, J.L. 1980. Premarital sex in the seventies. *Journal of Marriage and the Family* 42 (4):759–775.

Coles, R., and Stokes, G. 1985. *Sex and the American Teenager.* New York: Rolling Stone Press.

Crepsi, L.P., and Stanley, E.A., Jr. 1948. Youth looks at the Kinsey Report. *Public Opinion Quarterly* 12:687–696.

Cvetkovich, G., and Grote, B. 1976. Psychological factors associated with adolescent premarital coitus. Paper presented at the National Institute of Child Health and Human Development, Bethesda, Maryland, May.

Cvetkovich, G.; Grote, B.; Lieberman, E.J.; and Miller, W. 1978. Sex role development and teenage fertility-related behavior. *Adolescence* 13 (50):231–236.

Darling, C.A., and Hicks, M.W. 1982. Parental influence on adolescent sexuality: Implications for parents as educators. *Journal of Youth and Adolescence* 11 (3):231–245.

Davidson, J.K., and Leslie, G.R. 1977. Premarital sexual intercourse: An application of axiomatic theory construction. *Journal of Marriage and the Family* 39 (1):15–25.

Dawson, D.A. 1986. The effects of sex education on adolescent behavior. *Family Planning Perspectives* 18 (4):162–170.

Dedman, J. 1959. The relationship between religious attitude and attitude toward premarital sex relations. *Marriage and Family Living* 21:171–176.

Diepold, J., and Young, R.D. 1979. Empirical studies of adolescent sexual behavior: A critical review. *Adolescence* 14 (53):45–64.

Dornbusch, S.M.; Carlsmith, J.M.; Gross, R.T.; Martin, J.A.; Jennings, D.; Rosenberg, A.; and Duke, P. 1981. Sexual development, age and dating: A comparison of biological and social influence upon one set of behaviors. *Child Development* 52:179–185.

Dranoff, S.M. 1974. Masturbation and the male adolescent. *Adolescence* 9:169–175.

Ehrmann, W.W. 1955. Influence of comparative social class of companion upon premarital heterosexual behavior. *Marriage and Family Living* 21:48–53.

———. 1964. Marital and nonmarital sexual behavior. In H.T. Christensen (ed.), *Handbook of Marriage and the Family*. Chicago: Rand McNally.

Ellis, H. 1896. *Man and Woman: A Study of Human Secondary Sexual Characteristics* London: Scott.

———. 1936. *Studies in the Psychology of Sex*. New York: Random House.

Finkel, M.L., and Finkel, D.J. 1975. Sexual and contraceptive knowledge, attitudes and behavior of male adolescents. *Family Planning Perspectives* 7 (6):256–260.

Fisher, T.D. 1985. An exploratory study of parent-child communication about sex and sexual attitudes of early, middle, and late adolescents. *Journal of Genetic Psychology* 147 (4):543–557.

———. 1986. Parent-child communication about sex and young adolescents' sexual knowledge and attitudes. *Adolescence* 21 (83):517–527.

Forste, R.T., and Heaton, T.B. 1988. Initiation of sexual activity among female adolescents. *Youth and Society* 19 (3):250–268.

Fox, G.L. 1979. The family's influence on adolescent sexual behavior. *Children Today* (May–June):21–36.

———. 1981. The family's role in adolescent sexual behavior. In T. Ooms (ed.), *Teenage Pregnancy in a Family Context: Implications for Policy*, pp. 73–129. Philadelphia: Temple University Press.

Fox, G.L., and Colombo, M. 1984. Parental division of labor in adolescent sexual socialization. Paper presented at North Central Sociological Association meeting, Indianapolis, April.

Fox, G.L., and Inazu, J.K. 1980. Patterns and outcomes of mother-daughter communication about sexuality. *Journal of Social Issues* 36 (1):7–29.

Fox, G.L., and Medlin, C. 1986. Accuracy in mothers' perception of daughters' level of sexual involvement: Black and white single mothers and their teenage daughters. *Family Perspective* 20 (4):267–286.

Furstenberg, F.F., Jr.; Gordis, L.; and Markowitz, M. 1969. Birth control knowledge and attitudes among unmarried pregnant adolescents: A preliminary report. *Journal of Marriage and the Family* 31:34–42.

Furstenberg, F.F., Jr.; Moore, K.A.; and Peterson, J.L. 1985. Sex education and sexual experience among adolescents. *American Journal of Public Health* 75 (11):1331–1332.

Furstenberg, F.F., Jr.; Morgan, S.P.; Moore, K.A.; and Peterson, J.L. 1987. Race differences in the timing of adolescent intercourse. *American Sociological Review* 52:511–518.

Gagnon, J., and Simon, W. 1973. *Sexual Conduct: The Social Sources of Human Sexuality*. Aldine, Chicago.

Gilbert, M.A.; Bauman, K.E.; and Udry, R.A. 1986. A panel study of subjective expected utility for adolescent sexual behavior. *Journal of Applied Social Psychology* 16 (8):745–756.

Goldfarb, J.L.; Mumford, D.M.; Schum, D.A.; Smith, P.B.; Flowers, C.; and Schum, C. 1977. An attempt to detect "pregnancy susceptibility" in indigent adolescent girls. *Journal of Youth and Adolescence* 6 (2):127–144.

Groves, E.R. 1929. Adolescent strain and social pressure. *Social Forces* 7:342–350.

———. 1934. Courtship and marriage. *Mental Hygiene* 18:26–39.

Hall, M.D. 1966. Understanding adolescent sex behavior. *Mental Hygiene* 50:371–373.

Hampe, G.D., and Ruppel, H.J. 1974. The measurement of premarital sexual permissiveness: A comparison of two Guttman Scales. *Journal of Marriage and the Family* 36 (3):451–463.

Harris and Associates. 1986. *American Teens Speak: Sex, Myths, TV, and Birth Control*. New York: Louis Harris and Associates.

Hayes, C.D. 1987. *Risking the Future: Adolescent Sexuality, Pregnancy, and Childbearing*. Vol. 1. Washington, D.C.: National Academy Press.

Hepburn, E.H. 1983. A three level model of parent-daughter communication about sexual topics. *Adolescence* 18:523–534.

Hofferth, S.L. 1987. Initiation of sexual intercourse. In S.L. Hofferth and C.D. Hayes (eds.), *Risking the Future: Adolescent Sexuality, Pregnancy, and Childbearing*. Vol. 2. Washington, D.C.: National Academy Press.

Hofferth, S.L., and Hayes, C.D. (eds.). 1987. *Risking the Future: Adolescent Sexuality, Pregnancy, and Childbearing*. Vol. 2: *Working Papers and Statistical Appendixes*. Washington, D.C.: National Academy Press.

Hofferth, S.L.; Kahn, J.R.; and Baldwin, W. 1987. Premarital sexual activity among U.S. teenage women over the past three decades. *Family Planning Perspectives* 19 (2):46–53.

Hogan, D.P., and Kitagawa, E.M. 1985. The impact of social status, family structure, and neighborhood on the fertility of black adolescents. *American Journal of Sociology* 90 (4):825–855.

Jessor, R.; Costa, F.; Jessor, L.; and Donovan, J.E. 1983. Time of first intercourse: A prospective study. *Journal of Personality and Social Psychology* 44 (3):608–626.

Jessor, S.L., and Jessor, R. 1974. Maternal ideology and adolescent problem behavior. *Developmental Psychology* 10:246–254.

———. 1975. Transition from virginity to nonvirginity among youth: A social-psychological study over time. *Developmental Psychology* 11 (July): 473–484.

Kahn, J.R.; Kalsbeek, W.D.; and Hofferth, S.L. 1988. National estimates of teenage sexual activity: Evaluating the comparability of three national surveys. *Demography* 25 (2): 189–204.

Kahn, J.R.; Smith, K.W.; and Roberts, E.J. 1984. Familial communication and adolescent sexual behavior. Final report to the Office of Adolescent Pregnancy Programs, Department of Health and Human Services. Cambridge, Mass.: American Institutes for Research.

Kanin, E.J. 1960. Premarital sex adjustments, social class, and associated behavior. *Marriage and Family Living* 22:268–272.

Kantner, J.T., and Zelnik, M. 1972. Sexual experience of young unmarried women in the United States. *Family Planning Perspectives* 4 (4):9–18.

Kelley, J. 1978. Sexual permissiveness: Evidence for a theory. *Journal of Marriage and the Family* 40 (3):455–468.

Kinsey, A.C.; Pomeroy, W.B.; and Martin, C.E. 1948. *Sexual Behavior in the Human Male.* Philadelphia: W.B. Saunders Company.

Kinsey, A.C.; Pomeroy, W.B.; Martin, C.E.; and Gebhard, P.H. 1953. *Sexual Behavior in the Human Female.* Philadelphia: W.B. Saunders and Company.

Leigh, G.K.; Weddle, K.D.; and Loewen, I.R. 1988. Analysis of the timing of transition to sexual intercourse for black adolescent females. *Journal of Adolescent Research* 3 (3–4):333–344.

Lewis, R.A. 1963. Parents and peers: Socialization agents in the coital behavior of young adults. *Journal of Sex Research* 9:156–170.

Libby, R.W.; Gray, L.; and White, M. 1978. A test and reformulation of reference group and role correlates of premarital sexual permissiveness theory. *Journal of Marriage and the Family* 40 (1):79–92.

Maddock, J.W. 1973. Sex in adolescence: Its meaning and its future. *Adolescence* 8 (31):325–342.

Miller, B.C. 1988. Adolescent sexual intercourse: Behavior patterns and measurement issues. Paper presented at a workshop cosponsored by NICHHD, NIDA, CDC, Bethesda, Maryland, September 15–16.

Miller, B.C., and Bingham, C.R. 1989. Family configuration in relation to the sexual behavior of female adolescents. *Journal of Marriage and the Family* 51 (2):499–506.

Miller, B.C.; Christensen, R.B.; and Olson, T.D. 1987. Adolescent self-esteem in relation to sexual attitudes and behavior. *Youth and Society* 19:93–111.

Miller, B.C., and Fox, G.L. 1987. Theories of adolescent heterosexual behavior. *Journal of Adolescent Research* 2:269–282.

Miller, B.C.; Higginson, R.; McCoy, J.K.; Olson, T.D. 1987. Family configuration and adolescent sexual attitudes and behavior. *Population and Environment* 9:111–123.

Miller, B.C.; McCoy, J.K.; Olson, T.D.; and Wallace, C.M. 1986. Parental discipline and control attempts in relation to adolescent sexual attitudes and behavior. *Journal of Marriage and the Family* 48:503–512.

Miller, B.C., and Olson, T.D. 1988. Sexual attitudes and behavior of high school students in relation to background and contextual factors. *Journal of Sex Research* 24:194–200.

Miller, B.C.; Olson, T.D.; and McCoy, J.K. 1986. Dating age and stage as correlates of sexual attitudes and behavior. *Journal of Adolescent Research* 1:361–371.

Miller, B.C., and Sneesby, K.R. 1988. Parent and adolescent education as correlates of adolescent sexual attitudes and behavior. *Journal of Youth and Adolescence* 17 (6):521–530.

Miller, P.Y., and Simon, W. 1974. Adolescent sexual behavior: Context and change. *Social Problems* 22:58–75.

Miller, W.B. 1973. Sexuality, contraception and pregnancy in a high school population. *California Medicine* 119:14–21.

Mirande, A.M. 1968. Reference group theory and adolescent sexual behavior. *Journal of Marriage and the Family* 30:572–577.

Moore, K.A.; Peterson, J.L., and Furstenberg, F.F. 1986. Parental attitudes and early sexual activity. *Journal of Marriage and the Family* 48 (4):777–782.

Moore, K.A.; Simms, M.C.; and Betsey, C.L. 1986. *Choice and Circumstance: Racial Differences in Adolescent Sexuality and Fertility.* New Brunswick, N.J.: Transaction Books.

Morris, N.M., and Udry, J.R. 1980. Validation of a self-administered instrument to assess stage of adolescent development. *Journal of Youth and Adolescence* 9 (3):271–280.

Newcomb, M.D.; Huba, G.J.; and Bentler, P.M. 1986. Determinants of sexual and dating behaviors among adolescents. *Journal of Personality and Social Psychology* 50 (2):428–438.

Newcomer, S.F.; Udry, J.R.; and Cameron, F. 1983. Adolescent sexual behavior and popularity. *Adolescence* 18:515–522.

Newcomer, S.F., and Udry, J.R. 1984. Mothers' influence on the sexual behavior of their teenage children. *Journal of Marriage and the Family* 46:477–485.

———. 1985. Parent-child communication and adolescent sexual behavior. *Family Planning Perspectives* 17:169–174.

Offer, D. 1971. Sexual behavior of a group of normal adolescents. *Medical Aspects of Human Sexuality* 5:44–49.

Papini, D.R.; Farmer, F.L.; Clark, S.M.; and Snell, W.E., Jr. 1988. An evaluation of adolescent patterns of sexual self-disclosure to parents and friends. *Journal of Adolescent Research* 3 (3–4):387–401.

Papini, D.R., and Sebby, R.A. 1987. Adolescent pubertal status and affective family relationships: A multivariate assessment. *Journal of Youth and Adolescence* 16:1–15.

Porterfield, A.L., and Salley, H.E. 1946. Current folkways of sexual behavior. *American Journal of Sociology* 52:209–216.

Presser, H.B. 1978. Age at menarche, socio-sexual behavior and fertility. *Social Biology* 25 (2):94–101.

Reiss, I.L. 1956. The double standard in premarital sexual intercourse. *Social Forces* 34:224–230.

———. 1964. The scaling of premarital sexual permissiveness. *Journal of Marriage and the Family* 26:188–198.

———. 1967. *The Social Context of Premarital Sexual Permissiveness.* New York: Holt, Rinehart, and Winston.

Reiss, I.L., and Miller, B.C. 1979. Heterosexual permissiveness: A theoretical analysis. In W.R. Burr, R. Hill, F.I. Nye, and I.L. Reiss (eds.), *Contemporary Theories about the Family.* Vol. 1. New York: Free Press.

Roebuck, J., and McGee, M. 1977. Attitudes toward premarital sex and sexual behavior among black high school girls. *Journal of Sex Research* 13:104–114.

Rogers, J.L. 1983. Family configuration and adolescent sexual behavior. *Population and Environment* 6:73–83.

Schultz, B.; Bohrnstedt, G.W.; Borgatta, E.F.; and Evans, R.R. 1977. Explaining premarital sexual intercourse among college students: A causal model. *Social Forces* 56:148–165.

Shah, F., and Zelnik, M. 1981. Parent and peer influence on sexual behavior, contraceptive use, and pregnancy experience of young women. *Journal of Marriage and the Family* 43:339–348.

Smith, E.A., and Udry, J.R. 1985. Coital and non-coital sexual behaviors of white and black adolescents. *American Journal of Public Health* 75 (1):1200–1203.

Smith, E.A.; Udry, J.R.; and Morris, N.M. 1985. Pubertal development and friends: A biosocial explanation of adolescent sexual behavior. *Journal of Health and Social Behavior* 26:183–192.

Sorenson, R.C. 1973. *Adolescent Sexuality in Contemporary America.* New York: World.

Spanier, G.B. 1977. Sources of sex information and premarital sexual behavior. *Journal of Sex Research* 13 (2):73–85.

Thornburg, H.D. 1978. Adolescent sources of initial sex information. *Psychiatric Annals* 8 (8):70–77.

Thornton, A., and Camburn, D. 1987. The influence of the family on premarital sexual attitudes and behavior. *Demography* 24 (3):323–340.

Udry, J.R. 1988. Biological predispositions and social control in adolescent sexual behavior. *American Sociological Review* 53:709–722.

Udry, J.R.; Bauman, K.R.; and Morris, N.M. 1975. Changes in premarital coital experience of recent decade-of-birth cohorts of urban American women. *Journal of Marriage and the Family* 37:783–787.

Udry, J.R., and Billy, J.O.G. 1987. Initiation of coitus in early adolescence. *American Sociological Review* 52:841–855.

Udry, J.R.; Billy, J.O.G.; Morris, N.M.; Groff, T.R.; and Raj, M.H. 1985. Serum androgenic hormones motivate sexual behavior in adolescent boys. *Fertility and Sterilty* 43:90–94.

Udry, J.R.; Talbert, L.M.; and Morris, M.M. 1986. Biosocial foundations for adolescent female sexuality. *Demography* 23:217–230.

Vener, A.M., and Stewart, C. 1974. Adolescent sexual behavior in middle America revisited: 1970–1973. *Journal of Marriage and the Family* 36 (4):728–734.

Vener, A.M.; Stewart, C.; and Hager, D.L. 1972. The sexual behavior of adolescents in middle America: Generational and American-British comparisons. *Journal of Marriage and the Family* 34 (4):696–705.

Wagner, N.; Byron, F.; and Pion, R. 1973. Sexual behavior in high school: Data on a small sample. *Journal of Sex Research* 9:150–155.

Westney, O.E.; Jenkins, R.R.; Butts, J.D.; and Williams, I. 1984. Sexual development and behavior in black preadolescents. *Adolescence* 19:557–568.

Wile, I.S. 1930a. Sex problems of youth. *Social Hygiene* 16:413–427.

———. 1930b. Sex education in relation to mental and social hygiene. *Social Hygiene* 16:40–50.

Yankelovich, D. 1981. New rules in American life: Searching for self-fulfillment in a world turned upside down. *Psychology Today* 15 (4):35–42.

Zabin, L.S.; Hirsch, M.B.; Smith, E.A.; and Hardy, J.B. 1984. Adolescent sexual attitudes and behavior: Are they consistent? *Family Planning Perspectives* 16 (4):181–185.

Zabin, L.S.; Smith, E.A.; Hirsch, M.B.; and Hardy, J.B. 1986. Ages of physical maturation and first intercourse in black teenage males and females. *Demography* 23 (4):595–605.

Zelnik, M., and Kantner, J.F. 1977. Sexual and contraceptive experience of young unmarried women in the United States, 1976 and 1971. *Family Planning Perspectives* 9 (2):55–71.

Zelnik, M., and Kantner, J. 1980. Sexual activity, contraceptive use and pregnancy among metropolitan-area teenagers: 1971–1979. *Family Planning Perspectives* 12:230–237.

Zelnik, M.; Kantner, J; and Ford, K. 1981. *Sex and Pregnancy in Adolescence.* Beverly Hills: Sage.

Zelnik, M., and Kim, Y.J. 1982. Sex education and its association with teenage sexual activity, pregnancy and contraceptive use. *Family Planning Perspectives* 14 (3):117–126.

Zelnik, M., and Shah, F.K. 1983. first intercourse among young Americans. *Family Planning Perspectives* 15 (2):64–70.

3
Marital and Extramarital Sexuality

Ann B. Parkinson

This chapter reviews empirical research on the sexual relationship between married men and women and those sexual relationships outside marriage while a couple are still husband and wife. The time period covered is 1930 through 1989. Most of the studies include the American population, but a few were conducted in Europe and Great Britain.

The articles reviewed were identified by a search of *International Bibliography of Research in Marriage and the Family,* 1906–1964; *Research in Marriage and the Family,* vol. 2, *1965–1972; Inventory of Marriage and Family Literature,* 1973–1988; *Social Science Index,* 1969–1987; and *Psychological Abstracts,* 1970–1989; and by searching the references of research articles. Key words for identification were: *sexual, sexuality, marital sexuality, extramarital sexuality, sexual behavior, husband-wife relationships,* and *sexual relationships.*

The Decade 1930–1939

During the 1930s, sexuality was just beginning to be viewed as being apart from reproduction. The theme of most articles was marital adjustment.

Research Findings

Beliefs about Sexuality. Early in the decade, Watson and Green (1932) compared personal opinions about sex with findings from scientific studies by Hamilton (1929) and Davis (1929). After surveying 231 graduate students in an eastern city, Watson and Green found their subjects were in agreement with Hamilton and Davis: (1) regular intercourse contributes to efficiency in the labor force; (2) "unusually frequent intercourse" during the first year of marriage tends to be associated with marital happiness; (3) psychoneurosis is more common among the sexually inadequate; (4) a traumatic sex experience in childhood interferes with normal sexual development; and (5) women were becoming more promiscuous.

Marital Sexuality. Dickenson and Beam (1931) recorded and published the sexual histories of their patients in *A Thousand Marriages.* They reported that three in five women were sexually adjusted in their marriages.

The work of Havelock Ellis (1933) was directed to the helping professions. His major conclusions and contributions were that any sexual technique practiced by a couple that was "not injurious" could strengthen the marriage relationship; husbands were responsible for the frigidity of their wives, suggesting that poor technique of husbands rendered poor results in the sexual relationship; and a number of positions of intercourse should be practiced to enhance or expand the sexual experience of a couple (Ellis, 1933). Unconsummated marriages did exist ("many," he said, but gave no specific number) and Ellis noted that where there was mutual understanding between partners, these marraiges were not necessarily the least happy.

Terman (1938) studied 792 middle- and upper-middle-class couples in northern California and found that for both men and women, the frequency of marital sexual intercourse declined with increasing age. To assess the relationship of intercourse frequency to marital happiness, Terman compared 325 marriages in which the age of the husband was between 30 and 40 years. Sexual intercourse was almost as frequent in the unhappiest as in the happiest couples.

Terman's study also found that husbands who refused intercourse "frequently" or "sometimes" were only slightly less happy than those who "never" refused. Duration of intercourse was found to have very little influence on marital happiness. When the husband had complete lack of control over ejaculation, marital happiness was significantly lower. High incidence of the wife's achieving orgasm was positively related with marital happiness. Women whose desire for intercourse was greater than that of their husband's consistently rated themselves as unhappy.

The Decade in Review

Theory and Methodology. During the 1930s, most scholars made conclusions based on their impressions from clinical experience, not from empirical study (table 3–1).

Key Studies and General Findings. Terman's study in California provided the key empirical findings of the decade. Of most significance were findings that frequency of intercourse declined with age for both men and women and that frequency of intercourse was not related to marital happiness. Terman also made an important contribution by reviewing the methodology employed in the 1930s (Terman and Johnson, 1939). Questionnaires and interviews were the most common methods of data collection (Davis, 1929; Burgess and Cottrell, 1936; Hamilton, 1929; Dickenson and Beam, 1931; Mowrer, 1935). Both

Table 3–1
Overview of Research on Marital and Extramarital Sexuality, 1930–1939

Year	*Author*	*Topic*	*Theory*	*Method*[a]	*Sample*
1931	Dickenson and Beam	Sexual adjustment	None	Personal histories	1,000
1932	Watson and Green	Opinions on sex	None	Questionnaire-P	231
1933	Ellis	Sex psychology	None	Observation	
1937	Folsom	Sexual values	None	Other	1,250
1938	Terman	Sex and marital happiness	None	Interview-P	792

[a]P = primary data.

Terman's longitudinal California study and his evaluation of methodology contributed significiantly to methdology.

The Decade 1940–1949

Studies of sexuality were rare until the conclusion of World War II. Researchers mainly concerned themselves with sexual adjustment in marriage. Premarital sex still carried taboos, so researchers assumed sexual innocence among newly married couples.

Research Findings

Marital Sexuality. In a study of 409 married couples, Landis (1947) found that sexual adjustment was the most difficult of all areas of adjustment in marriage. When asked what problems were the greatest obstacle in achieving happiness in marriage, sex adjustment ranked second to spending the family income. Only about half the couples claimed that their sexual adjustment was satisfactory from the beginning, although all but 10 percent felt that they had made successful adjustment in the first year of marriage. More husbands than wives said sexual adjustment had never been satisfactory.

Brav (1947) studied the honeymoon period of fifty women in a small southern community. Forty-eight percent reported that they failed to achieve complete sexual harmony during their honeymoon; nevertheless, 74 percent described their honeymoon as a "complete success." Sixty-four percent of the women claimed that "a honeymoon is the achievement of all pre-marital romantic desires." Sexual adjustment was rated as the most frequent difficulty encountered on the honeymoon; "lack of adequate sex education" followed second. Only 10 percent claimed that premarital sex experience was helpful on a honeymoon. By contrast, 80 percent were sure that it was not. However, 70 percent felt that information on sex and love derived from a book helped a honeymoon's success.

The Kinsey Report. The landmark study during this period was *Sexual Behavior and the Human Male* (Kinsey, Pomeroy, and Martin, 1948). The authors obtained detailed sexual histories by interviewing 6,300 men from every state in the union. Their sample was mostly white, had about equal numbers of males and females, and included individuals from all social and educational levels and ages. Among the major findings in the Kinsey study were the following:

1. Frequency of sexual intercourse declined with age for men. Males who married between the ages of 16 and 20 had the maximum sexual perfor-

mance. Mean frequency of sexual outlet was 4.7 times per week, with many individuals reporting 10, 14, or even 20 times per week.

2. There were social class differences in the sexual practices of males. Educated men were more likely to employ manual manipulation, oral eroticism, and varied positions of intercourse, whereas men with low education levels regarded such techniques as unnecessary or perverted.
3. About half of the males had engaged in intercourse with women other than their wives at some time while they were married. Extramarital intercourse was highest among young men of low socioeconomic status, and it decreased with age. By age 40, about 45 percent of lower-class men who had married in their late teenage years were involved in extramarital intercourse, compared to 27 percent among the middle class. In rural areas and among devoutly religious males, the incidence of extramarital intercourse was considerably lower.

Extramarital Sexuality. Reinemann (1945) studied the relationship between employment in the war industries and extramarital relations. He examined the complaints filed with the domestic relations division of the municipal court where either husband or wife was employed in one of the war industries and associated with a fellow employee of the opposite sex. Eighty-nine cases were compared with a control group of 3,539 desertion and nonsupport cases handled by the domestic relations division. Extramarital relations among those in the war industries was similar to extramarital relations among the control sample. The war industries only added a new locale and another way of meeting people. Among men over age 30, however, the amount of extramarital sex was higher among war industry employees than among the control group.

The Decade in Review

Studies of sexuality within marriage dominated the decade of the 1940s, but extramarital sexuality began to be researched (table 3–2). Kinsey's study was the most significant contribution of the decade. Interviews became important in that decade because of the Kinsey study. Samples were biased toward white middle-class individuals.

Findings of the decade indicated that sexual adjustment within marriage was not immediate but in most cases was resolved early in the relationship. Different social classes expressed sexuality in different ways. It was estimated that about half of married men had engaged in extramarital intercourse. Many questioned the validity of Kinsey's results because the subjects had been volunteers, but the dramatic nature of many of his findings stimulated much interest in the scientific study of sexual behavior.

Table 3–2
Overview of Research on Marital and Extramarital Sexuality, 1940–1949

Year	*Author*	*Topic*	*Theory*	*Method*[a]	*Sample*
1945	Reinemann	Extramarital sexuality	None	Demographic	89
1947	Brav	Sex adjustment	None	Questionnaire-P	50
1947	Landis	Sex adjustment	None	Questionnaire-P	409
1948	Kinsey, Pomeroy, and Martin	Male sexuality	None	Interview-P	12,000

[a] P = primary data.

The Decade 1950–1959

The Kinsey Report appeared to be a stimulus to research during the 1950s. Marital and extramarital sexuality continued to be studied, and the most frequently studied topic was the relationship between sexual and marital adjustment.

Research Findings

Marital Sexuality. The effects of first pregnancy on the marital sexual relationship were studied by Landis, Poffenberger, and Poffenberger (1950). Couples who had a good sexual adjustment before pregnancy had a good adjustment after the birth of the child. In a minority of cases, the sexual relationship improved from poor to good. Sexual desire decreased with each trimester of pregnancy. Wives who were confident in the efficacy of contraceptives experienced better sexual adjustment after a birth. Wives whose health was good during the pregnancy experienced better adjustment following it.

Terman (1951), who examined the correlates of orgasm adequacy in a group of wives who were part of the longitudinal study he began in the 1930s, found that wives' orgasm adequacy was associated with many aspects of individual personality and with specific experiences stemming from childhood and family background. This adequacy, however, was only one of many factors contributing to wives' marital happiness, not the most important one, and it appeared to have almost no effect on the husband's marital happiness.

Stokes (1951) studied sixty cases of unconsummated marriages observed in his medical practice and concluded that although most reasons for postmarital virginity were medical, there was strong argument for psychological as well as physical treatment since the inability to consummate a marriage was in most cases traumatic.

The Second Kinsey Report. Five years after publishing their report of sexual behavior in males, Kinsey and coworkers (1953) reported on the sexual behavior of 5,700 women. They found that there were differences in the mode of arousal for women compared to men. Women were more stimulated by watching commercial movies, whereas men were more aroused by portrayals of sexual activity, burlesque shows, nude photos, or erotic stories.

Similar to men, frequency of intercourse declined with age. The mean frequency reported by married women ages 16–20 was 2.7 times per week compared to 0.5 time per week at ages 56–60.

Kinsey's study found that almost half of all women achieved orgasm within the first month of marriage and three-fourths within the first year. After that, a few more of the wives achieved orgasm each year until at the fifteenth year of marriage, 90 percent of the wives had experienced orgasm. Ten percent of the women never achieved orgasm. The women in Kinsey's era reported greater sexual responsiveness than women twenty to thirty years earlier. The number of women who admitted to extramarital intercourse by age 40 was about 20 percent.

Marital Sexuality. Using a sample of 466 black couples, King (1953) studied the association between satisfactory sexual relations in marriage and successful marital adjustment. Among women who reported "good" or "very good" adjustment to marriage, 52 percent reported their first sexual experience in marriage as enjoyable. Women whose first sex experience in marriage was "merely tolerable" had a 51 percent rate of "good" or "very good" marital adjustment. Sixty percent of the women who reported their first sex experience as "shocking and disgusting" had a "good" or "very good" marital adjustment. King concluded that continued sexual experience seemed to remedy initial poor experience, findings that were in agreement with those of Brav (1947).

Sexual complaints in divorce cases in Philadelphia were studied by Kephart (1954). Many divorces occurring in the first year of marriage were found to involve sexual complaints. The number of such complaints declined steadily with divorce filings in later years of marriage.

Contraception contributed to the rise in coital frequency. Reviews of Kinsey's data suggested that sexuality was becoming divorced from procreation. Because of correct use of condoms and diaphragms, family planning became possible. Sex was becoming "fun" or "recreational" (Foote, 1954).

Thomason (1955) hypothesized that couples would disagree more on sexual than nonsexual matters, but contrary to his hypothesis, there was 67 percent agreement in sexual matters compared to only 53 percent for nonsexual matters. Factors surrounding interpretation of spouses attitudes or feelings were more likely to be misunderstood.

Sex and marital adjustment still dominated the focus of research toward the end of the decade. In a study of 102 couples, Bowerman (1957) found sexual adjustment less satisfactory for women than men.

Kanin and Howard (1958) collected data from 177 wives of college students to examine the relationship between premarital sex and postmarital sexual adjustment during the honeymoon period, as well as contraceptive practices employed. They found that couples who had engaged in premarital intercourse were less likely to take a "wedding trip" (only 47 percent compared to 87 percent who had not had intercourse before marriage), subjects who had been involved in a premarital sexual relationship were less likely to use contraceptives after marriage, and wives who experienced sexual intercourse before marriage reported greater sexual difficulties after marriage.

The Decade in Review

Theory and Methodology. Studies conducted in the 1950s showed more sophistication than in previous decades, including more representative sampling (table 3–3). Some hypotheses were tested, but no theory was evident

Table 3-3
Overview of Research on Marital and Extramarital Sexuality, 1950–1959

Year	*Author*	*Topic*	*Theory*	*Method*[a]	*Sample*
1950	Landis, Poffenberger, and Poffenberger	Sex adjustment	None	Questionnaire-P	414
1951	Stokes	Unconsummated marriages	None	Case study	60
1951	Terman	Orgasm adequacy	None	Questionnaire-P	556
1953	Ellis	Incompatibility	None	Case study	
1953	King	Sex adjustment	None	Questionnaire-P	466
1953	Kinsey et al.	Female sexuality	None	Interview-P	5,300
1954	Foote	Sex as play	None	Other	
1954	Kephart	Maladjustment	None	Questionnaire-P	1,434
1955	Thomason	Sex agreement	None	Questionnaire-P	1,282
1957	Bowerman	Sex adjustment	None	Questionnaire-P	204
1958	Kanin and Howard	Sex adjustment	None	Questionnaire-P	177

[a] P = primary data.

regarding marital sexuality. Terman began to assess correlates of orgasm adequacy, and Kinsey's findings concerning orgasm and percentages of women involved in extramarital sex were cited for many years.

Key Studies and General Findings. During the 1950s, most couples who enjoyed satisfactory sexual adjustment prior to the birth of the first child resumed a satisfactory sexual relationship after the child was born. Women appeared to be more responsive sexually than in past decades. Better methods of contraception were associated with greater frequency of intercourse.

The Decade 1960–1969

Research Findings

Marital Sexuality. Study of the relationship between sex and marital adjustment continued. In previous decades, most scholars had examined the sexual adjustment of the wives; now Dentler and Pineo (1960) looked at the sexual satisfaction of husbands. The sample they used had been studied as engaged couples in 1937 and 1938 by Ernest W. Burgess and Leonard Cottrell. Their data were gathered in the fifth and fifteenth years of marriage. Dentler and Pineo found a strong relationship between sexual adjustment and marital adjustment. Couples who enjoyed successful sexual adjustment seemed to make satisfactory marital adjustment, and vice versa.

Whether orgasm was necessary to sexual enjoyment was challenged early in the decade (Wallin and Clark, 1963), based on the sample from the Burgess-Cottrell study. Although some women never or only occasionally achieved orgasm, they nevertheless experienced some sexual enjoyment. Of the 17 percent of women who had orgasm seldom or never, most enjoyed intercourse "very much." These women also preferred to have intercourse frequently. A similar association existed between enjoyment ratings and preferred frequency for women who had higher rates of orgasm achievement.

In contrast with Wallin and Clark, Gebhard (1966) found a correlation between female orgasm and marital happiness. The longer the marriage existed, the greater was the chance for orgasm. There was a moderate correlation between orgasm rate and duration of foreplay, as well as between orgasm rate and duration of intercourse.

In a study of college-educated wives, Bell (1964) asked 196 women to assess their sexual adjustment. Seventy-nine percent reported "very good" and "good," 17 percent "fair," and 4 percent "poor" and "very poor." Their husbands' ratings were almost identical.

Clark and Wallin (1965) studied the sexual responsiveness of women over time and its relation to the quality of the women's marriages. They found that 88 percent of those responsive in early years remained responsive in middle years. Fifty-two percent of those who were unresponsive in the early years became responsive in the middle years. Surprisingly, wives whose marriages changed from negative to positive had a lower percentage of responsiveness than those who changed from positive to negative. In constantly negative marriages, unresponsive women remained unresponsive. The number of women who became sexually responsive increased with time, as Kinsey (1953) had found.

Matthews and Mihanovich (1963) studied sexual maladjustment in 984 marriages among Catholics. They found that many of the same problems existed in intact marriages as in those that had ended in divorce. The adaptability of and willingness to live with sexual problems determined whether the marriage lasted.

Extramarital Sexuality. Strength of conscience was a determining factor in whether a person would engage in an extramarital affair or a fantasy involvement, according to Neubeck and Schletzer (1962), who studied forty couples. Those with high strength of conscience were less likely to attempt an affair. Their measurement of strength of conscience was derived from the Psychopathic Deviate Scale. Individuals who rated low in personal satisfaction were more likely to seek a fantasy outlet rather than actual sexual or emotional involvement.

Finding "strength of conscience" as a difficult variable for measurement, Whitehurst (1969) conceptualized his theoretical framework around sociological variables. He asserted that male extramarital sexual behavior (EMS) is more a product of the American socialization process than pathological deviance. He conceptualized EMS as "an expected outcome of alienation involving life-cycle variations, socialization, and changes in values." Of the 112 professional men in his study, 80 percent of EMS men were in the high-alienation group, and 41 percent of the sample saw high opportunity as a factor in their behavior. Whitehurst concluded that the hypothesis of alienation received support and that the factor of opportunity needed further investigation.

Social Class. Rainwater (1964) studied the marital sexual relationships of 250 women. He observed that women at the poverty level had the least satisfying sexual relationships of any other subgroup. Over half of the women in poverty had completely rejecting attitudes toward sexual relations.

In a study on family size, Rainwater (1965) found that social class influenced the enjoyment in marital sexual relationships. Attitudes toward sexual relations were very positive among almost two-thirds of blacks and whites in which husbands and wives shared decisions. Rainwater asserted that conjugal role organization was predictive of the wife's enjoyment of sexual relations. Strong rejection of sexual relationships was characteristic of lower-lower-class couples in segregated role relationships.

Unconsummated Marriages. Blazer (1964) reported fifteen reasons given by "married virgins" as to why their marriages remained "unconsummated":

> Fear of pain in the initial intercourse, the sex act was considered nasty or wicked, impotent husbands, fear of pregnancy or childbirth, small size of vagina, ignorance regarding the exact location of their organs, preference for a female partner, extreme dislike for the penis, intense dislike for intercourse without pregnancy, dislike of contraceptives, belief that submission implies inferiority, general dislike of men, desire to 'mother' their husbands only, fear of damaging the husband's penis.

His sample consisted of 1,000 women, ages 17–47, whose length of marriage and unconsummation ranged from one to twenty-one years.

Methodology. Two studies during the 1960s looked at the accuracy of reports of sexual behavior. Clark and Wallin (1964) found that agreement between husbands and wives as to frequency of intercourse varied with number of years married, mutual satisfaction of marriage, and whether one partner was more satisfied than the other.

Levinger (1966) applied Festinger's theory of cognitive dissonance to estimation of intercourse frequency by suggesting that attributing higher sexual desire to the female spouse would be "dissonant with one's adherence to the cultural norm. Thus respondents are inclined to deny instances of the wife's higher relative desire." He also concluded that it would be dissonant to determine an unpleasant activity as lasting only a short time and to report being satisfied with an experience that occurred infrequently. Such feelings would account for overestimation of the event.

Masters and Johnson. Masters and Johnson (1966) conducted an unprecedented firsthand observation of human sexual intercourse, observing and photographing in cinematography, 694 participants. Among their important findings are the following:

1. There is neither a purely clitoral nor a purely vaginal orgasm.
2. The female's physiologic responses to effective sexual stimulation develop with consistency regardless of the psychic or physical sexual stimulation.
3. Some women had several orgasms before full satiety.
4. The size of a man's penis was not related to sexual performance.

The Decade in Review

Theory and Methodology. Firsthand observation of the sexual experience emerged as a new methodology in sexual science. Levinger (1966) used cognitive dissonance to study husband-wife discrepancies, while Whitehurst studied extramarital sexuality using a social systems approach. (However, Whitehurst's glaring oversight of females in presenting a theory of human behavior attests to the sexist nature of studies of the decade.)

Key Studies and General Findings. Female sexuality was a central focus of study in the 1960s (table 3–4). The conflicting findings of the Wallin and Clark (1963) and Gebhard (1966) studies suggested a need for evaluation to determine what the women in the studies wanted from the sexual experience.

The myth of the vaginal orgasm was debunked, leaving women free of fears that they might not be experiencing all they should from the sexual experience. Other important findings of the decade were that strength of conscience deterred involvement in extramarital sexuality and that women of the lower-lower social class were likely to have a rejecting attitude toward sexual relationships.

The Decade 1970–1979

The new emphasis on female sexuality of the 1960s carried over into studies of the 1970s and became part of feminist scholarship. Alternate styles of marriage received much study during this decade.

Research Findings

Descriptive Studies. Athanasiou and Shaver (1970) analyzed data from 20,000 *Psychology Today* readers who responded to questions about sexual attitudes and activities both in and out of marriage. Americans, it turned out, were a little more conservative than popular media generally portrayed. Where Kinsey had estimated that about half of all men who had ever been married had engaged in extramarital intercourse, about 40 percent of Athanasiou and Shaver's sample reported extramarital sexual intercourse. The proportion of women was 36 percent compared to Kinsey's findings of 26 percent.

A similar study appeared in *Redbook*, a magazine geared to young married women (Bell, 1974). The results of the poll, to which 100,000 readers responded, were published a year later by another researcher (Levin, 1975). *The Hite Report* (Hite, 1977) appeared a few years later. It gained a great deal of public attention but was highly criticized for its methodology. All of these magazine surveys were limited in their validity because self-selected magazine readers are not representative of the population.

Johnson (1970) found that extramarital activity may not be accurately assessed in studies, since most people oppose extramarital activity in theory, if not in practice. He emphasized the importance of first giving a hypothetical rationale to respondents in case they feel the need to justify their behavior.

Table 3–4
Overview of Research on Marital and Extramarital Sexuality, 1960–1969

Year	*Author*	*Topic*	*Theory*	*Method*[a]	*Sample*
1960	Dentler and Pineo	Sex adjustment	None	Questionnaire-S	2,000
1962	Neubeck and Schletzer	Extramarital sexuality	None	Interview-P	80
1963	Matthews and Mihanovich	Sex adjustment	None	Questionnaire-P	984
1963	Wallin and Clark	Orgasm (mid-life)	None	Questionnaire-S	417
1964	Bell	Socioeconomic status and sexuality	None	Questionnaire-P	196
1964	Blazer	Unconsummated marriages	None	Interview-P	1,000
1964	Clark and Wallin	Sex frequency	None	Questionnaire-P	604
1964	Rainwater	Socioeconomic status and sexuality	None	Interview-P	250
1965	Clark and Wallin	Orgasm adequacy	None	Questionnaire-S	602
1966	Gebhard	Orgasm adequacy	None	Interview-S	8,000
1966	Levinger	Sex behavior	Dissonance	Questionnaire-S	120
1966	Masters and Johnson	Sex response	None	Observation	694
1969	Whitehurst	Extramarital sexuality	Social system	Questionnaire-P	112

[a] P = primary data; S = secondary data.

The Hunt Study. Hunt (1974) collected data from 2,026 subjects to examine changes in the attitudes and behaviors of Americans since Kinsey's time. Hunt found that frequency of marital intercourse had increased, extramarital sexuality was not as high as had been estimated by Kinsey, and sexual experimenting had expanded. Hunt also asked questions about incest, mate swapping, and sadomasochism, which had not been part of the Kinsey study, and compared marital and extramarital relationships on frequency of orgasm. His findings indicated that women experienced orgasm more frequently in their marriage relationships than in extramarital relationships.

Marital Sexuality. Although there was a scarcity of research on sex within marriage, Ard (1977) studied the sexual relationship of 161 long-term marriages from data collected in 1955. Most couples reported sexually satisfying marriages. Although sexual activity declined with time, feelings about sex and satisfaction from it remained positive. Novelty or need for a new sexual partner did not appear necessary for satisfaction among these couples.

Bell (1974) found that most wives, especially younger ones, were enjoying sex in their marriages. His initial data on 100,000 women suggested that younger women were more pleasure oriented and more experimental than older women, but Levin's (1975) detailed analysis of the data revealed that reports of orgasm achievement of the women were similar in percentages to Kinsey's (1953) findings two decades earlier: 17 percent "always," 42 percent "most of the time," 32 percent "some of the time," 8 percent "never," and 1 percent "don't know." The women citing high orgasm achievement reported a frequency of intercourse almost twice that of women who had never achieved orgasm. The women, however, claimed that whether they achieved orgasm had little effect on their desire for sex.

Levin's (1975) statistics were also similar to Kinsey's in reports that about 30 percent of the women had engaged in extramarital sexuality. In addition, Levin found that college-educated women were less likely than high school graduates to become involved in EMS until the age of 40, but women of that age group more frequently participated in EMS regardless of educational level. This study was another "newsstand" variety, so a specific audience had responded to the survey.

Heath (1978) studied the sexual enjoyment of fifty-nine married professional men and found that well-educated businessmen, as a group, scored high on the Minnesota Multiphasic Personality Inventory Femininity scale. These men were sensitive and caring of their partner's needs, and thus much of their own sexual enjoyment came from perceiving of their spouse's enjoyment. Heath determined that sexual pleasure or frustration is more psychologically complicated than can be expressed in data on intercourse frequency or orgasms.

Sexual Dysfunctions. Masters and Johnson contributed significantly to the field with the publication of *Human Sexual Inadequacy* (1970). The sexual dysfunctions most common to the 301 patients at the Masters and Johnson clinic were listed as premature ejaculation, ejaculatory incompetence, female orgasmic dysfunction, vaginismus, and male and female dyspareunia. These dysfunctions were all discussed with recommendations for treatment.

Extramarital Sexuality. Johnson (1970) studied 100 middle-aged couples and found that husbands who had experienced EMS had a lower degree of sexual satisfaction and marital adjustment. Sex differences existed in opportunity, perceived desire of others for involvement, potential involvement, justification of involvement, and marital sexual satisfaction involvement. Percentages who had participated in EMS were lower than Kinsey's (1948, 1953) findings; only 20 percent of these men and 10 percent of these women had engaged in EMS. These couples as a group were well educated and had stable marriages.

Bell, Turner, and Rosen (1975) found a correlation between general liberality and EMS. Females less rooted in religion, less traditional, more sexually experimenting, more oriented to use of drugs and alcohol, and more politically liberal tended to participate more readily in EMS. Among their sample, 26 percent of women were involved in extramarital affairs, identical to the Kinsey (1953) findings.

Singh, Walton, and Williams (1976) used the Reiss-Miller model of premarital sexual permissiveness (PSP) as the basis for a model of extramarital permissiveness (ESP). Using National Opinion Research Center data gathered in 1,484 interviews, they found that about three-fourths of Americans disapproved of sexual relations outside marriage. Causal variables of ESP were found to be general liberality and PSP. They concluded that "the more liberal the person, the greater the chances of his or her approval of ESP; and that the greater the approval of PSP, the greater the approval of ESP."

Maykovich (1976) found similar results within a different context. In a comparison of the attitudes and behavior of Japanese and American women toward extramarital sexuality, Japanese women were found to engage in EMS only slightly less than American women (27 percent compared with 32 percent), though the Japanese women were more opposed to EMS than the American women were.

Edwards and Booth (1976) suggested that EMS was more greatly affected by current situation than background. Interviews of 507 persons indicated that occupation, education, and religiosity were not associated with EMS; threats by either party to leave home were positively related to EMS.

In the psychoanalytic tradition, Strean (1976) reviewed some of the pathological reasons that people engage in EMS and described the following subtypes as most common among those who become involved extramaritally: "those who experience a spouse as an incestuous object, a punitive superego figure, a partner in bisexual conflicts, or a partner in symbiosis [one whose partner also suffers from unhealthy sexual patterns]." EMS was one way of externalizing the conflict.

In their analysis of Athanasiou's (1970) data, Glass and Wright (1977) found that women's affairs were largely emotional, whereas men more often had affairs centered on sexual pleasure. Some couples engaged in EMS regardless of marital satisfaction. Among those satisfied with their marriages, only younger women participated in EMS. Among men who perceived their marriages as satisfying, older men, in their late thirties or early forties, were more likely to engage in EMS than younger men.

Bukstel and co-workers (1978) predicted involvement in EMS among the 4,017 unmarried college students in their sample. Although a longitudinal study would be required to test if the numbers they projected actually engaged in EMS once they were married, these researchers predicted that the greater number of premarital sexual partners a person had, the greater was the likelihood for EMS. Bukstel concluded that many persons engage in extramarital sex in search of emotional satisfaction and a variety of sexual experiences rather than for pathological reasons.

Walster, Traupmann, and Walster (1978) used equity theory to study EMS. They predicted that the more emotionally deprived a person felt in a relationship, the greater was the likelihood that that person would risk EMS. The theory was tested using data gathered from readers of *Psychology Today* (Bercheid, Walster, and Bohrnstedt, 1973). They concluded that persons in a marriage who felt deprived were far more likely to engage in EMS than those who were treated equitably or who were overbenefited.

Sexually Open Marriages. Cole and Spanier (1973), exploring reasons that couples become involved in mate swapping, suggested that the mate swapper "is searching for an alternative set of meanings to redefine social reality." The most common independent variables related to mate swapping were poor relations with family of orientation and low evaluation of parents' marriage.

Denfield (1974) found the following reasons for discontinuing mate swapping among 965 respondents: jealousy, guilt, threat to marriage, development of outside emotional attachments, boredom and loss of interest, disappointment, divorce or separation, wife's inability to "take it," and fear of discovery.

Among the variations of sexually open marriages identified in research was intimate friendships (IF), distinguished from other forms of sexually open marriages because of the deeper level of commitment and the long-term nature of the relationships (Ramey, 1975). IF groups were likely to join each other in business ventures. They included singles, gays, lesbians, and one partner of a marriage whose partner did not want to be involved. An interesting finding of the activities of IF groups was that the level of sexual activity fell with the length of involvement in the group.

In one study, seventeen open marriages were examined to understand this popularized life-style (Knapp, 1976). About half of the couples had satisfactory, low-conflict marriages. In these marriages, both spouses believed in the rightness of the practice for them. Four couples were dealing with conflict; one, in which the wife had initiated the practice, eventually divorced. In over half of the sexually open marriages, women admitted to being influenced by the women's movement and felt they were achieving equal social and sexual rights with their husbands.

Coital Frequency and Contraception. Using a sample of over 10,000 individuals, Westoff (1974) reported that between 1965 and 1970, the frequency of intercourse rose among contraceptive-practicing individuals; however, there was an overall rise in frequency of intercourse for all women of all ages who were using any one of a number of contraceptive measures, as well as among women who were not using contraceptives. The highest frequencies of intercourse correlated with the most effective contraceptive use, which supported the idea that contraception influences intercourse frequency. However, the overall rise in frequency for all women was interpreted as more willingness to discuss the subject.

Coital frequency tends to decrease with age (Cleveland, 1976). For many years, it was believed that males, and not females, were responsible for the decline of coital frequency with age. Udry and Morris (1978) found, however, that female and male age contribute independently to the decline. Interest level decreases for both sexes.

Marital Rape. Gelles (1977) examined the question of forcible sexual abuse in marriage. Although forced sexual intercourse may take place within a marriage, most women do not view this as rape. In studies of marital violence, Gelles found that some women were forced into having sexual relations with their husbands through intimidation of physical force.

The Decade in Review

There was a considerable amount of research on extramarital sexuality in the 1970s, but research on marital sexuality did not receive much attention (table 3–5). There were several studies of mate swapping and alternatives to sexually exclusive monogamy. Westoff (1974) contributed significant findings on the impact of contraception on frequency of intercourse. Psychological factors were studied as influences on extramarital sexuality. Theory construction expanded somewhat during the 1970s. The Edwards and Booth (1976) study looked at the social forces relating to EMS, and equity theory was applied to EMS in the Walster (1978) study. Americans were found to be more conservative regarding extramarital sexual relationships than previously assumed.

Table 3–5
Overview of Research on Marital and Extramarital Sexuality, 1970–1979

Year	*Author*	*Topic*	*Theory*	*Method*[a]	*Sample*
1970	Athanasiou and Shaver	Sexuality	None	Questionnaire-P	20,000
1970a	Johnson	Extramarital sexuality	None	Questionnaire-P	100
1970b	Johnson	Extramarital sexuality	None	Questionnaire-P	100
1970	Masters and Johnson	Sex inadequacy	None	Interview-P	301
1973	Cole and Spanier	Mate swapping	None	Questionnaire-P	579
1974	Bell	Sex expression	None	Other	
1974	Denfield	Mate swapping	None	Questionnaire-P	965
1974	Hunt	Sexuality	None	Questionnaire-P	2,026
1974	James	Frequency	None	Other	5,000+
1974	Westoff	Contraception	None	Other	10,000+
1975	Bell	Marital and extramarital sexuality	None	Questionnaire-P	2,372
1975	Bell, Turner, and Rosen	Female extramarital sexuality	None	Questionnaire-P	2,262
1975	Levin	Extramarital sexuality	None	Questionnaire-P	100,000
1975	Ramey	Intimate friendships	Mini	Questionnaire-P	380
1976	Cleveland	Frequency	None	Other	
1976	Edwards and Booth	Sex behavior	Social	Interview-P	507
1976	Knapp	Open marriage	None	Mixed	34
1976	Maykovich	Extramarital sexuality attitudes	None	Interview-P	200
1976	Singh, Walton, and Williams	Extramarital sexuality attitudes	Mini	Questionnaire-S	1,484
1976	Strean	Extramarital sexuality	Freudian	Case Study	
1977	Ard	Marital sex	None	Questionnaire-S	454
1977	Bayer	Permissiveness	None	Questionnaire-P	4,017
1977	Gelles	Marital rape	None	Mixed	40
1977	Glass and Wright	Sexuality	None	Questionnaire-S	2,000
1978	Bukstel et al.	Extramarital sexuality attitudes	None	Questionnaire-S	4,017
1978	Heath	Marital sex	None	Questionnaire-P	59
1978	Udry and Morris	Frequency	None	Other	
1978	Walster, Traupmann, and Walster	Equity and extramarital sexuality	Equity	Questionnaire-S	20,000

[a]P = primary data; S = secondary data.

The Decade 1980–1989

After the exploration of alternate marriage styles and extramarital sex in the 1970s, the 1980s focused more on marital sexuality, particularly relationships and individual rights. Marital rape emerged as a topic of both sexuality and marital violence.

Research Findings

Marital Sexuality. Trussell and Westoff (1980) interviewed 440 individuals to replicate Westoff's 1974 study. They found that among persons using effective contraceptives, the rate of intercourse frequency was higher in 1975 than in 1965 or 1970. Similarly, a study on changes in sexual desire after voluntary sterilization reported that approximately the same proportion of males and females stated an increase in sexual desire following the surgery (Bean et al., 1980). Findings from the sample of 855 persons who had been sterilized in one of four military hospitals indicated that older women were less likely to report increased sexual desire than younger women and that better-educated men were less likely than other men to report increased sexual desire after sterilization. Both the Trussell and Westoff and Bean and associates studies suggest a causal relationship between effective contraception and frequency of intercourse.

In a study of eighty-five highly educated couples, Morris and Udry (1983) found that women prefer not to have intercourse during menstruation. Because a highly educated group is less likely to be as traditional, the results surprised the researchers.

Udry (1980) studied the coital frequency of 256 couples. Women, all of them under age 30 at the beginning of the study, were interviewed in 1974, 1977, and 1978, and their husbands were interviewed in 1977 and 1978. Most of the marriages showed a decline in coital frequency. In the cases where frequency of intercourse increased, unemployment, less likelihood of wanting more children, and either use of highly effective contraceptives or change from a less effective method to a more effective method were influencing factors. The declining rates of intercourse indicated that couples who had been married the shortest length of time showed the greatest decrease in coital rates.

James (1981) studied twenty-one couples and found a rapid decline of frequency of intercourse during the early years of marriage. He called this the "honeymoon effect" and concluded that it was due to the fact that a majority in his sample were virgins at marriage.

Equity theory was applied to sexual satisfaction in recently married couples by Hatfield and co-workers (1982). Results supported the predictions that the partners in equitable marriages have greater sexual satisfaction. Emotional satisfaction, feelings of intimacy, and closeness in the sexual experience are influenced by equity. The physical enjoyment of the sexual experience, however, did not appear to be influenced by the equity of the marriage.

Perlman and Abramson (1982) studied 148 subjects and found, as Terman (1938) had earlier, that frequency of intercourse was directly related to marital satisfaction.

Expectations of coital frequency in marriage of 203 unmarried college students indicated that actual frequency of marital intercourse tends to follow expectations prior to marriage (Zeiss, 1982). However, college students tended to underestimate sexual activity among persons in their forties and sixties and had rather inflated ideas about sexual activity among persons over age 70.

Declining coital rates after the first year of marriage has been a common finding in many studies of marital sexuality. Greenblat (1983) studied the salience of sexuality among eighty persons in the early years of marriage. She found that frequency of intercourse decreased sharply after the first year of marriage. Although some persons described sex as "very important" in a marriage, they stressed that closeness, tenderness, love, companionship, and affection are more important. Greenblat concluded that the quality of the relationship was more important to most persons than sexual activity.

James (1983) and Jasso (1985) found that frequency of intercourse dropped 50 percent after the first year of marriage and then continued to decline. Both studies drew from secondary longitudinal data. James analyzed data from 100 couples surveyed by Udry; Jasso used data from the 1970 and 1975 National Fertility Surveys, which included over 2,000 couples. A variety of factors influenced the frequency of intercourse, including birth of children, pressures of work, financial worries, and growing social commitments.

Schenk, Pfrang, and Rausche (1983) studied how personality traits affected the marital sexual satisfaction of 631 couples. Personality traits had small correlations with sexual satisfaction. The quality of the relationship and the amount of interaction of the couple had high correlations with sexual satisfaction.

About 4,200 men and women ages 50 to 93 responded to a Consumer's Union questionnaire, with the findings reported in *Love, Sex, and Aging* (Brecher, 1984). Ninety-eight percent of the men and 93 percent of the women in their fifties said they were sexually active. Among persons in their sixties, the percentages were 91 and 81 percent among men and women, respectively, and they were 70 and 65 percent, respectively, for men and women over age 70. The proportion of sexually active people who usually have orgasm remained constant for women but declined somewhat among men. Perhaps the most striking aspect of the book was that it reported how the elderly compensated for hormonal changes, declining health, menopause, and other factors that deter optimal sexual activity. In most cases, older persons were willing to make any accommodation possible in order to maintain some form of sexual activity.

Pregnancy often decreases coital frequency in a marriage. Elliott and Watson (1985) interviewed 128 couples and reported a gradual decline in frequency of intercourse during pregnancy, with the sharpest decline during the third trimester. Intercourse usually resumed within the first three months postnatally and frequency increased gradually until one year after birth. Women over 30 tended to postpone resuming sexual activity longer than younger women.

Weizman and Hart (1987) studied sexual behavior of eighty-one healthy men ages 60–71. Men ages 66–71 decreased in participation in sexual intercourse but increased in the practice of masturbation in comparison with the men ages 60–65. This study asserted that "the interest in sexuality continues in elderly men, although the form of sexual expression changes from active sexual intercourse to a self-pleasuring/auto-erotic form."

Morris and co-workers (1987) examined the effects of female midcycle testosterone levels on sexual activity by taking daily blood samples of forty-three women who had regular menstrual cycles in the middle ten to fourteen days of the cycle and having the women record their temperatures daily. Both the women and their husbands responded to questionnaires. Midcycle testosterone levels were shown to affect coital frequency, which the authors conclude "is indexing some unobserved process that affects the frequency of intercourse of couples."

Biological effects on sexuality cannot be completely removed from psychological effects and preferences. Age, length of marriage, and number of children are reported as factors that can reduce preferred frequency of marital intercourse according to Doddridge, Schumm, and Bergen (1987). They contended that couples should not misinterpret decline as disinterest. Fatigue and other actors are typical occurrences that make for decline in frequency of intercourse but not necessarily in satisfaction with sex or the marriage.

McCann and Biaggio (1989) examined how sexual satisfaction relates to life meaning. Forty-eight married couples who volunteered for the study were administered the Purpose of Life Test, Personal Orientation Inventory, Selfism Scale, Sexual Interaction Inventory, and Crowne-Marlowe Social Desirability Scale. The researchers found that purpose in life and self-actualization were related to sexual satisfaction, but gender differences influenced the nature of that relationship. All aspects of sexual satisfaction, with the exception of frequency of sexual activity, were related to purpose in life and self-actualization for females. In contrast, "males high in purpose in life" tended to be more accepting of their mates. Also, male self-actualization was related to one's own pleasure and self-acceptance.

Byers and Heinlein (1989) studied sexual initiations and refusals among seventy-seven married or cohabitating individuals. Males were found to initiate or consider initiating sexual activity more often than females; however, gender appeared to make no difference in how one responded to the initiations.

Extramarital Sexuality. Reiss, Anderson, and Sponaugle (1980) studied social and cultural influences on EMS. The independent variables in their model were education, gender, age, religiosity, gender equality, political liberality, marital happiness, and premarital permissiveness. Only education, gender equality, political liberality, and premarital sexual permissiveness were significantly associated with EMS.

Medora and Burton (1981) studied attitudes toward EMS among 200 unmarried college undergraduates. They found no difference among persons who had and had not belonged to a sorority or fraternity. Males showed a significantly higher acceptance of extramarital sex.

Consequences of EMS have largely been ignored, although Buunk (1982) studied jealousy as a coping skill in dealing with a spouse's infidelity. The sample consisted of fifty men and fifty women who were aware of their spouse's infidelity. Women tended to avoid an unfaithful spouse in order to reduce jealousy. Among both men and women, avoiding a confrontation or finding ways of retaliation were more likely to be used by persons with high neuroticism scores.

Spanier and Margolis (1983) studied the benefits of EMS in adjusting to a divorce or separation. They found no relationship between EMS and separation or divorce adjustment and no support for the notion that the number of coital partners or the quality of EMS positively influenced postmarital adjustment. EMS had little impact on a person's life once separation had occurred.

Thompson (1984) studied extramarital relationships without intercourse among 162 subjects. Women were just as likely as men to develop emotional attachments outside marriage, but fewer women became involved to the point of intercourse.

Beach, Jouriles, and O'Leary (1985) examined consequences of EMS for 120 couples who sought therapy at a New York clinic. Couples who reported EMS as one of their marital problems "reported higher rates of depression and lower levels of commitment to their marriages." The spouse who had the greater commitment to the marriage was usually the faithful partner and the one to initiate the idea of seeking therapy.

Open Marriages. Open marriages were not studied as much in the 1980s as they were in the 1970s. Two of the studies examined the psychological and sociological aspects of these arrangements. Wheeler and Kilmann (1983) measured the personalities of thirty-five couples who were involved in comarital sexual behavior (CMS) and compared them to thirty-five couples who had not been involved in CMS. The CMS couples had a higher need for social approval, were more liberal in their sexual attitudes, and reported greater pleasure in their sexual relationships. Control group couples (those who did not engage in CMS) showed better conflict-resolution skills.

Jenks (1985) compared 114 mate swappers with a group of 114 non–mate swappers. The former were less likely to identify with a religion, had changed residence more often in the last five years, and had lived in their communities fewer years than the latter.

Marital Rape. Following the *Rideout* case in Oregon in 1978 (state of Oregon vs. John Rideout for forcible sexual abuse of his wife), marital rape was studied by a few researchers, with work focused on reviewing laws regarding marital rape (Finkelhor and Yllo, 1982; Jeffords and Dull, 1982). The Jeffords and Dull survey found that only 35 percent of 1,300 respondents favored a law where a wife could sue her husband for rape.

Factors correlated with marital rape were absence of time spent in recreational activities together, great financial stress, and marriages in which the husband placed a low value on the children. It was estimated that marital rape was experienced by about one of eight battered wives (Bowker, 1983).

Frieze (1983), reported that women who suffered marital rape and wife battering were more severely damaged psychologically than women who had been battered but not raped by their husbands.

Jeffords (1984) reported that only twenty-nine of the fifty states had marital rape laws. He found that persons with traditional sex role attitudes were much less likely to believe that forced marital intercourse is undesirable. Jeffords claimed that such attitudes "prevent the needed social change of not allowing forced sexual relations under any circumstances."

Sigler and Haygood (1989) surveyed 166 college students about their attitudes toward marital rape laws. About 57 percent of the subjects endorsed "either the passage of a statute making forced marital intercourse a felony or a passage of a statute making it a misdemeanor offense."

The Decade in Review

Theory and Methodology. The Reiss model produced a framework for future theory building of causal factors of EMS. Many of the studies used secondary or demographic data, turning away from the newsstand magazine data collection. More integrity and less bias in studies was present in the 1980s. (Table 3-6 contains an overview of the research.)

Key Findings. Contraception was positively associated with frequency of intercourse. Frequency of intercourse declined with age. Frequency of intercourse was highest during the first year of marriage and declined to about half that in the second year of marriage, and about half of that by the twelfth year of marriage.

Table 3–6
Overview of Research on Marital and Extramarital Sexuality, 1980–1989

Year	*Author*	*Topic*	*Theory*	*Method*[a]	*Sample*
1980	Bean et al.	Sterilization	None	Interview-P	855
1980	Reiss, Anderson, and Sponaugle	Permissiveness	Mini	Interview-S	
1980	Trussell and Westoff	Frequency	None	Interview-S	440
1980	Udry	Frequency	None	Interview-P	512
1981	James	Frequency	None	Other	42
1981	Medora and Burton	Extramarital sexuality attitudes	None	Questionnaire-P	200
1982	Buunk	Extramarital sexuality coping	None	Questionnaire-P	100
1982	Hatfield et al.	Equity in marriage	Equity	Interview-P	236
1982	Finkelhor and Yllo	Marital rape	None	Interview-S	
1982	Jeffords and Dull	Marital rape	None	Questionnaire-P	1,300
1982	Perlman and Abramson	Marital sex	None	Questionnaire-P	148
1982	Zeiss	Sex and aging	None	Questionnaire-P	203
1983	Bowker	Marital rape	None	Interview-P	146
1983	Frieze	Marital rape	None	Interview-P	137
1983	Greenblat	Marital sex	None	Interview-P	80
1983	James	Frequency	None	Interview-S	200
1983	Morris and Udry	Marital sex	None	Case study	170
1983	Schenk, Pfrang, and Rausche	Personality and sex	None	Questionnaire-P	1,262
1983	Spanier and Margolis	Separation and extramarital coitus	None	Interview-S	205
1983	Wheeler and Kilman	Mate swapping	None	Questionnaire-P	140
1984	Jeffords	Marital rape	None	Questionnaire-P	267
1984	Thompson	Extramarital sexuality	None	Questionnaire-P	162
1985	Beach, Jouriles, and O'Leary	Extramarital sexuality	None	Questionnaire-P	240
1985	Elliott and Watson	Frequency	None	Mixed	256
1985	Jenks	Mate swapping	Mini	Questionnaire-P	228
1985	Jasso	Frequency	None	Other	2,000+
1985	Weingourt	Marital rape	None	Interview-S	930
1986	Buunk and Bosman	Attitude	None	Questionnaire-P	81
1987	Doddridge, Schumm, and Bergen	Frequency	None	Questionnaire-S	138
1987	Morris et al.	Frequency	None	Mixed	43
1987	Weizman and Hart	Sex and aging	None	Questionnaire-P	81
1988	Sigler and Haygood	Marital rape	None	Questionnaire-P	166

[a] P = primary data; S = secondary data.

Overall Review

Researchers of the past six decades have repeatedly discovered that sex in marriage tends to follow certain patterns: a decline in frequency of sexual intercourse as couples grow older and a marked decline after the first year of marriage. The level of satisfaction with sex in marriage may be just as great at older ages as it is among the young, however.

The majority of persons disapprove of sexual relations outside of the marriage. Kinsey's (1948) estimate that 50 percent of married men who had engaged in EMS appears a little high compared to Johnson's (1970) findings of 20 percent, Athanasiou, Shaver, and Travis's (1970) findings of 40 percent, and Hunt's (1974) findings of 41 percent. Studies of EMS among women show greater variation. Kinsey (1953) estimated 26 percent of women had engaged in EMS; Athanasiou, Shaver, and Travis (1970) found 36 percent; Johnson (1970), 10 percent; Hunt (1974), 18 percent; Bell, Turner, and Rosen (1975), 26 percent; Levin (1975), 39 percent; and Maykovich (1976), 32 percent of American women. Attitude toward EMS is the accommodating factor as to how it will affect the marriage. Whatever a couple agrees to, they seem to adapt to.

The following findings are significant:

1. Frequency of intercourse declines with age.
2. After the first year of marriage, frequency of intercourse declines by about half and then half again after about the twelfth year of marriage.
3. Declines in frequency of intercourse over time do not detract from sexual satisfaction.
4. Sexual satisfaction within marriage is a qualitative rather than a quantitative factor.
5. Factors affecting intercourse frequency are contraceptive practices, stress, birth of children, and career demands.
6. A greater percentage of men than women engage in extramarital sexual intercourse.
7. Factors positively related to EMS are greater liberality, younger age, lower education, male gender, and opportunity.
8. Most persons do not approve of EMS whether they have engaged in it or not.
9. EMS does not appear to help post-marital (after marriage has dissolved) adjustment.
10. Attitude seems to have the strongest predictive value in EMS behavior.

Future Research

More theory construction is needed in studies of sexuality. As findings become more systematically integrated, the possibility of theory construction is more feasible.

New findings in biology will undoubtedly influence sex research. As more is uncovered about hormonal influence and chemical imbalances, scientists will need to look at these influences, both physically and psychologically. The HIV virus causing AIDS, as well as the more than twenty other known venereal diseases, will most likely influence sexual behavior.

Much has been said about the causal factors of extramarital sexuality, but little has been investigated concerning the consequences, an area that offers many opportunities for exploration.

Work on issues, such as marital rape, is likely to continue, as well as a feminist focus on the quality of relationships. There will probably be a greater sorting out of the emotional, as opposed to the physical, aspects of sexuality. Scientific investigation will continue to have an impact on the sexual expression of human lives.

References

Ard, B.N., Jr. 1977. Sex in lasting marriages: A longitudinal study. *Journal of Sex Research* 13 (4):274–285.

Athanasiou, R., and Shaver, P. 1969. A questionnaire on sex. *Psychology Today* 3:64–69.

Athanasiou, R.; Shaver, P.; and Travis, C. 1970. Sex: A report to *Psychology Today* readers. *Psychology Today* 4:39–52.

Bayer, A.E. 1977. Sexual permissiveness and correlates as determined through interaction analysis. *Journal of Marriage and the Family* 39: 29–40.

Beach, S.R.H.; Jouriles, E.N.; and O'Leary, D. 1985. Extramarital sex: Impact on depression and commitment in couples seeking marital therapy. *Journal of Sex and Marital Therapy* 11 (2):99–108.

Bean, F.D.; Clark, M.P.; South, S.; Swicegood, G.; and Williams, D. 1980. Changes in sexual desire after voluntary sterilization. *Social Biology* 27 (3):186–193.

Bell, R.R. 1964. Some factors related to the sexual satisfaction of the college educated wife. *Family Life Coordinator* 13 (2):43–47.

———. 1974. Married sex: How uninhibited can a woman dare to be? *Redbook* 143 (5):75ff.

———. 1975. How do you really feel about sex? *Redbook* 143 (6):89–91.

Bell, R.R.; Turner, S.; and Rosen, L. 1975. A multivariate analysis of female extramarital coitus. *Journal of Marriage and the Family* 37:375–383.

Berscheid, E.; Walster, E.; and Bohrnstedt, G. 1973. The body image report. *Psychology Today* 7:119–131.

Blazer, J.A. 1964. Married virgins—a study of unconsummated marriages. *Journal of Marriage and the Family* 26 (2):13–14.

Bowerman, C.E. 1957. Adjustment in marriage: Over-all and in specific areas. *Sociology and Social Research* 41 (3):257–263.

Bowker, L.H. 1983. Marital rape in marriage. *Social Casework* 64 (6):347–348.

Brav, S. 1947. Notes on honeymoons. *Marriage and Family Living* 9 (3):237–240.

Brecher, E.M., and Editors of Consumer Reports Books. 1984. *Love, Sex, and Aging.* Boston: Little, Brown.

Bukstel, L.H.; Roeder, G.D.; Kilmann, P.R.; Laughlin, J.; and Sotile, W.M. 1978. Projected extramarital involvement in unmarried college students. *Journal of Marriage and the Family* 40 (2):337–340.

Burgess, E.W., and Cottrell, L.S. 1936. The prediction of adjustment in marriage. *American Sociological Review* 1:737–751.

Buunk, B. 1982. Strategies of jealousy: Styles of coping with extramarital involvement of the spouse. *Family Relations* 31 (1):13–18.

Buunk, B., and Bosman, J. 1986. Attitude similarity and attraction in marital relationships. *Journal of Social Psychology* 126 (1):133–134.

Byers, E.S., and Heinlein, L. 1989. Predicting initiations and refusals of sexual activities in married and cohabitating heterosexual couples. *Journal of Sex Research* 26 (2):210–231.

Clark, A.L., and Wallin, P. 1964. The accuracy of husbands' and wives' report of the frequency of marital coitus. *Population Studies* 18:165–173.

———. 1965. Women's sexual responsiveness and the duration and quality of their marriages. *American Journal of Sociology* 71 (2):187–196.

Cleveland, M. 1976. Sex in marriage: At 40 and beyond. *Family Coordinator* 25 (3): 233–240.

Cole, C.L., and Spanier, G. 1973. Introduction into mate swapping: A review. *Family Process* 12 (3):270–290.

Davis, K.B. 1929. *Factors in the Sex Life of Twenty-two Hundred Women.* New York: Harper & Brothers.

Denfield, D. 1974. Dropouts from swinging. *Family Coordinator* 23 (1):45–49.

Dentler, R.A., and Pineo, P. 1960. Marital adjustment and personal growth of husbands: A panel analysis. *Marriage and the Family* 22:45–48.

Dickenson, R.L., and Beam, L. 1931. *A Thousand Marriages.* Baltimore: Williams & Wilkins.

Doddridge, R.; Schumm, W.R.; and Bergen, B. 1987. Factors related to decline in preferred frequency of sexual intercourse among young couples. *Psychological Reports* 60:391–395.

Edwards, J.N., and Booth, A. 1976. Sexual behavior in and out of marriage: An assessment of correlates. *Journal of Marriage and Family Living* 38 (1):73–83.

Elliott, S.A., and Watson, J.P. 1985. Sex during pregnancy and the first postnatal year. *Journal of Psychosomatic Research* 29 (5):541–548.

Ellis, A. 1953. Marriage counseling with couples indicating sexual incompatibility. *Marriage and Family Living* 15 (1):53–58.

Ellis, H. 1933. *Psychology of Sex.* New York: Emerson Books.

Finkelhor, D., and Yllo K. 1982. Forced sex in marriage: A preliminary research report. *Crime and Delinquency* 28:459–478.

Folsom, J.K. 1937. Changing values in sex and family relations. *American Sociological Review* 2 (1):717–726.

Foote, N.N. 1954. Sex as play. *Social Problems* 1 (1):159–163.

Frieze, I.H. 1983. Investigating the causes and consequences of marital rape. *Signs* 8 (3):532–553.

Gebhard, P.E. 1966. Factors in marital orgasm. *Journal of Social Issues* 22:88–95.

Gelles, R.J. 1977. Power sex and violence: The case of marital rape. *Family Coordinator* 26 (4):339–347.

Glass, S.P., and Wright, T.L. 1977. The relationship of extramarital sex, length of marriage, and sex differences on marital satisfaction and romanticism: Athanasiou's data reanalyzed. *Journal of Marriage and the Family* 39 (4):691–703.

Greenblat, C.S. 1983. The salience of sexuality in the early years of marriage. *Journal of Marriage and Family Living* 45 (2):289–299.

Hamilton, G.V. 1929. *A Research in Marriage.* New York: Boni.

Hatfield, E.; Greenberger, D.; Traupmann, J.; and Lambert, P. 1982. Equity and sexual satisfaction in recently married couples. *Journal of Sex Research* 18 (1):18–32.

Heath, D.H. 1978. Marital sexual enjoyment and frustration of professional men. *Archives of Sexual Behavior* 7 (5):463–476.

Hite, S. 1981. *The Hite Report: A Nationwide Study of Female Sexuality.* New York: Dell.

Hunt, M. 1974. *Sexual Behavior in the 1970's.* Chicago: Playboy Press.

James, W.H. 1974. Marital coital rates, spouses' ages, family size, and social class. *The Journal of Sex Research* 10 (3):205–218.

———. 1981. The honeymoon effect on marital coitus. *Journal of Sex Research* 17 (2): 114–123.

———. 1983. Decline in coital rates with spouses' ages and duration of marriage. *Journal of Biosocial Science* 15 (1):83–87.

Jasso, G. 1985. Marital coital frequency and the effects of spouses' ages and marital duration, birth and marriage cohorts, and period influences. *American Sociological Review* 50:224–241.

Jeffords, C.R. 1984. The impact of sex-role and religious attitudes upon force marital intercourse norms. *Sex Roles* 2 (5–6):543–552.

Jeffords, C.R., and Dull, R.T. 1982. Demographic variations in attitudes toward marital rape immunity. *Journal of Marriage and the Family* 44 (3):755–762.

Jenks, R.J. 1985. Swinging: A test of two theories and a proposed new model. *Archives of Sexual Behavior* 12 (4):295–307.

Johnson, R.E. 1970a. Extramarital sexual intercourse: A methodological note. *Journal of Marriage and the Family,* 32 (2):279–282.

———. 1970b. Some correlates of extramarital coitus. *Journal of Marriage and the Family* 32 (3):449–455.

Kanin, E.J., and Howard, D.H. 1958. Postmarital consequences of premarital sex adjustments. *American Sociological Review* 23:556–562.

Kelly, E.L. 1937. A preliminary report on psychological factors in assortive mating. *Psychology Bulletin* 34:749.

Kephart, W.M. 1954. Some cases in reported sexual maladjustment. *Marriage and Family Living* 16 (3):241–243.

King, C.E. 1947. Notes on honeymoons. *Marriage and Family Living* 9 (3):60, 65.

———. 1954. The sex factor in marital adjustment. *Marriage and Family Living* 16 (3): 237–240.

Kinsey, A.C.; Pomeroy, W.B.; and Martin, C.E. 1948. *Sexual Behavior in the Human Male.* Philadelphia: W.B. Saunders.

Kinsey, A.C.; Pomeroy, W.B.; Martin, C.E.; and Gebhard, P.E. 1953. *Sexual Behavior in the Human Female.* Philadelphia: W.B. Saunders.

Knapp, J.J. 1976. An exploratory study of seventeen sexually open marriages. *The Journal of Sex Research* 12 (3):206–219.

Landis, J.T. 1947. Adjustments after marriage. *Marriage and Family Living* 9 (2):32–34.

Landis, J.T.; Poffenberger, T.; and Poffenberger, S. 1950. The effects of first pregnancy upon the sexual adjustment of 212 couples. *American Sociological Review* 15:766–772.

Levin, R.J. 1975. The *Redbook* report on premarital and extramarital sex. *Redbook* (October) 145:38ff.

Levinger, G. 1966. Systematic distortion of spouses' reports of preferred and sexual behavior. *Sociometry* 29 (3):291–299.

Masters, W.H., and Johnson, V.E. 1966. *Human Sexual Response.* Boston: Little, Brown.

———. 1970. *Human Sexual Inadequacy.* Boston: Little, Brown.

Matthews, V.D., and Mihanovich, C.S. 1963. New orientations on marital maladjustment. *Marriage and Family Living* 25 (3):300–304.

Maykovich, M.K. 1976. Attitudes versus behavior in extramarital sexual relations. *Journal of Marriage and the Family* 36 (4): 693–699.

McCann, J.T., and Biaggio, M.K. 1989. Sexual satisfaction in marriage as a function of life meaning. *Archives of Sexual Behavior* 18 (1):59–71.

Medora, N.P., and Burton, M.M. 1981. Extramarital sexual attitudes and norms of an undergraduate-student population. *Adolescence* 16 (62):251–262.

Morris, N.M., and Udry, R. 1981. Menstruation and marital sex. *Journal of Biosocial Science* 15:173–181.

Morris, N.M.; Udry, J.R.; Khan-Dawood, F.; Daywood, M.Y. 1987. Marital sex frequency and midcycle female testosterone. *Archives of Sexual Behavior* 16 (1):27–37.

Mowrer, H.R. 1935. *Personality Adjustment and Domestic Discord.* New York: American Book Co.

Neubeck, G., and Schletzer, V.M. 1962. A study of extra-marital relationships. *Marriage and Family Living* 24 (30):279–281.

Perlman, S.D., and Abramson, P.R. 1982. Sexual satisfaction among married and cohabitating individuals. *Journal of Consulting and Clinical Psychology* 50 (3): 458–468.

Rainwater, L. 1964. Marital sexuality in four cultures of poverty. *Journal of Marriage and the Family* 26 (4):457–466.

———. 1965. *Family Design.* Chicago: Aldine Publishing Co.

Ramey, J.W. 1975. Intimate groups and networks: Frequent consequence of sexually open marriage. *Family Coordinator* 24:515–530.

Reinemann, J.O. 1945. Extra-marital relations with the fellow employee in the war industry as a factor in the disruption of family life. *American Sociological Review* 10:399–404.

Reiss, I.L.; Anderson, R.E.; and Sponaugle, G.C. 1980. A multivariate model of the determinants of extramarital sexual permissiveness. *Journal of Marriage and the Family* 42 (2):395–409.

Rubin, A.M., and Adams, J.R. 1986. Outcomes of sexually open marriages. *Journal of Sex Research* 22 (3):311–319.

Saunders, J.M., and Edwards, J.N. 1984. Extramarital sexuality: A predictive model of permissive attitudes. *Journal of Marriage and the Family* 46 (1):825–836.

Schenk, J.; Pfrang, H.; and Rausche, A. 1983. Personality traits versus the quality of the marital relationship as the determinant of marital sexuality. *Archives of Sexual Behavior* 12 (1):31–42.

Sigler, R.T., and Haygood, D. 1988. The criminalization of forced marital intercourse. *Marriage and Family Review* 12:71–85.

Singh, B.K.; Walton, B.L.; and Williams, J.S. 1976. Extramarital sexual permissiveness: Conditions and contingencies. *Journal of Marriage and the Family* 38 (4):701–712.

Spanier, G.B., and Margolis, R.L. 1983. Marital separation and extramarital sexual behavior. *The Journal of Sex Research* 19 (1):23–48.

Stokes, W.R. 1951. A marriage counseling case: The married virgin. *Marriage and the Family* 13:29–34.

Strean, H.S. 1976. The extramarital affair: A psychoanalytic view. *Psychoanalytic View* 63 (1):101–113.

Terman, L.M. 1938. *Psychological Factors of Marital Happiness.* New York: McGraw-Hill.

———. 1951. Correlates of orgasm adequacy in a group of 556 wives. *Journal of Psychology* 32:115–172.

Terman, L.M., and Johnson, W.B. 1939. Methodology and results of recent studies in marital adjustment. *American Sociological Review* 4 (3):307–324.

Thomason, B. 1955. Extent of spousal agreement on certain non-sexual and sexual aspects of marital adjustment. *Marriage and Family Living* 17 (4):332–337.

Thompson, A.P. 1984. Emotional and sexual components of extramarital relations. *Journal of Marriage and the Family* 46 (10):35–40.

Trussell, J., and Westoff, C.F. 1980. Contraceptive practice and trends in coital frequency. *Family Planning Perspectives* 12 (5):246–249.

Udry, J.R. 1980. Changes in the frequency of marital intercourse from panel data. *Archives of Sexual Behavior* 9 (4):319–325.

Udry, J.R., and Morris, N.M. 1978. Relative contribution of male and female age to the frequency of marital intercourse. *Social Biology* 25 (2):128–134.

Wallin, P., and Clark, A.L. 1963. A study of orgasm as a condition of women's enjoyment of coitus in the middle years of marriage. *Human Biology* 35 (2):131–139.

Walster, E.; Traupmann, J.; and Walster, G.W. 1978. Equity and extramarital sexuality. *Archives of Sexual Behavior* 7 (2):127–142.

Watson, G., and Green, G. 1932. Scientific studies and personal opinion on sex questions. *Journal of Abnormal and Social Psychology* 27:130–146.

Weingourt, R. 1985. Wife rape: Barriers to identification and treatment. *American Journal of Psychotherapy* 39 (2):187–192.

Weizman, R., and Hart, J. 1987. Sexual behavior in healthy married elderly men. *Archives of Sexual Behavior* 16 (1):27–37.

Westoff, C.S. 1974. Coital frequency and contraception. *Family Planning Perspectives* 6 (3):136–141.

Wheeler, J., and Kilmann, P.R. 1983. Comarital sexual behavior: Individual and relationship variables. *Archives of Sexual Behavior* 12 (4):295–307.

Whitehurst, R.N. 1969. Extramarital sex: Alienation or extension of normal behavior. In G. Neubeck (ed.), *Extramarital Relations.* Englewood Cliffs, N.J.: Prentice-Hall.
Zeiss, A.M. 1982. Expectations for the effects of aging on sexuality in parents and average married couples. *Journal of Sex Research* 18 (1):39–45.

4
Family Interaction Patterns and Communication Processes

Gary L. Steggell
James M. Harper

Researchers who have studied family interaction and family communication have assumed that identifiable patterns and processes occur in the family system and influence the development and maintenance of normal and dysfunctional behaviors both inside and outside the family. The purpose of this chapter is to examine interaction and communication patterns, processes, and structures as they relate to the development of the individual and to the development of function and dysfunction within the family.

Several reviews of research in this area have been conducted, most of them focusing on family interaction patterns (Aldous, 1977; Eisler, Dare, and Szmukler, 1988; Glick, and Gross, 1975; Jacob, 1975; Portes, Mas, and Dunham, 1986), with others concerned specifically with family communication processes (Rausch, Greif, and Nugent, 1979). This review integrates family interaction and family communication concepts and evaluates the substance and methodology of reported research. Specific subtopics of review are family and marital interaction, communication, patterns, processes, structure, decision making, problem solving, husband-wife relations, parent-child relations, and interpersonal communication.[1]

The Decade 1930–1939

We found six articles that described family interaction research during this decade. The topics of research were the effect of family interaction on child development and adjustment, alcoholism, and success in the family.

Research Findings

Parent-Child Studies. Pressey (1931) examined 500 case records of college students who were on academic probation for deleterious psychological or sociological aspects of home life and concluded that these students had come from homes in which parents would not let their children grow up and away from them. These parents were too emotionally attached to their children, and the children, in turn, were too dependent on them.

Hattick and Stowell (1936) investigated the influence of parental overattentiveness on the performance and social adjustment of 146 elementary school children. They inspected school records for evidence of children who were being "babied" or unduly pushed by their parents and reported that these children had poorer social adjustment and poorer work habits than children who were not babied or pushed. The former also tended to develop more social difficulties and poorer work habits as they progressed through school.

DuVall (1936) probed for factors that influenced parent-child interaction among 458 "average" and "underprivileged" teenagers. Among the results reported were that average children were closer to their parents than underprivileged children, boys and girls were closer to their mothers than to their fathers, girls were closer to both parents than boys were, and younger children were closer to parents than older children were.

Stott (1939) surveyed 1,855 high school students from Nebraska in order to define important family life patterns and the relationship of these patterns to personality development. Two universal patterns were found: "confidence, affection and companionability" and "family discord." The author concluded that children from families characterized by the former pattern were superior in personal adjustment, independence, appreciatory attitude toward home life, and personality development in general. Children from families characterized by family discord were less well adjusted to life and were less appreciative of their home environment.

Family Studies. Using concepts from psychodynamic theory, Wittman (1939) descriptively analyzed differences between families of 100 male alcoholic hospital patients and 100 male nonalcoholic volunteers. The author deduced from the findings that chronic alcoholics were not a homogeneous group and that no one element was characteristic of the entire group. However, some family interactions did differentiate the alcoholic from the control group: a domineering but idealized mother and a stern, autocratic father whom the subject feared as a child; a marked degree of strict, unquestioning obedience demanded by the family; and a definitely expressed and disproportionately greater love for mother than for father.

Thurow (1934) examined 200 autobiographies of college students in order to establish some criteria for successful family interaction. Two general factors emerged from the analysis: "tension in the family" and "satisfaction with family pattern." Ten types of specific family interactions had high degree of association with the positive factor and were labeled as criteria for successful families: (1) little tension between parents and between parents and children, (2) much family affection, (3) much entertaining of friends and relatives in the house, (4) husband and wife attending social functions together, (5) much consensus on discipline, (6) little dominance of father in home, (7) medium to much family counseling, (8) little to medium disciplining, (9) medium supervision of child's activities by both parents, and (10) medium to much confidence of children in parents.

The Decade in Review

Theory and Methodology. The six studies reviewed from this period were based on survey questionnaires and case history analyses (table 4–1). Much is lacking methodologically in these studies in comparison to more recent research. For example, although the studies employed sample sizes ranging from 146 to 1,855 subjects, they were mainly convenience samples and not representative of any general population. Also, little information was provided in any of the articles concerning the demographic makeup of subjects; only Hattwick and Stowell (1936) speficied their sampling method.

Only two of the reviewed articles utilized statistical analyses of their data; Thurow (1934) used contingency analysis, and Stott (1939) utilized factor analysis. Both researchers outlined the specific components of their analyses and provided reference citations for more information as well. The other four authors provided no information concerning the statistical tests that they may have used and presented their results as either percentages or informed opinions.

For most of this early research, little reference was made to previous work. One of the articles had fifteen references (Wittman, 1939), one had eight (Stott, 1939), one had three (Thurow, 1934), and the others had none. Only Wittman (1939) employed theory in guiding the research.

Key Studies and General Findings. The most notable research from the decade was that reported by Stott (1939). Although no theory or sampling methods were described, this was not uncharacteristic of most of the research reviewed from the 1930s. Stott included questionnaire items used in the study and linked the project to previous research. Statistical analysis was also used to confirm the results, and specific limitations of the study were presented.

For the decade in general, specific interaction patterns were found to be associated with both positive and negative development within the family. Beneficial family patterns included little tension between parents, much affection, little dominance and controlling behavior by parents, husband-wife consensus on child discipline, and sharing of home and outside activities. Family interactions found to be negatively associated with development were chronic dissension, little or excessive expression of affection, and overattentiveness to and dominance by parents of children.

The Decade 1940–1949

Parent-child studies made up the bulk of the research reviewed in this decade. Twenty articles dealt with child development and adjustment, conflict, court-

Table 4–1
Overview of Research on Family Interaction Patterns, 1930–1939

Year	*Author*	*Topic*	*Theory*	*Method*	*Sample*[a]	*Strengths*[a]
1931	Pressey	Academic achievement	None	Case study	500	
1934	Thurow	Family success	None	Case study	200	St,I
1936	DuVall	Child-parent distance	None	Questionnaire–P	458	M
1936	Hatwick and Stowell	Social adjustment	None	Case study	146	St
1939	Stott	Personality development	None	Questionnaire–P	1855	S,M,St,I
1939	Wittman	Alcoholism	Psychodynamic	Interview–P	200	M,T,I

[a]S = sample; M = measurement of variables; St = statistics; T = use of theory; I = importance, uniqueness.

ship behavior, delinquency, mother-child behavior, psychiatric disorders, sex differences, and schizophrenia. There were also three marital interaction articles concerning authority patterns and conflict and three articles examining general family communication and interaction.

Research Findings

Child Adjustment. Lurie and co-workers (1943) explored the importance of specific exogenous home and neighborhood factors in producing behavior and personality disorders in 400 children referred to a child guidance home. Home factors were divided into two categories: medical and sociopsychological. In the majority of case records reviewed, they found nine or more pertinent home factors involved in the development of the child problems. The sociopsychological factors—lack of proper supervision, oversolicitation, rejection, poor problem-solving skills, low moral standards, sexual promiscuity, delinquency, and nonreligious status—outweighed medical ones by a four-to-one ratio.

Woolf (1943) ascertained the relationship between home adjustment and the behavior of 211 women college students. Home adjustment was defined by parental emotional stability, parental understanding of subjects, expressions of parental authority, and subjects' response to these parental factors. Women with poor home adjustment were observed to express hate more, mope by themselves more, cut class more, be more self-conscious, express more feelings of inferiority, express more prejudice, be unable to make friends as easily, express more fears, sulk and pout more, and be more spiteful than subjects with good home adjustment.

Baruch and Wilcox (1944), using seventy-six children and their parents as subjects, inquired into the effect of parental tensions on child adjustment. They described five wife-husband interactions negatively related to child adjustment: tensions over sex, lack of consideration, inability to talk over differences to a mutually acceptable solution, lack of expressed affection, and an ascendant-submissive relationship. These parental factors were reported to have a more pronounced effect on the adjustment of girls than of boys.

Banister and Ravden (1944) explored the association of home environment with the problems of 112 children at a child guidance clinic in England. They categorized homes into four types: accord—both parents alive and living amicably together; discord—both parents alive and living together but with evidence of discord; one parent dead; and other broken home—parents divorced, separated, or child adopted or in an institution. Child problems were also classified into four types: delinquent—stealing, pilfering, and lying; aggressive—destructive, angry, and "beyond control"; nervous—fearful, restless, unhappy, and having speech, feeding, and sex difficulties; and backward—daydreaming, unable to concentrate, sulky, and stupid. Inadequate or improper discipline was found in 66 percent of all cases, and lack of affection and overprotectiveness were identified with nervous problems. The authors concluded that nervous problems were associated with accord homes, and delinquency was associated with other broken homes.

Meyer (1947), with a sample of twenty-nine families, researched the relationship between parental behavior and children's behavior with peers. Children were more likely to show dominating, noncooperative peer behavior if in the home there was friction over discipline, restrictions on child behavior, general home discord, many coercive suggestions from parents, parental dissatisfaction with the children's behavior, little rapport between children and parents, little parental understanding, and an unwillingness of parents to give desired explanations to natural questions from the children.

Baldwin published four articles on the effects of parental behaviors on the developing child (Baldwin, Kalhorn, and Breese, 1945; Baldwin, 1946, 1947, 1948). Parent behavior was observed in the home and cooled using the Fels Parent Behavior Scales. The researchers focused on democracy in the home and how it influenced children. Three major conclusions were presented from the data. First, the predominant effect of parent-child interaction on the socialization of the child was to raise or lower the child's willingness and ability to behave actively toward the environment. Second, freedom and permissiveness with a high level of positive parent-child interaction permitted the child to become active, outgoing, and spontaneous. And third, habitual expressiveness in the child resulted when the parents spontaneously expressed warmth and emotionality and when the child's attempts to establish emotional contacts with other people were greeted with warmth and reciprocation.

Mother-Child Behavior. In the first experimental project of family interaction, Merrill (1946) investigated the consistency of mother-child behavior from one experimental session to another. Using stimulus-response learning theory as a framework, the author examined the effect of pressure applied to thirty mothers, in the form of increased motivation for their children to perform well, as well as individual differences in mother-child behavior. Mother's behavior was observed and coded in terms of the degree of contact between mother and child and the degree of maternal control. The major results were that the control group mothers' behavior did not change from the first to the second session; the experimental group mothers showed a significant increase at the second session in directing, interfering, criticizing, and structuring-a-change-in-activity types of behavior; and each mother presented a unique pattern of behavior.

Parent-Child Conflict. Dinkel (1943) analyzed the conflict between aged parents and their offspring and determined the factors associated with that conflict. It was found that twenty-one of the fifty parents interviewed reported conflicts that interfered with their relationship with at least one of their children. The attitude of these parents was noted as one of bitterness. The major conflict for subjects was a clash between rural and urban cultures, and families were found to have similar levels of conflict over the life span. Family interactions associated with reported conflicts were quarrels between parents and noncooperation between parents in child rearing techniques as their children were growing up.

Punke (1943) examined the frequency and subject matter of quarrels between the parents of youth and between youth and their parents, using as subjects 7,021 high school students from nine states. Three results stood out among the many descriptive findings presented: only one-third of the youths reported quarreling in their families; quarrels between parents centered on economic matters, the social life of children, and the parents' personal habits; and the most common causes of quarrels between youths and parents were economic matters and the youth's social life and friends.

Delinquency. Zucker produced two studies (1943a, 1943b) relating parent-child interaction to delinquency in children. The first evaluated emotional parental attachment and its relation to the delinquent behavior of twenty-five delinquent and twenty-five nondelinquent teenage boys. Delinquents were less attached to their parents than nondelinquents. It was also found that parental moral training was less effective in the delinquent group than the nondelinquent group, and weak attachment to parents resulted in less effective parental moral training in both groups.

Zucker (1943b) also explored the degree of affectional identification between children and their parents and the association between that identification and delinquent behavior. Major findings were that fewer delinquents showed affectional attachment to their parents than nondelinquents, parents of delinquents reacted more frequently to child problems in a manner that disturbed affectional relationships, and all subjects with poor affectional relationships with their parents reported that they responded to punishment by participating in activities that irritated their parents.

Schizophrenia. Tietze (1949) used a psychodynamic perspective to study the personality characteristics, maternal attitudes, and behavior patterns of twenty-five mothers of adult schizophrenic patients. All mothers were overprotective, obsessive, and domineering in their interactions with their schizophrenic child. They were restrictive in regard to the "libidinal gratification" of their children and were perfectionistic, oversolicitous, and dependent on the approval of others. Rejection of the child, either overt or "subtle," was the key negative factor found in the mother-child relationship.

Lidz and Lidz (1949) evaluated the frequency with which disturbed family environments were associated with schizophrenia by surveying hospital records of fifty schizophrenic patients for five factors: (1) deprivation of parent, (2) chronic instability of parent, (3) chronic hostility or serious friction between parents, (4) serious deviation from cultural norms in child rearing, and (5) mental illness in the history of the family. Only five of the fifty patients were raised in homes that seemed reasonably favorable and contained two stable parents. Of the remaining subjects, twenty had lost a parent by death or separation prior to their nineteenth birthday (in nine cases this loss was due to a serious emotional illness of one parent), twenty had parents who were "incompatible," twenty-three had at least one parent who was "grossly instable," and eighteen had been raised in a manner described as "clearly bizarre or deleterious."

Marital Authority Patterns. Ingersoll (1948) examined the process by which authority patterns were transmitted from the parental families of thirty-seven couples in their own present family patterns. The authority roles learned by individuals in their families of origin tended to be reenacted if expectations of both partners were complementary, influenced by other personal or situational factors, and modified through interaction if expectations differed in the subject's current family.

Marital Conflict. Pace (1940) investigated the areas of disagreement between 584 young adult husbands and wives. The three most frequent topics of disagreement were management of income (17 percent of males, 19 percent of females), relatives (16 percent of males, 20 percent of females), and recreation (16 percent of males, 14 percent of females).

Family Communication. Bossard (1943, 1945) proposed that family table talk was a form of family interaction, a vehicle for transmission of family culture, and an area for sociological study. Very little information was provided as to methodology and procedure. Although these two articles represent perhaps the weakest methodology of this decade, they were notable for two reasons. First, they were the first record of direct observation of family interaction as a method of sociological study, and second, they were the first to indicate that family communication is an important form of family interaction.

Family Interaction. Fitzsimmons and Perkins (1947) described the nature of interrelationships that prevailed in fifty prosperous farm families in Illinois. Four family interaction patterns were seen in over fifty percent of the families: the families shared in planning and management, they knew what they wanted and made plans to get it, there was marked family cohesiveness, and cooperation and team work predominated in management and planning.

The Decade in Review

Theory and Methodology. Some theory was identified in eight of the twenty-six reviewed articles, indicating that theory had become a more important element in the development of research in this decade. Psychodynamic theory was the most prevalent, with four researchers reporting its use (table 4–2).

Table 4–2
Overview of Research on Family Interaction Patterns 1940–1949

Year	*Author*	*Topic*	*Theory*	*Method*[a]	*Sample*	*Strengths*[b]
1940	Pace	Family conflict	None	Questionnaire-P	584	M
1941	Bolles, Metzger, and Pitts	Emotional adjustment	None	Interview-P	295	S
1942	Bates	Courtship behavior	None	Interview-P	201	
1943	Bossard	Family conversations	None	Direct observation	N.A.	I
1943	Dinkel	Older persons	None	Interview-P	50	St
1943	Lurie et al.	Personality disorders	None	Case study	400	S
1943	Punke	Family conflict	None	Questionnaire-P	7,021	S,M
1943	Winch	Courtship behavior	Psychodynamic	Questionnaire-P	435	S,M,St,T
1943	Woolf	Social adjustment	None	Questionnaire-P	211	M,St
1943a	Zucker	Delinquency	Social learning	Interview-P	50	St,T
1943b	Zucker	Delinquency	Psychodynamic	Interview-P	50	M,St,T,I
1944	Banister and Ravden	Disturbed behavior	None	Case study	112	
1944	Baruch and Wilcox	Social adjustment	None	Direct observation	76	S,M,St,I
1945	Baldwin, Kalhorn, and Breese	Personality development	None	Direct observation	125	M,St,I
1945	Bossard	Social development	None	Direct observation	82	I
1946	Baldwin	Age differences	None	Direct observation	153	M,St,I
1946	Merrill	Mother-child behavior	Behavior	Direct observation	30	M,St,T,I
1946	Winch	Courtship behavior	Psychodynamic	Questionnaire-P	435	S,M,St,T
1947	Baldwin	Age differences	None	Direct observation	46	M,St,I
1947	Fitzsimmons and Perkins	Farm families	None	Interview-P	50	
1947	Meyer	Social adjustment	None	Direct observation	29	M,St
1948	Baldwin	Personality development	None	Direct observation	67	M,St,I
1948	Ingersoll	Authority patterns	Role	Questionnaire-P	37	
1948	Jurovsky	Sex differences	Social learning	Questionnaire-P	775	S,M,T
1949	Lidz and Lidz	Schizophrenia	None	Case study	50	
1949	Tietze	Schizophrenia	Psychodynamic	Case study	25	T

[a] P = primary data.
[b] S = sample; M = measurement of variables; St = statistic; T = use of theory; I = importance, uniqueness.

The increase in number of research projects and improved methodology were the most noteworthy changes of the decade. Only four of the studies were strictly case studies; the remainder employed survey or direct observation or some combination of the three methods. The introduction of direct observation as a technique to learn about family interaction and communication processes was an important step in the development of later research.

Sample sizes ranged from 25 to 7,021 subjects. Although no information about sampling method was reported in two studies (Bossard, 1943; Ingersoll, 1948), most researchers explained their methods and described demographic characteristics of their sample.

Analytical methods were used in half of the studies in order to evaluate the data collected. Included in these methods were critical ratio tests, contingency and chi-square analyses, t-tests, syndrome analysis, analysis of variance, Pearson correlation, tetrachoric correlation, and multiple correlation.

Key Studies and General Findings. The most important research from this decade was produced by Baldwin and colleagues at the Fels Research Institute and reported in four articles. In each of these studies, direct observation of family interaction was coded in the home using the Fels Parent Behavior Rating Scales. Variables were clearly defined, and the reliability and validity of assessment instruments were reported. In addition, inferential statistics were clearly outlined and appropriately utilized. The authors offered alternative explanations for their results and gave suggestions for future research.

Both positive and negative family interaction patterns were described as influential in family development, and negative family interaction patterns were described more frequently than positive ones. Parent-child conflict, resulting in bitter feelings on the part of the parent, were associated with quarreling between the husband and wife and noncooperation between parents in child rearing techniques. Delinquency was related to lack of affection between parents and children, inadequate discipline techniques, and retaliation by the child when punished by parents.

Schizophrenia was reported to be connected with lack of husband-wife affection, parental conflicts, overprotectiveness, poor problem-solving skills, dominant and authoritative parents, and deleterious parenting practices. Various other child behavior problems were related to lack of proper parental supervision, oversolicitation and overprotectiveness, rejection, poor problem-solving skills, inadequate discipline, lack of affection, parental tensions over sex, inconsiderate husband-wife relations, and husband-wife conflict.

Positive interactions included whole families' sharing in planning and management; family cohesiveness, cooperation, and teamwork; a minimum of conflict between parents and children; mutual respect; and spontaneous expression of warmth and emotion by parents toward children. These types of interactions resulted in prosperous, successful families and in functional personality development in children.

Several topics of family disagreement were characterized. Conflict issues for husbands and wives were management of income, relatives, recreation, personal habits, and the social life of children. Conflict between parents and children revolved around rural and urban cultural differences and children's friends and social life.

The Decade 1950–1959

Thirty articles were reviewed for this decade. Because of the increase in the number of articles, we no longer looked at case studies with the exception of three research reports on family interaction and schizophrenia which analyzed large numbers of hospital case records. There were seventeen parent-child studies dealing with child adjustment, older parents, and schizophrenia and nine marital interaction articles.

Research Findings

Child Adjustment. Bishop (1951), in an experiment with thirty-four mothers and their children, observed mothers' facilitative and inhibitory behavior and the effect of those behaviors on children's behavior. The author found that mothers who exhibited high control behaviors by directing, interfering, and criticizing received noncooperation and reluctant acceptance of their control from their children.

Milner (1951) identified parent-child behaviors that were influential in the development of reading readiness in forty-two grade-school children. The children were placed into one of two groups on the basis of being a high scorer or low scorer on the Language I.Q. scale from the California Test of Maturity. Mothers of the children were also interviewed about their parenting behaviors and parent-child interaction. There were four important findings: high-scoring children were read to by parents and taken places by their mothers more than low scorers; high-scorers were subjected to controlling, preventing and prohibitive techniques by parents, while low scorers seem to be liberally treated to direct physical punishment administered by either or both parents; mealtime for the high scorers included interaction that was positive and permissive in emotional tone and had a high verbal content, while the opposite was true for low scorers; and parents of high scorers expressed their affection for their children in some overt manner on a consistent basis, while parents of low scorers did not.

Cass (1952) evaluated the relationships among parental awareness, parental control, parent-child conflict, and child social adjustment. Twenty-one seriously maladjusted adolescents were paired individually according to age, sex, race, and father's occupational level with a group of twenty-one adolescents who were selected by their school principal as being well adjusted. The major findings were that parental awareness was satisfying to the child and resulted in low parent-child conflict, parental overcontrol was associated with high parent-child conflict, and children who displayed poor social adjustment reported higher parental control and lower parental awareness than children with good social adjustment.

Stone and Landis (1953) related family authority patterns to the adjustment problems in 4,310 high school seniors. The families of each teenager were classified as authoritarian, intermediate, or democratic according to responses from a family interaction questionnaire. The researchers found that almost twice as many boys as girls placed their families in the democratic category, teenagers in democratic families reported more harmonious relationships with their parents than those in authoritarian families, and teenagers in democratic families reported fewer adjustment problems than teenagers in other families.

Highberger (1955) investigated the relationship between maternal behavior and childs early adjustment to nursery school. The mother-child interactions of thirty-eight children and their mothers were observed and rated using the Fels Parent Behavior Ratings and the interaction ratings were compared to children's school adjustment. Highberger found no significant correlations between mother's behavior and school adjustment.

Nakamura (1959) explored the relationship between children's expression of hostility and parental discipline. Seventy-eight female college students completed an autobiographical workbook, which was scrutinized for methods of parental discipline, parents' dominant and overprotective techniques, children's criticism of parents and family, and children's criticism of people other than family. Respondents whose parents used positive types of discipline had more favorable attitudes toward parents and family than those whose parents used negative methods. Subjects with overprotective parents criticized others more and parents less if their parents used positive methods of discipline.

Schizophrenia. McKeown and Chyatte (1954) compared the behaviors of fathers among 392 normal, 85 neurotic, and 157 schizophrenic persons. Case records of neurotics and schizophrenics were examined for data while the normals completed an unnamed questionnaire. Four types of parent behavior toward their children were coded: demanding-antagonistic, superficial, encouraging, and protective-indulgent. Normal females and males reported their father's behavior toward them as encouraging. Neurotic males and females reported their father's behavior as demanding-antagonistic. Schizophrenic females reported their father's behavior as superficial, while males reported equal amounts of demanding-antagonistic and superficial behavior.

Wahl (1954, 1956) explored the frequency with which certain family factors were associated with schizophrenia. In the first study, Wahl examined case records of 392 male and female schizophrenic patients, and in the second study, the sample was 568 male schizophrenics admitted consecutively to a U.S. naval hospital. The findings from the two studies were similar. About half of the schizophrenics came from homes where there was severe rejection and/or overprotection by one or both parents, more than 40 percent had lost one or both of their parents before age 15, and they came from larger-than-average families (the average number of children per family was 4 compared to a national average of 2.2).

Kohn and Clausen (1956) explored the differences in authority behavior of thirty-nine parents of schizophrenics and thirty-nine parents of nonschizophrenics. Families were interviewed about their family interaction during the period when the children were 13 to 14 years old. Overall, schizophrenic patients reported, more frequently than normals, that their mothers were strict, certain of themselves, restrictive of child's freedom, and dominating, whereas their fathers did not demonstrate these qualities. In addition, normal males and females reported different patterns of parental authority behavior, whereas schizophrenic males reported much of the same parental patterns as schizophrenic females.

Behrens and Goldfarb (1958) investigated differences in patterns of family interaction between twenty families with schizophrenic children and ten normal families. These families were observed in their homes, and their interactions were coded and scored. Families with schizophrenic children had lower family interaction scores than families with nonschizophrenic children. Homes with low-scoring families were characterized by a general absence of interest, isolation between father and mother or between one of them and other family members, lack of genuine communication with affection, absence of cooperation and common activities, absence of shared pleasure between family members, and confusion and disorganization. The high-scoring families were characterized by mutual support, shared pleasure, a sense of direction, and integration of all children into the family group.

Marital Decision Making. Strodtbeck (1951) investigated whether researchers could measure the balance of power in a marital relationship by using a decision-making interaction process. The decision-making interactions of ten couples from three geographically adjacent communities (Navajo Indians, Mormons, and Texas homesteaders) were recorded and analyzed. It was reported that Mormon women lose more decisions than Mormon men, Navajo women win more decisions than Navajo men, and the spouse who talked more won more decisions. There was no significant difference in the number of decisions won by either husband or wife among Texan homesteaders.

Kenkel conducted three studies in the 1950s using similar methodology. In each project, subjects were twenty-five couples who were told to assume they had received a gift of $300 and to determine how to spend this money. Their interaction was observed and coded using the Bales Interaction Process

Analysis. Kenkel and Hoffman (1956) investigated the extent to which husbands and wives were able to recognize their roles in the family decision-making process. The authors reported that neither husbands nor wives judged accurately the amount of time spent in talking during a decision-making exercise. They also stated that husbands and wives showed "no great ability" to judge beforehand what roles they would play and that there was only a slight tendency to judge more accurately what roles were played after the exercise was completed.

Kenkel (1957) determined how influence—"the degree to which a person is able to have his own wishes reflected in the decision of a group" (p. 19)—was distributed between spouses. It was reported that (1) 48 percent of the spouses expected husbands to have the greater share of influence, 10 percent expected wives to, and 42 percent expected equal distribution of influence; (2) 56 percent of the husbands and wives actually had a medium degree of influence, with 26 percent of husbands and 16 percent of wives demonstrating a high degree of influence; (3) high influence among males was related to high levels of talking, whereas wives achieved their degree of influence by saying and doing things that raised husband's status, showing affection, and keeping their interaction running smoothly during the exercise.

Kenkel (1959) investigated the relationship between certain personality characteristics and the roles that husbands and wives demonstrated in an observed decision-making session. Husbands and wives were divided into two groups, high and low, according to their scores on three subscales of the Traditional Family Ideology Scale. The two groups were then compared on the amount of time they spent in different types of interaction. Traditional family ideology did not have a consistent, predictable effect on husband-wife interaction.

Wolgast (1958) investigated husband and wife interaction in making major economic decisions with 959 subjects (454 males and 505 females). Wife and husband responses were not paired, resulting in separate responses for females and males. Males and females reported equality in decisions about handling money. With increased age and length of marriage, husbands reported a major role in automobile purchases and wives a major role in home appliance purchases. Women's plans for handling money were more frequently fulfilled than men's.

Marital Interaction. Lu (1952) investigated the association between 589 young couples' conflict attachment relationships with their own parents before marriage and their dominant-egalitarian-submissive roles in marriage. There were three major findings: (1) the husband played a more dominant role in husband-wife interactions if he experienced a conflict relationship with his father and mother and if his wife did not; (2) the egalitarian role was found in families in which the husband had an absence of conflict with his father and mother accompanied by attachment to his mother, and the wife experienced absence of conflict and presence of attachment with her mother; and (3) the wife played a more dominant role if she had experienced a conflict relationship with her mother.

Strodtbeck (1952) assessed the interaction patterns of a well-known married couple in a small Mormon community to see if the community perspective and the couple's actual interaction were congruent. The husband had been categorized as the most "henpecked" husband of the community after using a snowball referral process with town members. The couple's decision-making process was recorded and coded using the Bales Interaction Process Analysis. The author found that the wife was indeed more dominant than husband but that the couple was not unsatisfied with their interaction pattern, although the community perception was that their interaction was dysfunctional.

Family Decision Making. Strodtbeck (1954) investigated whether certain propositions developed from research on small ad hoc groups held true for forty-eight small family groups. Each family was presented with nine decision-making situations designed to allow for a potential coalition of two of the three family members against the other. Sessions were recorded and coded using the Bales Interaction Process Analysis. Results were then compared to results of another study of the same type that used a three-person ad hoc group. Decision-making power was associated with high participation. Families did not tend to group into two-person coalitions. In contrast to ad hoc groups, stability in the family remained high throughout the exercise.

Wilkening (1954) investigated whether differences in family interaction patterns affect decisions about changes in farm technology made by 170 farm families. Family interaction patterns were categorized on three scales: familism—the ascendance of family interests over the interests of individual family members; family integration—the degree to which the family functioned as a unit in attaining common goals; and the degree of father-centered decision making. Family integration, familism, and father-centered decision making were not predictive of changes in farm technology.

Johannis and Rollins (1959) investigated the extent to which family decision making reflected a pattern that included all family members. Subjects were 1,027 high school students who were asked who made most of the decisions in the family. In 63 percent of the families, the father and mother were considered a joint decision-making team; in 11 percent of the families, children were included in decision making; and more males saw their families as patricentric, and more females saw their families as egalitarian or democratic.

Family Interaction. Jansen (1952) measured solidarity in 284 families. Family solidarity was defined as the degree to which interaction between family members was marked by a drawing together of the individual members or by a minimizing of the social distance between family members. Subjects completed a questionnaire, and a family solidarity score was computed from their answers. Jansen found that family solidarity was negatively related to family size and age of children, except for families having one child, who scored higher than families with no children. Family solidarity was greater in families favoring authority equally distributed between wife and husband and also in families tending to favor dominance by husband.

The Decade in Review

Theory and Methodology. Only nine of the thirty articles reviewed did not identify some theory in connection with the hypotheses proposed. Psychodynamic, small group, and various mini theories were represented by six articles. Behavior, social learning, and systems theories were incorporated in one article each (table 4–3).

Direct observation techniques increased in importance, with twelve research projects employing their use. The remainder utilized questionnaire (ten articles), interview (four articles), and experimental (one article) techniques.

Sample sizes ranged from 1 to 4,310 subjects. As in the 1940s, most researchers explained their sampling method and described demographic characteristics of their sample.

In sixteen of the studies reviewed, analytical methods were utilized; in four studies (Jansen, 1952; Nye, 1957; Strodtbeck, 1951, 1954) mention is made of the use of some test of significance without clarification of which specific test. Similar types of statistical analysis were used in this decade as in the previous one. Only ten researchers used solely descriptive statistics.

Key Studies and General Findings. The most impressive research of the decade was that reported by Lasko (1954). The author tied theory to the hypotheses presented, capitalized on earlier research citing twenty-two previous articles, used reliable and valid scales, demonstrated a good grasp of statistics using both correlation and analysis-of-variance techniques, and presented the results clearly and concisely.

Highberger (1955) and Wilkening (1954) also used sound methodology. Each defined methods well, listed limitations, and provided alternative explanations for the results. Interestingly, they reported that family interaction had no observable influence on child's school adjustment (Highberger, 1955) or changes in the use of new farm technology (Wilkening, 1954).

As in the previous decades, both positive and negative family interaction patterns were described as influential in family development. The patterns of influence were similar to those previously reported.

The Decade 1960–1969

Because of the increase in the number of articles, we did not review studies with sample sizes fewer than fifty. (A list of these articles appears at the end of this

Table 4–3
Overview of Research on Family Interaction Patterns 1950–1959

Year	*Author*	*Topic*	*Theory*	*Method*[a]	*Sample*	*Strengths*[b]
1951	Bishop	Mother-child behavior	Behavior	Direct observation	34	M,St,T
1951	Milner	Reading readiness	None	Questionnaire-P	42	M,St
1951	Strodtbeck	Decision making	Small group	Direct observation	10	M,T,I
1952	Cass	Delinquency	Social learning	Questionnaire-P	21	M,St,T
1952	Jansen	Family solidarity	Systems	Questionnaire-P	384	M,T
1952	Lu	Husband-wife roles	Psychodynamic	Questionnaire-P	589	St,T
1952	Strodtbeck	Decision making	Small group	Direct observation	1	M
1953	March	Political decisions	Mini	Direct observation	8	
1953	Stone and Landis	Adolescent adjustment	None	Questionnaire-P	4,310	M,St
1954	Carter	Personality development	None	Questionnaire-P	305	M,St
1954	Lasko	Age differences	Mini	Direct observation	46	M,St,T
1954	McKeown and Chyatte	Schizophrenia	Psychodynamic	Case study	634	
1954	Stewart et al.	Colic in children	Psychodynamic	Direct observation	18	M
1954	Strodtbeck	Family coalitions	Small group	Direct observation	48	S,M,I
1954	Wahl	Schizophrenia	Psychodynamic	Case study	392	S,M,T
1954	Wilkening	Farm family decisions	None	Interview-P	170	S
1955	Highberger	School adjustment	Psychodynamic	Direct observation	38	M,St,T
1956	Kenkel and Hoffman	Decision making	Small group	Direct observation	25	M
1956	Kohn and Clausen	Schizophrenia	None	Interview-P	78	T
1956	Wahl	Schizophrenia	Psychodynamic	Case study	568	S,M,T,I,
1957	Kenkel	Decision making	Small group	Direct observation	25	M
1957	Nye	Divorce adjustment	None	Questionnaire-P	780	S,M,I
1958	Behrens and Goldfarb	Schizophrenia	None	Direct observation	30	M,St
1958	Brown	Older persons	Mini	Interview-P	161	S,M,St,T
1958	Wolgast	Decision making	None	Interview-P	959	
1959	Antonovsky	Mother-child behavior	Mini	Direct observation	9	M
1959	Johannis and Rollins	Decision making	None	Questionnaire-P	1,027	S,M
1959	Kenkel	Decision making	Small group	Direct observation	25	M,T
1959	Middleton and Putney	Social class	Mini	Questionnaire-P	40	S,St
1959	Nakamura	Child hostility	Mini	Case study	78	St,T

[a] P = primary data.
[b] S = sample; M = measurement of variables; St = statistic; T = use of theory; I = importance, uniqueness.

chapter.) Also, any project in which the behavior of only one family member was observed or measured was no longer regarded as family research.

We reviewed twenty-two articles for the 1960s. Parent-child studies made up the greatest proportion of the projects, which looked at aggressiveness, child development and adjustment, communication efficiency, decision making, general interaction, information exchange and silence, older parents, schizophrenia, and talking time. There were five marital interaction articles; they were concerned with communication efficiency, decision making, dominance, and general interaction patterns. Two articles looked at family interaction and social class differences.

Research Findings

Family Communication and Child Adjustment. Ferreira and Winter (1965) explored differences in family interaction during decision-making tasks between fifty normal and seventy-five abnormal (fifteen schizophrenic, sixteen delinquent, forty-four maladjusted in some other way) families. They found that normal families had greater agreement prior to discussion, spent less time in reaching decisions, and arrived at decisions that were more fulfilling to all family members than abnormal families did.

Ferreira, Winter, and Poindexter (1966) investigated whether fifty-six normal families differed from seventy-six abnormal families (sixteen schizophrenic, sixteen delinquent, forty-four maladjusted in some other way) in their decision-making interactions. Family triads were asked to complete stories from three cards of the Thematic Apperception Test (TAT). The authors reported that normal families took less time to make decisions, children in schizophrenic families talked less than children in other families, groups were no different in amount of overlap in speaking, and abnormal families had more silence than normal families.

Winter and Ferreira (1967) utilized the Bales Interaction Process Analysis to measure interaction and communication in family triads of thirty-five normal, thirty-three emotionally maladjusted, ten schizophrenic, and twelve delinquent families. Each family was asked to reach a consensus on three stories they had made up using nine cards from the TAT. The only group that could be differentiated from the normals was the schizophrenic one. Schizophrenic families interacted less and spent more time asking questions, stating opionions, and making suggestions than other families.

Ferreira and Winter (1968) investigated the amount of valid and explicit information and the amount of silence observed in seventy-five families (thirty normal, fourteen schizophrenic, fourteen delinquent, and seventeen maladjusted) engaged in decision-making tasks. Abnormal families exchanged significantly less information among themselves and remained silent considerably longer than normal families.

Gassner and Murray (1969) examined dominance and conflict interactions between parents of thirty neurotic and thirty normal children using Strodtbeck's revealed-differences technique. They found that neurotic boys and girls had homes with maternal domination, while there were no differences in the patterns of parental domination between normal boys and girls. Parents of neurotic children displayed more disagreement and aggression and failed to agree more times than parents of normal children. Cross-sex parental domination occurred for neurotics with high-conflict parents; for normal children, it occurred with low-conflict parents.

McCord, McCord, and Howard (1963) explored family interaction patterns of men who had manifested extreme aggressiveness as children and had criminal records as adults (aggressive-antisocial, $N = 26$), showed extreme aggressiveness as children but had no criminal record as adults (aggressive-socialized, $N = 25$), and were not aggressive as children and had no criminal record (nonaggressive, $N = 52$). They concluded that families in which there was extreme punishment and neglect, along with a paternal model of deviant-aggressiveness (criminal record or alcoholic), yielded aggressive-antisocial men; families with a pattern of moderate neglect and punishment and ineffective parental control produced aggressive-socialized men; and families with little punitive discipline but much parental agreement and consistent discipline generated nonaggressive men.

Family Interaction and Schizophrenia. Cheek (1964) explored the concept of the "schizophrenogenic mother" in terms of interaction within the family system. The interaction patterns of sixty-seven mothers of schizophrenics were compared to those of fifty-six mothers of nonpsychotics. Subjects responded to self-report questionnaires and were observed during decision-making discussions. Mothers of schizophrenics tended to be cold and withdrawn; and mothers of female schizophrenics were more withdrawn than mothers of male schizophrenics. Among the control mothers, high reported support was related to high support behaviors, whereas among mothers of schizophrenics, high reported support was related to low disagreement behavior rather than active support behavior.

Cheek (1965) also studied and compared the role performance and family structure of sixty-seven families containing a young adult schizophrenic and fifty-six families containing a nonpsychotic young adult in their adjustment to in-home convalescence after hospitalization. Both in-clinic and in-home family interactions were coded using the Bales Interaction Process Analysis, and the families filled out questionnaires concerning family relationships. In normal families, the father played an active role, father and mother approved of discipline rather than permissiveness in handling the child, and both fathers and mothers were high on negative sanctions, although fathers were somewhat lower on positive sanctions and mothers were higher on positive sanctions.

Farina, Holzberg, and Dies (1969) explored the relationship between family interaction and task performance of seventy-four hospitalized psychiatric patients (twenty-four nonschizophrenics, twenty-six schizophrenics classed as "good," and twenty-four schizophrenics classed as "poor") and their parents. The patients were given a task of making as many words as possible out of a given word, and then their reaction time was measured. There were no differences among groups in the initial analyses. In a subsequent analysis, the researchers reported that patients whose families expressed high levels of conflict in decision making made more errors and produced more words on the anagrams task.

Marital Communication and Decision Making. Larson (1967) determined which interpersonal interaction dimensions were the most critical correlates of effective communication in fifty-two married couples. The couples filled out self-report questionnaires designed to measure decision-making interaction and communication effectiveness. After a factor analysis of all items, the most clearly reported finding was that if married couples had patterns of interaction that included patience, trust, concern, reassurance, and a lack of arguing, they were more accurate and effective in their communication.

Kenkel (1961) investigated the relationship between husband-wife interaction and decision outcome with fifty married couples. Each couple was asked to imagine that they had received $300 and now had to reach an agreement on how to spend it. The Bales Interaction Process Analysis was used to code the amount of talking time, suggestions, and opinions (task actions) that were offered and what each partner did to keep the discussion going smoothly (social emotional actions). Kenkel found that when both partners talked equally (40 percent of the cases), they were more likely to choose wife-household items to spend the money on; when the husband spoke most (42 percent of the cases), they were more likely to choose husband-children items; 60 percent of the time, the husband contributed most of the suggestions and opinions and the couples were more likely to choose wife-husband and family items; and in 72 percent of the cases, the wife performed most of the socioemotional actions and the couples chose items that were for the children, family, and household.

Bauman and Roman (1966) examined dominance in a marital decision-making task. In each of fifty couples who were subjects, one partner was a psychiatric patient. Each couple was asked to answer the Comprehension and Similarities subtests of the Weschler-Bellevue individually and as a couple. Couple scores were compared to individual scores, and a dominance scale was devised. The dominance scores were compared according to sex, patient status, and recorder status (which partner recorded the answers). It was found that husbands, nonpatients, and recorders were more dominant than wives, patients, and nonrecorders, respectively. There were no significant interactions between any of these variables.

Ryder (1968) examined differences in the amount of agreement between sixty-four wife-husband and fifty-six married stranger dyads in a decision-making task. Couples were administered the Color Matching Test, and the groups were compared across thirteen variables. The author reported that people expected to have a pleasanter time with strangers than with their spouse. There were differences between the two types of dyads in seven of the thirteen variables measured. Three of the findings reported were that husbands were more likely to take the lead in conversations with their wives than with strangers, wives laughed less with spouses than with strangers, and wives showed more disapproval in interaction with husbands than with strangers.

Haley (1964) determined whether and on what dimensions the patterns of interaction between members in one family can be differentiated from those in another family. Forty disturbed families and forty control families participated in a discussion of questionnaire items and completed stories from TAT cards. The author found that normal families were characterized by random patterns of speech in their family conversations, while disturbed families had more nonrandom patterns of verbal interaction.

Straus (1967) examined the influence of communication patterns and creativity in problem-solving activities between middle- and working-class families in India ($N = 64$), Puerto Rico ($N = 45$), and the U.S. Midwest ($N = 64$). The author reported that working-class families in each of the three societies were less able to solve problems than middle-class families. Differences were attributed to less intrafamily communication and less creativity among the working-class families.

The Decade in Review

Theory and Methodology. Theory became a major part of research in the 1960s. Family systems theory was the predominant theory identified for the decade, with half of the researchers recognizing its use. Various mini theories dealing with integrated concepts of both communication and systems theory were also prevalent (table 4–4). A listing of research studies with sample sizes lower than fifty is shown in table 4–5.

Sample sizes of reviewed articles ranged from 50 to 923, and most researchers continued to explain their sampling method and to describe the demographic characteristics of their samples. Direct observation became the overwhelming method of choice; only four projects did not use it. Of these four, three utilized interview techniques (and the other) a self-report questionnaire.

The most noticeable change in methodology from the previous decade was the preponderance of the use of the family triad—mother, father, and child—in almost every direct observation project examining parent-child interaction.

Key Studies and General Findings. Cheek (1964) produced the most well-rounded research of the decade. He cogently linked his research hypotheses to theory and previous research findings, utilized a sample of families that represented fairly his population of interest, used multimethod assessment of parent-child interaction with reliable and valid instruments, appropriately applied analysis of variance statistics, and presented his results and conclusions

Table 4–4
Overview of Research on Family Interaction Patterns 1960–1969

Year	*Author*	*Topic*	*Theory*	*Method*[a]	*Sample*	*Strengths*[b]
1961	Kenkel	Decision making	Mini	Direct observation	50	M
1963	Ferreira	Decision making	Systems	Direct observation	50	
1963	McCord, McCord, and Howard	Male aggressiveness	Mini	Direct observation	103	S
1964	Cheek	Schizophrenia	Systems	Direct observation	123	S,M,St,T,I
1964	Haley	Communication patterns	Systems	Direct observation	80	M,T
1965	Burchinal and Bauder	Decision making	Mini	Interview-P	923	S,M,St
1965	Cheek	Schizophrenia	Systems	Direct observation	123	S,M,T,I
1965	Ferreira and Winter	Communication efficiency	Systems	Direct observation	125	M,St,T,I
1966	Bauman and Roman	Marital dominance	Mini	Interview-P	50	
1966	Ferreira, Winter, and Poindexter	Decision making	Systems	Direct observation	126	M,T
1967	Bee	Child distractibility	Mini	Direct observation	72	M,St,T
1967	Haley	Speech sequences	Systems	Direct observation	90	M,St,T
1967	Larson	Communication efficiency	Mini	Questionnaire-P	52	
1967	Straus	Social class	Mini	Direct observation	173	S,M,St,T
1967	Winter and Ferreira	Decision making	Systems	Direct observation	90	M
1968	Ferreira and Winter	Talking and silence	Systems	Direct observation	75	M,St,T,I
1968	Ryder	Married versus stranger	Mini	Direct observation	120	
1969	Alkire	Child behavior	Communication	Direct observation	54	T
1969	Bultena	Older persons	Mini	Interview-P	507	S,St,T
1969	Farina, Holzberg, and Dies	Schizophrenia	Systems	Direct observation	74	
1969	Gassner	Neurotic behavior	Systems	Direct observation	60	M,St,T
1969	Winter and Ferreira	Family talking time	None	Direct observation	127	

[a]P = primary data.
[b]S = sample; M = measurement of variables; St = statistic; T = use of theory; I = importance, uniqueness.

Table 4-5
Research on Family Interaction Patterns with Sample Sizes of Fewer than Fifty, 1960–1969

Year	*Author*	*Topic*	*Sample*
1960	Farina	Schizophrenia	36
1961	Kenkel	Decision making	25
1962	Baxter, Flood, and Hedgepath	Schizophrenia	18
1962	Schulman, Shoemaker, and Moelis	Parental behavior	41
1962	Scott	Social interaction	32
1963	Caputo	Schizophrenia	40
1964	Caldwell and Hersher	Mother-child behavior	35
1964	Walters and Connor	Social class	40
1965	Becker, Tatsvoka, and Carlson	Parental Speech	24
1965	Lennard, Beaulieu, and Embry	Schizophrenia	17
1965	Morris and Wayne	Schizophrenia	12
1965	Stabenau et al.	Schizophrenia	15
1966	Ferreira and Winter	Decision making	23
1966	Shere and Kastenbaum	Cerebral palsy	13
1967	Becker and McArdle	Nonlexical speech	38
1967	Haley	Abnormal families	46
1967	Hatfield, Ferguson, and Alpert	Socialization	40
1967	Levenstein and Sunley	Mother-child behavior	12
1967	Murrell and Stachowiak	Clinic/nonclinic families	22
1967	Navran	Marital communication	48
1967	Reiss	Schizophrenia	16
1968	Behrens, Rosenthal, and Chodoff	Schizophrenia	39
1968	Goodman and Ofshe	Marital communication	45
1968	Haley	Schizophrenia	44
1968	Levenstein and Sunley	Social class	11
1968	Reiss	Schizophrenia	15
1969	Beakel and Mehrabian	Psychopathology	8
1969	Becker and Finkel	Schizophrenia	45
1969	Kogan and Wimberger	Social class	20
1969	Reiss	Schizophrenia	15
1969	Sojit	Double-bind communication	46

in a manner that was clear and matched his presentation of hypotheses and methodology.

The most prolific researchers of the decade were Ferreira and Winter, with five articles published either one or both of their credits. Their sole use of the direct observation method led to its firm establishment as the workhorse of family interaction research.

The Decade 1970–1979

The 1970s saw a growth in research that compared family interaction patterns among various groups of people. Comparisons were made by ethnicity, gender, and social class. Of the twenty-two articles reviewed for this decade, seventeen were parent-child studies, and five were marital studies. In addition to ethnic, gender, and social class differences, other topics included enuresis, schizophrenia, sibling interaction, twinship, marital satisfaction, nonverbal interaction, older couples, and general family interaction.

Research Findings

Ethnic and Social Class Differences in Parent-Child Interaction. Levenstein (1970) conducted an experiment in which verbal interaction of thirty-three low-income mothers and their preschool children was stimulated, and then the cognitive development of the experimental children was compared with that of two groups of nonexperimental low-income controls ($N = 9$, $N = 12$). The families in the experimental condition were visited for seven months by a "toy demonstrator" who taught the mother how to interact with her child using twenty-eight toys and books (called Verbal Interaction Stimulus Materials, VISM) designed to increase mother-child verbal interaction. The families in one of the comparison groups also received visits from a toy demonstrator who brought non-VISM toys and did not encourage mother-child verbal interaction. The other control group received nothing. Children's cognitive skills were assessed before and after the seven-month period using the Cattell or Stanford-Binet Intelligence Scales and the Peabody Picture Vocabulary Test. A mean gain of 17.0 IQ points was demonstrated by children in the experimental condition, while the control children gained 1 and 2 points, respectively. On the Peabody test, the experimental children had a mean gain of 12.2 points while the controls had a mean gain of 4.0 and 4.7 points, respectively.

Miller (1972) explored racial differences in descriptive and judgmental verbalizations of 208 black and white mothers with their eighth-grade children. These family members completed two questionnaires designed to measure type of parental responses and child's self-esteem. The author stated that, overall, mothers who used descriptive verbalizations had children with higher self-esteem, while mothers who were more judgmental in their verbalization had children with lower self-esteem. Blacks were found to be more judgmental and have children with lower self-esteem when compared to whites, but there was a confounding of this latter result by the family's socioeconomic status.

Dickson and co-workers (1979) studied the relationship of mother-child communication accuracy to child's cognitive development. Sixty-seven American and 58 Japanese children and their mothers participated in a communication game during which mother and child alternated as sender and receiver. Communication accuracy was defined as correctness of listener responses. There were no differences in communication accuracy between the two cultures, and the greater the communication accuracy was, the higher was the child's level of cognitive development.

Tulkin and Kagan (1972) examined differences in verbal and nonverbal behavior of primiparous mothers and their infant daughters from middle-class ($N = 30$) and working-class ($N = 26$) homes. Mother-daughter interaction was observed in the home and coded across five scales of behavior. Middle-class mothers had more verbal interaction and provided a greater variety of stimulation for their daughters than working-class mothers did; the two groups were not different in any of the other coded behaviors. It appeared that the working-class mothers more often believed their infants were unable to understand anything that might be said and thus saw no reason to verbalize with them.

Gender Differences in Parent-Child Interaction. Tauber (1979) explored sex differences in parent-child interaction during free-play activities in a laboratory setting. The sample consisted of 145 children and one of their parents. Their interaction was coded with twenty-four parent and nineteen child categories, which were then factor analyzed into four parent scales (sociable play, active play, buoyant support, abrasive talk) and four child scales (active play, solitary play, buoyant mood, physical contact seeking). Major conclusions were that parents of girls tended to engage in sociable play and parents of boys in active play; mother-child interaction was similar for both sons and daughters; and fathers played more actively with sons and less actively with daughters.

Family Interaction and Schizophrenia. Cheek and Anthony (1970) compared the use of personal pronouns in schizophrenic ($N = 67$) and nonschizophrenic ($N = 56$) families. Family interaction was recorded during four fifteen-minute sessions in which behaviors of young adults were discussed. Schizophrenics used the first-person pronouns more than the young adult controls, indicating an overfocus on self. Parents of schizophrenics were no different from normals in their first-person pronoun usage, suggesting that schizophrenics did not learn their usage pattern from their parents. Parents of schizophrenics tended to use second-person pronouns more than controls, and schizophrenic youth used them less than normal youth. This suggests that parents of schizophrenics might be overfocusing on the behaviors of their schizophrenic child.

Friedman and Friedman (1970) studied differences in family interactions of forty families with a schizophrenic child (labeled "schizogenic") and twenty-two "normal" families. As the families made up stories from TAT cards, their interaction was observed and coded. Schizogenic families showed higher levels of conflict, failure, and confusion than the normal families and demonstrated more anxiety, depressive mood, and evasiveness than the control parents. These differences were evident even when the schizophrenic member was not present in the interaction task.

Waxler and Mishler (1971) compared the parent-child interaction of fifty-nine schizophrenic and nonschizophrenic families when one child was present (the patient in schizophrenic families) and when two children were present. Families participated in two revealed-differences problem-solving tasks, and their interactions were coded. There were no differences between the two types of families in interaction: overall family patterns did not change when there were two rather than one child present, parents did not behave differently toward their children from one session to the next, and parents did not act differently toward the well child than toward the patient child, either individually or as a parental pair.

Family Interaction and Child Adjustment. Prinz, Rosenblum, and O'Leary (1978) assessed differences in the affective communication patterns of thirty-eight distressed and forty nondistressed mother-adolescent dyads. Family members filled out a questionnaire evaluating their relationships and then participated in a joint problem-solving discussion, both rated according to various categories of negative and positive affect. Distressed parent-adolescent pairs produced written responses that evidenced more demands, personal attacks, anger, hostility, complaining, and disrespect and fewer compliments, less showing of appreciation, and less enjoyment than the nondistressed dyads. Correlations between written and observed interactions suggested that the written answers were predictive of actual family behaviors.

Lytton, Conway, and Sauvé (1977) compared the reciprocal influence of parents' child-rearing practices on level of child compliance, attachment, independence, speech, and activity of forty-six families with twins (seventeen monozygotic, twenty-nine dizygotic) and forty-four families with single-birth children. Families were observed in the home, and their interactions were coded using the Parent-Child Interaction Code. Parents of twins talked less to their children and gave fewer directions, fewer justification of rules, less praise, fewer refusals, fewer threats, and fewer expressions of affection than other parents. Twins spoke less and had a lower activity rate than single-birth children; the two groups were not different on the other child measures. The authors also assessed certain aspects of prenatal twin development and concluded that it was parents' reduced speech that was the causal factor in the twins' reduced level of verbal activity rather than the twins' vocalizations that elicited lower parental response.

Hetherington, Stouwie, and Ridberg (1971) examined patterns of family interaction and child-rearing attitudes among 200 families with an adolescent child classified as nondelinquent, neurotic delinquent (withdrawn, feels guilt and anxiety), psychopathic delinquent (rebellious, anti-authority, amoral), or social delinquent (acceptant of social norms of delinquent subculture). Parents responded to a child-rearing attitudes questionnaire, and family triads participated in a structured interaction task in which they were presented situations that included adolescent problem behaviors. Different patterns emerged for all four types of families. Neurotic delinquent sons and daughters were passive and inactive in family interaction, while psychopathic and social delinquent daughters were inappropriately assertive and disruptive. Psychopathic and social delinquent sons were passive and inactive. There was little correlation between parents' written responses and overt displays of behavior.

Marital Satisfaction. Gottman, Markman, and Notarius (1977) investigated differences in message content, nonverbal delivery (termed affect), and nonverbal reception (termed context) of fourteen distressed and fourteen nondistressed couples. Subject couples were asked to discuss and problem solve a salient marital issue, and their interactions were coded using the Couple Interaction Coding System. Nonverbal behavior was found to be a better discriminator of distress or nondistress than verbal behavior. Differences in interactional sequences were found for the two groups of couples. Nondistressed couples were more likely to begin with a validation sequence, to avoid negative exchange, and to end their discussion with a contract sequence; distressed couples were more likely to begin with a cross-complaining sequence, follow with a negative exchange loop, and end without a contract exchange. The data did not support the reciprocity model of interaction, perhaps the most popular of communication models of the time.

Beier and Sternberg (1977) looked at the effect of nonverbal cues on the marital discord and accord of fifty-one young married couples. Couples' touching, arm position, leg position, laughing, eye contact, and talking were rated during a conversation between spouses, and their level of discord was measured using the Beier-Sternberg Discord Questionnaire. The authors reported that couples who had the least amount of discord sat closer together, looked at each other more, touched each other more, touched themselves less, and sat with their legs in a more open position than couples reporting higher levels of discord. For couples in which one of the partners rated high on discord when compared to the spouse, there was more closeness when the partner was the husband than when the higher discord partner was the wife.

Social Class Differences in Marital Interaction. Tallman and Miller (1974) measured social class differences in problem-solving performance of fifty-five blue- and fifty-five white-collar families grouped according to power (husband decides, wife decides, shared decision making) and speech style (elaborate, restricted). The families participated in five problem-solving tasks. It was found that middle-class families were more efficient at problem solving than working-class families, speech style did not affect problem-solving ability, and blue-collar families performed best when the father was the decision maker and white-collar families performed best when both parents shared decision making.

Hawkins, Weisberg, and Ray (1977) assessed communication style differences in 110 married couples, grouped into three classes according to husband's education level, and compared differences among them. Preference, imputed use, and actual observed use of four communication styles (conventional, controlling, speculative, contactful) were observed and coded in both an individual interview and two joint couple problem-solving tasks. All three classes rank ordered their preference of styles the same way, although the higher class preferred the speculative and contactful styles to a greater degree than the other classes. In all classes, the majority of the couples believed that they handled emotional issues in speculative and contactful ways. There were no significant differences among the three classes in the observed use of communication styles.

Older Couples. Saunders (1974) examined relationships among the perceived levels of empathy, communication, and life satisfaction of sixty married couples whose children had grown up and were now living away from home. Responses from several self-report questionnaires revealed that frequency of marital communication was not related to life satisfaction; higher levels of self-disclosure were associated with lower levels of satisfaction, particularly among white-collar families; and only when empathy was reciprocated by both spouses did the couples define their satisfaction as better than the previous stage of their lives.

The Decade in Review

Theory and Methodology. Instead of focusing on broad assumptions of particular theories, researchers in the 1970s based their hypotheses on specific concepts. Most authors had specific research questions and provided logical explanations tied to previous research. This use of theory was a strength of most studies conducted in this decade (table 4–6).

Sample sizes of reviewed articles ranged from 54 to 208, with the exception of one study of unique value, which had only 28 couples as subjects (Gottman, Markham, and Notarius, 1977). Direct observation techniques continued to be the method of choice of researchers from 1970 to 1979. Of the twenty-two studies reviewed, nineteen used this method. Two of the others used questionnaire assessment, and the remaining one interview assessment. Table 4–7 lists studies with the sample sizes fewer than fifty.

Key Studies and General Findings. One of the major projects reported on in the 1970s was that of Gottman, Markham, and Notarius (1977). This study was distinctive for several reasons. First, couples were observed discussing and problem solving on marital issues that were present and salient instead of a standard prearranged topic. Second, the researchers implemented a new coding system that described both verbal and nonverbal delivery and reception behaviors. Finally, they analyzed not only discrete portions of the observed interaction but also sequential, reciprocal patterns of couple behavior using a new statistical procedure, lag sequential analysis.

There were many general findings gleaned from the parent-child interaction studies that added to knowledge about family interaction and communication. First, there were no inherent differences in family interaction as a result of ethnicity; rather, dissimilarity between groups was based on cultural and socioeconomic expectations. Mothers of lower socioeconomic status tended to

Table 4–6
Overview of Research on Family Interaction Patterns, 1970–1979

Year	*Author*	*Topic*	*Theory*	*Method*[a]	*Sample*	*Strengths*[b]
1970	Cheek and Anthony	Schizophrenia	Mini	Direct observation	123	M,St,T
1970	Friedman and Friedman	Schizophrenia	Systems	Direct observation	62	T
1970	Levenstein	Cognitive development	Mini	Direct observation	54	S,M,T,I
1970	Umphress et al.	Adolescent enuresis	None	Interview-P	73	S
1971a	Greenglass	Cultural differences	Mini	Direct observation	132	S,M
1971b	Greenglass	Cultural differences	Mini	Direct observation	132	S,M
1971	Hetherington, Souwie, and Ridberg	Delinquency	Mini	Direct observation	200	S,T
1971	Waxler and Mischler	Schizophrenia	Communi-cation	Direct observation	59	M,St,T,I
1972	Greenglass	Cultural differences	Mini	Direct observation	89	M,St
1972	Miller	Social class	Mini	Questionnaire-P	208	
1972	Tulkin and Kagan	Social class	Mini	Direct observation	56	M,St
1974	Saunders	Older couples	Mini	Questionnaire-P	60	S,St,T,I
1974	Tallman and Miller	Social class	Small group	Direct observation	115	M,St,T
1975	Cicirelli	Sibling presence	Mini	Direct observation	120	M
1977	Beier and Sternberg	Marital discord	Mini	Direct observation	51	
1977	Gottman, Markman, and Notarious	Interation sequences	Systems	Direct observation	28	M,St,T,I
1977	Hawkins, Weisberg, and Ray	Social class	Communi-cation	Direct observation	110	S,T
1977	Lytton, Conway, and Sauvé	Twinship	Mini	Direct observation	90	S,M,T
1978	Cicirelli	Sibling presence	Mini	Direct observation	80	M
1978	Prinz, Rosenblaum, and O'Leary	Cognitive development	Mini	Direct observation	125	S,M,St,T
1979	Tauber	Sex differences	Mini	Direct observation	145	M,St,T

[a]P = primary data.
[b]S = sample; M = measurement of variables; St = statistics; T = use of theory; I = importance, uniqueness.

Table 4–7
Research on Family Interaction Patterns with Sample Sizes of Fewer than Fifty, 1970–1979

Year	*Author*	*Topic*	*Sample*
1970	Feinsilver	Schizophrenia	12
1970	Hore	Social class	30
1970	McPherson	Disturbed adolescents	28
1970	Mishler and Waxler	Schizophrenia	35
1970	Sandler	Mother-child behavior	27
1970	Schuham	Disturbed families	28
1971	Alkire et al.	Disturbed adolescents	32
1971	Bugental, Love, and Gianetto	Nonverbal behavior	40
1971	Bugental, et al.	Disturbed children	30
1971	Gorad	Alcoholism	40
1971	Kogan	Disturbed children	10
1971	Leighton, Stollak, and Ferguson	Clinic-nonclinic	15
1971	Murrell	Adjustment	30
1971	O'Connor and Stachowiak	Mental retardation	24
1971	Odom, Seeman and Newbrough	Personality	23
1971	Rebelsky and Hanks	Father-child behavior	10
1971	Smith	Family role structure	12
1972	Aston and Dobson	Social adjustment	25
1972	Bugental, Love, and Kaswan	Disturbed children	30
1972	Kogan	Mother-child behavior	5
1972	Lewis	Mother-child behavior	32
1972	Lusk and Lewis	Cultural differences	10
1972	Mead and Campbell	Drug abuse	40
1972	Osofsky and O'Connell	Parent-child interaction	41
1972	Radin	Father-child behavior	42
1972	Schuerman	Marital interaction	22
1972	Schuham	Disturbed families	28
1972	Thoman, Leiderman, and Olson	Mother-child behavior	40
1973b	Alexander	Deviant families	20
1973a	Alexander	Family communication	21
1973	Hadley and Jacob	Family power	20
1973	Jacob and Davis	Family interaction	10
1973	Murphy and Mendelson	Marital adjustment	30
1973	Winter, Ferreira, and Bowers	Decision making	40
1974	Hassan	Disturbed families	46
1974	Jacob	Social class	44
1974	Liem	Schizophrenia	22
1974	Matteson	Self-esteem	40
1975	Birchler, Weiss, and Vincent	Marital communication	24
1975	Herschey and Werner	Woman's liberation	28
1975	Moerk	Mother-child behavior	20
1975	Seitz and Stewart	Mother-child communication	18
1975	Solvberg and Blakar	Schizophrenia	10
1975	Vincent, Weiss, and Birchler	Problem solving	24
1976	Alsbrook	Marital communication	40

Table 4–7 continued

Year	*Author*	*Topic*	*Sample*
1976	Becker and Miller	Alcoholism	12
1976	Cherry and Lewis	Mother-child behavior	12
1976	Cicirelli	Sibling interaction	40
1976	Doleys, Cartelli, and Doster	Mother-child behavior	27
1976	Lamb	Stress	20
1976	Reichle, Longhurst, and Stepanich	Mother-child behavior	24
1977	Als	Newborn communication	31
1977	Boyd and Roach	Marital communication	39
1977	Jacob	Social class	44
1977	Ponnuswami	Cognitive style	30
1977	Sternberg and Beier	Conflict	41
1977	Tronick, Als, and Brazetton	Mutuality	3
1978	Gantman	Drug abuse	30
1978	Pakizegi	Parent-child interaction	20
1978	Spinetta and Maloney	Cancer	16
1978	Steinberg and Hill	Family interaction	31
1978	Wilton and Barbour	Social class	20
1979	Belsky	Family interaction	40
1979	Billings	Conflict resolution	24
1979	Cunningham and Barkley	Hyperactive children	40
1979	Golinkoff and Arnes	Parent-child speech	12
1979	Lessin and Jacob	Delinquent families	10
1979	McAdoo	Self-esteem	36
1979	Vandell	Parent-child interaction	12
1979	Williams	Marital satisfaction	20
1979	Zuckerman and Jacob	Family interaction	30

display less verbal interaction and less stimulation and had lower expectations of the same for their children than mothers of higher socioeconomic status. Second, families with a schizophrenic child showed higher levels of conflict, failure, and confusion than normal families, and these family patterns were apparent not only in parent-child interaction with the patient child but also with other siblings. Third, fathers and mothers interacted differently with sons and daughters, and fathers were the discriminating element in parent-child interaction.

Findings from marital interaction studies were varied. First, wife-husband communication that contained negative affect contributed to marital distress. Satisfied couples were more likely to validate each other, avoid negative exchanges, and arrive at mutually agreeable solutions. Second, although couples of all socioeconomic classes appeared to handle problems in similar ways, middle-class couples were more efficient at problem solving than working-class couples. Communication and problem-solving efficiency was higher for working-class couples when they were more traditional in their decision-making styles, that is, when the father was the decision maker. Middle-class families tended to be more efficient with a more egalitarian style. Third, older couples were happier with their marriage when higher levels of self-disclosure were used and when empathy was reciprocated by both spouses.

The Decade 1980–1989

Parent-child interaction research was the topic of thirty-four studies of this decade. The subtopics included adolescent depression, anorexia and bulimia, child development and adjustment, ethnic differences, gender differences, hyperactivity, individuation, interaction sequence, parent-adolescent communication, peer interaction and health, preterm infants, sexual socialization, social class differences, and stepfamily interaction.

There were fifteen marital interaction studies; they looked at affective communication, cognitive styles, communication satisfaction, compliance, dual career couples, locus of control, marital satisfaction, married couples versus cohabitors, older couples, and sterilization methods.

Research Findings

Parent-Infant Interaction. Clarke-Stewart and Hevey (1981) noted changes in the interactions of seventy-seven mothers and their children, ages 12 to 30 months, over a year and a half and the effect of those changes on child attachment. Observations of the families were made in the home. Among the findings reported were that mothers initiated the majority of interactions with the child but this predominance declined over time, mother-child physical contact and proximity declined over time (this was more pronounced for children with higher levels of attachment), and children's communication and responsiveness increased, while mothers' first increased and then decreased.

Maccoby, Snow, and Jacklin (1984) observed fifty-seven mother-child dyads to determine the relationship between mothers' teaching style and children's disposition (difficulties and activity level). The family pairs were asked to participate in a mother-teaching task when the child was 12 months and then 18 months old. The authors reported no correlation between mother teaching style and child disposition at 12 months. At 18 months, the mothers of difficult boys had reduced their teaching efforts, and the sons of mothers who demonstrated high levels of teaching effort at 12 months were less difficult.

Cohn and Tronick (1987) examined the sequential structure of mother-infant face-to-face interaction with fifty-four mother-infant dyads at 3, 6, and

9 months. Interactions were coded using the Monadic Phases Manual during six minutes of play. At 6 and 9 months, mothers initiated engagement with their infant using positive affective expressions. At 3 and 6 months, the infant responded to mothers' engagement with positive expressions, and the mother continued this engagement until the infant became disengaged. At 9 months, the infant was positive before the mother was.

In a similar study, Cohn and Tronick (1988) investigated bidirectional influence in the face-to-face interactions of fifty-four mothers and their infants who were 3, 6, and 9 months old (eighteen each). Mother-infant interaction was coded using the Monadic Phases Manual and then analyzed using both time-series and cross-correctional analyses. Among several results presented, the authors found that mother-infant interactions were not periodic except when the child was 3 months old. Most interactions were stochastic, or nonrandom, in terms of their sequence. Mothers and babies were more likely to respond to changes in the other's behavior if the other was responsive to changes in their own behavior, indicating that their interaction was bidirectional in nature.

Stewart (1983) examined the effect of an older sibling on infant behavior in the presence of their mother and a stranger. Attachment, affiliation, fear, and coordinated play interactions were observed for all dyadic and triadic combinations of fifty-four mothers, infants, siblings, and strangers. Three major results were reported: (1) 52 percent of the siblings provided reassurance and comfort to their younger sibling when their mother was not present, (2) older brothers were most active in caring for younger sisters and older sisters were most active in caring for their younger brothers, and (3) older sisters gave more care than was sought by infants, whereas older brothers gave care that matched the requests for care made by infants.

Parenting and Child Adjustment. Loeb, Horst, and Horton (1980) examined the relationship between four types of parenting models—imitation/modeling, directive, rewarding/punishing, and warm/involved—and the self-esteem of ninety-eight preadolescent children. The children were categorized into high and low self-esteem groups according to their scores on the Self-Esteem Inventory and the Behavior Rating Form. Parents completed the Self-Esteem Scale; families participated in a joint interaction task and also were given the Family Rorschach. Results indicated that child self-esteem was not correlated with the parental behaviors of imitation/modeling; physically directive paternal behavior and verbally directive behavior of both parents were associated with low self-esteem of girls, while for boys, low self-esteem was related only to paternal physical directiveness; low self-esteem for sons and high self-esteem for daughters resulted when fathers made a high proportion of their rewards contingent on desired child behaviors; and high self-esteem in both sons and daughters was seen when mothers were highly supportive, but girls had higher and boys lower self-esteem when fathers demonstrated high levels of involvement.

Doane and colleagues (1982) examined the relationship between parental communication deviance and children's psychosocial competence. Sixty-two parent dyads in which one parent had been diagnosed with a psychiatric disorder participated with their 7- or 10-year-old child. Parent communication deviance was coded from individual, couple, and family Rorschach testing. Child psychosocial competency was rated using the Rochester Teacher Rating Scale, the Rochester Peer Rating Scale, and the Rochester Adaptive Behavior Inventory. The authors reported that, overall, communication deviance scores in the three settings were not related to each other or to child competence. However, the higher was the level of mothers' communication deviance in the individual and family Rorschach situations, the lower was the level of child psychosocial competence.

Webster-Stratton (1985) compared mother-child interactions of forty families with conduct-disordered children and twenty-eight nonclinic families. Behavior was measured with the Eyberg Child Behavior Inventory, the Interpersonal Behavior Construct Scale, and the Dyadic Parent-Child Interaction Coding System. Mothers of clinic children gave more criticisms, commands, and praises than nonclinic mothers, yet their children were no more noncompliant than nonclinic children. Nonclinic mothers expressed more submissions and positive affect behaviors than clinic mothers. Nonclinic children exhibited more dominance and positive affect behaviors than clinic children.

Wampler and Halverson (1990) and Wamper and colleagues (1989) reported on a five-year longitudinal study of 149 families in Georgia. Their purpose was to determine the relationship between congenital, parent-child, marital, parental, and whole family characteristics and behavior problems in children and family coping. They gathered multiple measures, which included both direct observation of parent-child, marital, and whole family interaction using both micro and macro level coding systems, as well as self-report measures. In general, it appeared that when children who were at risk for behavioral problems were members of poorly functioning families, the functioning of both children and families deteriorated over time. When children at risk were members of well-functioning families, the behavioral problems of the children were minimized, and the families did well over time. Their findings lend support to the conclusion that child and family characteristics mutually influence each other in reciprocal ways.

MacKinnon (1989) examined the influence of spousal/ex-spousal and parent-child relationships on sibling relationships between forty-eight mother-custody divorced and forty-eight biological two-parent married families. Sibling interaction was observed and coded while the children played a popular board game. Mothers completed the Family History Inventory, the Family Satisfaction Inventory, the Quality of Life Scale, and the Family Environment Scale. Sibling dyads from divorced families with an older male were more negative, more resistant, and less compliant than all other dyad combinations. As the quality of other dyadic relationships in the family became more positive, the quality of sibling relationship also became more positive. The quality of the spousal/ex-spousal relationship was more predictive than the marital status of parents in predicting negativity in sibling relationships.

Humphrey (1989) compared family interaction patterns among sixteen anorexic, eighteen bulimic-anorexic, sixteen bulimic, and twenty-four normal families. Parents and their teenage daughters were observed in a family discussion, and their interaction was coded using Benjamin's Structural Analysis of Social Behavior. The interaction of the three clinical types of families differed from the control families. Control families demonstrated patterns of helping, protecting, trusting, relying on, approaching, and enjoying each other; parents of anorexics were nurturing and comforting yet also ignoring and neglecting. The anorexic daughters were ambivalent in their disclosure of feelings and tended to be submissive or to defer to their parents. Bulimic family interaction was more hostile in nature and was characterized by mutual belittling and blaming, along with sulking and appeasing interactions.

Cognitive Development in Children. In a follow-up study from one previously described (Dickson et al., 1979), McDevitt and colleagues (1987) reported once again on the relationship between mother-child communication accuracy and child's cognitive development among forty-seven Japanese and forty-four American families. In this study, the children were now 12 years old. The effects of communication accuracy on child achievement in vocabulary and mathematics were examined. The authors reported that the higher was the level of communication accuracy, the higher was the level of child's proficiency in vocabulary and mathematics in both cultures. After controlling for the effects of children's age, socioeconomic status, and mother's IQ, communication accuracy predicted skill in vocabulary for American children and skill in mathematics for Japanese children.

Ditton, Green, and Singer (1987) asked whether parents of thirty learning disabled children exhibited higher frequencies of communication deviance than parents of thirty normally achieving students. As parents helped their child solve a picture-arranging task, their comments and instructions were coded according to five communication deviance categories. The authors reported that communication deviances accounted for 18 percent of the variance when predicting child language ability, and high levels of parental communication deviance were associated with a child's placement in a learning disability class.

Hunter and associates (1987) identified social-constructive interactions of fifty-two infants with their parents at 6 and 12 months of age and measured the influence of these interactions on child cognitive development. In-home observations were made of parent-child interactions at 6 and 12 months. The infants were also administered the McCarthy Scales of Children's Abilities at 30 months. Fathers demonstrated more object play with children than mothers, although all interactions increased over time. All mother-infant interactions and none of the father-infant interactions were positively related to all measured aspects of cognitive development.

Gender Differences in Parent-Child Interaction. Snow, Jacklin, and Maccoby (1983) examined sex differences in father-child interactions with 107 year-old children and their fathers. As the family dyads played in a laboratory setting, their interactions were coded across various behaviors. The researchers reported that fathers and daughters held each other and remained in close proximity to each other more than fathers and sons; fathers were more likely to give toys to girls than to boys and less likely to give dolls to boys than to daughters, although equally likely to give trucks to boys and girls; and there were no sex differences in the amount of father-child vocalization or in the amount of time fathers played with children.

Belsky, Gilstrap, and Rovine (1984) observed seventy-two families in a longitudinal study of developmental changes in mother- and father-child interactions. Families were observed in the home at 1, 3, and 9 months of child age. Both fathers' and mothers' interaction with their children changed over time, with overall engagement, caregiving, and positive affection decreasing and stimulating and responding increasing. Mothers displayed more engagement, responsiveness, stimulation, and positive affection than fathers did. The researchers found consistent positive association between father-infant and husband-wife interaction yet no relationship between mother-infant and husband-wife interaction.

Jacklin, DiPietro, and Maccoby (1984) examined parent-child interactions of fifty-four families for differences in sex-typed behavior on the part of fathers and mothers. Fathers and mothers participated separately with their child in free-play activity in their homes, and interactions were coded. Children initiated sex-typed play and played with toys that were sex appropriate. Fathers played more with both children, and mothers played more with daughters in sex-appropriate, cooperative thematic play. Mothers were equally as likely to play with masculine and feminine toys with their sons. Father-son dyads exhibited the greatest amount of rough-and-tumble play. The authors concluded that fathers were the discriminating factor in the determination of sex-appropriate play.

Hauser and colleagues (1987) investigated sex differences in the verbal interactions of forty normal and thirty-nine psychiatrically hospitalized adolescents and their parents. Families participated in a revealed-differences problem-solving task, and the family discussions were rated using the Constraining and Enabling Coding System. The two major findings were that (1) both sons and daughters spoke more to their fathers, including more affective and cognitive speech directed toward him, and engaged in more problem solving with him and (2) fathers demonstrated more cognitive enabling while the mothers exhibited more constraining communication.

Parent-Adolescent Communication. Barnes and Olson (1985) studied the relationship between parent-adolescent communication and a circumplex model of family systems in 426 "normal" families. Families completed several questionnaires: the Parent-Adolescent Communication Scale; the Family Adaptability and Cohesion Scales, Version II; the Family Inventory of Life Events; and F-COPES. For parents, high levels of communication were associated with Balanced families according to the circumplex model. For adolescents, high levels of communication were associated with families typed as Extreme, whereas low communication scores were found in connection with Balanced family types. When adolescent and parent scores were combined as a family score, families with better communication were higher in family cohesion, adaptability, and satisfaction.

Callan and Noller (1986) studied perceptions of family communication in fifty-four families with adolescents. The families were videotaped in their homes during the discussions. The researchers then watched those tapes and rated their perceptions of each family member's anxiety, involvement, dominance, and friendliness. Parents also completed the Dyadic Adjustment Scale. Adolescents consistently rated family members as less involved and less dominant, and they were rated by others as less dominant and less involved than other family members. In families with daughters, those with high levels of marital satisfaction rated family members as friendlier than families with low satisfaction. On the other hand, in families with sons, those with low marital satisfaction rated family members as more dominant and more involved than families with high satisfaction.

Sexual Socialization. Fox and Inazu (1980) analyzed the effects of direct verbal communication about sex between 449 mothers and their teenage daughters. Mothers and daughters were interviewed separately about the frequency, onset, and subject matter of mother-daughter communication about sexual topics. Higher frequencies of current mother-daughter communication resulted in more responsible patterns of daughter behavior.

Fisher (1987) examined the relationship between family communication and sexual attitudes of both parents and adolescents, as well as the relationship between family communication and adolescent sexual activity and contraceptive use. Sexual attitudes were measured using the Attitudes Toward Sexuality Scale and family communication by the Parent-Adolescent Communication Scale. Subjects were asked to specify which and how often nine sexual topics had been discussed in the home, and adolescents also responded to various questions about frequency of sex and use of contraception. Quality of family communication was unrelated to the degree of family sexual discussions. Contraceptive use among females was higher when there was more parent-child communication about sex as reported by the adolescent.

Social Class and Mother-Child Interaction. Harmon and Kogan (1980) looked at differences in mother-child interaction as a function of social class. Ninety-six families were categorized into three groups by social class. Family dyads were observed during a free-play exercise, and interactions were coded across eight major categories of behavior. Only two minor differences were found when the groups were compared. The authors concluded that social class could not be used to predict differences in mother-child behavior.

Marital Communication and Decision Making. Davis and associates (1988) investigated the affective components of marital interaction with sixty-four couples. The subjects participated in a discussion of a high-conflict issue in their marriage and also completed the Profile of Mood States, the Marital Research Inventory, and the Couples Problem Inventory. As subjects expressed higher levels of depression, fatigue, and confusion, they also recalled more intense emotions during the interaction. As couples expressed more vigor, they recalled less intense negative emotions in the interaction.

Allen and Thompson (1984) measured congruence between marital partners on perceptions, metaperceptions, and meta-metaperceptions and the influence of these perceptions on the communication satisfaction of sixty-five couples. Perceptions and satisfaction were measured using a questionnaire modeled after Laing's Interpersonal Perception Method. Greater levels of agreement and feeling understood led to higher communicative satisfaction in couples. Also, higher levels of realization and understanding on the part of wives was predictive of higher satisfaction for husbands.

Bean and co-workers (1983) measured the influence of marital communication and wife's employment on type of sterilization method (vasectomy for males and tubal ligation or hysterectomy for females) used by 313 couples. The amount of shared communication was reported by both husbands and wives on a self-report questionnaire. The researchers concluded that if the wife had worked since the birth of the last child and her assessment of marital communication was poor, she was more likely to be the one sterilized; if the wife had not worked and the couple disagreed on their perceptions of communication, the wife was likely to get sterilized; if they agreed, the husband was more likely to have a vasectomy.

Blechman and McEnroe (1985), with a sample of ninety-seven families, studied the effectiveness of family problem solving. The subjects participated in three problem-solving tasks, and their interactions were rated according to the number of strategies used, success at the task, and time to reach agreement. Families who were most effective at all three tasks tried more strategies, took longer to reach agreement, and reached more agreements that were satisfactory to all family members. Other family characteristic factors, such as education, occupational prestige, and social competence, were found to be only weak predictors of problem-solving effectiveness.

Shukla (1987) assessed decision-making power in forty-seven single- and fifty-four dual-career families in India. Spouses completed a questionnaire designed to assess who made the decisions in sixteen common family situations. Four major results were presented: husbands in the single-career families had more power than those in dual-career families, wives in dual-career families had more power than wives in single-career families, in dual-career families husbands and wives shared in decision making more often, and in single-career families, the husband was the more frequent decision maker.

Marital Satisfaction. Barnes and colleagues (1984), using partial correlation methods, compared the explanatory effects of positive regard and effective communications on the marital satisfaction of eighty-three rural and ninety-eight urban couples. All couple measures were obtained from a self-report questionnaire, the Barrett-Lennard Relationship Inventory. The authors reported that positive regard explained variations in marital satisfaction more effectively than marital communication.

Hansen and Schuldt (1984) examined the relationship between self-disclosure and marital satisfaction with fifty married couples. Subject couples completed Jourard's Self-Disclosure Questionnaire and the Dyadic Adjustment Scale. Interactions were coded according to thought units, total talking time, and level of intimacy. The authors reported that as husbands disclosed more, they were more satisfied in their marriage. As wives disclosed more, both their own and their husband's marital satisfaction increased. The greater was the discrepancy between husband and wife disclosure, the lower was the husbands' satisfaction. The shorter was the duration of husbands' self-disclosure, the lower were both husband and wife satisfaction scores.

Miller and colleagues (1986) examined locus of control, marital problem solving, and marital satisfaction among eighty-eight couples. Each couple completed Rotter's I-E Locus of Control Scale, the Miller Marital Locus of Control Scale, the Dyadic Adjustment Scale, and Edmond's Marital Conventionalization Questionnaire. Couples were typed as internal or external according to the marital locus of control scale and their interaction on a structured problem-solving task was coded using the Couple Interaction Coding System. Among the many results presented were that internals were more direct and active in their problem solving than externals, externals generated lower-quality solutions in problem solving, and internals were more effective in conveying and attaining their goals and were more satisfied in their marriage.

Yelsma and Athappilly (1988) compared marital satisfaction and communication practices of thirty-one American, twenty-eight Indian arranged-marriage, and twenty-five Indian love-marriage couples. The couples completed the Primary Communication Inventory and the Dyadic Adjustment Scale. Indian arranged-married couples reported the highest levels of marital adjustment, followed by the Indian love-marriage couples; American couples reported the lowest levels of adjustment. Nineteen of the thirty-eight communication items were significantly correlated with marital satisfaction for the American couples, while only six of the items correlated for the Indian love-marriage couples and only three items for the Indian-arranged marriage couples.

Gottman and Krokoff (1989) conducted a longitudinal study of the effect of various types of couple interaction on the marital satisfaction of fifty-five couples. Couples were observed during a discussion of areas of disagreement in their marriage, and the interaction was coded using the Specific Affect Coding System. Disagreement and anger were found to relate to concurrent unhappiness and negative interaction but were also predictive of improved marital satisfaction over time. Defensiveness, stubbornness, and withdrawal from interaction were identified as longitudinally dysfunctional, especially when exhibited by the husband.

White (1989) examined conflict resolution interactions and their effects on marital satisfaction among fifty-six couples. Couple interaction during a conflict discussion task was coded using the Coding Scheme for Interpersonal Conflict. Marital adjustment was measured using the Marital Adjustment Test. Both frequencies and sequences of interaction were analyzed, and it was reported that couples whose behavior was more coercive were more likely to be unhappy in their marriage. High rates of affiliative and coercive responses and increased reciprocity of the same differentiated unsatisfied from satisfied couples. Also, in response to dissatisfaction in marriage, husbands exhibited more coercive interactions, while wives demonstrated higher levels of affiliative interaction.

Older Couples. Dorfman and Heckert (1988) evaluated differences among 149 retired rural couples in their division of household tasks, decision-making patterns, and leisure activities. The couples were interviewed, and differences between answers for pre- and postretirement periods were examined. In both division of household tasks and decision-making patterns, couples reported more equal participation by both spouses after retirement. No differences were found in their level of leisure participation.

Stepfamilies. Anderson and White (1986) identified key interaction and relationship patterns that distinguished functional and dysfunctional nuclear families and stepfamilies. Families responded to the Family Concept Inventory and the Family Relations Test and participated in a family interaction task. Parents also completed the Marital Adjustment Test. The authors concluded that functional nuclear families were similar to functional stepfamilies in that both had good marital adjustment; strong positive relationships between biological child and parent; did not make exclusion-from-family statements like, "I wish that this family member would go away"; and made mutually compromising family decisions. These two types of families were different in that stepfamilies had a less intense interaction between stepfather and child, and there was a greater tendency for parent-child coalitions. The two types of dysfunctional families were similar in that both formed stronger parent-child coalitions than functional families, and they did not demonstrate mutual decision-making interactions.

The Decade in Review

Theory and Methodology. The use of theory in the 1980s was similar to that in the 1970s. Researchers continued to focus on specific concepts of more general theories and defined fairly precise hypotheses as they specified their research questions. Sample sizes ranged from 54 to 449. Direct observation assessment was used in fourteen of the articles reviewed, questionnaire assessment in five, and interview assessment in one. A listing of these studies is shown in table 4–8, and a listing of studies with sample sizes lower than 50 is shown in table 4–9.

Key Studies and General Findings. Four key studies were identified from this decade: (1) Anderson and White (1986) on interaction within stepfamilies, (2) Harmon and Kogan (1980) on social class and family interaction, (3) McDevitt and colleagues (1987) on communication accuracy, and Wampler and Halverson (1989) and Wampler and co-workers (1989) on reciprocity. Sampling methodology, measurement of variables, use of statistics, integration of theory, and uniqueness of their contribution were strengths in each of these research projects.

Among the additional findings for the 1980s from parent-child interaction research were that children were more likely to express more and problem solve more with fathers than with mothers; the higher was the level of parental communication deviance, the lower was the child's psychosocial competence, and, conversely, the higher was the level of communication accuracy, the higher was the level of child's proficiency; and families in which there were strong parent-child coalitions and weak mutual decision-making interactions were less functional than other types of families.

The major findings of marital interaction research were that spouses who had a more internal locus of control were better problem solvers and were happier in their relationships, women who were employed had more power in their marital relationship and dual-career couples shared power in their decisions, and older couples also participated more equally in both household and decision-making responsibilities.

Conclusion

Methodological Trends and Developments

Family interaction and communication research has passed through three phases of development. In its infancy there was little use of theory. Most samples were convenience samples, and most authors did not define their sampling methods or describe their sample characteristics. Most projects were

Table 4–8
Overview of Research on Family Interaction Patterns, 1980–1989

Year	*Author*	*Topic*	*Theory*	*Method*[a]	*Sample*	*Strengths*[b]
1980	Fox and Inazu	Sexual socialization	Mini	Direct observation	449	S
1980	Harmon and Kogan	Social class	Mini	Direct observation	96	S,M,St,T,I
1980	Loeb, Horst, and Harmon	Self-esteem	Mini	Direct observation	98	S,T
1981	Clarke-Stewart, and Hevey	Mother-child behavior	Mini	Direct observation	77	M,St,T
1982	Doane et al.	Communication deviance	Communication	Direct observation	62	M,T
1983	Arco	Sex differences	Mini	Direct observation	56	
1983	Bean et al.	Sterilization	Mini	Questionnaire-P	313	S,St,T,I
1983	Mash and Johnston	Hyperactivity	Mini	Direct observation	96	S,M
1983	Snow, Jacklin, and Maccoby	Sex differences	Mini	Direct observation	107	M
1983	Stewart	Sibling interaction	Mini	Direct observation	54	M,T
1984	Allen and Thompson	Communication satisfaction	Mini	Questionnaire-P	50	St
1984	Barnes et al.	Marital satisfaction	Mini	Questionnaire-P	181	S
1984	Belsky, Gilstrap, and Rovine	Parent-child interaction	Mini	Direct observation	72	S,M,St,T
1984	Hansen and Schuldt	Marital satisfaction	Communication	Direct observation	50	M,St
1984	Jacklin, DiPietro, and Maccoby	Sex differences	Mini	Direct observation	54	M,St,T
1984	Maccoby, Snow, and Jacklin	Child disposition	Mini	Direct observation	57	M,St,T
1985	Barnes and Olson	Circumplex model	Mini	Questionnaire-P	426	S,M,T
1985	Befera and Barkley	Hyperactive children	None	Direct observation	60	M
1985	Blechman and McEnroe	Problem solving	Mini	Direct observation	97	S,M,T
1985	Castan, Gallois, and Callan	Social class	Mini	Direct observation	54	M
1985	Grotevant and Cooper	Individuation	Mini	Direct observation	84	M,St,T
1984	Tyndall and Lichtenberg	Cognitive style	Communication	Questionnaire-P	60	M,T
1985	Webster-Stratton	Conduct-disordered children	Mini	Direct observation	68	M,St
1986	Anderson and White	Stepfamilies	Structure	Direct observation	63	S,M,St,T,I
1986	Brody, Pillegrini, and Sigel	Parent-child behavior	Mini	Direct observation	60	S,M
1986	Callan and Noller	Family communication	Mini	Direct observation	54	M,T
1986	Millet et al.	Locus of control	Mini	Direct observation	88	M,St,T,I

1986	Vuchinich	Family communication	Communication	Direct observation	52	M,St,T
1986	Witteman and Fitzpatrick	Relationship types	Mini	Direct observation	51	M,St,T
1986	Yelsma	Marital communication	Social exchange	Questionnaire-P	92	M,St,T
1987	Cohn and Tronick	Interaction sequence	Mini	Direct observation	54	St,T,I
1987	Ditton, Greene, and Singer	Communication deviance	Communication	Direct observation	60	M,St,T,I
1987	Fisher	Sexual socialization	Mini	Questionnaire-P	95	M,T
1987	Hauser et al.	Sex differences	Communication	Direct observation	79	M,St,T
1987	Hunter et al.	Cognitive development	Mini	Direct observation	52	M,T
1987	McDevitt et al.	Communication accuracy	Mini	Direct observation	91	S,M,St,T,I
1987	Shukla	Wife's employment	Mini	Questionnaire-P	101	
1988	Bridges, Connell, and Belsky	Parent-child behavior	Mini	Direct observation	50	M,St,T
1988	Cohn and Tranick	Mother-child behavior	Mini	Direct observation	54	S,M,St,T
1988	Davis et al.	Marital interaction	Communication	Direct observation	64	M,St,T
1988	Dorfman and Heckert	Older couples	Mini	Interview-P	149	S,M,St
1988	Fogel, Toda, and Kawai	Cultural differences	Mini	Direct observation	72	S,T
1988	Stivers	Adolescent depression	Mini	Questionnaire-P	53	
1988	Yelsma and Atheppilly	Marital satisfaction	Mini	Questionnaire-P	84	S,M,T
1988	Zarling, Hirsch, and Landry	Preterm infants	Mini	Direct observation	54	St,T
1989	Gottman and Krokoff	Marital satisfaction	Mini	Direct observation	55	M,St,T,I
1989	Gottman and Katz	Peer interaction and health	Pyshio-social	Direct observation	56	S,M,St,T,I
1989	Humphrey	Eating disorders	Psycho-dynamic	Direct observation	74	S,M,T
1989	Stocker, Dunn, and Plomin	Sibling interaction	Mini	Direct observation	96	M
1989	MacKinnon	Sibling interaction	Mini	Direct observation	96	S,M,St,T,I
1989	Wampler et al.	Reciprocity	Mini	Direct observation	149	S,M,St,T,I
1989	White	Marital communication	Communication	Direct observation	56	M,St,T
1990	Wampler and Halverson	Reciprocity	Mini	Direct observation	149	S,M,St,T,I

[a]P = primary data.
[b]S = sample; M = measurement of variables; St = statistics; T = use of theory; I = importance, uniqueness.

Table 4–9
Research on Family Interaction with Sample Sizes of Fewer than Fifty, 1980–1989

Year	*Author*	*Topic*	*Sample*
1980	Craddock	Problem solving	42
1980	Gottman	Marital interaction	38
1980	Greenberg	Deaf preschoolers	28
1980	Kaye and Fogel	Temporal structure	37
1980	Martlew	Control strategies	8
1980	Masur and Gleason	Parent-child interaction	14
1980	Noller	Marital communication	48
1980	Relich et al.	Abused children	26
1980	Schubert, Bradley-Johnson, and Nuttal	Maternal employment	30
1980	Wedell-Monnig and Lumley	Child deafness	12
1981	Barton	Teaching style	32
1981	Borduin and Henggeler	Social class	32
1981	Fash and Madison	Language interaction	9
1981	Gottman and Porterfield	Communicative competence	42
1981	Kaye and Charney	Conversational asymmetry	27
1981	Landerholm and Scriven	Parent-child interaction	22
1981	Lewis, Rodnick, and Goldstein	Schizophrenia	47
1981	Margolin and Wampold	Conflict and accord	39
1981	McCarrick, Manderscheid, and Silbergeld	Gender differences	5
1981	Resick et al.	Conflict and accord	19
1981	Steinglass	Alcoholism	31
1981	Wilkinson, Wiebert, and Rembold	Parental communication	18
1982	Asarnow et al.	Psychopathology	33
1982	Blotcky, Tittler, and Friedman	Double-bind	15
1982	Brody, Stoneman, and Mackinnon	Role assymetries	22
1982	Crawford	Premature infants	33
1982	Davis and Hathaway	Reciprocity	28
1982	Eheart	Mental retardation	16
1982	Eyberg and Robinson	Parent-child interaction	7
1982	Malone and Guy	Parental speech	10
1982	Masur	Parental speech	14
1982	McDonald and Pien	Mother behavior	11
1982	Noller	Channel consistency	48
1982	Olsen-Fulero	Mother behavior	11
1982	Pannabecker, Emide, and Austin	Father-child behavior	48
1982	Sabatelli, Buck, and Dreyer	Nonverbal communication	48
1982	Santrock et al.	Stepfamilies	36
1982	Stuckey, McGhee, and Bell	Maternal employment	40
1982	Warmbrod	Problem solving	44
1982	Webster-Stratton and Eyberg	Child temperament	35
1983	Arco	Temporal patterns	24
1983	Barkley, Cunningham, and Karlsson	Hyperactive children	36
1983	Bondurant, Romeo, and Kretschmer	Delayed language	28
1983	Broerse, Peltola, and Crassini	Perceptual paradox	36
1983	Cousins and Vincent	Marital interaction	42
1983	Davis and Graybill	Abused children	30
1983	Ewart, Burnett, and Taylor	Blood pressure	2
1983	Gordon	Child temperament	35
1983	Henggeler and Cooper	Deaf children	30
1983	Kniskern, Robinson, and Mitchell	Mother-child behavior	40

Table 4–9 continued

Year	*Author*	*Topic*	*Sample*
1983	Koegel et al.	Autistic children	49
1983	Kontos	Metacognition	37
1983	Levenson and Gottman	Physiology	30
1983	Lipscomb and Coon	Parental speech	40
1983	Loeber, Weissman, and Reid	Delinquent adolescents	33
1983	Mash and Johnston	Hyperactive children	46
1983	McLaughlin	Parental speech	24
1983	Sabatelli, Buck, and Dreyer	Nonverbal communication	48
1983	Slee	Emotional expression	4
1984	Adamson and Bakeman	Mothers' communication	28
1984	DeSalvo and Zucher	Parental communication	47
1984	Dixon et al.	Cultural differences	36
1984	Donnellan, Anderson, and Mesaras	Autistic children	7
1984	Giblin, Starr, and Agronow	Abused children	28
1984	Hladik and Edwards	Parental speech	10
1984	Kekelis and Andersen	Language development	6
1984	Lessin and Jacob	Delinquent families	18
1984	Rowland	Blind children	5
1984	Sass et al.	Schizophrenia	25
1984	Schnur and Shatz	Maternal gesturing	4
1984	Yelsma	Marital adjustment	46
1985	Banmen and Vogel	Sexual communication	44
1985	Barbarin and Tirado	Obesity	45
1985	Borduin et al.	Delinquent boys	36
1985	Frankenstein, Hay, and Nathan	Alcoholism	8
1985	Hsu, Tseng, and Ashton	Cultural differences	48
1985	Lester, Hoffman, and Brazelton	Rhytmic structure	40
1985a	Meyers and Freeman	Stuttering	24
1985b	Meyers and Freeman	Stuttering	24
1985	Mitchell	Home video games	20
1985	Mullis and Hollis	Parental speech	32
1985	Nienhuys, Hasborough, and Cross	Deaf children	32
1985	Phelps and Slater	Sequential interactions	24
1985	Schachter and O'Leary	Affective intent	28
1985	Venaki, Nadler, and Gershoni	Holocaust experience	15
1985	Wanska and Bedrosian	Conversational structure	30
1985a	Webster-Stratton	Conduct problem children	40
1985b	Webster-Stratton	Conduct problem children	30
1985	Weitzman, Birns and Friend	Mothers' communication	40
1985	Williamson and Fitzpatrick	Relational patterns	40
1986	Anderson, Lytton, and Romney	Conduct problem boys	32
1986	Bakeman and Adamson	Mother-child behavior	28
1986	Borduin et al.	Social class	32
1986	Cole and Rehm	Childhood depression	45
1986	Gjerde	Family interaction	44
1986	Hooley	Depression	30
1986	Jasnow and Feldstein	Temporal characteristics	29
1986	Langlois, Hanrahan, and Inouye	Stuttering children	16
1986	Meeks, Arnkoff, and Glass	Marital adjustment	36
1986	Murray and Trevathen	Mother-child communication	8

Table 4–9 continued

Year	*Author*	*Topic*	*Sample*
1986	Oldershaw, Walters, and Hall	Abused children	20
1986	Olson, Bayles, and Bates	Speech progress	40
1986	Sabatelli, Buck, and Kenny	Nonverbal communication	48
1986	Slater	Mental retardation	40
1986a	Stevenson et al.	Mothers' speech	25
1986b	Stevenson et al.	Vocal responsiveness	25
1986	Wanska and Bedrosian	Mother-child discourse	30
1987	Breznitz and Sherman	Depressed mothers	32
1987	Burggraf and Sillars	Sex differences	36
1987	Dunn, Bretherton, and Munn	Mother-child discourse	43
1987	Gardner	Conduct problem children	39
1987	Hardman, Hoopes, and Harper	Interaction style	35
1987	Holaday	Chronic illness	5
1987	Hornik, Risenhoover, and Gunner	Affective communication	48
1987	Jones and Adamson	Mother-child behavior	32
1987	Kowalik and Gotlib	Depression	20
1987	Lavin	Causal attribution	40
1987	Madden	Decision making	37
1987	Martinez	Mother-child communication	20
1987	Masur	Imitative interchange	18
1987	Oscarson, Mullis, and Mullis	Speech complexity	26
1987	Putallaz	Sociometric status	42
1987	Roopnarine and Adams	Child popularity	37
1987	Rutter and Durkin	Turn taking	18
1987	Shapiro, Frosch, and Arnold	Autistic children	6
1988	Barton, Alexander, and Turner	Defensive communication	32
1988	Jacob and Leonard	Alcoholism	49
1988	MacKay-Soroka, Trehub, and Thorpe	Deaf children	30
1988	McCarrick, Hunt, and Sobal	Schizophrenia	17
1988	Morikawa, Shand, and Kosawa	Cultural differences	40
1988	Pettit, Dodge, and Brown	Social competence	46
1988	Termine and Izard	Mother-child behavior	36
1989	Caldera, Huston, and O'Brien	Social interaction	40
1989	Hahlweg et al.	Schizophrenia	43
1989	Pettit and Bates	Family interaction	25

descriptive in nature and included measurement of only one individual within the family. A bright spot in this early period was that researchers began to attempt to recognize and explain patterns of behavior and interaction within families.

As inquiry in the field matured, researchers began to use theory to guide their investigations, mostly in broad and general terms. Larger, more representative samples were utilized, and descriptions of these samples were included in the various reports. Research also began to be more inferential in nature. The major impetus to growth and development in this period was the inclusion of more than one family member and the introduction of direct observation of family interaction. At this time, two camps of research began to be distinguished: those who concentrated mostly on parent-child interaction in relation to child development and those who focused on marital interaction and parent-child interaction in relation to dysfunction in the child and within the family.

Currently research in the field is in its adolescent stage. Many authors report the use of specific concepts of theory as they determine and test their hypotheses. There has been an explosion of studies that are similar in methodology. Direct observation assessment has become the most widely used procedure for measurement of interaction and communication, and various coding systems have been developed. Different types of statistics, such as lag sequential analysis, time-series analysis, log linear hazards and logit models, structural equation modeling and path analysis, and multivariate and covariate analysis of variance have been introduced, and the resulting family interaction picture has become more complex.

Major Findings

Parent-Child Interaction. In general, negative family patterns are associated with negative child development, and positive family patterns are associated with positive child development. Negative family interactions include dissension between parents; too much or too little expression of concern, support, and affection from parents toward their children; confusion in communication; and an inability to reach mutual decisions. Positive family interactions include consensus between father and mother on various aspects of family life, including their marriage relationship and parenting practices; a moderate level of parental supervision and expression of affection and concern; and communication accuracy and mutual agreement in decision making.

Marital Interaction. Satisfaction in the marital relationship is the result of several communication and interaction factors: validation of each spouse for the other, reciprocation of positive affect, lack of negative verbal exchanges with accompanying negative nonverbal cues, and problem resolution that is satisfactory to both partners.

Observations about Research. Much of the research reported continues to look for direct causal relationships between family interaction and child and family dysfunction, but most measurement techniques are unidirectional and assess interaction between only two people at a time. There is an absence of true family or dyadic measures in which the relationship patterns rather than individual behaviors are the target of measurement.

The emphasis on observation of interactional behavior has overshadowed the focus on perception and cognitive and affective styles in family relationships. Moreover, most measurement of family interaction occurs in contrived laboratory settings using structured, present tasks and with minimal samplings of interaction (usually one or two).

There are a number of other problems. Most coding schemes lack the development necessary to demonstrate strong validity and reliability, and they assess very micro levels of behavior. The child development and family interaction camps of researchers tend to overlook the work done by each other because they often identify with different disciplines and attend different research meetings. An unresolved problem is how to create relational data when individuals are the sources. And the target of measurement is often unclear. Is the target an individual with other family members acting as sources of information; or the relationship in which patterns that are truly relational are measured; or, one person's individual behavior in relation to another person's individual behavior?

There is no accepted method of analysis for looking at both simultaneous and sequential patterning in family interaction. The problem is confounded when a researcher wants to move beyond looking at one family or dyad to comparing differences in interaction patterns between specific groups of families or dyads.

Almost all of the research on family communication and interaction is cross-sectional. The nature of cross-sectional research does not permit one to answer whether individual family member problems occur first, with observed family interaction being subsequent, or whether patterns of family interaction are present before individual problems occur.

Suggestions for Future Research

The word *interaction* implies two- or more-way streams of action that are interrelated. Methods need to be developed to codify and analyze these types of data (for example, relationship patterns as opposed to individual behaviors in the relationship context). The use of new computer programs that record parallel behaviors might be an answer to the codification problem, but the problem most likely is related to the theory-building stage of what to observe. When the target of observation is individual behavior rather than a relationship pattern, the consequent results will tend to emphasize individual behaviors in the relationship context rather than true relational patterns or styles.

More naturalistic settings for collecting data, along with use of portable video camcorders and computers, may be a means of getting at a more accurate picture of family interaction. More than one sample of the dyad's or family's patterns needs to be taken. The interaction tasks themselves are also crucial and influence the results.

The development of true couple and family measurements would strengthen results immensely. New advances in statistical techniques such as confirmatory factor analysis and structural equation analysis might help in the development of such instruments.

Inclusion of more qualitative data, such as perceptions and feelings of family members during family interaction, might be a way to use more of a multimethod approach to interaction research. Since family behavior and interaction seems to be so complex, knowledge from other fields that predict consequences from a multitude of variables might be usefully incorporated into family interaction research. Weather prediction, economic forecasting, and actuarial science come to mind as worthwhile domains to investigate.

More studies need to investigate the interplay between biological factors and social interaction in families. Continued attention needs to focus on ways of analyzing simultaneous and sequential patterns of behavior, feelings, perceptions, beliefs, and thoughts in dyads. And a method for analyzing similar data in groups larger than two needs to be developed.

Coding schemes that access more macro levels of couple and family interaction need to be developed. The Georgia Family Q Sort (Wampler et al., 1989) and Georgia Marriage Q Sort (Wampler and Halverson, 1989) are good beginnings.

More longitudinal studies need to be conducted that investigate the reciprocal influences of individual family members, other units of the family, and the family as a whole.

Note

1. *Psychological Abstracts, Child Development Abstracts, Combined Retrospective Index to Journals in Sociology, Dissertation Abstracts, International Bibliography of Research in Marriage and the Family, Research in Marriage and the Family*, and the *Inventory of Marriage and Family Literature* were used as resource guides to published materials. In order to locate additional articles in the first three decades reviewed, each of the following journals was examined volume by volume by inspecting titles and topic listings found in respective indexes and table of contents: *American Journal of Sociology, American Sociological Review, Human Communication Research, Journal of Communication, Journal of Marriage and the Family, Social Forces*, and *Sociology and Social Research*. Some articles were unavailable to us; they are listed at the end of this chapter.

References

Aldous, J. 1977. Family interaction patterns. *Annual Review of Sociology* 3:105–135.

Alkire, A. 1969. Social power and communication within families of disturbed and nondisturbed preadolescents. *Journal of Personality and Social Psychology* 13 (4):335–349.

Allen, A., and Thompson, T. 1984. Agreement, understanding, realization, and feeling understood as predictors of communicative satisfaction in marital dyads. *Journal of Marriage and the Family* 46:915–921.

Anderson, J.Z., and White, G.D. 1986. An empirical investigation of interaction and relationship patterns in functional and dysfunctional nuclear families and stepfamilies. *Family Process* 25 (3):407–422.

Antonovsky, H.F. 1959. A contribution to research in the area of the mother-child relationship. *Child Development* 30:37–51.

Arco, C.M. 1983. Pacing of playful stimulation to young infants: Similarities and differences in maternal and paternal communication. *Infant Behavior and Development* 6 (2):223–228.

Baldwin, A.L. 1946. Differences in parent behavior toward three- and nine-year-old children. *Journal of Personality* 15:143–165.

———. 1947. Changes in parent behavior during pregnancy. *Child Development* 18:29–39.

———. 1948. Socialization and the parent-child relationship. *Child Development* 19 (3):127–136.

Baldwin, A.L.; Kalhorn, J.; and Breese, F.H. 1945. Patterns of parent behavior. *Psychological Monographs* 58 (3):1–75.

Banister, H., and Ravden, M. 1944. The problem child and his environment. *British Journal of Psychology* 34:60–65.

Barnes, H.L., and Olson, D.H. 1985. Parent-adolescent communication and the circumplex model. *Child Development* 56:438–447.

Barnes, H.L.; Schumm, W.R.; Jurich, A.P.; and Bolmann, S.R. 1984. Marital satisfaction: Positive regard versus effective communications as explanatory variables. *Journal of Social Psychology* 123:71–78.

Baruch, D.W., and Wilcox, J.A. 1944. A study of sex differences in preschool children's adjustment coexistent with interparental tensions. *Journal of Genetic Psychology* 64:281–303.

Bates, A. 1942. Parental roles in courtship. *Social Forces* 20:483–486.

Bauman, G.B., and Roman, M. 1966. Interaction testing in the study of marital dominance. *Family Process* 5:365–382.

Bean, F.D.; Clark, M.P.; Swicegood, G.; and Williams, D. 1983. Husband-wife communication, wife's employment, and the decision for male or female sterilization. *Journal of Marriage and the Family* 45 (2):395–403.

Beavers, W.R.; Blumberg, S.; Timken, K.R., and Weiner, M.F. 1965. Communication patterns of mothers of schizophrenics. *Family Process* 4:95–104.

Bee, H.L. 1967. Parent-child interaction and distractibility in 9-year-old children. *Merrill-Palmer Quarterly* 13:175–190.

Befera, M.S., and Barkley, R.A. 1985. Hyperactive and normal girls and boys: Mother-child interaction, parent psychiatric status and child psychopathology. *Journal of Child Psychology and Psychiatry and Allied Disciplines* 26 (3):439–452.

Behrens, M.L., and Goldfarb, W. 1958. A study of patterns of interaction of families of schizophrenic children in residential treatment. *American Journal of Orthopsychiatry* 28:300–312.

Beier, E.G., and Sternberg, D.P. 1977. Marital communication. *Journal of Communication* 27 (3):92–97.

Belsky, J.; Gilstrap, B.; and Rovine, M. 1984. The Pennsylvania Infant and Family Development Project, I: Stability and change in mother-infant and father-infant

interaction in a family setting at one, three, and nine months. *Child Development* 55 (3):692–705.
Bishop, B.M. 1951. Mother-child interaction and the social behavior of children. *Psychological Monographs* 65 (11):whole no. 328.
Blechman, E.A., and McEnroe, M.J. 1985. Effective family problem solving. *Child Development* 56:429–437.
Bolles, M.M.; Metzger, H.F.; and Pitts, M.W. 1941. Early home background and personality adjustment. *American Journal of Orthopsychiatry* 11:530–534.
Bossard, J.H.S. 1943. Family table talk—an area for sociological study. *American Sociological Review* 8:295–301.
———. 1945. Family modes of expression. *American Sociological Review* 10:226–237.
Bridges, L.J.; Connell, J.P.; and Belsky, J. 1988. Similarities and differences in infant-mother and infant-father interaction in the strange situation: A component process analysis. *Developmental Psychology* 24:92–100.
Brody, G.H.; Pillegrini, A.D.; and Sigel, I.E. 1986. Marital quality and mother-child and father-child interactions with school-aged children. *Developmental Psychology* 22 (3):291–296.
Brown, R.G. 1958. Family structure and social isolation of older persons. *Journal of Gerontology* 15:170–174.
Bultena, G.L. 1969. Rural-urban differences in the familial interaction of the aged. *Rural Sociology* 34:5–15.
Burchinal, L.G., and Bauder, W.W. 1965. Decision-making and role patterns among Iowa farm and nonfarm families. *Journal of Marriage and the Family* 27:525–530.
Callan, V.J., and Noller, P. 1986. Perceptions of communicative relationships in families with adolescents. *Journal of Marriage and the Family* 48:813–820.
Carter, D.C. 1954. The influence of family relations and family experiences on personality. *Marriage and Family Living* 16:212–215.
Cass, L.K. 1952. Parent-child relationships and delinquency. *Journal of Abnormal and Social Psychology* 47:101–104.
Castan, B.; Gallois, C.A.; and Callan, V.J. 1985. Problem-solving interactions between Greek mothers and children. *Journal of Social Psychology* 125 (3):335–340.
Cheek, F.E. 1964. The "schizophrenic mother" in word and deed. *Family Process* 3 (1):155–177.
———. 1965. Family interaction patterns and convalescent adjustment of the schizophrenic. *Archives of General Psychiatry* 13:138–147.
Cheek, F.E., and Anthony, R. 1970. Personal pronoun usage in families of schizophrenics and social space utilization. *Family Process* 9:431–447.
Cicirelli, V.G. 1975. Effects of mother and older sibling on the problem-solving behavior of the younger child. *Developmental Psychology* 11 (6):749–756.
———. 1978. Effect of sibling presence on mother-child interaction. *Developmental Psychology* 14 (3):315–316.
Clarke-Stewart, K.A., and Hevey, C.M. 1981. Longitudinal relations in repeated observations of mother-child interaction from 1 to 2 1/2 years. *Developmental Psychology* 17 (2):127–145.
Cohn, J.F., and Tronick, E.Z. 1987. Mother-infant face-to-face interaction: The sequence of dyadic states at 3, 6, and 9 months. *Developmental Psychology* 23:68–77.
———. 1988. Mother-infant face-to-face interaction: Influence is bidirectional and

unrelated to periodic cycles in either partner's behavior. *Developmental Psychology* 24 (3):386–392.

Davis, A.J., and Lange, G. 1973. Parent-child communication and the development of categorization styles in preschool children. *Child Development* 44 (3):624–629.

Davis, H.C.; Haymaker, D.J.; Hermecz, D.A.; and Gilbert, D.G. 1988. Marital interaction: Affective synchrony of self-reported emotional components. *Journal of Personality Assessment* 52 (1):48–57.

Dickson, W.P.; Hess, R.D.; Miyake, N.; and Azuma, H. 1979. Referential communication accuracy between mother and child as a predictor of cognitive development in the United States and Japan. *Child Development* 50 (1):53–59.

Dinkel, R.M. 1943. Parent-child conflict in Minnesota families. *American Sociological Review* 8:412–419.

Ditton, P.; Green, R.J.; and Singer, M.T. 1987. Communication deviances: A Comparison between parents of learning-disabled and normally achieving students. *Family Process* 26 (1):75–87.

Doane, J.A. 1978. Family interaction and communication deviance in disturbed and normal families: A review of the research. *Family Process* 17:357–371.

Doane, J.A.; Jones, J.E.; Fisher, L.; Ritzler, B.; Singer, M.; and Wynne, L.C. 1982. Parental communication deviance as a predictor of competence in children at risk for adult psychiatric disorder. *Family Process* 21 (2):211–223.

Dorfman, L.T., and Heckert, D.A. 1988. Egalitarianism in retired rural couples: Household tasks, decision making, and leisure activities. *Family Relations* 37:73–78.

DuVall, E.W. 1936. Child-parent social distance. *Sociology and Social Research* 21: 458–463.

Eisler, I.; Dare, C.; and Szmukler, G.I. 1988. What's happened to family interaction research? An historical account and a family systems viewpoint. *Journal of Marriage and Family Therapy.* 14 (1):45–65.

Farina, A.; Holzberg, J.D.; and Dies, R.C. 1969. Influence of the parents and verbal reinforcement on the performance of schizophrenic patients. *Journal of Abnormal Psychology* 74 (1):9–15.

Ferreira, A. 1963. Decision making in normal and pathologic families. *Archives of General Psychiatry* 8:68–73.

Ferreira, A., and Winter, W. 1965. Family interaction and decision making. *Archives of General Psychiatry* 13:214–223.

———. 1968. Information exchange and silence in normal and abnormal families. *Family Process* 7:251–276.

Ferreira, A.; Winter, W.; and Poindexter, E. 1966. Some interactional variables in normal and abnormal families. *Family Process* 5:60–75.

Fisher, T.D. 1987. Family communication and the sexual behavior and attitudes of college students. *Journal of Youth and Adolescence* 16 (5):481–495.

Fitzsimmons, C., and Perkins, N.L. 1947. Patterns of family relationships in fifty farm families. *Rural Sociology* 12:300–303.

Fogel, A.; Toda, S.; and Kawai, M. 1988. Mother-infant face-to-face interaction in Japan and the United States: A laboratory comparison using 3-month-old infants. *Developmental Psychology* 24 (3):398–406.

Fox, G.L., and Inazu, J.K. 1980. Patterns and outcomes of mother-daughter communication about sexuality. *Journal of Social Issues* 36 (1):7–29.

Friedman, C.J., and Friedman, A.S. 1970. Characteristics of schizogenic families during a joint story-telling task. *Family Process* 9:333–353.

Gassner, S., and Murray, E.J. 1969. Dominance and conflict in the interactions between parents of normal and neurotic children. *Journal of Abnormal Psychology* 74:33–41.

Glick, B.R., and Gross, S.J. 1975. Marital interaction and marital conflict: A critical evaluation of current research strategies. *Journal of Marriage and the Family* 37:505–512.

Gottman, J.M., and Katz, L.F. 1989. Effects of marital discord on young children's peer interaction and health. *Developmental Psychology* 25 (3):373–381.

Gottman, J.M., and Krokoff, L.J. 1989. Marital interaction and satisfaction: A longitudinal view. *Journal of Consulting and Clinical Psychology* 57 (1):47–52.

Gottman, J.M.; Markman, H.; and Notarius, C. 1977. The topography of marital conflict: A sequential analysis of verbal and nonverbal behavior. *Journal of Marriage and the Family* 39:461–477.

Greenglass, E.R. 1971a. A cross-cultural comparison of maternal communication. *Child Development* 42 (3):685–692.

———. 1971b. A cross-cultural study of the child's communication with his mother. *Developmental Psychology* 5 (3):494–499.

———. 1972. A comparison of maternal communication style between immigrant Italian and second-generation Italian women living in Canada. *Journal of Cross-Cultural Psychology* 3 (2):182–192.

Grotevant, H.D., and Cooper, C.R. 1985. Patterns of interaction in family relationships and the development of identity exploration in adolescence. *Child Development* 56:415–428.

Haley, J. 1964. Research on family patterns: An instrument measurement. *Family Process* 3 (1):41–65.

———. 1967. Speech sequences of normal and abnormal families with two children present. *Family Process* 6:81–97.

Hansen, J.E., and Schuldt, W.J. 1984. Marital self-disclosure and marital satisfaction. *Journal of Marriage and the Family* 46:923–926.

Harmon, D., and Kogan, K.L. 1980. Social class and mother-child interaction. *Psychological Reports* 46:1075–1084.

Hattwick, B.W., and Stowell, M. 1936. The relation of parental over-attentiveness to children's work habits and social adjustments in kindergarten and the first six grades of school. *Journal of Educational Research* 30 (3):169–176.

Hauser, S.T.; Book, B.K.; Houlihan, J.; Powers, S.; Weiss-Perry, B.' Follansbee, D.; Jacobson, A.M.; and Noam, G.G. 1987. Sex differences within the family: Studies of adolescent and parent family interactions. *Journal of Youth and Adolescence* 16 (3):199–220.

Hawkins, J.L.; Weisberg, C.; and Ray, D.L. 1977. Marital communication style and social class. *Journal of Marriage and the Family* 39 (3):479–490.

Hetherington, E.M.; Stouwie, R.J.; and Ridberg, E.H. 1971. Patterns of family interaction and child-rearing attitudes related to three dimensions of juvenile delinquency. *Journal of Abnormal Psychology* 78 (2):160–176.

Highberger, R. 1955. The relationship between maternal behavior and the child's early school adjustment. *Child Development* 26 (1):49–61.

Humphrey, L.L. 1989. Observed family interactions among subtypes of eating disorders using structural analysis of social behavior. *Journal of Consulting and Clinical Psychology* 57 (2):206–214.

Hunter, F.T.; McCarthy, M.E.; MacTurk, R.H.; and Vietze, P.M. 1987. Infants' social-constructive interactions with mothers and fathers. *Developmental Psychology* 23 (2):249–254.

Ingersoll, H.L. 1948. Transmission of authority patterns in the family. *Marriage and Family Living* 10:36.

Jacklin, C.N.; DiPietro, J.A.; and Maccoby, E.E. 1984. Sex-typing behavior and sex-typing pressure in child/parent interaction. *Archives of Sexual Behavior* 13 (5):413–425.

Jacob, T. 1975. Family interaction in disturbed and normal families: A methodological and substantive review. *Psychological Bulletin* 82:33–65.

Jansen, L.T. 1952. Measuring family solidarity. *American Sociological Review* 17:727–733.

Johannis, T.B., and Rollins, J.M. 1959. Teenager perception of family decision making. *Family Life Coordinator* 7:70–74.

Jones, J.E. 1977. Patterns of transactional style deviance in the TAT's of parents of schizophrenics. *Family Process* 16 (3):327–337.

Jurovsky, A. 1948. The relations of older children to their parents. *Journal of Genetic Psychology* 72:85–100.

Kenkel, W.F. 1957. Influence differentiation in family decision making. *Sociology and Social Research* 42:18–25.

———. 1959. Traditional family ideology and spousal roles in decision making. *Marriage and Family Living* 21:334–339.

———. 1961. Husband-wife interaction in decision making and decision choices. *Journal of Social Psychology* 54:255–262.

Kenkel, W.F., and Hoffman, D.K. 1956. Real and conceived roles in family decision making. *Marriage and Family Living* 18:311–316.

Kohn, M.L., and Clausen, J.A. 1956. Parental authority behavior and schizophrenia. *American Journal of Orthopsychiatry* 26:297–313.

Larson, C.E. 1967. Interaction patterns and communication effectiveness in the marital context: A factor analytic study. *Journal of Communication* 17 (4):342–353.

Lasko, J.K. 1954. Parent behavior toward first and second children. *Genetic Psychology Monographs* 49:97–137.

Levenstein, P. 1970. Cognitive growth in pre-schoolers through verbal interaction with mothers. *American Journal of Orthopsychiatry* 40 (3):426–432.

Lidz, R.W., and Lidz, T. 1949. The family environment of schizophrenic patients. *American Journal of Psychiatry* 106:332–345.

Loeb, R.C.; Horst, L.; and Horton, P.J. 1980. Family interaction patterns associated with self-esteem in preadolescent girls and boys. *Merrill-Palmer Quarterly* 26 (3):205–217.

Lu, Y. 1952. Parent-child relationship and marital roles. *American Sociological Review* 17:357–361.

Lurie, L.A.; Levy, S.; Rosenthal, F.M.; and Lurie, O.B. 1943. Environmental influences: The relative importance of specific exogenous factors in producing behavior and personality disorders in children. *American Journal of Orthopsychiatry* 13:150–162.

Lytton, H.; Conway, D.; and Sauvé, R. 1977. The impact of twinship on parent-child interaction. *Journal of Personality and Social Psychology* 35 (2):97–107.
Maccoby, E.E.; Snow, M.E.; and Jacklin, C.N. 1984. Children's dispositions and mother-child interaction at 12 and 18 months: A short-term longitudinal study. *Developmental Psychology* 20 (3):459–472.
McCord, J.; McCord, W.; and Howard, A. 1963. Family interaction as antecedent to the direction of male aggressiveness. *Journal of Abnormal and Social Psychology* 66 (3):239–242.
McDevitt, T.M.; Hess, R.D.; Kashiwagi, K.; Dickson, W.P.; Miyake, N.; and Azuma, H. 1987. Referential communication accuracy of mother-child pairs and children's later scholastic achievement: A follow-up study. *Merrill-Palmer Quarterly* 33 (2):171–185.
McKeown, J.E., and Chyatte, C. 1954. The behavior of fathers as reported by normals, neurotics, and schizophrenics. *American Catholic Sociological Review* 15:332–340.
MacKinnon, C.E. 1989. An observational investigation of sibling interactions in married and divorced families. *Developmental Psychology* 25 (1):36–44.
March, J.G. 1953. Husband-wife interaction over political issues. *Public Opinion Quarterly* 17:461–470.
Mash, E.J., and Johnston, C. 1982. A comparison of the mother-child interactions of younger and older hyperactive and normal children. *Child Development* 53:1371–1381.
Merrill, B. 1946. A measurement of mother-child interaction. *Journal of Abnormal and Social Psychology* 41:37–49.
Meyer, C.T. 1947. The assertive behavior of children as related to parent behavior. *Journal of Home Economics* 39:77–80.
Middleton, R., and Putney, S. 1959. Dominance in decisions in the family: Race and class differences. *American Journal of Sociology* 65:605–609.
Miller, P.C.; Lefcourt, H.M.; Holmes, J.G.; Ware, E.E.; and Salch, W.E. 1986. Marital locus of control and marital problem solving. *Journal of Personality and Social Psychology* 51 (1):161–169.
Miller, T.W. 1972. Cultural dimensions related to parental verbalizations and self-concept in the child. *Journal of Social Psychology* 87:153–154.
Milner, E. 1951. A study of the relationship between reading readiness in grade one school children and patterns of parent-child interaction. *Child Development* 22 (2):95–112.
Nakamura, C.Y. 1959. The relationship between children's expression of hostility and methods of discipline exercised by dominant overprotective parents. *Child Development* 30:109–117.
Nye, F.I. 1957. Child adjustment in broken and in unhappy unbroken homes. *Marriage and Family Living* 19:356–361.
Pace, C.R. 1940. Problems in family relationships among young married adults. *Living* 2:42–43, 68.
Parsons, T., and Bales, R.F. 1955. *Family, Socialization and Interaction Process.* Glencoe, Ill.: Free Press.
Portes, P.R.; Mas, C.; and Dunham, R.M. 1986. Problems and directions in family interaction research. *Family Therapy* 13 (3)291–297.
Pressey, L.C. 1931. Some serious family maladjustments among college students. *Social Forces* 10:236–242.

Prinz, R.J.; Rosenblum, R.S.; and O'Leary, K.D. 1978. Affective communication differences between distressed and nondistressed mother-adolescent dyads. *Journal of Abnormal Child Psychology* 6 (3):373–383.

Punke, H.H. 1943. High-school youth and family quarrels. *School and Society* 58:507–511.

Raush, H.L.; Greif, A.C.; and Nugent, J. 1979. Communication in couples and families. In W.R. Burr, R. Hill, F.I. Nye, and I.L. Reiss (eds.), *Contemporary Theories about the Family,* 1:468–489. New York: Free Press.

Ryder, R.G. 1968. Husband-wife dyads versus married strangers. *Family Process* 7:233–238.

Saunders, L.E. 1974. Empathy, communication, and the definition of life satisfaction in the postparental period. *Family Perspective* 8:21–35.

Shukla, A. 1987. Decision making in single- and dual-career families in India. *Journal of Marriage and the Family* 49:621–629.

Snow, M.E.; Jacklin, C.N.; and Maccoby, E.E. 1983. Sex-of-child differences in father-child interaction at one year of age. *Child Development* 54:227–232.

Stewart, A.H.; Weiland, I.H.; Leider, A.R.; Mangham, C.A.; Holmes, T.H.; and Ripley, H.S. 1954. Excessive infant crying (colic) in relation to parent behavior. *American Journal of Psychiatry* 110:687–694.

Stewart, R.B. 1983. Sibling attachment relationships: Child-infant interaction in the strange situation. *Developmental Psychology* 19 (2):192–199.

Stivers, C. 1988. Parent-adolescent communication and its relationship to adolescent depression and suicide proneness. *Adolescence* 23 (90):291–295.

Stocker, C.; Dunn, J.; and Plomin, R. 1989. Sibling relationships: Links with child temperament, maternal behavior, and family structure. *Child Development* 60:715–727.

Stone, C.L., and Landis, P.H. 1953. An approach to authority in parent-teen-age relationships. *Rural Sociology* 18:233–242.

Stott, L.H. 1939. Some family life patterns and their relation to personality development in children. *Journal of Experimental Education* 8 (2):148–160.

Straus, M.A. 1967. Communication, creativity, and problem-solving ability of middle- and working-class families in three societies. *American Journal of Sociology* 73:417–430.

Strodtbeck, F.L. 1951. Husband-wife interaction over revealed differences. *American Sociological Review* 16:468–473.

———. 1952. The interaction of a "henpecked" husband with his wife. *Marriage and Family Living* 14:305–308.

———. 1954. The family as a three-person group. *American Sociological Review* 19:23–29.

Tallman, I., and Miller, G. 1974. Class differences in family problem solving: The effects of verbal ability, hierarchal structure, and role expectations. *Sociometry* 37:13–37.

Tauber, M.A. 1979. Sex differences in parent-child interaction styles during a free-play session. *Child Development* 50 (4):981–988.

Thurow, M.B. 1934. A study of selected factors in family life as described in life history material. *Social Forces* 12:562–569.

Tietze, T. 1949. A study of mothers of schizophrenic patients. *Psychiatry* 12:55–65.

Tulkin, S.R., and Kagan, J. 1972. Mother-child interaction in the first year of life. *Child Development* 43 (1):31–41.

Tyndall, L.W., and Lichtenberg, J.W. 1985. Spouses' cognitive styles and marital interaction patterns. *Journal of Marital and Family Therapy* 11 (2):193–202.
Umphress, A.; Murphy, S.; Nichols, J.; and Hammar, S. 1970. Adolescent enuresis: A sociological study of family interaction. *Archives of General Psychiatry* 22:237–244.
Vuchinich, S. 1986. On attention in verbal family conflict. *Social Psychology Quarterly* 49:281–293.
Wahl, C.W. 1954. Some antecedent factors in the family histories of 392 schizophrenics. *American Journal of Psychiatry* 110:668–676.
———. 1956. Some antecedent factors in the family histories of 568 male schizophrenics of the United States Navy. *American Journal of Psychiatry* 113:201–210.
Wampler, K.S., and Halverson, C.F., Jr. 1990. The Georgia Marriage Q-sort: An observational measure of marital functioning. *American Journal of Family Therapy* 18 (2):169–178.
Wampler, K.S.; Halverson, C.F., Jr.; Moore, J.J.; and Walters, L.H. 1989. The Georgia Family Q-Sort: An observational measure of family functioning. *Family Process* 28 (2): 223–238.
Waxler, N.E., and Mishler, E.G. 1971. Parental interaction with schizophrenic children and well siblings: An experimental test of some etiological theories. *Archives of General Psychiatry* 25:223–231.
Webster-Stratton, C. 1985. Mother perceptions and mother-child interactions: Comparison of a clinic-referred and a nonclinical group. *Journal of Clinical Child Psychology* 14 (4):334–339.
White, B.B. 1989. Gender differences in marital communication patterns. *Family Process* 28:89–106.
Wilkening, E.A. 1954. Change in farm technology as related to familism, family decision making and family interaction. *American Sociological Review* 19:29–37.
Winch, R.F. 1943. The relation between courtship behavior and attitudes toward parents among college men. *American Sociological Review* 8:164–174.
———. 1946. Interrelations between certain social background and parent-son factors in a study of courtship among college men. *American Sociological Review* 11:333–343.
Winter, W.D., and Ferreira, A.J. 1967. Interaction process analysis of family decision making. *Family Process* 6:155–172.
———. 1969. Talking time as an index of intrafamilial similarity in normal and abnormal families. *Journal of Abnormal Psychology* 74 (5):574–575.
Witteman, H., and Fitzpatrick, M.A. 1986. Compliance-gaining in marital interaction: *Communication Monographs* 53 (2):130–143.
Wittman, M.P. 1939. Development characteristics and personalities of chronic alcoholics. *Journal of Abnormal and Social Psychology* 34:361–377.
Wolgast, E.H. 1958. Do husbands or wives make the purchasing decisions? *Journal of Marketing* 23:151–158.
Woodhouse, C.G. 1930. A study of 250 successful families. *Social Forces* 8:511–532.
Woolf, M.D. 1943. A study of some relationships between home adjustment and the behavior of junior college students. *Journal of Social Psychology* 17:275–286.
Yelsma, P. 1986. Marriage vs. cohabitation: Couples' communication practices and satisfaction. *Journal of Communication* 36:94–107.
Yelsma, P., and Athappilly, K. 1988. Marital satisfaction and communication practices: Comparisons among Indian and American couples. *Journal of Comparative Family Studies* 19:37–54.

Zarling, C.L.; Hirsch, B.J.; and Landry, S. 1988. Maternal social networks and mother-infant interactions in full-term and very low birthweight, preterm infants. *Child Development* 59 (1):178–185.

Zucker, H. 1943a. The emotional attachment of children to their parents as related to standards of behavior and delinquency. *Journal of Psychology* 15:31–40.

Zucker, H.J. 1943b. Affectional identification and delinquency. *Archives of Psychology* 286:1–60.

Articles with Sample Sizes Smaller Than Fifty

Adamson, L.B., and Bakeman, R. 1984. Mothers' communicative acts: Changes during infancy. *Infant Behavior and Development* 7 (4):467–478.

Alexander, J.F. 1973a. Defensive and supportive communication in family systems. *Journal of Marriage and the Family* 35:613–617.

———. 1973b. Defensive and supportive communications in normal and deviant families. *Journal of Consulting and Clinical Psychology* 40:223–231.

Alkire, A.A.; Goldstein, M.J.; Rodnick, E.H.; and Judd, L.L. 1971. Social influence and counterinfluence within families of four types of disturbed adolescents. *Journal of Abnormal Psychology* 77:32–41.

Als, H. 1977. The newborn communicates. *Journal of Communication* 27 (2):66–73.

Alsbrook, L. 1976. Marital communication and sexism. *Social Casework* 57 (8):517–522.

Anderson, K.E.; Lytton, H.; and Romney, D.M. 1986. Mothers' interactions with normal and conduct-disordered boys: Who affects whom? *Developmental Psychology* 22 (5):604–609.

Arco, C.M. 1983. Infant reactions to natural and manipulated temporal patterns of paternal communication. *Infant Behavior and Development* 6 (3):391–399.

Asarnow, J.R.; Lewis, J.M.; Doane, J.A.; Goldstein, M.J.; and Rodnick, E.H. 1982. Family interaction and the course of adolescent psychopathology: An analysis of adolescent and parent effects. *Journal of Abnormal Child Psychology* 10 (3):427–441.

Aston, P.J., and Dobson, G. 1972. Family interaction and social adjustment in a sample of normal school children. *Journal of Child Psychology and Psychiatry and Allied Disciplines* 13:77–90.

Bakeman, R., and Adamson, L.B. 1986. Infants' conventionalized acts: Gestures and words with mothers and peers. *Infant Behavior and Development* 9 (2):215–230.

Banmen, J., and Vogel, N.A. 1985. The relationship between marital quality and interpersonal sexual communication. *Family Therapy* 12 (1):45–58.

Barbarin, O.A., and Tirado, M. 1985. Enmeshment, family processes, and successful treatment of obesity. *Family Relations* 34 (1):115–121.

Barkley, R.A.; Cunningham, C.E.; and Karlsson, J. 1983. The speech of hyperactive children and their mothers: Comparison with normal children and stimulant drug effects. *Journal of Learning Disabilities* 16 (2):105–110.

Barton, C.; Alexander, J.F.; and Turner, C.W. 1988. Defensive communication in normal and delinquent families: The impact of context and family role. *Journal of Family Psychology* 1 (4):390–405.

Barton, K., and Ericksen, L.K. 1981. Differences between mothers and fathers in teaching style and child-rearing practices. *Psychological Reports* 49 (1):237–238.

Baxter, J.; Arthur, S.; Flood, C.; and Hedgepeth, B. 1962. Conflict patterns in the families of schizophrenics. *Journal of Nervous and Mental Disease* 135:419–424.

Beakel, N.G., and Mehrabian, A. 1969. Inconsistent communication and psychopathology. *Journal of Abnormal Psychology* 74:126–130.

Becker, J., and Finkel, P. 1969. Predictability and anxiety in speech by parents of female schizophrenics. *Journal of Abnormal Psychology* 74 (4):517–523.

Becker, J., and McArdle, J. 1967. Non-lexical speech similarities as an index of intrafamilial identifications. *Journal of Abnormal Psychology* 72 (5):408–414.

Becker, J.; Tatsuoka, M.; and Carlson, A. 1965. The communicative value of parental speech in families with disturbed children. *Journal of Nervous and Mental Disease* 141:359–364.

Becker, J.V., and Miller, P.M. 1976. Verbal and nonverbal marital interaction patterns of alcoholics and nonalcoholics. *Journal of Studies on Alcohol* 37 (11):1616–1624.

Behrens, M.; Rosenthal, H.; and Chodoff, P. 1968. Communication in lower class families of schizophrenics. II. Observations and findings. *Archives of General Psychiatry* 18:689–696.

Belsky, J. 1979. The interrelation of parental and spousal behavior during infancy in traditional nuclear families: An exploratory analysis. *Journal of Marriage and the Family* 41 (4):749–755.

Billings, A. 1979. Conflict resolution in distressed and nondistressed married couples. *Journal of Consulting and Clinical Psychology* 47:368–376.

Birchler, G.R.; Weiss, R.L.; and Vincent, J.P. 1975. A multimethod analysis of social reinforcement exchange between maritally distressed and nondistressed spouse and stranger dyads. *Journal of Personality and Social Psychology* 31:349–360.

Blotcky, A.D.; Tittler, B.I.; and Friedman, S. 1982. The double-bind situation in families of disturbed children. *Journal of Genetic Psychology* 141 (1):129–142.

Bondurant, J.L.; Romeo, D.J.; and Kretschmer, R. 1983. Language behaviors of mothers of children with normal and delayed language. *Language, Speech, and Hearing Services in Schools* 14 (4):233–242.

Borduin, C.M., and Henggeler, S.W. 1981. Social class, experimental setting, and task characteristics as determinants of mother-child interaction. *Developmental Psychology* 17 (2):209–214.

Borduin, C.M.; Henggeler, S.W.; Hanson, C.L.; and Pruitt, J.A. 1985. Verbal problem solving in families of father-absent and father-present delinquent boys. *Child and Family Behavior Therapy* 7 (2):51–63.

Borduin, C.M.; Henggeler, S.W.; Sanders-Walls, M.; and Harbin, F. 1986. An evaluation of social class differences in verbal and nonverbal maternal controls, maternal sensitivity and child compliance. *Child Study Journal* 16 (2):95–112.

Boyd, L.A., and Roach, A.J. 1977. Interpersonal communication skills differentiating more satisfying from less satisfying marital relationships. *Journal of Counseling Psychology* 24 (6):540–542.

Breznitz, Z., and Sherman, T. 1987. Speech patterning of natural discourse of well and depressed mothers and their young children. *Child Development* 58:395–400.

Brody, G.H.; Stoneman, Z.; and MacKinnon, C.E. 1982. Role asymmetries in interactions among school-aged children, their younger siblings, and their friends. *Child Development* 53:1364–1370.

Broerse, J.; Peltola, C.; and Crassini, B. 1983. Infants' reactions to perceptual paradox during mother-infant interaction. *Developmental Psychology* 19 (3):310–316.

Bugental, D.E.; Love, L.R.; and Gianetto, R.M. 1971. Perfidious feminine faces (videotaped verbal and nonverbal behavior of parents in interaction with their children). *Journal of Personality and Social Psychology* 17 (3):314–318.

Bugental, D.E.; Love, L.R.; and Kaswan, J.W. 1972. Videotaped family interaction: Differences reflecting presence and type of child disturbances. *Journal of Abnormal Psychology* 79 (3):285–290.

Bugenthal, D.; Love, L.; Kaswan, J.; and April, C. 1971. Verbal-non-verbal conflict in parental messages to normal and disturbed children. *Journal of Abnormal Psychology* 79:285-290.

Burggraf, C.S., and Sillars, A.L. 1987. A critical examination of sex differences in marital communication. *Communication Monographs* 54 (3):276–294.

Caldera, Y.M.; Huston, A.C.; and O'Brien, M. 1989. Social interaction and play patterns of parents and toddlers with feminine, masculine, and neutral toys. *Child Development* 60:70–76.

Caldwell, B.M., and Hersher, L. 1964. Mother-infant interaction during the first year of life. *Merril-Palmer Quarterly* 10:119–128.

Caputo, D.V. 1963. The parents of the schizophrenic. *Family Process* 2 (2):339–356.

Cherry, L., and Lewis, M. 1976. Mothers and two-year-olds: A study of sex-differentiated aspects of verbal interaction. *Developmental Psychology* 12 (4):278–282.

Cicirelli, V.G. 1976. Mother-child and sibling-sibling interactions on a problem-solving task. *Child Development* 47 (3):588–596.

Cole, D.A., and Rehm, L.P. 1986. Family interaction patterns and childhood depression. *Journal of Abnormal Child Psychology* 14 (2)297–314.

Cousins, P.C., and Vincent, J.P. 1983. Supportive and aversive behavior following spousal complaints. *Journal of Marriage and the Family* 45:679–682.

Craddock, A.E. 1980. Marital problem-solving as a function of couples' marital power expectations and marital value systems. *Journal of Marriage and the Family* 42 (1):185–196.

Crawford, J.W. 1982. Mother-infant interaction in premature and full-term infants. *Child Development* 53 (4):957–962.

Cunningham, C.E., and Barkley, R.A. 1979. The interactions of normal and hyperactive children with their mothers in free play and structured tasks. *Child Development* 50 (1):217–224.

Davis, A.J., and Hathaway, B.K. 1982. Reciprocity in parent-child verbal interactions. *Journal of Genetic Psychology* 140:169–183.

Davis, C.A., and Graybill, D. 1983. Comparison of family environments and abused versus non-abused children. *Psychology* 20 (1):24–37.

DeSalvo, F.J., and Zurcher, L.A. 1984. Defensive and supportive parental communication in a discipline situation. *Journal of Psychology* 117 (1):7–17.

Dixon, S.D.; LeVine, R.A.; Richman, A.; and Brazelton, T.B. 1984. Mother-child interaction around a teaching task: An African-American comparison. *Child Development* 55 (4):1252–1264.

Doleys, D.M.; Cartelli, L.M.; and Doster, J. 1976. Comparison of patterns of mother-child interaction. *Journal of Learning Disabilities* 9 (6):371–375.

Donnellan, A.M.; Anderson, J.L.; and Mesaros, R.A. 1984. An observational study of stereotypic behavior and proximity related to the occurrence of autistic child-family member interactions. *Journal of Autism and Developmental Disorders* 14 (2):205–221.

Dunn, J.; Bretherton, I.; and Munn, P. 1987. Conversations about feeling states between mothers and their young children. *Developmental Psychology* 23 (1):132–139.

Eheart, B.K. 1982. Mother-child interactions with nonretarded and mentally retarded preschoolers. *American Journal of Mental Deficiency* 87 (1):20–25.

Ewart, C.K.; Burnett, K.F.; and Taylor, C.B. 1983. Communication behaviors that affect blood pressure: An A-B-A-B analysis of marital interaction. *Behavior Modification* 7 (3):331–344.

Eyberg, S.M., and Robinson, E.A. 1982. Parent-child interaction training: Effects on family functioning. *Journal of Clinical Child Psychology* 11 (2):130–137.

Farina, A. 1960. Patterns of role dominance and conflict in parents of schizophrenic parents. *Journal of Abnormal and Social Psychology* 61 (1):31–38.

Fash, D.S., and Madison, C.L. 1981. Parents' language interaction with young children: A comparative study of mothers' and fathers'. *Child Study Journal* 11 (3):137–152.

Feinsilver, D. 1970. Communication in families of schizophrenic patients: Describing common objects as a test of communication between family members. *Archives of General Psychiatry* 22:143–148.

Ferreira, A., and Winter, W. 1966. Stability of interactional variables in family decision making. *Archives of General Psychiatry* 14:352–355.

Frankenstein, W.; Hay, W.M.; and Nathan, P.E. 1985. Effects of intoxication on alcoholics' marital communication and problem solving. *Journal of Studies on Alcohol* 46:1–6.

Frankenstein, W.; Nathan, P.E.; Sullivan, R.F.; Hall, W.M.; and Cocco, K. 1985. Asymmetry of influence in alcoholics' marital communication: Alcoholics' effects on interaction dominance. *Journal of Marital and Family Therapy* 11 (4):399–410.

Gantman, C.A. 1978. Family interaction patterns among families with normal, disturbed, and drug-abusing adolescents. *Journal of Youth and Adolescence* 7 (4):429–440.

Gardner, F.E. 1987. Positive interaction between mothers and conduct-problem children: Is there training for harmony as well as fighting? *Journal of Abnormal Child Psychology* 15 (2):283–293.

Giblin, P.T.; Starr, R.H.; and Agronow, S.J. 1984. Affective behavior of abused and control children: Comparisons of parent-child interactions and the influence of home environment variables. *Journal of Genetic Psychology* 144 (1):69–82.

Gjerde, P.F. 1986. The interpersonal structure of family interaction settings: Parent-adolescent relations in dyads and triads. *Developmental Psychology* 22:297–304.

Golinkoff, R.M., and Amers, G.J. 1979. A comparison of fathers' and mothers' speech with their young children. *Child Development* 50 (1):28–32.

Goodman, N., and Ofshe, R. 1968. Empathy, communication efficiency, and marital status. *Journal of Marriage and the Family* 30:597–603.

Gorad, S.L. 1971. Communicational styles and interaction of alcoholics and their wives. *Family Process* 10 (4):475–489.

Gordon, B.N. 1983. Maternal perception of child temperament and observed mother-child interaction. *Child Psychiatry and Human Development* 13 (3):153–167.

Gottman, J.M. 1980. Consistency of nonverbal affect and affect reciprocity in marital interaction. *Journal of Consulting and Clinical Psychology* 48 (6):711–717.

Gottman, J.M., and Porterfield, A.L. 1981. Communicative competence in the nonver-

bal behavior of married couples. *Journal of Marriage and the Family* 43 (4):817–824.
Greenberg, M.T. 1980. Social interaction between deaf preschoolers and their mothers. The effects of communication method and communication competence. *Developmental Psychology* 16 (5):465–474.
Hadley, T., and Jacob, T. 1973. Relationship among measures of family power. *Journal of Personality and Social Psychology* 27:6–12.
Hahlweg, K; Goldstein, M.J.; Nuechterlein, K.H.; Magana, A.B.; Mintz, J.; Doane, J.A.; Miklowitz, D.J.; and Snyder, K.S. 1989. Expressed emotion and patient-relative interaction in families of recent onset schizophrenia. *Journal of Consulting and Clinical Psychology* 57 (1):11–18.
Haley, J. 1967. Experiment with abnormal families: Testing in a restricted communication setting. *Archives of General Psychology* 17:53–63.
———. 1968. Testing parental instructions of schizophrenic and normal children. *Journal of Abnormal Psychology* 73:559–565.
Hardman, R.K.; Hoopes, M.H.; and Harper, J.M. 1987. Verbal interaction styles of two marital combinations: Based on a systems approach to sibling positions. *American Journal of Family Therapy* 15:131–144.
Hassan, S.A. 1974. Transactional and contextual invalidation between the parents of disturbed families: A comparative study. *Family Process* 13:53–76.
Hatfield, J.S.; Ferguson, L.R.; and Alpert, R. 1967. Mother-child interaction and the socialization process. *Child Development* 38:365–414.
Henggeler, S.W., and Cooper, P.F. 1983. Deaf child–hearing mother interaction: Extensiveness and reciprocity. *Journal of Pediatric Psychology* 8 (1):83–95.
Hershey, S., and Werner, E. 1975. Dominance in marital decision making in women's liberation and non–women liberation families. *Family Process* 14:223–233.
Hladik, E.G., and Edwards, H.T. 1984. A comparative analysis of mother-father speech in the naturalistic home environment. *Journal of Psycholinguistic Research* 13 (5):321–332.
Holaday, B. 1987. Patterns of interaction between mothers and their chronically ill infants. *Maternal Child Nursing Journal* 16 (1):29–45.
Hooley, J.M. 1986. Expressed emotion and depression: Interactions between patients and high- versus low-expressed-emotion spouses. *Journal of Abnormal Psychology* 95:237–246.
Hore, T. 1970. Social class differences in some aspects of the nonverbal communication between mother and preschool child. *Australian Journal of Psychology* 22 (1):21–27.
Hornik, R.; Risenhoover, N.; and Gunnar M. 1987. The effects of maternal positive, neutral, and negative affective communications on infant responses to new toys. *Child Development* 58 (4):937–944.
Hsu, J.; Tseng, W.; and Ashton, G. 1985. Family interaction patterns among Japanese-American and Caucasian families in Hawaii. *American Journal of Psychiatry* 142:577–581.
Jacob, T. 1974. Patterns of family conflict and dominance as a function of child age and social class. *Developmental Psychology* 10:1–12.
———. 1977. Verbal activity of middle- and lower-class parents when teaching their child. *Psychological Reports* 40 (2):575–578.
Jacob, T., and Davis, J. 1973. Family interaction as a function of experimental task. *Family Process* 12:415–425.

Jacob, T., and Leonard, K.E. 1988. Alcoholic-spouse interaction as a function of alcoholism subtype and alcohol consumption interaction. *Journal of Abnormal Psychology* 97:231–237.

Jasnow, M., and Feldstein, S. 1986. Adult-like temporal characteristics of mother-infant vocal interactions. *Child Development* 57 (3):754–761.

Jones, C.P., and Adamson, L.B. 1987. Language use in mother-child and mother-child-sibling interactions. *Child Development* 58 (2):356–366.

Kaye, K., and Charney, R. 1981. Conversational asymmetry between mothers and children. *Journal of Child Language* 8 (1):35–49.

Kaye, K., and Fogel, A. 1980. The temporal structure of face-to-face communication between mothers and infants. *Developmental Psychology* 16 (5):454–464.

Kekelis, L.S., and Andersen, E.S. 1984. Family communication styles and language development. *Journal of Visual Impairment and Blindness* 78 (2):54–65.

Kenkel, W.F. 1961. Dominance, persistence, self-confidence, and spousal roles in decision making. *Journal of Social Psychology* 54:349–358.

Kniskern, J.R.; Robinson, E.A.; and Mitchell, S.K. 1983. Mother-child interaction in home and laboratory settings. *Child Study Journal* 13 (1):23–39.

Koegel, R.L.; Schreibman, L.; O'Neill, R.E.; and Burke, J.C. 1983. The personality and family-interaction characteristics of parents of autistic children. *Journal of Consulting and Clinical Psychology* 51 (5):683–689.

Kogan, K.L. 1971. Behavior transactions between disturbed children and their mothers. *Psychological Reports* 2:395–404.

———. 1972. Specificity and stability of mother-child interaction styles. *Child Psychiatry and Human Development* 2 (4):160–168.

Kogan, K.L., and Wimberger, H.C. 1969. Interaction patterns in disadvantaged families. *Journal of Clinical Psychology* 25 (4)347–352.

Kontos, S. 1983. Adult-child interaction and the origins of metacognition. *Journal of Educational Research* 77 (1):43–54.

Kowalik, D.L., and Gotlib, I.H. 1987. Depression and marital interaction: Concordance between intent and perception of communication. *Journal of Abnormal Psychology* 96:127–134.

Lamb, M.E. 1976. Effects of stress and cohort on mother-and father-infant interaction. *Developmental Psychology* 12 (5):435–443.

Landerholm, E.J., and Scriven, G. 1981. A comparison of mother and father interaction with their six-month-old male and female infants. *Early Child Development and Care* 7 (4):317–328.

Langlois, A.; Hanrahan, L.L.; and Inouye, L.L. 1986. A comparison of interactions between stuttering children, nonstuttering children, and their mothers. *Journal of Fluency Disorders* 11 (3):263–273.

Lavin, T.J. 1987. Divergence and convergence in the causal attibutions of married couples. *Journal of Marriage and the Family* 49:71–80.

Leighton, L.A.; Stollak, G.E.; and Fergusson, L.R. 1971. Patterns of communication in normal and clinic families. *Journal of Consulting and Clinical Psychology* 36:252–256.

Lennard, H.; Beaulieu, M.; and Embry, N. 1965. Interaction in families with a schizophrenic child. *Archives of General Psychiatry* 12:166–183.

Lessin, S., and Jacob, T. 1979. Verbal-nonverbal congruence in normal and delinquent families. *Journal of Clinical Psychology* 35 (2):391–395.

Lessin, S., and Jacob, T. 1984. Multichannel communication in normal and delinquent families. *Journal of Abnormal Child Psychology* 12 (3):369–383.

Lester, B.M.; Hoffman, J.; and Brazelton, T.B. 1985. The rhythmic structure of mother-infant interaction in term and preterm infants. *Child Development* 56 (1):15–27.

Levenson, R.W., and Gottman, J.M. 1983. Marital interaction: Physiological linkage and affective exchange. *Journal of Personality and Social Psychology* 45:587–597.

Levenstein, P., and Sunley, R. 1967. An effect of stimulating verbal interaction between mothers and children around play material. *American Journal of Orthopsychiatry* 37:334–335.

———. 1968. Stimulation of verbal interaction between disadvantaged mothers and children. *American Journal of Orthopsychiatry* 38:116–120.

Lewis, J.M.; Rodnick, E.H.; and Goldstein, M.J. 1981. Intrafamilial interactive behavior, parental communication deviance, and risk for schizophrenia. *Journal of Abnormal Psychology* 90 (5):448–457.

Lewis, M. 1972. State as an infant environment interaction: An analysis of mother-infant interaction as a function of sex. *Merrill-Palmer Quarterly* 18 (2):95–121.

Liem, J.H. 1974. Effects of verbal communication of parents and children: A comparison of normal and schizophrenic families. *Journal of Consulting and Clinical Psychology* 42:438–450.

Lipscomb, T.J., and Coon, R.C. 1983. Parental speech modification to young children. *Journal of Generic Psychology* 143 (2):181–187.

Loeber, R.; Weissman, W.; and Reid, J.B. 1983. Family interactions of assaultive adolescents, stealers, and nondelinquents. *Journal of Abnormal Child Psychology* 11 (1):1–14.

Lusk, D., and Lewis, M. 1972. Mother-infant interaction and infant development among the Wolof of Senegal. *Human Development* 15 (1):58–69.

McAdoo, J.L. 1979. Father-child interaction patterns and self-esteem in black preschool children. *Young Children* 34 (2):46–53.

McCarrick, A.; Hunt, G.J.; and Sobal, J. 1988. Relational control patterns in families of schizophrenics. *American Journal of Family Therapy* 16:216–228.

McCarrick, A.K.; Manderscheid, R.W.; and Silbergeld, S. 1981. Gender differences in competition and dominance during married couple's group therapy. *Social Psychology Quarterly* 44:164–177.

McDonald, L., and Pien, D. 1982. Mother conversational behaviour as a function of interactional intent. *Journal of Child Language* 9 (2):337–358.

MacKay-Soroka, S.; Trehub, S.E.; and Thorpe, L.A. 1988. Reception of mother's referential messages by deaf and hearing children. *Developmental Psychology* 24 (2):277–285.

McLaughlin, B.; White, D.; McDevitt, T.; and Raskin, R. 1983. Mothers' and fathers' speech to their young children: Similar or different? *Journal of Child Language* 10 (1):245–252.

McPherson, S. 1970. Communication of intents among parents and their disturbed adolescent. *Journal of Abnormal Psychology* 76:98–105.

Madden, M.E. 1987. Perceived control and power in marriage: A study of marital decision making and task performance. *Personality and Social Psychology Bulletin* 13:73–82.

Malone, M.J., and Guy, R.F. 1982. A comparison of mothers' and fathers' speech to their 3-year-old sons. *Journal of Psycholinguistic Research* 11 (6):599–608.
Margolin, G., and Wampold, B.E. 1981. Sequential analysis of conflict and accord in distressed and nondistressed marital partners. *Journal of Consulting and Clinical Psychology* 49:554–567.
Martinez, M.A. 1987. Dialogues among children and between children and their mothers. *Child Development* 58 (4):1035–1043.
Martlew, M. 1980. Mothers' control strategies in dyadic mother/child conversations. *Journal of Psycholinguistic Research* 9 (4):327–347.
Mash, E.J., and Johnston, C. 1983. Sibling interactions of hyperactive and normal children and their relationship to reports of maternal stress and self-esteem. *Journal of Clinical Child Psychology* 12 (1):91–99.
Masur, E.F. 1982. Cognitive content of parents' speech to preschoolers. *Merrill-Palmer Quarterly* 28 (4):471–484.
———. 1987. Imitative interchanges in a social context: Mother-infant matching behavior at the beginning of the second year. *Merrill-Palmer Quarterly* 33 (4):453–472.
Masur, E.F., and Gleason, J.B. 1980. Parent-child interaction and the acquisition of lexical information during play. *Developmental Psychology* 16 (5):404–409.
Matteson, R. 1974. Adolescent self-esteem, family communication, and marital satisfaction. *Journal of Psychology* 86 (1):35–47.
Mead, E., and Campbell, S. 1972. Decision-making and interaction by families with and without a drug-abusing child. *Family Process* 11:487–498.
Meeks, S.; Arnkoff, D.B.; and Glass, C.R. 1986. Wives' employment status, hassles, communication, and relational efficacy: Intra- versus extra-relationship factors and marital adjustment. *Family Relations* 35:249–255.
Meyers, S.C., and Freeman, F.J. 1985a. Are mothers of stutterers different? An investigation of social-communicative interaction. *Journal of Fluency Disorders* 10 (3):193–209.
———. 1985b. Mother and child speech rates as a variable in stuttering and disfluency. *Journal of Speech and Hearing Research* 28 (3):436–444.
Mishler, E.G., and Waxler, N.E. 1970. Functions of hesitations in the speech of normal families and the families of schizophrenic patients. *Language and Speech* 13:102–117.
Mitchell, E. 1985. The dynamics of family interaction around home video games. *Marriage and Family Review* 8:121–135.
Moerk, E.L. 1975. Verbal interactions between children and their mothers during the preschool years. *Developmental Psychology* 11 (6):788–794.
Morikawa, H.; Shand, N.; and Kosawa, Y. 1988. Maternal speech to prelingual infants in Japan and the United States: Relationships among functions, forms and referents. *Journal of Child Language* 15 (2):237–256.
Morris, G., and Wynne, L. 1965. Schizophrenic offspring and parental styles of communication: A predictive study using excerpts of family therapy recordings. *Psychiatry* 28:19–44.
Mullis, R.L., and Mullis, A.K. 1985. Comparison of mothers' and fathers' speech with that of their school age children. *Perceptual and Motor Skills* 60 (2):567–574.
Murphy, D.C., and Mendelson, L.A. 1973. Communication and adjustment in marriage. *Family Process* 12:317–326.

Murray, L., and Trevarthen, C. 1986. The infant's role in mother-infant communications. *Journal of Child Language* 13 (1):15–29.

Murrell, S. 1971. Family interaction variables and adjustment of nonclinic boys. *Child Development* 42:1485–1494.

Murrell, S.A., and Stachowiak, J.G. 1967. Consistency, rigidity, and power in the interaction patterns of clinic and nonclinic families. *Journal of Abnormal Psychology* 72:265–272.

Navran, L. 1967. Communication and adjustment in marriage. *Family Process* 6:173–184.

Nienhuys, T.G.; Horsborough, K.M.; and Cross, T.G. 1985. A dialogic analysis of interaction between mothers and their deaf or hearing preschoolers. *Applied Psycholinguistics* 6 (2):121–139.

Noller, P. 1980. Misunderstanding in marital communication: A study of couples' nonverbal communication. *Journal of Personality and Social Psychology* 39 (6):1135–1148.

———. 1982. Channel consistency and inconsistency in the communications of married couples. *Journal of Personality and Social Psychology* 43:732–741.

O'Connor, W.A., and Stachowiak, J. 1971. Patterns of interaction in families with low adjusted, high adjusted, and mentally retarded members. *Family Process* 10:229–241.

Odom, L.; Seeman, J.; and Newbrough, J.R. 1971. A study of family communication patterns and personality integration in children. *Child Psychiatry and Human Development* 1 (4):275–285.

Oldershaw, L.; Walters, G.C.; and Hall, D.K. 1986. Control strategies and noncompliance in abusive mother-child dyads: An observational study. *Child Development* 57:722–732.

Olsen-Fulero, L. 1982. Style and stability in mother conversational behaviour: A study of individual differences. *Journal of Child Language* 9 (3):543–564.

Olson, S.L.; Bayles, K.; and Bates, J.E. 1986. Mother-child interaction and children's speech progress: A longitudinal study of the first two years. *Merrill-Palmer Quarterly* 32 (1):1–20.

Oscarson, R.A.; Mullis, R.L.; and Mullis, A.K. 1987. Speech complexity of parents and their school-age children. *Child Study Journal* 17 (1):67–76.

Osofsky, J.D., and O'Connell, E.J. 1972. Parent-child interaction: Daughters' effects upon mothers' and fathers' behavior. *Developmental Psychology* 7 (2):157–198.

Pakizegi, B. 1978. The interaction of mothers and fathers with their sons. *Child Development* 49 (2):479–482.

Pannabecker, B.J.; Emide, R.N.; and Austin, B.C. 1982. The effect of early extended contact on father-newborn interaction. *Journal of Genetic Psychology* 141:7–17.

Pettit, G.S., and Bates, J.E. 1989. Family interaction patterns and children's behavior problems from infancy to 4 years. *Developmental Psychology* 25 (3):413–420.

Pettit, G.S.; Dodge, K.A.; and Brown, M.M. 1988. Early family experience, social problem solving patterns, and children's social competence. *Child Development* 59:107–120.

Phelps, R.E., and Slater, M.A. 1985. Sequential interactions that discriminate high- and low-problem single mother-son dyads. *Journal of Consulting and Clinical Psychology* 53:684–692.

Ponnuswami, S. 1977. Mother-child interactions and cognitive style. *Indian Journal of Psychology* 52 (3):250–255.

Putallaz, M. 1987. Maternal behavior and children's sociometric status. *Child Development* 58 (2):324–340.

Radin, N. 1972. Father-child interaction and the intellectual functioning of four-year-old boys. *Developmental Psychology* 6 (2):353–361.

Rebelsky, F., and Hanks, C. 1971. Fathers' verbal interaction with infants in the first three months of life. *Child Development* 42:63–68.

Reichle, J.E.; Longhurst, T.M.; and Stepanich, L. 1976. Verbal interaction in mother-child dyads. *Developmental Psychology* 12 (4):273–277.

Reiss, D. 1967. Individual thinking and family interaction: Introduction to an experimental study of problem solving in families of normals, character disorders, and schizophrenics. *Archives of General Psychiatry* 16:80–93.

———. 1968. Individual thinking and family interaction, III: An experimental study of categorization performance in families of normals, those with character disorders, and schizophrenics. *Journal of Nervous and Mental Disease* 146 (5):384–403.

———. 1969. Individual thinking and family interaction, IV: A study of information exchange in families of normals, those with character disorders, and schizophrenics. *Journal of Nervous and Mental Disease* 149:472–490.

Relich, R.; Giblin, P.T.; Starr, R.H.; and Agronow, S.J. 1980. Motor and social behavior in abused and control children: Observations of parent-child interactions. *Journal of Psychology* 106 (2):193–204.

Resick, P.A.; Barr, P.K; Sweet, J.J.; Kieffer, D.M.; Ruby, N.L.; and Spiegel, D.K. 1981. Perceived and actual discriminators of conflict from accord in marital communication. *American Journal of Family Therapy* 9 (1):58–68.

Roopnarine, J.L., and Adams, G.R. 1987. The interactional teaching patterns of mothers and fathers with their popular, moderately popular, or unpopular children. *Journal of Abnormal Child Psychology* 15 (1):125–136.

Rowland, C. 1984. Preverbal communication of blind infants and their mothers. *Journal of Visual Impairment and Blindness* 78 (7):297–302.

Rutter, D.R., and Durkin, K. 1987. Turn-taking in mother-infant interaction: An examination of vocalizations and gaze. *Developmental Psychology* 23 (1):54–61.

Sabatelli, R.M.; Buck, R.; and Dreyer, A. 1982. Nonverbal communication accuracy in married couples: Relationship with marital complaints. *Journal of Personality and Social Psychology* 43:1088–1097.

———. 1983. Locus of control, interpersonal trust, and nonverbal communication accuracy. *Journal of Personality and Social Psychology* 44:399–409.

Sabatelli, R.M.; Buck, R.; and Kenny, D.A. 1986. A social relations analysis of nonverbal communication accuracy in married couples. *Journal of Personality* 54:513–527.

Sandler, L.W. 1970. Early mother-infant interaction and 24-hour patterns of activity and sleep. *Journal of the American Academy of Child Psychiatry* 9:103–123.

Santrock, J.W.; Warshak, R.; Lindbergh, C.; and Meadows, L. 1982. Children's and parents' observed social behavior in stepfather families. *Child Development* 53 (2):472–480.

Sass, L.A.; Gunderson, J.G.; Singer, M.T.; and Wynne, L.C. 1984. Parental communication deviance and forms of thinking in male schizophrenic offspring. *Journal of Nervous and Mental Disease* 172 (6):513–520.

Schachter, J., and O'Leary, K.D. 1985. Affective intent and impact in marital communication. *American Journal of Family Therapy* 13 (4):17–23.

Schnur, E., and Shatz, M. 1984. The role of maternal gesturing in conversations with one-year-olds. *Journal of Child Language* 11 (1):29–41.

Schubert, J.B.; Bradley-Johnson, S.; and Nuttal, J. 1980. Mother-infant communication and maternal employment. *Child Development* 51 (1):246–249.

Schuerman, J.R. 1972. Marital interaction and posthospital adjustment. *Social Casework* 53 (3):163–172.

Schuham, A.I. 1970. Power relations in emotionally disturbed and normal family triads. *Journal of Abnormal Psychology* 75:30–37.

———. 1972. Activity, talking time and spontaneous agreement in disturbed and normal family interaction. *Journal of Abnormal Psychology* 79:68–75.

Schulman, R.; Shoemaker, D.; and Moelis, I. 1962. Laboratory measurement of parental behavior. *Journal of Consulting Psychology* 26 (2):109–114.

Scott, F.G. 1962. Family group structure and patterns of social interaction. *American Journal of Sociology* 68:214–225.

Seitz, S., and Stewart, C. 1975. Imitation and expansions: Some developmental aspects of mother-child communications.*Developmental Psychology* 11 (6):763–768.

Shapiro, T.; Frosch, E.; and Arnold, S. Communicative interaction between mothers and their autistic children: Application of a new instrument and changes after treatment. *Journal of the American Academy of Child and Adolescent Psychiatry* 26 (4):485–490.

Shere, E., and Kastenbaum, R. 1966. Mother-child interaction in cerebral palsy: Environmental and psychosocial obstacles in cognitive development. *Genetic Psychology Monographs* 73:255–335.

Slater, M.A. 1986. Modification of mother-child interaction processes in families with children at-risk for mental retardation. *American Journal of Mental Deficiency* 91 (3):257–267.

Slee, P.T. 1983. Mother-infant vocal interaction as a function of emotional expression. *Early Child Development and Care* 11 (1):33–44.

Smith, R.C. 1971. Verbal discussion versus note passing tasks in the study of family role structure. *Journal of Nervous and Mental Disease* 152:173–183.

Sojit, C.M. 1969. Dyadic interaction in a doublebind situation. *Family Process* 8:235–260.

Solvberg, H., and Blakar, R. 1975. Communication efficiency in couples with and without a schizophrenic offspring. *Family Process* 14:515–534.

Spinetta, J.J., and Maloney, L.J. 1978. The child with cancer: Patterns of communication and denial. *Journal of Consulting and Clinical Psychology* 46 (6):1540–1541.

Stabenau, J.; Turpin, J.; and Pollin, W. 1965. A comparative study of families of schizophrenics, delinquents, and normals. *Psychiatry* 28:45–59.

Steinberg, L.D., and Hill, J.P. 1978. Patterns of family interaction as a function of age, the onset of puberty, and formal thinking. *Developmental Psychology* 14 (6):683–684.

Steinglass, P. 1981. The alcoholic family at home: Patterns of interaction in dry, wet, and transitional stages of alcoholism. *Archives of General Psychiatry* 38 (5):578–584.

Sternberg, D.P., and Beier, E.G. 1977. Changing patterns of conflict. *Journal of Communication* 27 (3):97–100.

Stevenson, M.B.; Leavitt, L.A.; Roach, M.A.; and Chapman, R.S. 1986. Mothers' speech to their 1-year-old infants in home and laboratory settings. *Journal of Psycholinguistic Research* 15 (5):451-461.

Stevenson, M.B.; ver-Hoeve, J.N.; Roach, M.A.; and Leavitt, L.A. 1986. The beginning of conversation: Early patterns of mother-infant vocal responsiveness. *Infant Behavior and Development* 9 (4):423-440.

Stuckey, M.F.; McGhee, P.E.; and Bell, N.J. 1982. Parent-child interaction: The influence of maternal employment. *Developmental Psychology* 18 (4):635-644.

Termine, N.T., and Izard, C.E. 1988. Infants' responses to their mother's expressions of joy and sadness. *Developmental Psychology* 24 (2):223-229.

Thoman, E.B.; Leiderman, P.H.; and Olson, J.P. 1972. Neonate-mother interaction during breast feeding. *Developmental Psychology* 6 (1):110-118.

Tronick, E.D.; Als, H.; and Brazelton, T.B. 1977. Mutuality in mother-infant interaction. *Journal of Communication* 27 (2):74-79.

Vandell, D.L. 1979. Effects of a playgroup experience on mother-son and father-son interaction. *Developmental Psychology* 15 (4):379-385.

Venaki, S.K.; Nadler, A.; and Cershoni, H. 1985. Sharing the holocaust experience: Communication behaviors and their consequences in families of ex-partisans and ex-prisoners of concentration camps. *Family Process* 24 (2):273-280.

Vincent, J.P.; Weiss, R.L.; and Birchler, G.R. 1975. A behavioral analysis of problem-solving in distressed and nondistressed married and stanger dyads. *Behavior Therapy* 6:475-487.

Walters, J., and Connor, R. 1964. Interaction of mothers and children from lower-class families. *Child Development* 35:433-440.

Wanska, S.K., and Bedrosian, J.L. 1985. Conversational structure and topic performance in mother-child interaction. *Journal of Speech and Hearing Research.* 28 (4):579-584.

———. 1986. Topic and communication intent in mother-child discourse. *Journal of Child Language* 13 (3):523-535.

Warmbrod, M.E.T. 1982. Alternative generation in marital problem solving. *Family Relations* 31:503-511.

Webster-Stratton, C. 1985a. Comparisons of behavior transactions between conduct-disordered children and their mothers in the clinic and at home. *Journal of Abnormal Child Psychology* 13 (2):169-183.

———. 1985b. The effects of father involvement in parent training for conduct problem children. *Journal of Child Psychology and Psychiatry and Allied Disciplines* 26 (5):801-810.

Webster-Stratton, C., and Eyberg, S.M. 1982. Child temperament: Relationship with child behavior problems and parent-child interactions. *Journal of Clinical Child Psychology* 11 (2):123-129.

Wedell-Monnig, J., and Lumley, J.M. 1980. Child deafness and mother-child interaction. *Child Development* 51 (3):766-774.

Weitzman, N.; Birns, B.; and Friend, R. 1985. Traditional and nontraditional mothers' communication with their daughters and sons. *Child Development* 56:894-898.

Wilkinson, L.C.; Hiebert, E.; and Rembold, K. 1981. Parents' and peers' communication to toddlers. *Journal of Speech and Hearing Research* 24 (3):383-388.

Williams, A.M. 1979. The quantity and quality of marital interaction related to marital satisfaction: A behavioral analysis. *Journal of Applied Behavior Analysis* 12 (4):665-678.

Williamson, R.N., and Fitzpatrick, M.A. 1985. Two approaches to marital interaction: Relational control patterns in marital types. *Communication Monographs* 52 (3):236–252.

Wilton, K, and Barbour, A. 1978. Mother-child interaction in high-risk and contrast preschoolers of low socioeconomic status. *Child Development* 49 (4):1136–1145.

Winter, W.D.; Ferreira, A.J.; and Bowers, N. 1973. Decision-making in married and unrelated couples. *Family Process* 12:83–94.

Yelsma, P. 1984. Marital communication, adjustment and perceptual differences between "happy" and "counseling" couples. *American Journal of Family Therapy* 12 (1):26–36.

Zuckerman, E., and Jacob, T. 1979. Task effects in family interaction. *Family Process* 18:47–53.

Articles That Were Unavailable to the Authors

Banks, E. 1979. Mother-child interaction and competence in the first two years of life: Is there a critical period? *Child Study Journal* 9 (2): 93–107.

Bates, J.E.; Maslin, C.A.; and Frankel, K.A. 1985. Attachment security, mother-child interaction, and temperament as predictors of behavior-problem ratings at age three years. *Monographs of the Society for Research in Child Development* 50 (1–2):167–193.

Belch, G.E.; Belch, M.A.; and Ceresino, G. 1985. Parental and Teenage child influences in family decision making. *Journal of Business Research* 13 (2):163–176.

Bodin, A. 1966. Family interaction, coalition, disagreement, and compromise in problem, normal, and synthetic triads. Ph.D. dissertation, State University of New York at Buffalo.

Bonnar, J.W., and McGee, R.K. 1977. Suicidal behavior as a form of communication in married couples. *Suicide and Life Threatening Behavior* 7 (1):7–16.

Bonnheim, M.L., and Korman, M. 1985. Family interaction and acculturation in Mexican-American inhalant users. *Journal of Psychoactive Drugs* 17 (1):25–33.

Boulton, M. 1985. Negative parental messages masquerading as positive parental messages. *Women and Therapy* 4 (4):59–65.

Cantwell, D.P.; Baker, L.; and Rutter, M. 1980. Families of autistic children and dysphasic children: Family life and interaction patterns. *Advances in Family Psychiatry* 2:295–312.

Coates, D.B., and Mallinson, T.J. 1967. Family interaction and schizophrenia. *Canadian Psychiatric Association Journal* 12:387–401.

Costello, A.J. 1969. Scientific investigations of relationships and communication within the family. *Proceedings of the Royal Society of Medicine* 69:900–901.

Cushman, D.P., and Cahn, D.D. 1986. A study of communicative realignment between parents and children following the parents' decision to seek a divorce. *Communication Research Reports* 3:80–85.

Dammann, C.A. 1970. Patterns of family communication and the ability of parents to administer accurate reinforcement. Ph.D. dissertation, Emory University.

Diesing, L. 1967. Observations on interactions between mothers and their children in the waiting room of an outpatient child psychiatric clinic. *Journal of the American Academy of Child Psychiatry* 6:1–14.

Drotar, D. 1977. Parent-child interaction and infantile autism. *Journal of Pediatric Psychology* 2 (4):167–171.

Dunham, R.M.; Portes, P.R.; and Williams, S. 1984. Identification of mother-child interaction patterns. A longitudinal evaluation of early age intervention effects on early adolescents. *Children and Youth Services Review* 6 (1):19–35.

Dunn, J.; Wooding, C.; and Hermann, J. 1977. Mothers' speech to young children: Variation in context. *Developmental Medicine and Child Neurology* 19 (5):629–638.

Dyk, R.B. 1969. An exploratory study of mother-child interaction in infancy as related to the development of differentiation. *Journal of American Academy of Child Psychiatry* 8:657–691.

Easton, K. 1966. Neonatal behavior, mother-baby interaction, and personality development. New York: Journal of Medicine 66:1874–1882.

Edwards, C.P.; Logue, M.E.; Loehr, S.; and Roth, S. 1986. The influence of model infant-toddler group care on parent-child interaction at home. *Early Childhood Research Quarterly* 1 (4):317–332.

Feiring, C.; Lewis, M.; and Jaskir, J. 1983. Birth of a sibling: Effect on mother-first born child interaction. *Journal of Developmental and Behavioral Pediatrics* 4 (3):190–195.

Field, T.M. 1978. The three Rs of infant-adult interactions: Rhythms, repertoires, and responsivity. *Journal of Pediatric Psychology* 3 (3):131–136.

Fisher, T.D. 1986. An exploratory study of parent-child communication about sex and the sexual attitudes of early, middle, and late adolescents. *Journal of Genetic Psychology* 147:543–557.

———. 1986. Parent-child communication about sex and young adolescents' sexual knowledge and attitudes. *Adolescence* 21 (83):517–527.

Fraser, B.C. 1986. Child impairment and parent/infant communication. *Child Care, Health and Development* 12 (3):141–150.

Gautam, S., and Kamal, P. 1986. Family typology and family interaction in psychiatric disorder. *International Journal of Social Psychiatry* 32:27–31.

Goldstein, M.J. 1984. Family affect and communication related to schizophrenia. *New Directions for Child Development* 24:47–62.

Guttman, H.A., and Eaton, W. 1986. Variables differentiating affective interaction in a family therapy and a control group: Father-child welfare and mother-child emergency affect. *Contemporary Family Therapy* 8 (4):316–327.

Haddock, B.L., and Sporakowski, M.J. 1982. Self-concept and family communication: A comparison of status and criminal offenders and non-offenders. *Journal of Offender Counseling, Services and Rehabilitation* 7 (2):61–74.

Hafner, R.J. 1982. Marital interaction in persisting obsessive-compulsive disorders. *Australian and New Zealand Journal of Psychiatry* 16 (3):171–178.

Hall, J.A., and Levin, S. 1980. Affect and verbal-nonverbal discrepancy in schizophrenic and non-schizophrenic family communication. *British Journal of Psychiatry* 137:78–92.

Hansen, D.J.; Tisdelle, D.A.; and O'Dell, S.L. 1985. Audio recorded and directly observed parent-child interactions: A comparison of observation methods. *Behavioral Assessment* 7 (4):389–399.

Hanson, P.G. 1968. Patterns of communication in alcoholic marital couples. *Psychiatric Quarterly* 42 (3):538–547.

Harris, M.; Jones, D.; Brookes, S.; and Grant, J. 1986. Relations between the nonverbal context of maternal speech and rate of language development. *British Journal of Developmental Psychology* 4 (3):261–268.

Haynes, S.N.; Chavez, R.E.; and Samuel, V. 1984. Assessment of marital communication and distress. *Behavioral Assessment* 6 (4):315–321.

Henggeler, S.W.; Watson, S.M.; and Cooper, P.F. 1984. Verbal and nonverbal maternal controls in hearing mother–deaf child interaction. *Journal of Applied Developmental Psychology* 5 (4):319–329.

Hirsch, S.R., and Leff, J.P. 1971. Parental abnormalities of verbal communication in the transmission of schizophrenia. *Psychological Medicine* 1:118–127.

Hooshyar, N. 1985. Language interactions between mothers and their nonhandicapped children, mothers and their Down Syndrome children, mothers and their language-impaired children. *International Journal of Rehabilitation Research* 8 (4):475–477.

Hsu, J. 1983. Asian family interaction patterns and their therapeutic implications. *International Journal of Family Psychiatry* 4 (4):307–320.

Hutchinson, J. 1967. Interaction patterns in families of severely disturbed and normal adolescents. Ph.D. dissertation, University of Chicago.

Jamuna, D., and Ramamurti, P.V. 1984. Age, adjustment and husband-wife communication of middle aged and older women. *Journal of Psychological Researches* 28 (3):145–147.

Kirschenbaum, M.; Leonoff, G.; and Maliano, A. 1974. Characteristic patterns in drug abuse families. *Family Therapy* 1 (1):43–62.

Kucia, C., et al. 1979. Home observation of family interaction and childhood adjustment to cystic fibrosis. *Journal of Pediatric Psychology* 4 (2):189–195.

Kulka, A.M. 1968. Observations and data on mother-infant interaction. *Israel Annals of Psychiatry and Related Disciplines* 6:70–84.

Kuthiala, S.K. 1972. Decision-making patterns of family planning among husbands and wives. *Journal of Family Welfare* 19 (1):11–22.

Kysela, G.M., and Marfo, K. 1983. Mother-child interactions and early intervention programmes for handicapped infants and young children. *Educational Psychology* 3 (3–4):201–212.

Liotti, G., and Guidano, V. 1976. Behavioural analysis of marital interaction in agoraphobic male patients.*Behaviour Research and Therapy* 14 (2):161–162.

Longhurst, T.M., and Stepanich, L. 1975. Mothers' speech addressed to one-, two-, and three-year-old normal children. *Child Study Journal* 5 (1):3–11.

McCraw, R.K. 1980. Epilepsy and the double bind. *Journal of Clinical Child Psychology* 9 (1):74–77.

McNeil, T.F.; Harty, B.; Thelin, T.; Aspegren-Jansson, E.; et al. 1986. Identifying children at high somatic risk: Long-term effects on mother-child interaction. *Acta Psychiatrica Scandinavica* 74 (6):555–562.

Messaris, P., and Kerr, D. 1983. Mothers' comments about TV: Relation to family communication patterns. *Communication Research* 10 (2):175–194.

Miller, T.W. 1971. Communicative dimensions of mother-child interaction as they affect the self-esteem of the child. *Proceedings of the Annual Convention of the American Psychological Association* 6 (Part 1):241–242.

Mitchell, D.R. 1987. Parents' interactions with their developmentally disabled or at-risk infants: A focus for intervention. *Australia and New Zealand Journal of Developmental Disabilities* 13 (2):73–81.

Nelson, C.D., and Stockdale, D.F. 1984. Maternal control behavior and compliance of preschool children. *Parenting Studies* 1 (1):11–18.

Noller, P. 1980. Gaze in married couples. *Journal of Nonverbal Behavior* 5:115–129.

Nurmi, J.E. 1987. Age, sex, social class, and quality of family interaction as determinants of adolescents' future orientation: A developmental task interpretation. *Adolescence* 22 (88):977–991.

O'Neill, M.S., and Alexander, J.F. 1971. Family interaction patterns as a function of task characteristics. *Journal of Applied Social Psychology* 1 (2):163–172.

Person-Blennow, I.; Naslund, B.; McNeil, T.F.; and Kaij, L. 1986. Offspring of women with nonorganic psychosis: Mother-infant interaction at one year of age. *Acta Psychiatrica Scandinavica* 73 (2):207–213.

Peterson, C., and Peterson, R. 1986. Parent-child interaction and daycare: Does quality of daycare matter? *Journal of Applied Developmental Psychology* 7 (1):1–15.

Phinney, J.S. 1986. The structure of 5-year-olds' verbal quarrels with peers and siblings. *Journal of Genetic Psychology* 147:47–60.

Podmore, V.N., and St. George, R. 1986. New Zealand Maori and European mothers and their 3-year-old children: Interactive behaviors in pre-school settings. *Journal of Applied Developmental Psychology* 7 (4):373–382.

Portes, P.R.; Dunham, R.M.; and Williams, S.A. 1986. Preschool intervention, social class, and parent-child interaction differences. *Journal of Genetic Psychology* 147 (2):241–255.

Portes, P.R.; Franke, S.; and Alsup, R. 1987. Parent-child interaction: Processes related to scholastic achievement in urban elementary children. *Journal of Human Behavior and Learning* 4 (1):2–9.

Rashkis, H.A., and Rashkis, S.R. 1981. An investigation of the influence of parental communications on adolescent ego development: I. *Adolescent Psychiatry* 9:227–235.

Rasku-Puttonen, H. 1983. Parent-child communication in families of different educational backgrounds. *Scandinavian Journal of Psychology* 24 (3):223–230.

Ravich, R.A. 1966. An experimental study of marital discord and decision-making. *Psychiatric Research Reports* 20:91–94.

Reiss, D. 1967. Individual thinking and family interaction. II. A study of pattern recognition and hypothesis testing in families of normals, character disorders and schizophrenics. *Journal of Psychiatric Research* 5:193–211.

Robin, M. 1980. Interaction process analysis of mothers with their newborn infants. *Early Child Development and Care* 6 (3–4):93–108.

Roopnarine, J.L., and Lamb, M.E. 1980. Peer and parent-child interaction before and after enrollment in nursery school. *Journal of Applied Developmental Psychology* 1 (1):77–81.

Roth, H., and Johnson, T. 1984. Interpersonal patterns of abusing parents and parent-child interactions. *Parenting-Studies* 1 (2):43–46.

Rubin, M.E.Y. 1977. Nonverbal communication between distressed and nondistressed couples in verbal and nonverbal communication codes. Ph.D. dissertation, Indiana University.

Sander, L.W. 1964. Adaptive relationships in early mother-child interaction. *Journal of the American Academy of Child Psychiatry* 3:231–264.

Savitsky, E., and Sharkey, H. 1972. Study of family interaction in the aged. *Journal of Geriatric Psychology* 5 (1):3–19.

Schaap, C., and Jansen-Nawas, C. 1987. Marital interaction, affect and conflict resolution. *Sexual and Marital Therapy* 2 (1):35–51.

Schindler, F., and Arkowitz, H. 1986. The assessment of mother-child interactions in physically abusive and nonabusive families. *Journal of Family Violence* 1 (3):247–257.

Searle, A. 1987. The effects of postnatal depression on mother-infant interaction. *Australian Journal of Sex, Marriage and Family* 8 (2):79–88.

Share, L. 1972. Family communication in the crisis of a child's fatal illness. *Omega* 3 (3):187–203.

Singer, M.T., and Wynn, L.C. 1966. Communication styles in parents of normals, neurotics, and schizophrenics. *Psychiatric Research Reports* 20:25–38.

Singh, M.B., and Kaur, S. 1981. Mother-child interaction in rural and urban areas. *Indian Psychological Review* 20 (2):7–16.

Thomas, D.R. 1978. Communication patterns among Pakeha and Polynesian mother-child pairs: The effects of class and culture. *New Zealand Journal of Educational Studies* 13 (2):125–132.

Weiner, M.F. 1967. Nonverbal communication in mothers of schizophrenics. *Texas Reports on Biology and Medicine* 25:607–612.

Winokur, G., and Gaston, W.R. 1961. Sex, anger, and anxiety: intrapersonal interaction in married couples. *Diseases of the Nervous System* 22:256–260.

Yalom, M.; Estler, S.; and Brewster, W. 1982. Changes in female sexuality: A study of mother/daughter communication and generational differences. *Psychology of Women Quarterly* 7 (2):141–154.

Zam, R.S. 1978. Communication and cognition in distressed and nondistressed marriages: Observer judgments versus on-line self-reports. Ph.D. dissertation, Pennsylvania State University.

5
Family Resource Management

Craig L. Israelsen

Much of family resource management research can be divided into two broad areas: financial resources and human and household resources. Studies of financial resources have examined issues such as income and expenditure, financial management, financial security and retirement planning, housing, saving, debt and credit, budgeting, financial support from kin, insurance, and financial satisfaction. Studies of human and household resources have dealt with division of household work, time usage and management, household production, household tasks, and household management styles.

This chapter provides an overview of family resource management research published between 1930 and 1990. It presents a chronological compilation of research abstracts, arranged by topic within each decade, with specific attention given to research methodology and theoretical orientations. Sample size, data acquisition methodology, and theoretical orientation of the studies are reported in summary tables at the end of each decade review.

The research abstracts were written and compiled after reviewing available family resource management literature. No attempt was made to review everything in print that could feasibly relate to family resource management. Major journals and social science indexes represent the literature base used to generate the research abstracts reported in this review.[1]

The Decade 1930–1939

The 1920s ended with noticeable research interest in the areas of family living standards and income and expenditure studies. The imminent economic depression soon provided fertile research soil for these two topics. Research conducted in the 1930s dealt with the effects of the Great Depression, unemployment, income and expenditure, credit use, determination of living standards, and women's employment.

Research Findings

Great Depression and Unemployment. Swerdloff (1933) studied the effects of unemployment on the family life of seventy-nine Baltimore families who had received public assistance between 1930 and 1932. Thirty-two individuals were employed, and eighty were unemployed. Of the unemployed people, sixty were male heads of households. All but seven families had exhausted all savings and credit and had become indebted beyond expectation ever to repay. Eighty percent of the families had lowered their food and clothing standards. Half of the families eliminated all forms of paid recreation. Forty-nine families (over half) reported strained relations between the husband and wife.

Gilboy (1937) studied income and expenditure data for 397 families receiving relief in Massachusetts during 1934–1935. Twenty-seven percent of the heads of families were unemployed, 58 percent part-time employed, and 15 percent steadily employed. Expenditure consistently exceeded income by 15 to 20 percent. Money taken from savings and liquidated insurance policies accounted for 7 percent of total expenditure, and unpaid bills accounted for almost 10 percent of expenditure. Bills most frequently left unpaid were rent, medical services, and food.

Conard (1939) studied the differential effects of the depression on 150 Iowa families. Laborers suffered the most severe losses in food, followed by businessmen, with farm families experiencing the least loss in food consumption. All three groups reduced expenditure for recreation. Laborers and farmers found new recreation within the community, and businessmen spent more leisure time at home. (See also Byrne, 1936; Gross and Pond, 1936.)

Standard of Living. The *Monthly Labor Review* (1930) reported a study of the minimum wage required in seventeen European cities for comparison with Ford employees in Detroit, Michigan, earning the minimum wage of $7 per day. Average total yearly salary for the 100 families in the study was $1,711, which included income from other sources. Average expenditure for the families was $1,719, resulting in an average deficit of $8. Food expenditures constituted 32 percent of the total budget, followed by housing (22 percent) and clothing (12 percent). Nineteen families were just able to meet expenses, forty-four had a surplus ($131 average), and thirty-seven ended the year with a deficit ($134 average).

Leiffer (1933) reported a one-year study of income and standards of living in the Methodist ministry. A questionnaire was sent to white, English-speaking Methodist ministers in the United States requesting information on the size of the minister's family, various sources of income, and a detailed report of expenditures. Approximately 1,200 questionnaires were returned, of which 1,038 were usable. In almost all cases, the minister's family income was supplemented by investment income, honoraria for professional services, and earnings of the wife and children. The average ministerial salary was $2,081 (which does not include the value of rent since in most cases a house was provided) was contrasted to the average physician's salary of $5,250 and that of office workers of $2,467 (see also Monroe, 1937).

Finance—Income and Expenditure. Clarke (1931) reported on a study of incomes, emergencies, and credit in seventy-five dependent families. Half of the families attempted to "augment" their income by using installment credit, three-fourths used charge accounts as a form of credit, and one-third of the families made use of loans. When controlling for the number of families in different income groups, families in the highest income groups had the largest proportion of charge accounts (see also Brady, 1938; Clark and Morton, 1930; Hyde, 1931; Kaplan, 1938; Saffian, 1933; Wright, 1932).

Women's Employment. Whittemore (1931) studied the reasons that homemakers sought employment and the impact of their work on family income. Data were obtained from 408 rural women living in Rhode Island. Nearly three-quarters of the women reported that they worked because they needed the money. Average income among the women was just over $16 per week.

The Decade in Review

Theory and Methodology. Of the sixteen research studies in this decade, eleven used primary data, and five used secondary data.[2] Research was conducted primarily by survey research—either mailed questionnaires or interviews. Research findings were generally reported descriptively in the body of the text and in tables. Cross-classification of variables was common, such as food expenditure as a function of income or family type. Theoretical orientation was essentially nonexistent, although one study made reference to psychoanalysis, and there were occasional references to the work of Ernst Engel (table 5-1).

General Findings. The Great Depression had a devastating impact on already poor families, causing economic and interpersonal turmoil in the lives of parents and children. Paid forms of recreation were severely curtailed, and a large majority of families suffered a reduction in food consumption and clothing purchases. Fifty percent of the families reported strained relationships between spouses (Wright, 1932; Swerdloff, 1933). In terms of reduction of food and increases in family tension, farm families were affected the least and families of laborers the most (Conard, 1939).

Expenditures consistently exceeded income by as much as 20 percent. Bills most often not paid were food, rent, and medical care (Saffian, 1933; Gilboy, 1937). Families with higher incomes used credit most often (Clarke, 1931). A large majority of women who worked outside the home did so because of economic need (Whittemore, 1931).

Table 5-1
Overview of Research on Family Resource Management, 1930–1939

Year	*Author*	*Topic Area*	*Theory*	*Method*[a]	*Sample*
1930	Clark and Morton	Finance—income and expenditure	None	Interview-S	29
1930	Monthly Labor Review	Standard of living	None	Questionnaire-P	100
1931	Clarke	Finance—income and expenditure	None	Interview-P	75
1931	Hyde	Finance—income and expenditure	None	Interview-P	20
1931	Whittemore	Women's employment	None	Questionnaire-P	408
1932	Wright	Finance—income and expenditure	None	Interview-S	550
1933	Leiffer	Standard of living	None	Questionnaire-P	1,038
1933	Saffian	Finance—income and expenditure	None	Records-P	42
1933	Swerdloff	Great Depression	Psychoanalytical	Case study-P	79
1936	Byrne	Great Depression	None	Interview-P	1,120
1936	Gross and Pond	Great Depression	None	Interview-P	144
1937	Gilboy	Great Depression	None	Interview-P	397
1937	Monroe	Standard of living	Engel	Government data-S	N.A.
1938	Brady	Finance—income and expenditure	None	Interview-S	>10,000
1938	Kaplan	Finance—income and expenditure	Engel	Government data-S	N.A.
1939	Conard	Great Depression	None	Questionnaire-P	150

[a] P = primary data; S = secondary data.

The Decade 1940–1949

Research in the 1940s was affected significantly by World War II. Dominant research themes during the 1930s continued into the 1940s: studies of income and expenditure and standards of living. The war effort, however, gave the research of this decade a specific slant by relating to the context of the wartime efforts—saving money and buying war bonds, and maintaining a reasonable standard of living despite a reduction in the availability of many consumer products. Other research topics in the decade included an analysis of children's use of money and a study of the financial aspects of marital adjustment.

Research Findings

Finance—Income and Expenditure. Leevy (1940) studied the contrasts between rural and urban family life. The sample consisted of 2,000 white Illinois families, half living in urban areas and half in rural settings. Sixty-three percent of the rural families owned their home compared to 54 percent of the urban families. Urban families used a family budget about two and a half times more frequently than rural families. Eighty-six percent of rural families produced some of their own food, compared to 4 percent of the urban families.

Standard of Living. Reed (1946) presented information on the Basic Maintenance Budget prepared by the Works Progress Administration. The budget, developed between 1935 and 1945 for seven U.S. cities, represents the actual amounts and kinds of goods required for industrial, service, and manual workers. In 1940, U.S. census data indicated that 29.7 percent of the families in the cities Reed studied (Cincinnati, Cleveland, Dallas, Detroit, Houston, New Orleans, and St. Louis) had annual incomes of less than $1,000. The average maintenance budget for those same cities was $1,336. In Cincinnati between 1939 and 1941, people in the lowest-income class died of pneumonia almost three times more often than people in the highest-income class, and for every infant death in the highest-income class there were three infant deaths in the lowest-income bracket. Clearly, families with higher incomes obtained better health care. (See also MacNaughton, 1948.)

Finance

Children. Lorimer (1940) studied the effect of children on the economic status of American families. As the number of children increased, families devoted a larger part of their available resources to food, even though they often restricted their diet. The amount spent for clothing in urban families was similar with or without children, due to the fact that increased expenditures for children's clothing was offset by reduced expenditures for parents' clothing. Urban families with one child or no children averaged net savings of 3 to 5 percent of income, while families with two or more children averaged less than 1 percent savings.

Saving. Monroe (1942) analyzed prewar savings and spending patterns of American families. Increased savings meant greater investments in war bonds, while decreased expenditures helped control inflation and free factories for war production. Monroe found that elderly families without children generally saved more than young families did. In the income range of $1,000 to $1,499, young families "just about broke even," while families in which the wife was 60 or older saved an average of $125.

Marital Adjustment. Landis (1947) studied the time required for 409 couples to adjust in six different areas—sex relations, spending the family income, social activities, in-law relationships, religious activities, and mutual friends—and the relationship between adjustment time and marital happiness. The second most difficult area of adjustment was spending the family income. Just over half of the couples acknowledged that a satisfactory agreement had been reached from the beginning of their marriage, but about 10 percent of the couples felt they had never made a satisfactory adjustment.

Household Management. Gross and Zwemer (1944) studied the management of money, time, and energy among 382 Michigan farm families. There was a lack of conscious planning, and when it did take place, it involved preparing menus, work plans, and saving money rather than planning current expenditures. Decisions on money use were made jointly by the couples in 50 to 75 percent of the homes. High-income groups were found to utilize recommended management practices more often than low-income groups, and families at the median income level made budget plans most frequently.

Adolescents and Money. In a study of 100 adolescents, Prevey (1945, 1946) found that parents of boys consistently employed better educational methods in relation to money than did parents of girls; more boys than girls had their own money; more boys than girls were having real earning experiences in the community; and more of the boys were informed about family resources, expenditures, and financial problems. Boys whose parents provided broad and varied experiences with money tended to become young adults who could manage financial affairs wisely. Girls generally had poor money management skills as young adults, perhaps reflecting the poor quality of the experiences provided them earlier in life.

The Decade in Review

Theory and Methodology. Theoretical research orientations in this decade were almost nil, with two exceptions. One study was implicitly based on economic theory (Cave, 1943), and another suggested that a socialized system of family allowances and subsidies, similar to the system in Sweden, could equalize the standard of living between large families and families with no children (Lorimer, 1940). Fifteen studies were identified. Eight used primary data, and seven utilized secondary data sources.

Statistical analysis was generally limited to percentages and frequency tables. One study used ordinary least-squares regression. Data were generally obtained from interviews, questionnaires, or government sources (table 5–2).

General Findings. Compared to urban families, rural families produced more of their own food, had a higher rate of home ownership, and used an annual budget less frequently (Leevy, 1940). Total expenditure was shown to be a more reliable indicator of "effective family income" at low and moderate income levels (Cave, 1943). Families living at or below the maintenance budget were more likely to experience serious illness and had higher rates of infant mortality (Reed, 1946). In 1944, 20 percent of city families and single persons had after-tax annual incomes of less than $1,500 (Brady, 1946).

As the number of children in a family increased, the percentage spent for food increased, clothing expenditures stayed about the same, and savings rates declined (Lorimer, 1940). Elderly families without children saved more than young families with children (Monroe, 1942). Spending the family income was found to be the second most difficult area of marital adjustment (Landis, 1947).

Among farm families, decisions regarding money use were made jointly a majority of the time, and families with median-level incomes used a formal budget more frequently than high- or low-income families (Gross and Zwemer, 1944). Boys consistently received better training in the use of money than did girls. Young adults with good money management skills generally had experience handling money in their youth (Prevey, 1945, 1946).

The Decade 1950–1959

Financial topics—financial management, income and expenditure, security and retirement, housing, budgeting, saving, and marital adjustment—comprised half of the research studies in the 1950s. Household research looked at time use, household production, and division of work. During the 1950s, there was no dramatic national event that influenced research as was the case in the 1930s (the Great Depression) and the 1940s (World War II). As a result, research was more eclectic than in the two previous decades. Additional topics that emerged during the 1950s included women's employment, adolescents and money, leisure, and decision making.

Table 5–2
Overview of Research on Family Resource Management, 1940–1949

Year	*Author*	*Topic Area*	*Theory*	*Method*[a]	*Sample*
1940	Leevy	Finance—income and expenditure	None	Interview-P	2,000
1940	Lorimer	Finance—children	None	Interview-S	N.A.
1941	Jones	Finance—income and expenditure	None	Government data-S	8,905
1942	Monroe	Finance—saving	None	Interview-S	N.A.
1943	Cave	Finance—income and expenditure	Economics	Interview-S	14,469
1943	Freeman and Crouch	Finance—income and expenditure	None	Case study-P	1
1943	Working	Finance—income and expenditure	None	Government data-S	N.A.
1944	Gross and Zwemer	Household management	None	Interview-P	382
1945	Prevey	Adolescents and money	None	Interview-P	100
1946	Prevey	Adolescents and money	None	Interview-P	100
1946	Brady	Finance—income and expenditure	None	Government data-S	N.A.
1946	Reed	Standard of living	None	Government data-S	N.A.
1947	Landis	Finance—marital adjustment	None	Questionnaire-P	818
1948	MacNaughton	Standard of living	None	Questionnaire-P	119
1949	Coles	Finance—income and expenditure	None	Interview-P	76

[a]P = primary data; S = secondary data.

Research Findings

Finance

Management. Thorpe (1951) studied the managerial practices of 484 married college students in Michigan. Eighty-four percent of the couples reported budgeting their money prior to spending it, and 74 percent kept a record of expenditures. Half of the couples were saving some money. Over three-fourths of the student husbands regularly helped with the housework.

Income and Expenditure. Merriam (1955) studied spending patterns among 171 families in which the husband was the only wage earner. On average, the families spent 37 percent of their income for food, 18 percent for housing, 9 percent on car payments, and 7.7 percent for income taxes. All of the families in the sample carried life insurance, compared to a national average of 75 percent. All but one family carried some form of hospital, health, or accident insurance. (See also Blankertz, 1950; Converse, 1950; Millican, 1959.)

Budget. Using data from the Bureau of Labor Statistics (BLS), Knapp (1951) estimated the budget for a family of four in thirty-four large cities in the United States during October 1950. Expenditures for food averaged 33 percent of the family budget, and 23 percent was spent for housing. The percentage paid in taxes ranged from 3.5 to 6 percent.

Housing. Freeman (1951) examined the amount of money spent on housing repairs and improvement by Illinois farm families over a seventeen-year period (1933–1949). Over 5,000 annual records of housing expenditures kept by 181 farm families were examined. In 1933, approximately 2 percent was spent on housing repair and improvement. By 1949 that amount had increased to 8 percent (including payments made by both landlord and tenant). It was also found that the value of the house increased as annual spendable income increased. As a result, the percentage spent on housing and related costs remained constant at 23 percent across income groups.

Marital Adjustment. Williamson (1952) studied the relationship between economic factors and marital adjustment among 210 white couples in Los Angeles. Couples in higher-class residences were more likely to be happily married. In the lower middle class, more women than men were unhappy. There was a higher percentage of happy marriages among those having a sizable amount of savings (at least $600). Couples who did not overspend their budget more than two months out of the year were happier than those who had a chronic budgeting problem.

Security and Retirement. Smith (1954) surveyed 490 households to explore problems in providing for later maturity and old age. To the question, "What bothers people most about old age?" 43 percent of the respondents mentioned the lack of financial security. When asked, "In your opinion whose responsibility is it to help older people?" 71 percent felt it was the family's responsibility, 61 percent said the government should help, and 33 percent felt that old people should be responsible for themselves. (Respondents often gave multiple responses; hence, the percentages add up to more than 100 percent.) Of those in the sample who had already retired, 42 percent had planned for retirement. A positive relationship between family income and the formulation of retirement plans was found. In other words, the rich planned more for retirement.

Household

Time Usage and Management. Cowles and Dietz (1956) studied the amount of time eighty-five Wisconsin women spent in homemaking activities. The average weekly time spent in homemaking activities was 53 hours. The authors cited research conducted in 1929 and 1940 that had found that 52 hours was the average weekly time women spent in homemaking. The combined total amount of weekly time spent in homemaking activities by other family members was 8 hours in the Cowles and Dietz study, 10 hours in the two 1929 studies, and 12 hours in the 1940 study. (See also Steidl, 1958.)

Division of Work. Blood (1958) investigated the division of labor among 731 Detroit families and 178 rural Michigan families. With the single exception of amount of time spent in paid employment outside the home, farm wives exceeded city wives in the work they performed in both traditional feminine spheres and many masculine areas. It was concluded that farm women perform a larger share of household tasks than city wives and that more of them help with the husband's work.

Women's Employment. Knoll (1955) studied the economic contributions of family members, primarily those members 14 years of age and older. Data were obtained through interviews with 202 randomly selected households in New York—half urban and half rural. Women who worked full time outside the home received more help than did other women. Interestingly, women working part-time jobs took greater responsibility for work in their homes and carried on more home production than did women who were homemakers only or those who had full-time jobs outside the home. Farm children more frequently worked without remuneration, and farm primary earners tended to turn over all their earnings to the household less often than did other primary earners.

Adolescents and Money. Dunsing (1956) studied the spending money of 738 adolescents. Irregular earnings was the source of almost two-thirds of the adolescents' spending money. Thirty-one percent of the youth received spending money from an allowance and 8 percent from the dole. (Allowance is receiving a fixed amount of money at regular intervals, usually for completing regular chores; a dole is receiving irregular amounts of money with no work being required.) More girls than boys received money from an allowance (38 percent compared to 21 percent). Eleven percent of the girls received a dole compared to only 4 percent of the boys.

Decision Making. Sharp and Mott (1956) examined who within the family makes certain economic decisions. Data were obtained from 749 Detroit housewives on decisions on purchase of the family car, purchase of life insurance, weekly food expenditures, selection of house or apartment, where to go on vacation, and if the wife should work. Husbands usually selected which car to buy but generally did not make the final decision on food expenditures. Also, in selecting a new home and deciding where to go on vacation, married couples relied largely on consensus rather than on unilateral decision making. As income increased, spouses were more likely to make joint decisions. (See also Kenkel and Hoffman, 1956; Wolgast, 1958.)

The Decade in Review

Theory and Methodology. A broader spectrum of research topics and theoretical orientations was investigated in the 1950s, including role theory, exchange theory, and life cycle theory. The overall quality of the research methodology (sample size, sampling procedures, description of demographics, association of variables, and awareness of research weaknesses) improved over previous decades. Interview was the most popular method of obtaining data (table 5-3). Eighteen of the twenty-four studies in the decade used primary data, and six used secondary data. Use of statistics was still primarily descriptive, relying on percentages and tabular cross-classification. One study used chi-square analysis, and another used factor analysis.

General Findings. Young families generally budgeted their money, kept records of expenditures, and shared housework between spouses (Thorpe, 1951). Families utilized more paid services as length of marriage increased (Wells, 1959). Food expenditures generally accounted for approximately one-third of the total family budget, and housing expenditures ranged from 18 to 23 percent (Knapp, 1951; Merriam, 1955). The savings rate of rural families was twice that of urban families (Liston, 1950). Among farm families, the amount of money spent on housing and related housing costs remained constant at 23 percent across income groups (Freeman, 1951).

Couples who had at least $600 in savings and did not overspend their budget tended to be happier (Williamson, 1952). People with higher incomes generally planned more for retirement (Smith, 1954). Hours spent each week by homemakers in household tasks remained constant between 1929 (52 hours)

Table 5-3
Overview of Research on Family Resource Management, 1950–1959

Year	*Author*	*Topic Area*	*Theory*	*Method*[a]	*Sample*
1950	Blankertz	Finance—income and expenditure	None	Interview-P	467
1950	Converse	Finance—income and expenditure	None	Secondary analysis	98
1950	Leevy	Leisure	None	Interview-P	1,250
1950	Liston	Finance—saving	None	Interview-P	163
1951	Freeman	Finance—housing	None	Records-P	181
1951	Knapp	Finance—budget	None	Survey-P	N.A.
1951	Thorpe	Finance—management	None	Questionnaire-P	484
1952	Williamson	Finance—marital adjustment	Exchange	Interview-P	210
1953	Pecheniuk and Liston	Finance—management	None	Interview-S	865
1954	Smith	Finance—security and retirement	Life cycle	Interview-P	447
1955	Brady	Finance—saving	None	Government data	N.A.
1955	Knoll	Women's employment	None	Interview-P	202
1955	Merriam	Finance—income and expenditure	None	Interview-P	171
1955	Schlaphoff and Burema	Household production	None	Interview-P	82
1956	Cowles and Dietz	Household time usage	None	Records-P	85
1956	Dunsing	Adolescents and money	None	Questionnaire-P	738
1956	Kenkel and Hoffman	Decision making	Role	Interview-P	50
1956	Sharp and Mott	Decision making	Role	Interview-S	749
1958	Blood	Household work division	Role	Interview-S	909
1958	Steidl	Household time usage	None	Laboratory-P	N.A.
1958	Wolgast	Decision making	Role	Interview-P	>900
1959	Johannis and Cunningham	Leisure	Role	Interview-P	>100
1959	Millican	Finance—income and expenditure	None	Records-S	59
1959	Wells	Finance—management	None	Interview-P	60

[a]P = primary data; S = secondary data.

and 1956 (53 hours). Roughly 37 percent of homemaking time was spent in meal preparation and meal cleanup (Cowles and Dietz, 1956).

Farm families raised two-thirds of all the vegetables they consumed, and over half preserved all their own food (Schlaphoff and Burema, 1955). Farm wives exceeded urban wives in the amount of work they performed, in both traditional feminine roles and many masculine role areas (Blood, 1958).

As income increased, couples were more likely to make joint purchasing decisions (Sharp and Mott, 1956). Economic decisions were generally made jointly by husbands and wives; however, men often took the lead in making car purchases while wives were responsible for planning home appliance purchases (Wolgast, 1958).

The Decade 1960–1969

The dominant research themes in the 1960s were adolescents and money, financial security and management, and women's employment. Other areas were financial management, decision making, insurance, economic support from family, expenditure, and household tasks. Thirty-five research articles were identified in this decade.

Research Findings

Adolescents and Money. Marshall and Magruder (1960) studied 512 children and 484 parents to determine how children learn financial skills. Educational status, age, IQ, parent education, and socioeconomic status had a positive, linear relationship with children's scores on a coin test and an experience-with-money scale. The authors rejected the commonly held belief that children who receive an allowance (money received at regular intervals) have more knowledge about money use than children who do not receive an allowance. They also found, however, that children who are given wide experience in the use of money have more knowledge of money and its use than children who lack such varied experiences. (See also Marshall, 1964.)

Zunich (1966) studied the influence of 294 teenagers on personal and family purchases. Sixty percent of the youth felt they had all the influence in the purchase of their clothing. By contrast, only 2 percent felt they had influence in the purchase of furniture and the family car. (See also Clare, 1963; Dunsing, 1960; Epstein, 1961; Fults and Zunich, 1967; Phelan and Schvaneveldt, 1969; Zunich and Fults, 1967.)

Finance

Security and Retirement. Cowles and Knothe (1960) studied financial security in 145 Wisconsin families, which included 208 men and women aged 65 years or older. They found that 14 percent of the elderly families had not paid off the mortgage on the farm and that 13 percent had made the last mortgage payment after their sixty-fifth birthday. For at least one-fourth of the families, farm debt was a life-long concern. Twenty-three percent of the families had life insurance on at least one of the spouses, 27 percent carried health insurance, and almost 25 percent had no written will. Only half of the families felt they could meet emergency expenditures. Moreover, thirty families indicated they could not even meet ordinary expenses.

Kundak and Fitzsimmons (1960) studied factors associated with financial security among 401 Indiana farm families. Using multiple regression, they found five factors correlated with financial security (beta coefficients are in parentheses): ability to meet emergency expenses (.16), ability to attain goals (.13), satisfaction with current economic conditions (.15), family size (−.05), and ability to meet current expenses (.48). (See also Larery, 1963.)

Morse (1962) studied the financial security of 200 rural Kansas families. Over 80 percent of the families surveyed had life insurance, and virtually all of the families had some form of casualty insurance (home, auto, health, or accident); however, only one in twenty carried major medical insurance. College education was viewed as important by 93 percent of the families. Over two-thirds of the families who felt financially secure tended to be those that felt they had the right amount of insurance. (See also Guthrie and Fitzsimmons, 1963; Lomberg and Krofta, 1965; White and Dunsing, 1963.)

Management. Hill (1963) studied the management of family resources among 300 Minnesota families. He identified four distinctive components of consumership: planning, efficiency of decision making (judgment), risk taking, and "planfulness" (actions preceded by plans). Efficiency of decision making had the highest positive association with consumer satisfaction. (See also Downs, 1968; Gover, 1964; Manning, 1960.)

Kin Support. Clark (1962) investigated the economic contributions made by 107 New York families to their newly married children during the first three years of their marriage. Contributions were classified into three types: goods, money, and services. Clark found that all the families gave some items in the first year, and almost all continued to give during the second and third years. The median total value of first-year contributions was $495, with food being the most frequently given item. The median frequency of giving some kind of contribution was once per week. Parents with higher incomes gave more.

Income and Expenditure. Bymers and Galenson (1968) found, using national data, that expenditures for medical care declined fairly consistently as income rose. By contrast, the percentage spent on education and gifts to organizations increased as income went up. The amount of income spent on reading material and library fees was constant at just less than 1 percent (0.8 percent) across all income groups. Expenditures for personal insurance rose moderately with income.

Debt. Ryan and Maynes (1969) conducted a study of consumer indebtedness using data from 1,223 debtor households. They found that installment credit use was most common among middle-income, young married families with children. Eleven percent of the households in the sample were found to be in economic trouble (a debt payment-to-income ratio of 20 percent or higher).

Women's Employment. Anderson and Fitzsimmons (1960) studied the use of time and money by 190 employed women in Virginia. Women employed full time spent 31 hours in homemaking activities, while the part-time employees spent 49 hours. On the average, women employed full time contributed 43 percent of total family income.

The *Monthly Labor Review* (1962) reported on a study that examined the net contribution to family income of 171 full-time employed wives. The wives' average work-related expenditures amounted to nearly half of their earnings, so that only 53 percent of their pay could be considered a net addition to the family income. If there were children under 17 years of age in the home, the amount was 49 percent; without children, it was 58 percent.

Rollins (1963) compared data on working wives in Rochester, New York, in 1920 and 1960. In 1920, 25 percent of married women worked for money, with 8 percent employed outside the home. By 1960, almost 37 percent of wives living with a husband were working for pay outside the home. In 1920, 5 percent of married women with children under 5 were employed outside the home. In 1960, 22 percent of married Rochester women with children under 6 worked outside the home.

Caudle (1964) studied the financial management practices of employed and nonemployed wives in Tallahassee, Florida. Subjects in the study were 205 state-employed clerical workers and 205 full-time homemakers. All of the women's husbands were employed full time. The money the working women earned contributed to total family income by an average of 32 percent. Monthly job-related expenditures for the working women ranged from 24 to 50 percent of their take-home pay. No statistical difference was found between the two groups of women in expenditures for laundry, drycleaning, recreation, church and charity, support of relatives, annual vacation, and clothing. (See also Hafstrom and Dunsing, 1965; Wenck, 1967.)

Decision Making. Schomaker (1963) studied financial decision making in 100 Michigan farm families. Families with heads under 45 years of age were more likely to carry out various decision-making practices, as were families in which the husband and wife had more education. In addition, families who perceived their financial decisions to be satisfactory generally discussed the problem as a family and consulted sources of information outside the family more often than families who viewed their financial decisions as unsatisfactory. (See also Schlesinger, 1962.)

Household Tasks. Maloch (1963) examined why homemakers like and dislike certain household tasks. The sample consisted of 120 New York homemakers with children no older than 8 years old. The most-liked household tasks were cooking (38 percent), cleaning (27 percent), and washing (20 percent). The three most disliked tasks were cleaning (43 percent), ironing (34 percent), and dishwashing (13 percent). Phrases most often used by homemakers in describing tasks they liked were "like time spent," "pride in results," "results appreciated by family," and "adequate equipment." By contrast, phrases such as "monotonous," "short-term results," "dislike time spent," and "tiring" were used to describe the least-liked tasks.

The Decade in Review

Theory and Methodology. Theoretical orientations were not a major influence in research in the 1960s, although some use of theory was evident, including life cycle, family development, economic, and role theory. As in prior decades, data were most often obtained by personal interview or questionnaire. Of the thirty-five studies identified, primary data were used in twenty-eight, and seven used secondary data. The size of the sample in most research projects exceeded 100 subjects (table 5–4).

Percentages and frequency tables continued to be the most common statistical techniques used in data analysis; however, more rigorous statistical methods started to appear. Chi-square was used in five studies, two studies utilized analysis of variance, and factor analysis and multiple regression were each used once.

General Findings. Girls received less financial training than boys and generally felt that saving and investing were not their concern (Clare, 1963). Children who received an allowance from parents did not have more knowledge about money use than children who did not receive an allowance. Youth who planned to save money and follow their plans had favorable spending patterns, regardless of the source of spending money (Marshall and Magruder, 1960; Marshall, 1964; Fults and Zunich, 1967; Phelan and Schvaneveldt, 1969). Irregular earnings or irregular amounts received from parents were the most common sources of money income among youth aged 13 to 15 (Dunsing, 1960; Rogerson and Whiteford, 1960).

Children in low-income families were more likely to enter the work force earlier than children from higher-income families (Epstein, 1961). Teenage marriages were typically burdened with high levels of installment debt (Herrmann, 1965). Teenagers generally felt they had some control over the purchases of their own clothing but not over the purchase of family furniture or car (Zunich, 1966).

Nearly half of farm families could not meet emergency expenditures, and two-thirds did not have wills (Cowles and Knothe, 1960). The length of time between the last child's leaving home and the parents' retirement was relatively short in many farm families, resulting in a lack of financial resources at retirement (Lomberg and Krofta, 1965).

Perceived financial security was characterized by the ability to meet emergency and current expenses, attainment of financial goals, size of family, job stability, past experience with financial distress, and stability of current income (Kundak and Fitzsimmons, 1960; Guthrie and Fitzsimmons, 1963). Families that tended to feel financially secure had proper amounts of insurance (Morse, 1962).

Satisfaction with the management of family resources was positively correlated with efficiency of decision making or judgment in the use of resources (Hill, 1963). Families commonly gave items (food most frequently) to newlywed children during their first three years of marriage (Clark, 1962). Percentage of income spent on reading material was fairly constant across different income groups, and expenditures for personal insurance rose with income (Bymers and Galenson, 1968). Installment credit use was most common among middle-income, young married families with children (Ryan and Maynes, 1969).

Full-time employed women spent 31 hours in homemaking activities each week and earned about 43 percent of the family income. Part-time employed women spent 49 hours each week in homemaking activities (Anderson and Fitzsimmons, 1960). Full-time employed mothers were generally satisfied with their performance in caring for children, caring for the house and clothing, and preparing meals (Wenck, 1967). Job-related expenditures for working women ranged from 25 to 50 percent of take-home pay (Monthly Labor Review, 1962; Caudle, 1964). Between 1920 and 1960, there was a substantial increase in the number of women with children under 6 years of age working outside the home (Rollins, 1963). Two-thirds of working wives in two-earner families worked to obtain a higher standard of living (Hafstrom and Dunsing, 1965).

Younger and better-educated farm families were more likely to utilize a variety of financial decision-making practices (Schomaker, 1963). Most housewives named lack of time as their biggest household management problem (Hunter, 1961). Having her efforts appreciated by her family had a positive relationship to homemaking tasks enjoyed by women (Maloch, 1963).

Table 5–4
Overview of Research on Family Resource Management, 1960–1969

Year	*Author*	*Topic*	*Theory*	*Method*[a]	*Sample*
1960	Anderson and Fitzsimmons	Women's employment	None	Questionnaire-P	191
1960	Cowles and Knothe	Finance—security and retirement	None	Interview-P	208
1960	Dunsing	Adolescents and money	None	Questionnaire-P	964
1960	Kundak and Fitzsimmons	Finance—security and retirement	None	Questionnaire-P	401
1960	Manning	Finance—management	None	Interview-P	35
1960	Marshall and Magruder	Adolescents and money	None	Interview-P	512
1960	Rogerson	Adolescents and money	None	Interview-P	504
1961	Epstein	Adolescents and money	None	Secondary analysis	N.A.
1961	Hunter	Household tasks	None	Interview-P	511
1962	Clark	Finance—kin support	None	Interview-P	107
1962	Monthly Labor Review	Women's employment	None	Interview-P	171
1962	Morse	Finance—security and retirement	None	Interview-S	200
1962	Schlesinger	Decision making	None	Survey-P	33
1963	Clare	Adolescents and money	None	Questionnaire-P	120
1963	Guthrie and Fitzsimmons	Finance—security and retirement	None	Interview-P	20
1963	Hill	Finance—management	Family development	Interview-P	300
1963	Larery	Finance—security and retirement	None	Interview-P	252

1963	Maloch	Household tasks	None	Interview-P	120
1963	Rollins	Women's employment	None	Census records	N.A.
1963	Schomaker	Decision making	None	Interview/Questionnaire-P	100
1963	White and Dunsing	Finance—insurance	None	Interview-P	50
1964	Caudle	Women's employment	None	Questionnaire-P	410
1964	Gover	Finance—management	None	Questionnaire-P	213
1964	Marshall	Adolescents and money	None	Interview-P	180
1965	Hafstrom and Dunsing	Women's employment	None	Interview-P	50
1965	Herrmann	Adolescents and money	None	Secondary analysis	N.A.
1965	Lomberg and Krofta	Finance—security and retirement	Life cycle	Interview-S	209
1966	Zunich	Adolescents and money	None	Questionnaire-P	294
1967	Fults and Zunich	Adolescents and money	None	Questionnaire-P	294
1967	Wenck	Women's employment	None	Questionnaire-P	445
1967	Zunich and Fults	Adolescents and money	None	Questionnaire-P	610
1968	Bymers and Galenson	Finance—income and expenditure	Economics	Interview-S	13,728
1968	Downs	Finance—management	None	Questionnaire-P	45
1969	Phelan and Schvaneveldt	Adolescents and money	None	Questionnaire-P	100
1969	Ryan and Maynes	Finance—debt	Economics	Interview-S	1,223

[a] P = primary data; S = secondary data.

The Decade 1970–1979

Prominent research topic areas in the 1970s were division of work in the home, household tasks, time usage and management, women's employment, expenditure, and debt and insurance. Thirty-three research articles were identified in this decade.

Research Findings

Household

Work Division. Walker (1973), who studied the household work time of 1,400 families in New York City, found that employed women averaged between 4 and 8 hours each day in housework. Unemployed women spent between 5 to 12 hours in household work. Men averaged 11 hours per week in housework, regardless of whether the wife worked outside the home. The three variables found to be most associated with housework time were number of children, age of the youngest child, and outside employment of the mother of more than 15 hours per week.

Nickols and Metzen (1978) found, using data from a sample of 1,156 families, that husbands contributed relatively little time to housework, family size had a negative effect on husband's housework time, and husbands whose wives had higher hourly earnings contributed more time to housework. (See also Lovingood and Firebaugh, 1978.)

Time Management. Hall and Schroeder (1970) obtained data from 229 Seattle homemakers to ascertain the amount of time they spent weekly in ten different household tasks, such as meal preparation, dishwashing, laundering, and transportation. They found that homemakers in 1968 spent slightly more total time on household tasks than did homemakers in 1920—49 hours in 1968 compared to 47 in 1920. The time spent at individual tasks shifted over time, however. For example, time spent in food preparation increased to 19 hours per week in 1968 from 13 hours in 1920. (See also Schaurer and Manning, 1973.)

Satisfaction. Hafstrom and Dunsing (1973) studied factors influencing homemakers' satisfaction with her family's level of living. Using data from a sample of 488 "typical" and 191 "disadvantaged" families, they found that adequacy of family income was the most important factor in explaining satisfaction with level of living among the "typical" families. In the "disadvantaged" sample, satisfaction with housing was the most important variable in determining the homemaker's satisfaction with her level of living.

Women's Employment. Williamson (1970) examined the scholastic performance of children of working mothers. Data were obtained on eighty children in the seventh grade, half of whom had mothers who had worked full time since the child began first grade. It was hypothesized that the children of employed mothers would have lower grade point averages and higher rates of absenteeism and that the attitude of the mother toward work or nonwork would be unrelated to the child's academic performance. Williamson found no statistical difference in grade point average or absenteeism between the two groups of children and thereby rejected the first two hypotheses. The third hypothesis was also rejected; a high, positive correlation was found between the mother's attitude toward her work or nonwork status and the child's scholastic achievement.

Metzen and Helmick (1975) studied the impact of the earnings of secondary workers on family income adequacy. From a diverse multistate sample of 1,559 families, they found that the impact of supplemental earnings was greatest in relatively poor families—the migrant families in California and black families in East Texas.

Szinovacz (1977) studied family structure and role allocation between spouses in 1,370 Austrian families in which the wife was employed outside the home. Reliance on outside help from relatives was related to a high degree of role segregation between spouses on both task allocation and decision making. Female employment did not necessarily result in the development of egalitarian role relations between spouses. (See also Sailor, Crumley, and Patterson, 1977.)

Finance

Debt. Kinsey and Lane (1978) studied the effect of debt on perceived household welfare. From a national sample of 1,425 U.S. families, they found that families tended to allocate their debts and assets within the constraints they face in order to maximize their utility, as economic theory suggests. The researchers concluded, in contrast to the advice found in traditional consumer credit literature, that use of consumer credit does not increase the probability of feeling worse off in terms of household welfare.

Wright (1978) studied the social and economic characteristics differentiating families that succeeded in repaying their debts from those that did not. They studied 2,800 families who used the Family Debt Counseling Service in Syracuse, New York, and found that a family's total debt load and number of creditors did not affect its success in resolving debt problems. Moreover, age and education of the primary wage earner were not related to a family's success in repaying debts. Factors associated with a family's ability to repay debts were monthly net income, ratio of debt payments to income, duration of marriage, and number of years in current job. It was also found that among families seriously in debt, the wife did not generally have an education beyond the ninth grade. Wright concluded, "If, as is true in many blue-collar marriages, the husband/wage earner gives the family paycheck to his wife to manage and spend wisely, she is severely handicapped by her lack of education" (p. 39).

Divorce. House (1976) conducted a study of how women fared financially following divorce. The sample was eighty-seven randomly selected female plaintiffs and defendants involved in divorce actions in Texas. Noticeable differences existed with respect to property settlements when the women were grouped according to ethnic background. No significant differences in property settlements were found when the women were grouped according to age, annual income, marital tenure, family size, and types of property disposition.

Adolescents and Money. Turner and Brandt (1978) simulated a market to test sixty-two children for selected consumer skills. Half of the children were 4 years old, and the other half were in fourth grade (9–10 years old). Children learned consumer skills by being given opportunities to participate in consumer decision making and by sharing family responsibilities. Too little or too much time spent in market search lessened the chance of obtaining a "best buy." Finally, although children learned to be consumers early in life, some skills depended on maturation and use of education. (See also Langrehr and Mason, 1978.)

Decision Making. Jeries (1977) conducted a study of wives' perceptions of marital decision making. The sample consisted of 163 families living in small southwestern Iowa towns. Marital satisfaction, going places together as a family, and the family income were positively related to joint decision making. Wife's employment outside the home, seeing and visiting with friends from work, wife's perception of income adequacy, not being able to meet large bills, and the wife's inclination toward authority versus equality with regard to education were all negatively related to joint decision making. (See also Gladhart, 1977.)

The Decade in Review

Theory and Methodology. Several theoretical orientations were evident in the research of this decade: systems and ecosystems, economic, role, and conjugal power theory (table 5–5). The majority of studies, however, did not have a stated or implied theory. Use of statistical methods increased during the 1970s. Multiple regression and percentage tables were the most common statistical methods, followed by chi-square, factor analysis, and analysis of variance. One study utilized logit analysis, a log-linear technique. Of the thirty-three research articles identified, twenty-one used primary data, and twelve used secondary data.

General Findings. Women spent more time in housework when there were more children in the home, when the children were younger, and when the women did not work outside the home. Men averaged 11 hours of housework per week, regardless of the employment status of the wife (Walker, 1973).

Table 5-5
Overview of Research on Family Resource Management, 1970–1979

Year	*Author*	*Topic Area*	*Theory*	*Method*[a]	*Sample*
1970	Hall and Schroeder	Household—time usage	None	Questionnaire-P	229
1970	Williamson	Women's employment	None	Questionnaire-P	80
1971	Ronald, Singer, and Firebaugh	Household—tasks	None	Interview-S	120
1972	Ater and Deacon	Household—interaction	Conjugal	Interview-P	104
1972	Morrison	Finance—income and expenditure	None	Secondary analysis	391
1972	Mumaw and Nichols	Household—management	None	Questionnaire-P	102
1972	Rudd and Dunsing	Finance—saving	None	Interview/Questionnaire-S	52
1972	Williamson and Manning	Finance—net worth	None	Records-P	60
1973	Hafstrom and Dunsing	Household—satisfaction	None	Interview-S	679
1973	Schaurer and Manning	Household—time usage	None	Interview-P	20
1973	Walker	Household—work division	None	Interview-S	1,400
1974	Maynes and Geistfeld	Finance—insurance	None	Interview-P	95
1975	Hall	Household—tasks	None	Court records-S	N.A.
1975	Metzen and Helmick	Women's employment	Economics	Interview-S	1,559
1975	Steidl	Household—tasks	None	Interview-P	208
1976	Geistfeld	Finance—insurance	None	Questionnaire-P	70
1976	House	Finance—divorce	None	Questionnaire-P	87
1977	Gladhart	Decision making	Ecosystem	Interview-S	216
1977	Hager and Bryant	Finance—income and expenditure	None	Interview-S	491
1977	Jeries	Decision making	Power	Interview-P	163
1977	Sailor, Crumley, and Patterson	Women's employment	Role	Questionnaire-P	175
1977	Szinovacz	Women's employment	Role	Questionnaire-P	1,370
1978	Arndt and Holmer	Finance—management	Economics	Questionnaire-P	222
1978	Kinsey and Lane	Finance—debt	Economics	Interview-S	1,425
1978	Langrehr and Mason	Adolescents and money	None	Examination-P	>100
1978	Lovingood and Firebaugh	Household—work division	Systems	Interview-P	100
1978	Nickols and Metzen	Household—work division	Time	Interview-S	1,156
1978	Turner and Brandt	Adolescents and money	None	Interview-P	62
1978	Winakor and Thomas	Finance—income and expenditure	None	Interview-P	1,140
1978	Wright	Finance—debt	None	Questionnaire-P	2,800
1979	Hogan and Paolucci	Finance—housing	Ecosystem	Interview/Questionnaire-S	157
1979	Pershing	Household—family policies	Systems	Questionnaire-P	279

[a]P = primary data; S = secondary data.

Variance in husband's household work time was best predicted by the wife's earnings—the higher was the wife's earnings, the more time husbands spent in housework. Family size was found to influence husband's household work time negatively (Nickols and Metzen, 1978). Wives tended to have more responsibility in implementing decisions in the home than did husbands (Lovingood and Firebaugh, 1978).

Cooking was the most-liked household task, cleaning and ironing the least liked (Ronald, Singer, and Firebaugh, 1971). Household tasks were made more complex because of inadequate time, lack of knowledge, and poor planning (Steidl, 1975b). Aspects of homemaking tasks most often liked were in the affective domain (Steidl, 1975a). Total time spent in housework in 1968 (49 hours) was slightly higher than in 1920 (47 hours). Time spent in some tasks, such as food preparation and house care, increased noticeably over the fifty-year period. Time spent in family care, clothing care, management and shopping, and "other" decreased over the same period (Hall and Schroeder, 1970).

Consensus between husband and wife, family income, and quality of housing were all positively correlated with the wife's satisfaction with level of living (Ater and Deacon, 1972; Hafstrom and Dunsing, 1973). Common family management policies (or family customs) included keeping records, eating meals together at a regular time, communication patterns among family members and with extended family, and household repair and maintenance (Pershing, 1979).

Academic grades and rates of absenteeism from school were not significantly different for children of employed mothers and children whose mothers did not work ouside the home (Williamson, 1970). The impact of supplemental earnings was greatest in relatively poor families (Metzen and Helmick, 1975). Employment of the wife did not necessarily lead to egalitarian role relations between husband and wife (Szinovacz, 1977).

Families generally defined savings as the accumulation of liquid reserves (Rudd and Dunsing, 1972). Use of consumer credit did not increase the probability of feeling worse off in terms of household welfare (Kinsey and Lane, 1978). In families with serious debt problems, the wife generally did not have more than a ninth-grade education. Factors associated with a family's ability to repay accumulated debt were amount of net income, ratio of debt payments to income, duration of marriage, and number of years in current job (Wright, 1978).

An estimated 50 percent of families had a life insurance deficit (Maynes and Geistfeld, 1974). Differences in property settlements existed when divorced women were grouped according to ethnic background but not when grouped by age, income, or family size (House, 1976). Families were more energy conscious when the parents had more education (Hogan and Paolucci, 1979). Children learned consumer skills by participating in consumer decision-making activities and by sharing in family responsibilities (Turner and Brandt, 1978). Joint decision making by married couples was positively related to family income, degree of marital satisfaction, and going places together as a family (Jeries, 1977).

The Decade 1980–1989

There was a marked increase in research within the field of family resource management in the 1980s; 112 research articles were identified. There was not a substantive increase in the number of topic areas investigated, but within each topic, more research was conducted. Major areas of research were women's employment, time usage and management, division of work within the home, household production, housing and energy conservation, financial management, adolescents and work, and studies of financial expenditure.

Research Findings

Women's Employment. Gordon and Kammeyer (1980) investigated the gainful employment of 735 women who had at least one child under the age of 4. Economic need was the most often cited reason for their decision to work for pay. Other variables correlated with the decision to work included previous employment, number of children, and beliefs about mothering. Sex role attitudes were slightly correlated with the decision to work, but wife's education level was not. Women whose husbands had lower incomes were less likely to believe that mothering was critically important for an infant.

Foster and Metzen (1981) examined the influence of the wife's earnings on family net worth. Data were obtained from a national sample of 807 women aged 30 to 44. Amount of family income—not its sources—had the most important influence on net worth. Home ownership status was positively associated with net worth, particularly among low- and moderate-income families. Wife's income was found to have no consistent impact on net worth position among low-, moderate-, and high-income families. (See also Foster and Metzen, 1981a; Foster, Abdel-Ghany, and Ferguson, 1981; Foster, 1988.)

Stafford (1983) studied the effects of wife's employment on her household work time using data collected in 1967–1968 from 362 wives in New York State. Increases in wives' daily nonphysical care time were greater than their decreases in physical care time for all families except those with only preschool-age children. The author suggested that in the light of the findings, employment status may not be a suitable substitute measure for daily time spent in paid employment. (For additional studies of women's employment, see the September 1988 issue of *Home Economics Research Journal,* which was devoted entirely to off-farm employment.)

Household Time Management. Hafstrom and Schram (1983) investigated the housework time of wives using a sample of 227 Illinois homemakers. Contributing factors that led to wives' devoting more hours to housework included spending fewer hours working outside the home, having a larger family, eating out less often, and a home that has more levels. Wives with a chronic illness spent more time in housework. The most important determinant of wife's time spent in housework was her labor force participation.

Tasker and co-workers (1983) studied the amount of time families spend in travel for specific activities. Data were collected from 2,100 two-parent, two-child families from selected communities in eleven states. Families spent the most time for social and recreational travel, followed by travel for paid work, shopping, school, and chauffeuring. Of all family members, husbands spent the most time in travel, the majority of it for paid work. Wives spent the largest amount of time traveling for shopping, social, and recreational activities. Family income was not a significant source of variation in the time spent for travel.

Lovingood and McCullough (1986) investigated the relationship of demographic variables, appliance ownership, and time spent in specific household tasks. Data were obtained from 2,100 two-parent, two-child households. Over 60 percent of the families owned seven of the eleven appliances studied. Appliance ownership was not associated with less time spent in household tasks. In fact, a positive relationship was found between the number of appliances owned that require continuous attention and time spent in related tasks.

Blaylock and Smallwood (1987) investigated the intrahousehold allocation of human resources to grocery shopping in a traditional male-female household. Data were obtained from a nationwide survey of 2,200 households conducted by the U.S. Department of Agriculture. About 75 percent of the households reported that the female usually performed the shopping, 5 percent the male, and 20 percent both the male and the female. Among the most important factors influencing a household's choice of a food shopper were hours of market labor supplied by the male and female and the age and education level of the male and female. Support was found for the premise that younger, better-educated couples are more likely to share household responsibilities than older, less-educated couples. (See also Ackerman, 1989.)

Dismukes and Abdel-Ghany (1988) investigated homemakers' household work time in single- and two-parent families. Data were obtained from households with two parents and two children under 18 and from households with one parent and two children (sample size was around 200). Employed homemakers (single or married) did not spend significantly less time in household work than nonemployed homemakers, except for time spent in dishwashing by homemakers in two-parent households. (See also Rowland, Nickols, and Dodder, 1986.)

Division of Household Work. Sanik (1981) studied the division of household work between 1967 and 1977, using a sample of 483 New York families with husband and wife present and two children. Even when employed outside the home, wives still spent more time in household production than other family members. Wives spent less time in dishwashing and clothing care in 1977 than in 1967, while children spent more time in shopping in 1977. The total input to all household production by the entire family remained approximately 10 hours per day over the ten-year period. (See also Coverman and Sheley, 1986.)

Abdel-Ghany and Nickols (1983) investigated the differential between husbands and wives in household work time among 421 dual-earner families. Four socioeconomic variables (wage rate, minutes in paid work, age, and education) explained 16 percent of the variation in husband's household work time and 25 percent of the variation in wife's household work time. The difference in minutes spent in housework between husbands and wives (149 minutes per day) was significant at the .001 level. Minutes in paid work was the most important variable in explaining each spouse's time spent in housework. Gender-based role expectations appeared to account for most of the variance in household work time.

Rexroat and Shehan (1987) studied the family life cycle and spouses' time in housework using data from 1,618 white couples. Salience of work and family roles was found to influence the amount of time that spouses allocated to household labor. For couples in which both spouses were employed full time, wives' total hours of work per week (housework, child care and full-time paid employment) were shown to exceed husbands' at each stage of the life cycle. In the second life cycle stage (oldest child aged 0–3), wives spent almost 90 hours in work each week, compared to just over 60 hours for the husband.

Hardesty and Bokemeier (1989) examined the distribution of household labor among 697 married couples in nonmetropolitan Kentucky. One-third of the women and most of the men were employed full time. Roughly three-fourths of the male and female respondents reported that the wife always or usually performs the grocery shopping, prepares breakfast, and makes doctor and dental appointments. In addition, 85 percent of the respondents indicated that the wife usually or always writes letters to relatives and takes care of general housecleaning. A high degree of agreement was found between spouses regarding who performs household tasks. (See also Barnett and Baruch, 1987; Benin and Agostinelli, 1988; Berardo, Shehan, and Leslie, 1987; Bird, Bird, and Scruggs, 1984; Broman, 1988; Dolan and Scannell, 1987; Rettig and Metzger, 1986.)

Household Production. Volker, Winter, and Beutler (1983) studied expenditures and level of satisfaction associated with household production of food among 470 Iowa households. Those producing more of their own food tended to have lower expenditures for food and a higher quantity and greater variety of it. However, household production of food was not significantly related to household satisfaction with its food. A significant positive relationship between food expenditure and satisfaction with food was discovered. (See also Owen and Beutler, 1981; Volker and Winter, 1988, 1989.)

Ormsby (1989) examined family choices in household production activities in 107 households in which the oldest child was between 6 and 12 years old. Rural wives perceived greater household production within their families than did urban wives. Dual-income households and households with higher incomes purchased more market goods and services and engaged in less home production than single-earner and lower-income households.

Weagley and Norum (1989) studied the household choice to purchase market commodities that could be substituted for home-produced commodities. Value of time, particularly the wife's time, was important in explaining household demand for some home-producible market commodities. (See also Henze, 1983; Norum, 1987.)

Adolescents and Work. White and Brinkerhoff (1981) studied the extent of children's involvement in household work among 790 families. They found that parents reported four rationales for involving children in work in the home: (1) developmental (doing chores helps build character), (2) reciprocal obligation (duty to help the family), (3) extrinsic reasons (parents need the help), and (4) task learning (children need to learn how to do tasks around the home).

Lawrence, Tasker, and Babcock (1983) examined the time urban adolescents spent in housework. The sample contained 517 adolescents between the ages of 12 and 17 living in two-parent, two-child families. Total time in household work averaged 71 minutes per day, with the most time being spent in shopping, maintenance of home, yard, car, and pets, housecleaning, and food preparation. Sex of the adolescent, education of the father, education and employment of the mother, income of the family, and season of the year were significantly related to adolescents' time spent in housework. Adolescents' age was not a statistically significant predictor. (See also Lawrence, Tasker, and Wozniak, 1988; Sanik and Stafford, 1986.)

Lovett and Abdel-Ghany (1988) studied children's contributions to household activities in single- and two-parent families. Data were obtained from 210 households with two children under the age of 18. Labor force participation of the mother and sex of the child did not significantly affect the total household work time of children. Girls spent more time in three particular tasks: food preparation, dishwashing, and housecleaning. Older children (ages 12–18) averaged 78 minutes in total household work time per day. Children aged 6–11 spent an average of 44 minutes in housework per day.

Finance

Income and Expenditure. Horton and Hafstrom (1985) studied changes in expenditure behavior of female-headed families and two-parent families with changes in income. Using national Consumer Expenditure Survey data, they assembled samples of 590 female-headed families and 4,881 two-parent families. They found that except for shelter, the expenditure behavior of female-headed families did not differ significantly from that of two-parent families.

Wagner (1986) analyzed family expenditures for textiles and textile home furnishings using data from 3,007 households. Expenditures for both household textiles and textile home furnishings were influenced positively by total consumption expenditure. Married couples spent more on household textiles and textile home furnishings than did households headed by single people. As the age of the household head increased, expenditures for textile home furnishings decreased. Home owners, with and without mortgages, spent more on textile home furnishings than did renters. (See also Abdel-Ghany and Foster, 1982; Wagner and Lucero-Campins, 1988; Nelson, 1989; Winakor, 1989.)

Management. Hira (1987) studied money management practices influencing household asset ownership. Data were obtained from 198 Midwest households. A majority of the households (70 percent or more) had checking and savings accounts, cars, and real estate. A minority owned certificates of deposit (22 percent), mutual funds (17 percent), stocks and bonds (26 percent), and individual retirement accounts (21 percent). Sociodemographic variables of age, net income, and length of housing tenure were positively related to total asset ownership among households, as were two money management practices: number of credit cards and the amount of money the household felt comfortable charging on the cards. (See also Godwin and Carroll, 1986.)

Johnson (1989) investigated the changes in the financial practices of 1,169 Southeast Asian refugees living in British Columbia, Canada, over a two-year period. The financial practice most frequently adopted by refugees was saving money; the least frequent were the purchase of property insurance and the use of credit cards. Employed male refugees between the ages of 18 and 45 who were privately rather than government sponsored and who were better educated used more financial practices (checking and saving accounts, credit, and so forth). (See also Schnittgrund and Baker, 1983; Heck, 1983; Berger and Drennen, 1985.)

Security and Retirement. McKenna and Nickols (1988) examined the retirement planning of 220 women between the ages of 40 and 55. The respondents had a high interest in retirement planning, but their level of planning raised serious concern for the future. The women who were most active in retirement planning had higher household income, expected a pension, had a positive orientation toward financial risk, perceived control over change, were comfortable with math, were older, and had an internal belief in the ability to control one's life.

Housing. Winter (1980) studied home ownership among 1,267 young families in Iowa. Young families that owned homes had higher incomes and higher monthly housing expenses than did non–home owners. However, the percentage of income devoted to housing did not differ between home owners and non–home owners. Home owners did not have a higher number of full-time workers per household than non–home owners.

Chen and Jensen (1985) used a national sample of 1,706 households to analyze the use of home equity to fund current consumption. Older households did not rely on dissaving from assets. In fact, older home owners were less likely to use home equity to fund current consumption than others. Low-income households demonstrated a greater propensity to use home equity.

Debt. Marlowe (1981) investigated the financial variables associated with successful debt liquidation. Data were obtained from 292 families involved in credit counseling in Tennessee. Families that successfully liquidated debts had lower debt-to-income ratios, lower living expenses, higher car payments, and higher medical bills than families that did not successfully liquidate debt. It was hypothesized that medical debt was largely unplanned and therefore did not represent poor money management habits. The association between higher car payments and successful debt repayment was unexpected.

Satisfaction. Davis and Helmick (1985) investigated the family financial satisfaction in 703 families in three midwestern states. Two reference point variables, perceived change in financial condition and aspirations for the future, exerted a significant direct impact on financial satisfaction. Other predictors of financial satisfaction were area of residence, family income, net worth, number of earners in family, remaining child-rearing years, and debt-to-income ratio. Use of the predictors in a regression model explained between 30 and 40 percent of the variance in family financial satisfaction. (See also Hira, 1987b; Titus, Fanslow, and Hira, 1989.)

Budget. Beutler and Mason (1987) investigated cash flow budgeting in a sample of 665 Iowa households. Formal budget planners were more likely to be young two-spouse households with more education and higher circumstantial demands. Total family income showed no systematic directional impact on budget formality, yet it was found to have an indirect negative effect on budget formality through home production. Over one-third of the families reported no planning for spending income and maintained no records of money spent.

Poduska (1988) made a comparative study of family budgets among eighteen countries using data from each country's equivalent of the U.S. Bureau of Labor and Statistics. The United States had the largest family budget (as of 1984), with an annual mean expenditure of $26,815; Italy had the lowest mean budget expenditure—$6,315. Food expenditure as a percentage of total family budget was substantially lower in the United States than in European and non-European foreign countries. The percentage spent on shelter and transportation was higher in the United States. (See also Mullis and Schnittgrund, 1982.)

Marital Conflict and Money. Williams and Berry (1984) studied the intensity of family disagreement over finances using data from 265 Indiana families. Approximately 25 percent of all husbands and wives reported intense disagreement over family finances. For husbands married fewer than eight years, the percentage was 50 percent. Disagreement over family finances was not associated with family income. Among men, disagreements over family finances were negatively related to family management practices and number of years married. Men whose wives worked part time reported more disagreement. Women reported fewer disagreements when there was more communication between spouses, when they were employed full time, and when they perceived future financial security.

Schaninger and Buss (1986) conducted a longitudinal study of the consumption patterns and finance handling arrangements of 311 happily married and divorced couples. Happily married couples were found to practice role specialization, with greater influence of wife and less husband dominance in family finance handling, and more joint decision making. They spent more for household appliances, their home, and recreational vehicles. Divorced couples spent more on stereos, color televisions, and living room furniture.

Marital Exchange. Rettig and Bubolz (1983) investigated interpersonal resource exchanges as indicators of the quality of marriage. The sample consisted of 224 husband-wife couples. Respondents provided information concerning feelings about perceived quality of marriage, resources received from spouse, and shared time. The study was designed to test resource exchange theory, developed by Uriel Foa and Edna Foa (1974). Results provided support for the theory in that the order of the resource classes on the particularism dimension corresponded to their effectiveness in contributing to marital satisfaction. The Foa and Foa model was best confirmed by the women's data, suggesting that husbands and wives experience marriage differently.

Saving. Hefferan (1982) studied the determinants and patterns of saving within families. Data were obtained from over 18,000 families using U.S. census data. Results of the study indicated that the decision to save and the level of saving are influenced by income, wealth, and family characteristics. In addition, a family's current wealth position was found to be a better indicator of their level of saving than their current income. (See also Davis and Schumm, 1987.)

Kin Support. Kennedy and Stokes (1982) examined the relationship between increasing housing costs and financial support from kin. It was hypothesized that social and financial help from kin is most often received by young, middle-class married couples and home owners rather than renters, and that the higher the cost is for housing, the more likely it is that kin will help. Data were obtained from 452 Canadian households. Results from the analysis found support for each hypothesis. The relationship between home ownership and kin support was not a function of socioeconomic status but of life-cycle stage and housing tenure. (See also Cheal, 1983.)

Women. Scholl (1985) examined married women's accessibility and ownership of credit and cash accounts by collecting data from a national sample of 2,405 married women living on farms. The majority of women were found to be partially or not involved with the family's financial accounts (based upon whether their name appeared on savings and checking accounts, credit cards, charge accounts, and bank loans). Women had more financial involvement when they had more education, had off-farm income, and were involved in farm decision making. Negatively related to financial involvement was wife's age.

Decision Making. Godwin and Scanzoni (1989) studied joint marital decision making among 188 couples. Spouses who reached higher levels of consensus had more equitable economic resources. Husbands were cooperative during conflict situations, and wives had less coercive communication styles.

Leisure Time. Nickols and Abdel-Ghany (1983) investigated the leisure time of 405 two-child families in which both the husband and wife were employed. Husbands were found to have significantly more daily leisure time per day than their wives—255 minutes compared to 220 minutes. Time spent in paid work and time spent in household work were negatively related to leisure time of both husband and wife. Leisure time of the spouse had a significant positive relationship to leisure time of both husband and wife. Age of youngest child was related positively to the wife's leisure time; that is, as the child gets older, the wife has more leisure time.

The Decade in Review

Theory and Methodology. Use of theory as a basis for research topics increased dramatically in this decade, with economic theory, role theory, and systems theory most prominent. Other theories or conceptual frameworks utilized by researchers included household production, equity, life cycle, household time allocation, family resource management, exchange, Marxist, feminist, kin support, communication, ecosystem, and resource exchange (table 5–6).

Use of multiple statistical procedures became the norm for researchers during the 1980s. In prior decades, researchers commonly employed one statistical test. In the 1980s, use of several statistical procedures to analyze data was a common practice. Multiple regression was the most frequently used method of analysis. Other statistical methods were percentage tables, correlation and contingency tables, analysis of variance, t-test, Fischer Z, chi-square, analysis of covariance, factor and path analysis, Pearson correlations, discriminant analysis, tobit analysis, logit analysis, Rotterdam regression, mutliple classification analysis, and LISREL. Of the 112 research studies identified, 46 utilized primary data, and 66 used secondary data.

There was a noticeable increase in the number of researchers who utilized secondary data collected from large, regional studies, among them, An Interstate Urban/Rural Comparison of Families' Time Use, 1978 (NE-113); 1977–78 Nationwide Food Consumption Survey; Panel Study of Income Dynamics; 1980 National Farm Women Survey; Quality of Life as Affected by Area of Residence (NC-128); 1965–1966 Multi-National Time Use Study; 1975–1976 Study of Americans' Use of Time; National Survey of Black Americans; National Longitudinal Surveys 1967, 1972; 1980–81 Consumer Expenditure Survey; and 1977 Consumer Credit Survey.

General Findings. Economic need was the most cited reason for mothers' gainful employment. Wife's education level was not correlated with the decision to work (Gordon and Kammeyer, 1980). Income received by the wife had no consistent impact on family net worth (Foster and Metzen, 1981). Expenditure levels differed between working-wife and non-working-wife families (Foster, 1988). Employment status may not be a suitable substitute measure for daily time spent in paid employment (Stafford, 1983).

Compared to nonemployed homemakers, employed homemakers spent less time in meal preparation and their families ate more meals away from home (Ortiz et al., 1981). Expenditures for meals purchased away from home did not differ by mother's employment status, whereas meal preparation time did (Goebel and Hennon, 1982, 1983).

Role management strategies of husbands and wives differed in dual-career families and career-earner families (Bird, Bird, and Scruggs, 1983). Among dual-earner families, combined number of hours a couple worked was not strongly related to quality of family life; however, a couple's work schedule generally affected the attitudes and behaviors of wives more than husbands (Kingston and Nock, 1985). In dual-earner families, husband's perceptions of his life were unrelated to the wife's level of strain, whereas the wife's perceptions of marital interaction and family conflict were associated with the role strain of both spouses (Galambos and Silbereisen, 1989).

Households allocated time and goods according to an explicit decision-making rule so as to maximize utility (Gerner and Zick, 1983). Time spent in housework by women increased when family size increased, the family ate out less often, the wife had a chronic illness, the wife worked fewer hours outside the home, and the husband worked outside the home more hours (Hafstrom and Schram, 1983; Schram and Hafstrom, 1984; Schram and Hafstrom, 1986). Families spent the most travel time for social and recreational activities, followed by travel for paid work, shopping, and school (Tasker et al. 1983). A positive relationship was found between the number of home appliances requiring continuous attention and the amount of time spent in related household tasks (Lovingood and McCullough, 1986).

Table 5–6
Overview of Research on Family Resource Management, 1980–1989

Year	*Author*	*Topic*	*Theory*	*Method*[a]	*Sample*
1980	Gordon and Kammeyer	Women's employment	Economic role	Interview-S	735
1980	Moschis, Lawton, and Stampfl	Adolescents and money	None	Experiment-P	26
1980	Schnittgrund	Household—time usage	Economics	Records-S	451
1980	Winter	Finance—housing	Systems	Interview-P	1,267
1981a,b	Foster and Metzen	Women's employment	Economics	Interview-S	807
1981b	Foster, Abdel-Ghany, and Ferguson	Women's employment	Economics	Interview-S	1,299
1981	Helmick and Jurich	Adolescents and work	None	Interview-S	149
1981	Marlowe	Finance—debt	Economics	Case study-P	292
1981	Matsushima	Household—time usage	None	Secondary data	N.A.
1981	Meeks and Oudekerk	Finance—housing	Family resource management	Questionnaire-P	571
1981	Ortiz et al.	Women's employment	None	Interview-S	210
1981	Owen and Beutler	Household—production	Economics	Interview-P	664
1981	Sanik	Household—work division	Role	Interview-S	483
1981	White and Brinkerhoff	Adolescents and work	None	Interview-P	790
1982	Abdel-Ghany and Foster	Finance—income and expenditure	Economics	Interview-S	6,679
1982	Goebel and Hennon	Women's employment	Role	Interview-S	206
1982	Hefferan	Finance—saving	Economics	Interview-S	18,903
1982	Kennedy and Stokes	Finance—kin support	Kin support	Interview-S	452
1982	Mullis and Schnittgrund	Finance—budget	Life cycle	Interview-P	199
1982	Purchase, Berning, and Lyng	Household—tasks	None	Interview-S	>10,000
1983	Abdel-Ghany and Nickols	Household—work division	Role	Interview-S	421
1983	Bird, Bird, and Scruggs	Women's employment	Role	Questionnaire-P	214
1983	Cheal	Finance—kin support	Life cycle	Government data-S	9,370
1983	Crawford and Beutler	Household—management	Economics and family resource management	Interview-P	664
1983	Gerner and Zick	Household—time usage	Economics	Interview-S	1,475
1983	Goebel and Hennon	Women's employment	Role	Interview-S	N.A.
1983	Guthrie and Brandt	Finance—housing	None	Questionnaire-S	8,430
1983	Hafstrom and Schram	Household—time usage	None	Interview/ Questionnaire-P	227

1983a	Heck	Household—management	Systems and family resource management	Interview-S	195
1983b	Heck	Finance—management	None	Questionnaire-P	912
1983	Henze	Household—production	Economics	Interview-S	320
1983	Lawrence and Tasker	Adolescents and work	None	Interview-S	517
1983	Matsushima and Suzuki	Household—time usage	None	Secondary data	>50,000
1983	Nickols and Abdel-Ghany	Leisure	Role	Interview-S	405
1983	Rettig and Bubolz	Finance—marital exchange	Resource exchange	Questionnaire-P	224
1983	Sanik and Stafford	Household—production	None	Interview-S	210
1983	Schnittgrund and Baker	Finance—management	None	Interview-P	199
1983	Stafford	Women's employment	Household time	Interview-S	362
1983	Tasker et al.	Household—time usage	Exchange	Interview-S	2,100
1983	Volker, Winter, and Beutler	Household—production	Household production	Questionnaire-P	470
1984	Bird, Bird, and Scruggs	Household—work division	Role	Questionnaire-P	166
1984	Goebel and Hennon	Household—work division	None	Interview-P	210
1984	Maret and Finlay	Women's employment	Role	Interview-S	1,223
1984	Schram and Hafstrom	Household—time usage	Household production	Interview-S	710
1984	Williams and Berry	Finance—marital conflict	Communications	Interview/ Questionnaire-S	265
1985	Berger and Drennen	Finance—management	None	Questionnaire-P	945
1985	Chen and Jensen	Finance—housing	Life cycle	Interview-S	1,706
1985	Davis and Helmick	Finance—satisfaction	Systems	Interview/ Questionnaire-S	703
1985	Horton and Hafstrom	Finance—income and expenditure	Economics	Interview-S	5,471
1985	Kingston and Nock	Women's employment	Role	Interview-S	668
1985	Rowland, Dodder, and Nickols	Finance—assessment	None	Questionnaire-P	520
1985	Scholl	Finance—women	Economics	Interview-S	2,405
1985	Skinner et al.	Women's employment	None	Records/ Questionnaire-P	211
1985	Urich and Hogan	Finance—housing	None	Interview-P	24
1986	Brandt and Olson	Finance—housing	None	Questionnaire-P	222
1986	Bryant	Finance—debt	Economics	Interview-S	2,191
1986	Buehler	Household—management	Systems	Questionnaire-P	203
1986	Coverman and Sheley	Household—work division	Role	Interview-S	912
1986	Garrison	Household—management	Systems	Interview-S	312

Table 5–6 continued

Year	*Author*	*Topic*	*Theory*	*Method*[a]	*Sample*
1986	Godwin and Carroll	Finance—management	Family resource management	Questionnaire-P	73
1986	Hoeflin and Bolsen	Household—investment	None	Questionnaire-P	52
1986	Iams, Steinfelt, and Wilhelm	Finance—management	None	Questionnaire-P	122
1986	Lovingood and McCullough	Household—time usage	Systems	Interview-S	2,100
1986	Rettig and Metzger	Household—work division	Equity	Interview/ Questionnaire-P	88
1986	Rowland, Nickols, and Dodder	Household—time usage	Ecosystem	Interview/ Questionnaire-P	89
1986	Sanik and Stafford	Adolescents and work	None	Interview-S	2,100
1986	Schaninger and Buss	Finance—marital conflict	Eclectic	Interview-S	311
1986	Schram and Hafstrom	Household—time usage	Economics	Interview/ Questionnaire-P	227
1986	Wagner	Finance—income and expenditure	Economics	Interview-S	3,007
1987	Barnett and Baruch	Household—work division	Role	Interview/ Questionnaire-P	160
1987	Berardo, Shehan, and Leslie	Household—work division	Role	Interview-S	1,565
1987	Beutler and Mason	Finance—budget	Systems	Questionnaire-P	665
1987	Blaylock and Smallwood	Household—time usage	Economics	Interview-S	2,200
1987	Davis and Schumm	Finance—saving	Systems	Interview-S	1,739
1987	Dolan and Scannell	Household—work division	None	Records-P	30
1987a	Hira	Finance—management	Economics	Interview-P	198
1987b	Hira	Finance—satisfaction	Economics	Interview-P	198
1987	Norum	Household—production	Household production	Interview-S	2,146
1987	Rexroat and Shehan	Household—work division	Role/life cycle	Interview-S	1,618
1987	Wilhelm, Iams, and Rudd	Finance—assessment	Economics	Questionnaire-P	114
1987	Zick and Gerner	Household—investment	Economics	Interview-S	N.A.
1988	Benin and Agostinelli	Household—work division	None	Questionnaire-P	148

1988	Broman	Household—work division	Role	Interview-S	876
1988	Dismukes and Abdel-Ghany	Household—time usage	None	Interview-S	210
1988	Douthitt and Zick	Household—time usage	Household production	Government data-S	N.A.
1988	Douthitt and Fedyk	Finance—children	Economics	Questionnaire-S	785
1988	Foster	Women's employment	None	Interview-S	3,595
1988	Lawrence, Tasker, and Wozniak	Adolescents and work	None	Interview-S	2,071
1988	Lovett and Abdel-Ghany	Adolescents and work	None	Interview-S	210
1988	McKenna and Nickols	Finance—security and retirement	Family resource management	Questionnaire-P	220
1988	Poduska	Finance—budget	Economics	Government data-S	N.A.
1988	Terzioglu and Safak	Women's employment	None	Interview-P	2,776
1988	Volker and Winter	Household—production	None	Interview-S	11,345
1988	Wagner and Lucero-Campins	Finance—income and expenditure	Economics	Interview-S	5,994
1989	Ackerman	Household—time usage	Economics	Questionnaire-P	420
1989	Floge	Women's employment	None	Interview-S	383
1989	Galambos and Silbereisen	Women's employment	Role	Questionnaire-S	314
1989	Godwin and Scanzoni	Decision making	Decision making	Observation-P	188
1989	Hardesty and Bokemeier	Household—work division	Marxist, feminist	Questionnaire-P	697
1989	Johnson	Finance—management	None	Interview-P	1,169
1989	Khan et al.	Household—time usage	None	Interview-S	2,100
1989	Nelson	Finance—income and expenditure	None	Government data-S	1,812
1989	Ormsby	Household—production	Economics	Questionnaire-S	107
1989	Ozgen and Gonen	Adolescents and money	Economics	Interview-P	300
1989	Roper and Darden	Finance—housing	None	Interview-P	445
1989	Swagler, Sweaney, and Marlowe	Adolescents and work	Economics	Content analysis-P	359
1989	Titus, Fanslow, and Hira	Finance—satisfaction	Systems	Interview-P	123
1989	Turner and Gruber	Finance—housing	None	Questionnaire-P	15
1989	Volker and Winter	Household—production	Economics	Interview-S	11,345
1989	Weagley and Norum	Household—production	Household production	Questionnaire-S	177
1989	Winakor	Finance—income and expenditure	None	Government data-S	N.A.

[a]P = primary data; S = secondary data.

In 75 percent of most households, the wife did the grocery shopping. Younger, better-educated couples were more likely to share household responsibilities (Blaylock and Smallwood, 1987). Home ownership, age, and number of meals eaten away from home best predicted the hours spent shopping by homemakers (Ackerman, 1989). In single-parent and two-parent families, employed homemakers spent about the same amount of time in household tasks (Dismukes and Abdel-Ghany, 1988).

Regardless of employment status, women spent more time in housework than other family members, averaging 7 hours per day. Total housework time by other family members (husband and children) averaged 3 hours per day in 1977 (Sanik, 1981). Husband's household work time changed little between 1965 and 1975. Important factors influencing men's housework time were paid-work time and leisure time (Coverman and Sheley, 1986). The best predictor of a woman's time spent in housework was the amount of time she spent in paid employment (Abdel-Ghany and Nickols, 1983).

Division of household work was not an important correlate of perceived quality of family life; however, less traditional couples tended to be more dissatisfied with the work each did in the home (Goebel and Hennon, 1984). The mother's perception of husband's support of child rearing was a good indicator of the quality of family life (Rettig and Metzger, 1986). Salience of household work and family roles affected the amount of time spouses allocated to household work. Wives spent more time in household labor than husbands in every stage of the life cycle (Bird, Bird, and Scruggs, 1984; Rexroat and Shehan, 1987).

Dual-career couples were not more egalitarian in their allocation of time to household labor than non-dual-career couples (Berardo, Shehan, and Leslie, 1987). Husbands in dual-earner couples were more satisfied with an equitable division of labor, while wives were more satisfied if the division of family work favored them, i.e., they did less work (Benin and Agostinelli, 1988). Women were almost twice as likely as men to feel overworked by household tasks. Employed spouses and men were less satisfied with their family life if they performed most of the household work (Broman, 1988). In single-earner families, attitude toward the quality of fathering he received as a child was the most reliable predictor of husband's participation in household work and child care (Barnett and Baruch, 1987).

Households that engaged in food production generally spent less money on food and had a higher quantity and greater variety of it (Volker, Winter, and Beutler, 1983). Household size and stage of the family life cycle contributed significantly to the amount of production taking place within the home (Owen and Beutler, 1981). Significant predictors of secondary household production (meals prepared and eaten at home) were household size and age of head of household (Volker and Winter, 1988). Living in an urban area and home ownership were the most important predictors of household production of food. Food expenditures were best predicted by household size after being adjusted for ages and composition (Volker and Winter, 1989). Value of food prepared at home was related to education of husband and wife and age of the youngest child (Sanik and Stafford, 1983). Value of time, particularly the wife's time, was important in explaining household demand for some home-producible market commodities (Weagley and Norum, 1989).

Rationales for children's involvement in housework included character development, reciprocal obligation, help needed, and task learning (White and Brinkerhoff, 1981). Adolescents between the ages of 12 and 17 averaged 71 minutes per day doing housework; children between the ages of 6 and 11 averaged 44 minutes per day (Lawrence, Tasker, and Babcock, 1983). First-born boys contributed significantly less time in housework than did first-born girls (Sanik and Stafford, 1986). Rural children spent more time in housework than urban children. Boys spent similar amounts of time regardless of residence, whereas rural girls spent more time in housework than urban girls (Lawrence, Tasker, and Wozniak, 1988). Labor force participation of the mother and sex of the child did not significantly affect total housework time of children (Lovett and Abdel-Gahny, 1988). Working adolescents generally reported that their job had a positive effect on their overall quality of life (Helmick and Jurich, 1981).

Expenditures by female-headed households did not differ materially from those of two-parent households, with the exception of shelter (Horton and Hafstrom, 1985). Expenditures for textile home furnishings decreased as people became older (Wagner, 1986). Level of wife's education was influential in determining family consumption expenditures (Abdel-Ghany and Foster, 1982). American consumers spent roughly 6 percent of their income on clothing and shoes in 1986, compared to 12 percent in 1933 (Winakor, 1989).

Women generally had more interest than men in retirement planning and life insurance, while families with children were more interested in information pertaining to financial management (Iams, Steinfelt, and Wilhelm, 1986). Women most active in retirement planning generally were older and had higher incomes, expected a pension, and were comfortable with math (McKenna and Nickols, 1988). Number of credit cards and amount of money charged on credit cards were positively associated with total asset ownership (Hira, 1987).

Number of years married, completion of a course in consumer education, and occupational status of the wife were the best predictors of positive financial management attitudes and behaviors (Godwin and Carroll, 1986). The financial practice most frequently adopted by foreign refugees living in Canada was saving money; the least frequent was use of credit cards and purchasing property insurance (Johnson, 1989). Keeping track of expenditures was more common than budgeting among white, black, and Mexican-American families (Schnittgrund and Baker, 1983).

The percentage of income devoted to housing did not differ between home owners and renters (Winter, 1980). Older home owners were less likely to use home equity to fund current consumption than younger families. Low-income families most frequently tapped into home equity as a source of funds (Chen and Jensen, 1985). Improvements in home energy efficiency were more common among higher-income Caucasian families (Roper and Darden, 1989). Implementation of residential energy conservation strategies was related to energy savings (Turner and Gruber, 1989). Factors influencing family energy consumption and efficiency included size of house, socioeconomic status, family size, and stage of the family life cycle (Urich and Hogan, 1985).

Families that successfully liquidated debt had lower debt-to-income ratios, lower living expenses, higher car payments, and higher medical bills (Marlowe, 1981). Financial satisfaction was directly influenced by perceived change in financial condition and aspirations for the future (Davis and Helmick, 1985). Households using optimum financial planning practices were more likely to have higher net worth (Titus, Fanslow, and Hira, 1989). Satisfied dual-earner families were generally smaller in size, saved more money, and had little or no credit card debt (Hira, 1987a).

Budgets were more commonly used by young two-spouse households with more education and higher circumstantial demands. Total family income had no consistent impact on budget usage (Beutler and Mason, 1987). Food expenditures, as a percentage of the family budget, were substantially lower in the United States than in European and non-European foreign countries (Poduska, 1988). Low-income families used informal, unwritten budgets almost exclusively, with no apparent relationship between stage of family life cycle and type of budget method used (Mullis and Schnittgrund, 1982).

Intense disagreement regarding family finances occurred within 25 percent of families and in 50 percent of families married fewer than eight years (Williams and Berry, 1984). Among happily married couples, the wife was generally involved in family financial decisions. Divorced couples generally spent more money on stereos, color televisions, and living room furniture, while happily married couples spent more on homes, household appliances, and recreational vehicles (Schaninger and Buss, 1986). Couples achieving high levels of consensus generally had equitable economic resources (Godwin and Scanzoni, 1989).

Husbands had more leisure time per day than their wives: 255 minutes compared to 220 minutes. Age of the youngest child was positively related to the wife's leisure time (Nickols and Abdel-Ghany, 1983).

Summary of Research, 1930–1990

Topic Review

A total of 235 research articles were identified during the period from 1930 to 1990 dealing with topics in the field of family resource management. The number of research articles identified over the sixty-year period, however, is less important than the distribution of research topics (table 5–7), for several reasons. First, the research abstracts reported in this chapter provide a representative sample of family resource management research rather than a compre-

Table 5-7
Research Topics in Family Resource Management, 1930–1990

Number of Articles	*Research Topic*
28	Finance—income and expenditure
28	Women's employment
19	Household—time usage
18	Adolescents and money
17	Household—work division
15	Finance—management
10	Finance—housing
10	Household—production
8	Decision making
8	Finance—security and retirement
7	Adolescents and work
7	Household—tasks
6	Finance—saving
6	Household—management
5	Great Depression
5	Marriage and money topics
5	Standard of living
5	Finance—debt
4	Finance—budget
3	Finance—support from kin
3	Finance—insurance
3	Leisure
3	Finance—satisfaction
2	Household—investment
2	Finance—assessment
2	Finance—children
1	Household—satisfaction
1	Finance—divorce
1	Finance—net worth
1	Finance—women
1	Family policies
1	Family interaction

hensive review of all published research. Second, much of the published research in the early decades (1930–1950) was descriptive rather than quantitative; hence it was not included in this review.[3] Last, fewer journals existed in the early decades, limiting the potential outlets for research. As a result, the number of articles identified in the early decades is substantially fewer than in later decades.

Prominent research topics in family resource management during the sixty-year period under review included (number of studies in parenthesis) women's employment (28), income and expenditure (28), time usage and management (19), adolescents and money (18), division of household work (17), financial management (15), financial security and retirement (8), housing (8), household tasks, household production, and decision making (7 each), and household management, saving, and adolescents and work (6 each).

Decade Review

Societal conditions have profoundly influenced family resource management research conducted in each of the past six decades. For instance, the social and economic impact of the Great Depression on families was staggering. Between 1929 and 1933 average family income in the United States declined 40 percent. In 1932, approximately 28 percent of the households in America, representing 34 million men, women, and children, lacked a wage earner (Mintz and Kellogg, 1988, p. 134). Assessing the impact of the depression on families was of primary interest to family resource management scholars in the 1930s. The majority of the research focused on income and expenditure patterns, studies specific to the economic depression, and living standards (table 5–8).

During the 1940s, shortages of consumer durables caused by World War II kept family resource management scholars' research attention focused on standards of living and consumer expenditure patterns. The war effort also focused research interest on consumer savings rates. During this period, the government sold war bonds to reduce the demand for consumer durables. In effect, the government was attempting to redirect consumer expenditures from consumption to saving. As a result, the aggregate consumer savings rate became of interest to researchers.

In the 1950s, research concerning financial expenditure and management, decision making, and household time use reflected the demands and opportunities faced by families in an expanding national economy. Following the Korean War, there was a boom in the production of capital goods in the United States. This increase in the production of consumer goods and services presented families with the "problem" of choosing—a problem not known during the years of scarce consumer goods during World War II (Hefferan, 1986). Additionally, studies of leisure time and activities followed the improved economic climate.

Four research areas—adolescents and money use, financial security, financial management, and women's employment—dominated the work done in the 1960s. The large number of studies investigating the use of money by adolescents is likely due to the fact that children born at the beginning of the baby boom were teenagers at this time. In fact, in 1967 there were approximately 25 million teenagers in the United States between the ages of 13 and 19. Large numbers of teen-agers, coupled with a growing national economy, meant that a lot of money was going through teenagers' hands. The topic of women's employment also became more visible, perhaps because as the divorce rate increased, more women went job hunting. From 1960 to 1970 the percentage of married women in the labor force went from 30.5 to 40.8 percent, and the divorce rate went from about 9 per 1,000 to 15 per 1,000 total population (Bahr, 1989, p. 342).

Research about women's employment continued into the 1970s, as did the increase in the national divorce rate. Research regarding the division of household work between spouses began in the 1970s, possibly reflecting a growing interest in the feminist perspective. There was an increase in the variety of

Table 5-8
Summary of Major Research Topics on Family Resource Management, by Decade, 1930–1990

Decade	*Number of Articles*	*Topic*
1930	16	Finance—income and expenditure (6) Great Depression (5) Standard of living (3)
1940	15	Finance—income and expenditure (7) Standard of living (2) Finance—saving (1)
1950	24	Finance—income and expenditure (4) Finance—management (3) Decision making (3) Household—time usage (2) Finance—saving (2) Leisure (2)
1960	35	Adolescents and money (11) Women's employment (6) Finance—security and retirement (6) Finance—management (4) Decision making (2) Household—tasks (2)
1970	33	Women's employment (4) Household—tasks (4) Household—work division (3) Finance—income and expenditure (3) Finance—debt (2) Decision making (2)
1980	112	Women's employment (16) Household—time usage (15) Household—work division (13) Household—production (9) Finance—housing (8) Finance—management (7) Adolescents and work (7) Finance—income and expenditure (6)

research too. One study dealt with household energy conservation as a direct result of the energy crisis of 1973–1974, another examined the formation of family policies, and another investigated the association between interpersonal relationships and managerial behavior in the family. Both studies seem to reflect a growing sensitivity toward a human rather than a task orientation.

In the 1980s, studies about time usage, division of household work between spouses, and women's employment represented 40 percent of the family resource management research conducted. The emphasis on family task sharing (division of household work) was likely due to traditional gender roles' being called into question by a growing body of feminist literature, converging work roles of men and women, a steady increase in the number of wives and two-earner families, changing employment options for husbands (such as flex-time), an increase in the number and variety of home appliances, and a lessening of traditional sex stereotypes in society.

Time use and management studies also increased in the 1980s, reflecting the value placed on time in a management-oriented society. Women's employment continued as a dominant research theme in response to the increasing number of women in the work force. In 1950, approximately 25 percent of married women worked outside the home; in 1988, over 60 percent did. The percentage of working mothers also increased. In 1950, 12 percent of mothers with school-age children worked outside the home; in 1988, over 50 percent of mothers with school-age children worked full or part time (Mintz and Kellogg, 1988). Household production surfaced as an important research theme in recognition of the fact that families are not solely consumers and that social and economic value of production within the home has long been ignored in our expenditure-oriented society. Finally, research about adolescents and work began in earnest during the 1980s, possibly due to a concern that as the number of single-parent families increases, the nature of children's household work will change.

A general trend over the sixty-year period was an increase in the number of researchers utilizing secondary data in their research rather than collecting data themselves. In the 1930s, 28 percent of the articles were based on secondary data. By the 1980s, 58 percent of the researchers utilized secondary data.

Key Findings, 1930–1990

Women's Employment. Women generally seek paid employment based on economic need and to obtain or maintain a higher standard of living. Their work-related expenses are between 25 and 50 percent of their take-home pay, with child care as the largest component for those who have young children. Working women provide one-third to one-half of total family income. Among couples in which both spouses work for paid employment, the wife appears to be more sensitive to and more aware of increased strain within the family. Women who work outside the home spend less time in meal preparation. Husbands of women who work outside the home do not significantly differ from husbands of full-time homemakers in terms of egalitarian attitudes.

Income and Expenditure and Budget. The percentage of the average family budget spent for food has decreased over time: from 32 percent in the 1930s and 37 percent in 1955 to 18 percent by 1988. The percentage of a family's budget spent on housing has fluctuated only slightly over the same time period: 22 percent in 1930, 23 percent in the early 1950s, and 24 percent in 1988. Except for shelter, expenditure patterns between single-parent and two-parent families do not differ significantly.

Time Usage and Management and Work Division. Total hours spent in homemaking tasks by women and other family members has changed only moderately since the early 1930s, with women currently spending as many as 50 hours per week in housework (less if employed outside the home); 11 hours are contributed by men and 8 hours by children. Regardless of employment status, women contribute significantly more time to housework and child care than their spouses or children. Variables commonly used to explain differences in husband-wife household work time have included each spouse's wage rate and hours spent in paid employment, age of each spouse, stage in family life cycle, education attainment of each spouse, and ages and number of children.

Adolescents and Money. Children who receive money to manage (regardless of the source), plan their expenditures, and participate in family responsibilities generally develop better financial management skills than children without such experiences. Irregular earnings is the most common source of children's money. Boys often receive better money management training than girls.

Other Topics. During times of financial strain, paid forms of recreation are often eliminated or severely reduced, credit debt increases, and bills are not paid. Financial management skills lessen the chance of marital discord. Formal budgeting is more often used by young, educated families with moderate incomes. Age, education, income, and degree of marital satisfaction affect decision making by couples; however, it is common for couples to make economic decisions together. Women have more interest in retirement planning and insurance than men do. Compared to urban families, rural households produce more of their own food, and rural children spend more time in housework. Newly married couples often receive economic assistance from other family members.

Suggestions for Future Research

Attempting to forecast the future direction and focus of family resource management research is nothing short of challenging; however, it is reasonable to assume that family resource management research will continue to be sensitive to national economic conditions, changing technologies, and dynamic societal trends that influence the stewardship and management of human and financial resources.

Inasmuch as "human resources research is inextricably tied to economics and social conditions" (Hefferan, 1986), it necessarily follows that any attempt to forecast the nature of family resource management research during the next decade is also an attempt to forecast economic and social conditions. Understanding the historical connection between economic and social conditions and the evolution of family resource management research aids in this process.

Previously in this chapter, I outlined the societal events and trends that have influenced family resource management research during the past sixty years. (Prominent research topics, which in essence represent underlying social and economic conditions, of the past six decades are shown in tables 5–7 and 5–8.) Certain research topics have received a good deal of attention over the past sixty years: women's employment, time usage and management, and division of household work. At the same time, topics such as the financial impact of children, determinants of family financial satisfaction, and financial impacts of divorce on women have received relatively less research attention. (Recall that tables 5–7 and 5–8 do not represent an exhaustive compilation of every research project in print but rather a representative sample of the quantity and variety of family resource management research.)

Three of the most prominent research topics since 1930 (women's employment, household time usage and management, and work division) are clearly related to a steadily increasing percentage of married women joining the work force, particularly those with school-age children still at home. It appears that the trend toward dual-career and dual-earner households will continue. As a result, research about women's employment, time usage and management, and work division within the home will likely remain of interest.

Other areas of research interest will likely center around our continually expanding and increasingly sophisticated economy. Such research topics might include the retirement planning of one-parent and two-parent households; insurance planning and alternative health maintenance and protection plans; flexible employee benefit plans and work hours; costs and benefits of an expanding financial services and investment industry; and the financial and social impact of increased public involvement in the rearing of children.

A great deal of work in the 1990s will build on the base of research already established, leading researchers to explore issues such as the financial impact of divorce on women and children, family use of leisure time, involvement of women in financial planning and management, family policies and traditions and their impact on family stability, variables associated with successful debt repayment, budgeting, and the economic role of the kin network.

Notes

1. The following sources were used to compile the research abstracts: *International Index to Periodicals* (1907–1965), *Social Science and Humanities Index* (1966–1973), *Social Science Index* (1974–1989), *International Bibliography of Research in Marriage and the Family* (1900–1964), *Research in Marriage and the Family* (1965–1972), *Inventory of Marriage and Family Literature* (1973–1989), *Psychological Abstracts* (1927–1989), *Journal of Marriage and the Family* (1938–1989), *Journal of Home Economics* (1930–1989), *Journal of Consumer Affairs* (1967–1989), and *Home Economics Research Journal* (1972–1989, with the exception of 1979, which was unavailable). Key words used in

searching the indexes included: *financial, management, money, resources, time, decision making, family, domestic finance, cost of living, and standard of living, budget (personal and household)*. Several important sources of family resource management literature are absent (either completely or largely) from this review: textbooks, dissertations and theses (in several instances, they were later published in journals and were included in this review), extension service and experiment station bulletins, conference proceedings (such as of the American Council on Consumer Interests, Association of Financial Counseling and Planning Education, and the Southeastern and Western Regional Family Economics/Home Management research groups), journals from other disciplines, and government reports. I believed that a representative sample of family resource management research topics could be attained by reviewing articles published in prominent journals. In the early decades (1930–1950), articles from a variety of journals were included in the review. In the later decades only the prominent journals were reviewed.

2. Primary data are defined as data obtained by the researchers who wrote the article. Secondary data include government data, data obtained in large regional research projects, and any other data source external to the researchers involved.

3. In reviewing the literature, I found a number of excellent articles that did not fit the criteria of this review. A number of these nonresearch articles (over two dozen) are included in the References.

References

Abdel-Ghany, M., and Foster, A.C. 1982. Impact of income and wife's education on family consumption expenditures. *Journal of Consumer Studies and Home Economics* 6:21–28.

Abdel-Ghany, M., and Nickols, S.Y. 1983. Husband/wife differentials in household work time: The case of dual-earner families. *Home Economics Research Journal* 12:159–167.

Ackerman, N.M. 1989. Money resources, time demands, and situational factors as predictors of shopping time. *Journal of Consumer Studies and Home Economics* 13: 1–19.

Anderson, E.S., and Fitzsimmons, C. 1960. Use of time and money by employed homemakers. *Journal of Home Economics* 52:452–455.

Arndt, J., and Holmer, O. 1978. Dimensions of household economic management. *Journal of Consumer Studies and Home Economics* 2:27–34.

Ater, E.C., and Deacon, R.E. 1972. Interaction of family relationship qualities and managerial components. *Journal of Marriage and the Family* 34:257–263.

Bagshaw, M. 1982. Domestic energy conservation and the consumer. *Journal of Consumer Studies and Home Economics* 6:183–190.

Bahr, S. 1989. *Family Interaction.* New York: Macmillan.

Baker, G. 1980. Household production: A cultural and cross-national view. *Journal of Consumer Studies and Home Economics* 4:71–86.

Barnett, R.C., and Baruch, G.K. 1987. Determinants of fathers' participation in family work. *Journal of Marriage and the Family* 49:29–40.

Benin, M.H., and Agostinelli, J. 1988. Husbands' and wives' satisfaction with the division of labor. *Journal of Marriage and the Family* 50:349–361.

Berardo, D.H.; Shehan, C.L.; and Leslie, G.R. 1987. A residue of tradition: Jobs, careers and spouses' time in housework. *Journal of Marriage and the Family* 49: 381–390.

Berger, P.S., and Drennen, N.H. 1985. Predictors of consumption cutback in response to increased energy costs. *Journal of Consumer Studies and Home Economics* 9: 185–205.

Beutler, I.F., and Mason, J.W. 1987. Family cash-flow budgeting. *Home Economics Research Journal* 16:3–12.

Beutler, I.F.; Owen, A.J.; and Hefferan, C. 1988. The boundary question in household production: A systems model approach. *Home Economics Research Journal* 16: 267–278.

Bird, G.W.; Bird, G.A.; and Scruggs, M. 1983. Role-management strategies used by husbands and wives in two-earner families. *Home Economics Research Journal* 12: 63–70.

———. 1984. Determinants of family task sharing: A study of husbands and wives. *Journal of Marriage and the Family* 46:345–355.

Blankertz, D.F. 1950. Shopping habits and income: A Philadelphia department store study. *Journal of Marketing* 14:572–578.

Blaylock, J.R., and Smallwood, D.M. 1987. Intrahousehold time allocation: The case of grocery shopping. *Journal of Consumer Affairs* 21:183–201.

Blood, R.O. 1958. Division of labor in city and farm families. *Journal of Marriage and the Family* 20:170–174.

Brady, D.S. 1938. Variations in family living expenditures. *Journal of the American Statistical Association* 33:385–389.

———. 1946. Expenditures and savings of city families in 1944. *Monthly Labor Review* 62:1–5.

———. 1955. Influence of age on saving and spending patterns. *Monthly Labor Review* 78:1240–1244.

Brandt, J.A., and Olson, G.I. 1986. Development of scales to assess homeownership consumption and investment attitudes. *Home Economics Research Journal* 14: 280–293.

Broman, C.L. 1988. Household work and family life satisfaction of blacks. *Journal of Marriage and the Family* 50:743–748.

Bryant, W.K. 1986. Assets and debts in a consumer portfolio. *Journal of Consumer Affairs* 20:19–35.

Buehler, C., and Hogan, M.J. 1986. Planning styles in single-parent families. *Home Economics Research Journal* 14:351–362.

Bymers, G.J., and Galenson, M. 1968. Time horizons in family spending. *Journal of Home Economics* 60:709–715.

Byrne, H.A. 1936. *Effects of the Depression on Wage Earners' Families.* U.S. Department of Labor, no. 108. Washington, D.C.: U.S. Government Printing Office.

Caudle, A.H. 1964. Financial management practices of employed and non-employed wives. Ph.D. dissertation, Florida State University, reported in *Journal of Home Economics* 56:723–727.

Cave, R.C. 1943. Variations in expenditures where families of wage earners and clerical workers are classified by economic level. *American Statistical Association* 38:445–452.

Cheal, D.J. 1983. Intergenerational family transfers. *Journal of Marriage and the Family* 45:805–812.

Chen, A., and Jensen, H.H. 1985. Home equity use and the life cycle hypothesis. *Journal of Consumer Affairs* 19:37–55.
Clare, M.P. 1963. Teen-age attitudes toward money management. *Journal of Home Economics* 55:124–126.
Clark, A.B. 1962. Economic contributions made to newly married children. Ph.D. dissertation, Cornell University, reported in *Journal of Home Economics* 54:229–230.
Clark, M.R., and Morton, G.M. 1930. Income and expenditure of women faculty at the University of Nebraska. *Journal of Home Economics* 22:653–656.
Clarke, H.I. 1931. A study of incomes, emergencies, and credit in dependent families. *Family* 12:92–94.
Coles, J. 1949. A study of family clothing expenditure. *Journal of Home Economics* 41:193–194.
Conard, L.M. 1939. Differential depression effects on families of laborers, farmers, and the business class: A survey of an Iowa town. *American Journal of Sociology* 44:526–533.
Converse, P.D. 1950. Family expenses in two centuries. *Journal of Home Economics* 42: 634–636.
Coverman, S., and Sheley, J.F. 1986. Change in men's housework and child-care time, 1965–1975. *Journal of Marriage and the Family* 48:413–422.
Cowles, M.L., and Dietz, R.P. 1956. Time spent in homemaking activities by a selected group of Wisconsin farm homemakers. *Journal of Home Economics* 48:29–35.
Cowles, M.L., and Knothe, M. 1960. Financial security among Wisconsin rural farm aged persons. *Journal of Home Economics* 52:99–102.
Crawford, C.E., and Beutler, I.F. 1983. Perceptions and misperceptions in consumer resource management. *Journal of Consumer Studies and Home Economics* 7:45–58.
Davis, E.P., and Helmick, S.A. 1985. Family financial satisfaction: The impact of reference points. *Home Economics Research Journal* 14:123–131.
Davis, E.P., and Schumm, W.R. 1987. Savings behavior and satisfaction with savings: A comparison of low- and high-income groups. *Home Economics Research Journal* 15:247–256.
Dickerson, M.D. 1980. The home economist as a financial planner: A career option. *Journal of Home Economics* 72:40–41.
Dismukes, D.L., and Abdel-Ghany, M. 1988. Homemakers' household-work time in single-parent and two-parent families. *Journal of Consumer Studies and Home Economics* 12:247–256.
Dolan, E.M. and Scannell, E. 1987. Husbands' and wives' household work: Moving toward egalitarianism? *Journal of Consumer Studies and Home Economics* 11:387–399.
Douthitt, R.A., and Fedyk, J.M. 1988. The influence of children on family life cycle spending behavior: Theory and applications. *Journal of Consumer Affairs* 22: 220–247.
Douthitt, R.A., and Zick, C.D. 1988. Taxes and the time allocation patterns of married women with children: Cross-cultural comparisons between the United States and Canada. *Journal of Consumer Studies and Home Economics* 12:141–157.
Downs, C. 1968. Money management attitudes and practices of some college women. *Journal of Home Economics* 60:737–738.
Dunsing, M. 1956. Spending money of adolescents. *Journal of Home Economics* 48: 405–408.

———. 1960. Money-management experiences of high school students. *Journal of Home Economics* 52:756–759.

Edwards, K.P. 1988. Using a systems framework for organizing family financial planning. *Journal of Consumer Affairs* 22:319–332.

Epstein, L.A. 1961. Effects of low income on children. *Social Security Bulletin* 24 (February):12–17.

Feldman, F.L. 1957. A new look at the family and its money. *Journal of Home Economics* 49:767–772.

Floge, L. 1989. Changing household structure, child-care availability, and employment among mothers of preschool children. *Journal of Marriage and the Family* 51:51–63.

Foa, U.G., and Foa, E.B. 1974. *Societal structures of the mind.* Springfield, Ill.: Charles Thomas.

Foster, A.C. 1988. Wife's employment and family expenditures. *Journal of Consumer Studies and Home Economics* 12:15–27.

Foster, A.C.; Abdel-Ghany, M.; and Ferguson, C.E. 1981. Wife's employment—its influence on major family expenditures. *Journal of Consumer Studies and Home Economics* 5:115–124.

Foster, A.C., and Metzen, E.J. 1981a. Wife's earnings and family net worth position. *Home Economics Research Journal* 10:192–201.

———. 1981b. The impact of wife's employment and earnings on family net worth accumulation. *Journal of Consumer Studies and Home Economics* 5:23–36.

Freeman, R.C. 1951. What farm families spend for housing. *Journal of Home Economics* 43:259–262.

Freeman, R.C., and Crouch, I. 1943. A tool for financial planning. *Journal of Home Economics* 35:346–348.

Fults, A.C., and Zunich, M. 1967. Money management of teenagers in low income families. *Journal of Home Economics* 59:45–47.

Galambos, N.L., and Silbereisen, R.K. 1989. Role strain in West German dual-earner households. *Journal of Marriage and the Family* 51:385–389.

Garrison, M.E., and Winter, M. 1986. The managerial behaviour of families with preschool children. *Journal of Consumer Studies and Home Economics* 10:247–260.

Geistfeld, L.V. 1976. An exploration of factors relating to life insurance holdings of families. *Journal of Consumer Affairs* 10:224–232.

Gerner, J.L., and Zick, C.D. 1983. Time allocation decisions in two-parent families. *Home Economics Research Journal* 12:145–158.

Gilboy, E.W. 1937. The unemployed: Their income and expenditure. *American Economic Review* 27:309–323.

Gladhart, P.M. 1977. Energy conservation and lifestyles: An integrative approach to family decision making. *Journal of Consumer Studies and Home Economics* 1: 265–277.

Gladhart, P.M., and Roosa, M.W. 1982. Family lifestyle and energy consumption: An energy adaptation model. *Journal of Consumer Studies and Home Economics* 6: 205–222.

Godwin, D.D., and Carroll, D.D. 1986. Financial management attitudes and behaviour of husbands and wives. *Journal of Consumer Studies and Home Economics* 10:77–96.

Godwin, D.D., and Scanzoni, J. 1989. Couple consensus during marital joint decision-making: A context, process, outcome model. *Journal of Marriage and the Family* 51:943–956.

Goebel, K.P., and Hennon, C.B. 1982. An empirical investigation of the relationship among wife's employment status, stage in the family life cycle, meal preparation time, and expenditures for meals away from home. *Journal of Consumer Studies and Home Economics* 6:63–78.

Goebel, K.P., and Hennon, C.B. 1983. Mother's time on meal preparation, expenditures for meals away from home, and shared meals: Effects of mother's employment and age of younger child. *Home Economics Research Journal* 12:169–188.

———. 1984. Husband-wife division of labour and quality of family life. *Journal of Consumer Studies and Home Economics* 8:61–72.

Gordon, H.A., and Kammeyer, K.C. 1980. Gainful employment of women with small children. *Journal of Marriage and the Family* 42:327–336.

Gover, D.A. 1964. Money management: Some implications for teaching. *Journal of Marriage and the Family* 26:231–233.

Gross, I.H., and Pond, J. 1936. *Changes in Standards of Living During a Depression.* Michigan Agricultural Experiment Station, Bulletin no. 274. July.

Gross, I.H., and Zwemer, E. 1944. *Management in Michigan Homes.* Michigan State College Agricultural Experiment Station, Technical Bulletin 196. June.

Guthrie, L.J., and Fitzsimmons, C. 1963. How do families perceive financial security. *Journal of Home Economics* 55:274–275.

Guthrie, L.A., and Brandt, J.A. 1983. Dwelling energy efficiency and home energy conservation policies: A western U.S. perspective. *Journal of Consumer Studies and Home Economics* 7:307–319.

Hafstrom, J.L., and Dunsing, M.M. 1965. Comparison of economic choices: One-earner and two-earner families. *Journal of Marriage and the Family* 27:403–409.

Hafstrom, J.L., and Dunsing, M. 1973. Level of living: Factors influencing the homemaker's satisfaction. *Home Economics Research Journal* 2:119–132.

Hafstrom, J.L., and Schram, V.R. 1983. Housework time of wives: Pressure, facilitators, constraints. *Home Economics Research Journal* 11:245–254.

Hager, C.J., and Bryant, W.K. 1977. Clothing expenditures of low income rural families. *Journal of Consumer Affairs* 11:127–132.

Hall, F.T. 1975. The case of the late Mrs. Smith: Preparing testimony for the court. *Journal of Home Economics* 67:30–33.

Hall, F.T., and Schroeder, M.P. 1970. Time spent on household tasks. *Journal of Home Economics* 62:23–29.

Hardesty, C., and Bokemeier, J. 1989. Finding time and making do: Distribution of household labor in non-metropolitan marriages. *Journal of Marriage and the Family* 51:253–267.

Heck, R.K.Z. 1983a. An analysis of the utilization of financial counselling services. *Journal of Consumer Studies and Home Economics* 7:271–285.

———. 1983b. A preliminary test of a family management research model. *Journal of Consumer Studies and Home Economics* 7:117–135.

Hefferan, C. 1982a. Determinants and patterns of family saving. *Home Economics Research Journal* 11:47–55.

———. 1982b. What is a homemaker's job worth?—Too many answers. *Journal of Home Economics* 74:30–33.

———. 1986. Human resources: Development in times of transition. In *Human Resources Research, 1887–1987 Proceedings.* Edited by Ruth E. Deacon and Wallace E. Huffman. Ames: College of Home Economics, Iowa State University.

Helmick, S.A., and Jurich, A.P. 1981. Employment behavior of adolescent family members. *Home Economics Research Journal* 10:21–31.

Henze, U. 1983. Household production—an example. *Journal of Consumer Studies and Home Economics* 7:287–298.

Herrmann, R.O. 1965. Expectations and attitudes as a source of financial problems in teen-age marriages. *Journal of Marriage and the Family* 27:89–91.

Heuer, L.A., and Shiras, S. 1951. Fashions in budgets. *Journal of Home Economics* 43:619–621.

Hill, R. 1963. Judgement and consumership in management of family resources. *Sociology and Social Research* 47:446–460.

Hira, T.K. 1987a. Money management practices influencing household asset ownership. *Journal of Consumer Studies and Home Economics* 11:183–194.

———. 1987b. Satisfaction with money management: Practices among dual-earner households. *Journal of Home Economics* 79:19–22.

Hoeflin, R., and Bolsen, N. 1986. Life goals and decision making: Educated women's patterns. *Journal of Home Economics* 78:32–35.

Hogan, M.J., and Paolucci, B. 1979. Energy conservation: Family values, household practices, and contextual variables. *Home Economics Research Journal* 7:210–218.

Horton, S.E., and Hafstrom, J.L. 1985. Income elasticities for selected consumption categories: Comparison of single female-headed and two-parent families. *Home Economics Research Journal* 13:292–303.

House, G. 1976. Divorced women: How they fare financially. *Journal of Home Economics* 68:36–38.

Hungerford, N., and Paolucci, B. 1977. The employed female single parent. *Journal of Home Economics* 60:10–13.

Hunter, S.M. 1961. Homemakers name their home problems. *Journal of Home Economics* 53:425–427.

Hyde, A.R. 1931. Where the money goes. *Harpers* 163:688–699.

Iams, D.R.; Steinfelt, V.; and Wilhelm, M.S. 1986. Needs assessments for financial management programs in extension. *Journal of Home Economics* 78:48–50.

Jeries, N. 1977. Wives' perceptions of marital decision making. *Home Economics Research Journal* 5:146–153.

Johannis, T.B., and Cunningham, K.R. 1959. Conceptions of use of non-work time: Individual, husband-wife, parent-child and family—a methodological note. *Family Life Coordinator* 8:34–36.

Johnson, P.J. 1989. Changes in financial practices: Southeast Asian refugees. *Home Economics Research Journal* 17:241–252.

Johnston, K.A. 1953. Research in family finance. *Journal of Home Economics* 45: 387–389.

Jones, D.C. 1941. Working-class earnings and expenditure. *Nature* 147:377–379.

Kaplan, A.D.H. 1938. Expenditure patterns of urban families. *American Statistical Association* 33:81–100.

Kenkel, W.F., and Hoffman, D.K. 1956. Real and conceived roles in family decision making. *Journal of Marriage and the Family* 18:311–316.

Kennedy, L.W., and Stokes, D.W. 1982. Extended family support and the high cost of housing. *Journal of Marriage and the Family* 44:311–317.

Key, R.J., and Firebaugh, F.M. 1989. Family resource management: Preparing for the 21st century. *Journal of Home Economics* 71:13–17.

Khan, S.; Ater, C.; Harp, S.; and Johnson, K. 1989. Resource use: The complexity of time and energy management in clothing maintenance. *Journal of Consumer Studies and Home Economics* 13:67–77.

Kingston, P.W., and Nock, S.L. 1985. Consequences of the family work day. *Journal of Marriage and the Family* 47:619–625.

Kinsey, J., and Lane, S. 1978. Effect of debt on perceived household welfare. *Journal of Consumer Affairs* 12:48–62.

Knapp, E.M. 1951. Family budget of a city worker, October 1950. *Monthly Labor Reivew* 72:152–155.

Knoll, M.M. 1955. Economic contributions to and from individual members of families and households. *Journal of Home Economics* 47:323–329.

Kundak, S.S., and Fitzsimmons, C. 1960. Factors in financial security of Indiana farm families. Ph.D. dissertation, Purdue University, reported in *Journal of Home Economics* 52:370–371.

Lamale, H.H. 1958. Changes in expenditures of urban families. *Journal of Home Economics* 50:683–687.

Landis, J.T. 1947. Adjustments after marriage. *Journal of Marriage and the Family* 9: 32–34.

Langrehr, F.W., and Mason, J.B. 1978. The effects of instruction in consumer education academic units on consumer economic proficiency. *Journal of Consumer Studies and Home Economics* 2:161–174.

Larery, D.A. 1963. Primary and secondary factors related to perceived financial security of urban families, Lafayette, Indiana. Ph.D. dissertation, Purdue University, reported in *Journal of Home Economics* 55:214.

Lawrence, F.C., Tasker, G.E., and Babcock, D.K. 1983. Time spent in housework by urban adolescents. *Home Economics Research Journal* 12:199–207.

Lawrence, F.C., Tasker, G.E., and Wozniak, P.H. 1988. Rural-urban differentials in children's household production time. *Journal of Consumer Studies and Home Economics* 12:39–47.

Leevy, J.R. 1940. Contrasts in urban and rural life. *American Sociological Review* 5: 948–953.

———. 1950. Leisure time of the American housewife. *Sociology and Social Research* 35:97–105.

Leiffer, M.H. 1933. Income and standards of living in the ministry. *Sociology and Social Research* 27:443–453.

Liston, M.I. 1950. Savings of farm and town families. *Journal of Home Economics* 42: 439–441.

Lomberg, D.E., and Krofta, J.A. 1965. Farm family finances in the middle years. *Journal of Home Economics* 57:123–128.

Lorimer, F. 1940. The effect of children on the economic status on American families. *Eugenical News* 25:28–31.

Lovett, S.B., and Abdel-Ghany, M. 1988. Children's contributions to household activities in single-parent and two-parent families. *Journal of Consumer Studies and Home Economics* 12:199–204.

Lovingood, R.P., and Firebaugh, F.M. 1978. Household task performance roles of husbands and wives. *Home Economics Research Journal* 7:20–33.

Lovingood, R.P., and McCullough, J.L. 1986. Appliance ownership and household work time. *Home Economics Research Journal* 14:326–335.

Lown, J.M. 1986. Family financial well-being: Guidance from research. *Journal of Home Economics* 78:5–8.

———. 1988. Home equity loans: Mortgaging the future? *Journal of Home Economics* 80:6–9.

McKenna, J.S., and Nickols, S.Y. 1986. Retirement planning strategies for midlife women. *Journal of Home Economics* 78:34–37.

———. 1988. Planning for retirement security: What helps or hinders women in the middle years? *Home Economics Research Journal* 17:153–164.

MacNaughton, M. 1948. Re the economic status of faculty families. *Journal of Home Economics* 40:133–134.

Maloch, F. 1963. Characteristics of most and least liked home tasks. Ph.D. dissertation, Cornell University, reported in *Journal of Home Economics* 55:413–416.

Manning, S.L. 1960. Financial management of fluctuating income families. Ph.D. dissertation, Cornell University, reported in *Journal of Home Economics* 52:274–275.

Maret, E., and Finlay, B. 1984. The distribution of household labor among women in dual-earner families. *Journal of Marriage and the Family* 46:357–364.

Marlowe, J. 1981. Financial variables associated with successful debt liquidation. *Home Economics Research Journal* 9:382–389.

Marlowe, J., and Sproles, G.B. 1986. Economic determinants of family development processes. *Journal of Consumer Studies and Home Economics* 10:59–75.

Marshall, H.R. 1964. The relation of giving children an allowance to children's money knowledge and responsibility and to other practices of parents. *Journal of Genetic Psychology* 104:35–51.

Marshall, H.R., and Magruder, L. 1960. Relations between parent money education practices and children's knowledge and use of money. *Child Development* 31: 253–284.

Matsushima, C. 1981. Time-input and household work-output studies in Japan—present state and future prospects. *Journal of Consumer Studies and Home Economics* 5:199–217.

———. 1981. Time-input and household work-output studies in Japan—present state and future prospects. *Journal of Consumer Studies and Home Economics* 5:199–217.

Matthews, W. 1978. Practical use of energy in the home. *Journal of Consumer Studies and Home Economics* 2:99–118.

Maynes, E.S., and Geistfeld, L.V. 1974. Life insurance deficit of American families. *Journal of Consumer Affairs* 8:37–60.

Meeks, C.B., and Oudekerk, E.H. 1981. Housing defects in newly purchased homes: Implications for family resource management. *Journal of Consumer Studies and Home Economics* 5:101–114.

Merriam, O. 1955. How young families spend their money. *Journal of Home Economics* 47:330–332.

Metzen, E.J., and Helmick, S.A. 1975. Secondary workers' earnings and their impact on family income adequacy. *Home Economics Research Journal* 3:249–259.

Millican, R.D. 1959. A factor analysis of expenditures of Illinois farm families. *Journal of Home Economics* 51:177–181.

Mintz, S., and Kellogg, S. 1988. *Domestic Revolutions: A Social History of American Family Life.* New York: Free Press.

Monroe, D. 1937. Levels of living of the nation's families. *Journal of Home Economics* 29:665–670.

———. 1942. Family saving and spending plans. *Journal of Home Economics* 34:659-661.

Monthly Labor Review. 1930. Standard of living of employees of Ford Motor Company in Detroit. *Monthly Labor Review* 30:1209–1252.

———. 1962. Net contribution of working wives. *Monthly Labor Review* 85:1383–1384.

Moore, D.F. 1953. Sharing in family financial management by high school students. *Journal of Marriage and the Family* 15:319–321.

Morrison, R.J. 1972. The standard of living in New York City in 1907: An early twentieth-century study of consumer expenditure patterns. *Journal of Consumer Affairs* 6:71–77.

Morse, R.L.D. 1962. Family financial security—survey of Kansas rural families. *Journal of Home Economics* 54:711–713.

Moschis, G.P.; Lawton, J.T.; and Stampfl, R.W. 1980. Preschool children's consumer learning. *Home Economics Research Journal* 9:64–71.

Mullis, R.J., and Schnittgrund, K.P. 1982. Budget behavior: Variance of the life cycle of low income families. *Journal of Consumer Studies and Home Economics* 6: 113–120.

Mumaw, C.R., and Nichols, A. 1972. Organizational styles of homemakers: A factor analytic approach. *Home Economics Research Journal* 1:35–43.

Nelson, J.A. 1989. Individual consumption with the household: A study of expenditures on clothing. *Journal of Consumer Affairs* 23:21–44.

Nickols, S.Y., and Abdel-Ghany, M. 1983. Leisure time of husbands and wives. *Home Economics Research Journal* 12:189–198.

Nickols, S.Y., and Metzen, E.J. 1978. Housework time of husband and wife. *Home Economics Research Journal* 7:85–97.

Norum, P.S. 1987. Empirically measuring household productivity: An application. *Home Economics Research Journal* 16:143–149.

Ormsby, T. 1989. Family choices in household production. *Journal of Consumer Studies and Home Economics* 13:359–368.

Ortiz, B.; MacDonald, M.; Ackerman, N.; and Goebel, K. 1981. The effect of homemakers' employment on meal prep time. *Home Economics Research Journal* 9: 200–206.

Owen, A.J., and Beutler, I.F. 1981. Household production and market employment: Dual avenues of consumer behavior. *Journal of Consumer Studies and Home Economics* 5:157–174.

Ozgen, O., and Gonen, E. 1989. Consumer behavior of children in primary school age. *Journal of Consumer Studies and Home Economics* 13:175–187.

Pecheniuk, O., and Liston, M. 1953. Selected indicators as measures of economic status of farm families in the north central region. *Journal of Home Economics* 45: 187–190.

Pershing, B. 1979. Family policies: A component of management in the home and family setting. *Journal of Marriage and the Family* 41:573–581.

Phelan, G.K., and Schvaneveldt, J.D. 1969. Spending and saving patterns of adolescent siblings. *Journal of Home Economics* 61:104–109.

Poduska, B. 1988. A comparative study of family budgets: An international perspective. *Journal of Home Economics* 80:16–23.

Preston, F. 1951. Financial counseling for families. *Journal of Home Economics* 43:19–22.

Prevey, E.E. 1945. A quantitative study of family practices in training children in the use of money. *Journal of Education Psychology* 36:411–428.

Prevey, E.E. 1946. Developing good habits in the use of money. *Journal of Home Economics* 38:79–81.

Price, D.Z. 1967. Research methodology for home management. *Journal of Home Economics* 59:433–437.

Purchase, M.E.; Berning, C.K.; and Lyng, A.L. 1982. The cost of washing clothes: Sources of variation. *Journal of Consumer Studies and Home Economics* 6:301–317.

Reed, E.F. 1946. Cost of living compared with family income in seven cities. *American Sociological Review* 11:192–197.

Rettig, K.D., and Bubolz, M.M. 1983. Interpersonal resource exchanges as indicators of quality of marriage. *Journal of Marriage and the Family* 45:497–509.

Rettig, K.D., and Metzger, N.M. 1986. Father's involvement in household activities. *Journal of Consumer Studies and Home Economics* 10:195–207.

Rexroat, C., and Shehan, C. 1987. The family life cycle and spouses' time in housework. *Journal of Marriage and the Family* 49:737–750.

Rogerson, L.C., and Whiteford, E.B. 1960. Money experiences of ninth grade pupils. *Journal of Home Economics* 52:44–45.

Rollins, M.A. 1958. The money we spend. *Journal of Home Economics* 50:514–516.

———. 1963. Monetary contributions of wives to family income in 1920 and 1960. *Journal of Marriage and the Family* 25:226–227.

Ronald, P.Y.; Singer, M.E.; and Firebaugh, F.M. 1971. Rating scale for household tasks. *Journal of Home Economics* 63:177–179.

Roper, L.L., and Darden, L.A. 1989. Energy conservation: Changes in heating practices by Alabama residents. *Journal of Consumer Studies and Home Economics* 13: 237–245.

Rowland, V.T.; Dodder, R.A.; and Nickols, S.Y. 1985. Perceived adequacy of resources: Development of a scale. *Home Economics Research Journal* 14:218–225.

Rowland, V.T.; Nickols, S.Y.; and Dodder, R.A. 1986. Parents' time allocation: A comparison of households headed by one and two parents. *Home Economics Research Journal* 15:105–114.

Rudd, N.M., and Dunsing, M.M. 1972. A three-pronged look at family saving. *Journal of Consumer Affairs* 6:35–46.

Rudd, N.M., and McKenry, P.C. 1980. Working women: Issues and implications. *Journal of Home Economics* 72:26–29.

Ryan, M.E., and Maynes, E.S. 1969. The excessively indebted: Who and why. *Journal of Consumer Affairs* 3:107–126.

Saffian, S. 1933. Income and expenditure of 42 unmarried social workers. *Journal of Home Economics* 25:563–566.

Sailor, P.J.; Crumley, W.; and Patterson, J. 1977. The working wife/mother home economist. *Journal of Home Economics* 69:26–27.

Sanik, M.M. 1981. Division of household work: A decade of comparison—1967–1977. *Home Economics Research Journal* 10:175–180.

Sanik, M.M., and Stafford, K. 1983. Product-accounting approach to valuing food production. *Home Economics Research Journal* 12:217–227.

———. 1986. Boy/girl differences in household work. *Journal of Consumer Studies and Home Economics* 10:209–219.

Schaninger, C.M., and Buss, W.C. 1986. A longitudinal comparison of consumption and finance handling between happily married and divorced couples. *Journal of Marriage and the Family* 48:129–136.

Schaurer, D.L., and Manning, S.L. 1973. Work time estimation for private household workers: Dusting. *Home Economics Research Journal* 2:82–92.

Schlaphoff, D., and Burema, J.P. 1955. Home production by farm families in a Nebraska county. *Journal of Home Economics* 47:400–404.

Schlesinger, B. 1962. A survey of methods used to study decision making in the family. *Family Life Coordinator* 11:8–14.

Schnittgrund, K.P. 1980. Productive time of household heads. *Journal of Consumer Studies and Home Economics* 4:239–248.

Schnittgrund, K.P., and Baker, G. 1983. Financial management of low-income urban families. *Journal of Consumer Studies and Home Economics* 7:261–270.

Scholl, K.K. 1985. Accessibility and ownership of financial accounts by married U.S. farm women. *Home Economics Research Journal* 14:208–217.

Schomaker, P.K. 1963. Financial decision-making as reported by 100 farm families in Michigan. Ph.D. dissertation, Michigan State University, reported in *Journal of Home Economics* 55:214.

Schram, V.R., and Hafstrom, J.L. 1984. Household production: A conceptual model for time-use study in the United States and Japan. *Journal of Consumer Studies and Home Economics* 8:283–292.

———. 1986. Family resources related to wife's time inputs to housework. *Journal of Consumer Studies and Home Economics* 10:235–245.

Sharp, H., and Mott, P. 1956. Consumer decisions in the metropolitan family. *Journal of Marketing* 21:149–156.

Skinner, J.D.; Ezell, J.M.; Salvetti, N.N.; and Penfield, M.P. 1985. Relationships between mothers' employment and nutritional quality of adolescents' diets. *Home Economics Research Journal* 13:218–225.

Smith, R.S. 1948. Economic aspects of marriage and family life. *Journal of Marriage and the Family* 10:64–65.

Smith, W.M. 1954. Family plans for later years. *Journal of Marriage and the Family* 16:36–40.

Staab, J.H. 1959. Historical development and trends of research in family economics. *Journal of Home Economics* 51:257–260.

Stafford, K. 1983. The effects of wife's employment time on her household work time. *Home Economics Research Journal* 11:257–266.

Steidl, R.E. 1958. Use of time during family meal preparation and cleanup. *Journal of Home Economics* 50:447–450.

———. 1975a. Affective dimensions of high and low cognitive homemaking tasks. *Home Economics Research Journal* 4:121–137.

———. 1975b. Complexity of homemaking tasks. *Home Economics Research Journal* 3:223–240.

Swagler, R.; Sweaney, A.; and Marlowe, J. 1989. Children's participation in household tasks as portrayed by national advertisements in the U.S.A. *Journal of Consumer Studies and Home Economics* 13:271–283.

Swerdloff, E.S. 1933. The effect of the depression on family life. *Family* 13:310–314.

Szinovacz, M.E. 1977. Role allocation, family structure and female employment. *Journal of Marriage and the Family* 39:781–791.

———. 1979. Women employed: Effects on spouses' division of household work. *Journal of Home Economics* 71:42–45.

Tasker, G.E.; Lawrence, F.C.; Purtle, V.S.; and Babcock, D.K. 1983. Values related to family travel time. *Home Economics Research Journal* 12:207–216.

Taylor, P.S. 1952. The employment of rural women. *Journal of Home Economics* 44:16–18.

Terzioglu, R.G., and Safak, S. 1988. Money use and purchases in families in which the wife works: A Turkish example. *Journal of Consumer Studies and Home Economics* 12:341–348;.

Thorpe, A.C. 1951. How married college students manage. *Journal of Marriage and the Family* 13:104–106, 130.

Titus, P.M.; Fanslow, A.M.; and Hira, T.K. 1989. Net worth and financial satisfaction as a function of household money managers' competencies. *Home Economics Research Journal* 17:309–318.

Turner, J., and Brandt, J. 1978. Development and validation of a simulated market to test children for selected consumer skills. *Journal of Consumer Affairs* 12: 266–276.

Turner, C.S., and Gruber, K.J. 1989. Occupant-use factors influencing optimal results from energy conservation strategies. *Journal of Consumer Studies and Home Economics* 13:219–235.

Urich, J.R., and Hogan, M.J. 1985. Measuring changes in family energy management: Consumption or efficiency. *Journal of Consumer Studies and Home Economics* 9: 161–172.

Volker, C.B., and Winter, M. 1988. Secondary household production of food: The influence of home meal preparation. *Journal of Consumer Studies and Home Economics* 12:321–340.

———. 1989. Primary household production of food, food expenditures, and reported adequacy of food. *Home Economics Research Journal* 18:32–46.

Volker, C.B.; Winter, M.; and Beutler, I.F. 1983. Household production of food: Expenditures, norms, and satisfaction. *Home Economics Research Journal* 11: 267–279.

Wagner, J. 1986. Expenditures for household textiles and textile home furnishings: An Engel curve analysis. *Home Economics Research Journal* 15:21–31.

Wagner, J., and Lucero-Campins, L. 1988. Social class: A multivariate analysis of its effect on expenditures for household services. *Journal of Consumer Studies and Home Economics* 12:373–387.

Walker, K.E. 1973. Household work time: Its implication for family decisions: *Journal of Home Economics* 65:7–11.

Warren, J. 1961. Income and housing expenditures. *Journal of Home Economics* 53: 349–351.

Weagley, R.O., and Norum, P.S. 1989. Household demand for market purchased, home producible commodities. *Home Economics Research Journal* 18:6–18.

Wells, H.L. 1959. Financial management practices of young families. *Journal of Home Economics* 51:439–444.

Wenck, D.A. 1967. Employed and non-employed homemakers—how they manage. *Journal of Home Economics* 59:737–738.

White, E.D., and Dunsing, M. 1963. Insurance practices of urban families with minor children. *Journal of Home Economics* 55:707–714.

White, L.K., and Brinkerhoff, D.B. 1981. Children's work in the family: Its significance and meaning. *Journal of Marriage and the Family* 43:789–798.

Whittemore, M. 1931. The wage-earning homemaker and the family income. *Journal of Home Economics* 23:998–1001.

Wilhelm, M.S.; Iams, D.R.; and Rudd, J. 1987. Husband and wife agreement on indicators of objective and subjective economic well-being. *Home Economics Research Journal* 16:13–22.

Williams, F.L., and Berry, R. 1984. Intensity of family disagreement over finances and associated factors. *Journal of Consumer Studies and Home Economics* 8:33–53.

Williams, F.L., and Manning, S.L. 1972. Net worth change of selected families. *Home Economics Research Journal* 1:104–113.

Williams, F.M. 1942. Consumer education and standards of living. *Journal of Marriage and the Family* 4:49–51.

Williamson, R.C. 1952. Economic factors in marital adjustment. *Journal of Marriage and the Family* 14:298–301.

Williamson, S.Z. 1970. The effects of maternal employment on the scholastic performance of children. *Journal of Home Economics* 62:609–613.

Winakor, G. 1989. The decline in expenditure for clothing relative to total consumption spending, 1929–1986. *Home Economics Research Journal* 17:195–214.

Winakor, G., and Thomas L. 1978. Standard budgets for household textiles: Farm and city families at two income levels and three family sizes. *Home Economics Research Journal* 7:2–19.

Winter, M. 1980. Managerial behavior of young families in pursuit of single-family home ownership. *Journal of Consumer Affairs* 14:82–95.

Wolgast, E.H. 1958. Do husbands or wives make the purchasing decisions? *Journal of Marketing* 23:151–158.

Working, H. 1943. Statistical laws of family expenditures. *American Statistical Association* 38:43–56.

Wright, H.R. 1932. A year's expenditures of ten railroad workers. *Social Science Review* 6:55–82.

Wright, L.A. 1978. Families in debt. *Journal of Home Economics* 70:38–39.

Zick, C.D., and Gerner, J.L. 1987. Family composition and investment in household capital: Contrasts in the behavior of the husband-wife and female-headed households. *Journal of Consumer Affairs* 21:21–39.

Zunich, M. 1966. Teen-agers' influence on personal and family purchases. *Journal of Home Economics* 58:483–484.

Zunich, M., and Fults, A.C. 1967. Teenage economic behavior: Earning and saving. *Journal of Home Economics* 59:739.

Research Topics on Family Resource Management, by Topic, 1930–1989

Year	*First Author*	*Research Topic*	*Reference*
1945	Prevey	Adolescents and money	JEP 36, 411–428
1946	Prevey		JHE 38, 79–81
1956	Dunsing		JHE 48, 405–408
1960	Marshall		CD 31, 253–284
1960	Rogerson		JHE 52 (1), 44–45
1960	Dunsing		JHE 52 (9), 756–759
1961	Epstein		SSB 24 (2), 12–17
1963	Clare		JHE 55 (2), 124–126
1964	Marshall		JGP 104, 35–51
1965	Herrmann		JMF 27, 89–91
1966	Zunich		JHE 58, 6, 483–484
1967	Fults		JHE 59, 45–47
1967	Zunich		JHE 59 (9), 739
1969	Phelan		JHE 61 (2), 104–109
1978	Turner		JCA 12, 266–276
1978	Langrehr		JCSHE 2, 161–174
1980	Moschis		HERJ 9, 64–71
1989	Ozgen		JCSHE 13, 175–187
1981	Helmick	Adolescents and work	HERJ 10, 21–31
1981	White		JMF 43, 789–798
1983	Lawrence		HERJ 12, 199–205
1986	Sanik		JCSHE 10, 209–219
1988	Lawrence		JCSHE 12, 39–47
1988	Lovett		JCSHE 12, 199–204
1956	Sharp	Decision making	JM 21, 149–156
1956	Kenkel		JMF 18, 311–316
1958	Wolgast		JM 23, 151–158
1961	Schomaker		JHE 55, 214
1962	Schlesinger		FLC 11, 8–14
1977	Jeries		HERJ 5, 146–153
1977	Gladhart		JCSHE 1, 265–277
1985	Rowland	Finance—assessment	HERJ 14, 218–225
1987	Wilhelm		HERJ 16, 13–22
1951	Knapp	Finance—budget	MLR 72, 152–155
1982	Mullis		JCSHE 6, 113–120
1987	Beutler		HERJ 16, 3–12
1988	Poduska		JHE 80, 16–23
1940	Lorimer	Finance—children	EN 25, 28–31
1988	Douthitt		JCA 22, 220–245
1978	Kinsey	Finance—debt	JCA 12, 48–62
1978	Wright		JHE 70, 38–39
1981	Marlowe		HERJ 9, 382–389
1986	Bryant		JCA 20, 19–35
1976	House	Finance—divorce	JHE 68, 36–38
1931	Clarke	Finance—expenditure	FAM 12, 92–94
1931	Hyde		*Harpers* 163, 688–699
1932	Wright		SSR 6, 55–82
1933	Saffian		JHE 25, 563–566
1938	Brady		ASA 33, 385–389
1938	Kaplan		ASA 33, 81–100

Year	*First Author*	*Research Topic*	*Reference*
1940	Leevy	Finance—expenditure	ASR 5, 948–953
1941	Jones		*Nature* 147, 377–379
1943	Working		ASA 38, 43–56
1943	Cave		ASA 38, 445–452
1943	Freeman		JHE 35, 346–348
1946	Brady		MLR 62, 1–5
1949	Coles		JHE 41, 193–194
1950	Converse		JHE 42, 634–636
1950	Blankertz		JM 14, 572–578
1955	Merriam		JHE 47, 330–332
1959	Millican		JHE 51, 177–181
1968	Bymers		JHE 60 (9), 709–715
1972	Morrison		JCA 6, 71–77
1977	Hager		JCA 11, 127–132
1978	Winakor		HERJ 7, 2–19
1982	Abdel-Ghany		JCSHE 6, 21–28
1985	Horton		HERJ 13, 292–303
1986	Wagner		HERJ 15, 21–31
1988	Wagner		JCSHE 12, 373–387
1989	Nelson		JCA 23, 21–44
1989	Winakor		HERJ 17, 195–214
1951	Freeman	Finance—housing	JHE 43, 259–262
1979	Hogan		HERJ 7, 210–218
1980	Winter		JCA 14, 82–95
1981	Meeks		JCSHE 5, 101–114
1983	Guthrie		JCSHE 7, 307–319
1985	Chen		JCA 19, 37–55
1985	Urich		JCSHE 9, 161–172
1986	Brandt		HERJ 14, 280–293
1963	White	Finance—insurance	JHE 55 (9), 707–714
1974	Maynes		JCA 8, 37–60
1976	Geistfeld		JCA 10, 224–232
1962	Clark	Finance—kin support	JHE 54 (3), 229–230
1982	Kennedy		JMF 44, 311–317
1983	Cheal		JMF 45, 805–812
1951	Thorpe	Finance—management	JMF 13, 104–106, 130
1953	Pecheniuk		JHE 45, 187–190
1959	Wells		JHE 51, 439–444
1960	Manning		JHE 52, 274–275
1963	Hill		SSR 47, 446–460
1964	Gover		JMF 26, 231–233
1968	Downs		JHE 60, 737–738
1978	Arndt		JCSHE 2, 27–34
1983a	Heck		JCSHE 7, 271–285
1983	Schnittgrund		JCSHE 7, 261–270
1985	Berger		JCSHE 9, 185–205
1986	Godwin		JCSHE 10, 77–96
1986	Iams		JHE 78, 48–50
1987b	Hira		JHE 79, 19–22
1989	Johnson		HERJ 17, 241–252
1947	Landis	Finance—marital adjustment	JMF 9, 32–34
1952	Williamson		JMF 14, 298–301
1984	Williams	Finance—marital conflict	JCSHE 8, 33–53
1986	Schaninger		JMF 48, 129–136
1983	Rettig	Finance—marital exchange	JMF 45, 497–509

Year	*First Author*	*Research Topic*	*Reference*
1972	Williams	Finance—net worth	HERJ 1, 104–113
1985	Davis	Finance—satisfaction	HERJ 14, 123-131
1987	Davis		HERJ 15, 247-256
1989	Titus		HERJ 17, 309-318
1942	Monroe	Finance—saving	JHE 34, 659-661
1950	Liston		JHE 42, 439–441
1955	Brady		MLR 78, 1240-1244
1972	Rudd		JCA 6, 35-46
1982a	Hefferan		HERJ 11, 47–55
1987a	Hira		JCSHE 11, 183-194
1954	Smith	Finance—security and retirement	JMF 16, 36-40
1960	Kundak		JHE 52, 370-371
1960	Cowles		JHE 52, 99-102
1962	Morse		JHE 54 (8), 711-713
1963	Guthrie		JHE 55, 274-275
1963	Larery		JHE 44, 214
1965	Lomberg		JHE 57 (2), 123-128
1988	McKenna		HERJ 17, 153-164
1985	Scholl	Finance—women	HERJ 14, 208-217
1933	Swerdloff	Great Depression	FAM 13, 310-314
1936	Gross		MAES 274
1936	Byrne		USDL, no. 108.
1937	Gilboy		AER 27, 309-323
1939	Conard		AJS 44, 526-533
1979	Pershing	Household—family policies	JMF 41, 573, 581
1972	Ater	Household—interaction	JMF 34, 257-263
1986	Hoeflin	Household—investment	JHE 78, 32-45
1987	Zick		JCA 21, 21-39
1944	Gross	Household—management	MAES 196 (June)
1972	Mumaw		HERJ 1, 35-43
1983	Crawford		JCSHE 7, 45-58
1983b	Heck		JCSHE 7, 117-135
1986	Buehler		HERJ 14, 351-362
1986	Garrison		JCSHE 10, 247-260
1955	Schlaphoff	Household—production	JHE 47, 400-404
1981	Owen		JCSHE 5, 157-174
1983	Henze		JCSHE 7, 287-298
1983	Sanik		HERJ 12, 217-227
1983	Volker		HERJ 11, 267-279
1987	Norum		HERJ 16, 143-149
1988	Volker		JCSHE 12, 321-340
1973	Hafstrom	Household—satisfaction	HERJ 2, 119-132
1988	Broman		JMF 50, 743-748
1961	Hunter	Household—tasks	JHE 53 (6), 425-427
1963	Maloch		JHE 55 (6), 413-416
1971	Ronald		JHE 63, 177-179
1975a	Steidl		HERJ 4, 121-137
1975b	Steidl		HERJ 3, 223-240
1975	Hall		JHE 67, 30-33
1982	Purchase		JCSHE 6, 301-317
1956	Cowles	Household—time	JHE 48, 29-35
1958	Steidl		JHE 50, 447-450
1970	Hall		JHE 62, 23-29
1973	Schaurer		HERJ 2, 82-92
1980	Schnittgrund		JCSHE 4, 239-248

Year	*First Author*	*Research Topic*	*Reference*
1981	Matsushima	Household—time	JCSHE 5, 199-217
1983	Gerner		HERJ 12, 145-158
1983	Hafstrom		HERJ 11, 245-254
1983	Matsushima		JCSHE 7, 229-246
1983	Tasker		HERJ 12, 207-216
1984	Schram		JCSHE 8, 283-292
1986	Lovingood		HERJ 14, 326, 335
1986	Rowland		HERJ 15, 105-114
1986	Schram		JCSHE 10, 235-245
1987	Blaylock		JCA 21, 183-201
1988	Dismukes		JCSHE 12, 247-256
1988	Douthitt		JCSHE 12, 141-157
1989	Ackerman		JCSHE 13, 1-19
1989	Khan		JCSHE 13, 67-77
1958	Blood	Household—work division	JMF 20, 170-174
1973	Walker		JHE 65, 7-11
1978	Lovingood		HERJ 7, 20-33
1978	Nickols		HERJ 7, 85-97
1981	Sanik		HERJ 10, 175-180
1983	Abdel-Ghany		HERJ 12, 159-167
1984	Bird		JMF 46, 345-355
1984	Goebel		JCSHE 8, 61-72
1986	Coverman		JMF 48, 413-422
1986	Rettig		JCSHE 10, 195-207
1987	Barnett		JMF 49, 29-40
1987	Berardo		JMF 49, 381-390
1987	Dolan		JCSHE 11, 387-399
1987	Rexroat		JMF 49, 737-750
1988	Benin		JMF 50, 349-361
1989	Hardesty		JMF 51, 253-267
1950	Leevy	Leisure	S&SR 35, 97-105
1959	Johannis		FLC 8, 34-36
1983	Nickols		HERJ 12, 189-198
1930	MLR	Standard of living	MLR 30, 1209-1252
1933	Leiffer		S&SR 27, 443-453
1937	Monroe		JHE 29, 665-670
1946	Reed		ASR 11 (2), 192-197
1948	MacNaughton		JHE 40, 133-134
1955	Knoll	Women's employment	JHE 47, 323-329
1960	Anderson		JHE 52 (6), 452-455
1962	MLR		MLR 85 (12), 1383-1384
1963	Rollins		JMF 25, 226
1964	Caudle		JHE 56, 723-727
1965	Hafstrom		JMF 27, 403-409
1967	Wenck		JHE 59, 9, 737-738
1970	Williamson		JHE 62, 609-613
1975	Metzen		HERJ 3, 249-259
1977	Sailor		JHE 69, 26-27
1977	Szinovacz		JMF 39, 781-791
1980	Gordon		JMF 42, 327-336
1981	Foster		JCSHE 5, 115-124
1981a	Foster		HERJ 10, 192-201
1981b	Foster		JCSHE 5, 23-36
1981	Ortiz		HERJ 9, 200-206
1982	Goebel		JCSHE 6, 63-78

Year	*First Author*	*Research Topic*	*Reference*
1983	Bird	Women's employment	HERJ 12, 63–70
1983	Goebel		HERJ 12, 169–188
1983	Stafford		HERJ 11, 257–266
1984	Maret		JMF 46, 357–364
1985	Kingston		JMF 47, 619–625
1985	Skinner		HERJ 13, 218–225
1988	Foster		JCSHE 12, 15–27
1988	Terzioglu		JCSHE 12, 341–348
1989	Floge		JMF 51, 51–63
1989	Galambos		JMF 51, 385–389

Note: AER, *American Economic Review;* AJS, *American Journal of Sociology;* ASA, *American Statistical Association;* ASR, *American Sociology Review;* CD, *Child Development;* EN, *Eugenics News;* FAM, *Family* (prior to 1947), *Journal of Social Casework* (after 1947); FLC, *Family Life Coordinator;* HERJ, *Home Economics Research Journal;* JCA, *Journal of Consumer Affairs;* JCSHE, *Journal of Consumer Studies and Home Economics;* JGP, *Journal of Genetic Psychology;* JHE, *Journal of Home Economics;* JM, *Journal of Marketing;* JMF, *Journal of Marriage and the Family;* MAES, *Michigan Agricultural Experiment Station;* S&SR, *Sociology and Social Research;* SSB, *Social Security Bulletin;* SSR, *Social Science Review;* USDL, U.S. Department of Labor (Bureau of Labor Statistics).

6
Religion and Families

Kip W. Jenkins

This chapter reviews the research on the relationship between family life experience and religious groups, organizations, or belief systems. Within this broad definition, I review the influences of the following on family life: religious beliefs, practices, and prejudices; general religiosity; effect of religious education on the family; religious affiliation and family experience; family customs and traditions as influenced by religion; family worship; influence of religious factors on marital success or failure; socialization of family values by means of religious factors; and religious aspects of family structure and functioning. The sources searched are listed in table 6–1.

The Decade 1930–1939

Research Findings

Fertility. Stouffer (1935) used census records to compare the birthrates of Catholics and non-Catholics. He found that from 1919 to 1933, fertility among Catholics had fallen and had dropped faster than the rate among non-Catholics.

Intermarriage. Using census records from 1910 to 1930, Resnick (1933) studied intermarriage between Jews and non-Jews. Intermarriage tended to occur among three different types of Jews: Jewish "risk-takers" who would gamble with intermarriage, nontraditional Jews who were not specifically interested in maintaining intra-Jewish marriages, and Jews who had specific wishes or desires to be achieved in intermarriage (freedom of expression, desire to lose association or identification with Jewish background, desire to be assimilated more quickly into American culture, and others).

Engelman (1935) studied the demographic characteristics of intermarriages among Jews in Germany from 1900 to 1930. He found that both sexes contributed to the increase of Jew–non-Jew marriages, though males contributed more to intermarriages than did females. Urban Jews intermarried more than rural Jews, and both male and female Jews were more likely to marry Protestants than Catholics.

Table 6–1
Literature Sources Used in Review

Source	*Years Reviewed*
Indexes	
International Bibliography of Research in Marriage and the Family	1900–1964
Research in Marriage and the Family, vol. 2	1965–1972
Inventory of Marriage and the Family Literature	1973–1986
American Doctoral Dissertation Index	1930–1951
Dissertation Abstracts	1951–1987
Dissertation Index	1951–1987
Academic journals	
American Journal of Sociology	1930–1988
American Sociological Review	1936–1988
Journal of Social Psychology	1930–1988
Social Forces	1930–1988
Marriage and Family Living	1939–1965
Journal of Marriage and the Family (formerly M&FL)	1966–1988
Family Process	1962–1988
Journal of Family Issues	1981–1988
Religious-oriented journals	
American Catholic Sociological Review	1940–1968
Sociological Analysis (formerly known as ACSR)	1969–1988
Journal of the Scientific Study of Religion	1961–1988
Review of Religious Research	1959–1988
AMCAP Journal (Association of Mormon Counselors and Psychotherapists)	1975–1988

Religion and Family Processes. Sturges (1937) collected information on religious beliefs and practices from a sample of college students and adults by asking specific questions about the religious significance of marriage, fidelity, the nature of marriage, religious devotion of parents, and adolescent religious feelings. The correlation between orthodoxy and piety was higher for religious than nonreligious individuals.

The Decade in Review

Theory and Methodology. The focus was on descriptive studies; no study was grounded in a major theory (table 6–2). An analysis of the research methods of the 1930s provides an interesting view of what was acceptable and important to scholars of that day. Of the seven studies of this period, four utilized census, court, or civil records to describe the research topic and offer analysis. Only Sturges (1937) utilized survey methods by selecting samples from available populations. Sample sizes in the studies tended to be rather large or unknown.

Key Studies and General Findings. None of the research findings of the 1930s were of general importance to the field. The studies describing Jewish and Catholic intermarriage were pioneering.

Table 6–2
Overview of Research on Religion and Families, 1930–1939

Year	*Author*	*Topic*	*Theory*	*Method*	*Sample*	*Analysis*
1933	Resnick	Intermarriage	None	Census/records	Unknown	Descriptive
1935	Engleman	Intermarriage	None	Census/records	Unknown	Descriptive
1935	Stouffer	Fertility	None	Census/records	40,000	Descriptive
1936	Robinson	Fertility	None	Census/records	Unknown	Descriptive
1937	Carrier	Religion and family process	None	Other (literature review)	Unknown	Descriptive
1937	Sturges	Religion and family process	None	Questionnaire-P	Unknown	Descriptive
1938	Mulvaney	Fertility	None	Census/records	5,000	Explanation

The Decade 1940–1949

Research Findings

Fertility. Mulvaney (1943) described the trends in fertility with specific concerns for how fertility practices affected family size, the correlation between fertility and Catholicity, and the social problems that could arise out of the fertility practices of the day. A survey of census records revealed that there was less than the anticipated decrease in family size. Mulvaney also found that Catholic fertility followed national trends but to a lesser degree.

Coogan (1946) described the characteristics of Catholic fertility in Florida by reviewing the census and church records of 4,891 Catholic families. He found that the more religiously oriented families had higher fertility rates. Other factors affecting birthrate were home ownership, occupation, educational level, place of birth of husband and wife (native versus foreign born), and the fertility of parents.

Christensen (1948) conducted a survey of 1,600 students enrolled in courtship and marriage classes at Brigham Young University. He discovered that Mormon fertility was influenced by religion and socioeconomic status and followed the general downward trend of national fertility yet remained consistently higher than national averages. Mormon students were found to desire larger families than the U.S. average (4.5 children as compared to 3) yet felt justified in the use of birth control devices. The expense of child rearing was the major reason cited for limiting family size. Most students desired smaller families than their parents.

Intermarriage. Kennedy (1944) studied the influences of religion and cultural group on intermarriage using census records in New Haven, Connecticut, from 1870 to 1940. She found that highly religious individuals tended to marry individuals of the same religion. When intermarriage occurred, religion still played a part in the attempt by one partner to "convert" the other, especially among Catholics. The result of her research was the formulation of the "triple melting pot" theory of intermarriage, which basically proposes that most marriages in the United States are homogamous, with the melting pot focusing more on intercultural melting rather than religion.

Landis (1949) studied intermarriage among the families of 4,108 students. Divorce was higher for interfaith than intrafaith marriages. Among interfaith marriages, the divorce rate was higher when the wife was a Protestant rather than a Catholic. Children tended to follow the religious preference of the mother.

Religion and Marital Stability. Somogyi (1941) studied the relationship between divorce and religion using Hungarian census records. The lowest divorce rates were among Catholics, and Jews had lower rates than Protestants.

Although religion had an impact on marital stability, its influence was less than that of educational and occupational factors.

Thomas (1949) studied factors that contributed to the dissolution of 7,000 Catholic families. The five most important factors were adultery (32 percent), drinking (24 percent), temperament (10 percent), war marriages (8 percent), and in-laws (6 percent).

The Decade in Review

Theory and Methodology. Most of the research conducted during the 1940s was descriptive; any theory was usually implied. The most common data sources were census, court, and church records (table 6–3).

Key Studies and General Findings. Somogyi (1941) documented that Catholics tend to have lower divorce rates than Jews or Protestants. Kennedy (1944) reported that highly religious individuals tend to marry within their religion, and Landis (1949) found that divorce is higher among interreligious marriages than among intrareligious marriages.

The Decade 1950–1959

Research Findings

Fertility. Samenfink (1958) examined the discrepancies between the teachings of the Roman Catholic church and the marital and family behavior of 100 church members. Young married couples who were Catholic tended to reject the church's teachings concerning contraceptives and the philosophy of marriage purity and indulged in premarital sexual relationships.

Intermarriage. Brown (1950) observed 391 people in a small Kentucky community to study class, intermarriage, and church membership. Compared to the lower class, higher-class residents tended to be long-time residents, morally strict, less isolated, more modern, and more prone to interfaith marriages. Lower-class residents tended to be newcomers, morally lax, isolated, old-fashioned, and backward, compared to the upper class. The lower-class residents were more likely to marry within their faith. Brown suggested that intermarriage occurred because the higher-class residents refused to have relationships with the lower-class residents in social and ecclesiastical settings and therefore had to accept marriage across religious lines.

Thomas (1951b) tested the triple melting pot theory proposed by Kennedy (1944). By using the *Official Catholic Directory of 1950,* he sent questionnaires to over 10,000 couples of mixed marriages that were sanctioned by Catholic

Table 6–3
Overview of Research on Religion and Families, 1940–1949

Year	*Author*	*Topic*	*Theory*	*Method*	*Sample*	*Analysis*
1940	Celestine	Religion and family process	None	Census/records	246	Descriptive
1940	Hulett	Religion and family process	Psychodynamic	Content analysis	47	Descriptive
1940	Neely	Religion and family process	None	Questionnaire-P	Unknown	Descriptive
1941	Alexander	Religion and family process	None	Observation	252	Descriptive
1941	DeHart	Fertility	None	Census/records	252	Explanation
1941	Somogyi	Religion and marital success	None	Census/records	Large	Descriptive
1942	Christina	Religion and family process	None	Questionnaire-P	1,680	Descriptive
1942	Cressman	Cleric family counseling	None	Questionnaire-P	242	Descriptive
1942	Slotkin	Intermarriage	None	Questionnaire-P	Unknown	Descriptive
1943	Hulett	Religion and family process	Symbolic Interaction	Content analysis	47	Descriptive
1943	Jones	Religion and family process	None	Questionnaire-P	880	Descriptive
1943	Mulvaney	Fertility	None	Census/records	Unknown	Descriptive
1944	Kennedy	Intermarriage	None	Census/records	Unknown	Descriptive
1944	Marie	Fertility	None	Questionnaire-P	1,085	Descriptive
1946	Coogan	Fertility	None	Census/records	4,891	Descriptive
1947	Lipscomb	Religion and family process	None	Other (literature review)	Unknown	Descriptive
1948	Christensen	Fertility	None	Questionnaire-P	1,600	Explanation
1949	Landis	Intermarriage	None	Questionnaire-P	4,108	Descriptive
1949	Thomas	Religion and marital success	None	Census/records	7,000	Descriptive

nuptials. He discovered a much higher mixed-marriage rate for Catholics than proposed by the triple melting pot theory and concluded that religion is only one of many factors determining intermarriage rate.

Kennedy (1952) utilized records to replicate her 1944 study. She observed that among Jews, British Americans, and Germans, the intermarriage rates had not changed from her previous study; intrafaith marriage rates had increased among Irish and Scandinavians as compared to her 1944 study; and interfaith marriage rates had also increased among Italians and Poles. Kennedy concluded that her data supported the hypothesis that religion continued to influence the marriage process for three broad groups: Protestant British Americans, Germans, and Scandinavians; Catholic Irish, Italians, and Poles; and Jews.

Religion and Family Processes. Christopherson (1956) studied patriarchal authority among thirty Mormon families. He found that patriarchal authority was still considered to be a part of Mormon family life, especially in the roles of parental discipline, recreation, decisions, finances, and religious observance. The traditional patriarchal role of the Mormon male was nevertheless changing to become more accommodating to the traditional female role, and there seemed to have been a decrease in traditional patriarchal authority behavioral patterns.

Cox (1957) studied formal religious practices in the family and found that religious identification and participation were highest in families where parents were highly educated and had professional careers. Participation was higher among Catholics than in any other religious denomination. There was a positive relationship between frequency of church attendance and formal religious activity in the home, with higher values placed on religion in church-attending families than in non-church-attending families.

Religion and Dating Behavior. Barta and O'Reilly (1952) studied the dating habits and attitudes toward marriage of 175 Catholic college students. Sixty-two percent of the men and 31 percent of the women discussed dating with their parents. A high percentage were willing to marry non-Catholics; however, only a small percentage were willing to give up their religion to preserve a mixed marriage. Eighteen percent planned on having three or fewer children, and 73 percent planned on having four or more.

Dedman (1959) studied the influence of religion on premarital sexual behavior. Questionnaires were obtained from a sample of freshmen and seniors attending a southern coeducational university. Those who were highly religious tended to participate less in premarital sex.

Religion and Mate Selection. Hollingshead (1950) studied cultural factors in mate selection and found that a large majority of people married within their own religion. Ninety-seven percent of the Jews married Jews, 94 percent of the Catholics married Catholics, and 74 percent of the Protestants married Protestants.

Bend (1952) performed content analysis of a Yiddish newspaper (the *Day*) in New York City to describe the marriage-offer advertisements in 1935 compared with 1950. Focusing on thirteen different terms used in the advertisement, he discovered that personal qualities dominated the ads in 1950, and economic factors were more prevalent in 1935. The desire to marry someone with similar Jewish background received insignificant attention in both periods.

Schnepp and Roberts (1952) tested the effect of propinquity on mate selection in a Catholic parish. Of the 205 marriages, 40 percent selected a mate from within a twenty-block radius. They found that the parish might not be as strong a force for mate selection as it had been. They also discovered the propinquity rates for mixed marriages in the parish followed the same pattern as for unmixed marriages and concluded that residential propinquity was not as important as an individual's desire to marry someone of the same religious background.

Religion and Marital Satisfaction. Schnepp and Johnson (1952) tested a number of religious factors as predictors of marital success. An implied theory of the researchers was that similarity in and strength of religiosity would predict marital success. The researchers utilized the predictive scales of Burgess and Cottrell (1939) and analyzed responses from about 600 individuals. Religious factors that correlated with marital success included: no parental quarrels over religious or moral matters, no premarital sex liberties, no parental quarrels over religious education, reception of the sacraments at the established age, two or more years' membership in a church organization, religion made childhood happier, first religious instruction was received in the home, parental approval of marriage, church periodicals in the home, and mother attended church regularly.

Wallin (1957) studied the effect of religiosity on the sexual gratification and marital satisfaction of 1,000 couples. He found that women with low sexual gratification were significantly more satisfied when religiosity was high rather than low; however, there was no significant difference between the marital satisfaction of religious and nonreligious women who were satisfied sexually.

The Decade in Review

Theory and Methodology. Most of the research articles had no specific theory to test, although some were based on an implied theory (table 6–4). Mini theories of propinquity and homogamy were tested as they related to religion and mate selection. Compared to previous decades, there was an increase in the use of survey methods and tests of significance.

Key Studies and General Findings. During the 1950s, intermarriage continued to be a popular research area. The major author was Ruby Jo Kennedy, who continued to test her triple melting pot theory of interreligious marriages.

Table 6–4
Overview of Research on Religion and Families, 1950–1959

Year	*Author*	*Topic*	*Theory*	*Method*	*Sample*	*Analysis*
1950	Barron	Intermarriage	None	Other (literature review)	Unknown	Descriptive
1950	Brown	Intermarriage	None	Observation	391	Descriptive
1950	Hollingshead	Religion and mate selection	None	Census/records/observation	523	Descriptive
1950	Marshall	Fertility	None	Census/records	Unknown	Descriptive
1950	Wade and Berreman	Cleric counseling	None	Questionnaire-P	135	Explanation
1951	Bulowski	Religion and marital stability	None	Census/records	Unknown	Descriptive
1951a	Thomas	Religion and family process	None	Questionnaire-P	16,500	Descriptive
1951b	Thomas	Religion and mate selection	None	Census/records	Large	Descriptive
1952	Barta and O'Reilly	Religion and dating behavior	None	Questionnaire-P	174	Explanation
1952	Bend	Religion and mate selection	None	Content analysis	700	Descriptive
1952	Kennedy	Intermarriage	None	Census/records	Unknown	Descriptive
1952	Schnepp and Johnson	Religion and marital satisfaction	Scale test	Questionnaire-P	600	Explanation
1952	Schnepp and Roberts	Religion and mate	Propinquity	Case study	205	Descriptive
1954	Cizon	Religion and dating behavior	None	Census/records	200	Descriptive
1954	Curtis	Religion and family process	None	Questionnaire-P	7,935	Explanation
1954	Hibbard	Cleric family process	None	Questionnaire-P	Unknown	Descriptive
1954	Monahan and Kephart	Religion and marital stability	None	Census/records	Unknown	Descriptive
1954	Reed	Religion and family process	None	Questionnaire-P	150	Descriptive
1955	Anders	Religion and marital stability	None	Census/records	417	Descriptive
1955	Chancellor and Monahan	Religion and marital stability	None	Census/records	22,000	Descriptive
1956	Bossard and Letts	Intermarriage	None	Questionnaire-P	382	Descriptive
1956	Christopherson	Religion and family process	None	Questionnaire-P	30	Descriptive
1956	Curtis and Mahan	Religion and marital success	Scale test	Census/records	1,050	Descriptive
1956	Samenfink	Fertility	None	Census/records	Unknown	Explanation
1957	Burchinal	Religion and marital satisfaction	Scale test	Questionnaire-P	256	Explanation
1957	Cox	Religion and family process	None	Questionnaire-P	Unknown	Descriptive
1957	Kanin	Fertility	None	Questionnaire	50	Explanation
1957	Mayer and Marx	Fertility	None	Census/records	Unknown	Descriptive
1957	Wallin	Religion and marital satisfaction	None	Questionnaire-P	Unknown	Explanation
1958	Christopherson and Walters	Religion and family process	None	Questionnaire-P	222	Descriptive
1958	Kiernan	Religion and marital stability	None	Census/records	Unknown	Explanation
1958	Samenfink	Religion and marital satisfaction	None	Questionnaire-P	200	Explanation
1959	Bell and Blumberg	Religion and dating behavior	None	Questionnaire-P	410	Explanation
1959	Dedman	Religion and dating behavior	None	Questionnaire-P	Unknown	Explanation
1959	Dohen	Religion and marital stability	None	Census/records	Unknown	Explanation

Thomas (1951) concluded that a single melting pot theory of intermarriage was more adequate for explanation. There was an increase in the study of dating and premarital sexual behavior. Other important research topics were religion and mate selection and religion and marital success.

The Decade 1960–1969

The 1960s saw a dramatic increase in fertility and intermarriage research. The influence of religion on dating behavior, mate selection, and marital satisfaction continued to be popular research topics.

Research Findings

Fertility. Freedman, Whelpton, and Smit (1961) examined social class, religion, and fertility. After controlling for socioeconomic factors, there was no difference between Protestant and Jewish fertility; however, Catholic-Jewish differences in fertility remained even when social class was held constant.

Hunt (1967) reviewed the findings of research on Catholic birthrates and found little evidence that being Catholic had much influence on fertility. White Catholics had birthrates only slightly higher than white non-Catholics.

Potvin, Westoff, and Ryder (1967) surveyed 5,600 Catholic wives to study the factors influencing conformity to Catholic birth control policy. They found that high religiosity and having parents of the same ethnic background contributed to higher levels of conformity. Nonconformity was associated with earlier ages at marriage and being educated in the 1960s.

Stycos (1967) described how Catholic birth control concerns in Latin America differ from U.S. characteristics. In a survey of over 2,000 Catholic women in Latin America, Stycos found that the persistence of high birthrates in Latin America was not due to Catholic teachings but rather to low socioeconomic level.

Potvin and Burch (1968) surveyed 1,028 married Catholic women to see how many children they planned to have and how many children they would have if they could have an ideal family. They concluded that religious practice influenced their expected and ideal family size.

Mayhew (1969) found that couples who were religiously homogamous tended to follow religious proscriptions about birth control; couples who were not religiously homogamous did not.

Intermarriage. Heiss (1961) compared 1,167 intrafaith marriages with 863 interfaith marriages. Among Catholics and Jews, intermarried couples had less satisfaction than intrafaith marriages. Among Protestants, marital satisfaction was not associated with intermarriage.

Barnett (1962) completed a comprehensive review of the research conducted on interreligious dating and marriage and summarized the general findings in the field. He identified six factors that fostered mixed marriages: (1) existence of the religious group as a minority; (2) an unbalanced sex ratio; (3) the development of cultural similarities; (4) disturbing psychological factors such as rebelliousness and rejection; (5) acceptance of certain cultural values; and (6) weakening of institutional controls over marriage.

In a study of 455 couples, Besanceney (1962) reported that intermarriage was more frequent among individuals who were highly educated and whose parents had mixed marriages. Contact with relatives and close generational ties with a foreign country tended to decrease the chance of intermarriage. Among Catholics and Protestants, intrafaith marriage was more common among those who attended church regularly.

Kenkel, Himler, and Cole (1965) analyzed how socialization and being devout affected the willingness of young adults to enter a mixed religious marriage. Data were obtained from 876 Catholic students at Iowa State University. Four factors tended to decrease the chance of intermarriage: (1) a devout childhood home; (2) attendance at a Catholic high school; (3) frequent attendance at Mass, Communion, and confession; and (4) current devoutness.

Prince (1966) measured the attitudes of Catholic college students concerning mixed religious marriages. Women appeared less willing to enter a mixed marriage than men, and most students believed marital satisfaction was more assured with a homogamous marriage than a mixed marriage. A large majority of students also believed that mixed marriages would lead to differences over religious matters, which in turn would lead to marital conflict. About 35 percent of students nevertheless believed it would be better to marry outside the faith than to remain single.

Christiansen and Barber (1967) reviewed over 42,000 marriage records to determine intermarriage characteristics. They found that only 11 percent of marriages were interfaith. Persons who were previously married, older, of higher status, urban dwellers, and from a religious minority were more likely to marry outside their religion. Many interfaith marriages involved premarital pregnancy. Interfaith marriages also showed only slightly higher divorce rates.

Greeley (1969) analyzed national data to study intermarriage. He found that denominational homogamy accounted for nearly 75 percent of all U.S. marriages. A review of Canadian records revealed that about 70 percent of marriages were of the same denomination.

In an effort to study how mixed marriages affect religion, religious identity, and conversion, Salisbury (1969) surveyed 2,524 college students in a New York university. He found that Protestant women converted to the religion of the spouse at a higher rate than did Catholic women, that women converted at a higher rate than men, and that conversion was in the direction of the spouse who brought the higher social status to the marriage.

Religion and Family Processes. Landis (1960) studied the relationship between family religiosity and family success among 2,654 students. Religious devoutness was associated positively with marital happiness, closeness to parents, and children's religiosity.

Fichter (1962) studied how religion influenced socialization among 1,069 families. Children from religious homes tended to be happier, less lonely, more alert, and outgoing and had a larger circle of friends than nonreligious children. Religious parents tended to be more concerned about children's behavior than nonreligious parents.

In a study of the differences between black Muslim and black Christian family relationships, Edwards (1968) selected matched families from each group. He found that differences were significant in husband-wife relationships, extended kin, parent-child, and family-community relationships. Overall, black Muslims tended to exhibit more American-type middle-class values and behaviors than did black Christian families.

Weigert (1968) examined parent-child interaction patterns and adolescent religiosity using a cross-cultural sample from New York City, St. Paul, San Juan, Puerto Rico, and Merida, Mexico. He found that high parental support and control were associated with high religiosity in children.

Religion and Dating Behavior. Cardwell (1969) studied religious commitment and attitudes toward premarital sex among 187 college students. High levels of religious commitment tended to be associated with less permissive premarital sexual behavior.

Heltsley and Broderick (1969) studied sexual norms and premarital sexual permissiveness among a sample of 1,435 college students. They found that when sexual abstinence was emphasized by a church, there was a negative association between religiosity and sexual permissiveness. When sexual abstinence was not emphasized by a church, there was no relationship between religiosity and premarital sexual permissiveness.

Using a sample of 437 university freshmen, Ruppel (1969) found an inverse relationship between religiosity and premarital sexual permissiveness. This relationship was stronger among groups with traditional values.

Religion and Marital Satisfaction. Carey (1967) studied the association between religion and marital happiness using a sample of 1,617 Catholics. Carey measured religiosity by use of five factors (devoutness, ethical concerns, religious attitudes, religious knowledge, and level of Catholic schooling).

Catholic schooling, devoutness, and ethical concerns were positively associated with marital happiness.

Religion and Marital Stability. Kunz (1964) studied the influence of Mormon ideology on divorce. In a study of 451 students (270 Mormon, 152 non-Mormon), he found that Mormons experienced a 5 percent divorce rate; non-Mormons experienced a 20 percent rate and mixed marriages a 13 percent rate. Kunz also found that Mormons divorce at a rate of 12 percent for civil marriages, 2 percent for "temple" marriages, and 3 percent for church marriages.

Crockett, Babchuk, and Ballweg (1969) conducted a study to see how change in religious affiliation affected family stability. They studied 388 families and found that, generally, religious homogamy between spouses promotes family stability. The authors also found that religious homogamy achieved as adults had the same effect on stability as homogamous marriages from the beginning of the union for both Catholic and Protestant spouses.

The Decade in Review

Theory and Methodology. During the 1960s, there was an increase in the testing of mini theories (table 6–5). Reiss's Premarital Sexual Permissiveness Theory was tested, and the findings were contradictory. Kennedy's triple melting pot theory continued to influence researchers. Besanceney (1965) recommended that researchers avoid the triple melting pot theory, while Christensen and Barber (1967) and Greely (1969) conducted research that supported it.

Research methods shifted dramatically in the 1960s. Fewer researchers used census and church records, and the use of questionnaires and interviews increased. Sample sizes tended to be large (over 200), and analysis of data shifted from descriptive to analytical.

Key Studies and General Findings. Potvin and his associates dominated research work done during the decade in the investigation of religion and fertility. Their samples tended to be large, and the factors investigated were well defined. Christiansen and Barber (1967) and Greeley (1969) reported that the majority of marriages in North America were religiously homogamous. Heltsley and Broderick's research on Reiss's Premarital Sexual Permissiveness theory was an important study that appeared to stimulate research on how religiosity is related to premarital sexual permissiveness.

Studies of intercultural religious influence on mate selection, marital adjustment, and family processes increased during the 1960s, perhaps because a section in the *Journal of Marriage and the Family* was dedicated to intercultural research.

Table 6–5
Overview of Research on Religion and Families, 1960–1969

Year	*Author*	*Topic*	*Theory*	*Method*[a]	*Sample*	*Analysis*
1960	Burchinal	Religion and dating behavior	None	Questionnaire-P	498	Explanation
1960	Landis	Religion and family process	None	Questionnaire-P	2,654	Explanation
1961	Dyer and Luckey	Religion and marital stability	None	Questionnaire-P	522	Explanation
1961	Freedman, Whelpton, and Smit	Fertility	None	Questionnaire-P	132	Descriptive
1961	Heiss	Intermarriage	None	Questionnaire-P	1,167	Explanation
1962	Barnett	Intermarriage	None	Other (research review)	N.A.	N.A.
1962	Besanceney	Intermarriage	None	Questionnaire-P	455	Explanation
1962	Burchinal and Kenkel	Religion and mate selection	None	Census/records	Large	Descriptive
1962	Fichter	Religion and family process	None	Questionnaire-P	1,069	Descriptive
1962	Heer	Intermarriage	None	Census/records	Large	Explanation
1962	Nash and Berger	Religion and family process	None	Questionnaire-P	Unknown	Descriptive
1962	Selfors, Kirk, and King	Religion and family process	None	Questionnaire-P	Unknown	Explanation
1963	Bell and Buerkle	Religion and marital stability	None	Questionnaire-P	150	Descriptive
1963	Bouma	Intermarriage	None	Questionnaire-P	100	Descriptive
1963	Burchinal and Chancellor	Religion and mate selection	None	Questionnaire-S	Large	Descriptive
1963	Christiansen	Religion and family process	None	Interview-P	154	Explanation
1963	Kunz	Religion and family process	None	Questionnaire-P	268	Explanation
1963	Willits, Bealer, and Bender	Intermarriage	None	Interview-P	1,829	Descriptive
1964	Jarrett	Fertility	None	Case study	478	Descriptive
1964	Jarrett	Intermarriage	None	Case study	478	Explanation
1964	Kunz	Religion and marital stability	None	Questionnaire-P	451	Descriptive
1964	Matras	Religion and family process	None	Interview-P	600	Explanation
1964	Wallin and Clark	Religion and marital satisfaction	None	Questionnaire-S	770	Explanation
1965a	Bescanceney	Intermarriage	None	Other (research review)	N.A.	N.A.
1965	Goering	Fertility	None	Questionnaire-P	605	Explanation
1965	Goldscheider	Fertility	None	Questionnaire-P	1,603	Descriptive
1965	Kenkel, Himler, and Cole	Intermarriage	None	Questionnaire-P	876	Explanation
1965	Reiber	Religion and family process	None	Questionnaire-P	137	Explanation
1965	Scanzoni	Cleric family process	None	Interview-P	31	Descriptive
1966	Goldscheider	Fertility	None	Questionnaire-P	1,420	Descriptive

1966	Prince	Intermarriage	None	Questionnaire-P	Unknown	Descriptive
1966	Westoff and Potvin	Fertility	None	Questionnaire-P	15,000	Descriptive
1967	Carey	Religion and marital satisfaction	None	Questionnaire-P	1,617	Explanation
1967	Christiansen and Barber	Intermarriage	None	Census	42,043	Descriptive
1967	Croog and Tede	Intermarriage	None	Questionnaire-P	2,300	Explanation
1967	Datta	Religion and creativity	None	Interview/Questionnaire	573	Explanation
1967	Goldscheider and Goldstein	Religion and family process	None	Interview-P	1,603	Descriptive
1967	Hershenson	Religion and family process	None	Questionnaire-P	162	Explanation
1967	Hunt	Fertility	None	Questionnaire-P	Unknown	Explanation
1967	Larson	Religion and family process	None	Questionnaire	1,400	Explanation
1967	Mogey	Religion and family process	None	Census/records	720	Explanation
1967	Potvin and Westoff	Religion and family process	None	Questionnaire-P	6,700	Explanation
1967	Potvin, Westoff, and Ryder	Fertility	None	Questionnaire-P	5,600	Descriptive
1967	Stycos	Fertility	None	Questionnaire-P	2,000	Descriptive
1968	Blair	Religion and family process	None	Questionnaire-P	2,300	Explanation
1968	Edwards	Religion and family process	None	Case study	Unknown	Descriptive
1968	Nash	Religion and family process	None	Census/records	Unknown	Explanation
1968	Potvin and Burch	Fertility	None	Questionnaire-S	1,028	Explanation
1968	Spaeth	Fertility	None	Questionnaire-S	10,000	Descriptive
1968	Vernon	Religion and marital satisfaction	None	Content analysis	Unknown	Descriptive
1968	Weigert	Religion and family process	None	Questionnaire-P	Large	Explanation
1969	Bean and Afzal	Religion and mate selection	None	Census/records	Unknown	Descriptive
1969	Cardwell	Religion and dating behavior	None	Questionnaire-P	187	Explanation
1969	Crockett, Babchuk, and Ballweg	Religion and marital stability	None	Questionnaire-P	328	Explanation
1969	Gockel	Religion and income	None	Questionnaire-P	7,518	Explanation
1969	Greeley	Intermarriage	None	Questionnaire-P	Large	Descriptive
1969	Haerle	Intermarriage	None	Questionnaire-S	360	Descriptive
1969	Heltsley and Broderick	Religion and dating behavior	Mini	Questionnaire-P	1,435	Explanation
1969	Korson	Religion and mate selection	None	Questionnaire-P	765	Descriptive
1969	Lee and Brattrud	Religion and family process	None	Case study	Unknown	Descriptive
1969	Mayhew	Fertility	None	Interview-P	99	Descriptive
1969	Mulhearn	Intermarriage	None	Questionnaire-S	10,000	Descriptive
1969	Ruppel	Religion and dating behavior	None	Questionnaire-P	437	Explanation
1969	Salisbury	Intermarriage	None	Questionnaire-P	2,524	Explanation

[a] P = primary data; S = secondary data.

The Decade 1970–1979

During the 1970s, there was increased interest in fertility, intermarriage, dating behavior, mate selection, and marital satisfaction.

Research Findings

Fertility. Neal and Groat conducted three studies (Neal and Groat, 1970; Groat and Neal, 1973; Groat, Neal, and Knisely, 1975) on the relationship between alienation and fertility among Protestant and Catholic women. The sample sizes of the three studies were 123, 700, and 336. Women who were high on alienation (powerlessness, meaninglessness) tended to have more children. They also found that low social class and high alienation resulted in greater fertility differences than either social class or alienation alone (Groat and Neal, 1973).

In a study of 973 couples, Bouvier (1973) reported that Catholics exhibited higher fertility than other affiliations, but differences were smaller than observed in previous studies. More Catholics were using birth control measures than previously.

In a study of contraceptive use among 412 Catholic women, Groat, Neal, and Knisely (1975) found ideal family size was the best predictor of contraceptive use. Feelings of alienation and religiosity were associated with contraceptive use; age was not.

Grindstaff and Ebanks (1975) studied 500 Catholic and Protestant couples in Canada who had decided to control fertility by a vasectomy. They found that Protestant men who were older, better educated, and had a high income were more likely to use vasectomy. Catholics desired more children than Protestants; both groups had more children than they desired due to contraceptive failures rather than to nonuse of contraceptives.

In a study to determine how religious differences influenced fertility, Stokes (1972) interviewed 304 couples. Controlling for duration of marriage, socioeconomic status, and education of wife, the data did not support the idea that Catholics and Protestants were moving toward a common fertility pattern. (See Freedman, Whelpton, and Smit, 1961.) Catholic couples desired, expected, and had more children.

Bean and Aiken (1976) studied religion, education, and age of interfaith married couples to determine which contributed most to unwanted fertility. There was an increase in unwanted fertility in interfaith versus intrafaith couples.

Using a sample of 1,941 college students, Brackbill and Howell (1974) found that religious affiliation was more predictive of preferred family size than race, sex, socioeconomic status, and school. Catholics generally desired larger families than Protestants.

Thornton (1979) studied Mormon fertility by analyzing a number of state and federal records and two national samples. He reported that Mormon fertility was significantly higher than other religious groups.

Abortion. Hertel, Hendershot, and Grimm (1974) interviewed about 800 nurses and social workers to study the relationship between religion and attitudes toward abortion. Liberal Christian denominational members were more likely to approve of abortion than conservative denominational members. Respondents who frequently attended church were more likely to disapprove of abortion. Religion was found to be the single best predictor of attitudes toward abortion.

In a survey of 821 college students, Clayton and Tolone (1973) found a negative relationship between religiosity and endorsement of abortions. The relationship was statistically significant for women but not for men.

Leon and Steinhoff (1975) reviewed the hospital records of 3,187 patients and found that Catholics chose to have abortions less often than non-Catholics and had more pregnancies. There was no difference between Catholic and non-Catholic women on the length of time from discovery of pregnancy to the decision to abort.

The impact of religious preferences and church attendance on the attitude of abortion was studied by McIntosh, Alston, and Alston (1979). Data were obtained from 1,050 white Catholics and Protestants. Frequent church attenders tended to have antiabortion attitudes, regardless of church affiliation.

Intermarriage. Rosenthal (1970) reviewed state marital records and found that divorced individuals had a higher rate of interreligious marriage in their second marriage than first marriages. Widows and widowers, however, tended to marry within their faith.

Barlow (1971) examined Mormon endogamy and exogamy in 282 Florida couples. He found that 61 percent of all Mormons in Florida had married outside their faith, but 34 percent of the non-Mormon spouses had converted to Mormonism.

Monahan (1971) reviewed many church and public records and found more intermarriage among Catholics than any other major denomination in the United States. Monahan postulated that intermarriage between major denominations is much greater than acknowledged due to sample inadequacy in the past. He then (1973) reviewed census and state marital records of 4,751 marriages in Indiana from 1962 to 1967 and found that religious intermarriage among non-Protestants was high and increasing. Of the major denominations, Jews were the most endogamous and Catholics the least endogamous. He concluded that religious constraint for interfaith marriage was lessening.

Winer (1977) questioned 304 Jews in a Connecticut syngogue to study causes and consequences of Jewish intermarriage. Intermarried Jews tended to come from more urban areas. He also found that more intramarried Jews had attended Hebrew school and knew more Hebrew language. The spouses of intermarried Jews tended to come from Protestant-Catholic or Protestant-Jewish parents. Jew and non-Jew spouses resembled each other in educational, occupational, and socioeconomic status.

Religion and Family Processes. Ritchie (1970) found a positive relationship between parental church attendance and adolescent church participation. The relationship between father's and son's attendance was particularly strong.

Weigert and Thomas (1974) extended their research on religiosity and adolescents to Mormons with a study designed to discover if parental support and control contributed to the development of religiosity in adolescents. They sampled fifty-six youth and found a positive association between parental support and a child's religious behavior and attitude.

In another study concerning adolescents and religion, Dickinson (1976) questioned 432 teenagers in a southern state and found that religious practices, such as reading the Bible and attending church, were declining, especially for males. Differences in religious practices were greater by sex than by race, but differences in saying grace were greater by race than by sex factors. Females and blacks displayed more religious behavior.

McReady (1972) studied the process of religious socialization in the family. In a secondary analysis of a large national sample of Catholics, McReady found that the Catholic father, rather than the mother, is the dominant source of religious socialization. Parental influence was greater than social class effect. McReady found that marital tension over religious activity affected sons more than daughters, and upward social mobility negatively affected religious devotion. Ethnicity and sex-linked factors also positively affected religious socialization processes.

Using a sample of 453 college students, Johnson (1973) found that students reported their parents as generally similar to themselves in religious commitment and that religious students tended to perceive their families as happier, warmer, and more accepting than nonreligious students.

Dodrill (1974) used the Guilford-Zimmerman Temperament Survey (1949) to study religious transfer among 340 freshmen. He found that five of six entering freshmen identified with their parents' religion. Tendencies toward independent thinking, social ascendance, introspectiveness, and reflectiveness tended to be attributed to students who did not affiliate with their parents' religion.

Alston (1974a) conducted a study concerning the attitudes of white Protestants and Catholics toward nonmarital sex. In a secondary analysis of National Opinion Research Center data, Alston found that respondents disapproved more strongly of nonmarital sex by women than by men; however, men were less likely to defend the double standard. Alston found that church affiliation was not related to sexual attitudes among women. Among men, however, Protestants were more likely than Catholics to disapprove of any kind of nonmarital sex.

In another examination of the same data set, Alston (1974b) examined how religion influences husbands' and wives' attitudes toward extramarital and homosexual relationships. He found a general dislike for any extramarital or homosexual relations by Catholic and Protestant men and women. Women tended to disapprove of extramarital affairs more strongly than men but were equal with men in their dislike of homosexual relationships.

Tanner (1975) studied 200 Mormon adolescents and found that church activity had a positive association with affection in family relationships. Participation in church-sponsored, family-related activities was related to more positive affection and family participation. Tanner's findings supported Homan's position that frequency of interaction leads to positive degrees of affection.

Religion and Dating Behavior. Middendopp, Brinkman, and Koomen (1970) tested Reiss's (1964) Premarital Sexual Permissiveness (PSP) theory. A secondary analysis of 1965 data collected in the Netherlands was analyzed. The authors found that religiosity and age were the strongest determinants of PSP. Less religious and older adolescents showed higher PSP than religiously active and younger adolescents. They also found that liberal adolescents showed more PSP, while conservative adolescents showed less.

In related research concerning PSP, Ruppel (1970) studied 437 college students at a midwestern university. His findings confirmed those of Heltsley and Broderick (1969). He suggested that the ritual dimensions of religiosity (church attendance, confessional) were not as important as intellect, ideology, and relevant experiences.

Hunter (1972) examined premarital sexual standards in a religiously conservative college. He found that Reiss's PSP theory could account only partially for factors leading to premarital sexual permissiveness and concluded that strong parental teachings and support from like-minded peer groups contributed significantly.

Religion and Marital Satisfaction. Herron (1976) used balance theory to study couple religious congruency in religiosity and marital satisfaction among 394 Lutheran and Catholic couples. Herron found that couple religiosity had no significant relationship with marital happiness; however, when religiosity was measured for the wife only, the relationship was positive and significant. As a result of his findings, Herron contended that balance theory could not be confirmed as a useful explanation of marital satisfaction.

Religion and Marital Stability. Snider (1971) studied the relationship of religious affiliation, religious practices, and marital adjustment and found a significant correlation between religious affiliation and marital adjustment. Sect groups were highest in this relationship, followed by evangelical groups, Catholics, and liberal groups. Bible reading, prayer, and church attendance were all positively correlated with marital adjustment. Snider also found that marital adjustment scores were higher among members of religions that emphasized conversion and that had greater emotional participation in public services.

Thornton (1978) described some of the factors that contributed to marital instability, employing a secondary analysis of a 1970 National Fertility Study of 13,715 respondents. Thornton found that religion was moderately related to marital instability. Fundamentalist and Baptist women were more maritally stable than women of other denominations.

Hunt and King (1978) examined the relationship between religion and marital stability. They tested sixty-four couples using the Locke-Wallace Marital Adjustment Scale and found that religiosity was correlated with marital success.

The Decade in Review

Theory and Methodology. The theoretical proposition that received the most interest was from Reiss's theory of premarital sexual permissiveness. Three researchers tested the relationship between religiosity and sexual permissiveness (Heltsley and Broderick, 1969, contains a discussion concerning the proposed relationship) and observed that Reiss's proposition did not make reliable predictions. Most of the other research with a theoretical foundation centered on testing different scales of religiosity and marital success (table 6–6).

Methodologies of the decade were quantitative and tended to have fairly large sample sizes. Descriptive studies tended to be associated with large sample sizes and were concerned with general trends in fertility, intermarriage, and the influence of religious activities on the family. Matras (1974) used a 60,000 sample, and Potvin and Lee (1974) and Thornton (1978) used sample sizes of 15,000 and 13,715, respectively.

Key Studies and General Findings. Researchers were still interested in the relationship between religious affiliation and fertility, but more researchers began to isolate the factors they believed interacted with religious activity to predict fertility. Neal and Groat conducted several studies (Neal and Groat, 1970; Groat and Neal, 1973; Groat, Neal, and Knisely, 1975) examining how feelings of alienation within religiously affiliated women interacted to promote or decrease fertility.

Studies of religion and the use of contraceptive devices became more popular in the 1970s. With the U.S. Supreme Court decision to legalize abortion in 1973, it also became popular for a number of family researchers to see how religion affected the decision to use abortion.

Intermarriage continued to be a major concern for researchers. Many of the studies were descriptive, especially with regard to foreign cultures and nationalities (Mol, 1970; Hassan, 1971). Cavan published three articles during the decade dealing with intermarriage and contended that in order to increase our

Table 6–6
Overview of Research on Religion and Families, 1970–1979

Year	Author	Topic	Theory	Method[a]	Sample	Strengths[b]
1970	Middendopp, Brinkman, and Koomen	Religion and dating behavior	None	Census-S	Unknown	M
1970a	Cavan	Intermarriage	Social distance	Questionnaire-P	848	M
1970b	Cavan	Intermarriage	None	Questionnaire-P	403	St
1970	Christianson	Religion and family processes	None	Questionnaire-P	Unknown	M
1970	Hicks	Religion and family process	None	Questionnaire-P	Unknown	S
1970	Mol	Intermarriage	None	Questionnaire/Interview/Census-P	2,607	S
1970	Neal and Groat	Fertility	None	Questionnaire-P	123	None
1970	Rhodes and Nam	Religion and family process	None	Census	Large	None
1970	Ritchie	Religion and family process	None	Questionnaire-P	Unknown	M
1970	Rosenthal	Intermarriage	None	Census	Large	S,St
1970	Ruppel	Religion and dating behavior	Mini	Questionnaire-P	437	None
1970	Weigert and Thomas	Religion and family processes	Mini	Questionnaire-S	Unknown	M
1971	Abramson	Intermarriage	None	Questionnaire-S	2,071	S
1971	Barlow	Intermarriage	None	Questionnaire-P	282	None
1971	Bell	Religion and family processes	None	Interview-P	60	M
1971	Cavan	Intermarriage	None	Other (literature review)	Unknown	I
1971	Clayton	Religion and dating behavior	Mini	Questionnaire-P	656	M,St
1971	Dahl	Religion and family processes	None	Questionnaire-P	405	None
1971	Hampe	Religion and dating behavior	Premarital sexual Permissiveness Test	Questionnaire-P	519	I
1971	Hassan	Intermarriage	None	Census	3,295	S
1971	Lambrechts	Fertility	None	Interview-P	838	None
1971	Monahan	Intermarriage	None	Other (literature review)	Unknown	None
1971	Sakran	Religion and family processes	None	Questionnaire-P	454	None
1971	Salisbury	Intermarriage	None	Questionnaire-P	2,524	S
1971	Snider	Religion and marital success	None	Questionnaire-P	Unknown	None
1972	Bouvier	Fertility	None	Interview-P	515	None

Table 6–6 continued

Year	*Author*	*Topic*	*Theory*	*Method*[a]	*Sample*	*Strengths*[b]
1972	Glass	Religion and dating behavior	None	Questionnaire-P	280	None
1972	Hong	Religion and family processes	None	Questionnaire-P	2,000	None
1972	Hunter	Religion and dating behavior	Mini	Questionnaire-P	Unknown	M
1972	McReady	Religion and family processes	None	Questionnaire-P	Unknown	None
1972	Nafzinger	Religion and family processes	None	Content analysis	Unknown	None
1972	Smith	Cleric family process	Mini	Questionnaire-P	181	M
1972	Stokes	Fertility	None	Interview-P	56	M
1972	Weigert and Thomas	Religion and family processes	None	Questionnaire-P	56	M
1972	Williams	Religion and family processes	None	Questionnaire-P	130	None
1973	Bouvier	Fertility	None	Interview-P	973	None
1973	Curcione	Cleric family processes	None	Interview-P	76	None
1973	Groat and Neal	Fertility	None	Questionnaire-P	700	M
1973	Johnson	Religion and family processes	None	Questionnaire-P	453	None
1973	Monahan	Intermarriage	None	Census-S	4,751	S
1973	Clayton and Tolone	Religion and abortion	None	Questionnaire-P	821	None
1974b	Alston	Religion and family process	None	Questionnaire-S	3,000	S
1974	Brackbill and Howell	Fertility	None	Questionnaire-P	941	None
1974	Dodrill	Religion and family processes	None	Questionnaire-P	344	None
1974	Hertel, Hendershot, and Grimm	Fertility	None	Questionnaire-P	448	M
1974	Matras	Fertility	None	Census	60,000	S
1974	Potvin	Fertility	None	Questionnaire-S	15,000	S
1974a	Weigert and Thomas	Religion and family processes	None	Questionnaire-S	Unknown	S,M
1975	Allen and Cole	Cleric family process	None	Questionnaire-P	265	None
1975	Bortnick	Religion and dating behavior	None	Questionnaire-P	511	None
1975	Cosper	Fertility	None	Records/Questionnaire-P	1,311	S
1975	Evans	Cleric marriage counseling	None	Interview/Observation/ Questionnaire-P	7	None
1975	Frank	Religion and family processes	None	Interview-P	27	St
1975	Grindstaff and Ebanks	Fertility	None	Questionnaire-P	500	St
1975	Groat, Neal, and Knisely	Fertility	None	Questionnaire-P	412	M
1975	Leon and Steinhoff	Fertility	None	Records	3,187	S
1975	Mueller and Johnson	Religion and family processes	None	Questionnaire-S	2,482	S,St

1975	Renzi	Fertility	None	Questionnaire-P	1,613	S,St,M
1975	Tanner	Religion and family processes	None	Questionnaire-P	223	None
1976	Alston	Intermarriage	None	Questionnaire-S	Unknown	S
1976	Bean and Aiken	Fertility	None	Questionnaire-S	Large	S
1976	Dickinson	Religion and family processes	None	Questionnaire-P	432	St
1976	Hsish	Cleric family processes	Mini	Questionnaire-P	78	M
1976	Herron	Religion and marital satisfaction	Mini	Questionnaire-P	394	M
1976	Hunsberger	Religion and family processes	None	Questionnaire-P	156	St
1976	Kourvetaris and Bobratz	Religion and mate selection	None	Questionnaire-P	264	None
1976	Nelsen and Everett	Cleric family process	None	Questionnaire-P	242	St
1976	Smith	Cleric family process	Mini	Questionnaire-P	259	M
1977	Cohen	Religion and family processes	None	Questionnaire-P	80	None
1977	Hartley and Taylor	Cleric family process	None	Questionnaire-P	448	M
1977	Schultz et al.	Religion and family processes	None	Questionnaire-P	1,903	S
1977	Winer	Intermarriage	None	Questionnaire-P	304	None
1978	Acock and Bergston	Religion and family processes	None	Questionnaire-P	653	St
1978	Becker	Religion and family processes	None	Questionnaire-P	959	None
1978	Chambers and Chalfant	Religion and family processes	None	Content analysis	Unknown	None
1978	Christensen	Religion and marital stability	None	Questionnaire-P	197	None
1978	Davis	Religion and family processes	None	Questionnaire-P	60	None
1978	Dudley	Religion and family processes	None	Questionnaire-P	400	St
1978	Hartley	Cleric family process	None	Questionnaire-P	448	M
1978a	Hoge and Petrillo	Religion and family processes	Mini	Questionnaire-P	451	M
1978b	Hoge and Petrillo	Religion and family processes	None	Questionnaire-P	451	None
1978	Hunt and King	Religion and marital success	None	Questionnaire-P	64	M
1978	Thornton	Religion and marital stability	None	Questionnaire-S	13,715	S,St,M
1978	Wicks and Workman	Religion and family processes	None	Questionnaire-P	318	None
1979	Farber	Religion and family processes	None	Interview-P	300	St
1979	Hutchison and Hutchison	Cleric family processes	None	Questionnaire-P	326	None
1979	McIntosh, Alston, and Alston	Fertility	None	Questionnaire-S	1,050	S,St
1979	Rout	Religion and family processes	None	Questionnaire-S	3,539	S
1979	Thornton	Fertility	None	Census-S	Unknown	None

[a] P = primary data; S = secondary data.
[b] M = methodology; St = statistical analysis; S = sample size; and I = interpretation of data.

understanding of intermarriage, researchers will need to go beyond simple identification of religious affiliation and look for additional factors that influence the attitude and decision-making process of intermarriage. Monahan reviewed many of the unpublished sources of data for intermarriage and proclaimed that intermarriage between major religious organizations was greater than acknowledged due to inadequacy of sample representativeness.

The interaction between family processes and religious activity was the major area of concern for researchers in this decade. Scholars were interested in knowing how religion influenced the use of power; the establishment and maintenance of generation gaps; child and adolescent religious value socialization; the expression of religiosity throughout the life cycle; family affection; child rearing; and family formation and size attitudes. More research was conducted, especially later in the decade, on the influence of family processes on religious affiliation and church activity, a theme that extended into the 1980s. An important study in this area was conducted by Weigert and Thomas (1970, 1973, 1974) who looked at how urbanization and secularization weakened adolescent religiosity.

Premarital sexual relationships continued to be the central focus of those interested in examining how religion influences dating behavior. A number of studies were conducted to test Reiss's PSP conceptualizations. Researchers were generally unconvinced that Reiss's propositions could predict premarital sexual attitudes.

The Decade 1980–1989

Religion and family researchers continued to study fertility, abortion, and intermarriage. As in the previous decade, many investigated how family and religion influence each other. Religion and dating behavior, mate selection, and marital satisfaction continued to be of interest. There were also a few studies on religion and suicide, sexual abuse in Christian homes, and the influence of religion on the establishment and maintenance of gender roles.

Research Findings

Fertility. In a study devoted to examining the role of religious affiliation on fertility, Mosher and Hendershot (1984) analyzed data from 14,000 women interviewed in the 1973 and 1975 National Survey on Family Growth (NSFG). Catholics had higher fertility rates than Protestants. White Catholics had higher rates than white Protestants, but black Protestants had the highest fertility rates of all, while Jews had the lowest.

A number of studies were conducted to investigate religion and fertility with women of different cultural backgrounds. Sabagh and Lopez (1980) interviewed 1,129 Chicana women and found that church activity had a positive impact on fertility of Chicanas reared in the United States but not on those reared in Mexico. The researchers contended that the characteristics of the country of upbringing may have to be considered as an intervening variable.

Heaton and Calkins (1983) examined the relationship between family size and contraceptive use among 258 Mormons from the 1965, 1970, and 1975 National Fertility Studies (NFS). Mormons were at least as likely to use contraceptive devices as other white Protestants but were less likely to be current users than either Catholics or Protestants. More devout Mormons had distinctive patterns of timing in contraceptive use compared to other religious groups.

Eckhardt and Hendershot (1984) analyzed data from the 1976 National Survey of Family Growth (Cycle II) and found that Catholics were less likely to be sterilized than those of other religious groups, but if they did decide on sterilization, females were less likely than males to be sterilized. The differences were not large, however, and might have resulted from nonreligious factors.

In a survey of 224 adolescents, Studer and Thornton (1987) found that adolescent religious commitment diminishes propensity to engage in sexual intercourse but is also associated with less effective contraceptive use when intercourse is engaged in. Teenage girls who were never married, sexually experienced, and regular attenders of religious services were less likely than any other group of use effective contraception.

Intermarriage. Glenn (1982) used national surveys conducted between 1957 and 1978 to study trends in religious intermarriage. He found that there were not strong attitudes against interreligious marriages and that endogamy was not as strong as thought. Still, religious endogamy was common, and more so for Catholics than Protestants. In a follow-up research note, Glenn (1984) utilized a new index for measuring religious endogamy for his sample and determined that there is virtually equal strength for Catholic and Protestant intrafaith marriages (one affiliation does not have more same-faith marriages than the other).

McCutcheon (1988) examined religious intermarriage of 13,626 white Americans and found that members of conservative Christian denominations have generally avoided increasing rates of interreligious marriage. He also found that college attendance was positively related to increases in intermarriage. College attendance did not appear to erode religious values, but, rather, college attendance was seen as a "marriage market." There was no support found for teenage marriages' being more exogamous than endogamous.

Bock and Radelet (1988) examined marriages of those who identified themselves as having no religious affiliation. A sample of 5,683 respondents from surveys gathered from 1973 to 1984 was analyzed, and the authors found that independents are less likely to marry, and if they do marry, they are more likely to divorce and remarry.

Religion and Family Processes. In a study designed to examine religious activity throughout the life cycle, Mueller and Cooper (1986) tested the hypothesis that church activity increases with marriage and young children and then declines as the family ages. Nearly 1,500 questionnaires were collected. The researchers found that the tested hypothesis was seen only in mainline Protestant young adults. The cycle was not evident with Catholics, and fundamentalists were seen to be active throughout the family life cycle.

Heaton and Goodman (1985) examined religious differentials in patterns of family formation. A sample of over 10,000 respondents showed that Catholics, Protestants, and Mormons were more likely to marry, less likely to divorce, and more likely to have larger families than those with no religious preference. Mormons had the highest rates of marriage, the highest fertility, and the lowest rates of divorce among the religious groups. Catholics had lower rates of marriage and divorce than Protestants. Heaton and Goodman also found that patterns are not altered by the frequency of church attendance or level of education.

In a study conducted to see if increased church attendance and other family dimensions (family solidarity) affect self-esteem and faith in other people, Bahr and Martin (1983) questioned 1,673 students and found little support for religiosity's building self-esteem, but church attendance was significantly related to developing one's faith in other people.

A number of studies examined how religion plays a part in the establishment of gender and family roles. Morgan and Scanzoni (1987) questioned a sample of 318 college women to see how religious devoutness affects a woman's decision to remain working after marriage or children. They found that greater devoutness depressed future work expectations. Regardless of the religious affiliation, being more devout even led to a reduction of expected continuity in the labor force.

Brinkerhoff and Mackie (1985) compared the findings of U.S. and Canadian student attitudes concerning religion and gender. Nearly 1,000 students were questioned. The researchers found that increased religiosity led to increases in traditional gender attitudes by both groups. Current religious identification was more important than childhood affiliation. People with no affiliation were more egalitarian, followed by Catholics, mainline Protestants, fundamentalists, and Mormons. Researchers also found that religious variables had more predictive power than demographic variables.

Rampey (1983) studied religiosity, purpose in life, and other factors related to family success. In a sample of 341 parents and 289 children, he found that parents tend to be more religious than their offspring and have more perceived purposes in life. Involvement in religious organizational activities leads to success for both parents and offspring; a clearly defined purpose in life also leads to family success.

Hunsberger (1985) studied parent-university student agreement on religious and nonreligious values. A sample of 1,000 subjects was given questionnaires. Hunsberger found no true generation gap, but there was a tendency for university students to agree to a greater extent with parents on religious concerns as compared with other areas. Parental estimates of students' attitudes were closer when parents and students shared similar religious orientations than when students had drifted away from parents.

Kiernen and Munro (1987) studied how parents influence adolescent religious activity. A secondary analysis of 1,140 families found that the sex of the adolescent plays an intervening role in religious socialization. Fathers were seen to be more influential on daughters than on sons; however, both paternal and maternal religious influence was positively and significantly related to male adolescent religiosity.

Nelson (1981a) examined how normal family processes interact with religious organization and societal climate to transmit religiosity from one generation to the next. A questionnaire survey was given to 3,000 fourth through eighth graders in public and Catholic schools. Nelson found that religious apostacy in adolescents occurs more in liberal mainline Protestant denominations than among conservative groups. Religious conformity was exhibited more by females and first-born sons than other sexes or siblings in the family.

Hunsberger and Brown (1984) examined how family background variables affect adolescent apostacy rates. Questionnaires were given to 836 college students. Researchers found that intellectual orientation and emphasis placed on religion in the childhood home were the best predictors of apostate-nonapostate status. Subjects believed the home was the most important to religious socialization and identified the mother as the most influential factor affecting religious orientation.

Religiosity and Adolescent Substance Use. A few studies examined the relationship of adolescent religiosity and substance abuse. Perkins (1985) studied religious traditions, parents, and peers as determinants of alcohol and drug abuse among college students. Over 1,500 college students completed questionnaires, and Perkins found that Jewish college students (and their families) showed the least drinking and drug use of any other religious affiliation. No relationship was found between religiosity and adolescent drug use. Parental attitudes did not play a significant role, but among peer influences, strong Judeo-Christian tradition was influential.

Perkins (1987) also studied parental religion and alcohol use problems of college youth. A sample of 860 students were given questionnaires. Perkins found that students are at a greater risk if they are not Jewish, are not strongly attached to a particular faith, and are a child of an alcohol abuser. Perkins also found a positive relationship between parent religiosity and offspring religiosity.

In a study designed to study religious factors and drug use among Seventh-Day Adventist youth, Dudley, Mutch, and Cruise (1987) questioned 801 youth and found that commitment to Christ was the strongest predictor of abstinence from tobacco, alcohol, and drugs. The researchers also found that religious practice was positively related to abstinence.

Kent (1987) constructed and tested a model of family religiosity and family socialization factors as explanations for adolescent substance abuse. In a survey of 143 families, Kent found that religious practice and family factors show strong independent effects to curb adolescent substance abuse.

Koplin (1987) also studied how family, religiosity, and peer group factors influence adolescent drug use. A survey of 2,626 returned questionnaires showed that of the family variables, parental monitoring was most significant among all drug groups; however, each family variable and religiosity were found to show direct, indirect, or interactive effects. Koplin suggested that substance abuse can be best understood by investigating the interaction of religion and family factors.

Religion and Dating Behavior. Woodroof (1984) studied religiosity and premarital sexual behavior among 477 students from several Christian colleges. Woodroof found an inverse relationship between religiosity and premarital sexual behavior. He also found that high intrinsic religious orientation was related to low premarital sexual behavior.

Religion and Mate Selection. Branch (1983) tested a hypothesis that churches provide a nonerotic social context that promotes intrafaith mate selection for marriage. Records of forty different Catholic and Lutheran churches were reviewed (1,803 marriages), and Branch found support for his theory.

Religion and Marital Satisfaction. Bahr and Chadwick (1985) described religiosity in Middletown fifty years following the famous study conducted by Lynd and Lynd. They found no real difference between Catholics and Protestants in regard to marital status. Religious affiliation was positively related to marital satisfaction, and increased church attendance led to increased marital satisfaction. Religious affiliation led to an increase in family size, as did an increase in church attendance.

In a study designed to reexamine Edmonds's (1967) marital conventionalization propositions (religiosity is a spurious artifact of social desirability), Schumm, Bollman, and Jurich (1982) interviewed and gave questionnaires to 181 couples. They found that religiosity is an important predictor of marital satisfaction even when using "marital conventionalization" scales. Religiosity cannot be considered as a simple aspect of social desirability.

Filsinger and Wilson (1984) studied religiosity, socioeconomic rewards, and family development as predictors of marital satisfaction. Over 200 couples from eight Protestant churches were questioned. The researcher found that religiosity was the most predictive factor for marital satisfaction and concluded that religosity facilitates the process of marital adaptation.

Heaton (1984) examined how religious homogamy affects marital satisfaction by conducting a secondary analysis of the 1982 GSS (NORC) data. Heaton found a positive association between religious homogamy and marital satisfaction. The presence of children did not account for lower satisfaction scores in heterogamous marriages; however, attendance at religious services did play a mediating role.

Hatch (1985) studied how marital adjustment and satisfaction relate to perceptions of religious practices and orientations. Questionnaires were received from 136 graduate and seminary students. Hatch found that church attendance and frequency of prayer led to marital satisfaction for both groups. Religious beliefs and shared devotional times led to marital satisfaction for seminary students. A lack of consensus about religious practices led to lower levels of marital satisfaction.

Religion and Marital Stability. Bahr (1981) investigated religious intermarriage and divorce in Utah and the Mountain States. A questionnaire was received from 1,199 individuals. Bahr found that same-faith marriages were more stable than interfaith marriages. Divorce rates for certain religious combinations were found to be as much as nine times higher than others (highest divorce rate was Catholic-Mormon, and where neither partner had religious preferences).

The Decade in Review

Theory and Methodology. The only testing of theory was a study conducted by Breault (1986) where Emile Durkheim's ideas concerning suicide were applied to religious factors. Most of the theory that guided research in this decade was implied by the researcher or existed in the assumptions proposed by research hypotheses. Over one-fourth of all the articles reviewed for the 1980s were secondary analysis of existing data sets (table 6–7). Availability of data, computer processing abilities, and availability of large nationwide or cross-cultural resources for analysis have made this methodological approach attractive for family researchers. The use of questionnaires was by far the most popular data collection technique, accounting for over 70 percent of the studies reviewed.

Key Studies and General Findings. Argument continues over religious affiliation and fertility rates. Researchers in the 1960s contended that Catholic-Protestant differences could be accounted for by other factors, but Mosher and Hendershot (1984) found that Catholic-Protestant differences continued to persist. They found that white Catholics had higher fertility than white Protestants, but black Protestants had the highest rate and Jews the lowest. An investigation into religious affiliation and cultural background was an interesting twist examined by a few scholars in the 1980s, while others continued to look

Table 6–7
Overview of Research on Religion and Families, 1980–1989

Year	*Author*	*Topic*	*Theory*	*Method*[a]	*Sample*	*Strengths*[b]
1980	D'Antonio and Stack	Fertility	Mini	Questionnaire-S	3,030	S,M,St,I
1980	Sabagh and Lopez	Fertility	None	Interview-P	1,129	M,S
1980	Wilkinson and Tanner	Religion and family processes	None	Questionnaire-P	223	None
1981	Bahr	Intermarriage	None	Questionnaire-P	1,199	S
1981a	Marcum	Fertility	None	Questionnaire-S	1,359	M
1981b	Marcum	Fertility	None	Questionnaire-P,S	5,617	S
1981	McKeon	Religion and family processes	None	Questionnaire-P	Unknown	None
1981a	Nelson	Religion and family processes	None	Questionnaire-P	3,000	M,S
1981b	Nelson	Religion and family processes	None	Questionnaire-P	2,774	S
1981	Patterson	Religion and family processes	None	Records	Unknown	None
1981	Warner	Religion and family education	None	Experimental-P	Unknown	St
1982	Bahr	Religion and family processes	None	Questionnaire-P	2,005	S,M
1982	Glenn	Intermarriage	None	Interview-S	1,500	S
1982	Hoge, Petrillo, and Smith	Religion and family processes	None	Questionnaire-P	254	M
1982	Schumm, Bollman, and Jurich	Religion and marital satisfaction	None	Questionnaire/Interview-P	181	M,St
1983	Bahr and Martin	Religion and family processes	None	Questionnaire-P	1,673	S,St
1983	Bean, Mineau, and Anderton	Fertility	None	Records	180,000	M,S
1983	Branch	Religion and mate selection	None	Records	1,803	None
1983	Cherlin and Celebuski	Religion and family processes	None	Questionnaire-S	Unknown	I
1983	Hartman and Hartman	Religion and family processes	None	Questionnaire-P	458	None
1983	Heaton and Calkins	Fertility	None	Questionnaire-S	258	M
1983	Rampey	Religion and marital success	None	Questionnaire-P	630	M,St
1983	Wickstrom and Fleck	Cleric family processes	None	Questionnaire-P	130	None
1983	Williams	Fertility	None	Interview-P	58	M,I
1984	Brutz and Ingoldsby	Religion and family processes	None	Questionnaire-P,S	288	None
1984	Eckhardt and Hendershot	Fertility	None	Questionnaire-S	Unknown	M,St
1984	Filsinger and Wilson	Religion and marital satisfaction	None	Questionnaire-P	208	None
1984	Glenn	Intermarriage	None	Interview-S	1,500	S,M
1984	Hartman	Fertility	None	Questionnaire-P	1,754	None

1984	Heaton	Religion and marital satisfaction	None	Questionnaire-S	Unknown	None
1984	Hunsberger and Brown	Religion and family processes	None	Questionnaire-P	836	St
1984	Jelen	Fertility	None	Questionnaire-S	Unknown	None
1984	Mosher and Hendershot	Fertility	None	Questionnaire-S	14,000	S
1984	Woodroof	Religion and dating behavior	None	Questionnaire-P	477	St,M
1985	Bahr and Chadwick	Religion and family processes	None	Questionnaire/Interview-P	Large	S
1985	Brinkerhoff and Mackie	Religion and gender roles	None	Questionnaire-P	938	M
1985	Harris and Mills	Fertility	None	Questionnaire-S	2,359	S,M,St
1985	Hatch	Religion and marital satisfaction	None	Questionnaire-P	136	None
1985	Heaton and Goodman	Religion and family processes	None	Questionnaire-P	10,000	S,St,I
1985	Hunsberger	Religion and family processes	None	Questionnaire-P	1,000	S,St
1985	Perkins	Religion and family processes	None	Questionnaire-P	1,154	St
1985	Potvin and Sloan	Religion and family processes	None	Interview-P	868	St,I
1985	Stack	Religion and suicide	None	Records	Unknown	M,St
1985	Toney, Golesorkhi, and Stinner	Fertility	None	Questionnaire-P	3,304	S
1985	Woodroof	Religion and dating behavior	None	Questionnaire-P	477	M,St
1986	Alwin	Religion and family processes	None	Research review	Unknown	None
1986	Breault	Religion and suicide	Mini	Records	200,000	S
1986	Christiano	Religion and family processes	Mini	Questionnaire-S	2,164	S,St
1986	Dudley and Dudley	Religion and family processes	None	Questionnaire-P	712	St,M
1986	Hart	Religion and family processes	None	Questionnaire-P	1,262	I
1986	Heaton	Fertility	None	Questionnaire-P	6,031	S,M,St
1986	Mueller and Cooper	Religion and family processes	None	Questionnaire-P	1,448	St,I
1986	Neuman and Ziderman	Fertility	None	Questionnaire-S	Unknown	S
1986	Woodroof	Religion and dating behavior	None	Questionnaire-P	477	M,St
1987	Austin and Jones	Cleric family processes	None	Content analysis	30	I
1987	Browning	Religion and marital satisfaction	None	Questionnaire-P	484	M,St
1987	Dudley, Mutch, and Cruise	Religion and family processes	None	Questionnaire-P	801	M
1987	Hertel and Hughes	Religion and family processes	None	Questionnaire-S	11,000	S,M
1987	Johnson and Burton	Fertility	None	Questionnaire-P	366	None
1987	Kent	Religion and family processes	None	Questionnaire-P	143	M,St
1987	Kiernen and Munro	Religion and family processes	None	Questionnaire-S	1,140	M
1987	Koplin	Religion and family processes	None	Questionnaire-P	2,626	S,St

Table 6–7 continued

Year	*Author*	*Topic*	*Theory*	*Method*[a]	*Sample*	*Strengths*[b]
1987	Morgan and Scanzoni	Religion and family processes	None	Questionnaire-P	318	None
1987	Perkins	Religion and family processes	None	Questionnaire-P	860	M
1987	Studer and Thornton	Fertility	None	Questionnaire/Interview-P	224	I
1987	Wilson, Simpson, and Jackson	Religion and family processes	None	Questionnaire-P	695	None
1988	Bock and Radelet	Religion and family processes	None	Questionnaire-S	5,683	I
1988	Clark, Worthington, and Danser	Religion and family processes	None	Questionnaire-P	68	M,St
1988	Dudley and Laurent	Religion and family processes	None	Questionnaire-P	390	M,St
1988	Gil	Religion and sex abuse	None	Questionnaire/Interview-P	35	M
1988	Homola	Religion and family processes	None	Questionnaire-S	12,120	S,St
1988	Johnson et al.	Religion and family processes	None	Questionnaire-P	313	M
1988	Lee	Intermarriage	None	Records	609,002	S
1988	McCutcheon	Intermarriage	None	Questionnaire-S	13,626	S
1988	Plutzer	Religion and family processes	None	Questionnaire-S	3,254	S
1989	Anderton and Emigh	Fertility	None	Secondary analysis of data	4,943	M,S

[a] P = primary data; S = secondary data.

[b] M = methodology; St = statistical analysis; S = sample size; and I = interpretation of data.

at specific religious affiliations and orientations (liberal versus conservative) within the denomination as a predictive factor of fertility. In conjunction with fertility concerns, the investigation into religion and contraceptive devices continued.

Glenn (1982, 1984) was the major researcher of intermarriage for the decade. His data showed there were no strong barriers to intermarriage and that endogamy was not as strong as previously thought. He also proposed that neither Catholics nor Protestants have more endogamous marriages than the other.

Examinations of religious factors and family process factors were major areas of inquiry in the 1980s. Bahr and his associates and Heaton and his associates were interested in Mormon families and the influence of religion, while others showed interest in church authority on family formation (Patterson, 1981), religious devoutness and women working (Morgan and Scanzoni, 1987), religious influence on gender roles (Brinkerhoff and MacKie, 1985), and religious socialization and the family (Hunsberger, 1985; Hoge, Petrillo, and Smith, 1982; Dudley and Dudley, 1986).

A new topic of interest centered on the religious alienation of adolescents (Nelson, 1981a, 1981b; Hunsberger and Brown, 1984). The role religion plays on adolescent substance abuse was a new topic (Perkins, 1985; Kent, 1987; Koplin, 1987). Denominational influence on family experiences was also a concern for researchers.

Studies concerning religion and dating behavior, mate selection, satisfaction, and stability were also represented during the decade, but the studies were few and reflective of work done in the past.

Some of the more interesting research came from work by Stack (1985) and Breault (1986) who investigated the role of religion and suicide and agreed that religion as a single explanative of suicide prevention is inadequate.

Conclusions

Methodological Trends and Developments

Research in religion and the family has followed the same path that other social science research has taken over the past sixty years. In the beginning, the majority of studies were conducted by reviewing census or other records, deploying descriptive statistical methods (averages and percentages in most cases), and drawing conclusions based on what the majority of the survey was doing. Advances in statistical analysis techniques, computer availability, and general awareness of accepted positions proposed by philosophers of science drew researchers to new methods of quantitative inquiry, including improved sample sizes, concerns for representativeness, advanced statistical analysis of data, and other quantitative orientations. The field today is firmly entrenched in quantitative analysis with much secondary analysis of data from NORC, GSS, and other data resources.

Theoretical Trends and Developments

There is no theory of religion and the family that has guided published research in major academic journals over the past sixty years. There are no general propositions or theoretical assumptions that have guided research concerning the role religion plays in the family or even how the family affects religion. A theory, strictly developed from research in the field, has not yet developed and may not be possible. However, there are a number of propositions that may lead other scholars toward a theory of religion and the family.

Major Findings

A review of the research covered in this study has been organized into propositions derived by collecting common findings and interpretations. Propositions are presented with three concerns. First, a general statement is presented regarding the relationship between religiously oriented activities and family concerns. Second, application to the general population or to specific denominations is given. Third, the strength of research evidence for the proposition is listed (S = Strong, M = Moderate, W = Weak, C = Conflicting). Propositions are given for the influence of religion on fertility (table 6–8), intermarriage (table 6–9), family processes (table 6–10), dating behavior (table 6–11), mate selection (table 6–12), marital satisfaction (table 6–13), and marital stability (table 6–14).

Table 6–8
Major Propositions Derived from Research Concerning Religion and Fertility

Proposition	*Applicable*	*Evidence*
High levels of religiosity increase fertility	General	C
High Catholic religiosity increases fertility	Catholics	M
Religious affiliation affects fertility	General	M
Catholic fertility is higher than non-Catholic fertility	Catholics	W
Mormon fertility is higher than non-Mormon fertility	Mormons	M
Jews have lowest fertility among major denominations	Jews	C
Major denominations follow national trends in fertility rates	General	S
Social processes negatively affect religiosity and fertility	General	M
High religiosity promotes lesser use of contraception	General	C
Interreligious marriages promote lesser use of contraception	General	M
Catholics are as likely to use birth control as non-Catholics	Catholics	W
High religiosity promotes less approval of abortion	General	S
Religious affiliation influences approval of abortion	General	W

Evidence key: C = conflicting; M = moderate support; W = weak; S = strong.

Table 6–9
Major Propositions Derived from Research Concerning Religious Intermarriage

Proposition	*Applicable*	*Evidence*
U.S. marriages are generally endogamous	General	M
Religious affiliation influences interreligious marriage	General	M
Protestants are most likely to intermarry	Protestants	M
Catholics are less likely to intermarry than Protestants	Catholics	M
Jews intermarry more than Protestants or Catholics	Jews	C
Jews intermarry more Protestants than Catholics	Jews	M
Highly religious individuals tend to marry interreligiously	General	M
Social processes promote intermarriage	General	C
Catholic-Protestant marriages are less stable than same-faith marriages	Protestants-Catholics	W
Most spouses will change religous affiliation in mixed marriages	General	M
Adolescent religious training inversely affects intermarriage	General	M
Offspring from mixed marriages tend to intermarry themselves	General	S

Evidence key: C = conflicting; M = moderate support; W = weak; S = strong.

Table 6–10
Major Propositions Derived from Research Concerning Religion and Family Processes

Proposition	*Applicable*	*Evidence*
Religious affiliation affects moral judgments	General	M
Catholics are more conservative in moral judgments	Catholics	W
Jews are more liberal in moral judgments	Jews	W
Protestants are mixed in moral judgments	Protestants	W
Catholics have higher religious participation than non-Catholics	Catholics	M
Religiosity of parent leads to similar religiosity in child	General	S
Positive parent communication promotes positive image of God	General	M
Parental support promotes religiosity in adolescents	General	C
Marital tension negatively affects adolescent religiosity	General	W
Secularization weakens adolescent religiosity	General	S
Social mobility negatively affects adolescent religiosity	General	W
High religiosity in home promotes family happiness and success	General	S
Religious thinking in children develops in stages	General	M
High religiosity promotes acceptance of traditional gender roles	General	M
Mormons are more traditional toward gender roles than non-Mormons	Mormons	M
Highly religious are more likely to marry than nonreligious	General	M
Highly religious are less likely to divorce than nonreligious	General	M
Highly religious have larger families than nonreligious	General	M
Catholics are less likely to divorce than non-Catholics	Catholics	M
Mormons are less likely to divorce than non-Mormons	Mormons	M
Children agree with parents more about religion than other topics	General	M
Daughters are less subject to religious apostasy than sons	General	M
High religiosity in adolescents promotes less substance abuse	General	S

Evidence key: C = conflicting; M = moderate support; W = weak; S = strong.

Table 6–11
Major Propositions Derived from Research Concerning Religion and Dating Behavior

Proposition	*Applicable*	*Evidence*
Religiosity does not significantly affect dating behavior	General	M
Males date interreligiously more than females	General	M
High religiosity promotes less premarital sexual permissiveness	General	C
High religiosity negatively affects use of contraceptive devices	General	M

Evidence key: C = conflicting; M = moderate support.

Table 6–12
Major Propositions Derived from Research Concerning Religion and Mate Selection

Proposition	*Applicable*	*Evidence*
U.S. marriages are generally endogamous	General	C
High religiosity promotes the desire for endogamous marriages	General	M
Church attendance promotes a desire for endogamous marriage	General	M

Evidence key: C = conflicting; M = moderate support.

Table 6–13
Major Propositions Derived from Research Concerning Religion and Marital Satisfaction

Proposition	*Applicable*	*Evidence*
Endogamy promotes marital satisfaction	General	M
High religiosity promotes marital satisfaction	General	C
Increased church attendance increases marital satisfaction	General	C

Evidence key: C = conflicting; M = moderate support.

Table 6–14
Major Propositions Derived from Research Concerning Religion and Marital Stability

Proposition	*Applicable*	*Evidence*
Religious endogamy promotes marital stability	General	S
Catholics divorce less than non-Catholics	Catholics	S
Mormons divorce less than non-Mormons	Mormons	S
High religiosity promotes marital stability	General	M

Evidence key: M = moderate support; S = strong.

Concerns for Future Research

A vast majority of the studies reviewed in this chapter were founded on quantitative methodological assumptions. Were qualitative methods unacceptable or unpublishable? Were researchers unaware of or untrained for qualitative research, or is the assumption by most researchers in the field that there is no room for qualitative research?

I recommend greater use of qualitative research methods in the study of religion and the family. There is much of religious process that remains unresearched due to dependency on questionnaires or interview schedules. Much more could be done to increase the variability of research methodologies, and the inclusion of qualitative methods is a good place to start.

Concerns for religion and fertility will certainly continue, as will intra- versus intermarriage effects. How religion and the family influence each other must be more extensively researched, and descriptions of denominationally specific activities must continue to catch the attention of researchers.

References

Abramson, H.J. 1971. Interethnic marriage among Catholic Americans and changes in religious behavior. *Sociological Analysis* 32:31–44.

Acock, A.C., and Bergston, V.L. 1978. On the relative influence of mothers and fathers: A covariance analysis of political and religious socialization. *Journal of Marriage and the Family* 40:519–530.

Alba, R.D., and Kessler, R.C. 1979. Patterns of interethnic marriage among American Catholics. *Social Forces* 57:1124–1140.

Alexander, F.D. 1941. Religion in a rural community of the South. *American Sociological Review* 53:241–251.

Allen, J.E., and Cole, L.P. 1975. Differences in predominant family planning attitudes and experiences of seminary students: A ten-year assessment. *Review of Religious Research* 13:68–74.

Alston, J.P. 1974a. Attitudes of white Protestants and Catholics toward nonmarital sex. *Journal for the Scientific Study of Religion* 13:73–75.

———. 1974b. Attitudes toward extramarital and homosexual relations. *Journal for the Scientific Study of Religion* 13:479–481.

———. 1976. Review of the polls: Three current religious issues: Marriage of priests, intermarriage, and euthanasia. *Journal for the Scientific Study of Religion* 15:75–78.

Alwin, D.F. 1986. Religion and parent-childrearing orientations: Evidence of a Catholic-Protestant convergence. *American Journal of Sociology* 92:412–440.

Anders, S.F. 1955. Religious behavior of church families. *Marriage and Family Living* 17:54–57.

Anderton, D.L., and Emigh, R.J. 1989. Polygynous fertility: Sexual competition versus progeny. *American Journal of Sociology* 94:832–855.

Austin, C.N., and Jones, B.V. 1987. Reentry among missionary children: An overview of reentry research from 1934–1986. *Journal of Psychology and Theology* 15:315–325.

Bahr, H.M. 1970. Aging and religious disaffiliation. *Social Forces* 49:59–71.

———. 1981. Religious intermarriage and divorce in Utah and the Mountain States. *Journal for the Scientific Study of Religion* 20:251–261.

———. 1982. Religious contrasts in family role definitions and performance: Utah Mormons, Catholics, Protestants and others. *Journal for the Scientific Study of Religion* 21:200–217.

Bahr, H.M., and Chadwick, B.A. 1985. Religion and family in Middletown, USA. *Journal of Marriage and the Family* 47:407–414.

Bahr, H.M., and Martin, T.K. 1983. And thy neighbor as thyself: Self-esteem and faith in people as correlates of religiosity and family solidarity among Middletown high school students. *Journal for the Scientific Study of Religion* 22:132–144.

Barlow, B.A. 1971. Mormon endogamy and exogamy in northern Florida. Ph.D. dissertation, Florida State University.

Barnett, L.D. 1962. Research in interreligious dating and marriage. *Marriage and Family Living* 24:191–194.

Barron, M.L. 1950. Research on intermarriage: A survey of accomplishments and prospects. *American Journal of Sociology* 57:249–255.

Barta, R., and O'Reilly, C.T. 1952. Some dating patterns and attitudes toward marriage of 174 Catholic college students. *American Catholic Sociological Review* 13: 240–248.

Bean, F.D., and Aiken, L.H. 1976. Intermarriage and unwanted fertility in the United States. *Journal of Marriage and the Family* 38:61–71.

Bean, L.L., and Afzal, M. 1969. Informal values in a Muslim society: A study of timing of Muslim marriages. *Journal of Marriage and the Family* 31:583–588.

Bean, L.L.; Mineau, G.; and Anderton, D. 1983. Residence and religious effects on declining family size: A historical analysis of the Utah population. *Review of Religious Research* 25:91–101.

Becker, T. 1978. Inter-faith and inter-nationality attitudinal variations among youth toward self, family and the collective. *Review of Religious Research* 20:68–81.

Bell, B.D. 1971. Church participation and the family life cycle. *Review of Religious Research* 13:57–62.

Bell, R.R., and Blumberg, L. 1959. Courtship and intimacy and religious background. *Marriage and Family Living* 21:356–360.

Bell, R.R., and Buerkle, J.V. 1963. Mothers and mother-in-laws as role models in relation to religious background. *Journal of Marriage and the Family* 25:485–486.

Bend, E. 1952. Marriage offers in a Yiddish newspaper, 1935 and 1950. *American Journal of Sociology* 58:60–66.

Besanceney, P.H. 1962. Unbroken Protestant-Catholic marriages among whites in the Detroit area. *American Catholic Sociological Review* 23:3–20.

———. 1965a. On reporting rates of intermarriage. *American Journal of Sociology* 70: 717–721.

———. 1965b. Interfaith marriage of Catholics in the Detroit area. *Sociological Analisis* 26:38–44.

Blair, M.J. 1968. Familism and style of participation in the Christian family movement in Canada. Ph.D. dissertation, University of Notre Dame.

Bock, E.W., and Radelet, M.L. 1988. The marital integration of religious independents: A reevaluation of its significance. *Review of Religious Research* 29:228–241.

Bortnick, D.M. 1975. Patterns of interfaith dating and religious observance among Jewish college students in Florida. Ph.D. dissertation, Florida State University.

Bossard, J., and Letts, H. 1956. Mixed marriages involving Lutherans—a research report. *Marriage and Family Living* 18:308-310.

Bouma, D.H. 1963. Religiously mixed marriages: Denominational consequences in the Christian Reformed church. *Journal of Marriage and the Family* 25:428-432.

Bouvier, L.F. 1972. Catholics and contraception. *Journal of Marriage and the Family* 34:514-522.

———. 1973. The fertility of Rhode Island Catholics. *Sociological Analysis* 34:124-139.

Brackbill, Y., and Howell, E. 1974. Religious differences in family size preferences among American teenagers. *Sociological Analysis* 35:35-44.

Branch, K.J. 1983. Mate selection and social context: Endogamy in midwestern religious congregations. Ph.D. dissertation, University of Nebraska.

Breault, K.D. 1986. Suicide in America: A test of Durkheim's theory of religious and family integration. *American Journal of Sociology* 92:628-656.

Brinkerhoff, M.E., and Mackie, M. 1985. Religion and gender: A comparison of Canadian and American student attitudes. *Journal of Marriage and the Family* 47:415-429.

Brown, J.S. 1950. Social class, intermarriage, and church membership in a Kentucky community. *American Journal of Sociology* 57:232-242.

Browning, P.K. 1987. Mormon marital satisfaction: A perceived congruence of expectations and outcomes and factors related to satisfaction and expectations. Ph.D. dissertation, University of California at Los Angeles.

Brutz, J.L., and Ingoldsby, B.B. 1984. Conflict resolution in Quaker families. *Journal of Marriage and the Family* 46:21-26.

Bulowski, A.F. 1951. The stability of the marriages of Catholic college graduates. *American Catholic Sociological Review* 12:11-16.

Burchinal, L.G. 1957. Marital satisfaction and religious behavior. *American Sociological Review* 22:306-310.

———. 1960. Membership groups and attitudes toward cross-religious dating and marriage. *Marriage and Family Living* 22:248-253.

Burchinal, L.G., and Chancellor, L.E. 1963. Social status, religious affiliation and ages at marriage. *Social Forces* 40:348-350.

Burchinal, L.G., and Kenkel, W. 1962. Comparison of state- and diocese-reported marriage data for Iowa, 1953-57. *American Catholic Sociology Review* 23:21-29.

———. 1966. Religious identification and occupational status of Iowa grooms, 1953-1957. *American Sociological Review* 27:526-532.

Cardwell, J.D. 1969. Religious commitment and premarital sexual permissiveness: A five dimensional analysis. *Sociological Analysis* 30:72-80.

Carey, R.G. 1967. Religion and happiness in marriage. *Review of Religious Research* 8:104-112.

Carrier, B. 1937. *Church Education for Family Life.* New York: Harper and Brothers.

Cavan, R. 1970a. A dating-marriage scale of religious social distance. *Journal for the Scientific Study of Religion* 10:93-100.

———. 1970b. Jewish student attitudes toward interreligious marriage and intra-Jewish marriage. *American Journal of Sociology* 76:1064-1071.

———. 1971. Concepts and terminology in interreligious marriage. *Journal for the Scientific Study of Religion* 10:311-320.

Celestine, S. 1940. Juvenile delinquency and the Catholic home: A study of juvenile court records in Duluth during the years 1934–1939, inclusively. *American Catholic Sociological Review* 1:198–216.

Chambers, P.P., and Chalfant, H.P. 1978. A changing role or the same old handmaidens: Women's role in today's church. *Review of Religious Research* 19: 192–197.

Chancellor, L.E., and Monahan, T.P. 1955. Religious preference and interreligious mixtures in marriages and divorces in Iowa. *American Journal of Sociology* 62: 383–390.

Chartier, M.R., and Goehner, L.A. 1976. A study of the relationship of parent-adolescent communication, self-esteem and God image. *Journal of Psychology and Theology* 4:227–232.

Cherlin, A., and Celebuski, C. 1983. Are Jewish families different? Some evidence from the general social survey. *Journal of Marriage and the Family* 45:903–910.

Christensen, H.T. 1948. Mormon fertility: A survey of student opinion. *American Journal of Sociology* 53:270–275.

Christensen, J.C. 1978. A descriptive study of the religious differences between divorced and non-divorced individuals. Ph.D. dissertation, Brigham Young University.

Christiano, K.J. 1986. Church as a family surrogate: Another look at family ties, anomie, and church involvement. *Journal for the Scientific Study of Religion* 25: 339–354.

Christiansen, H.J., and Barber, K.E. 1967. Interfaith versus intrafaith marriage in Indiana. *Journal of Marriage and the Family* 29:461–469.

Christiansen, J.R. 1963. Contemporary Mormons' attitudes toward polygamous practices. *Journal of Marriage and the Family* 25:167–170.

Christianson, R.A. 1970. The effect of reward and expert power on the distribution of influence on Mormon couples. Ph.D. dissertation, Brigham Young University.

Christina, M. 1942. A study of the Catholic family through three generations. *American Catholic Sociological Review* 3:144–153.

Christopherson, V.A. 1956. An investigation of patriarchal authority in the Mormon family. *Marriage and Family Living* 18:328–333.

Christopherson, V.A., and Walters, J. 1958. Responses of Protestants, Catholics, and Jews concerning marriage and family life. *Sociology and Sociological Review* 43:16–22.

Cizon, F.A. 1954. Interethnic and interreligious marriage patterns in parish x. *American Catholic Sociological Review* 15:244–254.

Clark, C.A.; Worthington, E.L.; and Danser, D.B. 1988. The transition of religious beliefs and practices from parents to first-born adolescent sons. *Journal of Marriage and the Family* 50:463–472.

Clayton, R.R. 1971. Religiosity and PSP: Elaboration of the relationship and debate. *Sociological Analysis* 32:81–92.

Clayton, R.R., and Tolone, W.L. 1973. Religiosity and attitudes toward induced abortion: An elaboration of the relationship. *Sociological Analysis* 34:150–167.

Cohen, J.L. 1977. A comparison of norms and behaviors of childrearing in Jewish and Italian-American mothers. Ph.D. dissertation, Syracuse University.

Coogan, T.F. 1946. Catholic fertility in Florida: Differential fertility among 4,891 Florida Catholic families. Ph.D. dissertation, Catholic University.

Cosper, R. 1975. Attendance at Mass and fertility in Caracas. *Sociological Analysis* 36:43–56.

Cox, C. 1957. A study of the religious practices, values, and attitudes in a selected group of families. Ph.D. dissertation, Cornell University.

Cressman, C.P. 1942. Ministers and marriage interaction. *Social Forces* 20:378–381.

Crockett, H.J.; Babchuk, J.; and Ballweg, J.A. 1969. Change in religious affiliation and family stability. *Journal of Marriage and the Family* 31:464–468.

Croog, S.H., and Teele, J.E. 1967. Religious identity and church attendance of sons of religious intermarriages. *American Sociological Review* 32:93–103.

Curcione, N.C. 1973. Family influence on commitment to the priesthood: A study of altar boys. *Sociological Analysis* 34:205–280.

Curtis, J.H. 1954. Group marginality and adherence to religious doctrine in an American community. Ph.D. dissertation, Stanford University.

Curtis, J.H., and Mahan, M.B. 1956. A pilot study in the prediction of success in Catholic marriages. *Marriage and Family Living* 18:145–150.

Dahl, P.E. 1971. Some factors which differ between married and never-married LDS males and females in relationship to their families of origin. Ph.D. dissertation, Brigham Young University.

D'Antonio, W.V., and Stack, S. 1980. Religion, ideal family size, and abortion: Extending Renzi's hypothesis. *Journal for the Scientific Study of Religion* 19: 397–408.

Datta, L. 1967. Family religious background and early scientific creativity. *American Sociological Review* 32:626–635.

Davis, R.F. 1978. Levels of religious thinking in young children and religious practices of their families. Ph.D. dissertation, University of North Carolina at Greensboro.

Dedham, J. 1959. The relationship between religious attitudes and attitude toward premarital sex relations. *Marriage and Family Living* 21:171–176.

DeHart, W.A. 1941. Fertility of Mormons in Utah and adjacent states. *American Sociological Review* 6:818–829.

Dickinson, G. 1976. Religious practices of adolescents in a southern community, 1964–1974. *Journal for the Scientific Study of Religion* 15:361–363.

Dodrill, C.B. 1974. Personality characteristics of students not identifying with their parents' denominations at entrance into a Christian college. *Journal of Psychology and Theology* 2:216–222.

Dohen, D. 1959. Religious practice and marital patterns in Puerto Rico. *American Catholic Sociological Review* 20:203–218.

Dudley, R.L. 1978. Alienation from religion in adolescents from fundamentalist religious homes. *Journal for the Scientific Study of Religion* 17:389–398.

Dudley, R.L., and Dudley, M.G. 1986. Transmission of religious values from parents to adolescents. *Review of Religious Research* 28:3–15.

Dudley, R.L., and Laurent, C.R. 1988. Alienation from religion in church-related adolescents. *Sociological Analysis* 49:408–420.

Dudley, R.L.; Mutch, P.B.; and Cruise, R.J. 1987. Religious factors and drug use among Seventh-Day Adventist youth in North America. *Journal for the Scientific Study of Religion* 26:218–223.

Dyer, D.T., and Luckey, E.B. 1961. Religious affiliation and selected personality scores as they relate to marital happiness of a Minnesota college sample. *Marriage and Family Living* 23:46–47.

Eckhardt, K.W., and Hendershot, G.E. 1984. Religious preference, religious participation, and sterilization decisions: Findings from the National Survey of Family Growth, Cycle II. *Review of Religious Research* 25:232–246.

Edwards, H. 1968. Black Muslim and Negro Christian family relationships. *Journal of Marriage and the Family* 30:604–611.

Engelman, U.Z. 1935. Intermarriage among Jews in Germany. *Sociology and Social Research* 20:34–39.

Evans, W.I. 1975. The pastor's role in working toward a corrective for the contemporary marital crisis. Ph.D. dissertation, Eastern Baptist Theological Seminary.

Farber, B. 1979. Kinship mapping among Jews in a midwestern city. *Social Forces* 57:1107–1121.

Fichter, J.H. 1962. Religion and socialization among children. *Review of Religous Research* 4:24–33.

Filsinger, E., and Wilson, M.R. 1984. Religiosity, socioeconomic rewards and family development: Predictors of marital adjustment. *Journal of Marriage and the Family* 46:663–670.

Fox, W.S., and Jackson, E.F. 1973. Protestant-Catholic differences in educational achievement and persistence in school. *Journal for the Scientific Study of Religion* 12:65–84.

Frank, B.B. 1975. The American Orthodox Jewish housewife: A generational study in ethnic survival. Ph.D. dissertation, City University of New York.

Freedman, R.; Whelpton, P.K.; and Smit, J.W. 1961. Socioeconomic factors in religious differentials in fertility. *American Sociological Review* 26:608–614.

Gil, V.E. 1988. In thy father's house: Self-report findings of sexually abused daughters from conservative Christian homes. *Journal of Psychology and Theology* 16:144–152.

Glass, J.C. 1972. Premarital sex standards among church youth leaders. *Journal for the Scientific Study of Religion* 11:361–367.

Glenn, N.D. 1982. Interreligious marriage in the United States: Patterns and recent trends. *Journal of Marriage and the Family* 44:555–568.

———. 1984. A note on estimating the strength of influence for religious endogamy. *Journal of Marriage and the Family* 46:725–727.

Gockel, G.L. 1969. Income and religious affiliation: A regression analysis. *American Journal of Sociology* 74:623–647.

Goering, J.M. 1965. The structure and processes of ethnicity: Catholic family size in Providence, Rhode Island. *Sociological Analysis* 26:129–136.

Goldscheider, C. 1965. Nativity, generation and Jewish fertility. *Sociological Analysis* 26:137–147.

———. 1966. Trends in Jewish fertility. *Sociology and Sociological Review* 50:173–186.

Goldscheider, C., and Goldstein, S. 1967. Generational changes in Jewish family structure. *Journal of Marriage and the Family* 29:267–276.

Greeley, A.M. 1969. Religious intermarriage in a denominational society. *American Journal of Sociology* 75:949–957.

Grindstaff, C.F., and Ebanks, L.E. 1975. Protestant and Catholic couples who have chosen vasectomy. *Sociological Analysis* 36:29–55.

Groat, H.T., and Neal, A.G. 1973. Social class and alienation correlates of Protestant fertility. *Journal of Marriage and the Family* 35:83–87.

Groat, H.T.; Neal, A.G.; and Knisely, E.C. 1975. Contraceptive nonconformity among Catholics. *Journal for the Scientific Study of Religion* 14:367–377.

Haerle, R.K. 1969. Church attendance patterns among intermarried Catholics: A panel study. *Sociological Analysis* 30:204–216.

Hampe, G.D. 1971. Interfaith dating: Religion, social class, and premarital sexual attitudes. *Sociological Analysis* 32:97–106.

Harris, R.J., and Mills, E.W. 1985. Religion, values, and attitudes toward abortion. *Journal for the Scientific Study of Religion* 24:137–154.

Hart, S. 1986. Religion and changes in family patterns. *Review of Religious Research* 28:51–70.

Hartley, S.F. 1978. Marital satisfaction among clergy wives. *Review of Religious Research* 19:178–191.

Hartley, S.F., and Taylor, M.G. 1977. Religious beliefs of clergy wives. *Review of Religious Research* 19:63–75.

Hartman, M. 1984. Pronatalistic tendencies and religiosity in Israel. *Sociology and Sociological Research* 70:178–180.

Hartman, M., and Hartman, H. 1983. Sex-role attitudes of Mormons vs. non-Mormons in Utah. *Journal of Marriage and the Family* 45:897–902.

Hassan, R. 1971. Interethnic marriage in Singapore: A sociological analysis. *Sociology and Social Research* 55:305–323.

Hatch, R.C. 1985. Marital adjustment and satisfaction as related to perceptions of religious practices and orientations: An examination of graduate and seminary student couples. Ph.D. dissertation, Kansas State University.

Heaton, T.B. 1984. Religious homogamy and marital satisfaction reconsidered. *Journal of Marriage and the Family* 46:729–733.

———. 1986. How does religion influence fertility? The case of the Mormons. *Journal for the Scientific Study of Religion* 25:248–258.

Heaton, T.B., and Calkins, S. 1983. Family size and contraceptive use among Mormons: 1965–1975. *Review of Religious Research* 25:102–113.

Heaton, T.B., and Goodman, K.L. 1985. Religion and family formation. *Review of Religious Research* 26:343–359.

Heer, D.M. 1962. The trends of interfaith marriages in Canada: 1922–1957. *American Sociological Review* 27:245–250.

Heiss, J. 1961. Interfaith marriage and marital outcome. *Marriage and Family Living* 23:228–233.

Heltsley, M.E., and Broderick, C.B. 1969. Religiosity and premarital sexual permissiveness: Reexamination of Reiss's traditional proposition. *Journal of Marriage and the Family* 31:167–169.

Herron, R.W. 1976. A study of couple congruency in religiosity and its relationship to marital satisfaction. Ph.D. dissertation, University of Minnesota.

Hershenson, D.B. 1967. Family religious background, secondary schooling and value orientation of college students. *Sociological Analysis* 28:93–96.

Hertel, B.; Hendershot, G.; and Grimm, J. 1974. Religion and attitudes about abortion: A study of nurses and social workers. *Journal for the Scientific Study of Religion* 13:23–34.

Hertel, B., and Hughes, M. 1987. Religious affiliation, attendance, and support for "pro-family" issues in the United States. *Social Forces* 65:858–882.

Hibbard, D.L., and Lee, J.P. 1954. Presbyterian ministers and widows in retirement. *Journal of Gerontology* 9:46–56.

Hicks, R.G. 1970. The Presbyterian ethic and the generation gap in the modern urban southern family. Ph.D. dissertation, Louisiana State University.

Hoge, D.R., and Petrillo, G.H. 1978a. Development of religious thinking in adolescence: A test of Goldman's theories. *Journal for the Scientific Study of Religion* 17:139–154.

———. 1978b. Determinants of church participation and attitudes among high school youth. *Journal for the Scientific Study of Religion* 17:359–379.

Hoge, D.R.; Petrillo, G.H.; and Smith, E.I. 1982. Transmission of religious and social values from parents to teen-age children. *Journal of Marriage and the Family* 44: 569–580.

Hollingshead, A.B. 1950. Cultural factors in the selection of marriage mates. *American Sociological Review* 15:619–627.

Homola, M.; Knudsen, D.; and Marshall, H. 1988. Status attainment and religion: A reevaluation. *Review of Religious Research* 29:242–258.

Hong, L.K. 1972. The association of religion and family structure: The case of the Hong Kong family. *Sociological Analysis* 33:50–57.

Hsish, T. 1976. Missionary family behavior, dissonance, and children's career decision. *Journal of Psychology and Theology* 4:221–226.

Hulett, J.E. 1940. Social role and personal security in Mormon polygamy. *American Journal of Sociology* 45:678–688.

———. 1943. The social role of the Mormon polygamist male. *American Sociology Review* 8:279–287.

Hunsberger, B. 1976. Background religious denomination, parental emphasis and religious orientation of university students. *Journal for the Scientific Study of Religion* 15:251–256.

———. 1985. Parent-university student agreement on religious and non-religious issues. *Journal for the Scientific Study of Religion* 24:314–320.

Hunsberger, B., and Brown, L.B. 1984. Religious socialization, apostasy, and impact of family background. *Journal for the Scientific Study of Religion* 23:239–251.

Hunt, C.L. 1967. Catholicism and the birthrate. *Review of Religious Research* 8:67–80.

Hunt, R.A., and King, M.B. 1978. Religiosity and marriage. *Journal for the Scientific Study of Religion* 17:399–406.

Hunter, T.L. 1972. Premarital sexual standards in a religiously conservative college. Ph.D. dissertation, University of Georgia.

Hutchison, I.W., and Hutchison, K.R. 1979. The impact of divorce upon clergy career mobility. *Journal of Marriage and the Family* 41:847–855.

Jarrett, W.H. 1964. Family size and fertility patterns of participants in family-planning clinics. *Sociological Analysis* 25:113–120.

Jelen, T.G. 1984. Respect for life, sexual morality, and opposition to abortion. *Review of Religious Research* 25:220–231.

Johnson, B.L.; Eberley, S.; Duke, J.T.; and Sartain, D.H. 1988. Wives' employment status and marital happiness of religious couples. *Review of Religious Research* 29:259–270.

Johnson, M.A. 1973. Family life and religious commitment. *Review of Religious Research* 14:165–180.

Johnson, N.E., and Burton, L.M. 1987. Religion and reproduction in Philippine society: A new test of the minority group status hypothesis. *Sociological Analysis* 48:217–233.

Jones, A.H. 1943. Sex, educational and religious influences on moral judgements relative to the family. *American Sociological Review* 8:622–624.

Kanin, E.J. 1957. Value conflicts in Catholic-device contraceptive usage. *Social Forces* 35:238–243.

Kaufman, D.R. 1985. Women who return to Orthodox Judaism: A feminist analysis. *Journal of Marriage and the Family* 47:543–551.

Kenkel, W.F.; Himler, J.; and Cole, L. 1965. Religious socialization, present devoutness, and willingness to enter a mixed religious marriage. *Sociological Analysis* 26:30–37.

Kennedy, R.R. 1944. Single or triple melting-pot? Intermarriage trends in New Haven, 1870–1940. *American Sociological Review* 49:331–339.

———. 1952. Single or triple melting-pot? *American Journal of Sociology* 58:56–59.

Kent, R.R. 1987. The religiosity and parent/child socialization connection with adolescent substance abuse. Ph.D. dissertation, Brigham Young University.

Kiernen, D.K., and Munro, B. 1987. Following the leaders: Parents' influence on adolescent religious activity. *Journal for the Scientific Study of Religion* 26: 249–255.

Kiernen, I.R. 1958. Annulments of marriage in the Roman Catholic church: A study in social change. Ph.D. dissertation, New York University.

Koplin, M.D. 1987. Family, religious, and peer influence on adolescent drug-use. Ph.D. dissertation, Brigham Young University.

Korson, J.H. 1969. Student attitudes toward mate selection in a Muslim society: Pakistan. *Journal of Marriage and the Family* 31:153–165.

Kourvetaris, G.S., and Bobratz, B.A. 1976. An empirical test of Gordon's ethclass hypothesis among three ethnoreligious groups. *Sociology and Social Research* 61: 39–53.

Kunz, P.R. 1963. Religious influence on parental discipline and achievement demands. *Journal of Marriage and the Family* 25:224–225.

———. 1964. Mormon and non-Mormon divorce patterns. *Journal of Marriage and the Family* 26:211–213.

Lambrechts, E. 1971. Religiousness, social status and fertility values in a Catholic country. *Journal of Marriage and the Family* 33:561–566.

Landis, J.T. 1949. Marriages of mixed and non-mixed religious faith. *American Sociological Review* 14:401–407.

———. 1960. Religiousness, family relationships, and family values in Protestant, Catholic, and Jewish families. *Marriage and Family Living* 22:341–347.

Larsen, L.E., and Johannis, T.B. 1967. Religious perspective and the authority structure of the family. *Pacific Sociological Review* 10:13–24.

Lee, S.C., and Brattrud, A. 1969. Marriage under a monastic mode of life: A preliminary report on the Hutterite family in South Dakota. *Journal of Marriage and the Family* 29:512–520.

Lee, S.M. 1988. Intermarriage and ethnic relations in Singapore. *Journal of Marriage and the Family* 50:255–265.

Leon, J.J., and Steinhoff, P.G. 1975. Catholics' use of abortion. *Sociological Analysis* 36:125–136.

Lipscomb, W.L. 1947. Status and Structure of the family in idealistic communities: A study of selected utopias, literary, religious and secular. Ph.D. dissertation, University of North Carolina at Chapel Hill.

McCutcheon, A.L. 1988. Denominations and religious intermarriage: Trends among white Americans in the twentieth century. *Review of Religious Research* 29:213–227.
McIntosh, W.A.; Alston, L.T.; and Alston, J.P. 1979. The differential impact of religious preference and church attendance on attitudes toward abortion. *Review of Religious Research* 2:195–213.
McKeon, D.M. 1981. Healthy family functioning as perceived by marriage and family therapists, rabbis, Roman Catholic priests, and Southern Baptist ministers. Ph.D. dissertation, East Texas State University.
McReady, W.C. 1972. Faith of our fathers: A study of the process of religious socialization. Ph.D. dissertation, University of Illinois.
Marcum, J.P. 1981. Explaining fertility differences among U.S. Protestants. *Social Forces* 60:532–543.
———. 1988. Religious affiliation, participation and fertility: A cautionary note. *Journal for the Scientific Study of Religion* 27:621–629.
Marcum, J.P., and Radosh, M. 1981. Religious affiliation, labor force participation and fertility. *Sociological Analysis* 42:353–362.
Marie, L. 1944. Is the Catholic birthrate declining? *American Catholic Sociological Review* 5:177–184.
Marshall, D.G. 1950. The decline in farm family fertility and its relationship to nationality and religious background. *Rural Sociology* 15:42–49.
Matras, J. 1964. Religious observance and family formation in Israel: Some intergenerational changes. *American Journal of Sociology* 69:464–475.
———. 1974. On changing matchmaking, marriage, and fertility in Israel: Some findings, problems, and hypotheses. *American Journal of Sociology* 79:364–388.
Mayer, A.J., and Marx, S. 1957. Social change, religion, and birth rates. *American Journal of Sociology* 62:383–390.
Mayhew, B.H. 1969. Behavioral observability and compliance with religious prescriptions on birth control. *Social Forces* 47:60–70.
Middendopp, C.P.; Brinkman, W.; and Koomen, W. 1970. Determinants of premarital sexual permissiveness: A secondary analysis. *Journal of Marriage and the Family* 32:369–379.
Mogey, J. 1967. Marriage, membership and mobility in church and sect. *Sociological Analysis* 28:205–214.
Mol, H. 1970. Mixed marriages in Australia. *Journal of Marriage and the Family* 32: 293–299.
Monahan, T.P. 1971. The extent of interdenominational marriage in the United States. *Journal for the Scientific Study of Religion* 10:85–92.
———. 1973. Some dimensions of interreligious marriages in Indiana, 1962–1967. *Social Forces* 52:195–204.
Monahan, T.P., and Kephart, W.M. 1954. Divorce and desertion by religious and mixed-religious groups. *American Journal of Sociology* 59:454–465.
Morgan, M.M., and Scanzoni, J. 1987. Religious orientations and women's expected continuity in the labor force. *Journal of Marriage and the Family* 49:367–379.
Mosher, W.D., and Hendershot, G.E. 1984. Religious affiliation and the fertility of married couples. *Journal of Marriage and the Family* 46:671–677.
Mueller, C.W., and Johnson, W. 1975. Socioeconomic status and religious participation. *American Sociological Review* 40:785–800.

Mueller, D.D., and Cooper, P.W. 1986. Religious interest and involvement of young adults: A research note. *Review of Religious Research* 27:245–254.

Mulhearn, J. 1969. Interfaith marriage and adult religious practice. *Sociological Analysis* 30:23–31.

Mulvaney, B.G. 1938. A correlational analysis of the relation between the Catholic composition of a population and its birth rate. Ph.D. dissertation, University of Illinois.

———. 1943. Recent trends in American child-bearing. *American Catholic Sociological Review* 4:41–46.

Nafzinger, J.M. 1972. The development of the twentieth century American Mennonite family as reflected in Mennonite writings. Ph.D. dissertation, New York University.

Nash, D. 1968. A little child shall lead them: A statistical test that children were the source of the American religious revival. *Journal for the Scientific Study of Religion* 8:238–240.

Nash, D., and Berger, P. 1962. The child, the family, and the religious revival in suburbia. *Journal for the Scientific Study of Religion* 2:85–93.

Neal, A.G., and Groat, H.T. 1970. Alienation correlates of Catholic fertility. *American Journal of Sociology* 76:460–473.

Neely, W.C. 1940. Family attitudes of denominational college and university students, 1929 and 1936. *American Sociological Review* 5:225–232.

Nelson, H.M. 1981a. Gender differences in the effects of parental discord on preadolescent religiousness. *Journal for the Scientific Study of Religion* 20:351–360.

———. 1981b. Religious conformity in an age of disbelief: Contextual effects of time, denomination and family processes upon church decline and apostasy. *American Sociological Review* 46:632–640.

Nelson, H.M., and Everett, R.F. 1976. Impact of church size on clergy role and career. *Review of Religious Research* 18:62–69.

Neuman, S., and Ziderman, A. 1986. How does fertility relate to religiosity: Survey evidence from Israel. *Sociology and Social Research* 70:178–180.

Patterson, J.E. 1981. Church control and family structure in a Moravian community of North Carolina: 1953–1957. Ph.D. dissertation, University of North Carolina.

Perkins, H.W. 1985. Religious traditions, parents, and peers as determinants of alcohol and drug use among college students. *Review of Religious Research* 27:15–31.

———. 1987. Parental religion and alcohol use problems as intergenerational predictors of problem drinking among college youth. *Journal for the Scientific Study of Religion* 26:340–357.

Plutzer, E. 1988. Work life, family life, and women's support of feminism. *American Sociological Review* 53:640–649.

Potvin, R.H., and Burch, T.K. 1968. Fertility, ideal family size, and religious orientation among U.S. Catholics. *Sociological Analysis* 29:28–34.

Potvin, R.H., and Lee, C.F. 1974. Catholic college women and family size preferences: A reanalysis. *Sociological Analysis* 35:24–34.

Potvin, R.H., and Sloane, D.M. 1985. Parental control, age, and religious practice. *Review of Religious Research* 27:3–14.

Potvin, R.H., and Westoff, C.F. 1967. Higher education and the family normative beliefs of Catholic women. *Sociological Analysis* 28:14–21.

Potvin, R.H.; Westoff, C.F.; and Ryder, N.R. 1967. Factors affecting Catholic wives' conformity to their church magisterium's position on birth control. *Journal of Marriage and the Family* 29:500–520.

Prince, A.J. 1966. Attitudes of a sample of Catholic students attending a Catholic university toward interfaith marriage. Ph.D. dissertation, Washington State University.

Rampey, T.S. 1983. Religiosity, purpose in life, and other factors related to family success: A national study. Ph.D. dissertation, University of Nebraska.

Reed, R.C. 1954. Catholic refugee families in St. Louis, 1948–1954. *American Catholic Sociological Review* 15:323–331.

Reiber, S.R. 1965. Perception of parents and children of Presbyterian related families as to the content of desirable religious behavior. Ph.D. dissertation, Florida State University.

Renzi, M. 1975. Ideal family size as an intervening variable between religion and attitudes toward abortion. *Journal for the Scientific Study of Religion* 14:23–27.

Resnick, R.B. 1933. Some sociological aspects of intermarriage of Jew and non-Jew. *Social Forces* 12:96–102.

Rhodes, A.L., and Nam, C.B. 1970. The religious context of educational expectations. *American Sociological Review* 35:253–267.

Ritchie, W.S. 1970. The relation of parental behavior to adolescent church participation. Ph.D. dissertation, University of Southern California.

Robinson, G.K. 1936. The Catholic birth rate: Further facts and implications. *American Journal of Sociology* 41:345–351.

Rosenthal, E. 1970. Divorce and religious intermarriage: The effect of previous marital status upon subsequent marital behavior. *Journal of Marriage and the Family* 32: 435–441.

Rout, W.C. 1979. Socioeconomic differentials among white socioreligious groups in the United States. *Social Forces* 58:280–289.

Ruppel H.J. 1969. Religiosity and premarital sexual permissiveness: A methodological note. *Sociological Analysis* 30:176–188.

———. 1970. Religiosity and premarital sexual permissiveness: A response to the Reiss-Heltsley and Broderick debate. *Journal of Marriage and the Family* 32:647–655.

Sabagh, G., and Lopez, D. 1980. Religiosity and fertility: The case of Chicanas. *Social Forces* 59:431–439.

Sakran, G.F. 1971. A comparative study of marriage and family perceptions and attitudes of professional students in law, medicine, ministry and social work. Ph.D. dissertation, University of North Carolina.

Salisbury, S. 1969. Religious identification, mixed marriage and conversion. *Journal for the Scientific Study of Religion* 8:125–129.

Salisbury, W.S. 1971. Religious identity and religious behavior of the sons and daughters of religious intermarriage. *Review of Religious Research* 12:128–140.

Samenfink, J.A. 1958. A study of some aspects of marital behavior as related to religious control. *Marriage and Family Living* 20:163–169.

Scanzoni, J. 1965. Resolution of occupational-conjugal role conflict in clergy marriage. *Journal of Marriage and the Family* 27:396–402.

Schnepp, G.J., and Johnson, M.M. 1952. Do religious background factors have predictive value? *Marriage and Family Living* 14:301–304.

Schnepp, G.J., and Roberts, L.A. 1952. Residential propinquity and mate selection on a parish basis. *American Journal of Sociology* 58:45–50.

Schulz, B.; Bohrnstedt, G.; Borgatta, E.; and Evans, R. 1977. Explaining premarital sexual intercourse among college students: A causal model. *Social Forces* 56: 148–165.

Schumm, W.R.; Bollman, S.R.; and Jurich, A.P. 1982. The marital conventionalization argument: Implications for the study of religiosity and marital satisfaction. *Journal for the Scientific Study of Religion* 10:236–241.

Selfors, S.A.; Keik, R.K.; and King, E. 1962. Values in mate selection: Education versus religion. *Marriage and Family Living* 24:399–401.

Slotkin, J.S. 1942. Jewish-Gentile intermarriage in Chicago. *American Sociological Review* 7:34–39.

Smith, H.W. 1972. Urbanization, secularization, and the roles of the professional's wife. *Review of Religious Research* 2:134–147.

Smith, T.R. 1976. The pastor-husband and wife: Correlates of theological perspectives, marital adjustment, job satisfaction, and wife's participation in church activities. Ph.D. dissertation, Florida State University.

Snider, A.G. 1971. A study of the relationships between religious affiliation, religious practices, and marital adjustment. Ph.D. dissertation, University of Southern California.

Somogyi, S. 1941. Differential divorce rates by religious groups. *American Journal of Sociology* 46:665–685.

Spaeth, J.L. 1968. Religion, fertility, and college type among college graduates. *Sociological Analysis* 29:155–159.

Stack, S. 1985. The effect of domestic/religious individualism on suicide, 1954–1978. *Journal of Marriage and the Family* 47:431–447.

Stokes, C.S. 1972. Religious differentials in reproductive behavior: A replication and extension. *Sociological Analysis* 33:26–33.

Stouffer, S.A. 1935. Trends in the fertility of Catholics and non-Catholics. *American Journal of Sociology* 41:512–518.

Studer, M., and Thornton, A. 1987. Adolescent religiosity and contraceptive usage. *Journal of Marriage and the Family* 49:117–128.

Sturges, H.A. 1937. Methods of comparing orthodoxy and piety. *American Sociological Review* 2:372–378.

Stycos, J.M. 1967. Contraception and Catholicism in Latin America. *Journal of Social Issues* 23:115–133.

Tanner, W.C. 1975. Participation in family-related activities and family affectional relationships as perceived by adolescent members of the Church of Jesus Christ of Latter-Day Saints. Ph.D. dissertation, Florida State University.

Thomas, J.L. 1951a. Religious training in the Roman Catholic family. *American Journal of Sociology* 57:178–183.

———. 1951b. The factor of religion in the selection of marriage mates. *American Sociological Review* 16:487–491.

Thomas, J.T. 1949. The urban impact on the American Catholic family. *American Catholic Sociological Review* 10:258–267.

Thornton, A. 1978. Marital instability differentials and interactions: Insights from multivariate contingency table analysis. *Sociology and Social Research* 62:572–595.

Thornton, A. 1979. Religion and fertility: The case of Mormonism. *Journal of Marriage and the Family* 41:131–142.

Toney, M.B.; Golesorkhi, B.; and Stinner, W.F. 1985. Residence exposure and fertility expectations of young Mormon and Non-Mormon women in Utah. *Journal of Marriage and the Family* 47:459–465.

Vernon, G.M. 1968. Marital characteristics of religious independents. *Review of Religious Research* 9:163–170.

Wade, A.L., and Berreman, J.V. 1950. Are ministers qualified for marriage counseling? *Sociology and Sociological Review* 35:106–112.

Wallin, P. 1957. Religiosity, sexual gratification, and marital satisfaction. *American Sociological Review* 22:300–305.

Wallin, P., and Clark, A. 1964. Religiosity, sexual gratification, and marital satisfaction in middle years of marriage. *Social Forces* 42:303–309.

Warner, M.D. 1981. Comparisons of a religious marriage enrichment program with an established communication training enrichment program. Ph.D. dissertation, Purdue University.

Weigert, A.J. 1968. Parent-child interaction patterns and adolescent religiosity: A cross-national analysis. Ph.D. dissertation, University of Minnesota.

Weigert, A.J., and Thomas, D.L. 1970. Secularization: Cross-national study of Catholic male adolescents. *Social Forces* 49:29–36.

———. 1972. Parental support, control, and adolescent religiosity: An extension of previous research. *Journal for the Scientific Study of Religion* 11:389–393.

———. 1974. Secularization and religiosity: A cross-national study of Catholic adolescents in five societies. *Sociological Analysis* 35:1–23.

Westfoff, C.F., and Potvin, R.H. 1966. Higher education, religion, and women's family-size orientations. *American Sociological Review* 31:489–495.

Wicks, J.W., and Workman, R.L. 1978. Sex-role attitudes and the anticipated timing of the initial stages of family formation among Catholic university students. *Journal of Marriage and the Family* 40:505–516.

Wickstrom, D.L., and Fleck, F.R. 1983. Missionary children: Correlates of self-esteem and dependency. *Journal of Psychology and Theology* 11:226–235.

Wilkinson, M.L., and Tanner, W.C. 1980. The influence of family size, interaction, and religiosity on family affection in a Mormon sample. *Journal of Marriage and the Family* 42:297–304

Williams, D. 1983. Religion, beliefs about human life and the abortion decision. *Review of Religious Research* 24:40–48.

Williams, J.L. 1972. An analysis of the similarities and disparities of religiosity between college students and their parents as related to family solidarity. Ph.D. dissertation, Louisiana State University.

Willits, F.K.; Bealer, R.C.; and Bender, G.W. 1963. Interreligious marriage among Pennsylvania rural youth. *Journal of Marriage and the Family* 25:433–438.

Wilson, J.; Simpson, I.H.; and Jackson, D.K. 1987. Church activism among farm couples: Measuring the impact of the conjugal unit. *Journal of Marriage and the Family* 49:875–882.

Winer, M.L. 1977. The demography, causes, and consequences of Jewish intermarriage. Ph.D. dissertation, Yale University.

Woodroof, J.T. 1984. Religiosity and reference groups: Toward a model of adolescent sexuality. Ph.D. dissertation, University of Nebraska.

———. 1985. Premarital sexual behavior and religious adolescents. *Journal for the Scientific Study of Religion* 24:343–366.

———. 1986. Reference groups, religiosity and premarital sexual behavior. *Journal for the Scientific Study of Religion* 25:436–460.

Unobtainable Dissertations and Additional Articles

Every effort has been made in this chapter to investigate doctoral dissertations with specific application to the study of religion and family. Readily available dissertations were reviewed and included in this chapter. However, because of interlibrary loan requirements and restrictions, copying costs, and, at times, the complete unavailability of cited material, a number of relevant dissertations are not reviewed in this chapter. Following is a list of doctoral dissertations that may have useful application to those interested in the history of religion-family research concerns.

The various indexes I used also list research material that is unavailable, many for the same reasons as for dissertations. References other than doctoral dissertations that have not been abstracted in this chapter yet were identified in the searching process are also listed.

Dissertations

Abdal-ati, H. 1970. The family structure in Islam. Princeton University.

Altman, L. 1935. The development and present status of the Jewish family. New York University.

Barber, K.E. 1969. An analysis of intrafaith and interfaith marriages in Indiana. Purdue University.

Bates, H.L. 1978. A church program for strengthening marriages: A critical analysis of a marriage encounter week-end. Louisville Presbyterian Theological Seminary.

Beck, R.W. 1986. The subjective well-being of widowed men and women: The influence of social support, social integration, and religion. University of Florida.

Besanceney, P.H. 1963. Factors associated with Protestant Catholic marriages in the Detroit area: A problem of social control. Michigan State University.

Byrne, A.M. 1961. An evaluation of a Catholic family life survey. St. Louis University.

Chambers, V.J. 1986. A test of the effect of parental religious socialization on second generation adult offspring. Brigham Young University.

Cressman, C.P. 1951. A study of the marriage counseling practices of selected Protestant pastors in the period between June, 1946 and June, 1949. University of Pennsylvania.

Currie, C. 1946. The association of marital adjustment with marital education, religious activities, and other factors. Ohio State University.

DeBlanc, I.A. 1974. A study of the father-role concept as found in a selected group of Catholic fathers and mothers. Catholic University.

Donovan, J.J. 1938. The pastors' obligation in the prenuptial investigation. Catholic University.

Dortzbach, E.M. 1975. The role of clergy in the life of the aged. University of Colorado.
Dunn, H.E. 1956. The self-ideal of selected married Catholics. Catholic University.
Endedrook, D.N. 1956. The parental obligation to care for the religious education of children within the home with special attention to the training of the preschool child. Catholic University.
Engel, U.Z. 1953. Jewish population trends since the Industrial Revolution. University of Buffalo.
Enns, R. 1979. Establishing a new tradition: Protestantism and family modernization in Japan. University of California at Santa Barbara.
Farthing, E.D. 1984. A course of study in marriage enrichment for couples in a local church. Drew University.
Flinchbaugh, J.E. 1951. The role of the pastor with preschool children. University of Boston.
Garcia-Marenko, E. 1978. Selected variables related to and content dimensions of the family concept of Seventh-day Adventist parents in Costa Rica. Andrews University.
Goad, R.L. 1987. The effect of a Christian family course on marital readiness. Oklahome State University.
Goldman, H.S. 1977. Role clarification in the Jewish two-career family. Crozer Theological Seminary.
Greene, J.T. 1956. The role of religiosity in marital success. University of North Carolina.
Haspel, E.C. 1971. Sociocultural factors in the development of guilt: Jewish parents and children in Chicago. University of Chicago.
Hawkins, J.E. 1988. A plan for aiding Christian leaders in identifying dysfunctional marriage and strategies for intervention and prevention. Fuller Theological Seminary.
Heer, D.M. 1958. The role of the working wife in Catholic families. Harvard University.
Heltsley, M.E. 1966. Religiosity and premarital sexual permissiveness. Pennsylvania State University.
Hey, R.M. 1963. Dissimilarity of religious background of marital partners as a factor in Marital conflict. Columbia University Teachers College.
Hicks, R.G. 1969. The Protestant ethic and the generation gap in the modern southern family. Louisiana State University.
Howington, N.P. 1948. The historic attitude of the Christian churches concerning marriage, divorce, and remarriage. Southern Baptist University.
Hulett, J.E. 1939. The sociological and social psychological aspects of the Mormon polygamous family. University of Wisconsin.
Irving, G.J. 1959. Some factors and characteristics of marriage separations in five Midwest dioceses. University of Notre Dame.
Jacobson, P.E. 1963. The dynamics of interfaith marriages. University of Minnesota.
Jacoby, G.P. 1941. Child-care in the 19th century: With a correlated summary of public and Protestant child welfare. Catholic University.
Jensen, G.O. 1974. Antecedents and consequences of non-Marriage in a selected Mormon population. Utah State University.
Johnson, R.A. 1979. Religious assortative marriage in the United States. University of Michigan.

Kleis, C.M. 1979. The God-person covenant and husband-wife role expectations. Eastern Baptist Theological Seminary.

Langlois, L.K. 1984. Mormons and the family. University of Southern California.

Larson, H.R. 1954. Familism in Mormon social structure. University of Utah.

Lenski, G.E. 1936. Marriage in the Lutheran church: A historical study. American University.

McAuliffe, M.F. 1954. Catholic moral teaching on the nature and object of conjugal love. Catholic University.

Mahan, M.B. 1955. Selected factors in the prediction of success in Catholic marriages. University of St. Louis.

Manjos, T.D.M. 1965. An investigation of the relationship between acceptance of disability and religious involvement of adults with cerebral palsy. New York University.

Matthews, V.D. 1962. A study on the nature and frequency of marital problems and their relationship to certain sociological factors in Catholic marriages. St. Louis University.

Mernissi, F. 1974. The effects of modernization of the male-female dynamics in a Muslim society: Morocco. Brandeis University.

Nelson, L. 1930. The Mormon village. A study in social origins. Brigham Young University.

Olson, L.J. 1985. Family life education in Bible colleges: Curriculum survey and program models. Kansas State University.

Onwurah, P.E.C. 1982. Marriage: Christian and traditional: A social and theological study of the interaction of ethical values in the Igbo society of Nigeria. Columbia University.

Peterson, J.A. 1951. An inquiry into the relation of objective and subjective religious factors to adjustment and maladjustment in marriage. University of Southern California.

Pierce, A. 1950. Fertility differentials among confessional groups. Harvard University.

Powell, M.L. 1984. Evaluation of a church-based sexuality program for adolescents. Texas Technical University.

Pratto, D.J. 1971. Socialization outcomes: A study of intergenerational agreement and disagreement in Catholic-American families. University of Colorado.

Quisenberry, L.T. 1978. Demographic variables related to response differences of Catholic students on specified moral values. University of Houston.

Rajah, M.S. 1987. The Mauritain Muslim family in transition: Structural and ideological changes: A cultural diffusion approach. University of California at San Diego.

Raschke, V.J. 1972. Religiosity and sexual permissiveness. University of Minnesota.

Reilly, E.W. Psychosocial aspects of Catholic faith life. St. Louis University.

Ruark, K.L. 1977. Clergy divorce and subsequent career mobility. Florida State University.

Shea, G.A. 1975. The parish priest and family planning: Focus on the United States, 1969. Brown University.

Smith, J.P. 1978. A program of premarital preparation in the local church: Design, implementation, and evaluation of a skill model. Louisville Presbyterian Theological Seminary.

Stiles, J. 1942. The marriage reform movement in the United States. Southern Baptist University.

Szekely, H. 1975. Perceptual accuracy in issues related to marriage, parenthood, and religion among engaged couples planning a Catholic wedding. University of Southern California.

Taylor, K.W. 1978. Church and family. Hartford Seminary Foundation.

Thomas, J.L. 1949. Factors involved in the breakdown of Catholic marriage. University of Chicago.

Thompson, V.L. 1979. Family communication seminar: A seven session, group-learning process to assist church-related families in developing and practicing communication skills. Lancaster Theological Seminary.

Towne, R. 1959. Early adjustment of two and three-year-old children in church nurseries under different induction procedures. Oregon State University.

Troutner, E.J. 1961. Optimal factors in marital decision-making with 140 Methodist ministers and their wives. Boston University.

Tubbs, A.L. A critical analysis of marriages between Roman Catholics and Protestants. Columbia University Teachers College.

West, R. 1934. The Mormon village family: A study of 400 Mormon families in Utah. University of Wisconsin.

Wieting, S.G. 1971. Family factors and the religious belief systems of adolescents. University of Minnesota.

Other Publications

Diel, A.E. 1954. "Dutch Reformed and neo-Calvinist women and future family size." *Sociological Bulletin* 8:42–53.

Free, R. 1950. "Fertility and religion." *Milbank Memorial Fund Quarterly* 28:294–343.

Gustafson, J. 1957. "Protestant sociology of the family." *Religious Education* 52:89–93.

Harris, L. 1950. "African marriage survey." *International Review of Missions* 39:94–99.

Karer, L. 1950. "Attitudes on religion, sex, and love." *American Psychologist* 5:468.

Pattison, E.M. (ed.). 1969. "Clinical psychiatry and religion." *International Psychiatry Clinics* 5, no. 4.

Thomas, J.L. 1952. "Marriage breakdown in Catholic cases." *Social Order* 4:445–457.

———. 1954. "The Catholic family in a complex society." *Social Order* 5:162–168.

———. 1955. "The Catholic family in a complex society: Fundamental requisites." *Social Order* 5:162–168.

———. 1956. *The American Catholic Family.* New York: Prentice-Hall.

7
Family Stress and Coping

I-Chiao Huang

Research on family stress and coping has examined how various life events and hardships affect families. The most frequently studied life events are chronic illness, drug abuse, sudden divorce, death, disaster, war, unemployment, parenthood, captivity, and rape. Stressor events, transitions, and related hardships produce tension, which calls for management (Antonovsky, 1979). When tension is not overcome, stress emerges. Family stress (as distinct from stressor) is defined as a state that arises from an actual or perceived imbalance between a stressor (e.g., challenge, threat) and capability (e.g., resources, coping) in the family's functioning.

This chapter provides a comprehensive review of family stress and coping research conducted between 1930 and 1990.[1] The research reports discussed are those that identify the hardships experienced by families that undergo stress, such as parenthood, a chronically ill child, unemployment, war, rape, and delinquency; examine the effect of family resources, perception, and coping in this crisis; and assess the successful or unsuccessful coping behaviors of individuals and families.

The reviews are organized by decade. The purpose of the research, theoretical orientations, sample size, sampling procedure, and other methodological issues relevant to research are reported if they were noted in the publication. Unless their findings appear particularly noteworthy, studies with unspecified sample sizes or fewer than twenty-five cases are not reviewed in the text. These studies are listed in the summary tables, however.

The Decade 1930–1939

The most significant event during the 1930s was the Great Depression. The growing unemployment and the increasing need of family relief stimulated research on the effect of the depression on the individual and the family.

Research Findings

Angell (1936) studied the histories of fifty families before and during the depression to determine the effect of the depression on family life. Integrated and adaptable families remained so during unemployment, and previously disorganized families became more disorganized. The loss of the provider role for men was a key influence in those families where the husband lost his authority in relation to his wife and adolescent children. His sense of failure was intensified when wives and adolescents took jobs or when family members held rigidly traditional sex role norms.

Cavan and Ranck (1938) interviewed 100 white families to determine ways in which families and individual members adjusted or failed to adjust to the depression. They reported three major findings: well-organized families met the depression with less catastrophic consequences than families that were disorganized prior to unemployment; families and their members tended to react to the depression in much the same way they had reacted to previously encountered crisis; and a period of unadjustment and disorganization typically was manifest in the early stages of the depression and was characterized by emotional strain. It generally was succeeded by a period of recovery or even more serious maladjustment. Attempts by families to adjust were similar, but the final outcomes in terms of organization or disorganization of family life were different. Well-organized families, though greatly affected by the depression, continued to be organized; unorganized families became more disorganized. Adjustment appeared to be influenced as much by prior family organization as by the degree of external pressure exerted by the depression.

Besides Angell's and Cavan and Ranck's studies, seven other research articles were found dealing with family stress and coping during the 1930s (Waller, 1933; Mack, 1935; Lenroot, 1935; Kirkpatrick, 1934; Zawadzki and Lazarsfeld, 1935; Conard, 1936; Young, 1933). All examined the effect of the depression on either individual or family depression.

Waller (1933) conducted case studies of 162 families that had applied to the Associated Charities between October 1, 1929, and April 1, 1930. Most of the families had made earnest and varied efforts to meet their situations themselves before applying to the relief agency. Two important effects of unemployment on the individual and the family were that the father or the family was no longer the breadwinner, and there was a rapid deterioration in morale following loss of work and income.

Mack (1935) studied sixty-one families helped by the Unemployment Relief Service. The material was presented in a series of case stories, grouped together according to type of problems experienced. The sixty-one families appeard to benefit from the work assignments and help in the maintenance of morale. When the program came to an end, the hardship increased for many of the families, and they were forced to reapply for assistance. Also, it was found that difficulties arising from alcoholism, domestic incompatibility, emotional dependence, and other family problems that did not arise out of unemployment were not materially affected by employment in the program.

Lenroot (1935) attempted to present a picture of some of the families on relief or on the borderline of destitution, to illuminate popular understanding of the social consequences of the economic cataclysm, and to indicate the points of greatest stress, where the social and health agencies of the community should reinforce the efforts of individual families and the general relief program. This was descriptive research with case examples. A total of 259 families—197 white and 62 black—were studied.

Lenroot's study found, first, that 80 percent of the families had suffered a reduction in income, and 50 percent were living on half or less than half the amount they formerly earned. Most families suffered severe financial losses. Second, 41 percent had never been on relief at any other time; 47 percent had relief during the period of the depression only; 10 percent were chronic relief cases, who had been on the relief rolls continuously or intermittently since before 1930. Third, larger proportion of the black than of the white families were on relief. Finally, many boys and girls of working age were unemployed and out of school or, if attending school, lacked needed clothing and schoolbooks.

In an effort to learn something of the functioning of farm families confronted by emergencies, Kirkpatrick (1934) conducted a longitudinal study of 143 Wisconsin families. Sharp decreases in income, due mainly to reduction in receipts, necessitated marked adjustments in their consumption habits and their participation in certain activities.

Zawadzki and Lazarsfeld (1935) examined how the unemployed perceived their own lot. The Institute for Social Economy in Warsaw held a contest for autobiographies of the unemployed. Of the 774 biographies received, 57 biographies of Polish unemployed (51 men and 6 women) were selected and analyzed in this study. The researchers found that all of the unemployed had reached a stage of extreme distress. The mental distress of the unemployed was produced not only by physical sufferings. Many people lost their sense of human dignity and suffered intensely.

Conard (1936) interviewed sixty-six families in Grinnell, Iowa, about how the depression had affected them. These families, each with one or more children of school age, had received relief at some time during the year but were not relief cases before the depression. Conard found a reduction in the quantity and quality of the food they ate. Other findings were that the depression led to the development of new skills in working-class families and that the loss of the car contributed to the breakdown of morale of the family, and particularly, to the discouragement and loneliness of the mother. Most important, it was found that the effect of the depression was quite different for different families. It resulted in increased family conflict in some families and; strengthened the family bonds and stimulated greater cooperation in others.

The Decade in Review

Theory and Methdology. Only Angell (1936) and Cavan and Ranck (1938) attempted to test a theory. Most of the other research was mainly descriptive or exploratory (see table 7–1).

Table 7–1
Overview of Research on Family Stress and Coping, 1930–1939

Year	*Author*	*Topic*	*Theory*	*Method*[a]	*Sample*	*Strengths*[b]
1933	Young	Depression/unemployment	None	Case studies	N.A.	
1933	Waller	Unemployment/stress	None	Interview-P	162	
1934	Kirkpatrick	Depression/farm	None	Interview-P	143	
1935	Zawadzki and Lazarsfeld	Unemployment/coping	None	Content analysis	57	
1935	Lenroot	Depression/stress	None	Interview-P	259	
1935	Mack	Depression/family	None	Interview-P	61	
1936	Angell	Depression/family	Mini	Case studies	50	St,T,I
1936	Conard	Depression/family	None	Interview-P	66	
1938	Cavan and Ranck	Depression/adjustment	Mini	Interview-P	100	T,I

[a]P = primary data.
[b]S = sample; M = measurement of variables; St = statistical analysis; T = theory; I = Important.

Key Studies and General Findings. During the Great Depression unemployed husbands were most likely to lose authority based on economic need or fear and least likely to lose authority based on love and respect. Integrated and adaptable families remained so during unemployment, and previously disorganized families became more disorganized. Of the research conducted during the 1930s, two were cited most frequently: Angell's *The Family Encounters the Depression* and Cavan and Ranck's *The Family and the Depression.*

The Decade 1940–1949

During the 1940s, attention shifted from the depression to the consequences of war and the adaptation of individuals and families to it. Of the twenty-eight articles found, only six of them were research articles, five dealt with the effect of war and one with unemployment.

Research Findings

Komarovsky (1940) conducted case studies of fifty-eight families to study how unemployment influences family authority. The following were some of the major findings: (1) Unemployment tended to lower the status of the husband. (2) Unemployment intensified the predepression parent-child relations rather than changed their quality. (3) The increased concern with the children on the part of the father brought about improvement in father-child relations only when such relations were satisfactory prior to unemployment. (4) The unemployed father fared less well with adolescent children than those under 12. (5) Unemployment rudely shattered the man's feeling of economic and social security. (6) For the unemployed man and his wife, social life outside the family, both formal club affiliations and informal social life, dimished greatly.

Hoffer (1945) surveyed 275 farm families to determine the impact of war on them. He found that war conditions did not disturb farm family life except when members of a family engaged in military service. The demands of war on the family strengthened rather than disrupted its internal relationships and its contacts with the local neighborhood and community.

Igel (1945) studied the effect of war-caused separations using ninety cases from the Bureau of Child Welfare and the City of New York, an agency engaged in providing for children who needed care away from their own homes. She found that war separation represented a real test of family and individual strength, and people reacted according to their own life experience. The war, like any other crisis, precipitated breakdown for many families that might have functioned adequately without this additional strain or tension.

Levy (1945) observed fifty families and concluded that war had both stabilizing and demoralizing influences on the individuals and the families. Among the stabilizing influences, family members were drawn together more closely, maternal feelings were strengthened, and fathers and sons showed increased interest and responsibility in their homes. In some cases the adjustments made to the privation served as a strengthened influence in family life. Numerous beneficial effects were seen as a result of participation in voluntary activities and industrial and military service. Emotional tension was reduced in certain families by the induction of male members into military service or by outside employment of mothers or fathers. As an indirect result of the war, jobs became available to many previously unemployed because of their age (too young or too old), personality difficulties, or physical handicaps.

On the other hand, the same type of privation that helped strengthened family ties in some instances weakened them in others. Increased incomes had deteriorative effects in certain families. The absent or derelict mother was the most frequent cause for the demoralization in these families. Among adolescents, high wages often resulted in hitherto unheard-of wealth. This weakened parental influence and precipitated unstable and delinquent behavior of the adolescents. The strain resulting from absence or change in the role of any member of the family group required various shifts in the adjustment of others.

Koos (1946) studied sixty-two low-income families for three years and found evidence of permanent demoralization—a blunting of the family's sensitivity and a tendency to be more vulnerable to future stresses. Koos argued that once families had been defeated by a crisis, they were not able to marshal their forces sufficiently to face the next crisis. Five periods during the process of adjustment to a crisis were identified: (1) the precrisis family situation; (2) the anticipatory reactions to crisis; (3) the immediate reaction to the departure of the husband and father; (4) the long-run reaction and readjustment process, with the wife taking over or failing to take over her responsibilities; and (5) the final readjustment of the family to the husband's absence, with a new role structure.

Hill (1949) interviewed 135 Iowa families with a father in the service to examine family adjustment to the crises of war-born separation and reunion. They discovered that crisis proneness—the tendency to define hardships as crises—was disproportionately found among families of low family adequacy, and it may run in families. There were many types of successful adjustment patterns to crisis, but for most families, the course of adjustment to separation followed a roller-coaster path of disorganization, recovery, and readjustment. Social time, not chronological time, determined the importance a particular event or experience had on family adjustment behavior, particularly among the child-rearing families. Previous history with crisis proved to be the best prediction of family behavior in new crisis. Many different types of hierarchical control succeed in the face of crisis; all shared the consultative process in decision making. The dynamics of family adjustment and recovery in the crises of impoverishment, bereavement, divorce, and other critical troubles found in other research (Angell, 1936; Cavan, 1938; Koos, 1946) were found to apply to the war-born crisis situations of separation and reunion.

The Decade in Review

Theory and Methodology. Most studies conducted during the 1940s were not theoretically oriented. Other than those of Koos (1946) and Hill (1949), none had a clearly defined theoretical orientation. Interviews and case studies were the primary methods of research conducted in this decade. Research findings were reported without mentioning the statistical methods employed.

Key Studies and General Findings. During the 1940s, research focused primarily on the effect of war on the individual and family (table 7–2). In general, the dynamics of family adjustment to war crises were similar to those from the crises of impoverishment, bereavement, divorce, and other stressors.

Among the research conducted in the 1940s, Hill's (1949) study of family adjustment to the crises of war separation and reunion had the most influence on the later research. The ABCX family crisis model was developed. In ABCX model, *A*, which represents the stressor event, interacts with *B*, which represents the family's crisis-meeting resources, and interacts with *C*, which represents the definition the family makes of the event, to produce *X*, the crisis. Hill's ABCX model focused primarily on precrisis variables that account for differences in family ability to cope with the impact of a stressor event and the degree to which the outcome is a crisis for the family. His family crisis model outlined a set of major variables and their relationships that have remained virtually unchanged for over thirty years.

The Decade 1950–1959

In the 1950s, the total number of entries related to family stress and coping was forty-four, of which only ten were research. The topics treated between 1930 and 1949, depression and war, were ignored as researchers turned to studies of reactions to illness, disaster, alcoholism, and parenthood.

Research Findings

Physical or Mental Illness of a Family Member. When confronted with a physically or mentally ill family member, some families appear to grow stronger and thrive. Others grow weaker with repeated crises, which can lead to dissolution of the family group. In the 1950s, two journal articles and three dissertations were found that studied the effect of chronic illness on the family and its members.

Yarrow, Schwartz, and Murphy (1955) examined the cognitive and emotional problems encountered by thirty-three wives in coping with the mental illness of their husbands. The major focus was on factors that lead to the reorga-

Table 7–2
Overview of Research on Family Stress and Coping, 1940–1949

Year	*Author*	*Topic*	*Theory*	*Method*[a]	*Sample*	*Strengths*[b]
1940	Komarovsky	Unemployment	None	Case studies	58	
1945	Igel	War/father/son	None	Case study	90	
1945	Hoffer	War/family	None	Interview-P	275	
1945	Levy	War/family	None	Case studies	50	
1946	Koos	Poverty	Mini	Case studies	62	T
1949	Hill	War/separation	Mini	Interview-P	135	M,St,T,I

[a] P = primary data.
[b] S = sample; M = measurement of variables; St = statistical analysis; T = theory; I = Important.

nization of the wife's perceptions of her husband from a well to a mentally ill man. The factors that influence her perceptions were the kind and intensity of the symptoms, their persistence over time, the husband's interpretation of his problems, and interpretations and defining actions of others, including professionals. Social pressure and expectations kept not only behavior in line but, to a great extent, perceptions of behavior as well.

Using interviews and observations, Kramm (1958) studied reactions and adjustments of fifty families that had a Down's syndrome child. The child's birth became a major point of reference in the lives of all members of the family. Families demonstrated outstanding capacity to adjust and adapt themselves to the prolonged infancy of the child. Reactions of parents to the diagnosis of Down's syndrome included short-term violent reactions followed by continuing adjustments and prolonged secondary reactions followed by growing awareness and continuing adjustments.

Parents commented on the negative attitude of the doctor who first diagnosed and interpreted the child's condition to them. "Acceptance" of the child emerged as a process that varied in intensity from family to family and took place over a period of time. About half of the families placed their child on a waiting list for custodial care but primarily to give him or her protection. Parents wanted their child home while he or she was young because they felt they could give more love and care to the child and because they felt the child contributed to character building of their normal siblings. Many changes in family organization were made in order to adjust to the child. Families were educated toward a reorientation of social values as part of the adjustment process. Many parents felt emotionally closer to one another after the birth of the child. The child had no adverse effect on a marriage that was strong prior to his birth. Marital adjustment depended on the family's mutual orientation to a system of religious beliefs that saw purpose in the child, the mother's health and ability to care for the child, and her consistent use of discipline.

Kelman (1959) investigated how twenty families related to a Down's syndrome child. A control group of families of normal children known to two nonsectarian community centers was utilized. Families were individually matched for significant variables related to the status of the child and the family. Kelman (1959) concluded that the presence of the Down's syndrome child need not have a damaging effect and may produce certain beneficial consequences.

Siporin (1959) examined the nature and content of the family roles of schizophrenic patients prior to the onset of their illness. The research consisted of an exploratory-descriptive study of fourteen schizophrenic patients and their families. Fifty family members, including the fourteen patients, were interviewed by the investigator in the dual role of psychiatric social worker and research worker.

Prior to the onset of illness, the roles played by the patients included the following types: the Fussy Mother Hen, the Domestic Tyrant, the Hen-Pecked Husband, and the Self-Sacrificing Mother. Each of these family roles was found to be severely disturbed in conception and performance and the subject of severe role conflict. Each patient had attempted to achieve new and more satisfying roles, but these efforts were unsuccessful. Prior to the precipitating crisis, the patients and their families had experienced a large number of family problems, which had accumulated to become chronic stress situations. Each patient and his or her family then experienced stressful events, which precipitated acute and severe family and personal crisis situations. The data indicated that the definitions and the effects of these crisis situations were related to the role conflicts and to the development of the schizophrenic illness.

Parenthood. If the family is conceived as a small social system of interrelated roles and statuses, then it follows that the addition or removal of a family member necessitates changes and reorganization, which may produce stress. LeMasters (1957) examined the hypothesis that the arrival of the first child would constitute a crisis, forcing the married couple to move from an adult-centered pair to a child-centered triad. To test this hypothesis, forty-eight couples were interviewed, using a relatively unstructured interviewing technique. The author found that more than two-thirds of the forty-eight couples reported "extensive" or "severe" crisis in adjusting to the first child. There was strong evidence that this crisis reaction was not the result of not wanting children, however. On the contrary, thirty-five of the thirty-eight pregnancies in the crisis group were either planned or desired. The data suggested that the crisis pattern occurs whether the marriage is good or poor. Moreover, the crisis pattern in the thirty-eight cases was not the result of "neurosis" or other psychiatric disability on the part of these parents. The thirty-eight couples in the crisis group appeared to have almost completely romanticized parenthood, and the mothers with professional training and extensive professional work experience (eight couples) all suffered "extensive" or "severe" crisis. LeMaster's study generated numerous replication researches in the 1960s and 1970s.

Disaster. The dissertations of Crawford (1957) and Fogleman (1958) described the effects of and adjustments after disaster. Crawford analyzed those factors that were influential in producing family crises and subsequent readjustments following tornadoes that struck Waco and San Angelo, Texas. Three hundred forty-nine white families were interviewed. Theories developed by Koos, Hill, and others formed the general foundation of this study.

Emotional stress was found to be associated with the death of a parent, severe injury, severe damages, and extreme disruptions of family life. When the only impact of the disaster was financial debt, families were not as severely affected as those that faced death or injury. Families facing economic stress usually had marginal economic status prior to the disaster.

Fogleman (1959) examined the social life of an area that was subjected to a hurricane and traced the effects of the disaster experience on individuals and groups within the impact zone. Residents of seventy-five households were interviewed twice. The predisaster social structure was thoroughly permeated by familistic, primary-type values. The family, as the most important group, was shown to dominate the lives of the people and to include within its effective organization the concepts and practices of an extended family system. Behavior during the entire disaster experience (threat, impact, isolation, rescue, evacuation, and rehabilitation) was family oriented. Family roles were altered during the rebuilding phase, although there were no indications of changes in the values upon which predisaster roles rested.

Alcoholic Family Members. During the 1950s, several articles discussed alcoholism and its impact on family. Only one of them was a research paper, and it focused primarily on the wives of alcoholics.

Jackson (1956) researched the way in which the wife of the alcoholic defines the situation and her resulting behavior from the first signs of bizarre behavior to the end of her husband's hospitalization. The onset of alcoholism in a family member precipitated a cumulative crisis for the family. Seven critical stages were delineated: (1) attempts to deny the problem, (2) attempts to eliminate the problem, (3) disorganization, (4) attempts to reorganize in spite of problem, (5) efforts to escape the problem (the decision to separate from the alcoholic husband), (6) reorganization of the family without the alcoholic, and (7) reorganization of the whole family including the alcoholic.

Each stage affected the form that the following stage took. The families found themselves in unstructured situations undefined by the culture and were forced to evolve techniques of adjustment through trial and error. The unpredictability of the situation, because of its lack of structure, created anxiety in family members, which gave rise to personality difficulties. Factors in the culture, in the environment, and within the family situation prolonged the crisis and deterred the development of permanent adjustment patterns. With the arrest of the alcoholism, the crisis entered its final stage. The family then attempted to reorganize to include the ex-alcoholic and to make adjustments to the changes that had occurred in him.

The Decade in Review

Theory and Methodology. The 1950s provided a broad spectrum of research topics and theoretical orientation (table 7–3). Besides crisis theory, role theory and life cycle theory were employed directly or indirectly. Researchers that were more theoretical were also more sophisticated methodologically. Most of research in this decade, however, was still descriptive or exploratory. The interview was the most frequently used method of obtaining data.

Key Studies and General Findings. The studies by Crawford (1957) and LeMasters (1957) were innovative. Crawford's study of family adjustment to

Table 7–3
Overview of Research on Family Stress and Coping, 1950–1959

Year	*Author*	*Topic*	*Theory*	*Method*[a]	*Sample*	*Strengths*[b]
1953	Barrabee and Von Mering	Illness/stress	None	Interview-P	439	M
1954	Young	Disaster/coping	None	Case Studies	N.A.	
1955	Yarrow, Schwartz, and Murphy	Illness/coping	None	Interview-P	33	
1956	Jackson	Alcoholic/stress	Mini	Case studies	75	T
1957	LeMasters	Parenthood/stress	Mini	Interview-P	48	T,I
1957	Crawford	Disaster/coping	Crisis	Interview-P	349	S,M,St,T,I
1958	Kramm	Illness/coping	None	Interview-P	50	St
1959	Fogleman	Disaster/life	None	Interview-P	75	St
1959	Kelman	Illness/stress	None	Interview-P	40	St
1959	Siporin	Illness/stress	Mini	Case studies	50	St,T,M

[a] P = primary data.
[b] S = sample; M = measurement of variables; St = statistical analysis; T = theory; I = Important.

tornadic disasters provided an understanding of family reactions in disaster situation. Crawford found that family stress associated with severe injury or damages produce extreme disruptions of family life.

LeMaster's study of the birth of the first child introduced concern with critical transition points in the normal development of the family life cycle: marriage, birth of the first child, children going to school, death of a spouse, and children leaving home.

The studies of Kramm (1958), Siporin (1959), and Kelman (1959) were noteworthy also. All found that the presence of a sick family member in the home need not necessarily prove to have a uniformly damaging effect on family living and may produce certain beneficial consequences.

Kramm (1958) also found that the adjustment depended on the presence of certain sociocultural, psychological, and biological factors, including the family's mutual orientation to a system of religious beliefs that saw purpose in the child, the mother's health, and her ability to care for the child.

There was an interesting difference between stresses caused by the disability of a spouse and stresses from disasters or the disability of a child. Stresses caused by the disability of a spouse often resulted in separation or divorce; in contrast, stresses from the disability of children or from disasters did not usually threaten the stability of the marital relationship.

The Decade 1960–1969

During the 1960s, the total number of entries related to family stress and coping was forty-four, of which only eighteen were of research (fourteen journal articles and four dissertations). The topics treated in the 1950s continued to attract interest in the 1960s, and delinquency and imprisonment appeared as new topics.

Research Findings

Physical or Mental Illness of a Family Member. In the 1960s, seven studies were found dealing with physical or mental illness of family member. Most of them emphasized the impact of stress caused by the disability of the family member; only two studied the adjustment or coping behavior of family members.

Parad and Caplan (1960) investigated how fifty-five families coped with a premature birth, congenital abnormality, or tuberculosis. They examined the family life-style, intermediate problem-solving mechanisms, and response patterns. They found that the stressful events posed a problem that was by definition insoluble in the immediate future, overtaxed the psychological resources of the family, since its solution was beyond their traditional problem-solving methods, and was perceived as a threat or danger to the life goals of the family members. The crisis period was characterized by tension that reached a peak and then fell, awakening unresolved problems from both the near and distant past.

Caldwell and Guze (1960) studied the adjustment of parents and siblings of institutionalized and noninstitutionalized retarded children. Thirty-two mothers and thirty-two siblings of retarded children were interviewed. Sixteen of the retarded children lived in their own homes, and sixteen lived in a state-maintained institution. Mothers and siblings of retarded children living at home were not significantly different in adjustment from those of retarded children who had been institutionalized.

Cummings, Bayley, and Rie (1966) studied the effects of the child's mental deficiency on the mother. They recruited 240 mothers through the cooperation of twelve clinics and social agencies and a group of community physicians. The mothers of mentally retarded children experienced greater psychological stress than mothers of chronically ill children.

Fowle (1968) examined the marital integration and sibling role tension in families in which a severely mentally retarded child had been either retained in the home (245 families) or placed in an institution (83 families). No significant difference in marital integration was found in the two samples; however, role tension of the retardates' siblings was higher when the retardates were kept at home, and the oldest female sibling was more adversely affected than was the oldest male sibling.

Jacobson (1963) studied the impact of heart disease of the husband-father on the family and the ways in which families coped with this problem. Data were secured from structured interviews with 400 active or retired farmers, half of them cardiacs and half of them noncardiacs, and from open-ended interviews with a subgroup of wives of fifty-four cardiacs. A field theory approach was used. Some wives had difficulty in defining husbands as sick or well, especially if there were no obvious symptoms. Many men did not care to talk about their diseases, and half kept the symptoms to themselves. The major problems discerned were changes in the husband's behavior, including dependency, aggressiveness, fear of crowds, pessimism, and increased conflicts with others. Some wives reported that husbands disliked being helped with work and being reminded about the illness.

Wives were more likely than husbands to report financial worries. Work problems included getting the work done, giving up or changing work, uncertainty about how much work could be done, and conflicts about the work situation. Patterns of work adjustment included retiring, finding nonfarm work, and continuing to farm. Where wives assumed a more dominant role in management and income earning, there was sometimes a loss of the man's status. Other problems included changes in diet, effects on children's lives, changes in values and outlook toward life, and fears related to death.

The family was the most common source of help. Relatively few of the women named the doctor as a source of help. The majority of the women said they learned through experience how to cope with the changes in behavior. The impacts and modes of adjustment depended on the stage of the family life cycle.

Delinquency. Browning (1960) was primarily concerned with the impact of family organization and disorganization on adolescent boys. The data were collected from probation records, school records, and home interviews with mothers or stepmothers. The total sample included 180 boys (60 truancy, 60 auto thefts, and 60 nondelinquent boys). Families high in solidarity and with good marital adjustment had fewer boys who were truants. The hypothesized stress variable, broken homes, was not significantly related to truancy or delinquency.

Robey and associates (1964) studied forty-two runaway girls and consistently found that a family stress preceded running away. The stresses included a disturbed marital relationship, inadequate control by the parents over their own and the girl's impulses, deprivation of maternal love, and subtle pressure by the mother for the daughter to take over the maternal role.

Alcoholism. Lemert (1960) examined the impact of alcoholism upon the family using a sample of 112 families (105 wives, 4 husbands, and 3 immediate relatives). Adjustment events were found to cluster rather than to fall into well-defined stages. The nature of the clustering suggests that there may be early, middle, and late phases in family adjustment.

Kogan, Fordyce, and Jackson (1963) examined personality disturbance in wives of alcoholics. The data were from fifty wives of alcoholics and a comparable group of wives of nonalcoholics. Measures from Minnesota Multiphasic Personality Inventory (MMPI) indicated that significantly more wives of alcoholics exhibited personality dysfunction than did wives of nonalcoholics; however, the total number of disturbed subjects was less than half on any measure.

Parenthood. In a replication of LeMasters's (1957) study, Dyer (1963) used a sample of thirty-two couples to investigate the level of the family organization prior to the crisis, the impact of the crisis on the family, and recovery and subsequent level of family reorganization. A majority of couples experienced extensive or severe crisis. The degree to which the birth of the first child was a crisis appeared to be related to the state of the marriage and family organization at the birth of the child, the couple's preparation for marriage and parenthood, the couple's marital adjustment after the birth of the child, and certain social background and situational variables, such as the number of years married and whether the pregnancy was planned.

Hobbs (1965) used a random sample of fifty-three first-time parents to test LeMasters's findings. Eighty-seven percent of the couples were classified in the "slight" crisis category, and there were no couples in the "extensive" or "severe" crisis categories. Women had a significantly higher mean crisis score than men. Unlike findings by LeMasters (1957) and Dyer (1963), none of the thirteen middle-class couples were found to have experienced "extensive" or "severe" crisis. Pregnancy was desired by 96 percent of the couples, all of whom perceived the addition of the first child as a rewarding, as well as a somewhat difficult, experience. Ninety-one percent of the fathers and 70 percent of the mothers reported their marriages as happier and more satisfying than before the arrival of the baby.

Meyerowitz and Feldman (1966) studied the marital satisfaction of 400 couples having their first child and reported results similar to those of Hobbs (1965). Data were collected at three different times: five months before delivery, five weeks after delivery, and five months after delivery. Marital satisfaction reported by both spouses was slightly higher when the baby was one month old than during pregnancy. When the baby was five months old, both sexes reported a decline in marital satisfaction.

Hobbs (1968) again tested the crisis of first parenthood with a random sample of twenty-seven couples in a Florida city. Nearly 20 percent of the mothers but only 4 percent of the fathers experienced "severe" difficulty in adjusting to the first child. Over 90 percent of the fathers and 80 percent of the mothers reported no more than "moderate" difficulty.

Imprisonment. Anderson (1966) interviewed fifty-nine prisoners' wives in Melbourne, Australia, to determine how imprisonment of the father affected families. The major effects were economic hardships, new roles, changed relationships, and stigma. The absence of the husband-father left no one to perform some family tasks, such as decision making and disciplining the children. The two most frequent complaints of wives were loneliness for the husband and financial worries. Marital bonds decreased, while bonds between mother and child were often strengthened. In two-thirds of the sample, the stigma of having one's husband or father in jail deterred association outside the family.

The Decade in Review

Theory and Methodology. There was some improvement in theory and research methods during the 1960s; however, about half of the research was still exploratory and lacked theoretical guidelines. The most prominent methods of obtaining data were by personal interview and questionnaire. A few studies used a secondary analysis or case studies.

Key Studies and General Findings. The topic of physical or mental illness of a family member was a major focus in the 1960s (see table 7–4). Families with a mentally retarded or chronically ill member experienced higher levels of stress than other families. Role tensions were higher for siblings of the disabled child, especially the oldest female sibling.

Table 7–4
Overview of Research on Family Stress and Coping, 1960–1969

Year	*Author*	*Topic*	*Theory*	*Method*[a]	*Sample*	*Strengths*[b]
1960	Browning	Disorganization	None	Interview-P	180	S
1960	Caldwell and Guze	Illness/coping	Mini	Interview-P	64	M,St,T
1960	Parad and Caplan	Illness/coping	Mini	Interview-P	55	M
1960	Lemert	Alcoholism/wives	Mini	Interview-P	112	S,M,St
1962	Graliker, Fishler, and Koch	Illness/coping	None	Interview-P	21	M
1962	Hansen	Delinquency/stress	Mini	Interview-P	11	M,St,T
1963	Dyer	Parenthood/coping	None	Interview-P	32	St,I
1963	Jacobson	Illness/stress	Field	Interview-P	454	S
1963	Kogan, Fordyce, and Jackson	Alcoholism/crisis	Mini	Interview-P	100	M
1964	Nealon	Illness/crisis	Mini	Case studies	25	
1964	Veen, Huebner, and Jorgens	Adjustment	Mini	Interview-P	20	M
1964	Robey et al.	Stress/delinquency	None	Interview-P	42	
1965	Hobbs	Parenthood/stress	None	Interview-P	53	St
1966	Anderson	Imprisonment/coping	Mini	Interview-P	59	M,St
1966	Cummings, Bayley, and Rie	Illness/stress	None	Questionnaire-P	240	S,St,M
1966	Meyerwitz and Feldman	Parenthood/stress	None	Interview-P	400	S,M
1968	Fowle	Illness/stress	Mini	Interview-P	328	S,St,T,M,I
1968	Hobbs	Parenthood/stress	None	Interview-P	27	St

[a]P = primary data.
[b]S = sample; M = measurement of variables; St = statistical analysis; T = theory; I = Important.

Two key studies in this decade were done by Dyer (1963) and Hobbs (1965). Dyer found, as did LeMasters (1957), that a majority of middle-class couples experienced ''extensive or severe'' crisis on the birth of the first child. However, Hobbs (1965) observed lower levels of crisis experienced by new parents than either LeMasters or Dyer had found. These controversial findings promoted a series of studies in the following decade.

The Decade 1970–1979

Twenty-eight studies on family stress and coping were found in the 1970s—twenty-five journal articles and three dissertations. The research ranged over a broad array of topics, including war-related stress, physical and mental illness, drug abuse, rape, inprisonment, parenthood, alcoholism, and disaster.

Research Findings

War-Related Stress. Bey and Lange (1974) interviewed forty-five wives of noncareer army men who had been sent to Vietnam. All of the women felt varying degree of numbness, shock, disbelief when first told of their husbands' orders. Many felt anger and frustration toward their husband for having gone to Vietnam and leaving them in the stressful situation; however, they recognized their husbands' lack of choice in the matter and felt guilty for harboring these angry feelings.

McCubbin and associates (1975) interviewed a sample of forty-eight families of returned American prisoners of war from the Vietnam conflict. The amount of family integration twelve to sixteen months after reunion was associated with the length of the marriage before the separation, the wife's retrospective assessment of the quality of marriage before the separation, and the wife's emotional distress during the separation period.

Cohen and Dotan (1976) explored the effects of war-related stress on communication patterns in the family. They conducted two waves of interviews with 188 wives of servicemen—the first during the October 1973 Middle East war and the second eight months later. During the war, there was more interpersonal communication, family stress, and attention to the mass media than during peacetime.

McCubbin and co-workers (1976) investigated the adjustment of forty-seven families of servicemen missing in action in the Vietnam conflict. Findings were explained in terms of both psychological and sociological theories of coping. Six coping behavior patterns were found: (1) seeking resolution and expression feelings, (2) maintaining family integrity, (3) establishing autonomy and maintaining family ties, (4) reducing anxiety, (5) establishing independence through self-development, and (6) maintaining the past and dependence on religion. The husband's and wife's background, the history of the marriage, the development of the family, and the stresses of separation were found to determine the family's response to separation.

Boss (1977) collected data from a representative sample of forty-seven families of servicemen missing in action. A negative relationship was found between family functionality and psychological father presence as proposed. However, psychological presence helped family functioning if it was for financial reasons. Psychological father presence was established as a viable concept with regard to father absence.

Physical or Mental Illness of a Family Member. Cumming (1970) studied the reaction of the family unit to the disability of the male head of the family. The data were from a sample of seven-two couples composed of disabled male wage earners and their wives. The author found that the male perception of self and the wife's perception of her mate were modified as the result of the husband's disability. Couples who had handled prior crises successfully tended to be successful in handling the new crisis situation. For the male, personal adjustment was directly related to his adjustment to the family crisis. The severity of the disability was directly related to the male's success in adjusting to the crisis. Families did not consistently interpret stressor events as family crises.

Gath (1972) examined the hypothesis that an abnormal child may adversely affect the mental health of the siblings. A group of thirty-six school-age siblings of children with Down's syndrome and another group of thirty-six school-age siblings of children with cleft lip or palate were compared with seventy-one individually matched school children. No significant differences in behavioral ratings were found between the siblings of handicapped children and their controls.

Kaplan and associates (1973) studied the impact of serious illness on the family using a clinical sample of fifty families with a child treated for leukemia. Coping demands were not static but changed. Parents who refused to accept the diagnosis of leukemia occasionally displayed overt hostility to members of the health center staff. The family's ability to manage the illness depended on successful coping by both parents. When the parents had different emotional reactions to leukemia and when they disagreed about the illness—how to define it, when to discuss, it, and what to tell others about it—individual and family coping were less adequate. Eighty-seven percent of the families failed to cope adequately with the consequences of leukemia.

Holroyd (1974) conducted three pilot studies with forty-three parents to assess the degree and variety of response to a physically or mentally handicapped family member. Mothers more than fathers described themselves as less able to experience personal development or freedom, more limited in how they could use their time, poorer in health or mood, more sensitive to how the child fit into the community, and more aware of disharmony within the family. Single mothers experienced more problems than married mothers, including excess time demands, lack of family integration, and financial problems. Mothers of retarded children were more concerned about overprotection or dependency problems and limited school or occupational opportunities than were mothers of emotionally disturbed children.

Cummings (1976) studied how a handicapped child affects the psychological life of the father. The subjects for this research were 240 fathers: 60 fathers each of mentally retarded children, chronically physically ill children, neurotic children, and healthy children. Fathers of retarded and chronically ill children had significant stress associated with parenting. Some appeared to have a pattern of neuroticlike constriction, with lowered self-esteem, depressive feelings, little sense of themselves as competent fathers, few satisfactions from family relationships, a need for compulsive ordering of their experience, and tight control of social and sexual interests.

Gayton and associates (1977) interviewed forty-three families who had children with cystic fibrosis. There were no evidence of an increased incidence of emotional disturbance in children with cystic fibrosis. Evidence for negative psychological impact of chronic illness on sibling development was also lacking. However, personality testing of the parents showed that 32 percent of the fathers and 22 percent of the mothers obtained scores in the range suggestive of emotional disturbance.

Friedrich (1979) examined a large number of psychosocial and demographic variables to determine which were the best predictors of coping behaviors of mothers of handicapped children. Subjects were ninety-eight mothers of children with a wide variety of handicapping conditions. Marital satisfaction was the best overall predictor, accounting for 70 percent of the predictive ability of all the items.

Lavigne and Ryan (1979) also studied the psychological adjustment of siblings of children with chronic illness. The specific illness groups were pediatric hematology (N = 62), cardiology (N = 57), and plastic surgery patients (N = 37), who were compared with siblings of healthy children (N = 46). The siblings of patient groups were more likely to show symptoms of irritability and social withdrawal, and the differences between illness groups approached significance on measures of fear and inhibition. No group differences were noted on measures of aggression or learning problems.

Leifson (1979) studied forty-seven families with handicapped children. She interviewed them within two weeks after the birth of the child and again six months later. She found that the couples' initial reactions were shock, grief, guilt, and depression; some expressed anger and resentment. Couples who had affectionate, satisfying marriages were able to adjust to the crisis and could function better as a couple. A second variable related to couple functioning was adaptability; couples who were flexible and able to adjust their roles were doing better six months after the birth than couples who were fairly rigid. Age, education, and insurance also were found to be related to functioning. Couples who were older had a harder time adjusting to the handicapped child. Individuals with more education were able to adjust more easily than individuals with less education. Finally, having adequate insurance eased the financial and emotional stress associated with the birth of a handicapped child.

Disaster. Penick, Powell, and Sieck (1976) interviewed twenty-six tornado victims to determine the mental health consequences of a natural disaster. The results, based on retrospective accounts, indicated that, five months later, approximately three-fourths of the victims suffered increased psychological discomfort, characterized by anxiety, nervousness, and, less frequently, mild somatic complaints. The disaster did not produce severe emotional impairment, and few of the victims felt the need for professional mental health assistance.

Drabek (1975) conducted a quasi-experimental study that permitted comparisons between victim and nonvictim families three years after a tornado. A sample of 1,354 was used to explore the patterns in kin relationships prior to and immediately following the event and three years later. Three years after the tornado, victim families (compared to nonvictim families) reported higher interaction frequencies with immediate kin, more often designated relatives as future help sources, and visited more with relatives than friends. Nonvictim families reported more frequent participation in exchange transactions with relatives such as borrowing or lending.

Parenthood. Leveen (1970) explored changes in fifty-eight first-child couples in terms of degrees of idealization of the infant, levels of anxiety, hostility, and depression, stress between themselves, and the emergence of love toward the baby. Couples were interviewed at three different stages. The data did not indicate that idealization diminished over time or that anxiety, hostility, and depression were more prevalent during pregnancy and parturition than when the baby was 5 months old. The data did not sustain the LeMasters hypothesis that couples feel undue stress in their caring relationships during pregnancy and immediately after birth. The results supported the hypothesis that love develops out of the interpersonal situation and as a consequence of interaction.

Ryder (1973) used a sample of 112 couples, ages 18 to 27, to examine the effect of children on marital satisfaction. Having a child contributed to feelings of wives that their husbands pay too little attention to them. Tyder concluded that this effect is one major component of the postpartum consequences observed by LeMasters (1957), Dyer (1963), Hobbs (1965), and Feldman (1971).

Hobbs and Cole (1976) used a random sample of sixty-five couples to replicate a study by Hobbs (1965). Their findings largely confirmed those of Hobbs: there were only slight amounts of difficulty in adjusting to the first child, and mothers reported significantly greater amounts of difficulty than did fathers. They concluded that it is more accurate to refer to beginning parenthood as a transition rather than a crisis.

Russell (1974) extended the focus of parenthood research to include a variety of subjectively positive as well as negative outcomes of becoming a parent for the first time. A total of 511 couples who lived in Minneapolis were included in this study. Respondents perceived that their first year of parenthood was moderately stressful yet rewarding. Few respondents saw their marriage as deteriorating since becoming parents.

Fein (1976) conducted an exploratory study of men's perinatal experiences that did not rely on a "crisis" perspective. Thirty men who attended childbirth preparation classes were interviewed with their wives before and after the birth of a first child. The data suggested that the "crisis" for these men came before the birth and in the first two weeks after the baby came home from the hospital. By six weeks after the birth, anxiety had decreased, and most men were adapting to their parental role.

Alcoholism. The impact of alcoholism on the family received much attention in the 1970s. Research on family stress and coping focused on the alcoholic's spouse, with emphasis on personality traits and characteristics, and the alcoholic's children's functioning, with emphasis on their psychological health. From the many studies on alcohol abuse (Booz-Allen and Hamilton, 1974; Busch et al., 1973; Chafetz et al., 1971; Edwards et al., 1973; El-Guebaly and Offord, 1977; Gorad, 1971; Hoffman and Noem, 1975; James and Goldman, 1971; Kammeier, 1971; Mik, 1970; O'Gorman, 1975; Orford, 1976; Paolino et al., 1976; Rimmer, 1974; Rimmer and Winokur, 1972; Rouse, Waller and Ewing, 1973; Tarter, 1976; Templer, 1974; Wiseman, 1975), four are reviewed here.

Rouse, Waller, and Ewing (1973) studied the impact of paternal drinking on adolescent stress levels. They interviewed 186 randomly selected adolescents and found significantly higher rates of depression and broken homes in children of heavy drinkers than in those of moderate drinkers or abstainers. Among black adolescents, there was a significant positive correlation between severity of fathers' drinking and the children's stress; in white adolescents, the correlation, also significant, was negative. There were no significant intergroup differences in the children's coping style or the quantity and frequency of drinking.

Templer (1974) examined thirty-three male alcoholics, from 26 to 67 years, at Western State Hospital. Being raised in a family with alcoholism was found to lead to greater severity of alcoholism and a generally less adeuate level of functioning.

Busch and associates (1973) reported on a sample of nineteen husbands of alcoholics in treatment and a control group of nineteen husbands matched for age and social class. Psychopathology was no more prevalent among the alcoholic than the nonalcoholic husbands, but the alcoholic husbands were less sociable and extroverted and had a more feminine self-concept than did the controls.

Wiseman's (1975) data from seventy-five wives of alcoholics in Helsinki, Finland, indicated that although all wives attempted to help their husbands stop drinking, 40 percent escaped an existence of increasing isolation and despair when he continued to imbide. A substantial minority of wives experienced a change in perspective; they increased their work and hobby skills, gained job promotions, scheduled their time to avoid contact with husbands, and made their own friends and social plans. Recovered husbands sometimes found wives torn between marital duty and this new separate existence.

Rape. Sutherland and Scherl (1970) studied a group of thirteen young victims of rape, in most instances within 48 hours of the rape incident, to identify a specific predictable sequence of responses to the rape. The women ranged in age from 18 to 24, and each had a background consistent with accomplishment, independence, and apparent psychological health. A clear pattern of responses to the assault emerged. In the initial phase of the response, including the time immediately following the assault, the victim exhibited signs of acute distress. Phase 2, often mistakenly thought to represent a successful resolution of the reaction to rape, included denial of the impact of the assault and was characterized by pseudo-adjustment and a return to usual activity. Denial, suppression, and rationalization replaced shock and dismay. This phase, frequently unrecognized or misdiagnosed, included depression and the need to talk. There were often obsessive memories of the rape at this time, and the victim had concerns about the influence of the assault on her future life.

Imprisonment. Love (1970) investigated the effects of involuntary separation due to the imprisonment of the husband-father. Data were collected from ninety-five inmates and fifty-six wives of the inmates. The adjustment of the family to the separation was influenced by the nature of the crime, the length of separation, background factors, marital relations, and economic and social life. It was anticipated that the better the marital relationship had been, the greater would be the initial impact on the wife. However, the middle marital integration group experienced the highest impact; while adjustment was easier for women low or high in marital integration.

The Decade in Review

Theory and Methodolgy. The research of family stress and coping in the 1970s yielded new findings and extended the theory of previous decades (table 7-5). Researchers clarified and added empirical support to the conceptualizations of Burgess (1926), Angell (1936), Cavan and Ranck (1938), Koos (1946), and particularly Hill's (1949) classic research on war-induced separation and reunion; improved the definition and measurement of variables; and elaborated the components of stress and resources.

Table 7–5
Overview of Research on Family Stress and Coping, 1970–1979

Year	*Author*	*Topic*	*Theory* [a]	*Method* [b]	*Sample*	*Strengths* [c]
1970	Cumming	Disabled/stress	None	Interview-P	72	M,St
1970	Leveen	Parenthood/stress	System	Interview-P	58	M
1970	Love	Imprisonment	Crisis	Questionnaire-P/ Interview-P	151	St
1970	Sutherland and Scherl	Rape/crisis	None	Case studies	13	I
1972	Gath	Illness/stress	Mini	Questionnaire-P/ Interview-P	71	M
1973	Kaplan	Illness/stress	None	Case studies	50	
1973	Ryder	Parenthood/stress	None	Interview-P	112	St
1974	Bey and Lange	War-related stress	None	Interview-P	40	
1974	De Forest	Drug abuse/stress	None	Interview-P	31	M,St
1974	Hadley	Crisis/stress	Development	Interview-P	90	M,St,T
1974	Holroyo	Illness/coping	None	Questionnaire-P	43	M
1974	Russell	Parenthood/stress	Mini	Interview-P	511	M,St
1974	Templer	Alcoholic	None	Interview-P	33	S,St
1975	McCubbin et al.	War-related stress	Mini	Questionnaire-P	48	M,St
1975	Drabek	Disaster/coping	Mini	Interview-P	1354	S,T
1975	Wiseman	Alcoholics/stress	None	Interview-P	75	
1976	Cohen and Dotan	War-related stress	Communi.	Interview-P	118	T
1976	Commings	Illness/stress	Mini	Interview-P	240	S,M
1976	McCubbin et al.	War-related stress	Coping	Interview-P	47	S,M,St,T,I
1976	Fein	Parenthood/stress	None	Interview-P	30	St
1976	Hobbs and Cole	Parenthood/stress	None	Interview-P	65	S
1976	Penick	Disaster/stress	None	Interview-P	26	M
1977	Boss	Absence/stress	Sys-symb	Interview-P	47	M
1977	Cohen	Absence/stress	Mini	Interview-P	42	M,T
1977	Gayton et al.	Illness/stress	None	Questionnaire-P	43	T
1979	Colletta	Divorce/support	Mini	Interview-P	72	M,St,P
1979	Friedrich	Illness/coping	None	Questionnaire-P	98	M,St
1979	Lavign	Illness/stress	System	Observation/ Interview-P	222	S,M,St,T
1979	Leifson	Illness/coping	ABCX	Interview-P	47	M,I

[a] Sys-symb.: combination of system theory and symbolic ineraction; communi.: communication theory.
[b] P = primary data.
[c] S = sample; M = measurement of variables; St = statistical analysis; T = theory; I = Important.

Compared to previous decades, the methodology used in the 1970s was more sophisticated. Longitudinal data were used to examine the transition to parenthood, and more advanced techniques of data analysis were utilized. Interiews were the primary method of collecting data.

Key Studies and General Findings. There were three important findings in the 1970s. First, changes from one life stage to another can be viewed as a family crisis, which might cause the onset of symptoms in family members. Second, the degree to which a family is integrated into the community is an important factor in evaluating stress tolerance, for it determines the number and quality of resources the family can count on for support and assistance. Third, the processes of adjustment involved in family reunions after prolonged separations were determined by several factors: the family's history, characteristics of family members, their adjustment to the separation period, and family dynamics at the time reunion occurred.

The key studies of the 1970s were conducted by Lavigne and Ryan (1979) and Hobbs and Cole (1976). Lavigne and Ryan (1979) studied the psychological adjustment of siblings of children with chronic illness. The siblings were found to be more likely than controls to show symptoms of irritability and social withdrawal. No group differences were noted on measures of aggression or learning problems.

Because Hobbs and Cole (1976) used a random sample of couples, their results appear to be more valid than those reported by other researchers. On the basis of their findings, Hobbs and Cole concluded that beginning parenthood should be viewed as a transition rather than a crisis. This statement has influenced the direction of research on family stress and coping in the 1980s. More research studied normative family stress and positive coping.

The Decade 1980–1989

Research conducted in the 1980s was more theoretically oriented than that conducted previously. The topics found in the 1980s were similar to those of 1970s: physical and mental illness of a family member, drug abuse, delinquency, rape, imprisonment, parenthood, alcoholism, disaster, absence of father, and divorce. A total of thirty-four entries related to family stress and coping—seventeen journal articles and nineteen dissertations—were found in this period.

Research Findings

Physical Illness of a Family Member. Waisbren (1980) compared thirty families with a developmentally disabled child to thirty families with a nonhandicapped child. Half the families lived in California, and half lived in Denmark. Compared to parents with normal children, the parents with a developmentally disabled child saw themselves more negatively after the baby's birth and expressed more negative feelings about their child.

Kazak (1983) studied fifty-three families with a child with spina bifida and fifty-six matched comparison families. There were no differences between the two groups in family cohesion, family adaptability, marital satisfaction, or sibling self-concept. Families with handicapped children visited less with outsiders, and their social support networks were smaller, more family dominated, and more concentrated.

Patterson and McCubbin (1983) examined the relationship between cumulated family stresses and changes in the health status of a child family member with cystic fibrosis. The data were collected from 100 parents and from clinic records. A decline in pulmonary functioning was associated with a pile-up of family stresses.

Lapham (1984) studied fifty-four families who had a severely handicapped child or young adult member. Over 40 percent of the mothers said the overall stress of having a deaf-blind child is comparable or worse than the death of a spouse. Having a deaf-blind child negatively affected the marital relationship and created strains in the relationships with their nonhandicapped children. There was a negative relationship between stress and physical health status.

Barbarin, Hughes, and Chesler (1985) used a sample of thirty-two married couples to study how they coped with their children's cancer. Family cohesion was strengthened by initial experiences with childhood cancer and spouses were the most important source of social support. As the number of the child's hospitalizations increased, however, perceptions of support from spouse and assessments of marital quality decreased.

Holroyd and Guthrie (1986) examined family stress resulting from having a child with a chronic illness (cystic fibrosis, neuromuscular disease, or renal disease). Parents of children with neuromuscular disease (N = 16), cystic fibrosis (N = 16), and renal disease (N = 11) were compared with parents of control subjects matched by age. Parents of children with neuromuscular disease experienced much greater stress than the other two clinical samples. Parents of children with cystic fibrosis also experienced extensive stress but less than anticipated. Parents of children with renal disease reported less stress.

Peyrot, McMurry, and Hedges (1988) examined the adjustment to diabetes among twenty adult patients and their spouses. The findings supported Hill's ABCX model of family adjustment to stress. While families may be disrupted by chronic illness, after a period of adjustment some families achieved a positive adaptation. The impact of diabetes on spouses was mediated by the perception of the illness as difficult and severe, as well as by the way in which the family brought its resources to bear in dealing with the illness. And interpersonal congruence was crucial in mediating the impact on individual perceptions and behavior. Differences in perceptions of severity affected satisfaction, regardless of the degree of severity perceived by the spouse.

Antonovsky and Sourani (1988) used coping theory to study family adaptation using a sample of sixty married Israeli males who were disabled by injury or illness and their wives. The theory proposed that a strong sense of coherence, particularly one shared by the spouse, provided the motivational, perceptual, and behavioral basis for successful resolution of the problems posed by stressors. Such resolution, not the absence of stressors, provided one with a sense of satisfaction about family life.

Mental Illness of a Family Member. Noh (1984; Noh and Avison, 1988) studied the burden of living with a psychiatric patient among 211 adults who were spouses or parents of adult patients who had been hospitalized with functional psychoses. Although family members experienced a substantial amount of burden, mastery ability and social support were found to have much greater impact on the mental health status of family members than family burden had.

Death of a Family Member. Cook (1982) examined parents' descriptions of their experiences in the first year after a child's death from cancer or a blood disorder. Data were gathered from 145 parents of these children. Compared to men, women reported greater difficulty adjusting to the death and were more likely to describe a sense of distance in their marital relationships. Men reported fewer sources of emotional support and were less likely to discuss their grief with others. Five major factors were found to influence the parents' ability to cope: (1) respondent's sex, (2) number of years since the death, (3) whether other problems were present in the marriage, (4) whether the respondent reported increased worry about the health of surviving siblings, and (5) self-perception.

Coping with Separation and Divorce. McLanahan, Wedemeyer, and Adelberg (1981) examined the relationships among network structure, social support, and psychological well-being in the single-parent family. Data were from forty-five divorced mothers. Three network types were identified: the family-of-origin network, the extended network, and the conjugal network. Findings indicated that network structure was associated with type of support received. The effects of structure and support on psychological well-being were mediated by a third variable, role orientation of the mother. In other words, the development of an adaptive support network depended not only on the availability of friends and/or relatives but also on the fit between the role orientation of the woman and the way in which her network was organized.

Berman and Turk (1981) examined two important aspects of divorce: the effect of divorce-related problems on distress and the effect of various coping strategies in mediating distress. The subjects had at least one child and were volunteers from chapters of Parents Without Partners (sixty-five females and twenty-five males). In addition, sixteen females were selected randomly from the superior courts records of all women who had received a divorce within the past two years and who had at least one minor child at home. Only interpersonal and familial problems had a major effect on overall emotional distress. Involvement in social activities, expressing feelings, and developing autonomy were highly related to better postdivorce adjustment.

Abelsohn (1985) explored the adjustment of forty-five adolescents during the first eighteen months of their parents' separation. Significant relationships were found between postseparation family structure and adolescent adjustment. Enmeshment and disengagement (the extremes of cohesion) were associated with increased adolescent difficulties with social relationships and activities. Extensive chaos (an extreme lack of adaptability) was associated with greater adjustment difficulties.

Using a random sample of young adult members from a large health maintenance organization, Baker (1985) found that family structure was correlated with stress: those who grew up in intact families reported less relationship-related stress than those who grew up in nonintact families. The current quality of connectedness to parents emerged as the powerful mediator between stress and symptoms of illness. Those with a friendly, autonomous relationship with parents reported fewer symptoms and less stress than those who were cut off from parents.

War-related Stress. Bardwell (1987) studied the functioning of marital pairs of Vietnam veterans diagnosed with posttraumatic stress disorder (PTSD). The sample included thirty veteran families in which a husband was diagnosed with PTSD; thirty nonveteran families were used as a comparison group. Veteran families showed significantly lower levels of adaptability in therapy compared to nonveteran families. Veteran families also displayed a lack of effective coping strategies, lower marital satisfaction, and less adaptability.

Lavee, McCubbin, and Olson (1985) examined the relationships among the major variables of the double ABCX model of family stress and adaptation. They used data on army families' adaptation to the crisis of relocation overseas. The sample of 288 families was drawn from the total enlisted population of U.S. Army families who were located in West Germany. Family life stresses significantly influenced postcrisis strain. Family system resources and social support facilitated adaptation but in different ways: family resources affected adaptation directly, whereas social supports reduced the postcrisis strain.

Pregnancy and Parenthood. Snowden and colleagues (1988) studied the marital satisfaction of a sample of 106 pregnant women. With sociodemographic variables controlled, coping resources and pregnancy decision making were related to marital satisfaction, both early and late in the pregnancy. Uncertainty and conflict in becoming pregnant were found to be negatively associated with marital satisfaction at the beginning of pregnancy. The consequences of these difficulties appeared to endure. Wantedness, intendedness, and agreement in deciding to become pregnant continued to predict marital satisfaction when assessed immediately prior to the scheduled delivery. Self-confidence was positively associated with marital satisfaction.

Wright (1985) studied coping strategies of 202 parents who had experienced the birth of a child in the last eighteen months. Mothers experienced significantly more stress than fathers in their individual and marital lives. Men and women also used different coping strategies. Mothers used social contacts (friends, neighbors, community, and relatives) substantially more than fathers did.

Alcohol and Drug Abuse. Wiseman (1980) examined how 152 wives of alcoholics reacted to their husband's drinking problem. Seventy-six wives of alcoholics were interviewed. The wife of an alcoholic usually attempted to treat her husband by herself before seeking professional help. The unsuccessful attempts at home treatment contributed to emotional stress and the ultimate alienation of the wife of an alcoholic.

Sellitto (1988) examined levels of stress and coping among wives of alcoholics and opiate addicts. The sample contained thirty wives of alcoholics and thirty wives of opiate addicts. No significant differences were found between the levels of stress and coping experiences of the spouses. As stress increased, the spouses of alcoholics showed a greater tendency to self-control and seeking social support than did the spouses of opiate addicts. For the spouses of male opiate addicts, as stress increased, coping decreased.

Scavnisky-Mylant (1988) studied the coping process and emotional development of young adult children of alcoholics. The sample consisted of thirty young adults between the ages of 18 and 28 who were raised in an alcoholic home. Three major methods of coping (confrontative, emotive, and palliative) were identified. Confrontive measures of coping were undeveloped until young adulthood, and then only after therapeutic intervention.

Other Stress Research. Olson, Lavee, and McCubbin (1988) examined the pileup of stressors and strains that families face across the life cycle, changes in family system types across the family life cycle, and responses of families with different system types to the normal range of life events and changes. The sample consisted of 1,251 families. The data indicated that interfamily strain and family well-being can best be explained by both the family system type and its developmental stage. Young couples and older couples showed higher levels of well-being than families with children. Flexible connected families tended to have the highest level of well-being, followed by structured connected families. Families with adolescents who were flexibly connected showed a high level of well-being despite the low level of well-being that families with adolescents generally showed as a group.

Based on systems and symbolic interaction theories, Bolsen (1985) constructed a life stages framework to examine the impact of life stressors on family satisfaction. Data were obtained from sixty women and fifty-four men who were married, middle-aged, and had at least one child. Intervening variables were locus of control, family adaptability, family cohesion, coping, coping networks, and perception of disturbance. Women more than men perceived that life stressor events were more disturbing. Believing that they could control events strengthened family satisfaction of women experiencing life stressor events. None of the variables in the model predicted men's family satisfaction.

Lavee, McCubbin, and Olson (1987) studied the effect of several types of stress on the family well-being of 1,140 families. Life events and transitions negatively affected marital adjustment and perceived well-being and intensified intrafamily strain. Contrary to the authors' hypothesis, family strain was positively associated with a more optimistic appraisal of the situation. Both marital adjustment and appraisal of the situation were positively related to well-being, thereby counteracting the effect of the pileup of demands.

Mays (1987) examined accumulation of family stresses, family social support, and coping strategies in relation to family satisfaction and infant immunization status of forty unwed adolscents and their mothers. The double ABCX model of family stress and adaptation (McCubbin and Patterson, 1982) was adapted. For mothers of unwed adolescents, family social support was negatively related to the accumulation of family stressors. For unwed adolescents, family social support was predictive of family satisfaction and infant immunization status. Family support accounted for 60 percent of the variance in family satisfaction and 10 percent of the variance in immunization compliance.

Goedeke (1984) investigated the contingent influence of "claims and control" on the relationship between the perceived rate of family stress and level of family satisfaction. Two hundred and two randomly selected Missouri husband-wife couples in the launching and launched stages of the family life cycle provided data for this study. A conceptual model for mediating family stress was presented. The findings supported the following propositions: (1) The influence of family stress on family satisfaction was mediated by the perceived ability of the family to achieve (control) its wants and meet needs and expectations (claims); (2) families were less able to cope with the effects of family stress on family satisfaction when wants, needs, and expectations were significantly greater than their ability to satisfy them; (3) husbands and wives responded differently to the contingent influences of claims; and (4) claims and control acted together to influence coping responses that mediate the effects family stress has on family satisfaction.

The Decade in Review

Theory and Methodology. In the 1980s, a larger proportion of researchers than in previous decades formulated hypotheses for testing and used multivariate stratistical techniques. As a result, studies yielded new findings and extended the theory of previous decades. For example, Olson, Lavee, and McCubbin (1988) integrated ideas within three areas of study: developmental stage, system frameworks, and stress theory. Samples size increased over earlier decades, but most of the samples were still not selected randomly.

Key Studies and Important Findings. Research in the previous five decades had focused on specific dimensions of family resources as mediating factors between stressor events and family adaptation. Olson, Lavee, and McCubbin (1988) focused on a multidimensional typology of family dynamics in an attempt to identify the types of family systems that are more resilient than others. They found that level of family cohesion accounted for level of family strain and well-being. "Connected" (more cohesive) families had lower levels of strain and higher levels of well-being than did "separated" (less cohesive) families.

Another key study of the 1980s was that of Lavee, McCubbin, and Olson (1985). Their examination of the relationships among the major variables of the double ABCX model of family stress and adaptation indicated that family life events significantly influence postcrisis strain. Family system resources and social support facilitate adaptation but in different ways: family system resources affect adaptation directly, whereas social support reduces the postcrisis strain. (Table 7–6 contains a complete listing of the research conducted during the 1980s.)

Overview of Sixty-Year Period

Methodological Trends and Development

Research conducted in the 1930s and 1940s was mainly descriptive or exploratory. Most samples were fewer than 100 and were not randomly selected. Research findings were frequently reported without mentioning the statistical methods employed. Interviews and case studies were the primary methods of research conducted in this decade.

In the 1950s and 1960s, research efforts concentrated on the adjustment of families to stresses such as alcoholism, disaster, illness, and delinquency. The major methods of data collection were personal interviews and questionnaires. A few studies used a secondary analysis or case studies. There was considerable improvement in the application of methodology during the 1950s and 1960s as compared to the 1930s and 1940s. For example, instruments were used to measure concepts, chi-square and t-tests were used to examine the differences between groups, and control variables were used to estimate the true effects of independent variables.

Methodologies used in the 1970s and 1980s were still more sophis-

Table 7–6
Overview of Research on Family Stress and Coping, 1980–1989

Year	*Author*	*Topic*	*Theory*[a]	*Method*[b]	*Sample*	*Strengths*[c]
1980	Cleveland	Illness/coping	Mini	Questionnaire-P	19	
1980	Waisbren	Illness/stress	None	Questionnaire-P/ Interview-P	120	S,M,St
1980	Wiseman	Alcoholic/stress	Mini	Interview-P	152	
1981	Bermand and Turk	Divorce/stress	Stress	Interview-P	90	M,St
1981	Greenstein	Disaster/coping	Stress	Interview-P	N.A.	
1981	McLanahan, Wedemeyer, and Adelberg	Coping/newwork	Stress	Interview-P	45	M,St
1981	Venters	Illness/coping	Stress	Interview-P	100	S,M,T
1982	Cook	Illness/coping	None	Questionnaire-P/ Interview-P	145	St
1983	Kazak	Illness/stress	Mini	Interview-P	109	M,St,T
1983	Patterson and McCubbin	Illness/stress	ABCX model	Interview-P	100	M,St,T
1984	Goedeke	Stress/coping	Stress	Questionnaire-P	202	S,M,St,T
1984	Lapham	Illness/stress	Stress	Questionnaire-P	54	M,St,T
1984	McGinn	Illness/stress	Stress	Questionnaire-P	200	M,St,T
1984	Noh	Illness/stress	Mini	Interview-P	211	St
1984	Ricker	Stress/resource	Double ABCX	Questionnaire-P	75	M,St,T
1984	Rubin	Parenthood/stress	Stress	Questionnaire-P	N.A.	M,St,T
1985	Abelsohn	Stress/adolescents	None	Interview	45	M,St
1985	Baker	Illness/stress	System	Interview-P	N.A.	M,St

1985	Barbarin, Hughes, and Chesler	Illness/stress	Mini	Questionnaire-P/ Interview-P	32	St
1985	Bolsen	Life event/stress	Sys-sym-life	Questionnaire-P	114	S,M,St,T
1985	Lavee, McCubbin, and Olson	Stress/coping	Double ABCX	Interview-P	288	S,M,St,T,I
1985	Wright	Parenthood/coping	Coping	Interview-P	202	M,St
1986	Holroyd and Guthrie	Illness/stress	None	Questionnaire-P	43	M,St,I
1987	Bardwell	War-stress/coping	Mini	Questionnaire-P	60	M,St
1987	Lavee, McCubbin, and Olson	Life events/stress	Mini	Questionnaire-P	1,140	S,M,St,T,I
1987	Mays	Parenthood/coping	Double ABCX	Questionnaire-P Interview-P	40	M,St,T
1988	Antonovsky and Sourani	Family adaptation	Coping	Interview-P	60	M,St,T
1988	Erickson	Illness/coping	Coping	Interview-P	37	M,St,T
1988	Olson, Lavee, and McCubbin	Stress/coping	Develop. sys.	Questionnaire-P	1,251	S,M,St,T,I
1988	Peyrot, McMurry, and Hodges	Stress/coping	ABCX	Interview-P	20	M,T
1988	Pittman and Lloyd	Stress/coping	Stress	Tele-Interview	810	S,M,St,T
1988	Sellitto	Alcoholic/coping	Mini	Interview-P	60	M,St
1988	Scanvisky-Nylant	Alcoholic/coping	Coping	Questionnaire-P/ Interview-P	30	M,St
1988	Snowden et al.	Parenthood/stress	Mini	Interview-P	106	St

[a] P = primary data; S = sample; M = measurement of variables; St = statistical analysis; T = theory; I = important.

[b] Development-system: Combination of family development theory and family system theory.

[c] S = sample; M = measurement of variables; St = statistical analysis; T = theory; I = importance.

ticated. More control groups were used, and definition and measurement of variables improved. Quantification increased, and multivariate and regression analyses were used extensively.

There still needs to be better linkages between theory construction and methodological techniques. The development of testable theoretical frameworks, combined with the use of proper statistical procedures, are the important tasks for future researchers. Although the size of the samples has increased, most of them are still nonrandomly selected.

Theoretical Trends and Developments

The majority of research conducted in the 1930s and 1940s was not theoretically oriented. Except for the studies of Angell (1936) and Cavan and Ranck (1938), most studies in the 1930s did not attempt to propose or support a theory. In the 1940s, only Hill's ABCX model study had a clearly defined theoretical orientation.

There was some improvement in theoretical frameworks during the 1950s and 1960s; however, about half of the research was still exploratory and lacked theoretical guidelines.

The research of family stress and coping in the 1970s yielded new findings and extended the theory of previous decades. The two important efforts carried out by the researchers of family stress and coping in the 1970s added empirical support to the conceptualizations of Angell (1936), Cavan and Ranck (1938), Koos (1946), and particularly to Hill's (1949) classic research on war-induced separation and reunion and elaborated on the components of stress, resources, and so forth.

In the 1980s, a larger proportion of researchers formulated hypotheses for testing. As a result, research in the area of family stress and coping extended the theory and the original models of the previous decades. For example, Olson, Lavee, and McCubbin (1988) integrated ideas, and knowledge advanced within three areas of study: developmental stage, system frameworks, and stress theory.

Major Findings

1. Unemployed husbands tend to lose authority based on economic need or fear.
2. Unemployed husbands tend not to lose authority based on love and respect.
3. Integrated and adaptable families remain so during unemployment; previously disorganized families become more disorganized.
4. The dynamics of family adjustment to war crises are similar to those from the crises of unemployment, impoverishment, bereavement, and divorce.
5. There is no significant change in marital integration among families with a mentally retarded or chronically ill member.

6. Mothers of a disabled child experience greater stress than mothers without a disabled child and more stress than fathers experience.
7. Siblings of a disabled child, especially the oldest female sibling in the family, experience more tension than siblings of a normal child.
8. While stresses caused by the disability of a spouse may break up the marriage, stresses from the disability of children or from disasters do not usually threaten the stability of marital relationships.
9. Social support networks of families with handicapped children are smaller, more family dominated, and more dense.
10. Family members of a mentally ill patient tend to experience a substantial degree of burden. However, mastery ability and social support have a much greater impact on the mental health status of family members than family burden has.
11. Changes from one life stage to another can be viewed as a family crisis, which might cause the onset of symptoms in family members.
12. Couples with difficulty adjusting to the birth of their child tend to be those who had difficulty throughout pregnancy and in deciding to have a child.
13. Mothers perceived more negative stress in their individual and marital lives following the birth of a child than fathers.
14. There are differences between mothers and fathers with respect to their use of coping strategies. Mothers use social support (friends, neighbors, community and relatives) substantially more than fathers do.
15. Major decisions in points of transition merely exacerbate underlying weaknesses and tensions in the family.
16. The degree to which a family is integrated into the community is an important factor in evaluating stress tolerance, for it determines the number and quality of resources the family can count on for support and assistance.
17. The family's history, characteristics of family members, their adjustment to the separation period, and the family dynamics at the time of reunion are the important determinants of the adjustment processes involved in family reunions after prolonged separations.
18. Postdisaster emotional stress is associated with the death of a parent, severe injury, severe damages, and extreme disruptions of family life. Families with only financial debt are not as severely affected.
19. The onset of alcoholism in a family member precipitates a crisis for the family.
20. Families of alcoholics are forced to evolve techniques of adjustment through trial and error. The unpredictability of the situation, because of its lack of structure, creates anxiety in family members, which can give rise to personality difficulties.
21. More cohesive families have lower levels of strain and higher levels of well-being than less cohesive families.

22. Family system resources and social support facilitate adaptation but in different ways; family system resources affect adaptation directly, whereas social support reduces the postcrisis strain.
23. The structure of the family in which young adults live is significantly correlated with their experiences of stress; those who grew up in intact families report less current life stress and relationship-related stress than those who grew up in nonintact families.
24. The development of an adaptive support network depends not only on the availability of friends and/or relatives but also on the fit between the role orientation of the woman and the way in which her network is organized.
25. The influence of family stress on family satisfaction is mediated by the perceived ability of family to achieve its want, needs, and expectations.
26. Families are less able to cope with the effects of family stress on family satisfaction when wants, needs, and expectations are significantly greater than their ability to satisfy them.
27. Husbands and wives respond differently to the contingent influences of claims.
28. Claims and control act together to influence coping responses that mediate the effects of family stress on family satisfaction.
29. Previous family life stresses significantly influence postcrisis strain.
30. A strong sense of coherence, particularly one shared by the spouse, provides the motivational, perceptual, and behavioral basis for successful resolution of problems posed by stressors. Not the absence of stressors but their successful resolution provides one with a sense of satisfaction about family life.
31. Life stressor events tend to influence family life satisfaction of men and women differently.
32. High locus of control—believing in their ability to control events—strengthens family satisfaction of women experiencing life stressor events.

Most Influential Studies

Of the research conducted during the 1930s, two were cited most frequently: Angell's *The Family Encounters the Depression* and Cavan and Ranck's *The Family and the Depression.*

Among the work conducted in the 1940s, Hill's (1949) study of family adjustment to the crises of war separation and reunion had the most influence on the later research. The ABCX family crisis model was developed. In the model, *A*, which represents the stressor event, interacts with *B*, which represents the family's crisis-meeting resources. *B* interacts with *C*, which represents the definition the family makes of the event, to produce *X* (the crisis).

The ABCX model focused primarily on precrisis variables that account for differences in family ability to cope with the impact of a stressor event and the degree to which the outcome is a crisis for the family. Hill's model outlined a set of major variables and their relationships that has remained virtually unchanged for over thirty years.

Research in the 1950s on family stress and coping was innovative in scope and in area of interest. The studies by Crawford (1957) and LeMasters (1957) were the most intriguing and innovative. Crawford's study of family adjustment to tornadic disasters provided the understanding of the action at the family level that occurs in disaster situation. Crawford found family stress associated with the death of parent, severe injury, severe damages, and extreme disruptions of family life. The families that had been less severely affected were fairly successful in their postcrisis adjustment.

LeMasters's (1957) study of the birth of the first child raised the concern about transition points in the normal development of the family life cycle: getting married, the birth of the first baby, children's going to school, death of a spouse, and children's leaving home.

The studies of Kramm (1958), Siporin (1959), and Kelman (1959) were noteworthy also. All found that the presence of an ill family member in the home need not necessarily prove to have a uniformly damaging effect on family living and may produce certain beneficial consequences for some families. Kramm (1958) also found that the adjustment depended on the presence of certain sociocultural, psychological, and biological factors, a few of which were the family's mutual orientation to a system of religious beliefs that saw purpose in the child and the mother's health and ability to care for the child.

Two key studies in the 1960s were done by Dyer (1963) and Hobbs (1965). Dyer found, as did LeMasters (1957), that a majority of middle-class couples experienced "extensive or severe" crisis on the birth of their first child. Hobbs (1965) found lower levels of crisis experienced by new parents than either LeMasters or Dyer had found. Variables that earlier had been found to differentiate couples in the slight to moderate crisis category from those in the extensive severe category were not statistically significant. Hobbs stated, "Measure of crisis proved to be a central problem and so became an added objective." These controversial findings stimulated a series of research in the following decade.

The key studies of the 1970s were conducted by Lavigne and Ryan (1979) and Hobbs and Cole (1976). Lavigne and Ryan (1979) studied the psychologic adjustment of siblings of children with chronic illness. In their sudy, control groups were used, and areas of difference between groups were identified. Siblings of children with chronic illness were found to be more likely to show symptoms of irritability and social withdrawal. No group differences were noted on measures of aggression or learning problems.

The samples of previous studies on the impact of the birth of the first baby were not randomly selected. Since Hobbs and Cole (1976) used a random sample of couples for their analysis, the results of their study were accepted with greater confidence. Hobbs and Cole concluded that beginning parenthood should be viewed as a transition rather than a crisis. This statement has influenced the direction of research on family stress and coping in the 1980s.

There was considerable improvement in theory and method during the 1980s. Olson, Lavee, and McCubbin (1988) developed a multidimensional typology of family dynamics in an attempt to identify what types of family systems are more resilient than others. They found that "connected" (more cohesive) families had lower levels of strain and higher levels of well-being than do "separated" (less cohesive) families.

Another key study of the 1980s was that of McCubbin, and Olson (1985). They examined the relationships among the major variables of double ABCX model of family stress and adaptation. The results indicated that family life events significantly influenced postcrisis strain. Family system resources and social support facilitated adaptation but in different ways: family system resources affected adaptation directly, whereas social support reduced the postcrisis strain.

Needed Future Research

The research over the last six decades provides useful information for future research and theory building. McCubbin and his associations extended the ABCX model (Hill, 1949) to the double ABCX model (McCubbin and Figley, 1983) and FAAR (Family Adjustment and Adaptation Response) model (McCubbin and Figley, 1983).

The research observations and theory building of the future depend on the empirical results generated from current knowledge and theories. Some recent research has not utilized adequate samples or current data analysis techniques. As a result, more attention should be directed to sampling, measurement issues, and analytical techniques.

While McCubbin and his associates attempted to clarify the relationships among the major variables of the double ABCX model, the task has not yet been completed. Not all of the theoretical constructs of the model have been measured and entered into the structural model. There is room for more exploration of new latent variables in the equation. And the relationships among stressors, resources, perception, and adaptation should be examined in other sets of pileup demands and in other populations (McCubbin et al. 1985).

The purpose of the research on family stress and coping is to understand the responses of the family to stress and eventually provide useful information on the prevention and effective management of family stress. To do this, it requires an integration of findings into a predictive model. Isolated findings of a relationship between two variables among a particular sample at a specific time do not provide sufficient knowledge for developing an effective program prevent or manage family stress. Also, more precise operationalizations of the concepts of family stress, social support, and family resources are needed to increase the power of the explanation.

Previous research in the area of family stress and coping has focused on families with severe and acute stressor events, and rather small samples of people were used. As research attention to family stress and coping shifts from the study of family dysfunction to the study of positive family-oriented coping, efforts should be made to obtain nationally random samples to understand family behavior in response to stress and positive efforts to avoid family stress. McCubbin and his associates were the pioneers in using a national random sample to study family response to stress. More data directly focused on the area of family stress and coping need to be collected with national random samples.

There should be studies designed to investigate efforts at applying research findings to family adaptation and coping. Such studies could include the following:

1. Different communication and problem-solving patterns should be evaluated to detemine what patterns are more effective in coping with or eliminating stress. Effective patterns could then be taught.
2. Methods to help families understand and cope with transitional stages of family life should be investigated.
3. Research on programs developed to incorporate families into communities should be conducted.

Note

1. The following indexes were used to identify articles on family stress and coping over the sixty-year period: *International Bibliography of Research in Marriage and Family* (1900–1964), *Research in Marriage and the Family*, vol. 2 (1965–1972), *Inventory of Marriage and the Family Literature* (1973–1986), *Psychological Abstracts* (1965–1989), and *Dissertation Abstracts International* (1930–1989). In each index words searched were: *adaptation, adjustment, alcoholics, anxiety, coping, crisis, disaster, disorder, disorganization, divorce, drug abuse, delinquency, illness, stress, unemployment,* and *war.* A volume-by-volume search was also conducted on the content of the following journals: *American Journal of Sociology, American Sociological Review, Social Forces, Rural Sociology, Journal of Social Psychology,* and *Journal of Marriage and the Family.* Due to several limitations, such as unavailable journals and dissertations, it was impossible to include all the research conducted. It was done as completely as possible. A list of those publications, which are relevant but were not available, is found in appendix 7–A.

References

Abelson, D. 1985. Adolescent adjustment to parental divorce: An investigation from the theoretical perspective of structural family therapy. Ph.D. Dissertation, University of Cape Town.

Anderson, Nancy N. 1966. Prisoners' families: A study of family crisis. Ph.D. dissertation, University of Minnesota.

Angell, R.O. 1936. *The Family Encounters the Depression.* New York: Charles Scribner.

Antonovsky, A. 1979. *Health, Stress, and Coping.* San Francisco: Jossey-Bass.

Antonovsky, A., and Sourani, T. 1988. Family sense of coherence and family adaptation. *Journal of Marriage and the Family* 50:79–92.

Baker, K.G., 1985. Perceptions of current stressful life events. Family stress/support factors, and selected health factors in young adults. Ph.D. disseration, Catholic University of America.

Barbarin, O.A.; Hughes, D.; and Chesler, M.A. 1985. Stress, coping, and marital functioning among parents of children with cancer. *Journal of Marriage and the Family* 44:473–480.

Bardwell, B. 1987. Analysis of marital cohesion and adaptability of Vietnam veteran families. Ph.D. dissertation, Washington State University.

Barrabee, P., and Von Mering, O. 1953. Ethnic variations in mental stress in families with psychotic children. *Social Problems* 1:48–53.

Berman, W.H., and Turk, D.C. 1981. Adaptation to divorce: Problems and coping strategies. *Journal of Marriage and the Family* 43:179–189.

Bey, D.B., and Lange, J. 1974. Waiting wives: Women and stress. *Journal of Psychiatry* 131 (3):283–287.

Bolsen, N.R. 1985. The influence of stressful life events upon subjective family satisfaction among rural Kansas families in the middle years: A path model. Ph.D. dissertation, Kansas State University.

Booz-Allen and Hamilton, Inc. 1974. *An Assessment of the Needs and Resources for Children of Alcoholic Parents.* Prepared for the U.S. National Institute on Alcohol Abuse and Alcoholism. Rep. No. PB-241-119. Springfield, Va.: National Technical Information Service.

Boss, P. 1977. A clarification of the concept of psychological father presence in families experiencing ambiguity boundary. *Journal of Marriage and the Family* 39 (February):141–151.

Browing, C.J. 1960. Differential impact of family disorganization on male adolescents. *Social Problem* 8:37–44.

Busch, H.; Kormendy, E.; and Feuerlein, W. 1973. Partners of female alcoholics. *British Journal of Addiction* 68:179–184.

Caldwell, B.M., and Guze, S. 1960. A study of the adjustment of parents and siblings of institutionalized and noninstitutionalized retarded children. *American Journal of Mental Deficiency* 64:845–861.

Cavan, R., and Ranck, K.R. 1938. *The Family and the Depression.* Chicago: University of Chicago Press.

Chafetz, M.E.; Blane, H.T.; and Hill, M.T. 1971. Children of alcoholics; observations in a child guidance clinic. *Quarterly Journal of Studies on Alcoholics* 32:687–698.

Cleveland, M. 1980. Family adaptation to traumatic spinal cord injury: Response to crisis. *Family Relations* 29:558–565.

Cohen, A.A., and Dotan, J. 1976. Communication in the family as a function of stress during war and peace. *Journal of Marriage and the Family* 38:141–148.

Cohen, G. 1977. Absentee husbands in spiralist families. *Journal of Marriage and the Family* 49:595–605.

Colletta, N.D. 1979. Support systems after divorce: Incidence and impact. *Journal of Marriage and the Family* 41:837–845.

Conard, L.M. 1936–1937. Some effects of the depression on family life. *Marriage and the Family* 15:76–80.

Cook, J.A. 1982. The adjustment of parents following the death of a child from a terminal illness. Ph.D. dissertation, Ohio State University.

Crawford, F.R. 1957. Patterns of family readjustment to tornadic disasters: A sociological case study. Ph.D. dissertation, University of Texas.

Cumming, G.H. 1970. A study of adjustment to a family crisis in the form of a disability to the male wage earner. Ph.D. dissertation, University of Southern California.

Cummings, S.T. 1976. The impact of the child's deficiency on the father: A study of fathers of mentally retarded and of chronically ill children. *American Journal of Orthopsychiatry* 46 (2):246–255.

Cummings, T.B.; Bayley, H.C.; and Rie, R.E. 1966. Effects of the child's deficiency on the mother: A study of mothers of mentally retarded, chronically ill and neurotic children. *American Journal of Orthopsychiatry* 36:595–608.

De Forest, J.W. 1974. Drug abuse: A family affair. *Journal of Drug Issues* 4 (2):130–134.

Drabek, T.E. 1975. The impact of disaster on kin relationships. *Journal of Marriage and the Family* 37 (3):481–494.

Dyer, E.D. 1963. Parenthood as crisis: A restudy. *Marriage and Family Living* 25:196–201.

Edwards, P.; Harvey, C.; and Whitehead, P. 1973. Wives of alcoholics; A critical review and analysis. *Quarterly Journal of Studies on Alcohol* 34:112–132.

El-Guebaly, N., and Offord, D.R. 1977. The offspring of alcoholics; A critical review. *American Journal of Psychiatry* 134:357–365.

Erickson, J.R. 1988. Coping with uncertainty for parents of ill infants. Ph.D. dissertation, University of Arizona.

Fein, R.A. 1976. Men's entrance to parenthood. *Family Coordinator* 25:341–348.

Fogleman, Charles Willard. 1958. Family and community in disaster: A socio-psychological study of the effects of a major disaster upon individuals and groups within the impact area. Ph.D. dissertation, Louisiana State University.

Fowle, C.M. 1968. The effect of the severely mentally retarded child on his family. *American Journal of Mental Deficiency* 72:468–473.

Friedrich, W.N. 1979. Predictors of the coping behavior of mothers of handicapped children. *Journal of Consulting and Clinical Psychology* 47:1140–1141.

Gayton, W.F.; Friedman, S.B.; Tavormins, J.F.; and Tucker, F. 1977. Children with cystic fibrosis: I. Psychological test findings of patients, siblings, and parents. *Pediatrics* 59:888–894.

Gath, A. 1972. The mental health of siblings of congenitally abnormal children. *Journal of Child Psychology, Psychiatry, and Allied Disciplines* 13:211–218.

Goedeke, D.A. 1984. Mediating family stress: Effects of claims/control. Ph.D. dissertation, University of Missouri.

Gorad, S.L. 1971. Communicational styles and interaction of alcoholics and their wives. *Family Process* 10:474–489.

Graliker, B.V.; Fishler, K.; and Koch, R. 1962. Teenage reaction to a mentally retarded sibling. *American Journal of Mental Deficiency* 66:838–843.

Greenstein, M.A. 1981. A log-linear test of a theory of family stress in natural disaster: The northeast Brazil drought. Ph.D. dissertation, University of Colorado.

Hadley, T.R. 1974. The relationship between family developmental crisis and the appearance of symptoms in a family member. *Family Process* 13:207–214.

Hansen, D.A. 1962. The impact of middle class delinquency on the family: An exploratory study. Ph.D. dissertation, University of Minnesota.

Hill, R. 1949. *Families under Stress: Adjustment to the Crises of War Separation and Reunion.* New York: Harper and Bros.

Hobbs, D. 1965. Parenthood as crisis: A third study. *Journal of Marriage and the Family* 27:367–372.

———. 1968. Transition to parenthood: A replication and an extension. *Journal of Marriage and the Family* 30:413–417.

Hobbs, D.F., and Cole, S.P. 1976. Transition to parenthood: A decade replication. *Journal of Marriage and the Family* 38:723–731.

Hoffer, C.R. 1945. The impact of war on the farm family. *Rural Sociology* 10:151–156.

Hoffmann, H., and Noem, A.A. 1975. Alcoholism among parents of male and female alcoholics. *Psychological Report* 36:322.

Holroyd, J. 1974. The questionnaire on resources and stress: An instrument to measure family response to a handicapped family member. *Journal of Community Psychology* 2:92–94.

Holroyd, J., and Guthrie, D. 1986. Family stress with chronic childhood illness: Cystic fibrosis, neuromuscular disease, and renal disease. *Journal of Clinical Psychology* 42:552–561.

Igel, A. 1945. The effects of war separation on father-child relations. *Family* 26:3–9.

Jackson, J.K. 1956. The adjustment of the family to alcoholism. *Marriage and Family Living* (November):361–369.

Jacobson, Margaret M. 1963. Coping with heart disease: A study of farm families. Ph.D. dissertation, University of Purdue.

James, J.E., and Goldman, M. 1971. Behavior trends of wives of alcoholics. *Quarterly Journal of Studies on Alcoholics* 32:373–381.

Kammeier, M.L. 1971. Adolescents from families with and without alcohol problems. *Quarterly Journal of Studies on Alcoholics* 32:364–372.

Kaplan, D.M.; Smith, A.; Grobstein, R.; and Fischman, S. 1973. Family mediation of stress. *Social Work* 18 (4):60–69.

Kazak, A.E. 1983. Family stress and social support networks: An analysis of families with handicapped children. Ph.D. dissertation, University of Virginia.

Kelman, H.R. 1959. The effects of a group of non-institutionalized mongoloid children upon their families as perceived by their mothers. Ph.D. dissertation, New York University.

Kirkpatrick, E.C. 1934. Adaptations of farm families to emergencies. *American Journal of Sociology* 40:495–502.

Kogan, K.L.; Fordyce, W.E.; and Jackson, J.K. 1963. Personality disturbance in wives of alcoholics. *Quarterly Journal of Studies on Alcoholics* 24:226–238.

Komarovsky, M. 1940. *The Unemployed Man and His Family: The Effect of Unemployment upon the Man in Fifty-nine Families.* New York: Dryden PR.

Koos, E. 1946. *Families in Trouble.* New York: King's Crown Press.

Kramm, E.R. 1958. Reactions and patterns of adjustment of the family to its mongoloid child. Ph.D. dissertation, University of Pittsburgh.

Lapham, E.V. 1984. Health, stress, and coping of families with deaf-blind (rubella) children. Ph.D. dissertation, University of Maryland.

Lavee, Y.; McCubbin, H.I.; and Olson, D.H. 1987. The effect of stressful life events and transitions on family functioning and well-being. *Journal of Marriage and the Family* 49:811–825.

Lavee, Y.; McCubbin, H.I.; and Patternson, J.M. 1985. The double ABCX model of family stress and adaption: An empirical test by analysis of structural equations with latent variables. *Journal of Marriage and the Family* 47:811–825.

Lavigne, J.V. and Ryan, M. 1979. Psychologic adjustment of siblings of children with chronic illness. *Pediatrics* 63 (4):616–627.

Leifson, J. 1979. Family crisis: The handicapped child. Ph.D. dissertation, Brigham Young University.

LeMasters, E.E. 1957. Parenthood as crisis. *Journal of Marriage and the Family* 17:352–355.

Lemert, E.M. 1960. The occurrence and sequence of events in the adjustment of families to alcoholics. *Quarterly Journal of Studies on Alcohol* 21:679–697.

Lenroot, K.F. 1935. Children of the depression: A study of 259 families in selected areas of five cities. *Social Service Review* 9:212–242.

Leveen, L. 1970. On becoming a Parent: Attitude and feeling changes. Ph.D. dissertation, University of Southern California.

Levy, D.M. 1945. The war and family life: Report for the War Emergency Committee, 1944. *American Journal of Orthopsychiatry* 15:140–152.

Love, J.P. 1970. Conjugal family's adjustment to the crisis of imprisonment. Ph.D. dissertation, Florida State University.

McCubbin, H.I.; Dahl, B.B.; Lester, G.R.; Benson, D.; and Robertson, M.L. 1975. The returned prisoner of war: Factors in family reintegration. *Journal of Marriage and the Family* 37:471–478.

——— 1976. Coping repertoires of families adapting to prolonged war-induced separations. *Journal of Marriage and the Family* 38:461–471.

McCubbin, H.I. and Figley C.R. 1983. *Stress and the Family*. New York: Brunner/Mazel.

McGinn, C.B. 1984. The relationship among family stressors, cohesion, adaptability, satisfaction, and illness or injury. Ph.D. dissertation. Brigham Young University.

McLanahan, S.S.; Wedemeyer, N.V.; and Adelberg, T. 1981. Network structure, social support, and psychological well-being in the single-parent family. *Journal of Marriage and the Family* 43:601–612.

Mack, D. 1935. Psychological and emotional values in C.W.A. assignment. A study of 61 families on relief before and after C.W.A. *Social Service Review* 9:256–268.

Mays, R.M. 1987. Family adaptation to unwed adolescent parenthood: The relationships of family stressors, social support and coping strategies to family satisfaction and infant immunization status. Ph.D. dissertation, University of Texas.

Meyerowitz, J.H.; and Feldman, H. 1966. Transition to parenthood. *Psychiatric Research Report* 20:78–84.

Mik, G. 1970. Son of alcoholic father. *British Journal of Addiction* 65:305–515.

Nealon, J. 1964. The adolscent's hospitalization as a family crisis. *Archives of General Psychiatry* 11:302–311.

Noh, S. 1984. Living with psychiatric patients: The relationship between family burden and mental health among family members. Ph.D. dissertation, University of Western Ontario.

Noh, S., and Avison, W.R. 1988. Spouses of discharged psychiatric patients: Factors associated with their experience of burden. *Journal of Marriage and the Family* 50:377–389.

O'Gorman, P.A. 1975. Self-concept, locus of control, and perception of father in adolescents from homes with and without severe drinking problems. Ph.D. dissertation, Fordham University.

Olson, D.S.; Lavee, Y.; and McCubbin, H.I. 1988. Types of families and family response to stress across the family life cycle. In D.M. Klein and J. Aldous (eds.), pp. 16–43. New York: Guildford Press.

Orford, J. 1976. A study of the personalities of excessive drinkers and their wives, using the approaches of Leary and Eyeseneck. *Journal of Consulting Clinical Psychology* 44:534–545.

Paolino, T.J.; McCrady, B.; Diamond, S.; and Longabaugh, R. 1976. Psychological disturbances in spouses of alcoholics. *Quarterly Journal of Studies on Alcohol* 37:1600–1608.

Parad, H.J., and Caplan, E. 1960. A framework for studying families in crisis. *Social Work* 5:3–15.

Patterson, J.M., and McCubbin, H.I. 1983. The impact of family life events and changes on the health of a chronically ill child. *Family Relations* (April):255–264.

Penick, E.C.; Powell, B.J. and Sieck, W.A. 1976. Mental health problems and natural disaster: Tornado victims. *Journal of Community Psychology* 4:64–67.

Peyrot, M.; McMurry, J.F.; and Hedges, R. 1988. Marital adjustment to adult diabetes: Interpersonal congruence and spouse satisfaction. *Journal of Marriage and the Family* 50:363–376.

Pittman, J.F., and Lloyd, S.A. 1988. Quality of family life, social support, and stress. Journal of Marriage and the Family 50:53–67.

Ricker, M.D. 1984. Application of the double ABCX model to predict changes in perception of stresses associated with a child's growth problem. Ph.D. dissertation, University of Main.

Rubin, M. 1984. A general stress model of the adjustment to pregnancy. Ph.D. dissertation, University of Wisconsin.

Rimmer, J. 1974. Psychiatric illness in husbands of alcoholics. *Quarterly Journal of Studies on Alcoholics* 35:281–283.

Robey, A.; Rosenwald, R.J.; Snell, M.D.; and Lees, R.E. 1964. The runaway girl: A reaction to family stress. *American Journal of Orthopsychiatry* 34:762–767.

Rouse, B.A.; Waller, P.F.; and Ewing, J.A. 1973. Adolescents' stress levels, coping activities and father's drinking behavior. *Proceedings of the American Psychological Association* 81:681–681.

Russell, C.S. 1974. Transition to parenthood: Problems and gratifications. *Journal of Marriage and the Family* 36:294–302.

Ryder, R.G. 1973. Longitudinal data relating marriage satisfactions. *Journal of Marriage and the Family* 35:604–607.

Scanvisky-Mylant, M. 1988. The process of coping and emotional development of young adult children of alcoholics: A nursing study. Ph.D, dissertation, University of Texas.

Sellitto, L.A. 1988. A comparison of stress and coping by spouses of alcoholics and spouses of opiate addicts. Ph.D. dissertation, University of Pittsburgh.

Siporin, M. 1959. The family role of the schizophrenic patient prior to the onset of illness. Ph.D. dissertation, University of Pittsburgh.

Snowden, L.R.; Schott, T.L.; Awalt, S.J.; and Gillis-Knox, J. 1988. Marital satisfaction in pregnancy: Stability and change. *Journal of Marriage and the Family* 50:325–333.
Sutherland, S., and D.J. Scherl. 1970. Patterns of response among victims of rape. *American Journal of Orthopsychiatry* 40 (3):503–511.
Tarter, R. 1976. Personality of Wives of alcoholics. *Journal of Clinical Psychology* 32:741–743.
Templer, D.I.; Ruff, C.F.; and Ayers, J. 1974. Essential alcoholism and family history of alcoholism. *Quarterly Journal of Studies on Alcohol* 35:655–657.
Veen, V.; Huebner, B.; and Jorgens, B. 1964. Relationships between parents' concept of the family and family adjustment. *American Journal of Orthopsychiatry* 34:45–55.
Venters, M. 1981. Familial coping with chronic and severe childhood illness: The case of cystic fibrosis. *Social Science and Medicine* 15a:289–297.
Waisbren, S.E. 1980. Parents' reactions after the birth of a developmentally disabled child. *American Journal of Mental Deficients* 84:345–351.
Waller, H.M. 1933. Some data regarding 162 families affected by unemployment known to the Cleveland Associated Charities. *Family Supplement* 14:131–135.
Wiseman, J.P. 1975. An alternative role for the wife of an alcoholic in Finland. *Journal of Marriage and the Family* 37:172–179.
———. 1980. The "home treatment": The first steps in trying to cope with an alcholic husband. *Family Relations* 29:541–549.
Wright, C.A. 1985. The relationship between self-reported stress and coping strategies during early parenting. Ph.D. dissertation, Oregon State University.
Yarrow, M.R.; Schwartz, C.G.; and Murphy, H.S. 1955. The psychological meaning of mental illness in the family. *Journal of Social Issues* 11:12–24.
Young, M. 1954. The role of the extended family in a disaster. *Human Relations* 7:383–391.
Young, P.V. 1933. The new poor. *Sociology and Social Research* 17:234–242.
Zadawzki, B., and Lazersfeld, P. 1935. The psychological consequences of unemployment. *Journal of Social Psychology* 6:224–251.

Relevant Reports Unavailable for Review

Bogdanoff, K.P. 1974. Method of childbirth and its relationship to marital adjustment and parental crisis. Master's thesis, Virginia Polytechnical Institute and State University.
Dahl, B., and McCubbin, H. 1975. Children of returned prisoners of war: The effect of long-term father absence. Paper presented at the annual meeting of the American Psychological Association, Chicago.
Fagen, S.; Janda, E.; Baker, S.; Fischer, E.; and Cove, L. 1967. *Impact of Father Absence in Military Families: II. Factors Relating to Success of Coping with Crisis.* Technical Report. Washington, DC: Walter Reed Medical Center.
Lumpkin, K. Du Pre, and Douglas, D.W. 1933. The effect of unemployment and short-time during 1931 in the families of 200 Alabama child workers. *Social Force* 11:548–558.
McCubbin, H.I., and Dahl, B.B. 1987. The returned prisoner of war: Factors in family

adjustment. Paper presented at the first international conference on psychological stress and adjustment in times of war and peace, Tel Aviv, January.

Price-Binham, S. 1970. A study of 32 wives whose husbands are missing in action in Vietnam. Paper presented at the Annual Meeting of the National Council on Family Relations, Chicago, October.

Tooke, S. 1974. Adjustment of parenthood among a select group of disadvantaged parents. Master's thesis, Montana State University.

Uhlenberg, B.T. 1970. Crisis factors in transition of college students to parenthood. Master's thesis, Ohio State University.

8
Violence in the Family

Dean M. Busby

Research on family violence is a relatively new phenomenon of the last two decades. Prior to 1960, researchers only hinted at deeper problems by using terms such as *corporal punishment* or *harsh discipline* in their work. Although it is difficult to determine why family violence was ignored for so long, at least two reasons are evident: antiquated attitudes allowed adults a tremendous amount of latitude in applying "punishment" to other family members (Pagelow, 1984), and the laws governing confidentiality before 1960 prohibited professionals from divulging information about their clients, regardless of the severity of their behavior. Nevertheless, with changes in attitudes and in legislation that require professionals to report suspected violence and protect them from damage suits from family members, research on family violence exploded during the mid-1960s and 1970s. This review reports and evaluates the empirical research during the last six decades.

Defining violence as it applies to families is no small task; researchers have struggled with the boundaries of the term *violence* for years (Gil, 1971). A main source of difficulty with research in this area has been the confusion of the terms *neglect*, *abuse*, and *violence* (Gelles, 1980). At times, scholars have used the three terms as if they were interchangeable, which has resulted in nebulous meanings for each word. The definition chosen for this chapter is the following: Violence in the family is the intentional use of physical force by one family member that is aimed at hurting or injuring another family member. The strength of this definition is that physical force is termed violence regardless of the severity of the outcome if it was used intentionally to inflict harm or injure another. The weakness is that it is often impossible to determine which acts were accidental and which were intentional.

Adopting such a definition implies that topics like parent-child violence, physical punishment, violence between spouses, and violence between siblings will be addressed. Topics that will not be covered in this chapter but sometimes include physical force are incest and other forms of sexual abuse, such as marital rape. My opinion is that sexual abuse is distinct from other types of abuse, and it is inappropriate to discuss physical and sexual abuse as if they were equivalent (Gelles and Cornell, 1985). Therefore, although physical abuse will

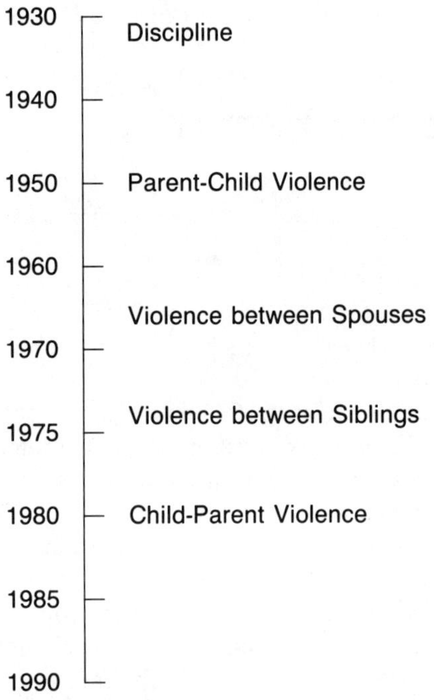

Figure 8–1. Approximate Dates That Subtopics of Family Violence Emerged in the Research.

be reviewed, this is not a comprehensive work on abuse or neglect in the family. When the term *abuse* is used in this chapter, it refers to physical abuse.

Historically, the earliest subtopic to receive attention in the literature on family violence was parent-child violence. Figure 8–1 presents a time line of when the subtopics of family violence emerged in the research literature. In the review by decade, the subtopics of family violence will be addressed in the same order that they occurred chronologically: parent-child violence, violence between spouses, violence between siblings, and child-parent violence.

Research Prior to 1930

Before 1930 the term *family violence* did not exist. Caseworkers, psychologists, and medical professionals knew that violence was occurring in families because they had to deal with its effects on a daily basis (Mower, 1928). Even Sigmund Freud (1919) was aware of the deleterious effects that violence had on children, as was evident in his early work about sexual perversions, "A Child Is Being

Beaten—A Contribution to the Study of the Origin of Sexual Perversions." Nevertheless, actual empirical research on the scope of the problem had not been done prior to 1930 (Van Hasselt et al. 1988).

Although research on family violence did not emerge before 1930, there were some important events that occurred that put the problem of parent-child violence on the map. The famous case of Mary Ellen, who had to be protected by the Society for the Prevention of Cruelty to Animals in 1875 because there was no similar organization to protect children, was one of these events (Pfohl, 1977). Her vicious abuse by foster parents was reported in newspapers around the country and led to the creation of the New York Society for the Prevention of Cruelty to Children.

The Decade 1930–1939

Research Findings

Early research on parent-child relationships only hinted at deeper problems by mentioning harsh punishment and cruelty (Martin, 1932; Brenneman, 1932). Even when the parent-child relationship was examined in detail, physical punishment or abuse would be mentioned only as a possible problem and rarely researched directly (Symonds, 1937).

A notable exception to this trend was an article by Ayer and Bernreuter (1937), which explored the relationship between discipline and personality traits in young children. Without any particular theory to guide their efforts, they collected information from a sample of forty preschool children (twenty-two from the merchant and professional class and eighteen from homes on the minimum-subsistence level). They found that the parents of lower-class children used physical punishment more than any other discipline technique. Middle-class parents used other types of discipline more often, although physical punishment was still one of the top four methods used. In addition, as physical punishment was used more, the children tended to face reality less and showed more dependence on adult affection and attention.

A study by Stagner (1933) represented a different view of physical punishment. Using a sample of 250 college freshmen, the author obtained biographical information about their homes to evaluate the role of parents in the development of emotional stability. Stagner addressed the proposition of psychoanalysts that parents play a large role in the personality development of the child. Stagner concluded that children coming from homes where the father did not resort to physical punishment were more likely to develop emotional instability than children who came from homes where the father used physical punishment.

The last study on parent-child violence reviewed in this decade was by Watson (1934). A sample of 230 graduate students completed questionnaires

Table 8–1
Overview of Research on Family Violence, 1930–1939

Year	*Author*	*Topic*	*Theory*	*Method*[a]	*Sample*	*Strengths*[b]
1933	Stagner	Discipline	Freud	Questionnaire-P	250	S
1934	Watson	Discipline	None	Questionnaire-P	230	S
1937	Ayer and Bernreuter	Discipline	None	Observation	40	I

[a] P = primary data; S = secondary data.
[b] S = sample; I = importance.

about the type of home training they received, as well as self-descriptions. The purpose of the study was to see if strict home training produced different effects from lax home training. The students who had experienced strict home training generally reported lower levels of functioning. They showed a greater tendency than the students from lax homes to feel that the world was "out to get them," were more dependent and socially maladjusted, had weaker support systems, and experienced more guilt, worry, and anxiety.

The Decade in Review

Theory and Methodology. None of the three studies reviewed during this decade had a theory that was being tested. The methodology was similar to other research during the 1930s in that simple percentages or descriptions were reported without any details on statistical significance.

Major Authors and Research Pieces. Table 8–1 presents a summary of the research during this decade. Of the three studies that were found from the 1930s, Ayer and Bernreuter's (1937) was the most carefully conducted. None of the three studies was designed to study violence directly; in fact, violence was more of a controlling or background variable in these studies. All three articles dealt with parental discipline rather than the more serious problem of child abuse. Nevertheless, with the exception of Stagner's (1933) study, the results suggested that physical punishment in large amounts was detrimental to those who experienced it.

Although there was little direct research on violence between parents and children, the theme was evident in the literature of the 1930s. Psychologists, social workers, and sociologists were consistent in their denouncement of physical punishment. An example is a study by Erik Erikson (1937) among the Sioux Indians. After extensively studying the families, he made the following statement about "parental aggression": "On the other hand, the Sioux considered the white settlers' slapping and beating of their own children as one of the most damaging pieces of evidence against their being adults at all" (p. 140). Other researchers were just as severe in condemning parents for using physical punishment or abuse (Levy, 1931).

The Decade 1940–1949

With the exception of three studies, the neglect of the topic of family violence continued into the 1940s. Violence was raging abroad during the decade and probably had something to do with the inattention to violence within the walls of the home.

Research Findings

The first study on parent-child violence was done by Stott (1940), who used a sample of 1,878 Nebraska high school students to assess the home punishment of adolescents. Stott found that few respondents were slapped, and only three were whipped. Most of the punishment was termed "scolding" and was done by the mothers. The findings suggest that physical punishment was less common in urban areas and decreases as the child gets older.

Wittman and Huffman (1945) compared psychotic, psychoneurotic, delinquent, and normal children's adjustment and personality characteristics. Violence was measured indirectly through open-ended questions about fathers and mothers. The sample contained 552 youths who were questioned extensively on background characteristics, personality characteristics, and adjustment. This was the earliest article discovered that used the term *violent* when referring to the parent-child subsystem. The fathers of the delinquent girls were labeled *violent disciplinarians* by the girls.

Perhaps the most important work of the 1930s and 1940s was Caffey's (1946) medical case study. This study was important in the development of research on violence in the family not because the findings were related to violence but because the article promoted a great deal of research that resulted in the explosion of child abuse issues in the medical and social science communities (Pfohl, 1977).

Caffey (1946) linked long bone fractures in children to what he called "unspecific origins." Although he suspected that some medical cause would be discovered for the fractures, his work prompted other researchers to investigate bone injuries and skeletal trauma in young children. This research led pediatric radiology to shift its diagnosis from internal medical explanations to external social causes, such as parental mistreatment (Pfohl, 1977). As a result of the discovery that many of the injuries of young children were caused by parents, doctors began to publish articles on what they called the "battered-child syndrome" (Kempe et al., 1962).

The Decade in Review

Theory and Methodology. Theory on family violence was still nonexistent during the 1940s. The methodology continued to suffer as a result of small samples and simple descriptive statements that were not supported through statistical tests.

Major Authors and Research Pieces. Table 8–2 summarizes the research conducted during the 1940s. While Caffey's article was the most influential, none of the three articles dealt directly with family violence. Nevertheless, reports of violence against individual children continued to show up in popular magazines and newspapers, as well as in the journals of clinical professionals

Table 8–2
Overview of Research on Family Violence, 1940–1949

Year	*Author*	*Topic*	*Theory*	*Method*[a]	*Sample*	*Strengths*[b]
1940	Stott	Discipline	None	Questionnaire-P	1,878	S
1945	Wittman and Huffman	Delinquency	None	Questionnaire-P	552	S
1946	Caffey	Physical injury	None	Case study	—	I

[a] P = primary data; S = secondary data.
[b] S = sample; I = importance.

(Smith, 1944), an indication that many were aware of family violence, though it was not a topic of empirical research.

The Decade 1950–1959

Research Findings

Parent-Child Violence. In the 1950s, research on parental discipline continued but with little attention to the physical abuse of children. Nevertheless, a few researchers started to make connections between harsh punishment or abuse and the development of dysfunction later in life. At the same time, the medical researchers spurned by Caffey's article (1946) entered the field in greater numbers to determine the causes of traumatic injuries suffered by children.

Social Class and Child Rearing Methods. Four of the articles in this decade dealt with the socialization of children in different social classes (Maccoby and Gibbs, 1954; Havighurst and Davis, 1955; Littmen, Moore, and Pierce-Jones, 1957; Miller and Swanson, 1958). The only connection that they had with violence in the family is that each had a brief section on physical punishment. The authors attempted to compare the child rearing techniques used by the parents to the middle and lower classes. Although the four studies did not produce conclusive evidence that middle-class parents used corporal punishment more or less often than lower-class parents, they did show that physical punishment was a commonly used method of discipline. In addition, these four studies were some of the earliest to demonstrate that social class was an important variable in the study of families.

Discipline and Dysfunctions Later in Life. Two other articles were important during the 1950s because the authors linked the types of discipline used on children to dysfunctions later in life. Gold (1953), using census data as well as data from other authors, found that whites committed suicide more often than blacks and blacks committed homicide more often than whites. The author found that physical punishment was used less often with whites than with blacks and presented this as a possible explanation for the different rates of homicide and suicide. The assumption was made that blacks were socialized to be aggressive through homicide, while whites were socialized to be aggressive through suicide.

The second study linking early discipline in the home to homicide was conducted by a group of doctors trying to understand the etiological factors in first-degree murder (Duncan et al. 1958). They questioned six prisoners convicted of murder and found that four of them had been subjected to physical brutality at the hands of their parents. They then interviewed the parents of the convicts and found them to be evasive as well as dishonest with respect to the brutality, even when confronted with evidence of it. They suggested that physicians working with children who have been injured should investigate brutality in order to prevent violent acts later in life.

Medical Personnel and Children with Physical Injuries. The last three articles that were reviewed during the 1950s were follow-ups on Caffey's (1946) work with children suffering physical injuries. Silverman's (1953) article was an early landmark study in specifying injuries of children that were probably a result of parental mistreatment. Three case studies of children who were suffering from "unrecognized skeletal trauma" were presented, as well as some of the reactions of parents when interviewed about the child's injuries. Although Silverman chided doctors for their laxity in obtaining reliable histories, the suggestion was given that interviews not be conducted with questionable parents so as not to precipitate a crisis in an already difficult family situation.

An article similar to Silverman's was published by Bakwin in 1956. Bakwin also used three case examples of children with multiple skeletal lesions and again suggested that rather than overwhelm the parents with guilt, it might be better to omit explanations of the causes of the bone trauma so as not to precipitate a family crisis.

The most important article of the decade was published by Woolley and Evans (1955). Using a sample of twenty-five consecutive babies admitted with the diagnosis of acute subdural hematoma, they found that twelve of them fit into the category of trauma most likely resulting from "injury-prone environments." They presented detailed histories and concluded that it was surprising how large a part parental misconduct played in the injuries of the children and that not a single stable family was found among the twelve cases. They also noticed that when these infants were removed from the families, no new lesions developed. They concluded by making four important points: (1) Since detailed histories were impossible to obtain and often chased parents away, it was best, if possible, to remove the child from the home first and then obtain information about the environment. (2) The general environments of the children were characterized by aggressive, immature, or emotionally ill adults. (3) There was no evidence to suggest that the repeated injuries were a result of fragile bones. (4) Many of the children came from unstable homes characterized by misconduct of the parents, and when the children were removed from these homes, they improved rapidly.

The Decade in Review

Theory and Methodology. The research of the 1950s was still not guided by any particular theory. The studies linking early discipline to disorders later in life, though, represented a beginning in the development of relationships between variables that could be used to develop more complex theories.

Table 8–3
Overview of Research on Family Violence, 1950–1959

Year	*Author*	*Topic*	*Theory*	*Method*[a]	*Sample*	*Strengths*[b]
1951	Hartogs	Discipline	Freud	Case study	—	T
1953	Gold	Aggression	None	Census-S	—	
1953	Silverman	Physical injury	None	Case study	3	I
1954	Maccoby and Gibbs	Discipline	None	Survey-P	372	S
1955	Havighurst and Davis	Discipline	None	Questionnaire-P	92	
1955	Woolley and Evans	Physical injury	None	Case study	25	I
1956	Bakwin	Physical injury	None	Case study	25	I
1957	Littmen, Moore, and Pierce-Jones	Discipline	None	Questionnaire-P	412	S
1958	Duncan et al.	Murder	None	Case study	6	
1958	Miller and Swanson	Discipline	None	Questionnaire-P	528	

[a] P = primary data; S = secondary data.
[b] S = sample; T = theory; I = importance.

The methodology of the researchers who were investigating social class and child rearing practices was an improvement over previous decades; the sample sizes increased, and statistical methods were used to compare groups. Still, the research on social class was only indirectly related to violence in the family, and not a single study used statistical methods for directly studying family violence.

Major Authors and Research Pieces. Table 8–3 summarizes the research during the 1950s. Woolley and Evans's (1955) article helped reduce much of the secrecy surrounding many of the abused children seen by practitioners and was the first research article to investigate child abuse directly, without evading the issues. Because of Woolley and Evans's research, previous articles by physicians or roentgenologists, and changes in the laws that forced physicians to report abuse, the literature on parent-child violence exploded during the 1960s and 1970s.

The Decade 1960–1969

Although there were few studies with adequate samples and appropriate methods during the previous three decades, they were generally articles on discipline. None of the articles that dealt with abusive violence in the home were empirical; rather they were descriptions of abused children seen by medical personnel. The medical articles were extremely important in putting child physical abuse in the public eye so that it could not be ignored, but the plethora of case studies and discussions of abuse produced during the 1960s added little to the information that had already been presented (Elmer, 1960; Adelson, 1961; Boardman, 1962; Morris and Gould, 1963; Caffey, 1965; Cohen, Rapling, and Green, 1966). Therefore, the research that will be reviewed from the 1960s through the 1980s will not include case studies or discussions on abuse from any field. The focus will be on presenting research that is empirical in nature.

Research Findings

Parent-Child Violence. In the early 1960s, researchers in the medical field continued to publish descriptive cases of abused children until the movement culminated in the creation of a new term for child abuse, the *battered child syndrome* (Kempe et al., 1962). In their study, which surveyed seventy-one hospitals, Kempe and associates found 302 cases of child abuse over a one-year period. Of the 302 cases, 33 of the children died, and 85 suffered permanent brain injury. In addition, Kempe and associates surveyed seventy-seven district attorneys who knew of 447 cases of child abuse in the same one-year period. In the reports of district attorneys, there were 45 deaths and 29 cases of permanent brain damage. Kempe and associates reported that the syndrome could occur at any age but was largely affecting children who were younger than 3 years. The influence of this article cannot be overestimated. It not only forced society to recognize a serious problem but also helped create a change in legislation that required professionals working with children to report suspected cases of abuse (U.S. Department of Health, Education, and Welfare, 1963, 1966). The change in laws made it very difficult for professionals to ignore child abuse (Bain, 1963). The legal mandate to report child abuse was applied to other areas such as social work, psychiatry, and education and probably opened the door for scholars on the family to become involved in the study of domestic violence.

In 1963 another group of professionals undertook a survey of child abuse (Bryant et al., 1963). They sent out questionnaires to seventeen district offices of the Massachusetts Society for the Prevention of Cruelty to Children. From the responses of these offices, they collected 115 cases involving 180 abused children. Most of the abusive families were not well integrated into the community, and 90 percent of them had serious social problems (marital discord, financial difficulties, faulty communication). Almost half of the mothers had conceived prior to marriage. Child abuse was committed equally by father and mother, who typically were young at the time of marriage and young during the abusive episodes.

Young (1964) used records from eight public welfare departments and two private agencies from which 300 families were selected to represent typical clinical families. The author found that 55 percent of the families abused their children, and 40 percent had been on public assistance. Sixty percent of the parents had problems of alcoholism, 35 percent were diagnosed as psychotic, and over half of the ones who were given psychological examinations were found to be mentally retarded. Young concluded that even though the sample was largely lower class, there were people from other classes represented, suggesting that abuse occurs in families from all economic groups.

In 1967 Elmer and Gregg attempted to determine the negative developmental effects abuse had on children. This was the first study to follow up on children who had been abused. The length of time between the initial hospital treatment and the reevaluation was from one to ten years. The authors found that only two out of twenty children were normal in all five areas in which they were studied (physical, intellectual, emotional, speech, and physical defects) and concluded that only a few of the twenty children showed promise of becoming self-sufficient adults. Elmer and Gregg suggested that because of the serious impairments that were likely to result from child abuse, it was essential to intervene in abusive situations as early as possible. A major limitation of their study was that there were no comparison groups and other important variables that could have contributed to the children's poor development were not controlled.

Elmer (1967) produced the second book on child abuse using the same sample that she used in the previous study with Gregg (Elmer and Gregg, 1967). Elmer's (1967) study validated some of the findings of Bryant and colleagues (1963) and Young (1964) in that abusive parents were found to be multiproblem parents who were suffering from a variety of stresses. In many of the families, she noticed that the abusing parents had been estranged from their families at a young age because of conflict and ended up involved in poor marriages or premaritally pregnant before they were mature enough to handle such responsibilities. She concluded that the "abused children of today become the abusing parents of tomorrow."

The third book of the decade was also the most influential one on child abuse for many years (Helfer and Kempe, 1968). This book contained the first extensive history of child abuse, a study of the radiological aspects of abused children, chapters on the role of the physician, social worker, and law enforcement officer, and discussions on the legal aspects of abuse. The only chapter that was applicable to this review was that by Steele and Pollock on the psychiatric study of abusive parents.

Steele and Pollock's (1968) results were distinct from previous results, though most differences were likely due to nonrandom samples. They studied sixty parents who had seriously abused their children. They did not find that most of the marriages were unstable, that alcoholism was a problem, that more of the abusers were from ethnic-minority groups, or that poverty was a problem, as had Elmer (1967) and Young (1964). Steele and Pollock found that almost all of the abuse in their sample occurred by the mother and that both parents had emotional problems of sufficient severity to be accepted at a clinic or psychiatrist's office. They also found that the parents expected and demanded a great deal more from their children than they could feasibly give and that many of the parents had themselves been abused.

In 1968, an additional study was done by members of the Denver's welfare department (Johnson and Morse, 1968). An important finding of the study, also found by Elmer (1967), was that 70 percent of the 101 children who were abused were hard to care for. The authors admitted that the abuse could have contributed to the difficult personalities of the children, but overall they determined that the children who were overly active and the most difficult to supervise were most likely to be abused. They studied the discipline techniques that the parents used and found that they frequently used corporal punishment and that the injuries to their children were the result of attempts to punish them physically.

A unique study was conducted by Gil and Noble in 1969 to determine the public's knowledge of and attitudes about child abuse. Their study was the first to use a standard representative sample rather than a sample from a hospital or public agency. Using responses from 1,520 people, they found that half of them lacked knowledge of child protective agencies. Most of the respondents had heard or read about child abuse in the last year, and their information was generally obtained through the media. The respondents thought that anyone was capable at some time of injuring their children and that children should be removed from the home only as a last resort.

Another study on the incidence of child abuse in a particular geographical area (Los Angeles) was conducted by Paulson and Blake (1969). Their three-year study employed a sample of ninety-six abused children who had been seen in a hospital over a three-year period. They reported that abused children were typically under 3 years of age, as the children could not escape from the parents. Mothers were more likely to abuse daughters, whereas fathers were just as likely to abuse sons as daughters. As in other hospital samples, the respondents were poor and suffering from many stressors, which Paulson and Blake thought contributed to the likelihood of abuse.

A study conducted in 1969 by Melnick and Hurley was the first to use a control group. They carefully matched ten nonabusive mothers with ten mothers who had abused their children. A limitation of their study was that the sample consisted largely of lower-class blacks. The authors found that the abusive mothers scored low on the need to be nurturing and on self-esteem and higher than the control group in pathogenicity and dependency frustration. They concluded that the abusive mothers studied were not (in contrast to other findings) chronically hostile, overwhelmed, or domineering. They reported that the abusive mothers were characterized by an inability to empathize, having frustrated dependency needs, and probable histories of emotional deprivation.

The last study on parent-child violence reviewed from the 1960s was by Gil (1969). It was the first to utilize the legally reported incidents of child abuse that were a consequence of legislative changes. In 1967, 5,993 cases of physically abused children were reported to the Children's Bureau. Many of Gil's findings were similar to hospital samples in that the majority of the families were poor and had more than four children, and the abusive incident developed out of disciplinary actions. He also found that 30 percent of the families were single-parent, female-headed households. Extrapolating from his statistics, Gil determined that it was a myth that child abuse was a major cause of death in the United States. He also proposed that abuse was a multidimensional problem caused by five factors: the culturally sanctioned use of physical force, child rearing traditions that made physical punishment acceptable, chance environmental circumstances, environmental stress factors, and physical, intellectual, emotional, and social deviance of the family members.

Violence between Spouses. The research on violence in the marital dyad was similar to that of the parent-child subsystem; violence was known about and talked about but not studied directly. Groves's (1927) and Mowrer's (1932) studies were characteristic of the types of studies that touched on violence between spouses during the 1930s, 1940s, and 1950s. In discussing divorce and its causes, they presented a number of tables showing that cruelty was the leading cause of divorce. Although mental and physical cruelty were common grounds for divorce in the early decades of this century, there were no attempts to study the problem in detail. From the absence of research during the 1930s, 1940s, and 1950s, it is apparent that there was a reluctance to investigate violence between spouses even in the face of statistics suggesting there was a problem.

In the 1960s two research articles on violence between spouses appeared. The first article, written in 1964 by three doctors (Snell, Rosenwald, and Robey, 1964), was based on case descriptions of women who had been abused by their husbands. The purpose was to explain why these women finally sought help after twelve to twenty years of marriage. They found a family structure in which the husband was passive, sexually inadequate, and indecisive and the wife was aggressive, masculine, frigid, and masochistic. Snell, Rosenwald, and Robey concluded that the women were coming in for help because of the involvement of an older son in the problem of the husband-wife abuse.

In 1966 Levinger attempted to understand the sources of marital unhappiness of couples applying for divorce; hence, violence was not the main focus of the article. The only finding of significance for this review was that among the 600 couples sampled, wives were eleven times as likely as men to report that their partner hurt them physically. Approximately 37 percent of the women filing for divorce in the Ohio county surveyed reported that they were physically abused, while only 3 percent of the men reported this. Levinger's study was similar to the one done by Mowrer (1932), except that the categories of cruelty were more specific so that it was apparent many women who were divorcing were in actuality suffering from more than mental cruelty.

The Decade in Review

Theory and Methodology. Theory was still not an important part of the study of family violence during this decade. Researchers were generally trying to understand the extent of the problem and its effects on the victims rather than explaining it.

The trend that was evident was that most studies had serious methodological problems in at least one area. Typically the research had inadequate samples and statistical procedures that offered little explanation of violence and its effects. Nevertheless, considering the difficulty of studying such a volatile issue and the limited resources that were available, the work was important in starting to unravel the complex issue of violence in families.

Major Authors and Research Pieces. Table 8–4 summarizes the research during the 1960s. Choosing the best research of the 1960s is difficult and would likely be a combination of two or three of the articles reviewed. Gil and Noble's (1969) sample would be used with Melnick and Hurley's (1969) methods and Johnson and Morse's (1968) questions. In addition, the three books written during the decade—by Young (1964), Elmer (1967), and, especially, Helfer and Kempe (1968)—were influential since they carried the topic of parent-child violence to a wider audience than those reading scholarly journals.

Table 8–4
Overview of Research on Family Violence, 1960–1969

Year	*Author*	*Topic*	*Theory*	*Method*[a]	*Sample*	*Strengths*[b]
1962	Kempe et al.	Physical injury	None	Questionnaire-P	77	S,I,
1963	Bryant et al.	Family patterns	None	Questionnaire-P	115	
1964	Snell, Rosenwald, and Robey	Abused wives	None	Case study	12	I
1964	Young	Family patterns	None	Questionnaire-P	300	I
1966	Levinger	Divorce	None	Questionnaire-S	600	I
1967	Elmer and Gregg	Effects of abuse	None	Questionnaire-P	33	I
1968	Steele and Pollock	Abusive parents	None	Observation	60	I
1968	Johnson and Morse	Injured children	None	Questionnaire-P	101	I
1969	Gil and Noble	Public attitudes	None	Questionnaire-P	1,520	S,M,I
1969	Paulson and Blake	Prevention	None	Questionnaire-P	96	
1969	Melnick and Hurley	Violent mothers	None	Experiment	20	St
1969	Gil	Violence patterns	None	Questionnaire-S	5,993	S,M,T,I

[a] P = primary data; S = secondary data.
[b] S = sample; M = measurement of variables; St = statistical analysis; T = theory; I = importance.

The Decade 1970–1979

The number of articles on family violence published during the 1960s was fewer than thirty; during the 1970s, this number more than tripled. The subtopics of violence between spouses and parent-child violence experienced the greatest increases in volume; the other subtopics, such as violence between siblings and child-parent violence, received limited attention.

I adapted more stringent criteria for use in choosing articles from the 1970s for this review. The first criterion, which was used in the 1960s and continued into the next two decades, was to eliminate case studies. The second criterion was to eliminate articles that did not deal directly with the family. This meant that the articles that discussed police intervention in family violence or changes in legislation were eliminated from consideration. The third criterion was to eliminate articles that were thought pieces, reviews, or theory presentations without data. The final criterion was to eliminate articles that contained data but did not contain methods more advanced than descriptive statistics. During the 1970s and 1980s, improved methods available to researchers allowed them to evaluate data more extensively than simply presenting means or percentages.

Research Findings

Parent-Child Violence. In 1971 the *Journal of Marriage and the Family* produced an issue devoted to violence in the family. Though many of the articles in it were not empirical research, the issue was nevertheless important because it was the first time a family journal had focused exclusively on violence. The researchers represented in it were not clinicians and as such moved the focus from sick parents to sociological theories in an attempt to explain family violence. Many of the authors who contributed to the issue were to lead the field in studying family violence for years to come (Gil, 1971; Straus, 1971; Steinmetz, 1971).

Gil (1971) used data from several national public opinion and press surveys to present the rates of abuse as well as the characteristics of the abused and abuser. Children of all ages were abused, and more of the abusers came from poor ethnic minority families. Fathers tended to abuse more than mothers, and most of the abuse was performed by a parent. Almost one-third of the families in which abuse occurred were female-headed, single-parent families. The author concluded that abuse is a multidimensional phenomenon.

In a similar vein, Straus (1971) used a sample of 229 college students to investigate some of the social antecedents to physical punishment. The most important finding in this study, which contradicted past studies, was that the social class of the parents did not influence the rate of physical punishment. Straus proposed that physical punishment is influenced by the parent's conception of the role the child would play in adulthood. If the parent perceived the child was moving up in social class, less physical punishment was used.

In 1978 Gelles reported results from the first representative random sample of families who were interviewed about violence. A considerable amount of effort was exerted to obtain a sample of 2,143 family members. This sample was used extensively in the future to produce many articles and an influential book on family violence (Straus, Gelles, and Steinmetz, 1980).

Gelles (1978) reported that at least one form of violence occurred in 63 percent of the homes surveyed during the past year. Milder forms of violence, such as slaps and pushes, were the most common form of violence in families. Gelles estimated that 1.0 million to 1.9 million children were punched, kicked, or bitten during 1975. Between 1.4 million and 2.3 million children had been "beat up" while growing up, and up to 1.8 million children between the ages of 3 and 17 had a gun or knife used on them by their parents. Male children were more likely to be victims than female children, and as children grew older, they were less likely to be physically abused.

Characteristics of Violent Parents. An article on the severest form of parent-child violence, neonaticide, was published in 1970 by Resnick. Resnick proposed that neonaticide referred to killing of the newborn baby on the day of birth and was distinct from filicide, the killing of a son or daughter older than 24 hours. Thirty-five mothers who committed neonaticide were compared with 88 mothers who committed filicide. The author found that 83 percent of the neonaticide mothers killed their child because he or she was unwanted, while only 11 percent of the filicide mothers killed the infant for this reason. The neonaticide mothers reported that they killed the child as a result of "extramarital paternity," while the filicide mothers murdered their children out of "altruistic" motives designed to relieve the victim of real or imagined suffering. Most of the filicide mothers (71 percent) were depressed or psychotic (33 percent), while only a few of the neonaticide were depressed (10 percent) or psychotic (17 percent).

In 1974 Paulson and colleagues measured 60 parents from "abusive" families on the Minnesota Multiphasic Personality Inventory and compared them to 100 parents in nonabusive homes. They found that the abusive parents did not demonstrate any consistent pathology. They also found that the women who did not abuse their children but were passive in attempting to stop the abuse were more pathological than the abusive mothers.

An additional study on the characteristics of abusing mothers was done by Gaines and associates (1978). They measured eighty abusing mothers, eighty neglectful mothers, and eighty normal mothers on personality characteristics and stress. Stress discriminated neglectful mothers better than personality factors or infant risk. Stress, personality, and risk of the child accounted for only 12 percent of the variance and were thus not highly predictive of abusive mothers.

Altemeier and colleagues (1979) tried to identify which of 1,400 pregnant women were most likely to abuse their future children. This was one of the earliest studies to follow a parent and child longitudinally over a period of years to see which factors were most likely to contribute to physical abuse. Through the use of multiple measures, the authors were able to identify a group of 273 mothers who were high risk. Seventy-five percent of the abuse reported during the one-year period following the birth of the children occurred in this high-risk group. The mother's nurture during her childhood, support systems, parenting skills, substance abuse, and life stressors were the most important variables in placing the mothers in the high-risk group.

Egeland and Brunnquell (1979) produced the second article on at-risk mothers. They followed 275 mothers through the first year of their child's life. The authors found that 10 percent of the mothers had abused their children to the extent that they were reported to local agencies. After going into the homes and interviewing the mothers, they found "considerably" more abuse than was reported. The variables that were most important in distinguishing between the abusing and nonabusing groups were related to the early mother-child relationship, such as mother's interest in the child, mother's understanding of the complexity of the infant, life stressors, empathy, and the early interactions of mother and infant during feeding.

Characteristics of Physically Abused Children. Herrenkohl and Herrenkohl (1979) compared to 295 abused children with 284 of their nonabused siblings to try to uncover why certain children in the family are abused. The authors found no evidence to suggest that abused children were different at birth from their nonabused siblings. They did find that the mothers perceived the abused children to be more difficult to raise, as well as to exhibit more behavioral problems. In addition, the mothers perceived that the abused children reminded them in negative ways about themselves and others.

In 1979 George and Main observed and coded ten abused toddlers and ten nonabused toddlers who came from families who were stressed. They determined that the abused children more frequently assaulted their peers, harassed the caregivers, and avoided friends or peers when approached with friendly overtures. The authors suggested that the abused children were already resembling their abusive parents by their aggressive and avoidant behaviors.

In contrast, Bolton, Reich, and Gutierrez (1977) found that 774 children who were physically abused as children were less likely to be reported for aggressive crime than their siblings who were only witnesses of violence. The abused children were more likely to be reported for escapist crimes (runaway, truancy, and so forth) than a control group of delinquents or their nonabused siblings. Their results did not support the cycle of violence theory.

Violence between Spouses. Straus in 1974 tested the hypothesis that leveling or giving free expression to aggressive feelings would reduce physical aggression. Using a sample of 385 students, Straus found that as verbal aggression increased, the physical aggression from the mother to the father and the father to the mother increased dramatically. The findings did not support claims from therapists that expressing anger verbally would reduce physical aggression. A weakness of the study was that college students rated the physical and verbal aggression of their parents rather than having direct data from the parents.

In 1976 Gelles, using a sample of forty-one women, tried to find out why abused wives stayed in their relationships. Gelles found three factors that influenced the actions of abused wives: (1) the less severe and less frequent the violence, the more wives remained with their husbands; (2) the more wives were struck as a child by their parents, the more likely they were to remain with abusive husbands; and (3) the fewer resources wives had and the less power they had, the more likely they were to stay with violent husbands. In addition, Gelles found that women with more education tended to seek help from a social service agency, while those with lower levels of education sought help through the police.

In a similar vein, Rounsaville (1978) tried to determine why some abused women sought follow-up services while others did not. The sample consisted of thirty-five women who sought help in a hospital emergency facility. Rounsaville found that the women who went to the follow-up sessions were distinct from those who did not in that they had already taken steps to end the relationship, had been in a longer relationship with the abusive partner, and were more likely to have contacted the police. Rounsaville concluded that abused women first responded with disbelief that the abuse was happening; second, they realized that the problem was severe; and third, they decided to leave after promptings from someone outside the relationship, such as a child, relative, or coworker.

Hilberman and Munson (1978) studied sixty battered women to investigate personality characteristics and other factors that made them unique. They found that the women were similar to rape trauma victims in the symptoms they exhibited. In addition, the women had many psychological problems, including alcoholism, depression, and schizophrenia. A limitation of this study was that it was difficult to tell whether the psychological problems were a result or a cause of the abuse. Interactive or longitudinal research would improve the ability of the researchers to understand the complex problem of violence between spouses.

One of the better estimates of the national incidence of spouse abuse was reported by Gaquin (1978). The National Crime Survey (NCS) produced a stratified multicluster sample of approximately 60,000 households between 1973 and 1975 from which Gaquin reported results. The spouse abuse (generally referring to assaults or attacks) rates per 1,000 people were 3.9 for women and 0.3 for men, a result suggesting that females are at a much higher risk for being assaulted by a spouse than men are. The NCS estimate of the total number of victimizations over the three year period was 1,058,500. Women were more likely to be injured by spouse abuse than by other forms of assault.

Steinmetz (1978) had a different perspective from Gaquin (1978) on the occurrence of husband abuse. The article by Steinmetz was probably the most controversial one to date in the family violence arena. Using samples from a number of past studies, Steinmetz concluded that it was husband, not wife, abuse that was the most underreported form of family violence. This and other statements in the article provoked a number of family scholars, who felt that the numbers were misinterpreted (Pleck et al., 1978; Field and Kirschner, 1978; Pagelow, 1984).

Both sides of the fence seem to have a point with the issue of violence to husbands. Steinmetz (1978) is correct in bringing to the light the fact that wives are not the sole recipients of violence in the marital system. Nevertheless, violence to women does appear to be more severe (Pleck et al., 1978) and to occur at higher rates than it does for men (Gaquin, 1978).

Violence between Siblings. In an excellent work on dysfunctional interactions in families, Steinmetz (1977a) studied violence between siblings. With a representative sample of fifty-seven families in Delaware, the author found that parents generally had difficulty discussing sibling violence because they did not consider it abnormal. Steinmetz had forty-nine of the families record the incidence of violence between siblings during a one-week period and found that 131 sibling conflicts occurred during the week. Sibling abuse became less frequent as the children grew older.

Child-Parent Violence. Two studies were done in the 1970s on the abuse of the elderly. The first was by O'Malley and associates (1979), who surveyed professionals regarding their knowledge of abuse or neglect of the elderly. Their response rates were poor (34 percent); only 332 questionnaires were returned. They found that the victims were generally female, older, or more frail elderly persons. The perpetrators were usually suffering from some form of stress, such as alcohol or drug abuse. The professionals reported that the elderly were generally afraid of divulging their abuse because they feared retaliation.

In 1979 Block and Sinnott undertook the second study of abuse of the elderly by their caretakers. This study was plagued by poor response rates, nonrepresentative samples, and inconclusive statistical techniques. Psychological abuse was more common than physical abuse, and the abuse most often was done by the victim's female relative, who was under stress. The victims were not helped in most of the cases, which were reported to authorities. The abused elders were generally over 75 and were in poor physical health.

A different type of child-parent abuse was studied by Harbin and Madden (1979). They found fifteen families in which a child between the ages of 14 and 20 was physically abusing a parent. The authors found that the families had some form of disturbance in the authority structure of the household, with the child often making parental decisions. Male adolescents were the abuser more often than female adolescents, and mothers were abused more than fathers. Harbin and Madden also found that the families were unwilling to discuss this form of abuse, did not punish the adolescent for the abuse, and did not seek outside help.

Family Violence in General. In 1971 Bourdouris analyzed the homicide records of Detroit during the years 1928–1968 to determine how many of the homicides involved family relations as well as some of the causes behind the family homicides. The largest category of homicides involved family members (29.5 percent). The highest rate of homicides tended to be among 25–44-year-old nonwhite males and females. Bourdouris concluded that these high rates of homicide in families suggested problems in family interaction.

O'Brien (1971) investigated violence in divorce-prone families. Fifteen percent of the individuals reported violence that was delivered primarily by husbands. O'Brien found that the violent husbands were underachievers in the work-earner role and were not equal to their wives in status characteristics. The interpretation was given that the results supported conflict theory: violence was used by males in a superordinate status when they found their stature threatened.

Steinmetz produced another article on family violence (1977b) after measuring seventy-eight college students on the extent of violence in their homes. There was a relationship between the method used to solve marital conflict and the method used to solve parent-child conflict. Children were also likely to use the same methods to resolve conflict between themselves. Steinmetz concluded that few families are conflict free and that there was evidence suggesting that social learning theory was applicable to family violence because parents taught their children to be aggressive.

Burgess and Conger (1978) compared seventeen abusive, seventeen neglectful, and nineteen normal families. They found that the abusive and neglectful parents demonstrated lower levels of interaction and emphasized the negative more than the normal families did. The neglectful families had less positive physical and verbal interactions than either the abusive or normal families. The relatively high rate of positive interactions for the abusive families (though much lower than the normal families) could help explain why families were so resistant to reporting the abuse. Perhaps the positive behavior from parents made the abuse harder to admit and helped the victims see reasons for not reporting the abuse. Another interesting finding was that the fathers did not differ from the control group but the mothers did.

Cazenave and Straus (1979) examined the relationship of race, class, and support systems to family violence. They found that although black respondents were more likely than whites to approve of violence and report the use of it in their families, when social class and social network embeddedness were controlled, black violence was lower than white violence. The authors suggested that the social networks of blacks are an important component in preventing family violence.

Measuring Family Violence. Straus (1979) published an expanded form of the instrument he used in 1974 and presented reliability and validity information on the Conflict Tactics Scales (CTS), the first reliable and valid scales measuring family violence (they are still widely used in the family science area). The CTS measures reasoning, verbal aggression, and physical violence on a continuum. The reliability of the subscales ranges from .50 for the Reasoning subscale to .88 for the Violence subscale. Additional information was presented supporting the construct validity of the CTS scales.

In 1975 Bulcroft and Straus compared parent and student reports of family violence with a sample of 105 students and 121 parents. The correlations between parent and student reports were low for the Reasoning subscale, moderate on the Verbal subscale, and relatively high on the Violence subscales. In addition, the students had higher correlations with their fathers than they did with their mothers. When comparing the violent acts in the home, the students reported more violent acts by the father than the father reported for himself and less violent acts for the mother than the mother reported for herself.

The Decade in Review

Theory and Methodology. Theory started to receive more attention during the 1970s as researchers moved beyond presenting violence rates to suggesting causes and effects of family violence. Several studies specifically investigated tenets of conflict theory (O'Brien, 1971; Bulcroft and Straus, 1975; Straus, 1979), and other related violence to social learning theories (Steinmetz, 1977b) or systems theories (Straus, 1973).

Many studies during the 1970s corrected the methodological errors of the previous decades by using valid instruments and large, representative samples (Gelles, 1978; Gaquin, 1978; Straus, 1979). Nevertheless, a large majority of research on family violence was plagued by serious methodological errors, and much of the published material consisted of thought pieces that had no empirical data. Bolton and colleagues (1981) reported that the child abuse literature they surveyed consisted of 71 percent thought pieces, 6 percent reviews, and 20 percent empirical research. Half the studies used samples with fewer than sixty subjects (Bolton et al., 1981).

Major Studies and Findings. Table 8-5 summarizes the research during the decade. The major authors during this decade were Steinmetz, Straus, and Gelles, who worked both together on many projects and separately. Their national survey is probably one of the best studies on family violence as far as methods, sample, instrumentation, and importance to the field are concerned.

Table 8–5
Overview of Research on Family Violence, 1970–1979

Year	*Author*	*Topic*	*Theory*	*Method*[a]	*Sample*	*Strengths*[b]
1970	Resnick	Neonaticide	Freud	Interviews	123	
1971	Bourdouris	Family homicides	None	Census	6,389	St
1971	Gil	Violence patterns	Mini	Questionnaire-S	—	M,St,T,I
1971	O'Brien	Divorce families	Conflict	Interview	150	T
1971	Steinmetz	Punishment	Mini	Questionnaire-P	17	
1971	Straus	Punishment	Mini	Questionnaire-P	229	M,T,I
1974	Paulson et al.	Violent parents	None	Questionnaire-P	169	M
1974	Straus	Aggressive spouse	None	Questionnaire-P	385	M,T,I
1975	Bulcroft and Straus	Measurement	Conflict	Questionnaire-P	226	M,St
1976	Wright	Violent parents	None	Questionnaire-P	26	
1976	Gelles	Abused wives	None	Interviews	41	I
1977	Bolton, Reich, and Gutierrez	Abused children	None	Questionnaire-P	774	S,St,I
1977	Elmer	Abused children	None	Interview	34	
1977a	Steinmetz	Sibling violence	None	Interview	57	S,M,I
1977b	Steinmetz	Family conflict	Social learning	Questionnaire-P	78	St,T
1978	Burgess and Conger	Family interaction	None	Observation	53	St
1978	Gaines et al.	Violent mothers	Mini	Questionnaire-P	240	M,St
1978	Gaquin	Spouse abuse	None	Questionnaire-S	436	S,I
1978	Gelles	Abused children	None	Interview	2,143	S,M,St,I
1978	Hilberman and Munson	Battered women	None	Interview	60	
1978	Rounsaville	Battered women	None	Interview	35	
1978	Spinnetta	Violent mothers	None	Questionnaire-P	—	I
1978	Steinmetz	Abused husbands	None	Questionnaire-P	—	I
1979	Altemeier et al.	Predicting abusers	None	Interview	1,400	S,St
1979	Block and Sinnott	Abused elders	None	Questionnaire-P	26	I
1979	Cazenave and Straus	Support systems	Mini	Questionnaire-P	2,143	S,M,St
1979	Egeland and Brunnquell	Violent mothers	None	Questionnaire-P	275	St,I
1979	George and Main	Abused children	None	Interview	20	M,St
1979	Harbin and Madden	Parent abuse	None	Interview	15	I
1979	Herrenkohl and Herrenkohl	Abused children	None	Interview	579	
1979	O'Malley et al.	Abused elders	None	Questionnaire-P	332	I
1979	Straus	Measurement	Conflict	Questionnaire-P	2,143	S,M,St,I

[a] P = primary data; S = secondary data.
[b] S = sample; M = measurement of variables; St = statistical analysis; T = theory; I = importance.

The Decade 1980–1989

During the 1980s, family violence research continued to expand rapidly. Researchers generally became more thorough and utilized advanced statistical methods to test hypotheses. The topic of violence between spouses increased dramatically, and parent-child violence continued to receive a great deal of attention. Still, there continued to be more thought pieces than empirical research.

One additional criterion will be imposed on the research reviewed for this decade: studies with sample sizes below fifty will not be reviewed. A sample size below fifty can seriously impair the generalizability of a study, especially when the sample consists of different groups that are compared to one another, such as a violent and a nonviolent group.

Research Findings

Parent-Child Violence. Egeland and Vaughn (1981) hypothesized that infants who were hospitalized for a length of time for birth complications or prematurity would not have bonded well to their mothers and would therefore be more likely to be abused or neglected. They compared thirty-three mothers who provided "inadequate" care with thirty-three mothers who provided "adequate" care and found that bonding failure was not significantly different for the two groups.

In 1982 Martin and Walters studied a sample of 489 families in which the children had been abandoned, physically abused, neglected, sexually abused, or emotionally abused. The interaction in families in which the children had been physically abused was distinct from the other families. Different family variables were related to each type of maltreatment, which suggests that researchers use caution when grouping different types of abuse.

Characteristics of Violent Parents. Perry, Wells, and Doran (1983) compared fifty-five abusing parents with fifty-five nonabusing parents. They found that fathers and mothers from abusing families expected slower development from their children, experienced less family cohesion, and had higher levels of family conflict. The mothers from abusing families also had lower self-esteem and reported more anxiety than the control group. The perpetrators of the abuse experienced greater anxiety and stress as well as feelings that they were not supported. In addition, when education was controlled, the history of abuse as a child did not differentiate between the two groups of parents.

In 1984 Estroff and colleagues compared thirty-five mothers of abused and neglected children with thirty-five matched controls who had children with psychiatric problems. They found that the abusive group had higher levels of psychopathology and perceived that the abused child was more maladjusted than the nonabused siblings. The authors suggested that the perception that the abused child was maladjusted was more a result of the psychopathology of the mother than a deficit in the child.

One of the best interaction studies in family violence was done by Herrenkohl and associates (1984). This study was one of the few in which the father's characteristics, as well as those of the mother and child, were examined. The authors analyzed 439 separate parent-child interactions of abusive and nonabusive families and found that cultural support of corporal punishment and isolation of the family contributed to violence, as did specific deficits in parenting skills. Income was an important correlate of parent behavior, and when it was controlled, the other differences between abusive and nonabusive parents were reduced. Even with income controlled, though, the abusive parents were more rejecting and the children showed less warmth than children in the control group.

Characteristics of Physically Abused Children. Kinard (1980) studied the emotional development of physically abused children. There were significant differences between the thirty physically abused children and the thirty control children on the measures of self-concept, aggression, and the ability to socialize with peer groups. In general, the abused children were more aggressive and had lower self-esteem, in addition to having more difficulty separating from their mothers and socializing.

Wolfe and Mosk (1983) compared the behavior of thirty-six abused children with thirty-five children who were not abused but came from distressed families and thirty-five control children from the community. The abused children displayed a significantly greater number of behavior problems and fewer social competencies than the control group, but they were not significantly different from the distressed children. The authors suggested that dysfunctions were more a result of poor interaction patterns in the home rather than isolated events of physical abuse.

The last two studies on the characteristics of abused children used samples of adolescents rather than the younger children used in the previous studies. Tarter and associates (1984) used a sample of twenty-eight juvenile delinquents who were physically abused and seventy-three delinquents who were not abused. They found that the abused sample performed less well on the intellectual, cognitive, educational, and neuropsychological measures and were also more likely to commit assaultive crimes. The families of the abused children were characterized by parental alcoholism, criminality, and separation. It appeared that certain deficits in the child interacted with certain characteristics of the family to produce abusive situations.

The adolescents in Monane, Leichter, and Lewis's (1984) study were 166 adolescent patients in a psychiatric hospital. Forty-two percent of the patients had been abused, and they were distinct from the nonabused patients in a number of ways. The abused patients were significantly more violent and had more homicidal ideations than the nonabused patients. The abused patients also came from homes where there was more spousal violence as well as violence to people outside the home.

Violence between Intimate Partners. In 1980 Coleman, Weinman, and Bartholomew compared thirty couples involved in marital violence with thirty couples who were not violent but were seeking therapy. They found that the variables that were important for identifying battered wives were the frequent use of alcohol by their husbands, frequent marital arguments, low education, and frequent legal drug use. Abusing husbands were identified by a background of family violence, frequent alcohol use, low education, and marital arguments.

An examination of the relationship between status inconsistency, defined as a situation where one's occupation and education are not consistent, and spouse abuse was done by Hornung, McCulough, and Sugimoto (1981). Using a random sample of 1,793 Kentucky wives, they found that status inconsistency was associated with an increased risk of psychological abuse, an even greater risk of physical abuse, and a still greater risk of life-threatening violence. The specific types of inconsistency that contributed to increased rates of violence were underachievement in occupation by the husband with the woman employed in a higher-status occupation than her husband was. At least one type of inconsistency—overachievement in occupation by the husband—decreased the chances of spouse abuse.

Yllo and Straus (1981) compared the violence rates of married and cohabitating couples. Using a representative sample of 2,143 adults, they found that cohabitating couples had higher rates of violence than married couples. Severe violence was almost five times as likely in cohabitating relationships.

Hudson and Mcintosh (1981) provided an important addition to the assessment instruments available for violence between spouses: the Index of Spouse Abuse (ISA), which has two subscales with high reliabilities that measure the nonphysical and physical abuse in a relationship.

Snyder and Fruchtman (1981) attempted to establish a taxonomy of wife abuse using data from a sample of 119 abused women who had sought refuge in shelters. They were able to identify five distinct types of battered women:

1. Women in stable relationships with low rates of violence who are more likely to instigate violence and more likely to stay with their husbands.
2. Women in very unstable relationships with the most severe type of violence that often includes a sexual component. These women were the most likely to experience physical beatings if they did return.
3. Victims of the most chronic and severe type of abuse who also had to see their children abused. They had little history of abuse in their families of origin and were the least likely to be living with the assailant later.

4. Women who were not abused often but whose children were. These women stayed at a shelter for only short periods of time and were not very likely to remain with the assailant.
5. Women with extensive histories of violence in their lives and had grown to expect it. They were one of the most likely to stay with the assailant.

In another study of women in shelters, Berk, Newton, and Berk (1986) found that shelters were beneficial only to women who were already taking control of their lives. By helping these women move out of the violent situation, the shelter dramatically decreased the chance of more violence. For the women who were not already taking control of their lives, a stay at a shelter seemed to encourage retaliation from the perpetrator.

Rosenbaum and O'Leary (1981) determined that some of the differences obtained in previous studies between violent and nonviolent couples could be a result of marital discord because the abusive couples in their study were not significantly different from the distressed, nonviolent couples, though they were different from the nondistressed couples. The authors found that abusive husbands were different from the other two groups in that they were less assertive with their wives, more likely to have been abused as children, and more likely to have witnessed parental spouse abuse.

Assertion and marital violence was also investigated by O'Leary and Curely (1986), who measured seventy-two couples who were abusive, distressed, or happily married on aggression and assertion. O'Leary and Curely found that both the abusive and distressed couples had lower levels of assertion than the happily married couples. The abusive couples were not significantly different from the distressed couples, a finding that suggested that the lack of assertion was a characteristic of distress in marriage rather than abuse. As in previous studies, spousal violence in the family of origin was an important discriminator of abusive men.

Another study comparing samples of abusive, distressed, and nondistressed individuals was done by Goldstein and Rosenbaum (1985). They compared the self-esteem of twenty maritally violent men, eighteen maritally distressed men, and twenty happily married men. The violent men were significantly lower on self-esteem than the other two groups of men. The violent men also perceived their wives' behavior to be more damaging to self-esteem, which suggests that the males' perception of behavior is an important component in the abusive cycle.

The relationship between wives' dependency and conjugal violence was investigated by Kalmuss and Straus (1982). The wives' subjective marital dependency was correlated with minor but not severe violence, and objective dependency was associated with severe violence. The researchers concluded that it was economic, not psychological, dependency that kept women in severely abusive marriages.

Strube and Barbour (1983, 1984) studied the relationship between economic dependence and psychological commitment on a battered woman's decision to leave the relationship. Both objective and subjective measures of economic dependence and psychological commitment influenced the decision to leave. The more committed and financially dependent the woman was, the more likely she was to stay in the relationship. The subjective measures were somewhat better than the objective measures; they accounted for twice as much variance in the dependent variable.

Another study on the decision to leave an abusive relationship was done by Aguirre (1985), who administered a questionnaire to 312 women in "family violence centers." Wives' economic dependence almost always ensured that they would return to the abusive relationship. Women who found the centers helpful had a greater probability of returning to their husbands. This finding debunked the myth that the effect of shelters for battered women was destruction of families.

In 1983 Walker studied 403 battered women and found that there were consistent symptoms developed by abused women constituting a battered woman syndrome. The symptoms were a survival technique and included learned helplessness and fear that separation would cause the violence to worsen. Violence in childhood and in the current relationship had an impact on the woman's ability to stop the batterer's violence after he initiated it.

Gentemann (1984) assessed women's attitudes toward wife beating using a random telephone survey of 422 women. Virtually none of the women approved of wife beating, although approximately 20 percent of them felt that beatings were justified in some situations. The same percentage of women blamed the victim for the beatings. Education and social class were significant predictors of attitudes that justified beatings.

In 1984 Rouse studied the relationship of self-esteem, locus of control, and family-of-origin violence to spouse abuse in a sample of seventy-nine men. The major finding was that exposure to violence as a child had more influence on spouse abuse than participating in violence as a child. Self-esteem and locus of control were only slightly related to marital violence.

Kalmuss and Seltzer (1986) undertook a study with a national sample of 2,143 to investigate violence rates in remarried spouses. Marriages in which at least one of the spouses was previously divorced had higher rates of violence than never-divorced marriages. This was true even when childhood family violence was controlled. The rates of violence for remarried adults who were not exposed to family-of-origin violence were still twice as high as those for never-divorced adults.

A unique study on the annual rhythm of spouse abuse was done in 1986 by Michael and Zumpe. Using reports from twenty-three shelters, they observed that the battering of women occurred with the highest frequency in the summer. This finding is similar to findings on assaults and rapes and was closely related to changes in temperature. Michael and Zumpe proposed that the higher rates during the summer could be a result of increased irritability from higher temperatures or some unknown neuroendocrine mechanism that is affected by seasons.

In 1987 Mason and Blankenship studied the relationship of power, affiliation motivation, stress, and abuse in a sample of 165 college students. They found that high power was related to physical abuse of their partners by men but not by women. Women who were highly stressed and had high affiliation and low activity inhibition were the most likely to inflict abuse. Abuse also occurred more often with committed couples. Another important finding was that when women hit, they were hit in return, while the same did not hold true for men.

The last study reviewed on violence between spouses was written by Gelles (1988) using data from the Second National Family Violence Survey of 6,002 representative homes. The study was designed to investigate whether pregnant women were truly at a higher risk for being physically abused. The results showed that although pregnant women did experience violence at higher rates, the relationship disappeared when age was controlled. The implication is that women under 25 years are both more likely to be abused and more likely to be pregnant.

Premarital Violence. Three of the articles reviewed in the 1980s were concerned with the occurrence of premarital violence. Makepeace's (1981) was one of the earliest published reports on this phenomenon. In his sample of 202 college students, 21 percent of the couples had experienced premarital violence. Jealousy was given as the most important factor leading to violence. Of those couples experiencing violence, 44 percent were still involved in the abusive relationship.

Cate and associates (1982) studied 355 college students and reported results similar to Makepeace's (1981): premarital abuse was substantial and reciprocal in nature. Twenty-two percent of the respondents were victims or perpetrators of abuse, which usually started after some degree of commitment was gained in the relationship. The abuse was seen as usually being caused by anger and was not always viewed by the partners as detrimental to the relationship. The authors found support for the social exchange proposition that those who stay in abusive relationships had fewer alternatives.

Laner and Thompson (1982) found much higher rates of violence with their college sample of 371. Sixty-eight percent of the women and 64 percent of the men had at least one violent episode in their courtships. They also found that violence was more likely to occur as the relationships became more serious. Men rated the violence as more of a mutual phenomenon than the women did.

Roscoe and Benaske (1985) studied the relationship between courtship violence and spouse abuse with eighty-two women in protective shelters. They found that 49 percent of the abused wives had been abused in their dating relationships and that 30 percent of the victims eventually married the perpetrator. Jealousy, alcohol, and money were reported by the women to be the primary causes of violence. Roscoe and Benaske suggested that premarital violence might be a more important predictor of spouse abuse than family-of-origin violence.

Effects on Children of Witnessing Marital Violence. Hughes and Barad (1983) studied the self-concept, anxiety level, and problem behaviors of sixty-five children who were members of maritally abusive families. The preschool children scored below average on the self-concept measure, and the school-age boys were more aggressive than the girls. The mothers also rated their children more negatively than outside observers.

Kalmuss (1984) investigated how witnessing marital violence between parents contributed to marital aggression later in life. Kalmuss found that witnessing parental marital violence was more strongly related to involvement in relationship aggression than being hit by parents. Observing one's father hitting one's mother increased the likelihood that sons and daughters would be perpetrators and victims of marital violence. This implies that the transmission of violence across generations is more role specific than previously thought.

In 1985 Forsstrom-Cohen and Rosenbaum explored how witnessing marital violence affected the emotional health of young adults. With their sample of 164, they were able to demonstrate that males who had viewed parental violence were more anxious than males who had parents with satisfactory relationships. Women who had witnessed marital violence, on the other hand, were more depressed and aggressive than both the women in conflictual but not violent families and the women in happily married families.

A group of four researchers teamed up to do four studies during the 1980s on witnessing marital violence (Wolfe et al., 1985, 1986; Jaffe et al., 1986a, 1986b). They found that boys who were exposed to family violence were similar to abused boys in their adjustment problems. Exposure to violence appeared to have effects similar to being physically abused. In addition, witnessing marital violence was related to internalizing behavior problems (depression and anxiety) in the girls and to both internalizing and externalizing problems in boys. Boys appeared to be more vulnerable to conjugal violence than girls.

Child-Parent Violence. Douglas, Hickey, and Noel (1980) surveyed 228 professionals about their knowledge of abuse of the elderly. Most of the professionals knew of consistent problems with neglect of the elderly but not of actual physical abuse. Other researchers, however, found evidence that physical abuse of the elderly was occurring. Pillemer and Sinkelhor (1988) reported that about 3 percent of the elderly suffered abuse.

Cornell and Gelles (1982) studied child-to-parent violence. They found that this type of family problem was as prevalent as marital violence. Four percent of the sample of male youths reported using serious violence on their mothers, and 2 percent reported father-directed serious violence. They proposed that child violence toward parents might be the missing link between violence in the family of origin and violence in the family of procreation. Perhaps adolescents began to use violence before leaving their homes and continued it in their new relationships.

An investigation of teenage violence toward parents was conducted in 1985 by Peek, Fisher, and Kidwell. They used a national probability sample of 1,545 adolescents who were measured during their sophomore, junior, and senior years of high school. The incidence of this type of violence was between 7 and 11 percent and did not increase over time. In contrast to Cornell and Gelles (1982), they found that violence toward fathers was higher than it was toward mothers.

Family Violence in General. In 1980 Straus, Gelles, and Steinmetz produced what has probably been the most widely read book on family violence. They reviewed the results from their national family-violence survey of 2,143 households that were collected in 1975. Many of the findings presented in this book were also examined in journal articles, so only a brief summary will follow.

The rate of wife and husband beatings was almost 6.1 per 1,000 couples, involving approximately 2 million marriages a year. The researchers proposed that violence to children was a serious problem and resulted from cultural norms that allowed certain forms of "normal violence" to be used as disciplinary methods. Violence between siblings occurred at far higher rates than other forms of violence.

Violence appeared to be transmitted from generation to generation. The more violent the grandparents had been, the more violent husbands were to their wives and parents were to their children. Children who grow up in homes where their parents hit each other and used a great deal of physical punishment had the highest chance of becoming violent adults. Nevertheless, violence was also learned from other sources; children who did not have violent parents often became violent.

The social factors that were strongly related to violence were age, income, and work status. Other variables that influenced violence rates were religion, urban or rural residence, region of the country, and race. Straus, Gelles, and Steinmetz (1980) reported that the safest homes as far as domestic violence was concerned were those in which there were fewer than two children, the parents had few life stressors, and a democratic system was used to make decisions.

In 1980 Dibble and Straus studied how attitudes and patterns of interaction affected domestic violence. Using the national sample of 2,143 adults, they found that social variables such as income, sex, and education were related to violence rates. They also found that attitudes were related to violence rates but that violent behavior by the spouse had a much greater impact on the respondent's violence than attitudes. The consistency between attitudes and behavior was strongest in people who had pro-violent attitudes and a violent spouse. The authors concluded that patterns of interaction between spouse and kin were at least as important as attitudes in explaining violence rates.

One of the better attempts at testing the cycle of violence proposition was done by Miller and Challas (1981). They studied 118 parents over a twenty-five-ear period who were either abused as children or not abused. They found that the abused parents, who in turn abused their children, were from multiproblem families, had poor socialization, were financially dependent, and were emotionally unstable. While more of the abused parents were rated as potential abusers of their children, 47 percent of the persons who were not abused as children had some potential for child abuse and 45 percent of the persons abused as children were rated as not abusive. The authors concluded that child abuse does not determine the next generation's fate but that poverty, ignorance, and unstable parental careers may.

Gully, Pepping, and Dengerink (1982) studied the effect of the gender of the respondent on recollections of parent-to-parent violence. They asked a sample of 108 students about their recollections of previous violence between their parents. The results of two subsamples demonstrated that females reported more violence than males. These differences in violence rates implied that reports of family violence were influenced by gender and should be taken from as many family members as possible.

A study exploring the effects of discipline experienced as a child on adult attitudes about discipline was done by Herzberger and Tennen (1985). The results from the 139 students who were measured illustrated that those who experienced a particular disciplinary method saw it as less harsh than those who did not. This result held for moderate forms of spanking to more severe forms of disciplinary actions.

An analysis of the relationship between family violence and adolescents' perceptions of family conflict was published by Martin and associates (1987). From a sample of 181 rural and urban adolescents, they found that families with nonviolent parents were better able to solve conflicts than families in which either verbal or physical violence was used. Adolescent compliance was unrelated to violence, suggesting that it is an ineffective form of control of adolescents. As violence increased, the adolescents had more anger toward the parents and lower levels of satisfaction with the family.

Using two national probability samples, Straus and Gelles (1986) estimated how family violence had changed over a decade. The rate of severe violence to children declined from 140 per thousand children in 1975 to 107 per thousand in 1985. The husband-to-wife severe violence declined from 38 per thousand couples to 30, a decrease of 22 percent. The wife-to-husband severe violence decreased only slightly and illustrated that wives were about as violent as men; still, female violence was less damaging than male violence. Straus and Gelles proposed that the decrease in violence demonstrated by the two surveys was either a result of a change in reporting behavior or an actual reduction in violence.

Straus and Gelles's article stimulated a response from one researcher (Stocks, 1988) who disagreed with their statistical methods and conclusions. Stocks felt that the decrease in violence demonstrated by the two data sets was an artifact of the different interview methods that were used (in-person interviews versus telephone interviews). Stocks also found a number of errors in Straus and Gelles's calculations and determined that their statistics were inappropriate for the types of data analyzed. Gelles, Straus, and Harrop (1988) responded to Stock (1988) by admitting that they had made a few calculation errors but that none made a difference in the main conclusions. They also provided evidence that telephone and in-person interviews were relatively equivalent and that Stocks's criticisms were largely out of context and inappropriate.

The Decade in Review

Theory and Methodology. Theory became a much more important part of the study of family violence in the 1980s. Researchers used social learning theory, social structural theory, systems theory, ecological theory, personality theory, and cognitive theory to explain their results.

Methodology also improved during the decade. Small, nonrepresentative samples were still frequent but were being replaced by large probability samples. In addition, many researchers working with dysfunctional populations exerted the effort to obtain comparison samples for use as control groups. The statistical procedures were representative of most other areas of family science in that multivariate analyses were used much more frequently, as were other advanced statistical methods. Nevertheless, many studies were still plagued by the use of the univariate analysis of variance techniques when other methods would have been more appropriate. In general, the quality of the measures used in the research also improved considerably, though a large proportion of the researchers continued to use instruments without evidence of validity or reliability.

Major Authors and Research Pieces. Table 8–6 summarizes the research during the 1980s. Groups of researchers began to partition themselves off as they studied specific aspects of family violence. Straus, Gelles, Steinmetz, Kalmuss, Yllo, and others continued to study violence with their large samples and sociological variables. Wolfe, Jaffe, Wilson, and Zak worked extensively with child witnesses of violence using smaller comparison groups. Rosenbaum, O'Leary, and their colleagues worked in the area of spouse abuse and also used small comparison groups.

Table 8–6
Overview of Research on Family Violence, 1980–1989

Year	*Author*	*Topic*	*Theory*	*Method*[a]	*Sample*	*Strengths*[b]
1980	Coleman, Weinman, and Bartholomew	Conjugal violence	None	Questionnaire-P	60	
1980	Dibble and Straws	Family violence	Social structure	Questionnaire-S	2,143	S,M,St,T,I
1980	Douglas, Hickey, and Noel	Elder abuse	None	Questionnaire-P	228	I
1980	Kinard	Abused children	Personality	Questionnaire-P	30	M
1981	Barahal, Waterman, and Martin	Abused children	None	Interview-P	33	M
1981	Egeland and Vaughn	Bond formation	None	Observation	66	
1981	Hornung, McCulough, and Sugimoto	Conjugal violence	Mini	Questionnaire-P	1,793	S,M,St,T,I
1981	Hudson and Mcintosh	Instrumentation	None	Questionnaire-P	693	M,St,I
1981	Makepeace	Premarital violence	None	Questionnaire-P	202	M,I
1981	Miller and Challas	Cycle of violence	Social learning	Questionnaire-P	118	S,M,St,T,I
1981	Rosenbaum and O'Leary	Conjugal violence	None	Questionnaire-P	112	M
1981	Snyder and Fruchtman	Conjugal violence	None	Questionnaire-P	116	M,St,I
1981	Yllo and Straus	Cohabitor violence	None	Interview-S	2,143	S,M
1982	Cate et al.	Premarital violence	Social exchange	Questionnaire-P	355	M,T,I
1982	Cornell and Gelles	Violence to parents	None	Questionnaire-S	2,143	S,M,I
1982	Gully, Pepping, and Dengerink	Gender and violence	None	Questionnaire-P	108	M
1982	Kalmuss and Straus	Marital dependency	Mini	Interview-P	1,183	S,M,St,I
1982	Kinard	Abused children	None	Questionnaire-P	30	
1982	Laner and Thompson	Courtship violence	Mini	Questionnaire-P	337	S,M,St,I
1982	Martin and Walters	Abused children	None	Interview-S	489	St,I
1983	Camras, Grow, and Ribordy	Abused children	None	Questionnaire-P	34	M
1983	Egan	Treatment	Social interaction	Experiment	41	S,M,St,T
1983	Hughes and Barad	Witnessing violence	None	Questionnaire-P	65	
1983	Mash, Johnston, and Kovitz	Family interaction	None	Observation	36	M
1983	Perry, Wells, and Doran	Abusive parents	Mini	Questionnaire-P	110	M
1983	Perry	Abused children	None	Questionnaire-P	42	M
1983	Rosenberg and Reppucci	Parent perceptions	Mini	Interview-P	24	M,St
1983	Strube and Barbour	Conjugal violence	None	Interview-P	98	
1983	Walker	Battered women	Social learning	Interview-P	403	S,T

Table 8–6 continued

Year	*Author*	*Topic*	*Theory*	*Method*[a]	*Sample*	*Strengths*[b]
1983	Wolfe and Mosk	Abused children	None	Interview-P	106	M,St
1983	Yllo	Women's status	None	Interview-S	2,143	S,M,St
1984	Bousha and Twentyman	Family interaction	None	Observation	36	M,St
1984	Centerwall	Domestic homicide	None	Census-S	222	
1984	Estroff et al.	Abusive parents	None	Questionnaire-P	422	S,St
1984	Gentemann	Public attitudes	Social learning	Interview-P	422	S,St
1984	Herrenkohl et al.	Family interaction	Ecological	Observation	439	S,St,I
1984	Kalmuss	Witnessing violence	Mini	Interview-S	2,143	S,M,T
1984	Lahey et al.	Abusive mothers	None	Observation	24	M,St
1984	Monane, Leichter, and Lewis	Abused adolescents	None	Case records	166	
1984	Rouse	Conjugal violence	Social learning	Questionnaire-P	79	
1984	Strube and Barbour	Conjugal violence	None	Interview-P	251	St
1984	Tarter et al.	Abused delinquents	None	Questionnaire-P	101	M
1984	Telch and Lindquist	Conjugal violence	None	Questionnaire-P	100	St
1985	Aguirrez	Abused wives	None	Questionnaire-P	312	S,St
1985	Forsstrom-Cohen and Rosenbaum	Witnessing violence	None	Questionnaire-P	164	M,St,I
1985	Goldstein and Rosenbaum	Violent husbands	None	Questionnaire-P	58	M
1985	Hasselt, Morrison, and Bellack	Alcohol use	None	Questionnaire-P	134	
1985	Hershorn and Rosenbaum	Witnessing violence	None	Questionnaire-P	45	M,St
1985	Herzberger and Tenner	Discipline	Mini	Questionnaire-P	139	T

1985	Peek, Fisher, and Kidwell	Violence to parents	Mini	Questionnaire-P	1,545	S,St,T,I
1985	Roscoe and Benaske	Premarital abuse	None	Questionnaire-P	82	M,I
1985	Shorkey and Armendariz	Abusive mothers	Cognitive	Questionnaire-P	36	M,St,T
1985	Webster-Stratton	Abusive families	Mini	Interview-P	40	M,St,T
1985	Wolfe et al.	Witnessing violence	None	Questionnaire-P	198	M,St
1986	Berk, Newton, and Berk	Shelters	None	Interviews-P	155	St
1986	Browning	Measurement issues	None	Questionnaire-P	60	M
1986a	Jaffe et al.	Witnessing violence	None	Questionnaire-P	65	M
1986b	Jaffe et al.	Witnessing violence	None	Questionnaire-P	126	M
1986	Kalmuss and Seltzer	Conjugal violence	None	Interview-S	2,143	S,M,St
1986	Michael and Zumpe	Seasonal changes	None	Questionnaire-P	23	
1986	O'Leary and Curely	Conjugal violence	None	Questionnaire-P	142	
1986	Straus and Gelles	Family violence	None	Interview-P	6,002	S,M,St,I
1986	Wolfe et al.	Witnessing violence	None	Questionnaire-P	63	M,St
1986	Jouriles, Darling, and O'Leary	Witnessing violence	None	Questionnaire-P	45	M,St
1987	Martin et al.	Family violence	None	Questionnaire-P	181	S,M,St,I
1987	Mason and Blankenship	Conjugal violence	Mini	Questionnaire-P	165	St
1988	Gelles, Straus, and Harrop	Pregnancy violence	None	Interviews-P	6,002	S,M,St,I
1988	Gelles	Family violence	None	Interviews-S	6,002	S,M,St
1988	Pillemer and Sinkelhor	Elder abuse	None	Questionnaire-P	—	S,M,St,I
1988	Stocks	Family violence	None	Interviews-S	—	

[a]P = primary data; S = secondary data.

[b]S = sample; M = measurement of variables; St = statistical analysis; T = theory; I = importance.

Conclusions from Sixty Years of Family Violence Research

Methodological Trends and Developments

Over the course of sixty years, research on family violence has improved from the early case studies of Caffey (1946) and others to the large national samples of Straus (1980) and his colleagues. This improvement paralleled other areas of family research and developed in the following manner:

1. Birth of the Topic: Case studies with no statistics.
2. Preschool Period: Nonrandom samples with descriptive statistics.
3. Grade School Stage: Nonrandom samples with t-tests, chi-square, and invalid measures.
4. Junior High Stage: Nonrandom samples with ANOVA, regression, and invalid measures.
5. High School Stage: Random samples, control groups with ANOVA, MANOVA, regression, log-linear, valid measures.
6. College Stage: Just starting, it consists of random samples, experiments, and interaction designs analyzed with structural models, sequential analysis, and multivariate analysis.

Theoretical Trends

Most of the early studies used either no explicit theory or a personality theory that assumed violent people were flawed. In the late 1960s and early 1970s, researchers started to investigate family and social characteristics that influenced violence. Recently they have tried to explain violence with commonly known theories as well as some mini theories. The empirical research, though, has usually been weak in that only small components of theories have been tested in any particular study.

Many authors have proposed general models that are difficult to test; few have proposed middle-range testable theories (Pagelow, 1984). An example of a middle-range theory derived from some of the findings from the last six decades is presented in figure 8–2. Such a model could be testable with the structural equations that researchers in other areas use (Lavee, 1988). As the field of family violence enters the college years and advanced methods for theory testing are utilized, theory development and testing should become more common.

Major Findings

A. Parent-Child Violence
   1. The physical abuse of children is a multidimensional problem that is a combination of societal and individual forces.

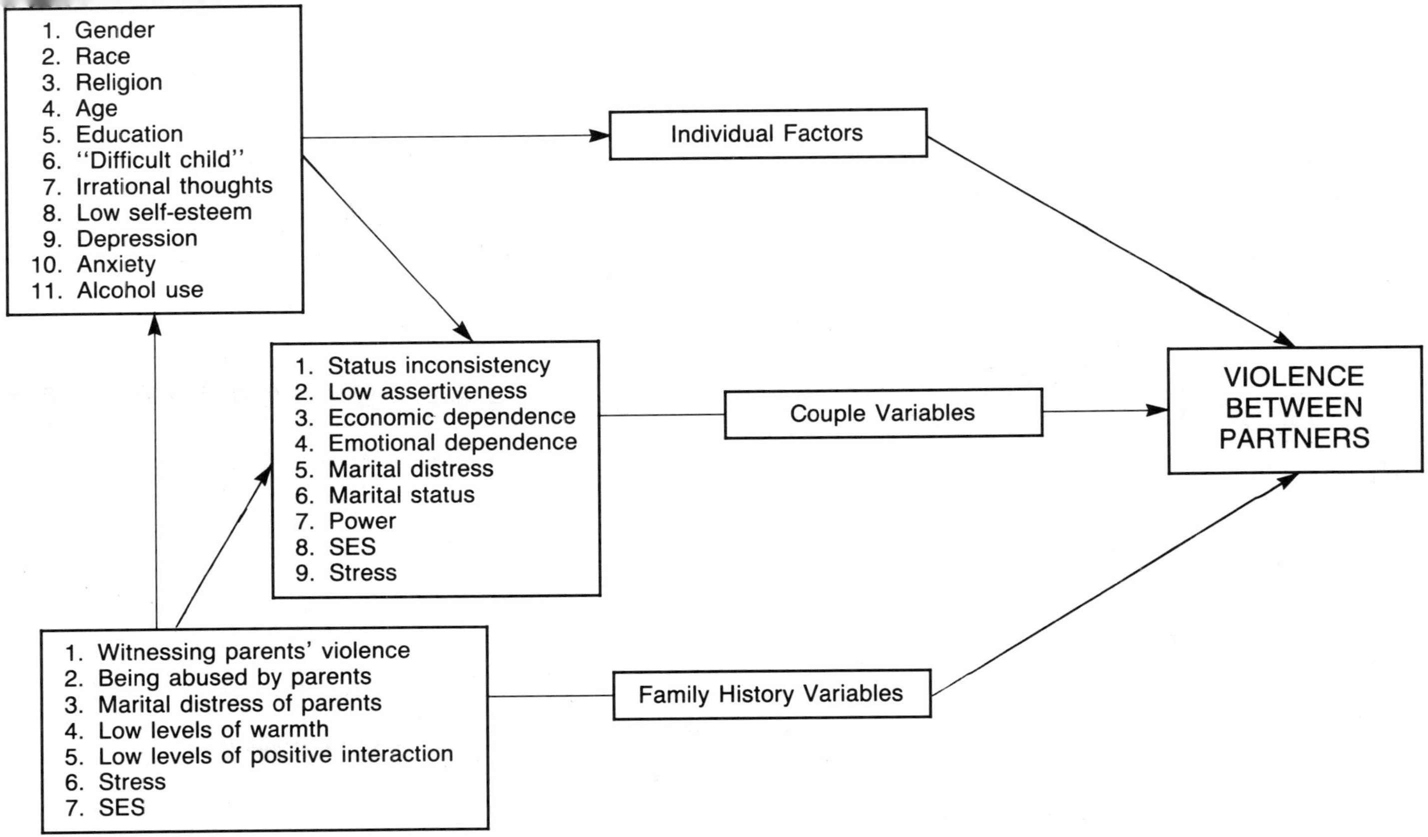

Figure 8–2. An Example of a Midrange Theory of Violence between Intimate Partners

2. Parent-child violence is not a discrete act; rather, it is a continuum of behaviors ranging from verbal aggression to life-threatening aggression with weapons.
3. At least one form of physical violence (slaps and pushes) occurs in more than half of the homes in the United States.
4. Different types of maltreatment, such as sexual abuse, physical abuse, and neglect, have unique causes and effects and should not be considered together.
5. The chances of parent-child violence are greater in homes where there is violence between parents.
6. Stress is an important factor in explaining parent-child violence.
7. Specific personality variables or syndromes are not good predictors of abuse by a parent.
8. The interaction patterns between parent and child are important in explaining which parents abuse and which do not.
9. Abusive and abused mothers are more depressed and anxious than nonabused mothers and also have lower self-esteem.
10. Abusive fathers have lower self-esteem and use alcohol more than nonabusive fathers.
11. Abusive mothers have more irrational thought patterns than nonabusive mothers and are more likely to view their children negatively.
12. Abusive parents interact differently from nonabusive parents in that they demonstrate less warmth and less positive behavior toward their children.
13. Children who are victims of parental violence show higher rates of aggression and lower rates of self-esteem and are not as socially skilled.
14. Girls are affected by abuse differently from boys; they are more likely to have internal problems, such as depression and anxiety, while boys are likely to have external problems like aggression and noncompliance.
15. Victims of parental violence are more likely to have school problems, a lower sense of control over their lives, and to be less adept at empathy than children who are not victims.
16. Abused children are similar to children who come from maritally distressed homes, which implies that the distinctions between abused and nonabused children might be the result of marital distress.
17. "Difficult children" are more likely to be abused.
18. There is a curvilinear relationship between age and violence rates. As children grow older, violence toward them decreases. The violence then begins to increase as children reach the age when they prepare to leave home.

B. Violence between Intimate Partners

1. Abusive husbands are more likely to have come from violent homes and to use alcohol.
2. Occupational and educational status inconsistency between husbands and wives contributes to violence.
3. Cohabitating couples experience more violence than married couples.
4. Abusive husbands often come from abusive homes where they were victims of or witnesses to family violence.
5. Spouses in an abusive relationship are less assertive than other married persons.
6. Many of the differences that are found between abusive and non-abusive couples disappear when abusive couples are compared to distressed couples.
7. Violent marriages are characterized by less stability than distressed, nonviolent marriages.
8. Economic dependence, emotional dependence, and commitment are important factors in keeping abused wives in their relationships.
9. A woman who was abused as a child is more likely to stay in an abusive relationship.
10. Wife abuse occurs more often in the summer.
11. Remarriages have higher rates of violence than first marriages.
12. Males report that they and their wives tend to be similar in violent acts, while females see the husbands as being more violent than themselves.
13. When women hit, they are more likely to be hit back than men.
14. Pregnant women are not more likely to be abused, but younger women are.
15. Violence to husbands by their wives is less frequent than husband-to-wife violence, is often in response to the husband's violence, and has less serious physical consequences than violence to wives.
16. Premarital violence is common and reciprocal.
17. Many women in premaritally violent relationships tend to marry the assailant.
18. Premarital violence is a better predictor of marital abuse than family of origin violence.

C. Effects of Witnessing Violence

1. Witnessing marital violence is related to males' becoming violent in their own marriages.
2. Witnessing marital violence is correlated with poor emotional health of children and behavioral problems.
3. Boys are affected by marital violence in different ways than girls are.

D. Other Types of Family Violence

1. Child-to-parent violence has been reported to be as common as conjugal violence.
2. It is unclear whether mothers or fathers are more often victims of their children's violence.
3. Adolescent boys are usually the perpetrators of child-parent violence.
4. Violence between siblings is the most prevalent type of violence and is viewed as the most acceptable form.
5. When parents are violent toward each other, their children are more likely to be violent among themselves.
6. The largest category of homicides involves people who are related.
7. When social class is controlled, blacks do not have higher rates of violence than whites.

E. Family Violence in General

1. Many violent families are multiproblem families
2. Whether a spouse is violent is more important in determining personal violence than attitudes against violence.
3. Violent families exhibit lower levels of interaction and are more negative than nonviolent families.
4. Women remember higher rates of violence in their homes than do men, but violence appears to be transmitted to men of the next generation more than to women.
5. Education, income, age, sex, race, religion, region of the country, and urban or rural residence are the demographic characteristics associated with abuse.
6. Individuals are more likely to rate severe types of violence as acceptable if they experienced it in their homes.
7. Violent families are less capable of solving conflicts than nonviolent families.
8. Violence toward children does not produce better compliance.
9. More children who are abused do not grow up to abuse their children than those who do. There is weak support for the cycle of violence theory.
10. Family dysfunction is as important as violence in explaining dysfunctions of children and parents.
11. There is evidence that violence has decreased in the United States in the last ten years.
12. Although statistics suggest that blacks are more violent within their families, when social class and social networks are controlled, blacks have lower rates of violence than whites.

Directions for the Future

Areas that have received little attention and need to be investigated more thoroughly are abuse of the elderly, violence between siblings, and child-to-parent violence. In addition, more attention should be paid to the perpetrators and what makes them unique; an inordinate amount of research has already been devoted to abused wives and abusive mothers. Males, the most serious perpetrators of violence, have been largely ignored.

Research should be shifted to focus on those members of a family who are abused and who do not abuse their own children. The individuals who break the cycle of violence are a rich source of information for designing prevention and rehabilitation programs. In addition, members of violent families who are skipped and not abused could provide social scientists with information on other family dynamics that are being overlooked.

It will be important to assess violence by measuring as many family members as possible. Since rates of violence differ according to the respondent, it is inadequate to use one family member's perception to measure violence. It has been disconcerting to realize that much of what we know about family violence is based on one family member's ratings of events that have occurred between other family members anywhere from one to twenty years ago. In addition, the possibility that violence is the cause of child deviance should be questioned. It is possible that poor family interactions, marital distress, children with difficult temperaments, or other variables are as important as the acts of violence in producing dysfunction.

Social class is related to both violent and deviant behaviors and should be included in all family violence research as a control variable. There is also a need to check the validity of the concept of violence. Is it a unitary phenomenon, or are there separate, not closely related concepts of corporal punishment, violence producing serious injury, and emotional abuse? Do the same independent variables predict all equally well?

Interactions in violent families have not been studied or statistically analyzed adequately, although methods are available that allow the assessment of interaction patterns (Gottman, 1982). The nature of violence is extremely complex and probably will not be fully understood until violent families are studied through interaction research. It is important to employ more longitudinal designs for following children and parents for longer periods of time to understand better the factors that are most influential in producing violence.

Another method that could be utilized by the numerous practitioners who work with victims and perpetrators of violence is the single-case experimental design (Robinson, 1981). This method could be the only way to show how individuals actually respond to witnessing violence or to being abused. The single-case design may result in more accurate results than the retrospective reports of violence from nonrandom clinical samples.

Another need is to combine more of the important variables into one study. Many researchers investigate psychological variables, others investigate sociological variables, and still others investigate family variables. If more studies with as many of the important variables as possible were conducted, important interactions and other hidden relationships would probably emerge.

Researchers in family violence have contributed greatly to helping us understand violence in the family. In twenty-five years, they have produced a considerable amount of literature that rivals many other areas of family research that were not shrouded in secrecy for centuries. With continued efforts like those that have been expended during the last few decades, family violence will be understood much more clearly by the end of the 1990s.

References

Adelson, L. 1961. Slaughter of innocents: A study of forty-six homicides in which the victims were children. *New England Journal of Medicine* 264:1345–1349.

Aguirre, B.E. 1985. Why do they return? Abused wives in shelters. *Social Work* 30: 350–354.

Altemeier, W.A., III; Vietze, P.M.; Sherrod, K.B.; Sandler, H.M.; Falsey, S.; and O'Connor, S. 1979. Prediction of child maltreatment during pregnancy. *Journal of the American Academy of Child Psychiatry* 18:205–218.

Ayer, M.E., and Bernreuter, R.G. 1937. A study of the relationship between discipline and personality traits in little children. *Journal of Genetic Psychology* 50:165–170.

Bain, K. 1963. The physically abused child. *Pediatrics* 31:895–897.

Bakwin, H. 1956. Multiple skeletal lesions in young children due to trauma. *Journal of Pediatrics* 49:7–15.

Barahal, R.M.; Waterman, J.; and Martin, H.P. 1981. The social cognitive development of abused children. *Journal of Consulting and Clinical Psychology* 49:508–516.

Berk, R.A.; Newton, P.J.; and Berk, S.F. 1986. What a difference a day makes: An empirical study of the impact of shelters for battered women. *Journal of Marriage and the Family* 48:481–490.

Block, M.R., and Sinnott, J.D. 1979. *The Battered Elder Syndrome: An Exploratory Study.* College Park: University of Maryland.

Boardman, H. 1962. Project to rescue children. *Social Work* 7:43–49.

Bolton, F.G., Jr.; Laner, R.H.; Gai, D.S.; and Kane, S.P. 1981. The study of child maltreatment: When is research research? *Journal of Family Issues* 2:531–539.

Bolton, F.G., Jr.; Reich, J.W.; and Gutierrez, S.E. 1977. *Delinquency Patterns in Maltreated Children and Siblings.* Phoenix, Ariz.: Community Development for Abuse and Neglect.

Bourdouris, J. 1971. Homicide and the family. *Journal of Marriage and the Family* 33:667–676.

Bousha, D.M., and Twentyman, C.T. 1984. Mother-child interactional style in abuse, neglect, and control groups: Naturalistic observations in the home. *Journal of Abnormal Psychology* 93:106–114.

Brennemann, J. 1932. The infant ward. *American Journal of Diseases of Childhood* 43: 577–584.

Browning, J., and Dutton, D. 1986. Assessment of wife assault with the conflict tactics scale: Using couple data to quantify the differential reporting effect. *Journal of Marriage and the Family* 48:375–379.

Bulcroft, R., and Straus, M.A. 1975. Validity of husband, wife, and child reports of intrafamily violence and power. Unpublished paper V16. Durham: University of New Hampshire, Family Violence Research Program.

Burgess, R.L., and Conger, R.D. 1978. Family interaction in abusive, neglectful, and normal families. *Child Development* 49:1163–1173.

Bryant, H.D.; Billingsley, A.K.; Kerry, G.A.; Leefman, W.V.; Merrill, E.J.; Senecal G.R.; and Walsh, B.G. 1963. Physical abuse of children: An agency study. *Child Welfare* 42:125–130.

Caffey, J. 1946. Multiple fractures in the long bones of infants suffering from chronic subdural hematoma. *American Journal of Roentology* 56:163–173.

———. 1965. Significance of the history in the diagnosis of traumatic injury to children. *Journal of Pediatrics* 67:1008–1014.

Camras, L.A.; Grow, J.G.; and Ribordy, S.C. 1983. Recognition of emotional expression by abused children. *Journal of Clinical Child Psychology* 12:325–328.

Cate, R.M.; Henton, J.M.; Koval, J.; Christopher, F.S.; and Lloyd, S. 1982. Premarital abuse: A social psychological perspective. *Journal of Family Issues* 3:79–90.

Cazenave, N.A., and Straus, M.A. 1979. Race, class, network embeddedness and family violence: A search for potent support systems. *Journal of Comparative Family Studies* 10:281–299.

Centerwall, B.S. 1984. Race, socioeconomic status and domestic homicide, Atlanta, 1971–1972. *American Journal of Public Health* 74:813–815.

Cohen, M.I.; Rapling, D.L.; and Green, P.E. 1966. Psychological aspects of the maltreatment syndrome of childhood. *Journal of Pediatrics* 69:179–284.

Coleman, H.H.; Weinman, M.L.; and Bartholomew, P.H. 1980. Factors affecting conjugal violence. *Journal of Psychology* 105:197–202.

Cornell, C.P., and Gelles, R.J. 1982. Adolescent to parent violence. *Urban and Social Change Review* 15:8–14.

Dibble, U., and Straus, M.A. 1980. Some social structure determinants of inconsistency between attitudes and behavior: The case of family violence. *Journal of Marriage and the Family* 42:71–80.

Douglas, R.L.; Hickey, T.; and Noel, C. 1980. A study of maltreatment of the elderly and other vulnerable adults. Final report to the U.S. Administration on Aging and the Michigan Department of Social Services. Washington, D.C.: U.S. Government Printing Office.

Duncan, G.M.; Frazier, S.H.; Litin, E.M.; Johnson, A.M.; and Baron, A.J. 1958. Etiological factors in first-degree murder. *Journal of the American Medical Association* 168:1755–1758.

Egan, K.J. 1983. Stress management and child management with abusive parents. *Journal of Clinical Child Psychology* 12:292–299.

Egeland, B., and Brunnquell, D. 1979. An at-risk approach to the study of child abuse. *Journal of the American Academy of Child Psychiatry* 18:219–235.

Egeland, B., and Vaughn, B. 1981. Failure of "bond formation" as a cause of abuse, neglect, and maltreatment. *American Journal of Orthopsychiatry* 51:78–84.

Elmer, B. 1960. Abused young children seen in hospitals. *Social Work* 5:98–102.

Elmer, E. 1967. *Children in Jeopardy: A Study of Abused Minors and Their Families.* Pittsburgh: University of Pittsburgh Press.

Elmer, E., and Gregg, G. 1967. Developmental characteristics of abused children. *Pediatrics* 50:596–602.

Elmer, Elizabeth. 1977. A follow-up study of traumatized children. *Pediatrics* 59: 273–279.

Erikson, E.H. 1937. Observation on Sioux education. *Journal of Psychology* 7:101–156.

Estroff, T.W.; Herrera, C.; Gaines, R.; Shaffer, D.; Gould, M.; and Green, A.H. 1984. Maternal psychopathology and perception of child behavior in psychiatrically referred and child maltreatment families. *Journal of the American Academy of Child Psychiatry* 23:649–652.

Field, M., and Kirschner, R.M. 1978. Services for battered women. *Victimology* 3: 216–222.

Forsstrom-Cohen, B., and Rosenbaum, A. 1985. The effects of parental marital violence on young adults: An exploratory investigation. *Journal of Marriage and the Family* 47:467–472.

Freud, S. 1919. A child is being beaten—A contribution to the study of the origin of sexual perversions. In *Collected Papers* 2:172–202. London: Nogarth Press.

Gaines, R.; Sandgrund, A.; Green, A.H.; and Power, E. 1978. Etiological factors in child maltreatment: A multivariate study of abusing, neglecting, and normal mothers. *Journal of Abnormal Psychology* 87:531–540.

Gaquin, D.A. 1978. Spouse abuse: Data from the National Crime Survey. *Victimology: An International Journal* 2:632–643.

Gelles, R.J. 1976. Abused wives: Why do they stay? *Journal of Marriage and the Family* 38:659–668.

———. 1978. Violence toward children in the United States. *American Journal of Orthopsychiatry* 48:580–592.

———. 1980. Violence in the family: A review of research in the seventies. *Journal of Marriage and the Family* 42:873–885.

———. 1988. Violence and pregnancy: Are pregnant women at greater risk of abuse. *Journal of Marriage and the Family* 50:841–847.

Gelles, R.J., and Cornell, C.P. 1985. *Intimate Violence in Families.* Beverly Hills, Calif.: Sage Publications.

Gelles, R.J.; Straus, M.A.; and Harrop, J.W. 1988. Has family violence decreased? A response to J. Timothy Stocks. *Journal of Marriage and the Family* 50:286–291.

Gentemann, K.M. 1984. Wife beating: Attitudes of a non-clinical population. *Victimology: An International Journal* 9:109–119.

George, C., and Main, M. 1979. Social interactions of young abused children: Approach, avoidance, and aggression. *Child Development* 50:306–318.

Gil, D.G. 1969. Physical abuse of children: Findings and implications of a nationwide survey. *Pediatrics* (Supplement) 44:857–864.

———. 1971. Violence against children. *Journal of Marriage and the Family* 33:637–648.

Gil, D.G., and Noble, J.H. 1969. Public knowledge, attitudes, and opinions about physical child abuse in the U.S. *Child Welfare* 48:395–401.

Gold, M. 1953. Suicide, homicide, and the socialization of aggression. *American Journal of Sociology* 63:651–661.

Goldstein, D., and Rosenbaum, A. 1985. An evaluation of the self-esteem of maritally violent men. *Family Relations* 34:425–428.

Gottman, J.M. 1982. Temporal form: Toward a new language for describing relationships. *Journal of Marriage and the Family* 44:943–962.

Groves, E.R. 1927. *Social Problems of the Family.* Philadelphia: J.B. Lippincott Company.

Gully, K.J.; Pepping, M.; and Dengerink, H.A. 1982. Gender differences in third-party reports of violence. *Journal of Marriage and the Family* 44:497–498.

Harbin, H., and Madden, D. 1979. Battered parents? A new syndrome. *American Journal of Psychiatry* 136:1288–1291.

Hartogs, R. 1951. Discipline in the early life of sex-delinquents and sex-criminals. *Nervous Child* 9:167–173.

Hasselt, V.B.; Morrison, R.L.; and Bellack, A.S. 1985. Alcohol use in wife abusers and their spouses. *Addictive Behaviors* 10:127–135.

Havighurst, R.J., and Davis A. 1955. A comparison of the Chicago and Harvard studies of social class differences in child rearing. *American Sociological Review* 20: 439–442.

Helfer, R.E., and Kempe, C.H. (eds.). 1968. *The Battered Child.* Chicago: University of Chicago Press.

Herrenkohl, E.C., and Herrenkohl, R.C. 1979. A comparison of abused children and their nonabused siblings. *Journal of the American Academy of Child Psychiatry* 18:260–269.

Herrenkohl, E.C.; Herrenkohl, R.C.; Toedter, L.; and Yanushefski, A.M. 1984. Parent-child interactions in abusive and nonabusive families. *Journal of the American Academy of Child Psychiatry* 23:641–648.

Hershorn, M., and Rosenbaum, A. 1985. Children of marital violence: A closer look at the unintended victims. *American Journal of Orthopsychiatry* 55:260–266.

Herzberger, S.D., and Tennen, H. 1985. The effect of self-relevance on judgments of moderate and severe disciplinary encounters. *Journal of Marriage and the Family* 47:311–318.

Hilberman, E., and Munson, K. 1978. Sixty battered women. *Victimology* 2:460–470.

Hornung, C.A.; McCulough, B.C.; and Sugimoto, T. 1981. Status relationships in marriage: Risk factors in spouse abuse. *Journal of Marriage and the Family* 42: 675–692.

Hudson, W.W., and Mcintosh, S.R. 1981. The assessment of spouse abuse: Two quantifiable dimensions. *Journal of Marriage and the Family* 42:873–885.

Hughes, H.M., and Barad, S.J. 1983. Psychological functioning of children in a battered women's shelter: A preliminary investigation. *American Journal of Orthopsychiatry* 53:525–531.

Jaffe, P.; Wolfe, D.; Wilson, S.; and Zak, L. 1986a. Similarities in behavior and social maladjustment among child victims and witnesses to family violence. *American Journal of Orthopsychiatry* 56:142–146.

———. 1986b. Family violence and child adjustment: A comparative analysis of girls' and boys' behavioral symptoms. *American Journal of Psychiatry* 143:74–76.

Johnson, B., and Morse, H.A. 1968. Injured children and their parents. *Children* 15:147–152.

Jouriles, E.N.; Darling, J.; and O'Leary, K.D. 1987. Predicting child behavior problems in maritally violent families. *Journal of Abnormal Child Psychology* 15:165–173.

Kalmuss, D. 1984. The intergenerational transmission of marital aggression. *Journal of Marriage and the Family* 46:11–19.

Kalmuss, D., and Seltzer, J.A. 1986. Continuity of marital behavior in remarraige: The case of spouse abuse. *Journal of Marriage and the Family* 48:113–120.

Kalmuss, D.S., and Straus, M.A. 1982. Wife's marital dependency and wife abuse. *Journal of Marriage and the Family* 44:277–286.

Kempe, C.H.; Silverman, F.N.; Steele, B.F.; Droegemueller, W.; and Silver, H.K. 1962. The battered-child syndrome. *Journal of the American Medical Association* 181:17–24.

Kinard, E.M. 1980. Emotional development in physically abused children. *American Journal of Orthopsychiatry* 50:686–696.

———. 1982. Experiencing child abuse: Effects on emotional adjustment. *American Journal of Orthopsychiatry* 52:82–91.

Lahey, B.B.; Conger, R.D.; Atkenson, B.M.; and Treiber, F.A. 1984. Parenting behavior and emotional status of physically abusive mothers. *Journal of Consulting and Clinical Psychology* 52:1062–1071.

Laner, M.R., and Thompson, J. 1982. Abuse and aggression in courting couples. *Deviant Behavior* 3:229–244.

Lavee, Y. 1988. Linear structural relationships (LISREL) in family research. *Journal of Marriage and the Family* 50:937–948.

Levinger, G. 1966. Sources of marital dissatisfaction among applicants for divorce. *American Journal of Orthopsychiatry* 36:803–807.

Levy, D. 1931. Maternal overprotection and rejection. *Archives of Neurology and Psychiatry* 25:886–889.

Littmen, R.A.; Moore, R.C.A.; and Pierce-Jones, J. 1957. Social class differences in child rearing: A third community for comparison with Chicago and Newton. *American Sociological Review* 22:694–704.

Maccoby, E.E., and Gibbs, P.K. 1954. Methods of child-rearing in two social classes. In W.E. Martin and C.B. Stendler (eds.), *Readings in Child Development*, pp. 380–396. New York: Harcourt, Brace and Company.

Makepeace, J. 1981. Courtship violence among college students. *Family Relations* 30: 97–102.

Martin, M..F. 1932. The training and ideals of two adolescent groups. *Mental Hygiene* 16:277–280.

Martin, M.J.; Schumm, W.R.; Bugaighis, M.A.; Jurich, A.P.; and Bollman, S.R. 1987. Family violence and adolescents' perceptions of outcomes of family conflict. *Journal of Marriage and the Family* 49:165–171.

Martin, M.J., and Walters, J. 1982. Familial correlates of selected types of child abuse and neglect. *Journal of Marriage and the Family* 44:267–276.

Mash, E.J.; Johnston, C.; and Kovitz, K. 1983. A comparison of mother-child interactions of physically abused and non-abused children during play and task situations. *Journal of Clinical Child Psychology* 12:337–346.

Mason, A., and Blankenship, V. 1987. Power and affiliation motivation, stress, and abuse in intimate relationships. *Journal of Personality and Social Psychology* 52: 203–210.

Melnick, B., and Hurley, J.R. 1969. Distinctive personality attributes of child-abusing mothers. *Journal of Consulting and Clinical Psychology* 33:746–749.

Michael, R.P., and Zumpe, D. 1986. An annual rhythm in the battering of women. *American Journal of Psychiatry* 143:637–640.

Miller, D., and Challas, G. 1981. Abused children as adult parents: A twenty-five year longitudinal study. Paper presented at the National Conference of Family Violence Researchers, Durham, N.H.

Miller, D.R., and Sanson, G.E. 1958. *The Changing American Parent.* New York: Wiley.

Monane, M.; Leichter, D.; and Lewis, D.O. 1984. Physical abuse in psychiatrically hospitalized children and adolescents. *Journal of the American Academy of Child Psychiatry* 23:653–658.

Morris, M.G., and Gould, R.W. 1963. Neglected child. *American Journal of Orthopsychiatry* 33:298–299.

Mowrer, E.R. 1928. *Domestic Discord.* Chicago: University of Chicago Press.

———. 1932. *The Family.* Chicago: University of Chicago Press.

O'Brien, J.E. 1971. Violence in divorce prone families. *Journal of Marriage and the Family* 33:692–698.

O'Leary, K.D., and Curley, A. 1986. Assertion in family violence: Correlates of spouse abuse. *Journal of Marital and Family Therapy* 12:281–290.

O'Malley, H.; Segars, H.; Perrez, R.; Mitchell, V.; and Kneupfel, G.M. 1979. *Elder Abuse in Massachusetts.* Boston: Legal Research and Services for the Elderly.

Pagelow, M.D. 1984. *Family Violence.* New York: Praeger.

Paulson, M.J., and Blake, P.R. 1969. The physically abused child: A focus on prevention. *Child Welfare* 48:86–95.

Paulson, M.J.; Afifi, A.A.; Thomason, M.L.; and Chaleff, A. 1974. The MMPI: A descriptive measure of psychopathology in abusive parents. *Journal of Clinical Psychology* 30:387–390.

Peek, C.W.; Fisher, J.L.; and Kidwell, J.S. 1985. Teenage violence toward parents: A neglected dimension of family violence. *Journal of Marriage and the Family* 47: 1051–1058.

Perry, M.A.; Doran, L.D.: and Wells, E.A. 1983. Developmental and behavioral characteristics of the physically abused child. *Journal of Clinical Child Psychology* 12: 320–324.

Perry, M.A.; Wells, E.A.; and Doran, L.D. 1983. Parent characteristics in abusing and nonabusing families. *Journal of Clinical Child Psychology* 12:329–336.

Pfohl, S.J. 1977. The discovery of child abuse. *Social Problems* 24:310–323.

Pillemer, K.A., and Sinkelhor, D. 1988. The prevalence of elder abuse: A random sample survey. *Gerontologist* 28:51–57.

Pleck, E.J.; Pleck, M.; Grossman, M.; and Bart, P. 1978. The battered data syndrome: A comment on Steinmetz's article. *Victimology* 2:680–683.

Radbill, S.X. 1968. A history of child abuse and infanticide. In Ray E. Helfer and Henry C. Kempe (eds.), *The Battered Child,* pp. 3–17. Chicago: University of Chicago Press.

Resnick, P.J. 1970. Murder of the newborn: A psychiatric review of neonaticide. *American Journal of Psychiatry* 10:58–64.

Robinson, P.W. 1981. *Fundamentals of Experimental Psychology.* Englewood Cliffs, N.J. Prentice-Hall.

Roscoe, B., and Benaske, N. 1985. Courtship violence experienced by abused wives: Similarities in patterns of abuse. *Family Relations* 34:419–424.

Rosenbaum, A., and O'Leary, K.D. 1981. Marital violence: Characteristics of abusive couples. *Journal of Consulting and Clinical Psychology* 49:63–71.

Rosenberg, M.S., and Reppucci, N.D. 1983. Abusive mothers: Perception of their own and their children's behavior. *Journal of Consulting and Clinical Psychology* 51: 674–682.

Rounsaville, B.J. 1978. Battered wives: Barriers to identification and treatment. *American Journal of Orthopsychiatry* 48:487–497.

Rouse, L.P. 1984. Models of self-esteem, and locus of control as factors contributing to spouse abuse. *Victimology: An International Journal* 9:130–141.

Rue, A.W. 1937. The case work approach to protective work. *Family* 18:277–282.

Shorkey, C.T., and Armendariz, J. 1985. Personal worth, self-esteem, anomia, hostility, and irrational thinking of abusing mothers: A multivariate approach. *Journal of Clinial Psychology* 41:414–421.

Silverman, F.N. 1953. The roentgen manifestations of unrecognized skeletal trauma in infants. *American Journal of Roentgenology, Radium Therapy and Nuclear Medicine* 69:413–427.

Smith, A.E. 1944. The beaten child. *Hygeia* 22:386–388.

Snell, J.E.; Rosenwald, R.J.; and Robey, A. 1964. The wifebeater's wife. *Archives of General Psychiatry* 11:167–113.

Snyder, D.K., and Fruchtman, L.A. 1981. Differential patterns of wife abuse: A data-based typology. *Journal of Consulting and Clinical Psychology* 49:878–885.

Spinnetta, J.J. 1978. Parental personality factors in child abuse. *Journal of Consulting and Clinical Psychology* 46:1409–1414.

Stagner, R. 1933. The role of parents in the development of emotional instability. *Psychology Bulletin* 30:696–697.

Steele, B.F., and Pollock, C.B. 1968. A psychiatric study of parents who abuse infants and small children. In Ray E. Helfer and C. Henry Kempe (eds.), *The Battered Child.* Chicago: University of Chicago Press.

Steinmetz, S.K. 1971. Occupation and physical punishment: A response to Straus. *Journal of Marriage and the Family* 33:664–666.

———. 1977a. *The Cycle of Violence: Assertive, Aggressive, and Abusive Family Interaction.* New York: Praeger.

———. 1977b. The use of force for resolving family conflict: The training ground for abuse. *Family Coordinator* 26:19–26.

———. 1978. The battered husband syndrome. *Victimology* 2:499–509.

Stocks, T.J. 1988. Has family violence decreased? A reassessment of the Straus and Gelles data. *Journal of Marriage and the Family* 50:281–285.

Stott, L.L. 1940. Home punishment of adolescents. *Journal of Genetic Psychology* 57: 415–428.

Straus, M.A. 1971. Some social antecedents of physical punishment: A linkage theory interpretation. *Journal of Marriage and the Family* 33:658–663.

———. 1973. A general systems approach to a theory of violence between family members. *Social Science Information* 12:105–125.

———. 1974. Leveling, civility, and violence in the family. *Journal of Marriage and the Family* 36:13–29.

———. 1979. Measuring intrafamily conflict and violence: The conflict tactics (CT) scales. *Journal of Marriage and the Family* 41:75–88.

Straus, M.A., and Gelles, R. 1986. Societal change and change in family violence from 1975 to 1985 as revealed by two national surveys. *Journal of Marriage and the Family* 48:465–479.

Straus, M.A.; Gelles, R.J.; and Steinmetz, S.K. 1980. *Behind Closed Doors: Violence in the American Family.* Garden City, N.Y.: Doubleday.

Strube, M.J., and Barbour, L.S. 1983. The decision to leave an abusive relationship:

Economic dependence and psychological commitment. *Journal of Marriage and the Family* 45:785–793.

———. 1984. Factors related to the decision to leave an abusive relationship. *Journal of Marriage and the Family* 46:837–844.

Symonds, P.M. 1937. Some basic concepts in parent-child relationships. *American Journal of Psychology* 50:195–206.

Tarter, R.E.; Hegedus, A.M.; Winsten, N.E.; and Alterman, A.I. 1984. Neuropsychological, personality, and familial characteristics of physically abused delinquents. *Journal of the American Academy of Child Psychiatry* 23:668–674.

Telch, C.F., and Lindquist, C.U. 1984. Violent versus nonviolent couples: A comparison of patterns. *Psychotherapy: Theory, Research and Practice* 21:242–248.

U.S. Department of Health, Education and Welfare. Children's Bureau. 1963. *The Abused Child.* Washington, D.C.: U.S. Government Printing Office.

———. 1966. *The Child Abuse Reporting Laws.* Washington, D.C.: U.S. Government Printing Office.

Van Hasselt, V.B.; Morrison, R.L.; Bellack, A.S.: and Hersen, M. 1988. *Handbook of Family Violence.* New York: Plenum Press.

Walker, L.E. 1983. Victimology and the psychology perspectives of battered women. *Victimology: An International Journal* 8:82–104.

Watson, G. 1934. A comparison of the effects of lax versus strict home training. *Journal of Social Psychology* 5:102–105.

Webster, Stratton, C. 1985. Comparison of abusive and nonabusive families with conduct-disordered children. *American Journal of Orthopsychiatry* 55:59–69.

Wittman, M.P., and Huffman, A.V. 1945. A comparative study of developmental, adjustment, and personality characteristics of psychotic, psychoneurotic, delinquent, and normally adjusted teenaged youths. *Journal of Genetic Psychology* 66: 167–182.

Wolfe, D.A., and Mosk, M.D. 1983. Behavioral comparison of children from abused and distressed families. *Journal of Consulting and Clinical Psychology* 51:702–708.

Wolfe, D.A.; Jaffe, P.; Wilson, S.K.; and Zak, L. 1985. Children of battered women: The relations of child behavior to family violence and maternal stress. *Journal of Consulting and Clinical Psychology* 53:857.

Wolfe, D.A.; Zak, L.; Wilson, S.K.; and Jaffe, P. 1986. Child witnesses to violence between parents: Critical issues in heavioral and social adjustment. *Journal of Abnormal Child Psychology* 14:95–104.

Woolley, P.V., Jr., and Evans, W.A., Jr. 1955. Significance of skeletal lesions in infants resembling those of traumatic origin. *Journal of the American Medical Association* 158:539–543.

Wright, Logan. 1976. The "sick but slick" syndrome as a personality component of parents of battered children. *Journal of Clinical Psychology* 32:41–45.

Yllo, K. 1983. Sexual equality and violence against wives in American States. *Journal of Comparative Family Studies* 14:67–85.

Yllo, K., and Straus, M.A. 1981. Interpersonal violence among married and cohabitating couples. *Family Relations* 30:339–347.

Young, L.R. 1964. *Wednesday's Children: A Study of Child Neglect and Abuse.* New York: McGraw-Hill.

9
Recreation in the Family

Steven R. Hawks

In the study of family recreation, researchers have been primarily interested in assessing the impact that family use of nonworktime has on patterns of family living. In general, relationships between leisure-time behavior and family structure have been analyzed in terms of marital stability and satisfaction; general family satisfaction or family strength; and the creation of new parental, spousal, and parent-child roles in the realm of family recreational planning and decision making. Independent variables that have been studied include the types of leisure activity engaged in; with whom leisure time is shared; the quantity of leisure time available; leisure attitudes and satisfaction; and the decision-making process that precedes recreation choices.

In addition, researchers have sought explanations for and predictors of family recreation in terms of certain family factors. Independent family variables that have been used to explain variations in family recreation include such items as family life cycle, number of children and family size, family type, gender orientations, socioeconomic status, early (parental) family influences, and spouse-parent employment.

Several reviews of the literature involving various aspects of family leisure and recreation have been previously undertaken (Cunningham and Johannis, 1960; Parker, 1976; Carlson, 1979; Wilson, 1980; Orthner and Mancini, 1980; Holman and Epperson, 1984). The value of the review in this chapter lies in its discussion of the chronological development of family recreation research in terms of purpose, theory, methodology, findings, and process. Studies are discussed within their historical context, and I provide an overall evaluation of major studies in each decade from 1930 through the 1980s. In addition, I identify current issues that are critical to family recreation and offer suggestions for future research.

This review focuses on sociological research with a direct bearing on recreation in the family. Accordingly, research on the following topics has not been considered directly: organized voluntary associations, professional recreational topics (recreation planning and development, recreation personnel development, and leisure counseling, for example), the psychology of parent-child play interactions, and the influence of television in the home. Each of these related topics warrants separate treatment. In addition to the list of references for studies cited in the text, a section at the end of the chapter cites other related research, as well as some of the most relevant theoretical literature.

Leisure has been defined primarily in two different ways: as a portion of one's time not specifically set aside for other obligatory duties or as a quality of experience unconfined to particular times (Wilson, 1980).

No studies dealing specifically with concerns related to recreation in the family were noted in the periodical literature prior to 1930. A few commentaries and essays recognizing the importance of family togetherness and family recreation were identified (e.g., Skolsky, 1929), but none was more than anecdotal in nature.

In their classic study of Middletown, however, Lynd and Lynd (1929) used informant interviews, questionnaires, personal diaries, available historical and written information, and direct observation to produce a descriptive analysis of activities and trends in the leisure-time behavior of "typical" midwestern Americans during the early to mid-1920s. With regard to family recreation, Lynd and Lynd concluded that the family was "declining as a unit of leisure-time pursuits" (p. 272). They saw formal clubs and organizations replacing the role of less formal neighborhoods and families as centers for individual recreation. In terms of leisure research, the value of their study lies in the descriptive baseline data and suggested trends that it provided for future comparisons.

The Decade 1930–1939

Two studies were identified in the literature during this decade that contributed to an understanding of recreation in the family. The earlier, and more important, study was that by Lundberg, Komarovsky, and McInerny (1934), *Leisure: A Suburban Study.*

Research Findings

In many respects, the study by Lundberg, Komarovsky, and McInerny (1934) was very similar to that of Middletown. The authors used similar methods, including systematic direct observation, informant interviews, questionnaires, personal diaries, schedules, and pertinent secondary data, and their objective was to describe the leisure habits of "typical" suburban Americans.

While Lundberg, Komarovsky, and McInerny recognized the increasing role of formal organizations in determining the use of individual leisure time (as described in the Middletown study), they nevertheless concluded that "the home and the family figure more prominently in the leisure and recreation of a larger proportion of the population than any other major institution" and that "the family is still the most stable nucleus of recreational activities in the suburb" (pp. 187–189). They also concluded that income was the single largest determinant for the type of recreation in which the family engaged. Most of the study's results were descriptive in nature and sought to provide detail as to the amount of leisure time available to, and the types of activities engaged in by, family members on the basis of age and gender.

Much of the information relating to family recreation patterns was obtained from a convenience sample of 470 families living in Westchester County, New York. The study's major weaknesses included the use of nonrandom sampling methods and data collection techniques that tended to treat individual subjects somewhat superficially. Along with the Middletown study, this one can be considered a pioneer effort in providing baseline descriptive data for future research.

In the mid-1930s, Conard (1939) used personal interviews and questionnaires to collect data from 150 families in a central Iowa town in an attempt to determine the differential impact of the Great Depression on families of laborers, farmers, and the business class. An attempt was made to contact all complete families in the town (containing school-age children) whose incomes had been reduced by at least 20 percent. One finding was that all classes of families reduced expenditures for recreation and that farm and labor families engaged in more recreation in the community while business families tended to develop new forms of leisure at home.

The Decade in Review

Family recreation research through 1939 was limited to descriptive studies and several methodological weaknesses were present. Sampling methods were either nonrandom convenience samples (Lynd and Lynd, 1929; Lundberg, Komarovsky, and McInerny, 1934) or were inadequately described (Conard, 1939). None of the research used statistical analyses to interpret the data collected, little or no mention was made of previous research, and the studies were atheoretical. (See table 9–1.)

In spite of these shortcomings, however, research up through the 1930s was valuable in providing important baseline data that attempted to describe how Americans spent their leisure time. A common theme during the decade was the impact that socioeconomic status had on determining the choice and location of an individual's or family's recreational activities. Lower-income families tended to stay home more often, visiting and listening to the radio, while high-income families were more likely to eat out and be involved in formal clubs.

The Decade 1940–1949

Five studies with relevance to recreation in the family were found in the literature for this period. The studies covered individual versus family social participation, the relation between childhood and adult leisure activities, socio-

Table 9–1
Overview of Research on Recreation in the Family, 1930–1939

Year	*Author*	*Topic*	*Theory*	*Method*[a]	*Sample*	*Strengths*[b]
1934	Lundberg, Komarovsky, and McInerny	Suburban leisure	None	Direct observation	470	I
1939	Conard	Income and families	None	Interview-P	150	

[a]P = primary data.
[b]I = important study.

economic status and leisure pursuits, and status self-ratings as a determinant of family social participation.

Research Findings

Anderson (1943) tested the hypothesis that the social participation of an individual tends to be a function of the social participation of that individual's family. Chapin participation scores were computed for 1,176 farm families in New York State and the 2,014 individuals over 10 years of age were included in those families. The correlation between individual and family participation scores was computed. Based on high correlations and other indicators of family unity, Anderson concluded that his hypothesis was confirmed. In addition, in the majority of cases, either all family members participated together in a given organization or no member participated. Anderson's findings added support to the conclusion of Lundberg, Komarovsky, and McInerny (1934) that the family was the most stable nucleus for individual recreation.

Although Anderson's (1943) study was not specifically limited to family participation in recreational activities, the results suggested that individual social participation, if not recreation, tended to be a function of family participation and that family unity in social participation was the norm. Using the same data, Anderson and Palmbeck (1943) found that upper-class families were more likely to be socially active than lower-class families.

Patrick (1945) attempted to determine the influence of childhood leisure activities on the use of adult leisure time by administering questionnaires to 120 adult subjects in a midwestern city with a population of 500,000. The sampling method and target population were not identified. Adult leisure time activities were not highly correlated with those of childhood.

Anderson (1946) further tested the hypothesis that family social participation is an expression of felt status on the part of the participating or nonparticipating family. Status and social participation self-ratings were obtained from 344 New York farm families through the use of questionnaires. Family social participation depended on the opinions families held concerning their own position in the community. Families appeared to accept a status position for themselves and then participated socially in accordance with that perception.

Another study during the period (MacDonald, McGuire, and Havighurst, 1949) supported the hypotheses that the quality and quantity of leisure time activities of children was determined by socioeconomic status and that children whose behavior was not typical of their class culture patterns prepared for social mobility by interacting with children from families at other class levels, thereby learning techniques and ways of thinking that would prepare them for upward advancement. The data were collected through the use of daily self-report diaries (over two separate, one-week periods), and the findings were interpreted in terms of social learning theory, with the suggestion that children learned the appropriate ways and beliefs of their class in part through class-specific leisure activities. The major weakness of the study was the use of children aged 10–12 from only a single school (N = 223). No mention was made of a specific target population.

The final study for the period was conducted by Hollingshead (1949) using a sample of 735 adolescents from 535 families residing in a midwestern community of 10,000 people. The sample represented a complete cross-section of the high school generation under study. In order to evaluate the relationship between social class and adolescent behavior, Hollingshead used participant-observation, informant interviews, schedules, official records, tests, autobiographies, and visits to collect data on the subjects. Based on chi-square tests for statistical independence, Hollingshead concluded that signficiant differences in leisure time behavior existed for subjects depending on which of the five social classes they had been assigned to (on the basis of reputational rankings determined by selected judges).

Individuals in the higher classes tended to be more socially active, with involvement in extensive travel, country clubs, exclusive cliques, and community organizations, while the lower classes tended to rely on public parks and visiting for leisure time recreation, with much less involvement in organized community activities. Upper-class adolescents tended to spend more of their time than lower-class youths in adult-supervised activities (often with parents). These findings generally support those of Anderson (1943, 1946) in terms of the impact of socioeconomic status on social participation. Although the findings of Hollingshead (1949) provide valuable descriptive information on the relationship between social class and adolescent leisure activity, the research was primarily focused on the individual, and the implications for family recreation behavior can only be inferred.

The Decade in Review

Theory and Methodology. While studies during this period continued to be largely descriptive in nature, there was more interest in testing specific hypotheses and, at least in one case (MacDonald, McGuire, and Havighurst, 1949), interpreting the results within a theoretical framework. Some of the studies during this decade also used more complex statistical methods to analyze the obtained data. Specifically, Pearson product moment correlation coefficients were used to determine significant relationships between variables (Anderson, 1943, 1946; Anderson and Palmbeck, 1943; Patrick, 1945), and the chi-square test of significance was used to compare frequencies between categorical data (Hollingshead, 1949; MacDonald, McGuire, and Havighurst, 1949). No new data collection techniques were used in the study of family recreation during this period, but validated and reliability-tested questionnaire instruments, such as the Chapin formal participation scale used by Anderson (1943), began to be employed.

A major weakness of most of the studies reported for this decade was the lack of a clear description of the target population. In addition, studies either failed to describe adequately the sampling method used or simply used convenience samples, and samples tended to be geographically isolated sample sizes ranged from 120 to 2,014. Because of the inadequate sampling techniques used, the statistical validity and the generalizability of results for studies during this period are limited. (See table 9–2)

Key Studies and General Findings. Anderson's studies (Anderson, 1943, 1946; Anderson and Palmbeck, 1943) of social participation among rural New York farm families provided the greatest contribution to our knowledge of family recreation for this period. Anderson found that families tend to participate socially as a unit rather than individually, upper-class families tend to have more social participation than lower-class families, and family participation is determined in part by how a family perceives its status within the community. The finding that families participate socially as a unit was not consistent with findings from an earlier descriptive study (Lynd and Lynd, 1929), at least in terms of family recreation. The difference may be due to the fact that the earlier study was based on a nonrural population while Anderson's work was based on rural farm families. Anderson's studies did support, however, the findings of another descriptive study by Lundberg, Komarovsky, and McInerny (1934), which was also based on a nonrural population.

Along with the studies by Anderson (1943, 1946), the research of Hollingshead (1949) and MacDonald, McGuire, and Havighurst (1949) added to the growing base of knowledge concerning the impact of socioeconomic status on leisure pursuits. The MacDonald, McGuire, and Havighurst study was also important in that, for the first time, it attempted to interpret family recreation findings within a theoretical framework.

The Decade 1950–1959

Studies conducted during this period can be categorized into individual-, couple-, and family-focused research. Three studies were concerned primarily with the recreation activities of a single family member (mother, wife, or child), another study looked at the leisure interests of couples, and twelve studies analyzed various aspects of recreation within the family as a whole.

Research Findings

Individual

Children. Cramer (1950) described the leisure activities of sixty-eight economically privileged students 6–14 years of age who were enrolled in a private day

Table 9–2
Overview of Research on Recreation in the Family, 1940–1949

Year	*Author*	*Topic*	*Theory*	*Method*[a]	*Sample*	*Strengths*[b]
1943	Anderson	Social participation	None	Questionnaire-P	2,014	M,I
1945	Patrick	Childhood leisure	None	Questionnaire-P	120	
1946	Anderson	Social participation	None	Questionnaire-P	344	M,I
1949	Hollingshead	Class and leisure	None	Direct observation	735	M,I
1949	McDonald, McGuire, and Havighurst	Status and leisure	Social learning	Questionnaire-P	223	T

[a] P = primary data.
[b] M = measurement of variables; T = theory; I = important study.

school located in Erie, Pennsylvania. Data concerning leisure activity were collected by questionnaire. The top five activities engaged in by the students were dancing lessons, choir, dramatics, art lessons, and ceramics, in that order. In addition, one-third of the students spent an average of 6 hours daily with their parents, while less than 6 percent spent 1 hour or less. These findings added to the growing body of evidence that children from high-socioeconomic-status families were more likely to be engaged in organized, supervised leisure activities and to spend more time with their parents.

Mother/Wife. Leevy (1950) utilized his self-designed Household Information Schedule to obtain leisure activity information from 820 urban and 430 rural housewives during personal interviews conducted by graduate students. The purpose of the study was to determine the quantity and type of leisure time available to the American housewife and to determine the impact of family size and modern conveniences on the housewife's leisure time activities. Sixty percent of urban wives and over 80 percent of rural wives indicated an average of 1 to 2 hours of leisure per day; reading, radio listening, and club attendance were the three most often mentioned forms of leisure for both urban and rural housewives. It was speculatively concluded that since urban housewives, who had smaller families and more conveniences, had somewhat more leisure time than rural housewives, modern conveniences were positively associated and family size negatively associated with leisure time for housewives; however, no correlation coefficients were calculated.

Nye (1958) tested the hypothesis that employed mothers would engage least in recreational activities requiring the most time (such as visiting) and most in activities requiring the least time (such as movie attendance). Data were obtained by mailed questionnaires from 1,993 urban mothers in three Washington towns. Based on chi-square tests for statistical independence, it was found that employed mothers participated significantly less than unemployed mothers in recreational activities involving time commitment (specifically, social relations outside the home) but participated equally with nonworking mothers in commercial recreation. It was also noted that family recreation activities, such as card and game playing at home or family picnics and vacations, did not diminish significantly when the mother became employed.

Couples. Up through the early 1950s, several studies had suggested that mutual interests were an important element of marriage adjustment (Clifford, 1937; Burgess and Cottrell, 1939; Locke, 1951; Burgess and Wallin, 1953). Benson (1952) examined the relationship between mutuality of interests and marriage adjustment using data from 1,000 engaged couples collected by Burgess and Wallin (1953). Data were obtained at the time of engagement and then several years later from the same couples who had actually married and were willing to participate (two-thirds of the original 1,000). Benson failed to find any relationship between the number of common leisure time interests and engagement or marital adjustment. There was, however, a significant relationship between perceptions that all or most activities and interests were engaged in together and adjustment. Mutuality of interest in home, children, romantic love, sexual relations, and religion was more prevalent among well-adjusted, happy couples, and the numerical total of common leisure time interests was not significantly related to either present or future adjustment. Benson concluded that it was unclear whether familistic or individualistic interests were actual causes or simply concomitants of family harmony or discord.

Family. While earlier studies had looked at the voluntary associations of individual urban dwellers (Komarovsky, 1946), Dotson (1951) attempted to describe the voluntary associations of urban, working-class families. Fifty working-class families were chosen at random from the New Haven City Directory. Data were obtained during personal interviews with both parents of study families. Eighty percent of the families had no participation in formal organized associations. Of those families that did, membership in organizations was concentrated in athletic and church-affiliated groups. Most families had an active, informal social life within the kin group. The social and leisure time activities of forty-three of the fifty families were dominated by visiting and other associations with relatives. While this study confirmed earlier findings that organized social participation was dominated by the upper classes, the study was also important in that it concentrated on the family as a unit (rather than individual family members) and described for the first time the social participation patterns of lower-class families. In terms of theory, the study was important in that it challenged the belief that urbanization results in the displacement of primary kin groups by secondary nonkin groups.

Hawkins and Walters (1952) administered a self-designed questionnaire, the Family Recreation and Leisure Time Activities Questionnaire, to eighty-five families from Stillwater, Oklahoma, in an effort to test the reliability of their instrument, determine the activities that families enjoyed most, and ascertain the correlation between selected factors concerning family relationships and the total number of activities families had engaged in during the previous year. It was determined that on the basis of several reliability measures, the instrument was reliable; that families enjoyed movies, picnicking, church, fishing, and visiting the most; and that the total number of activities engaged in during the previous year was not significantly related to the types of relationships maintained in the family. This study was one of the first to look at recreation from the standpoint of the family as a unit and to mention the reliability of the instrumentation used.

Wylie (1953) used questionnaires to obtain data from a representative national sample of 504 families (2,184 members) from thirty-eight states. Information concerning the reliability and validity of the instrument was provided. Wylie found that the most participated in activities were nature and outing activities, spectator activities, and social activities; the most common family activities were informal and not highly organized; 51 percent of recreation took place away from home; 60 percent of all families felt that they had achieved stronger unity as the result of participation in family recreation programs; 58 percent of families felt that they had an unsatisfactory family recreation program; and there was a mean increase in the number of family recreational activities as income approached $7,000 per year but a tapering off of activities as income exceeded $7,000. This study was important because of the large, representative sample used, the documented instrumentation, and the important descriptive findings.

Anderson (1953a, 1953b) looked at family social participation as a function of life cycle and status. Four hundred and twenty-four farm families in Ontario County, New York, were categorized into one of six life cycle stages and one of two status levels (owner or tenant) and then interviewed concerning their levels of informal and formal social participation. Owners were found to have higher levels of formal social participation during all stages of the life cycle, while tenants had higher levels of informal social participation during all life cycle stages. It was also found that both owner and tenant families with some or all children over the age of 10 had the highest levels of informal social participation, while families with all children under the age of 10 had the highest average formal participation and membership scores. The most common informal activities were visiting, automobile riding, movie attendance, and picnicking; the most common formal participation activities were church attendance and membership in the Farm and Home Bureau. This was the first study to look at family social participation in terms of family life cycle.

White (1955) interviewed 673 families randomly selected from a single county in Ohio to determine the relationship between social class and family leisure activities. In support of earlier findings, White found that upper-middle-class families selected the library, home diversions, and lecture-study groups more often than other classes, and the two lowest classes took advantage of public parks, playgrounds, and commercial entertainment.

Connor, Johannis, and Walters (1955) used questionnaires to collect data from a random sample of fifty tenth-grade students and their parents concerning the types of family activities engaged in, the perceptions of individual family members concerning the amount of activity engaged in with other members, and the amount of family recreation engaged in by "traditional" and "developmental" oriented parents. Developmental parents organize family life to promote personality growth and development among all family members, while traditional parents organize family life so that the father earns the living, the mother cares for the home, and the children are responsible for obedience to their parents. It was determined that the most enjoyed types of family activities were away from the home, there was considerable variation in perceptions of parent-child recreation levels between parents and adolescents, and there was no difference in family activity level between traditional and developmental oriented parents. The major contribution of this study was that it demonstrated the large differences (60–70 percent agreement) in perceived level of recreation activity between parents and their adolescent children.

Johannis (1958) asked 1,027 high school sophomores from unbroken homes in Tampa, Florida, to indicate family member participation in ten social activities. It was found that eight of the ten social activities were shared by family members in nearly 80 percent of the families, and the remaining two activities were shared in more than 50 percent of the families (belonging to a club was shared 57 percent of families and going on outings in 94 percent). There was, however, considerable variation by sex and age in the proportion of fathers, mothers, and teenage offsprings who participated in the ten activities.

In order to describe the recreational activities of large families (eight or more children), Amatora (1959) obtained questionnaire data from 672 large families in forty-eight states. In addition to demographic information, data were obtained on individual family members in the areas of recreational activity (including organizations, travel, and camps) and recreational interests (including pets and hobbies). A statistically significant correlation between activities and interests was noted. In addition, there were significant correlations between interests and the following variables: number of magazine subscriptions, family health, and religious practices. Activities were positively correlated with home ownership, religious practices, and family health. The study may have been more useful had interests and activities been obtained in relation to family interactions rather than only for individual family members.

The Decade in Review

Theory and Methodology. Only one study during the decade, Dotson (1951), attempted to interpret family activity findings in terms of theory. While the theoretical framework for urbanization suggest that "primary" family-oriented ties will be replaced by "secondary" workplace ties, Dotson found that for urban working-class families, the kin group continued to be the major source of social support.

Although many studies during this period continued to use poorly defined, nonrepresentative samples, there were some notable improvements. Six studies had relatively large, well-defined, representative samples. Sample sizes ranged from 50 to 1,993.

Another notable improvement for the decade was the use of validated, reliability-tested instruments to collect data in some key studies. A weakness was the use of a large number of dissimilar instruments that categorized leisure activities in such different ways and used such different wording that a comparison of results would be difficult at best and completely invalid at worst. A study near the end of the decade by Johannis and Cunningham (1959), for example, demonstrated the variability of results that can arise from the differential use of such terms as *leisure, recreation,* and *social activity* in the construction of instruments.

Personal interviews and questionnaires continued to be the dominant data collection methods during this period. Studies also continued to be primarily descriptive in nature, with approximately half of the studies using such analytical methods as chi-square tests, t-tests, and Pearson correlations. (See table 9–3.)

Key Studies and General Findings. The most important development during this period was the shift from an individual to a family focus. For the first time, recreation was analyzed in terms of the family unit. Perhaps the most impressive research of the decade, and a leader in the trend toward a family focus in recreation research, was that of Wylie (1953). The research was based on a relatively large, well-defined, national sample; a valid, reliable instrument was used; and the study used t-tests to analyze the data in addition to providing valuable descriptive information. Other key studies included Dotson (1951), who interpreted his findings within a theoretical framework and provided valuable descriptive information about the leisure activities of urban, working-class families; Hawkins and Walters (1952), whose research represented a pioneering effort toward the development of a standardized family recreation instrument and who provided valuable family recreation descriptions; and Anderson (1953a, 1953b), who continued to use analytic methods and reliable instrumentation to provide valuable information about the social participation of rural farm families.

Several new variables were looked at during the period including the impact of family size (negative), modern conveniences (positive), and the employment status of the mother (neutral) on the quantity, type, and quality of family leisure time. In addition, the correlation of the quantity and quality of family recreation with marital adjustment and family interactions was analyzed, with the determination that the relationship was weak. Finally, family member role conceptions toward leisure activity were analyzed, and the relationship between family life cycle and family social participation was studied. More descriptive data were added during the period, and the relationship between status and leisure activity continued to be a common theme.

The Decade 1960–1969

There were ten pertinent articles identified for this decade. Three studies related to camping and outdoor recreation reflected a continuing expansion in research interests in relation to family recreation. Two studies analyzed the leisure activities of couples in relation to occupational status and marital adjustment, and three other studies added to the growing knowledge base concerned with role conceptions and recreation. Two final studies looked at various

Table 9-3
Overview of Research on Recreation in the Family, 1950–1959

Year	*Author*	*Topic*	*Theory*	*Method*[a]	*Sample*	*Strengths*[b]
1950	Cramer	Status and leisure	None	Questionnaire-P	68	
1950	Leevy	Housewife leisure	None	Interview-P	1,250	S
1951	Dotson	Status and leisure	Mini	Interview-P	50	T,I
1952	Benson	Interests of couples	None	Questionnaire-P	1,000	S,I
1952	Hawkins and Walters	Family recreation	None	Questionnaire-P	85	M,I
1953	Anderson	Social participation	None	Interview-P	424	M,I
1953	Wylie	Family recreation	None	Questionnaire-P	504	S,M,I
1955	Connor, Johannis, and Walters	Role conceptions	None	Questionnaire-P	50	
1955	White	Class and leisure	None	Interview-P	673	
1958	Johannis	Family participation	None	Questionnaire-P	1,027	S
1958	Nye	Mother's employment	None	Questionnaire-P	1,993	S,I
1959	Amatora	Large family activity	None	Questionnaire-P	672	S

[a] P = primary data.
[b] S = sample; M = measurement of variables; T = theory; I = important study.

aspects of family characteristics and family cohesion in relation to recreation patterns.

Research Findings

Outdoor Family Recreation. In an effort to identify the social characteristics and recreational values of public campground users, Etzkorn (1964) used questionnaires to obtain data from sixty-four campsite users at a campground 100 miles north of Los Angeles. Although the sampling method was nonrandom and not representative of any particular population, the campground user demographics were well matched with those reported in other studies cited in an exhaustive review of outdoor recreation research (Sessoms, 1963). Etzkorn found that camping is a group activity, and the involved group is almost always the family; campground users represented higher-than-average educational and occupational levels; campers represented the higher fertility sector of society, with an average of 2.98 children; and campers were residentially stable, residing primarily in semirural and suburban areas. Campers indicated that the aspects of camping they liked most were rest and relaxation, socializing with family and others, and enjoying nature and that they intended to swim, read, listen to the radio, and play with their children during their stay in the camp. The study's main contribution is the description of family camping group characteristics and recreational values.

Burch (1965) analyzed camper activity in terms of play-action systems theory. Specifically, camper activities were analyzed in terms of conjugal solidarity and the division of play and the continuities and discontinuities in player identities. Twelve campgrounds in three national forest in Oregon were systematically observed, and interviews were conducted with 288 family camping groups in seven other campgrounds. Burch identified six categories of play and then analyzed the type of play by participant gender. He found that symbolic play (hunting and fishing) and organized play (football, horseshoes) were dominated by males, while free play (relaxing, drawing, reading) was dominated by females. Combined male and female participation was more likely in expressive play (water skiing and swimming) and sociability (conversation, singing, and walking). Burch argued that individual identities were shaped, expressed, and reestablished through camping play. The major contribution of the study was the innovative analysis of family camping in terms of play-action systems theory.

In 1969 Burch obtained questionnaire data from a systematic sample of 740 families who had camped overnight at the Three Sisters Wilderness Area in Oregon. Based on responses, families were categorized into one of three camping styles: auto access (N = 254), combination of wilderness and automobile access (N = 424), or wilderness only (N = 62). Burch hypothesized that the type of camping style represented a specific social meaning for the family that would transcend the particular activity of camping. Burch found evidence for the compensatory hypothesis and personal community hypothesis of social activity but not for the familiarity hypothesis. As such, Burch concluded that the influence of social circles and the desire for nonroutine (compensatory) activities have an important impact on the choice of camping style. The importance of the study was to suggest motivational factors for family camping activities and specific hypotheses that might be tested for other types of family recreation.

Couples. Gerson (1960) used a random sample of fifty couples selected from the population of married students at Montana State University to identify attitudes toward leisure time activity as reported by questionnaire. It was concluded that while there was not a significant relationship between marriage happiness and the amount of leisure time spent with the spouse, several attitudes concerning the use of leisure time were significantly related to marital happiness (more so for males than females). Specifically, kinds of leisure activity engaged in (positive), adjustments to the spouse's leisure behavior (positive), financial restrictions on leisure (negative), and disagreements about leisure activities (negative) were most closely correlated with marital happiness. The importance of this study was that it began to look at attitudes about leisure rather than simply emphasizing types and amounts of leisure activity.

Adams and Butler (1967) used random block sampling to obtain interview data from 788 white, married individuals living in Greensboro, North Carolina, with regard to occupational status and husband-wife social participation. They found (as did earlier studies) that upper-middle-class and managerial couples tended to be more involved in the community, including commercial recreation, churchgoing, and family entertaining and recreation, while the dominant social activity of working-class couples was kin-related visiting.

Recreational Role Perceptions. Johannis and Rollins (1960) analyzed the perceptions held by teenagers about decision making as it relates to family social participation. Questionnaire data were obtained from 1,027 adolescents from white, nonbroken homes in Tampa, Florida. In general, it was determined that decision making was shared equally between parents for such activities as going on outings, vacations, and using the living room radio. Both male and female teenagers participated in these decisions equally but at a lower level than parents, indicating that age is an important factor in decision making. The data also supported the idea that decision making in other areas is a function of gender. Fathers and sons were most concerned with who uses the family car, while mothers and daughters decided on the entertainment of guests.

In order to assess the relationships of leisure activity to demographics and leisure role perceptions to homemaking tasks, Searls (1966) obtained questionnaire data from 181 female college graduates who were married, had at least one child, and were unemployed. It was determined that age and family of orientation had significant positive relationships to community welfare activity, number of years married was positively related to total leisure, and family size was positively related to community welfare activity. It was further noted that perceived mastery of homemaking tasks and enjoyment of homemaking had significant positive correlations with total leisure, self-enrichment, and recreational activity.

Angrist (1967) hypothesized that the amount and type of leisure activity available to women was a function of life cycle stage with its related constellation of roles (based on marital, familial, and employment status). Questionnaire data were obtained from 245 female college alumnae who were categorized into one of five role constellations on the basis of marital, familial, and employment status. It was found that the amount of leisure time available did not differ significantly between role constellations, nor did the type of leisure engaged in differ between role constellations with respect to self-enrichment and recreation activities. Community welfare scores, however, tended to increase as the role constellation moved from single employed women to unemployed married women whose children were all in school.

Family Recreation. Scheuch (1960) presented information obtained as part of a cumulative community survey at the University of Cologne involving a representative sample of 1,500 individuals. In addition, data collected by the German opinion research institute (EMNID) during interviews with 1,757 respondents were used for comparison and supplementation. The research used both traditional descriptive categories and abstract categories related to theoretical conceptions to describe leisure activities. Major findings from the study suggested that the prevailing pattern for spending leisure time involved staying inside the home, leisure activities inside the home that involved interaction usually involved several family members, not just the spouse, and although outdoor activities were much rarer, they too were most often engaged in by several family members.

Evidence obtained also suggested that family interaction was actually preferred and not forced on members, the time period specifically set aside for the family was the weekend (working-day leisure primarily served the function of diversion and restoration), and for almost all family types, the family continued to be the center of recreational activity. The study concluded by noting that the social status and authority structure of the family were also factors that influenced the family recreation program. In terms of theory, the study suggested that transference of the leisure function from families to other societal institutions was not necessarily a result of industrialization, as had been suggested. In addition, the study used open-ended questions, precoded questions, and extensive (but partially guided) probing to classify activities rather than relying solely on traditional multiple-choice type questionnaires.

In her analysis of the characteristics of families with socially active teenagers, Stone (1960, 1963) obtained questionnaire data from 653 high school students in Pacific County, Washington. She found that most teenagers enjoyed recreational activities with their families and that over half (58 percent) indicated that they would like more. Fifty-one percent indicated that they participated in family recreational activities at the rate of once or more per week. Stone also noted that students who indicated the highest level of family participation also indicated the highest levels of school and out-of-school activities. Students with the highest levels of family activity reported the most desirable levels of responsibility at home and indicated that they enjoyed more parental understanding. She concluded by noting that teenagers generally desired greater levels of family recreation and that families with high levels of family recreation tended to have other desirable characteristics.

The Decade in Review

Theory and Methodology. Theory was not a significant part of most research reported during this 1960s. Only two studies actually tested theory-based hypothesis, and the others made only passing, if any, mention of the theoretical implications of their findings. A major continuing theoretical shift was the realization by some researchers that leisure functions, even for industrialized, urban societies, continued to be family based. In earlier decades, leisure in industrial societies had been looked at as being a function provided by societal institutions outside the family with a focus on individual, rather than family, participation.

Several large, representative samples were used during this period, ranging in size from 50 to 1,500. Most studies obtained random samples and made an attempt to identify specific target populations and provide descriptions of the obtained sample and the sampling method.

Statistical analyses continued to be dominated by descriptive studies. The remainder of the studies cited for this period continued to employ correlation statistics and/or t-tests of significance. (See table 9–4.)

Most instruments used in this and earlier periods simply attempted to classify leisure-related responses into descriptive categories based on distinctions made in everyday usage (such as reading, going for a walk, or listening to the radio). During the 1960s, however, some studies began to use open-ended questions, attitudinal scales, and other devices in an attempt to understand better the social meaning that participants attached to the various activities they engaged in and to determine if more than one activity might be occurring at the same time (such as listening to the radio while conversing with another family member). In addition, several instruments focused more on describing the leisure time activity of the family unit rather than on the activity of individual family members.

Key Studies and General Findings. Perhaps the most important study of the decade was that conducted at the University of Cologne and reported by

Table 9–4
Overview of Research on Recreation in the Family, 1960–1969

Year	*Author*	*Topic*	*Theory*	*Method*[a]	*Sample*	*Strengths*[b]
1960	Gerson	Leisure of couples	None	Questionnaire-P	50	
1960	Johannis and Rollins	Decision making	None	Questionnaire-P	1,027	S
1960	Scheuch	Family cohesion	Mini	Questionnaire-P	1,500	S,M,T,I
1963	Stone	Teenagers and leisure	None	Questionnaire-P	653	
1964	Etzkorn	Leisure and camping	None	Questionnaire-P	64	
1965	Burch	Outdoor recreation	Mini	Direct observation	288	T
1966	Searls	Leisure of homemakers	None	Questionnaire-P	181	
1967	Adms and Butler	Status and leisure	None	Interview-P	788	S
1967	Angrist	Women's roles	None	Questionnaire-P	245	
1969	Burch	Leisure and camping	Mini	Questionnaire-P	740	S,T

[a] P = primary data.
[b] S = sample; M = measurement of variables; T = theory; I = important study.

Scheuch (1960). The sample was large and representative, the measurement of variables was accomplished through the use of sophisticated instruments that sought the meaning behind responses, and the findings challenged the theory that industrialization and urbanization resulted in the loss of the leisure function from the family.

During the 1960s, the scope of family recreation research was broadened to include the meaning of camping and outdoor recreation, and several related studies reported interesting findings in these areas. In addition, various roles and role perceptions, as they related to family recreation, were analyzed, including the decision-making role, the homemaker role, and various life-cycle-related roles. In general, it was found that the family still provided the leisure function for most individuals in the industrialized, urban samples studied. Moreover, it was found that happiness and adjustment in marriage and family living were more related to individual perceptions regarding the adequacy of the family recreation program than to the actual amount or types of recreation engaged in by the family or couple. Nevertheless, it was not determined whether adjustment and happiness were the result of positively perceived recreation programs or whether happiness and adjustment might be the cause of positive perceptions.

The Decade 1970–1979

The breadth of topics being researched in relation to recreation in the family continued to grow during this decade. For the purpose of analysis, articles have been categorized into the areas of adjustment, roles and decision making, family life cycle, outdoor recreation and family cohesiveness, and leisure socialization.

Research Findings

Marital Satisfaction. A significant amount of research was conducted during the 1970s in the area of marital adjustment in relation to leisure time use. Presvelou (1971) investigated the relationship between different types of leisure activity and intraspousal dynamics, including verbal communication, gestural communication, areas of autonomy, and empathy between spouses. Seventy-one recently formed Belgian couples, who were enrolled in the University of Louvain, were interviewed. It was found that visiting friends together was positively associated with the intensity of empathy between spouses, participation in leisure activities as a whole was positively associated with gestural communication, and participation in joint cultural activities was positively associated with gestural communication and conjugal tenderness. Presvelou concluded that "in a society which gradually withdraws from a work-ethics culture, leisure could become a force for intra-familial cohesion." The major contribution of the study was in the measurement of variables that involved an attempt to understand the meaning behind leisure activity choices rather than merely the categorization of activities.

Based on data collected from 205 British couples, Rapoport, Rapoport, and Thiessen (1974) found that the enjoyment of activities by husbands and wives resembled one another, the enjoyment of activities by husbands and wives influenced each spouse's enjoyment in a positive way, symmetrical couples had a higher level of everyday enjoyment, and more activities were enjoyed by both spouses if the husband was family oriented.

Orthner (1975) not only looked at the influence of leisure activity on marital satisfaction but also took into consideration the influence of the marital "career period." He hypothesized that individual activities would be negatively associated, joint activities positively associated, and parallel activities not associated with satisfaction at each period of the marital career. Based on questionnaire data from 442 randomly selected, upper-middle-class respondents, he found that joint activities were positively associated with marital satisfaction for both husbands and wives in periods I (married 0–5 years) and IV (married 18–23 years). Individual activities were negatively associated with marital satisfaction in period I for husbands and in period IV for wives, and parallel activities were negatively associated with satisfaction for both husbands and wives in period IV. There was no correlation between the activity type and marital satisfaction for husbands or wives during periods II (married 6–11 years), III (married 12–17 years), or V (married 24 or more years). In general, it was concluded that periods I and IV were the most critical for couples in terms of marital satisfaction and joint leisure participation. This was an important study because it utilized a clear conceptual framework based on previous research with testable hypotheses, and it controlled for socioeconomic status and length of marriage.

In a second report using the same data, Orthner (1976) used symbolic interaction theory to link the concept of leisure to that of marital interaction. It was hypothesized that there would be a positive relationship between joint leisure activity and interaction (communication and task sharing), a negative relationship between individual activity and interaction, and a neutral relationship between parallel activity and interaction. The hypotheses generally held true for type of leisure activity and communication but not for type of leisure and task sharing. Again, periods I and IV seemed to be the most critical. Other variables, such as the degree of mutual interest in leisure activities, cultural factors, and the amount of exclusive attention shown to one another during leisure activities, must be accounted for in the development of a theoretical model that can adequately explain the relationship between leisure and marital interaction.

In a third report using the same data, Orthner and Mancini (1978) found that perceived sociability in the parental family was not associated with current marital leisure patterns of the respondents. In a fourth, and final, report using the data, Mancini and Orthner (1978) found that a preference for engaging in sexual or affectional activities declined with number of years married. At the same time, husbands' preferences for other joint activities increased proportionally, and wives' preferences for independent activities increased.

Employment Status and Leisure Adjustment. In a study of ninety-two married male employees, Willmott (1971) found that the spheres of family, work, and leisure were not exclusive, as previously hypothesized. Compared to junior staff and workers, senior staff employees were more likely to have high levels of involvement in all three spheres of activity.

Jorgenson (1977) predicted that the social position of fathers and the employment status of mothers would affect the leisure time for husbands and wives, fathers and children, the conjoint family, and the total family. Based on questionnaire data from a nonrepresentative sample of forty-five fathers representing three social positions, it was found that the social position of the father had the strongest positive associations with father-child leisure time and total family leisure time but no association with husband-wife leisure time. A significant inverse relationship was found for wife-mother employment and husband-wife leisure time, but wife-mother employment was positively related to conjoint family leisure time.

Clark, Nye, and Gecas (1978) studied the relationship between husbands' work involvement and performance of other marital roles, including the recreational role. Questionnaire data from a random sample of 390 Seattle couples were obtained to test the hypotheses that the greater the husband's worktime, the less time he will spend in each marital role and the less competent he will be in each role. They found that as worktime increased, husbands spent less time organizing recreational activities. However, there was no significant association between husbands' worktime and perceived competence in the recreational role. The study was important because multivariate analysis was used, and it challenged several myths concerning the relationship between husbands' worktime and the performance of marital roles.

These three studies support earlier research findings (Nye, 1958) to the effect that the amount of recreation available to the family and the quality of the family's recreational program are not necessarily influenced negatively by the amount of time parents devote to their formal employment.

Family Recreation and Child Adjustment. Hume, O'Connor, and Lowrey (1977) studied the typical week's total activity pattern for thirty male children and their parents. The thirty boys were either unusually well adjusted or poorly adjusted. It was hypothesized that the home environment would be different for high- than for low-adjusted students. Among the boys, low-adjusted subjects tended to watch significantly more television (especially alone), spend less recreational time (especially within the home and with the father), and have fewer social contacts overall (especially with the father and with other siblings).

The fathers of low-adjusted boys watched more television, engaged in less recreation (especially with other family members), and had fewer social contacts within the home, outside the home, and with other family members. The pattern was similar for the mothers of low-adjusted boys. The authors concluded that low adjustment among children may be a reflection of the low social adjustment of their parents, especially in the areas of discretionary time use. In contrast, Wilson (1971) found that for high socioeconomic families, the use of leisure time had no differential impact on the reading achievement of children.

The Recreational Role. Kelly (1975) obtained interview data from a random sample of seventy-eight households in Eugene, Oregon. It was hypothesized that there were four broad categories of leisure that could be differentiated on the basis of perceived obligation and relation to work activities. It was found that almost 90 percent of leisure activity could be placed into two categories: unconditional leisure (low obligation, low work relation), engaged in for its intrinsic value, with 42.1 percent, or complementary leisure (high obligation, low work relation), engaged in to satisfy role obligations, with 46.2 percent. Further, the nature of the obligation in complementary leisure was based primarily on family norms and expectations rather than on work-related expectations, with the most important factor being the presence of children. The findings provided modest support for both the dualistic and holistic approaches to leisure. As such, leisure was seen as being separate from work (dualistic) yet integrated into the role expectations of the family and community (holistic).

Based on questionnaire data obtained from 409 respondents, Carlson (1976) reported that providing family recreation was considered either a responsibility shared equally between spouses or an optional responsibility to be carried out by either spouse as long as it got done. Most husbands and wives rated themselves and their spouse as being fairly competent in performing the recreational role and indicated fairly high levels of satisfaction with their participation in family recreation. Approximately 75 percent of husbands and wives indicated that they seldom or never argued about recreation. A final finding was that the desired amount of participation in family recreation for wives was affected only by the wife's work status and was positively associated. The data supported the hypothesis that a distinct recreational role was emerging in the family but that the norms, expectations, and sanctions associated with the role remained flexible.

Expanding on his earlier work, Kelly (1978a) conducted interviews with 374 respondents, randomly selected from three different communities, to obtain data concerning with whom leisure time is spent, the extent to which family role constraints determine leisure decisions, and the extent to which the positive satisfactions of family recreation influence leisure decisions. It was found that 70 percent of the recreational activities under investigation involved other family members and that marriage and parenthood tended to increase an individual's orientation toward family recreation. Also, although role constraints were an important determinant of family recreational activities, the positive satisfactions of family recreation were seen as being equally important. This study demonstrated the importance of investigating family interaction variables in relation to leisure decision making.

In a further analysis of questionnaire data obtained during the same study, Kelly (1987b) found that situational variables were more predictive of leisure activity choices than social position or immediate community variables. Kelly also found further support for previous findings that leisure is dualistic in that it is usually separate from work relations but holistic in that it is closely related to other roles and meanings in the family and community. As such, the term *pluralistic* was suggested as being more appropriate. Finally, it was found that the type of leisure activity engaged in was the most significant element in the meaning derived from participation.

Family Life Cycle. Three studies considered various aspects of the family life cycle in relation to leisure activity. Bollman, Moxley, and Elliott (1975) hypothesized that six factors—resource level, stage of family life cycle, presence of a preschool child, family size, geographic mobility, and mother's employment status—affect the nonwork activities of families with children. They interviewed 155 rural, nonfarm families about twenty-one measures of nonwork activity. The families participating in voluntary organizations had been in the community more than a year, had no preschool-age children, and were in the upper resource group. Home- and family-centered activities were associated with the presence of preschool children and an unemployed mother.

Roberts and associates (1976) interviewed 474 economically active males in suburban Liverpool in an attempt to analyze the influence of the family life cycle on leisure activity. They found that 65 to 75 percent of all activities were done with other members of the household, the events of marriage and parenthood shifted leisure orientation toward the family, family togetherness was a major factor in making decisions about leisure, wife's employment did not significantly alter the amount or type of family leisure available. A study by Schoolmaster (1979) further demonstrated the importance of marriage, parenthood, and the presence of children in the home on leisure decision making.

Outdoor Recreation. West and Merriam (1970) interviewed 306 randomly selected families camping at St. Croix State Park, Minnesota, to test the hypothesis that family camping increases family cohesiveness. In order to measure differences in the amount of intimate communications and moods (as reflections of cohesiveness), families were interviewed during the summer and then responded to questionnaires sent in the fall. As such, the study used an expost facto experimental design in which the dependent variable (cohesiveness) was measured before and after the occurrence of the independent variable (outdoor recreation). Although the results were not statistically significant, the trends were in the expected directions and provided moderate support for the hypothesis. The primary value of the study was in its employment of an experimental design and its measurement of variables, including initial interviews with the father, mother, and oldest child over the age of 12 years. Previous studies usually had failed to obtain the input of children.

Based on questionnaire data from a random sample of 158 apartment and single-family residences, Hendricks (1971) found that the type of residence was a useful predictor of outdoor recreation activity. Urban apartment residents made comparatively less use of traditional outdoor leisure than single-family-home dwellers.

Ragheb (1975) added support to the hypothesis of West and Merriam (1970). Based on questionnaire data obtained from 131 families, Ragheb used univariate correlation, analysis of variance, and multiple regression analysis to test the relationship of the amount of leisure time shared by a family, the satisfaction associated with leisure time use, and family cohesiveness. It was found that both the amount of time spent together and the perception of satisfaction with leisure time were significantly associated with cohesiveness. There were no major differences between families with younger children, compared to those with older children, or between Protestant and Catholic families. Of four categories of leisure time use, only satisfaction with outdoor and social recreation was significantly associated with cohesiveness. Neither the satisfaction with nor the quantity of mass media or sports leisure activities was associated with cohesiveness.

Finally, on the basis of questionnaire data obtained from 141 fathers who had registered at one of three East Coast campgrounds, Dynes (1977) found that respondents tended to favor excursions over home-centered activities, there was an unexpected tendency for the family to participate together in excursion activities relatively more often than alone, and most of the respondents were categorized as family centered in that they exhibited a pronounced tendency to interact with family members in nonwork activities. These findings added support to the role of outdoor recreation in the promotion of family cohesion.

Leisure Socialization. In an exploratory study, Yoesting and Burkhead (1973) tested five hypotheses in relation to the impact that the level of childhood activity has on the level of adult recreation activity. Interview data were collected from a stratified area sample of 137 rural respondents. It was found that the level of participation in activities as a child has a direct impact on the level of adult participation, individuals active in outdoor recreation as children will continue to be active as adults, and childhood residence has little impact on adult activity.

Based on interview data from seventy-eight adults in Eugene, Oregon, Kelly (1974) studied whether adult leisure was learned and carried over from childhood. He found that current activities were evenly divided between those begun in childhood and those begun in adulthood, family associations were primary in learning 63 percent of current activities, and leisure socialization is a lifelong process.

Using data from a midwest mill town and an eastern suburban new town, Kelly (1977) replicated the results of the Oregon study. He found the same equal division between adult and child initiation of leisure activities and the same 65 percent level of family association in leisure learning. In contrast, the school was not found to be an important context of beginning adult-preferred leisure. Overall, the additional data supported the concept that leisure socialization is an ongoing, lifelong process.

The Decade in Review

Theory and Methodology. Most samples used during this period were selected randomly, but many were not representative of a specific target population. Sample sizes ranged from 45 to 474. Use of questionnaires continued to be the dominant instrument used to measure variables (fourteen studies), but increased use was also made of interviews (nine studies), and one study employed direct observation. The expanded use of interviews may have been representative of increased efforts to measure the meanings attached to leisure and the elements of family interaction more accurately rather than merely categorizing leisure activities.

Statistical analyses during this decade expanded to include analysis of variance and multiple regression. In addition, experimental designs were used for the first time in an attempt to demonstrate causality rather than simple correlation.

There was more use of theory in the formation of hypotheses and in the interpretation of results. Nine of the ten studies making use of theory used theoretical frameworks that were specifically confined to the phenomenon under study; the other study attempted to test hypotheses and interpret results in terms of specific concepts from the more general theory of symbolic interaction. During this period, new theoretical frameworks were developed for explaining leisure choices, explaining family interaction as a function of recreational activity, and categorizing types of leisure on the basis of meaning. (See table 9-5.)

Key Studies and General Findings. The two most important groups of studies during this decade were those of Orthner (1975, 1976, 1978) and of Kelly (1974, 1975, 1977, 1978a, 1978b). Both groups built on previous research and used sound theoretical frameworks to generate hypotheses and interpret results. Instrumentation was valid and reliable, confounding variables were controlled, and the samples were fairly large and representative of specific populations. Orthner's work led to valuable insights concerning the positive relationship of leisure activity to marital interaction and marital satisfaction, and

Table 9–5
Overview of Research on Recreation in the Family, 1970–1979

Year	*Author*	*Topic*	*Theory*	*Method*[a]	*Sample*	*Strengths*[b]
1970	West and Merriam	Family cohesiveness	None	Interview-P	306	M,St,I
1971	Hendricks	Residence and leisure	None	Questionnaire-P	158	
1971	Presvelou	Intraspousal dynamics	None	Interview-P	71	M
1971	Willmott	Work and leisure	None	Interview-P	92	
1971	Wilson	Reading achievement	None	Questionnaire-P	114	
1973	Yoesting and Burkhead	Leisure sozialization	None	Interview-P	137	
1974	Kelly	Leisure socialization	Mini	Interview-P	78	T,I
1974	Rapoport, and Thiessen	Couple symmetry	None	Questionnaire-P	205	
1975	Bollman, Moxley, and Elliott	Family life cycle	None	Interview-P	155	
1975	Kelly	Leisure decisions	Mini	Interview-P	78	T,I
1975	Orthner	Marital satisfaction	Mini	Questionnaire-P	442	S,M,T,I
1975	Ragheb	Family cohesiveness	None	Questionnaire-P	131	St
1976	Carlson	Recreational role	None	Questionnaire-P	409	
1976	Orthner	Marital interaction	Symbolic interaction	Questionnaire-P	450	S,M,T,I
1976	Roberts et al.	Family life cycle	None	Interview-P	474	
1977	Dynes	Outdoor recreation	Mini	Questionnaire-P	141	
1977	Hume, O'Connor and Lowrey	Child adjustment	Mini	Direct observation	30	M,T
1977	Jorgenson	Wives' employment	None	Questionnaire-P	45	
1977	Kelly	Leisure socialization	Mini	Questionnaire-P	291	S,St,T
1978	Clark, Nye, and Gecas	Husbands' employment	Mini	Questionnaire-P	390	S,St,T
1978a	Kelly	Family leisure	Mini	Interview-P	374	S,M,T,I
1978b	Kelly	Leisure decisions	Mini	Questionnaire-P	215	S,St,T,I
1978	Mancini and Orthner	Leisure sexuality	None	Questionnaire-P	450	
1978	Orthner and Mancini	Family sociability	None	Questionnaire-P	450	

[a] P = primary data.
[b] S = sample; M = measurement of variables; T = theory; I = important study.

Kelly provided important theoretical clarifications and frameworks for the investigation of family recreation. Specifically, Kelly found that the family provides the recreational focus for most individuals.

In general, it was found that recreation in the family was positively associated with marital and child adjustment, the role of providing individual recreation remained largely with the family and was becoming an increasingly important marital role, family recreation decisions were based equally on role expectations and on the satisfactions that come with family interaction, the family life cycle was an important factor in determining recreational orientation, outdoor recreation was positively associated with family cohesiveness, and the leisure activity of adults could largely be explained by childhood activity.

The Decade 1980–1989

During this decade, the types of studies being conducted and the variables being measured were similar to those of the 1970s. For the purpose of analysis, articles again have been categorized into the topical areas of family adjustment, roles and decision making, the family life cycle, family cohesiveness, and leisure socialization. In addition, descriptive studies concerning the family recreation program will be reviewed. Because of the large number of studies available, the review for this decade is limited to studies that involve more than one family member and that have more than an incidental interest in family recreation. By far the greatest volume of research for the decade was concerned with the relationship between leisure activity and the quality of the marital relationship, as well as factors that might affect that relationship, such as employment status.

Research Findings

Employment Status and Leisure Time. Orthner and Axelson (1980) obtained data from 219 randomly selected households to examine the relationship between the wife's employment status and the sociability of the couple. There were no significant differences in marital sociability between employed and unemployed wives; however, when the length of the workweek and the family life cycle were controlled, marital sociability tended to be higher among those with full-time employment in a high-status occupation and among mothers who were not employed outside the home. Low marital sociability was more common when the wife was employed part-time or when childless wives were unemployed. The results were interpreted in the light of the role scarcity and the role expansion models of marital interaction.

Based on questionnaire data obtained from thirty-eight dual-career couples, Schramm (1985) found a significant positive relationship between intimacy and the amount of shared leisure time, as a percentage of total leisure time, and satisfaction with leisure time. The variable most highly correlated with couples' intimacy was satisfaction with leisure time.

Shaw (1985, 1988) used time budget data and interviews with sixty randomly selected married couples living in Halifax, Nova Scotia, to assess the relationships among employment status, gender, and availability of leisure time. Males and females had similar amounts of leisure time during weekdays, but on weekends males had significantly more leisure time than females. In addition, wives' employment status was only moderately related to the quality and the amount of leisure time experienced by females. Quantity slightly decreased, but quality increased. There was no change in the amount of leisure time spent as a family. The results were interpreted in terms of the dependent labor and resource participation theories of gender inequality. Measuring variables on the basis of the qualitative responses of subjects was a strength of the study.

In a similar study of dual-career families, Nickols and Abdel-Ghany (1983) observed that husbands had more leisure time than wives. Time spent in paid work, time spent in household work, and leisure time of spouse were significantly related to the leisure time of both husband and wife.

Crouter and associates (1987) interviewed twenty dual-earner and twenty single-earner families to assess the impact of parents' employment on the leisure-time involvement of the father with his spouse and children. In dual-earner (as opposed to single-earner) families, the father's involvement with child care activities significantly increased (along with marital negativity), but the amount of leisure time spent with the children and with the wife remained unchanged.

Marital Satisfaction. New (1980) compared the leisure activity patterns of fifty couples involved in marital therapy with fifty matched couples not in therapy. It was found that both groups had similar leisure activity patterns and that there was no significant difference in the amount of time spent in joint leisure activities. Couples in therapy, however, reported more time engaged in parallel activities with others, but not with spouse, and fewer common hobbies. The shortcoming of the study was that it failed to measure satisfaction with leisure time activities, a more important predictor of marital satisfaction than time spent engaging in joint leisure activity.

Leoni (1985) obtained questionnaire and time budget data from 190 couples to test the hypothesis that the quality and quantity of couples' leisure time activity were related to marital satisfaction. Leoni concluded that the frequency of free-time activity and marital adjustment were not correlated, but the quality of participation in free-time activity produced statistically significant relationships for six of the ten variables used in the study. Richards (1985) also found that for couples who jogged together, the couples' perception as to the meaning of their running activity (individual, parallel, or joint leisure) was significantly related to their marital satisfaction.

In order to assess the stability of leisure preferences over time, Crawford, Godbey, and Crouter (1986) conducted interviews with 126 couples shortly after marriage and again two years later. Results indicated that individual leisure preferences for specific activities were significantly and positively correlated over a two-year time span; the average reported preference for specific activities generally declines over time, more so for men than for women; and husbands and wives show no pattern of joint increased leisure preference over the first two years of marriage. The strength of the study was in its longitudinal approach.

In their analysis of leisure activity patterns and marital satisfaction, Holman and Jacquart (1988) obtained questionnaire data from a convenience sample of 159 couples. They found that the direction and strength of the relationship between leisure and marital satisfaction depended on the perceived level of communication during the activity. As such, joint leisure was positively associated with marital satisfaction if communication was high but negatively associated if communication levels were perceived as being low. Various marital career stages were of little use in explaining the magnitude of the relationship between leisure activity patterns and marital satisfaction. High- and low-stress wives differed substantially in the magnitude of the relationship between leisure and marital satisfaction, but husbands showed little difference.

Smith and colleagues (1988) obtained similar results: individual pursuits and pursuits with others in exclusion of the spouse were predictive of marital discord, the family life cycle (marital career) concept was not useful in predicting marital satisfaction, the most important predictor of marital satisfaction was the proportion of leisure time spent with the spouse alone, and leisure activity patterns were more correlated with wives' satisfaction than husbands'.

Hill (1988) also found that the amount of leisure time shared by couples, especially outdoor recreation, is an important indicator of marital stability. This supported her attachment hypothesis that spouses' shared time is a form of pleasurable interaction that strengthens attachment. Finally, Crawford (1988) found that "love for spouse" was significantly related to the duration of joint participation in all leisure activities and mutually preferred activities.

Adjustment and Achievement of Children. Griswold (1986) obtained questionnaire data concerning family outings from 1,715 fourth-grade students and then correlated the activities with achievement scores. Griswold found that family activities differed across racial groups, and average achievement scores were higher for individuals who participated in family outdoor activities than for nonparticipators.

Roles and Decision Making. Allen and Donnelly (1985) collected questionnaire data from a systematic random sample of 213 adults residing in Laramie,

Wyoming, in order to determine the predominant social units in which individuals participate during their two most enjoyable recreation activities and whether a relationship exists between the social units and the reasons for participating in those activities. It was found that outdoor-oriented activities accounted for the first and second choices for most respondents' recreational preferences and that there was a statistically significant relationship between the most enjoyable activity and the social unit of participation, which primarily included the family alone or family and other friends. The reasons for participation in one's favorite activities remained fairly constant regardless of the social unit in which participation occurred (including family togetherness, relation with nature, escape from pressure, and physical fitness).

Darley and Lim (1986) investigated the impact of parental locus of control, age of child, and parental type (single versus dual earner) in relation to the perceived child influence on family decision making for three specific leisure activities (movie attendance, family outings, and participant sports). Data were obtained by questionnaires from a convenience sample of 106 parents in the Washington, D.C., area. Using multivariate analysis of variance, the authors found that perceived child influence was positively associated with an external locus of control orientation, higher for single-earner parents, and positively associated with the child's age (the greater the child's age, the greater the perceived influence). These associations were fairly consistent across activities.

Family Life Cycle. Preston and Taylor (1981) obtained questionnaire data from 103 randomly selected married women living in Hamilton, Ontario, in order to test their hypothesis that the family life cycle affects residential area aspirations (residential settings they considered desirable) through changes in the frequency and location of leisure activities. Eight residential area attributes varied significantly with life cycle status and participation in leisure activities varied with life cycle stage, but the original hypothesis was not confirmed.

Witt and Goodale (1981, 1982) analyzed the relationship between barriers to leisure enjoyment and family stages using questionnaire data obtained from a random sample of 535 individuals living in three different Ontario communities. It was found that barriers showing a U-shaped pattern over the family life cycle primarily involved family obligations, barriers showing an inverted U-shaped pattern over the family life cycle primarily involved lack of certainty about the types of family recreation to engage in, and barriers that showed a constant rise across the family life cycle were related to daily stress.

In their analysis of the effects of retirement on the activities of rural couples, Dorfman and Heckert (1988) obtained interview data from 149 retired couples residing in two rural counties in Iowa. They found that after retirement, household role segregation decreased significantly, joint decision making increased significantly, and couples participated in a larger number of joint activities.

Family Cohesiveness. In an attempt to define the characteristics that are associated with a strong family, Stinnett and associates (1982) obtained questionnaire data (utilizing the Family Strengths Inventory) from a national sample of 283 families. Families indicated that their six most important family strengths were love, religion, respect, communication, individuality, and doing things together. Concerning perceptions as to what the family does that makes it strong, respondents indicated their six most important activities were enjoying outdoors together, vacations, church, sports, eating together, and cultural interests.

Lynn (1983) examined the relationship between leisure activity participation and levels of family strength using questionnaire data from 500 men and women in forty-two states. Significant positive relationships were found for family strength and eight leisure activity subscales: mass media, social activities, outdoor recreation, sports activities, cultural activities, hobbies, parallel activities, and joint activities.

In contrast, Gustafson (1986) obtained somewhat different results when he examined the degree of relationship between leisure participation and family cohesiveness among 263 Protestant families. There was no relationship between leisure participation and family cohesiveness, but significant relationships did exist for family cohesiveness and special family times and leisure attitude. Gustafson concluded that certain types of leisure activity are associated with family cohesiveness while others are not, depending on the perceptions and attitudes related to the activity. Adkins (1987) concluded that the value of church recreation programs, as perceived by families, was that they provided opportunities for family togetherness.

Leisure Socialization. Weiss and Bailey (1985) interviewed eighty-seven sons or daughters of randomly selected members of a suburban senior club in order to analyze the extent to which the elderly parents serve as models, or leisure educators, for their middle-aged children. For the ten categories of activity analyzed, middle-aged children were likely to have the same leisure interests as their parents, especially the same-sex parent.

In an initial effort to explain the antecedents of children's playful behavior, Barnett and Chick (1986) tested the hypothesis that a child's play style is influenced by the messages that parents give from their own leisure. Thirty-two preschool children were observed by their teachers while parents responded to various questionnaires on leisure. It was found that the play style of male children was related to the leisure activity of the mother but not the father, and the play style of female children was unrelated to the leisure of either parent. Overall, parents' satisfaction with their own leisure was more predictive of their child's play style than was their actual leisure activity.

Yoshioka (1981) found that parents or related family groups were involved with an individual's initial introduction to a recreational activity 83 percent of the time. Individuals were introduced to family recreation activities as children more often than as adults.

Family Recreation. A descriptive survey by General Mills (1981) found that, in relation to family recreation, teenagers (32 percent), especially females (38 percent), felt that their fathers spent too little time with them; teenagers wanted to spend more time with their parents going on vacations, talking, and going to the movies; and there was little difference between teenagers in dual-earner and single-earner families in the amount of time spent with parents and in the desire for more time in various activities.

Adams and Lockard (1982) examined the age and sex composition of 3,838 family groups exiting shopping malls and the zoo in order to determine patterns in parental accompaniment of children. It was found that both-parent accompaniment was more likely for groups at the zoo and for groups with young children, and for single-parent groups, the mother was likely to accompany a single child or a daughter, especially to the shopping mall.

Based on survey data from a national sample of 400 self-selected psychiatrists with regard to their perceptions of the family recreational attitudes and activities of their clients, Pietropinto (1985) reported that friends should be included in family recreation activities often (46 percent) or occasionally (46 percent); television has had a mildly negative (48 percent) or strongly negative (30 percent) effect on families' recreation programs; the major obstacles to positive family recreation are tension between family members (48 percent), incompatibility of interests (25 percent), or preoccupation with work (22 percent); couples are most likely to enjoy family recreation in their twenties and sixties and least likely to enjoy it in their thirties, forties, and fifties; holidays should be spent with the extended family occasionally (52 percent) or very often (40 percent); couples should spend leisure time away from their young children often (35 percent) or regularly (32 percent); and several short vacations are preferable to one long one (57 percent).

The Decade in Review

Theory and Methodology. For this period there seemed to be a fairly even mix of large, representative samples and small, nonrepresentative samples. Sample sizes ranged from to 30 to 3,838. Most studies provided adequate demographic information in describing the samples used and explained the sampling method.

Statistical analysis for this period was more intense and varied than the previous decade. Such methods as univariate and multivariate analysis of variance, analysis of covariance, multiple regression, Pearson product-moment correlation, Wilcoxan tests, chi-square tests, and Spearman rank correlation analysis were used regularly.

In contrast to earlier decades, there was a definite trend toward the use of standardized (reliable and valid) scales in measuring variables. Such scales as the Leisure Activity-Interaction Index, the Inventory of Rewarding Activities, the Leisure Attitude Scale, the Leisure Satisfaction Scale, the Dyadic Adjustment Scale, the Marital Satisfaction Inventory, the Miller Social Intimacy Scale, the Recreation Experience Preference Scale, and the Family Strength Inventory were used in various studies during this decade. There was an increasing awareness of the need to understand leisure attitudes, perceptions, and satisfactions, in addition to the quantity and types of activities engaged in. Questionnaires continued to be the dominant method of data collection.

The use of theory in family recreation for this decade was sparse, with only seven of thirty studies making any substantial use of it. Many of the theoretical orientations used were very specific, with limited application outside the immediate topic of study. A notable exception was the use of small group theory to explain various patterns of recreation (Allen and Donnelly, 1985). (See table 9–6.)

Key Studies and General Findings. The study by Allen and Donnelly (1985) was important in that it provided significant insight as to the types of activities individuals enjoy most, who they enjoy doing them with, and the motivation behind doing them. The authors' conclusions have significant implications for family recreation. In addition, the study used a random sample, various statistical analyses, and small group theory to obtain and interpret the results. Research by Hill (1988) and Holman and Jacquart (1988) also provided new insights into the relationship between marital satisfaction and leisure.

With regard to employment status, it was found during this decade that the wife's employment is not correlated with marital sociability, the amount of leisure time available to working women is not significantly less than those who stay at home full time, and fathers from dual-career families tend to have more child care responsibilities but similar family leisure interactions when compared to single-earner fathers. In terms of marital satisfaction and adjustment, it was determined that couples' intimacy is related to their perceived satisfaction with leisure, the quantity of leisure activity is not related to marital satisfaction, but the perception of leisure quality is, an important factor in the quality of leisure for couples is the amount of communication and time spent alone together, and the concept of family life cycle or marital career is not important in explaining the relationship between marital satisfaction and leisure.

In the area of family recreation decision making, it was found that decisions are influenced by the age of children, parental employment status, and parental locus of control. In addition, it was determined that many barriers to family recreation are significantly related to the family life cycle. With regard to family strength and cohesiveness, it was reported that the quantity of family recreation was not as important as specific types of recreation, especially outdoor activity, or as important as the attitudes and satisfactions that family members attributed to family recreation activities. Finally, it was found that the family is a powerful source of leisure socialization across the life cycle.

Conclusion

Methodological Trends and Developments

In terms of methodology, family recreation research has matured considerably but still has some significant improvements to make. Initially samples were small and nonrepresentative, and much recent research has not improved sampling significantly. However, considerable progress has been made over the decades in describing sample characteristics and methods. The trend is toward large, representative samples with clear descriptions of sampling methods and characteristics of the population.

The data collection method used in this field of study has been predominantly the questionnaire. Early questionnaire data were collected using a variety of noncomparable, author-designed instruments that were not adequately described or tested for reliability or validity. More recent research has seen the widespread use of standardized scales and inventories that are reliable, valid, and comparable. Early research was primarily interested in the quantity and type of leisure activity being engaged in by family members. During the 1970s and 1980s, however, interest shifted to the meaning and attitudes associated with the leisure activity rather than the activity itself. In terms of data collection, the focus has also shifted during the last twenty years from the individual to the family. Most researchers during the 1970s and 1980s recognized the importance of gathering information from at least both husband and wife, if not from all family members.

Statistical analysis has matured over the decades. Early studies were almost exclusively descriptive in nature and involved minimal analysis. Later studies began to use correlational methods, and most studies conducted in the 1980s employed a wide variety of more powerful, inferential statistical methods. The future trend is toward analyses that can explain greater variance and suggest causation rather than merely association.

A major weakness of family recreation research throughout the decades reviewed has been the sparse use of theory in formulating hypotheses and interpreting results. Only a handful of studies reviewed used theory to any great extent, and even then the theory employed was often specific to the study, with little carry-over to future research efforts.

Major Findings

Marital Satisfaction. There have been fairly consistent findings throughout the decades reviewed that show a positive relationship between marital adjustment and the use of leisure time by couples. Rather than the quantity or types of leisure time activity, however, it has been demonstrated that couples' perceptions as to the quality of their leisure is the most useful predictor of marital

Table 9–6
Overview of Research on Recreation in the Family, 1980–1989

Year	*Author*	*Topic*	*Theory*	*Method*[a]	*Sample*	*Strengths*[b]
1980	New	Couples' leisure time	None	Questionnaire-P	100	St
1980	Orthner and Axelson	Work and leisure	Mini	Questionnaire-P	219	T
1981	General Mills	Family reaction	None	Questionnaire-P	235	
1981	Preston and Taylor	Family life cycle	None	Questionnaire-P	103	
1981	Witt and Goodale	Family life cycle	None	Questionnaire-P	535	S,St
1981	Yoshioka	Leisure socialization	None	Questionnaire-P	na	
1982	Adams and Lockard	Family leisure groups	None	Direct observation	3838	S,M
1982	Stinnett et al.	Family strength	None	Questionnaire-P	283	M
1983	Lynn	Family strength	None	Questionnaire-P	500	S
1983	Nickols, and Abdel-Ghany	Couples' leisure time	None	Questionnaire-P	405	S
1985	Allen and Donnelly	Social participation	Small group	Questionnaire-P	213	S,St,T,I
1985	Leoni	Marriage and leisure	None	Questionnaire-P	190	
1985	Pietropinto	Family recreation	None	Questionnaire-P	400	
1985	Richards	Marriage and jogging	None	Questionnaire-P	353	St
1985	Schramm	Intimacy and leisure	None	Questionnaire-P	38	M

1985	Shaw	Gender and leisure	Mini	Interview-P	60	M,T
1985	Weiss and Bailey	Leisure socialization	None	Interview-P	87	
1986	Barnett and Chick	Leisure socialization	Mini	Direct observation	32	M,T
1986	Crawford, Godbey, and Crouter	Leisure stability	Mini	Interview-P	126	M
1986	Darley and Lim	Decision making	None	Questionnaire-P	106	M,St
1986	Griswold	Family outings	None	Questionnaire-P	1715	
1986	Gustafson	Family cohesiveness	None	Questionnaire-P	263	M,St
1987	Adkins	Church recreation	None	Questionnaire-P	30	
1987	Crouter et al.	Father involvement	None	Interview-P	40	
1988	Crawford	Leisure companionship	None	Interview-P	126	M
1988	Dorfman and Weckert	Family life cycle	None	Interview-P	149	
1988	Hill	Spouses' shared time	Mini	Interview-S	280	S,M,T,I
1988	Holman and Jacquart	Marital satisfaction	None	Questionnaire-P	159	M,I
1988	Shaw	Work and leisure	Mini	Interview-P	60	M,T
1988	Smith et al.	Marital satisfaction	None	Questionnaire-P	251	M

[a] P = primary data.

[b] S = sample; M = measurement of variables; T = theory; I = important study.

satisfaction. In defining quality, there is evidence that the amount of communication and the amount of time spent alone together are important aspects of high-quality leisure for couples. It also appears that the perceived quality of leisure is more important for the marital satisfaction of wives than for husbands. In conclusion, it has been shown that perceived satisfaction with leisure time use is positively associated with marital sociability, marital satisfaction, marital stability, and marital intimacy.

Family Cohesiveness and Strength. It has been demonstrated that family strength or cohesiveness is related to the family's use of leisure time. Studies have consistently found that some types of family recreation are more related to family cohesiveness than others. Specifically, outdoor activities and camping have been associated with family cohesiveness. In addition, studies have found that, as in marital adjustment, perceptions as to the adequacy of the family recreation program are as important as the activities actually engaged in. Children whose families have high levels of recreation activity and satisfaction tend to have higher nonfamily sociability ratings, higher school achievement, and better overall adjustment.

The Recreational Role. In spite of early concerns to the contrary, it has been shown that the family continues to be the most important base for individual recreation and that most recreation is engaged in with other family members. Further, the recreational role has become an important marital role that is often shared equally by spouses. Several scholars have analyzed the recreational role from a decision-making perspective with attention to the motivations behind family recreation decisions.

Family Life Cycle. Recent research has refuted the idea that the family life cycle (or marital career) is an important factor in influencing the relationship between marital satisfaction and leisure activity. Other research, however, has suggested that the family life cycle is important in terms of recreational decision making and barriers to recreation. In other words, the quantity and types of recreation engaged in vary with different stages of the family life cycle. Marriage, parenthood, and retirement produce an impact on the types and quantity of family recreation engaged in. Finally, most individuals are introduced to new recreational activities within the context of the family, and most adult recreation continues activities begun in childhood.

Socioeconomic Status. A variable that received a great deal of attention during the earlier, but not the later, decades of family recreation research was socioeconomic status. Whether defined by occupation, income, or education, virtually every study that addressed the topic concluded that socioeconomic status is an important variable in determining family recreational activity. Basic conclusions are that higher-socioeconomic-status families are more active in formal, organized, or expensive recreational activities, while lower-socioeconomic-status families tend to rely on more informal and inexpensive activities, such as visiting relatives.

Spouse and Parent Employment. Several studies looked at the relationship between wife's employment status and the family recreation program and concluded that while the wife's employment alters her individual leisure activities, it has little impact on the amount of time available for family recreation. In addition, it was shown that fathers who spend more time at work do not necessarily spend less time in family recreation. A more important factor tends to be the orientation toward family centeredness rather than spouse-parent employment status.

Methodological Assessment

1. Use of questionnaires tends to be the primary data collection method used in family recreation research.
2. The use of standardized scales, inventories, and other devices has become the norm for measuring variables related to family recreation.
3. Many samples in family recreation research continue to be convenience samples that are not representative of a specific target population.
4. Family recreation research is largely atheoretical.
5. Most family recreation research is cross-sectional rather than longitudinal.
6. Most family recreation research is correctional, and therefore direct cause-and-effect conclusions generally have not been possible.
7. Within family recreation research, there is little consistent use of standardized, accepted definitions for such key terms as *leisure, recreation,* and *home,* and in spite of the increasing use of standardized scales and inventories, there is still a great deal of variability in defining categories of leisure activity and types of leisure patterns.

Suggestions for Future Research

Since the relationship of family recreation to other variables is largely a function of the meaning the individual places on his or her leisure program, future research that uses participant observation and other qualitative research methods would be beneficial in understanding that meaning.

Experimental designs and statistical analyses that can suggest causality and explain greater variance should be employed more often. In addition, more prospective, longitudinal research needs to be done in order to assess family outcomes in relation to their recreational programs.

The use of general and specific theories of family behavior could be used more profitably in the development of hypotheses and the evaluation of results. Specific theories that could be used profitably include exchange theory, attitude theory, family development theory, symbolic interaction theory, small group theory, and social learning theory.

The trend toward the use of more representative samples should be encouraged, and research that investigates a wider range of variables, such as family types and family size, and the meaning of leisure for all family members (rather than just for one or both parents) is necessary.

It would be beneficial to use accepted operational and theoretical definitions for leisure, recreation, and home as they relate to family recreation.

References

Adams, B.N., and Butler, J.E. 1967. Occupational status and husband/wife social participation. *Social Forces* 45 (4):501–507.

Adams, R.M., and Lockard, J.S. 1982. Age and sex composition of family groups on shopping and recreational settings. *Ethology and Sociobiology* 3:131–134.

Adkins, K.D. 1987. The meaning of church recreation programs as perceived by families. Ph.D. dissertation, Indiana University.

Allen, L.R., and Donnelly, M.A. 1985. An analysis of the social unit of participation and the perceived psychological outcomes associated with most enjoyable recreation activities, *Leisure Sciences* 7 (4):421–441.

Amatora, M. 1959. Analyses of certain recreational interests and activities and other variables in the large family. *Journal of Social Psychology* 50:225–231.

Anderson, W.A. 1943. The family and individual social participation. *American Sociological Review* 8 (4):420–424.

Anderson, W.A. 1946. Family social participation and social status self-ratings. *American Sociological Review* 11 (3):253–258.

———. 1953a. *Rural Social Participation and the Family Life Cycle: Part I. Formal Participation.* Memoir 314. Ithaca, N.Y.: Agricultural Station, Department of Rural Sociology, Cornell University.

———. 1953b. *Rural Social Participation and the Family Life Cycle: Part II. Informal Participation.* Memoir 318. Ithaca, N.Y.: Agricultural Experiment Station, Department of Rural Sociology, Cornell University.

Anderson, W.A., and Palmbeck, H. 1943. *The Social Participation of Farm Families.* Bulletin 8. Ithaca, N.Y.: Agricultural Experiment Station, Department of Rural Sociology, Cornell University.

Angrist, S.S. 1967. Role constellation as a variable in women's leisure activities. *Social Forces* 45 (3):423–431.

Barnett, L.A., and Chick, G.E. 1986. Chips off the ol' block: Parent's leisure and their children's play. *Journal of Leisure Research* 18 (4):266–283.

Benson, P. 1952. The interests of happily married couples. *Marriage and Family Living* 14 (4):276–280.

Bollman, S.R.; Moxley, V.M.; and Elliot, N.C. 1975. Family and community activities of rural nonfarm familiies with children. *Journal of Leisure Research* 7 (1):53–62.

Burch, W.R., Jr. 1965. The play world of camping: Research in the social meaning of outdoor recreation. *American Journal of Sociology* 70 (5):604–612.

———. 1969. The social circles of leisure: Competing explanations. *Journal of Leisure Research* 1 (2):125–147.

Burgess, E.W., and Cottrell, L.S. 1939. *Predicting Success or Failure in Marriage.* New York: Prentice-Hall.

Burgess, E.W., and Wallin, P. 1953. *Engagement and Marriage.* Chicago: J.B. Lippincott Company.

Carlson, J.E. 1976. The recreational role. In F.I. Nye (ed.), *Role Structure and Analysis of the Family,* pp. 131–214. Beverly Hills, Calif.: Sage Publications.

———. 1979. The family and recreation: Toward a theoretical development. In W.R. Burr et al. (eds.), *Contemporary Theories about the Family,* New York: Free Press.

Clark, R.A.; Nye, F.I.; and Gecas, V. 1978. Husbands' work involvement and marital role performance. *Journal of Marriage and the Family* 40 (1):9–21.

Clifford, K. 1937. Community of interest and the measurement of marriage adjustment. *Family* 18:133–137.

Conard, L.M. 1939. Differential depression effects on families of laborers, farmers, and the business class: A survey of an Iowa town. *American Journal of Sociology* 44 (4):526–533.

Connor, R.; Johannis, T.B., Jr.; and Walters, J. 1955. Family recreation in relation to role conceptions of family members. *Marriage and Family Living* 17 (4):306–309.

Cramer, M.W. 1950. Leisure time activities of economically privileged children. *Sociology and Social Research* 34 (6):444–450.

Crawford, D.W., Jr. 1988. The patterns of leisure companionship during the early marital relationship. Ph.D. dissertation, Pennsylvania State University.

Crawford, D.W.; Godbey, Geoffrey, G.; and Crouter, A.C. 1986. The stability of leisure preferences. *Journal of Leisure Research* 18 (2):96–115.

Crouter, A.C.; Perry-Jenkens, M.; Huston, T.L.; and McHale, S. 1987. Processes underlying father involvement in dual-earner and single-earner families. *Developmental Psychology* 23 (3):431–440.

Cunningham, K.R., and Johannis, T.B., Jr. 1960. Research on the family and leisure: A review and critique of selected studies. *Family Life Coordinator* 9 (1–2):25–32.

Darley, W.K., and Lim, J.S. 1986. Family decision making in leisure-time activities: An exploratory investigation of the impact of locus of control, child age influence factor and parental type on perceived child influence. *Advances in Consumer Research* 13:370–374.

Dorfman, L.T., and Heckert, D.A. 1988. Egalitarianism in retired rural couples: Household tasks, decision making, and leisure activities. *Family Relations* 37 (1):73–78.

Dotson, F. 1951. Patterns of voluntary association among urban working-class families. *American Sociological Review* 16 (5):687–693.

Dynes, W. 1977. Leisure location and family centeredness. *Journal of Leisure Research* 9 (4):281–290.

Etzkorn, K.P. 1964. Leisure and camping: The social meaning of a form of public recreation. *Sociology and Social Research* 49 (1):76–89.

General Mills American Family Report. 1981. *Families at Work.* Minneapolis: General Mills.

Gerson, W.M. 1960. Leisure and marital satisfaction of college married couples. *Marriage and Family Living* 22 (4):360–361.

Griswold, P.A. 1986. Family outing activities and achievement among fourth graders in compensatory education funded schools. *Journal of Educational Research* 79 (5):261–266.

Gustafson, J.D. 1986. The relationship between leisure participation and family cohesiveness among Protestant church families. Ph.D. dissertation, Temple University.

Hawkins, H., and Walters, J. 1952. Family recreation activities. *Journal of Home Economics* 44 (8):623–626.

Hendricks, J. 1971. Leisure participation as influenced by urban residence patterns. *Sociology and Social Research* 55 (4):414–427.

Hill, M.S. 1988. Marital stability and spouses' shared time: A multidisciplinary hypothesis. *Journal of Family Issues* 9 (4):427–451.

Hollingshead, A.B. 1949. *Elmtown's Youth: The Impact of Social Classes on Adolescents.* New York: Wiley.

Holman, T.B., and Epperson, A. 1984. Family and leisure: A review of the literature with research recommendations. *Journal of Leisure Research* 16 (4):277–294.

Holman, T.B., and Jacquart, M. 1988. Leisure-activity patterns and marital satisfaction: A further test. *Journal of Marriage and the Family* 50 (1):69–77.

Hume, N.; O'Connor, W.A.; and Lowery, C.R. 1977. Family, adjustment, and the psychosocial ecosystem. *Psychiatric Annals* 7 (7):345–355.

Johannis, T.B., Jr. 1958. Participation by fathers, mothers and teenage sons and daughters in selected social activity. *Coordinator* 7 (2):24–25.

Johannis, T.B., Jr., and Cunningham, K.R. 1959. Conceptions of use of non-work time: Individual, husband-wife, parent-child and family—a methodological note. *Family Life Coordinator* 8 (2):34–36.

Johannis, T.B., Jr., and Rollins, J.M. 1960. Teenager perceptions of family decision making about social activity. *Family Life Coordinator* 8 (3):59–60.

Jorgenson, S.E. 1977. The effects of social position, and wife/mother-employment on family leisure-time: A study of fathers. *International Journal of Sociology of the Family* 7 (2):197–208.

Kelly, J.R. 1974. Socialization toward leisure: A developmental approach. *Journal of Leisure Research* 6 (3):181–193.

———. 1975. Leisure decisions: Exploring intrinsic and role-related orientations. *Society and Leisure* 7 (4):45–61.

———. 1977. Leisure socialization: Replication and extension. *Journal of Leisure Research* 9 (2):121–132.

———. 1978a. Family leisure in three communities. *Journal of Leisure Research* 10 (1):47–60.

———. 1978b. Situational and social factors in leisure decisions. *Pacific Sociological Review* 21 (3):313–330.

Leevy, J.R. 1950. Leisure time of the American housewife. *Sociology and Social Research* 35:97–105.

Leoni, E.L. 1985. The relationship of frequency and quality participation in free-time activity and marital adjustment. Ph.D. dissertation, Indiana University.

Locke, H.J. 1951. *Predicting Adjustment in Marriage.* New York: Henry Holt.

Lundberg, G.A.; Komarovsky, M.; and McInerny, M.A. 1934. *Leisure: A Suburban Study.* New York: Columbia University Press.

Lynd, R.S., and Lynd, H.M. 1929. *Middletown: A Study in American Culture.* New York: Harcourt, Brace.

Lynn, W.D. 1983. Leisure activities in high-strength, middle-strength, and low-strength families. Ph.D. dissertation, University of Nebraska.

MacDonald, M.; McGuire, C.; and Havighurst, R.J. 1949. Leisure activities and the socioeconomic status of children. *American Journal of Sociology* 54 (6):505–519.

Mancini, J.A., and Orthner, D.K. 1978. Recreational sexuality preferences among middle-class husbands and wives. *Journal of Sex Research* 14 (2):96–106.

New, D.C. 1980. A study of leisure activity patterns of couples in marital therapy. Ph.D. dissertation, Auburn University.

Nickols, S.Y., and Abdel-Ghany, M. 1983. Leisure time of husbands and wives. *Home Economics Research Journal* 12 (2):189–198.

Nye, I.F. 1958. Employment status and recreational behavior of mothers. *Pacific Sociological Review* 1 (1):69–72.

Orthner, D.K. 1975. Leisure activity patterns and marital satisfaction over the marital career. *Journal of Marriage and the Family* 37 (7:91–102.

———. 1976. Patterns of leisure and marital interaction. *Journal of Leisure Research* 8 (2):98–111.

Orthner, D.K., and Axelson, L.J. 1980. The effects of wife employment on marital sociability. *Journal of Comparative Family Studies* 11:531–545.

Orthner, D.K., and Mancini, J.A. 1978. Parental family sociability and marital leisure patterns. *Leisure Sciences* 1 (4):365–372.

———. 1980. Leisure behavior and group dynamics: The case of the family. In S.E. Iso-Ahola (ed.), *Social Psychological Perspectives on Leisure and Recreation,* pp. 307–328. Springfield, Ill.: Charles C. Thomas.

Parker, S. 1976. *The Sociology of Leisure.* New York: International Publications Service.

Patrick, C. 1945. Relation of childhood and adult leisure activities. *Journal of Social Psychology* 21:65–79.

Pietropinto, A. 1985. Recreation and the family. *Medical Aspects of Human Sexuality* 19 (1):197–201.

Preston, V., and Taylor, S.M. 1981. The family life cycle, leisure activities, and residential area evaluation. *Canadian Geographer* 25 (1):47–59.

Presvelou, C. 1971. Impact of differential leisure activities on intra-spousal dynamics. *Human Relations* 24 (6):565–574.

Radheb, M.G. 1975. The relationship between leisure-time activities and family cohesiveness. Ph.D. dissertation, University of Illinois.

Rapoport, R.; Rapoport, R.; and Thiessen, V. 1974. Couple symmetry and enjoyment. *Journal of Marriage and the Family* 36 (6):588–591.

Roberts, K.; Cook, F.G.; Clark, S.C.; and Semeonoff, E. 1976. The family life-cycle, domestic roles and the meaning of leisure. *Society and Leisure* 8 (3):7–20.

Scheuch, E.K. 1960. Family cohesion in leisure time. *Sociological Review* 8 (1):37–61.

Schoolmaster, F.A. III. 1979. A spatial investigation into the effects of the family life cycle and household location on urban recreation behavior. Ph.D. dissertation, Kent State University.

Schramm, M.L. 1985. The relationship of intimacy to use of leisure time in dual-career couples. Ph.D. dissertation, Texas A&M University.

Searls, L.G. 1966. Leisure role emphasis of college graduate homemakers. *Journal of Marriage and the Family* 28 (1):77–82.

Sessoms, H.D. 1963. An analysis of selected variables affecting outdoor recreation patterns. *Social Forces* 42 (1):112–115.

Shaw, S.M. 1985. Gender and leisure: Inequality in the distribuion of leisure time. *Journal of Leisure Research* 17 (4):266–282.

———. 1988. Leisure in the contemporary family: The effect of female employment on the leisure of Canadian wives and husbands. *International Review of Modern Sociology* 18:1–16.

Skolsky, A.F. 1929. A recreational approach to family case work. *Family* 10 (4):107–109.

Smith, G.T,; Snyder, T.J.; and Monsma, B.R. 1988. Predicting relationship satisfaction from couples' use of leisure time. *American Journal of Family Therapy* 16 (1):3–13.

Stinnett, N.; Sanders, G.; DeFrain, J.; and Parkhurst, A. 1982. A nationwide study of families who perceive themselves as strong. *Family Perspective* 16 (1):15–22.

Stone, C.L. 1960. Some family characteristics of socially active and inactive teenagers. *Family Coordinator* 8:53–57.

———. 1963. Family recreation—a parental concern. *Family Life Coordinator* 12 (3–4):85–87.

Weiss, C.R., and Bailey, B.B. 1985. The influence of older adults' activity selection on their progeny's expectations for their own future. *Activities, Adaptation and Aging* 6 (4):103–114.

West, P.C., and Merriam, L.C., Jr. 1970. Outdoor recreation and family cohesiveness: A research approach. *Journal of Leisure Research* 2 (4):251–259.

White, R.C. 1955. Social class differences in the uses of leisure. *American Journal of Sociology* 61 (1):145–150.

Willmott, P. 1971. Family, work and leisure conflicts among male employees. *Human Relations* 24 (6):575–584.

Wilson, C.B. 1971. An exploratory study of certain leisure time activities of high socio-economic parents in relation to their child's reading achievement. Ph.D. dissertation, University of Virginia.

Wilson, J. 1980. Sociology of leisure. *Annual Review of Sociology* 6:21–40.

Witt, P.A., and Goodale, T.L. 1982. Stress, leisure, and the family. *Recreation Research Review* 9:28–32.

———. 1981. The relationships between barriers to leisure enjoyment and family stages. *Leisure Sciences* 4 (1):29–49.

Wylie, J.A. 1953. A survey of 504 families to determine the relationships between certain factors and the nature of the family recreation program. *Research Quarterly* 24 (2):229–243.

Yoesting, D.R., and Burkhead, D.L. 1973. Significance of childhood recreation experience on adult leisure behavior: An exploratory analysis. *Journal of Leisure Research* 5 (1):25–35.

Yoshioka, C.F. 1981. Leisure socialization and adult and child related decision-making interactions in family recreational activities. Ph.D. dissertation, University of Oregon.

Related Literature

Allen, P.G. 1951. Evening activities in the home. *Sociological Review* 43:127–141.

Arndt, J.; Gronmo, S.; and Hawes, D.K. 1980. Allocation of tie to leisure activities:

Norwegian and American patterns. *Journal of Crosscultural Psychology* 11 (4):498–511.

Berk, R.A., and Berk, S.F. 1979. *Labor and Leisure at Home: Content and Organization of the Household Day.* Beverly Hills: Sage.

Bernard, M. 1984. Leisure-rich and leisure-poor. The leisure patterns of young adults. *Leisure Studies* 3:343–361.

———. 1988. Leisure-rich and leisure-poor: Leisure lifestyles among young adults. *Leisure Sciences* 10 (2):131–149.

Better Homes and Gardens. 1978. *A Report on the American Family.* Des Moines, Iowa: Meredith Corporation.

Blood, R.O., and Wolfe, D.M. 1960. *Husbands and Wives: The Dynamics of Married Living.* Clencoe, Ill.: Free Press.

Brail, R.K., and Chapin, F.S., Jr. 1973. Activity patterns of urban residents. *Environment and Behavior* 5 (2):163–190.

Burgess, N.J.B. 1986. Race, wives' employment and social psycholocial well-being: Patterns of black/white differences among U.S. women. Ph.D. dissertation, North Carolina State University.

Clarke, A.C. 1956. The use of leisure and its relation to levels of occupational prestige. *American Sociological Review* 21 (3):301–307.

Critchton, A.; James, E.; and Wakeford, J. 1962. Youth and leisure in Cardiff, 1960. *Sociological Revies* 10 (2):203–220.

Crompton, J.L. 1981. Dimensions of the social group role in pleasure vacations. *Annals of Tourism Research* 8 (4):550–568.

Davey, A.J., and Paolucci, B. 1980. Family interaction: A study of shared time and activities. *Family Relations* 29 (1):43–49.

Donald, M.N., and Havighurst, R.J. 1959. The meanings of leisure. *Social Forces* 37 (4):355–360.

Dumazedier, J. 1967. *Toward a Society of Leisure.* New York: Free Press.

Glyptis, S.A., and Chambers, D.A. 1982. No place like home. *Leisure Studies* 1:247–262.

Goldstein, B., and Eichhorn, R.L. 1961. The changing Protestant ethic: Rural patterns in health, work, and leisure. *American Sociological Review* 26 (4):557–565.

Goodman, N.C. 1969. Leisure, work, and the use of time: A study of adult style of time utilization, childhood determinants and vocational implications. Ph.D. dissertation, Harvard University.

Groves, D.L., and Lastovica, A.M. 1977. A quality of life framework for family life leisure activities. *International Journal of Family Counseling* 5 (2):59–65.

Haavio-Mannila, E. 1971. Satisfaction with family, work, leisure and life among men and women. *Human Relations* 24 (6):585–601.

Hantrais, L.; Clark, P.A.; and Samuel, N. 1984. Time-space dimensions of work, family and leisure in France and Great Britain. *Leisure Studies* 3:301–317.

Havighurst, R.J. 1957. The leisure activities of the middle-aged. *American Journal of Sociology* 63 (2):152–162.

Havighurst, R.J., and Feigenbaum, K. 1959. Leisure and life-style. *American Journal of Sociology* 64 (4):396–404.

Hornby, M.C. 1986. The influence of television and family on children's leisure time reading. Ph.D. dissertation, Stanford University.

Johannis, T.B., Jr. 1973. The future of the sociology of leisure: Households and families. *Society and Leisure* 5 (1):155–158.

Kaplan, M. 1960. *Leisure in America: A Social Inquiry.* New York: Wiley.

Keith, P.M.: Goudy, W.J.; and Powers, W.A. 1984. Salience of life areas among older men: Implications for practice. *Journal of Gerontological Social Work* 8 (1/2):67–82.
Kelly, J.R. 1975. Life styles and leisure choices. *Family Coordinator* 24 (2):185–190.
Kelly, J.R.; Steinkemp, M.W.; and Kelly, J.R. 1987. Later-life satisfaction: Does leisure contribute? *Leisure Science* 9:189–200.
Komarovsky, M. 1946. The voluntary associations of urban dwellers. *American Sociological Review* 11:686–698.
McGeown, M. 1982. The concept of families in planning. *Journal of Leisurability* 9 (4):24–29.
McKay, J. 1986. Leisure and social inequality in Australia. *Australian and New Zealand Journal of Sociology* 22 (3):343–367.
Mancini, J.A., and Orthner, D.K. 1982. Leisure time, activities, preferences, and competence: Implications for the morale of older adults. *Journal of Applied Gerontology* 1:95–103.
Marsden, P.V., and Reed, J.S. 1983. Cultural choice among southerners. *American Behavioral Scientist* 26 (4):479–492.
Oldenburg, R.A. 1968. Companionship and identity as reflected in marital leisure patterns. Ph.D. dissertation, University of Minnesota.
Orden, S.R., and Bradburn, M. 1968. Dimensions of marriage happiness. *American Journal of Sociology* 73 (6):715–731.
Orthner, D.K. 1978. Leisure, work and the family: Life cycle changes and patterns. *Leisure, Work and the Family* 2:1–9.
———. 1985. Conflict and leisure interaction in families. In B.G. Gunter, Jay Stanley, and Robert St. Clair (eds.), *Transitions to Leisure*, pp. 133–139. New York: University Press of America.
Rapoport, R., and Rapoport, R.N. 1975. *Leisure and the Family Life Cycle.* London: Routledge and Kegan Paul.
Raymond, L.C.P. 1985. The effects of unemployment on the leisure behavior of unemployed steelworkers. Ph.D. dissertation, University of Illinois.
Reissman, L. 1954. Class, leisure, and social participation. *American Sociological Review* 19 (1):76–84.
Richards, P.E. 1985. Perceptions of running as styles of leisure interaction and marital relationships. Ph.D. dissertation, University of Northern Colorado.
Robins, E.J. 1985. A theoretical and empirical investigation of compatibility testing in marital choice. Ph.D. dissertation, Pennsylvania State University.
Rosenblatt, P.C., and Russell, M.G. 1975. The social psychology of potential problems in family vacation travel. *Family Coordinator* 24 (2):209–215.
Rowland, V.T.; Nickols, S.Y.; and Dodder, R.A. 1986. Parents' time allocation: A comparison of households headed by one and two parents. *Home Economics Research Journal* 15 (2):105–114.
Sagi, M. 1986. Motivational background of cultural activities in leisure. *Leisure Studies* 5:103–108.
Shank, J.W. 1984. Leisure in the lives of dual career women. Ph.D. dissertation, Boston University.
Slusher, B.J. 1982. Work and leisure: A study of family values. Ph.D. dissertation, University of Missouri.
Staines, G.L., and O'Connor, P. 1980. Conflicts among work, leisure, and family roles. *Monthly Labor Review* 103 (8):35–39.

Standlee, L.S., and Popham, W.J. 1958. Participation in leisure time activities as related to selected vocational and social variables. *Journal of Psychology* 46:149–154.
Stockmann, P. 1974. More leisure for employed mothers. *Society and Leisure* 6 (1):141–153.
Stone, A.A. 1987. Event content in a daily survey is differentially associated with concurrent mood. *Journal of Personality and Social Psychology* 52 (1):56–58.
Trafton, R.S. 1977. Measuring life satisfaction and its relation to satisfaction with work, family, and leisure. Ph.D. dissertation, Southern Illinois University.
United Media Enterprises. 1983. *Where Does the Time Go?* New York: United Media Enterprises.
Vanek, J. 1980. Work, leisure, and family roles: Farm households in the United States, 1920–1955. *Journal of Family History* 5 (4):422–431.
Volger, A.; Ernst, G.; Nachreiner, F.; and Hanecke, K. 1988. Common free time of family members under different shift systems. *Applied Ergonomics* 19 (3):213–218.
Williams, R.M. 1959. Friendship and social values in a suburban community: An exploratory study. *Pacific Sociological Review* 2 (1):3–10.
Willits, W.L., and Willits, F.K. 1986. "Adolescent participation in leisure activities: 'The less, the more' or 'the more the more.' " *Leisure Sciences* 8 (2):189–206.
Woolf, S.J. 1980. Relationship of family structure and leisure-time activities to middle grade students' voluntary reading. Ph.D. dissertation, Boston University.
Young, T.R. 1964. "Recreation and family stress: An essay in institutional conflicts." *Journal of Marriage and the Family* 26 (1):95–97.

10
Gender Roles in the Family

Julio C. Caycedo
Gabe Wang
Stephen J. Bahr

Perhaps no other characteristic is more important in family life than gender. Males and females have some distinct biological and social differences, and many family roles are assigned according to gender. Men have tended to specialize in the provider role, while women have tended to become heavily involved in the child care, child socialization, and housekeeping roles.

This chapter reviews empirical research on gender roles in the family for the period 1930 to 1989. Hochschild observed in 1973 that research on gender roles could be categorized into four groups. First, there is a vast research on differences between males and females on a wide variety of physical, psychological, and social characteristics. Second, the roles women and men play in the family and in the larger society have been the focus of much research. Third, some scholars have examined women as a minority group. A fourth focus has been an examination of women from the politics of caste perspective. In this chapter, the focus is on the second type of research: the roles women and men play in the family. We have excluded the many studies that examine differences between men and women unless there is a specific reference to the family. We are particularly interested in power, decision making, and division of labor in the family.

We attempted to locate and review all empirical research dealing with roles of spouses, parents, and children. Some of the key words we used to locate research in indexes were *gender roles, sex roles, division of labor, discrimination, equal rights, family, men, women, sex differences, social role, socioeconomic status—conditions of women, family life, employment of women, sex (psychology), marriage, married women, married men,* and *power.*

The Decade 1930–1939

During this decade, most of the literature on gender roles dealt with the increased participation of women in paid employment. Three of the seventeen articles identified were not accessible. Of the fourteen pieces retrieved, only three were empirical research. One examined the employment of women, one studied family power, and the other reported trends in gender role attitudes.

Research Findings

Davis (1931) described the participation of women in paid employment in Great Britain. He compared statistics on employed people from the Census Returns (1911 and 1921), the Ministry of Labour (1921 and 1929), State Health Insurance (1912 and 1928), and the Home Office (1890 and 1928). There was an increase in the rate of female employment, and Davis concluded that women were gradually replacing men in the industries.

Popenoe (1933) studied 2,596 families of college students at three universities and categorized participants into three groups: husband dominant, wife dominant, and democratic co-partnership where both spouses were equally dominant. Families with democratic partnerships were the most prevalent and the happiest. Families where the wife was dominant were the least common and least happy.

Kirkpatrick (1936) administered a questionnaire on feminism to 241 male and 312 female students at the University of Minnesota. The students were asked to have their parents complete the questionnaires, and responses were obtained from 152 fathers and 165 mothers. The data showed that the students were more egalitarian than their parents, and women were more egalitarian than the men. However, when education was held constant, the college students were not more feministic than their same-sex parent. Gender differences in attitudes were greater for the students than for the parents.

The Decade in Review

Theory and Methodology. None of these three studies on gender roles in the family tested a particular theory. Davis used census data, and Popenoe and Kirkpatrick used questionnaires. The Davis study was descriptive. Popenoe examined the relationship between marital decision making and marital happiness, and Kirkpatrick looked at generational and gender differences in attitudes toward feminism. (See table 10–1.)

Key Studies and Findings. Popenoe's (1933) study was important because it correlated type of family decision making with happiness in families. It was the first study located on the topic of family power and used a large sample. Kirkpatrick's (1936) work was a pioneering examination of attitudes toward feminism. He found that after controlling for education, college students were not more egalitarian than their parents. His study was the basis for a replication that took place in 1977 by Roper and Labeff.

Table 10–1
Overview of Research on Gender Roles in the Family, 1930–1939

Year	*Author*	*Topic*	*Theory*	*Method*	*Sample*	*Strengths*[a]
1931	Davis	Women's employment	None	Census	N.A.	
1933	Popenoe	Family power	None	Interview	2,596	S
1936	Kirkpatrick	Trends in attitude	None	Questionnaire	553	I

[a] S = sample; I = importance.

The Decade 1940–1949

Only one of the eleven articles identified was not able to be located and reviewed. Six of the ten articles were empirical research. These six studies dealt with the dating behavior of men and women, the roles family members played in social participation, gender roles and cultural conflict, and legal rights of married women.

Research Findings

Carter (1941) examined the attitudes of men and women regarding appropriate dating behavior. Females were more forceful than males in expressing their attitudes of approval or disapproval. Both females and males approved more of the male who dated many women than the male who dated only one woman. Both men and women thought it was improper for a man to get engaged frequently, object to a woman wearing shorts, and urge women to smoke. Of all the behaviors disapproved of by women, the worst was a man who became engaged frequently. Although men mildly disapproved of a man's kissing a woman on the first date, women strongly disapproved of this behavior. Both men and women disapproved of a woman's asking a man to go on a date with her. Contrary to popular opinion, men were more concerned than women about keeping homes clean and in order.

Seward (1945) administered a questionnaire to 147 female psychology students to assess their attitudes toward feminine roles in various aspects of social life. She compared liberals and conservatives with respect to performance on Kirkpatrick's Feminism-Antifeminism scale, the Terman-Miles' masculinity-femininity test, Maslow's inventory of dominance feeling, and the College Board Scholastic Aptitude test. She searched the backgrounds of her subjects for possible differences within the areas of family and sex relationships as well as religion.

Seward found that both liberal and conservative females favored equality between men and women in educational and vocational opportunities, working conditions, community activities, and social contacts. She also found that women expected equality in the jurisdiction of family property and in the solution of family problems. However, women said marriage was based on a need for love and for social and material security, did not feel free to propose marriage, did not want to retain their maiden names after marriage, expected their husbands to support them, and wanted to stop paid employment after the birth of a child. The liberal women conformed less to established mores and were less secure emotionally. The conservative women had more brothers and were more religious than the liberals.

Komarovsky (1946) studied 153 college women and observed that they were exposed to two contradictory roles, "feminine" and "modern." According to the feminine role, women were expected to be less dominant and aggressive than men, as well as more emotional and sympathetic. The modern role was more egalitarian and demanded similar attitudes and behaviors of women and men. The conflict between these two roles centered around vocational plans, excellence in specific fields, and social life. The main sources of inconsistency between the ideal of being a homemaker and that of being a career woman were family and male friends. Forty percent of the women reported they had "played dumb" on dates by concealing their academic honors, pretending they were ignorent of some subject, or permitting men to have the last word in an intellectual conversation.

Patrick (1946) used records from Germany, Great Britain, Sweden, the Soviet Union, and the United States to compare women's legal rights. Women in the Soviet Union had the most legal rights, while women in Germany had the least. Women in the United States, Great Britain, Sweden, and the Soviet union could make contracts and own and control their own property, and they had guardianship over their children. In Germany husbands had absolute authority over their wives and wives' property, children, and household. In Sweden and the Soviet Union both spouses had equal responsiblity to support the family financially, while in the United States, Great Britain, and Germany, this was the husband's responsibility.

The Decade in Review

Theory and Methodology. During this decade, functionalism emerged as a systematic approach to study gender roles. More experimental and analytical studies were conducted during the 1940s than during the previous decade, and methodology improved. The study of Seward (1945) was the most sophisticated of the decade. Using various means of control, she conducted an experiment on 147 subjects and used chi square to analyze the data. (See table 10–2.)

Key Studies and Findings. The study by Patrick (1946) was important because it examined the legal rights of women in five countries. Women in Germany had the fewest legal rights, while women in the Soviet Union, Sweden, Great Britain and the United States could make contracts, dispose of their own property, and have legal guardianship of their children. In all five countries, husbands had the legal obligation to support their families, although in Sweden and the Soviet Union, wives and husbands were equally responsible for financial support.

Komarovsky (1946) identified the contradictions college women faced between the emerging modern and the traditional feminine roles and observed that women viewed themselves at as equals to men, although they were expected to act inferior intellectually. This study was widely quoted and replicated during later decades.

Table10–2
Overview of Research on Gender Roles in the Family, 1940–1949

Year	*Author*	*Topic*	*Theory*	*Method*	*Sample*	*Strengths*[a]
1945	Seward	Attitudes	Psychology	Questionnaire	147	
1948	Fernberger	Attitudes	None	Experiment	271	
1941	Carter	Dating	None	Questionnaire	N.A.	
1943	Anderson	Social participation	None	N.A.	1,176	
1946	Komarovsky	Role conflict	None	Case study	153	I
1946	Patrick	Legal rights	None	Records	N.A.	I

[a] I = importance.

The Decade 1950–1959

The issue of gender roles produced more research studies during the 1950s than during the 1930s of 1940s. Of the thirty-three pieces identified, three were not accessible. Of the thirty studies retrieved, fourteen were empirical research conducted mostly on middle-class college students. Some of the major topics studied were role expectations, women's employment, division of labor, marital conflict, and marital adjustment.

Research Findings

Marital Quality. Utilizing role theory, Ort (1950) interviewed fifty young couples to examine how marital role expectations were related to marital happiness. He found that the more unmet role expectations there were, the lower was the marital happiness; husbands reported more unrealized role expectations for themselves than did wives; husbands experienced more conflicts from unrealized role expectations than wives; and both husbands and wives revealed more conflicts from unrealized role expectations for themselves than for their spouses.

Lu (1952) investigated the relationship between marital adjustment and dominant, egalitarian, and submissive marital roles. He collected data from 603 white, middle-class couples who lived in Chicago. In one-third of the couples, the husband was more dominant, in one-third the spouses were egalitarian, and in one-third the wife was more dominant. Couples who exhibited egalitarian gender roles had higher marital adjustment than couples in which one spouse was dominant.

Buerkle and Badgley (1959) hypothesized that couples who were receiving counseling for their marital problems would display significantly less role-taking ability than religious couples whose marriages were not in trouble. Data were collected from 222 married couples; 36 were troubled marriages receiving counsel at the Margaret Sanger Research Bureau in New York City, and 186 were stable marriages attending meetings of their religion-affiliated couples' clubs in New Haven. Spouses from troubled couples displayed significantly less reciprocal role-taking patterns than spouses from nontroubled couples.

Hobart and Klausner (1959) studied empathy, communication, marital role disagreement, and marital adjustment among fifty-nine college couples and found that communication and marital role empathy were positively related to marital adjustment. Spouses who were more empathic were less likely to experience role disagreement; however, no relation was found between role disagreement and marital adjustment.

Jacobson (1952) tested the hypothesis that divorced couples exhibited greater disparity in their attitudes toward the roles of the husband and wife in marriage than did married couples. Using records from divorced and married couples in Chillicothe, Ohio, Jacobson randomly selected and interviewed 200 divorcees and 200 married persons. The data supported the hypothesis. Divorced women were more egalitarian than their former husbands, while married women tended to be similar to their husbands but somewhat less egalitarian.

Gianopulos and Mitchell (1957) studied 134 marriages to determine the extent to which a husband's approval of his wife's employment influenced marital conflict. They classified their participants into three groups: those in which the wife worked and the husband disapproved, those in which the wife worked and the husband approved, and those in which the wife did not work. They found support for their hypothesis. Spouses in the group in which the wife worked and the husband disapproved perceived more areas of conflict between them than did spouses in either of the other two groups. Spouses in the group in which the husband approved of the wife's working perceived less conflict and more agreement among them.

Socialization. Komarovsky (1950) used a functionalist theoretical orientation to study gender role socialization among 20 middle-class, married women who were college students. Women with brothers reported that their parents tended to speed up the emancipation of sons from the family and slow it for daughters. Sons had more opportunities for independent action, a higher degree of privacy in personal matters, and a more relaxed code of filial and kinship obligations. These differential patterns of gender socialization were considered functionally oriented to their adult roles of husband-provider and mother-homemaker. However, Komarovsky reported that the differential training of the sexes had a "latent dysfunction." The strong ties women developed with their family of orientation made it difficult for them to adjust psychologically and socially to marriage.

Wallin (1950) replicated Komarovsky's (1946) study on incompatible gender roles of college women. The sample was 163 unmarried females who were undergraduates at a university in the United States. A substantial proportion of college women felt that occasionally they were called upon to pretend they were inferior to men, although they viewed themselves as being equal or even superior to men. He also found contradictions between many women and their parents regarding how they should spend their time in college.

Hartley and Klein (1959) described the gender role concepts of thirty-eight elementary school children from the upper-middle class. Contrary to popular beliefs of the time, the children had explicit ideas about appropriate behaviors of men and women, and their ideas tended to be traditional and congruent with adult expectations. Girls accepted for themselves the role behaviors they perceived in women and anticipated implementing these behaviors in their own adult lives. They rejected role behaviors characterizing men. Girls whose mothers were homemakers had more traditional views toward gender roles than girls whose mothers were employed. Girls tended to assign child-care tasks more to women, but boys tended to assign these tasks to both sexes.

McKee and Sherriffs (1959) examined gender role stereotypes among 200 single men and women. The women believed that, from men's point of view, the ideal female was markedly sex typed. Men felt, from the women's point of view, that both male and female characteristics were equally desirable. When asked to describe the ideal man, women used both "male" and "female" characteristics. Men were more likely than women to describe the ideal women using favorable female characteristics rather than favorable male characteristics. The women's real self was more sex typed and less favorable than the men's ideal self, but the women's ideal self was less sex typed than the men's. The authors concluded that the differences between the real and ideal selves were due to changing attitudes regarding gender roles and the dual socialization given to women.

Marital Roles. Rose (1951) studied the marital role expectations of 256 sociology students. He hypothesized that the role expectations of women would be more ambiguous than the men's. Rose found that there was a lack of consistency, definiteness, and realism in the adult role expectations of the women. Women were not as career oriented as the men and desired more children. Upon marriage, the women planned to give up their paid employment and devote most of their time to household tasks and raising children. Although women expected to participate in as many spare-time activities and join as many organizations as men upon finishing college, they expected to engage in more social-, group-, and service-oriented activities than did men. Women were unrealistic in that they expected to do more than their time permitted them to.

Heath (1958) studied the gender division of labor in subsistence activities of 556 cultures. Heath observed that the involvement of women in economic activity was related to the mode of production in a society.

Decision Making. Kenkel and Hoffman (1956) analyzed the decision making of twenty-five couples during a hypothetical task. Each couple was asked how they would spend a gift of $300. Neither husbands nor wives were able to identify who did the more talking, contributed more ideas and suggestions, and kept the conversation going smoothly.

The Decade in Review

Theory and Methodology. The study of gender roles in the family was significantly improved over previous decades. A majority of the studies used some type of theoretical framework. Interviews and questionnaires were the most frequently used methods of data collection, and most sample sizes were greater than 100. Analysis techniques such as correlation, factor analysis, and difference of means tests began to be used. Perhaps the biggest methodological limitation of the decade was that most samples consisted of white, middle-class, young respondents and were not chosen randomly. (See table 10–3.)

Table 10–3
Overview of Research on Gender Roles in the Family, 1950–1959

Year	*Author*	*Topic*	*Theory*	*Method*	*Sample*	*Strengths*[a]
1950	Ort	Marital quality	Role theory	Interview	100	T,I
1952	Lu	Marital quality	None	N.A.	1,206	S,I
1959	Buerkle and Badgley	Marital quality	Role theory	Questionnaire	444	
1959	Hobart and Klausner	Marital quality	Role theory	Interview	118	
1950	Komarovsky	Socialization	Functional	Case study	20	I
1950	Wallin	Socialization	None	Questionnaire	163	
1959	Hartley and Klein	Socialization	None	Questionnaire	38	
1959	McKee and Sherriffs	Socialization	Role theory	Other	200	I
1951	Rose	Role expectations	Role theory	Questionnaire	256	
1952	Jacobson	Role conflict	Role theory	Interview	400	I
1956	Kenkel and Hoffman	Decision making	None	Content analysis	50	
1957	Gianopulos and Mitchell	Wife's employment	Social perception	Interview-S	268	
1958	Heath	Division of labor	Functional	Other	556	
1958	Weiss and Samuelson	Self-worth	None	Interview	569	

[a] S = Secondary data.

[b] S = sample; T = use of theory; I = importance.

Key Studies and Findings. Lu (1952) conducted a pioneering study on family power and found that egalitarian marriages were more satisfying than either husband-dominant or wife-dominant marriages. The study by Jacobson (1952) was one of the most sophisticated of the decade. Random sampling, linear correlations, and difference of means tests were used to compare 200 divorced and 200 married couples. The divorced couples had more disparity than the married couples in their conceptions of gender roles in marriage. Divorced women were more egalitarian than their former husbands, and married women tended to be somewhat more traditional toward gender roles than their husbands.

Several interesting studies explored gender role socialization of men and women. Komarovsky (1950) documented differences in the way sons and daughters are socialized and suggested that this may be functional for some adult roles but dysfunctional for marital adjustment. Wallin (1950) identified contradictions women face in their adult roles, while Mckee and Sheriff (1959) observed that the real self is more sex typed and unfavorable for women than men. Although the 1950s is often described overall as a period of stability, the research suggests that changes in gender roles were taking place and produced contradictions and ambiguities in the roles of women.

The Decade 1960–1969

The 1960s produced substantially more literature on gender roles than any previous decade. Some of the major topics studied were division of labor, employment of women, marital satisfaction, and family decision making.

Research Findings

Division of Labor. Blood and Wolfe (1960) interviewed a random sample of 909 married women living in Detroit to study the division of labor among the couples. Husbands were much more involved than wives in repairs, lawn care, and shoveling snow. Wives were much more involved in cooking, doing dishes, and house cleaning. Handling the finances tended to be egalitarian, although women were more heavily involved than the men. Husbands with high incomes tended to do less work around the house than middle- or low-income husbands. When the wife was employed, husbands tended to become more involved in traditionally feminine tasks such as cooking and cleaning. Overall, the authors found that the husbands specialized in the heavy, technical, outside tasks, while the wives were more heavily involved in inside housework and child care.

Hurvitz (1961) examined the husband-father and wife-mother roles of 104 middle-class couples. Both men and women expected their spouses to be companions and sexual partners. Child socialization, family decision making, and management of income were expected to be shared activities. Both spouses tended to expect the husband to be the provider of the family income, and the wife's employment was viewed as a supplement for times of financial need. The primary role of the wife was to take care of the home and the daily needs of the children. It was expected that the husband would do yard work and repairs but not inside housework and child care except when the wife was ill.

Joseph (1961) assessed the attitudes toward marriage and work among 600 adolescent females in England. Data were obtained through autobiographical essays and questionnaires. Most of the girls said homemaking was the primary vocation they would carry on throughout their married lives. They viewed full- or part-time employment as a secondary activity they would engage in only if there were no children in the home.

Haavio-Mannila (1967) examined the gender role expectations and performance of a random sample of 550 Finnish men and women. Although most Finnish females were highly educated and frequently engaged in paid employment, a traditional gender division of labor existed in most families. Husbands were expected to get ahead in their careers, while wives were to take care of the home. The wives were relatively unsatisfied with the participation of their husbands in household tasks.

Pfeil (1968) interviewed a random sample of 1,000 young adults from Hamburg, West Germany, to study role expectations and role behaviors of young adults entering marriage. Although the traditional view of men as being providers and women as being homemakers predominated, both men and women tended to favor and practice an equal partnership marriage. Women were expected to limit their employment during the early years of marriage, particularly when small children were in the home. Most husbands approved of their wives' working when there were economic needs.

Harrell-Bond (1969) studied the segregation of conjugal roles in eighty-five families in England. Most partners shared their domestic duties and financial arrangements. In smaller-size households, there was more sharing of domestic chores and child care.

Employment of Women. Axelson (1963) investigated the attitudes of 152 husbands toward working wives and the association of the wife's employment with the husband's marital adjustment. Compared to husbands of employed women, husbands of nonemployed women were more likely to view employment of the wife as a threatening situation, have less egalitarian attitudes, state that their wives should not work except in an emergency, believe that mothers should not work until the children complete high school, and say that employment of women interferes with their role as companion to their husbands. Marital adjustment tended to be higher among husbands of nonemployed women than among husbands of employed women.

Kosa and Coker (1965) studied the role conflicts experienced by a sample of 525 physicians, 5 percent of them women. Because of role conflicts, the women physicians were more likely than the men to defer marriage, interrupt their work career, take part-time positions, and change positions. It was also difficult for female physicians to accept some aspects of the physician role that were not compatible with the traditional female role, such as being self-employed. To reduce role conflict, women tended to practice in specialties that were more compatible with the traditional female role, such as pediatrics, public health, and psychiatry.

Angrist (1966) studied the gender role attitudes of 188 single women who were attending college and 192 married women who had graduated from college and had at least one child. The employed married women were less traditional in their gender role attitudes than the unemployed married women. Similarly, the single women who desired employment were less traditional in their gender role attitudes than the single women who wanted to be homemakers. There were no differences between the homemakers and employed women in their attitudes about husband-wife relationships.

There was a common belief during this decade that the economic status of women was improving as more women became employed. Knudsen (1969) analyzed U.S. Census data from 1940 to 1964 and found women's relative socioeconomic status had actually declined. Compared to men, women had experienced a gradual and persistent decline in their occupational, economic, and educational achievements.

Decision Making. Blood and Wolfe (1960) examined the power and authority among 909 couples in Detroit, Michigan. Their hypothesis—that the power to make decisions in marriage depends on the comparative resources of the husband and wife—became known as the resource theory of marital power. They also suggested that marital power is influenced by the norms regarding who ought to decide. They asked their respondents who made the decisions in eight common areas and who usually gave in when there was a disagreement. They found that a majority of marriages were egalitarian. The husbands usually made decisions regarding his job and the car, while wives were more involved in decisions regarding food, medical care, and her employment. Decisions regarding what house to buy and where to go on vacation tended to be joint. Insurance decisions tended to be egalitarian, although there was more husband than wife involvement. When there were disagreements, the wives tended to give in to their husbands somewhat more than husbands gave in to their wives, although an egalitarian compromise was the most common outcome. Decision making was found to be influenced by the comparative resources of husband and wife, as hypothesized.

Burchinal and Bauder (1965) compared Iowa farm and urban spouses in regard to their relative dominance in family decision making and task performance. In a majority of families, decision making was egalitarian. There were no consistent differences between the urban and farm families in decision making.

Marital Quality. Blood and Wolfe (1960) also examined the relationship between gender roles in the family and marital satisfaction. They found that egalitarian marriages tended to be more satisfying than other types of marriages. When the husband and wife were equal in education, they had higher satisfaction than couples in which one spouse had more education than the other. Marital satisfaction was substantially higher in couples who made decisions together (syncratic) than those in which one spouse dominated. Marital satisfaction was lowest when decisions were dominated by the wife and only somewhat higher when they were dominated by the husband. When couples were egalitarian but did not make decisions together (husbands decides in some areas while the wife decides in other areas), marital satisfaction was higher than in husband- or wife-dominant marriages but considerably lower than in syncratic marriages. And marital satisfaction tended to increase as the number of shared household tasks increased.

Kotlar (1965) compared the attitudes toward gender roles of fifty satisfied and fifty unsatisfied couples. The satisfied couples were more likely to perceive that they and their spouse had similar attitudes regarding gender roles in marriage.

Socialization. Kammeyer (1966, 1967) studied how birth order was related to gender role attitudes of 232 single women who were college students. Compared to later-borns, women who were first-borns were more likely to have traditional attitudes toward gender roles, choose marriage over graduation from college, agree with their parents on gender role attitudes, and be religious. Kammeyer also observed that females with older brothers had less traditional gender role attitudes than females without older brothers.

Papanek (1969) studied socialization into gender roles by examining 486 adolescents and 201 of their parents. When the authority roles of husbands and wives were highly differentiated, there also tended to be more gender differentiation in the roles of the children. Fathers of families experiencing high marital role differentiation were less likely to encourage their daughters to be achievers and had more difficulty expressing their feelings to them.

The Decade in Review

Theory and Methodology. One of the major advances during the 1960s was the use of theory to guide research on gender roles. Most of the studies used some type of conceptual framework—usually role or symbolic interaction theory. Most of the researchers used questionnaires or interviews to collect their data. Sample sizes were larger than in previous decades, and more random samples were used. (See table 10–4.)

Key Studies and Findings. The major study of the decade was conducted by Blood and Wolfe (1960), who examined the division of labor, marital power,

Table10–4
Overview of Research on Gender Roles in the Family, 1960–1969

Year	*Author*	*Topic*	*Theory*	*Method*	*Sample*	*Strengths*[a]
1960	Blood and Wolfe	Division of labor	Resource	Interview	909	S,M,T,I
1961	Hurvitz	Division of labor	Functional	Interview	208	
1967	Haavio-Mannila	Division of labor	None	Interview	550	S,I
1968	Pfeil	Division of labor	None	Interview	1,000	
1968	Tharp et al.	Division of labor	Functional	Interview	250	
1969	Harrell-Bond	Division of labor	None	Interview	170	
1969	Mowrer	Division of labor	Role	Interview	1,200	
1969	Parker and Kleiner	Division of labor	Functional	Interview	2,913	
1961	Joseph	Women's employment	None	Questionnaire	600	
1963	Axelson	Women's employment	Functional	Questionnaire	152	
1965	Kosa and Coker	Women's employment	Role theory	Questionnaire	525	S,I
1966	Angrist	Women's employment	Role	Questionnaire	420	
1961	Buerkle, Anderson, and Badgley	Marital quality	Role	Questionnaire	444	
1965	Kotlar	Marital quality	Interaction	Questionnaire	200	
1967	Kammeyer	Socialization	None	Questionnaire	232	
1969	Papanek	Socialization	None	Qustionnaire	687	
1968	Strodtbeck and Creelan	Family size	Psychological	Questionnaire	572	
1965	Burchinal and Bauder	Family power	Functional	Interview	N.A.	
1969	Knudsen	Female status	Functional	Census	237,256	S,M,I
1965	Schmitt	Status congruence	None	Questionnaire	153	
1965	Wise and Carter	Homemaker role	None	Questionnaire	216	
1966	Kammeyer	Birth order	None	Questionnaire	232	

[a]S = sample; M = measurement; T = use of theory; I = importance.

and marital quality among a large, random sample of married women. Their study was a benchmark that stimulated considerable research during the 1970s. The research by Kosa and Koker (1965) was important because it examined family conflicts faced by women professionals.

Several scholars observed that the division of labor in marriages continued to be traditional; men were expected to be the primary providers, while women took care of the house and children. Even when women were employed, they remained primarily responsible for child care and housekeeping. Haavio-Mannila (1967) found that although most Finnish females were highly educated and engaged in paid employment, they still experienced a rigid division of labor by gender at home.

Blood and Wolfe (1960) reported that the majority of marriages were egalitarian in terms of decision making, and egalitarian marriages were more satisfying than those dominated by one spouse. Similarly, couples who participated in household tasks together were happier than those with segregated role responsibilities.

Kosa and Coker (1965) observed the role conflict faced by female physicians, which caused them to defer marriage, interrupt their career, or take part-time positions. Although attitudes about gender roles remained rather traditional during the 1960s, there was an increase in female employment, and employed women had less traditional attitudes about gender roles in the family. Still, Knudsen (1969) found that from 1940 to 1964, women's occupational, economic, and educational achievements declined relative to men.

The Decade 1970–1979

During the 1970s, gender became an important social issue. In 1971 the U.S. Supreme Court ruled that gender discrimination violated the equal protection clause of the Fourteenth Amendment (*Reed v. Reed*). After *Reed*, a series of Supreme Court decisions outlawed many existing laws that treated men and women differently. The equal rights amendment (ERA) passed both houses of Congress in 1972 and became the focus of much debate. A number of other laws were passed to eliminate gender discrimination, including Title IX of the Educational Amendments (1972), the Equal Credit Opportunity Act (1975), and the Pregnancy Discrimination Act (1978). In 1974 Executive Order 11375 mandated affirmative action to increase the employment opportunities of women and minorities. Research on the division of labor and female employment expanded, and there continued to be research on gender role socialization and marital power. A review of gender role research was conducted by Hochschild (1973).

During the decade, sixty-one empirical studies were identified. Division of labor, marital power, and wife's employment were the three most popular topics.

Research Findings

Trends. Roper and Labeff (1977) assessed the attitudes toward feminism of 282 students and their parents and compared their responses with data obtained by Kirkpatrick (1936) from 553 students and their parents. In both surveys, women were more egalitarian than men, and students were more egalitarian than their parents. The data showed a general trend toward egalitarian attitudes from 1936 to 1974; however, both generations were more egalitarian with regard to the economic and legal status of women than the domestic role of women.

Parelius (1975) compared the gender role attitudes of a sample of 147 women college students in 1969 and a sample of 200 in 1973 and found a marked shift toward feminism over the four-year period.

Ichilov and Rubineck (1977) gathered questionnaire data from fifty-three lower-class Israeli girls ages 16 to 18. They were asked about their own gender role attitudes and the role allocation in their families of orientation. The patterns they desired in their own lives were more egalitarian than the patterns existing in their families of origin. The girls expected that their husbands would share responsibility for raising children, school contacts, and family finances. Compared to their mothers, the girls desired to marry later and have fewer children and were more committed to working outside the home. Nevertheless, they viewed household chores, such as cooking and cleaning, as the woman's responsibility.

Albrecht, Bahr, and Chadwick (1979) studied 759 married couples at different points in the life cycle to determine changes in gender roles. The provider role had become egalitarian, and there was a trend toward greater involvement of men in child care, although wives continued to do most of this work. There was no evidence of change in the housekeeper or kinship roles. Decision making in the child care role was more likely to be shared among young couples, who were more supportive of nontraditional modes of sharing the provider, housekeeper, and child care roles.

Lopata (1971) studied 571 housewives and observed a trend to egalitarian attitudes over three generations. Husband-wife relationships were described as closer and more democratic than in previous generations, and wives had become more like an equal partner with the husband in the marriage.

Division of Labor. The topic that received the most attention during the 1970s was division of labor in the family. In the study by Lopata (1971), 571 married women were interviewed about the division of household work. Forty-one percent of the women said their husbands provided some help with cooking and dishes. Forty-seven percent of the women stated that their husbands never helped in household tasks such as making beds and dusting. Cooking, dishes, laundry, and cleaning were tasks largely done by the wives. The bills and money tended to be handled by the husband. Child care and shopping for food were women's tasks, but a substantial minority of husbands were involved. Twenty percent of the women said that she and her husband did the food shopping together, and another 12 percent said she received help from her husband. About one-fourth of the women indicated significant husband involvement in child care.

Nye (1976) obtained data on attitudes and behavior in family roles from a sample of 210 married couples in Washington. Almost half the men and women felt that the provider role should be shared by the wife, although it was considered to be primarily the man's responsibility. Over half of both men and women said that housekeeping should be a shared responsibility, although it was viewed primarily as the woman's responsibility. Care of children was seen as somewhat more the wife's than the husband's responsibility, but socialization of children was considered to be as much the father's as the mother's responsibility. Behavior was found to be less egalitarian than attitudes. About two-thirds of the men said they should share in household tasks, but only one-half actually helped with the housework. In attitude, the socialization role was the most egalitarian, while behaviorally it was dominated by women.

Berk and Berk (1979) studied the division of labor of 750 American households with a husband and wife. The wives were interviewed twice a week apart and kept a 24-hour time diary over a random day. About half of the husbands were also interviewed. The presence of young children affected the women much more than the men. The wives usually washed, dressed, fed, and talked to the children, while the husbands did a small amount of talking to and playing with the children. The wife's employment or the presence of children had little effect on the morning activities of the men; in the evening, about a third of the husbands did after-dinner chores and watched the children. The wives typically carried most of the burden for housework and child care, even when employed full time.

Fogarty, Rapoport, and Rapoport (1971) studied 865 men and women who had graduated from British universities in 1960. A majority of both men and women preferred a division of labor where the wife did most of the cooking, cleaning, and child care. It was accepted that the wife's career would be secondary to the husband's career. The actual division of labor was consistent with their attitudes. Women performed most of the cooking, cleaning, child care, and food shopping. The men did minor repairs, and budgeting, gardening, arranging social activities, and clothes shopping tended to be joint activities.

Incongruence between attitudes and behavior was the subject of a study of more than 1,000 husbands and wives studied by Araji (1977). Although both men and women expressed egalitarian attitudes regarding the performance of family roles, women did the majority of tasks in all of the roles except the provider role, which was performed mainly by the men. More women than men expressed egalitarian attitudes toward family roles.

Using a representative national sample of 1,575 employed persons, Pleck (1979) reported that employed wives averaged 31 hours per week in housework compared to 15 among employed husbands. Husbands with children under age 18 spent about 20 hours per week in child care compared to 33 hours for employed wives. Husbands of employed wives spent about 2 hours more per week in housework and 3 hours more per week in child care than did husbands with nonemployed wives. Although this increment was not large, it showed that men became somewhat more involved in housework and child care when their wives were employed outside the home.

Ericksen, Yancey, and Ericksen (1979) interviewed more than 1,700 households in Philadelphia and found that the higher the husband's income, the less likely it was that family roles would be shared. The higher the education of the wife, the more likely it was that the family roles would be shared. Black couples were more likely to share roles than white couples.

Scanzoni (1975) sampled 3,100 households in the northeast United States and found that blacks were more egalitarian than whites in gender role behavior but less egalitarian in gender role attitudes.

Mason and Bumpass (1975) examined women's gender role attitudes among a national sample of over 6,000 ever-married women. They found that women's attitudes toward gender roles were not organized around a single dimension. One dimension was their attitudes about women's labor market rights, and another was their attitudes about the division of labor between men and women. Women tended to be egalitarian regarding women's rights in the labor force but supported a traditional domestic division of labor based on beliefs about the needs of children and women.

In a study of 480 college students, Osmond and Martin (1975) examined gender role attitudes of men and women. Both men and women tended to be most traditional regarding family roles and most modern in macrosocial change issues.

Employment of Women. Although some of the research already cited on division of labor included information on women's employment, it did not focus on it. In this section, we examine research that focused directly on the employment of women and how it affects families.

Szinovacz (1977) interviewed 1,370 Austrian women who were employed. She found that reliance on help from relatives was related to role segregation between the spouses and concluded that the woman's employment does not necessarily result in the development of egalitarian role relations between the spouses.

Safilios-Rothschild (1970) collected data from 549 nonemployed and 347 employed women in Athens, Greece. Women with high work commitment were more satisfied in their marriage than women with low work commitment. The high-commitment women perceived themselves as having more freedom and decision-making power than women with low work commitment.

Several studies suggest that gender role attitudes influence the employment of women. Scanzoni (1979) reported that women favoring traditional patterns of family roles were less oriented toward occupational involvement, while women preferring greater role interchangeability became more active in the labor force. Fine-Davis (1979) found that employed women compared to nonemployed women were less traditional in gender role attitudes and less likely to perceive that women were inferior to men. Spitze (1978) used a national sample of 5,000 women ages 14 to 24 to study how employment affects gender role attitudes. She found that the experiences of paid employment, occupational training, and college attendance before marriage altered the taste for employment but did not affect gender role attitudes. In a study of 469 husbands, Brown (1970) found that the probability of the wife's employment increased as the attitude of the husband toward her employment became more favorable.

Burke and Weir (1976) compared personality characteristics of 189 one- and two-career couples. The housewives were more passive in relating to others than the employed wives, and the husbands of housewives were more active than husbands of employed wives. The dual-career couples also had lower needs for social interchange in the areas of affection and control.

Poloma (1970) studied educated, professional women and observed that family demands and the husband's career impinged on the practice of the women's profession. Nearly all of these women did not have a career in the same sense as their male colleagues because the traditional role of wife and mother was important in their role constellation.

Marital Power. Marital power and decision making were important research topics during the 1970s. Larson (1974) studied marital power among more than 500 couples and their children. Most respondents perceived family power as egalitarian. Both mothers and fathers attributed more power to themselves than to their spouses. Sons and daughters tended to assign more power to the father than the mother.

Christenson (1970) conducted a laboratory study of reward, expert, and legitimate power among fifty couples. He found that in a crisis situation husbands with legitimate power resisted attempts to be replaced as leader, even though he had no solution to crisis the couple was facing. Christenson suggested that marital power might be more resistant to change than power in other groups.

Bahr (1977) studied attitudes toward marital equality and the women's movement among 2,000 respondents. A favorable attitude toward the women's movement had a positive association with education of the wife, income of the wife, and number of children. These variables, however, had little effect on attitudes toward marital equality.

The resource theory of family power was a frequent topic of study during the decade. Lewis (1970) interviewed husbands and wives from fifty families in the southern Appalachians and received questionnaires from 1,077 sixth-grade children from the area. Although coal miners usually had more resources than their wives, they made few family decisions and scored low on family power. Contrary to resource theory, coal mining fathers were not dominant and participated less in family activities than fathers from other families in the area.

Gillespie (1971) reanalyzed published data and concluded that resources that provide power are denied to women. Therefore, differences in marital power are due to discrimination against women in the larger society and not to individual resources as predicted by the resource theory of family power.

Fox (1973) studied the marital power of 803 married women in Turkey. She found that the absolute power of the husband diminished when either the husband or the wife came in contact with modern egalitarian ideas through education. Her findings suggested that education and egalitarian ideals affected marital power more than relative resources did.

Another examination of resource theory was conducted by Richmond (1976). She interviewed 120 wives and 30 husbands from intact, exile families in Miami, Florida. She found that the wife's individual resources were less important in determining power than the joint effects of the dyad's resources and the adherence to an egalitarian ideology.

Szinovacz (1978) used a sample of 1,370 employed Austrian women to test the normative resource theory. She found that the social status of the couple but not the relatively resources of spouses was related to marital decision making.

Data supportive of resource theory were reported in a study of 334 college women by Vanfossen (1977). The relative occupation and educational resources of the father and mother were related to their perceived power within the family.

Studies of couples in different classes and ethnic groups produced results inconsistent with common stereotypes. Cromwell and Cromwell (1978) interviewed 274 Anglo, black, and Chicano couples to study decision making and conflict resolution. The data did not support the stereotype that black families were matriarchal or that Chicano families were patriarchal.

Similarly, McCurdy (1978) studied 256 Anglo, black, and Chicano couples. Anglo couples were not more egalitarian than the other couples, and the adherence to traditional role relationships was not associated with male dominance in decision making. All three types of couples tended to report an egalitarian marital power structure.

Dietrich (1975) studied 525 black families and found that wife dominance did not exist in attitudes or in actual decision making. Husbands were heavily involved in decision making in a majority of the families.

Finally, Hawkes and Taylor (1975) interviewed seventy-six women in Mexican and Mexican-American farm labor families. Husband dominance and wife submission were much less common than often assumed.

Socialization. A number of studies have explored how socialization in the family influences gender roles. Rosen and Aneshensel (1976) obtained questionnaires from 3,049 teenagers in upstate New York. Girls who were more traditional in their sex role attitudes were more likely to have had parents who were restrictive and controlling and emphasized interpersonal relationships.

Tomeh (1978) collected data from 642 college students in Ohio on gender role orientation. Having a mother and a father with nontraditional attitudes and behaviors was related to more modern gender role attitudes among the respondents. And Meier (1972) noted that college students tend to have more egalitarian attitudes if their mothers have some individual achievements.

Cronkite (1977) used data from 681 families in the Denver Income Maintenance Experiment. Earnings by the wife were associated with less traditional gender role attitudes among both spouses. Both spouses adjusted according to the attitudes of the spouse, implying that each spouse is a strong socializing agent for the other. The husband's preferences did not dominate the wife's.

Fertility and Gender Roles. Scanzoni (1976a) examined the birth intentions of 754 never-married undergraduates at a large midwestern university. Students who were more modern in their gender role attitudes and more favorable toward female employment had lower birth expectations.

In another study of fertility, Scanzoni (1976b) examined the intended and desired births among a sample of 157 couples. The wife's education, egalitarian marriage, and the positive reaction of the husband toward her job were all negatively correlated with the number of intended births.

Wicks and Workman (1978) obtained questionnaires from about 200 never-married undergraduates at a private, Catholic university. They found that those with more traditional gender role attitudes tended to plan for an earlier marriage and first birth.

The Decade in Review

Theory and Methodology. During the 1970s, there was a large increase in research on gender roles in the family (table 10–5). Although most of the research was not based on an explicit theory, most had a set of hypotheses with an implicit theoretical orientation. The most popular theory was the resource theory of family power, which a number of studies tested and refined. A few studies were based on exchange theory, and many were implicitly based on assumptions from role theory (symbolic interaction).

Sample sizes tended to be rather large; several of the samples were over 1,000. Many of the studies used unrepresentative samples, but several used national probability samples. Statistical techniques varied widely, although multivariate testing of models was relatively common.

Key Studies and Findings. The research demonstrated that gender role attitudes had become more egalitarian. However, attitudes were more egalitarian than behavior. The most popular research topic was the division of labor within the family. There was evidence that men had become somewhat more involved in child care and housework, but women still performed most of the household tasks, even if they were employed full time. Women had more egalitarian attitudes than men. Most couples perceived that they were egalitarian in their relationships. Research did not support the stereotype that black couples tend to be dominated by the wife or that Chicano couples are dominated by the husband.

The research tended not to support the resource theory of family power. Marital power and decision making were influenced more by education of the partners, egalitarian ideology in the culture, and the joint resources of the couple than by the comparative resources of the individual partners.

The study by Roper and Labeff (1977) was important because it demonstrated a trend toward egalitarian attitudes across several decades. Berk and Berk (1979) did the most thorough and intensive study of division of labor in the family. They used time diaries to document division of labor in the family. Pleck (1979) compared the hours that men and women spend in domestic labor and compared dual- and single-earner couples. Mason and Bumpass (1975) used a national sample to show that gender role attitudes are not a single dimension. They found that attitudes toward women's rights in the labor force were separate from attitudes about domestic roles. Attitudes toward women's domestic roles were more traditional than attitudes toward women's involvement in roles external to the home. This finding helped explain the rather traditional division of labor within the family, though attitudes had become more egalitarian.

The Decade 1980–1989

During the 1980s, a large amount of research was conducted on gender roles in the family; we identified 128 empirical studies on this topic. Atkinson (1987) and Thompson and Walker (1989) reviewed the extensive research that had accumulated and made recommendations for needed improvements in conceptualization and methodology.

Research Findings

Trends. One of the major questions addressed by scholars was change in gender role attitudes. Using three national data sets, Thornton (1989) examined changes from about 1960 to 1985. The data sets he used were the General Social Survey (N = 1,500), an annual survey of high school seniors (N = 6,000), and the Study of American Families (N = 867). Thornton reported that for both men and women, gender role attitudes became much more egalitarian between

Table 10–5
Overview of Research on Gender Roles in the Family, 1970–1979

Year	*Author*	*Topic*	*Theory*	*Method*	*Sample*	*Strengths*[a]
1973	Holmstrom	Trends	None	Interview	286	
1975	Touba	Trends	None	Interview	216	
1975	Parlius	Trends	None	Questionnaire	347	
1977	Ichilov and Rubineck	Trends	None	Questionnaire	53	
1977	Roper and Labeff	Trends	None	Questionnaire	568	I
1977	Schlesinger	Trends	None	Interview	N.A.	
1979	Albrecht, Bahr, and Chadwick	Trends	None	Questionnaire	1,518	M,I
1971	Lopata	Division of labor	Role	Interview	571	M,I
1971	Fogarty, Rapoport, and Rapoport	Division of labor	Developmental	Questionnaire	865	S
1972	Holmstrom	Division of labor	None	Interview	20	
1975	Scanzoni	Division of labor	None	Interview	3,100	S
1976	Stafford, Backman, and Dibona	Division of labor	None	Questionnaire	113	
1976	Nye	Division of labor	Exchange	Questionnaire	210	M,T,I
1978	Thrall	Division of labor	None	Interview	198	
1978	Osako	Division of labor	None	Interview	33	
1979	Ericksen, Yancey, and Ericksen	Division of labor	None	Interview	1,780	S
1979	Pleck	Division of labor	None	Interview	1,027	
1979	Berk and Berk	Division of labor	Economic	Interview	750	S,S,T,I
1970	Poloma	Division of labor	None	Interview	53	I
1973	Rice	Division of labor	None	Questionnaire	130	
1975	Hawkes and Taylor	Power	None	Interview	76	
1975	Dietrich	Power	None	Interview	525	S
1978	McCurdy	Power	None	Questionnaire	256	
1978	Cromwell and Cromwell	Power	None	Interview	274	
1970	Lewis	Power	Resource	Questionnaire	1,077	T
1978	Szinovacz	Power	Resource	Questionnaire	1,370	S,T,I
1976	Richmond	Power	Resource	Interview	120	T
1973	Fox	Power	Resource	Interview	803	St,T
1971	Gillespie	Power	Resource	N.A.	N.A.	T

1970	Christensen	Power	Exchange	Experiment	50	M,T
1974	Larson	Power	None	Questionnaire	571	
1975	Duberman and Azumi	Power	None	Interview	521	
1970	Campbell	Power	None	Questionnaire	1,242	
1972	Epstein and Bronzaft	Attitudes	None	Questionnaire	1,063	
1975	Mason and Bumpass	Attitudes	None	Interview	6,740	S.M.I
1975	Osmond and Martin	Attitudes	None	Questionnaire	480	
1977	Araji	Attitudes	Role	Questionnaire	1,154	S
1979	Mueller	Attitude	None	Interview	1,257	S,I
1977	Bahr	Attitudes	Exchange	Questionnaire	2,005	
1987	Russell and Rush	Attitudes	None	Questionnaire	320	
1987	Bridges	Attitudes	None	Experiment	322	
1983	Tomeh and Gallant	Attitudes	None	Questionnaire	415	
1977	Brown, Perry, and Harburg	Attitudes	None	Interview	253	
1972	Meier	Socialization	None	Interview	219	
1978	Tomeh	Socialization	None	Questionnaire	642	
1977	Cronkite	Socialization	Role	Interview	681	S
1978	Balkwell, Balswick, and Balkwell	Socialization	Role	Questionnaire	1,190	
1976	Rosen and Aneshensel	Socialization	None	Questionnaire	3,049	
1977	Vanfossen	Socialization	None	Questionnaire	334	
1971	Arnott	Socialization	Congruency	Questionnaire	NA	
1977	Szinovacz	Wife's employment	None	Interview	1,370	S
1979	Scanzoni	Wife's employment	None	Interview	427	M
1979	Fine-Davis	Wife's employment	None	Interview	240	
1970	Brown	Wife's employment	None	Questionnaire	469	
1978	Siperstein	Wife's employment	None	Questionnaire	150	
1978	Spitze	Employment	Economic	Interview	5,000	S,M,T,I
1976	Burke and Weir	Employment	None	Interview	378	M
1970	Safilios-Rothschild	Work commitment	None	Interview	896	
1972	Kando	Role strain	Role	Interview	34	
1977	Balswick and Avertt	Expressiveness	None	Questionnaire	523	

[a] S = sample; M = measurement; St = statistics; T = use of theory; I = importance.

1960 and 1985. The changes were particularly striking during the 1960s and 1970s, while there was less change during the 1980s.

Several other scholars documented similar changes. Weeks and Botkin (1987) examined marriage role expectations of female students at the University of Kentucky from 1961 to 1984. The 1978 and 1984 groups were significantly more egalitarian than the 1961 group. There was no difference between the 1978 and 1984 groups.

Tallichet and Willits (1986) examined the gender role attitudes of a sample of 294 young women. The women completed questionnaires in 1970 and again in 1981. Their attitudes became more egalitarian over the eleven-year period. Education, employment, income, and mother's education were all positively associated with more egalitarian attitudes.

Dambrot, Papp, and Whitmore (1984) compared forty-three female college students, their mothers, and their maternal grandmothers on attitudes toward women. Of the three groups, the students were the least traditional and the grandmothers the most traditional. Profeminist attitudes were negatively correlated with age and positively correlated with education.

Several scholars reported that a trend toward egalitarian attitudes also occurred in other countries. Long (1987) examined family change in Japan and reported increases in the education and employment of married women and greater equality among couples. Husbands of employed wives did slightly more housework than husbands of nonemployed wives, and employed wives had greater input in family decisions than wives who were not employed.

In a study of 183 Dutch families, Tavecchio and co-workers (1984) observed a trend toward egalitarianism, particularly in the higher socioeconomic strata. Yao (1987) studied 341 women in fourteen Taiwanese villages and found that attitudes and household division of labor had become more egalitarian. Women's education and employment had increased with attitude changes, but most household tasks continued to be performed by women. Counihan (1988) reported an increase in employment among Italian women but noted that most employed women tried to maintain their roles as administrators of the home and family. Because of time and identity conflicts, they had difficulty maintaining both roles and were losing some of their traditional influence over the children and family.

Although attitudes became more egalitarian during the 1980s, behavioral changes in family roles appeared to be small. Coverman and Sheley (1986) compared samples of married men taken in 1965 (N = 541) and in 1975 (N = 371). Over the ten-year period, there were no significant changes in the average amount of time husbands spent in housework and child care. However, men with young children devoted somewhat more time to child care in 1975. The data did not support the idea that men's and women's family roles were converging.

Sex Ratios and Gender Roles. One of the important studies during the decade was Guttentag and Secord's (1983) *Too Many Women?* They used exchange theory to explain the effect of imbalanced sex ratios on gender roles. They noted a decrease in the sex ratio between 1960 and 1970. Among unmarried men and women of marriageable age, the number of men to 100 women decreased from 93 in 1960 to 67 in 1970. They hypothesized that this undersupply of men would decrease the willingness of men to commit themselves and would make sexual freedoms more advantageous to men than to women. The persistence of such circumstances would leave many women hurt and angry and impel them to seek more power in society. In short, they theorized, the imbalance in the sex ratio would lead to later marriage, more divorce, more single-parent families, and more unwed births and would help stimulate a movement toward gender equality. Existing data were consistent with their theory.

South and Trent (1988) tested and refined the theory of Guttentag and Secord. Using a sample of 117 countries, they found that the expected correlations between sex ratio and women's roles tended to exist when the level of socioeconomic development was controlled. The effect of sex ratio on women's roles was more pronounced in developed than developing countries.

In another extension and test of the theory, South (1988) hypothesized that the influence of imbalanced sex ratios on women's roles was contingent on women's economic power. He tested the theory using data from 111 countries. High sex ratios (undersupply of women) were positively associated with the proportion of women who married and the fertility rate and inversely associated with age at marriage and the divorce rate. When sex ratios were low (undersupply of men), marriage and fertility rates tended to be low, while age at marriage and divorce tended to be high. However, when women's labor force participation was high, the correlations were considerably weaker. South concluded that women's economic power may counteract the tendency for high sex ratios to preserve women's traditional roles.

Social Characteristics and Gender Roles. A variety of scholars identified some of the social characteristics associated with various gender role attitudes and behaviors. In general, women, the young, and the highly educated had more egalitarian attitudes than men, the old, and the less educated.

Quarm (1983) used National Opinion Research Center data from 1974 through 1978 to examine gender role attitudes. Age and education were significant predictors of gender role attitudes. Gender differences were larger for items pertaining to caring for children than for items pertaining to women's roles in the public sphere.

Morgan and Walker (1983) examined the gender role attitudes of a national sample of 1,522 women. Consistent with predictions from exchange theory, women with traditional attitudes were older and less educated and had lower incomes and lower feelings of personal competence than women with more egalitarian attitudes.

Mirowsky and Ross (1987) interviewed 680 married couples and found that more husbands than wives believe in innate gender role differences. They also found mutual socialization in that each partner's beliefs directly influenced the other's beliefs.

Plutzer (1988) hypothesized that various aspects of women's family and work life would influence their attitudes toward gender roles and support for feminist issues such as approval of abortion and the equal rights amendment. Using data from the General Social Survey from 1977 through 1985, Plutzer found consistent support for her hypotheses. Women's attitudes were consistently more feminist when they were divorced, never married, childless, employed, had a high income, and were committed to work; however, the correlations tended to be small. Variables such as education, religion, race, and age were better predictors of gender role attitudes than family and work situations.

Morgan (1987) surveyed 318 college women and found that religious devoutness was negatively correlated with egalitarian gender role attitudes. Self-esteem, mother's employment, and mother's education tended to be positively associated with egalitarian attitudes, although the correlations were smaller and less consistent than the correlations between devoutness and gender role attitudes.

Division of Labor. During the 1980s, division of labor continued to be the most frequently studied topic in the broad area of gender roles and the family. Early in the decade Miller and Garrison (1982) conducted a review of existing literature on the sexual division of labor. Because of the large volume of research on this topic, only a selected number of studies are reviewed here.

Geerken and Gove (1983) analyzed the division of labor among a national sample of 1,225 married couples. Regardless of the wife's employment status, she usually did most of the housework. Compared with husbands of housewives, husbands of employed wives spent slightly more time on housework and slightly less time on the job. The differences were very small, however. Overall, the time allocation of men was essentially the same whether or not their wives were employed. There were two major differences between dual-earner and single-earner families. First, women who were employed spent substantially less time on housework than women who were not employed. Second, women who were employed had significantly fewer hours for relaxation than women who were housewives. The more educated the husband was, the more he helped with the housework. Still, no matter what the family circumstances, it was the wife who did most of the household chores.

Pleck (1985) used two national surveys to study marital division of labor: the Study of Time Use, which obtained time diaries from 2,406 persons, and the Quality of Life Survey, which collected interviews from 1,515 individuals. Pleck found that employed wives did much more household work than employed husbands and that the employment of the wife had little impact on the overall amount of housework performed by men. Low family participation by the husband led the wife to be dissatisfied with the division of labor.

Although there was this imbalance, men were doing more housework and child care in 1981 than in 1965.

Using a sample of 1,565 couples from the Panel of Study of Income Dynamics, Berardo and associates (1987) found that dual-career couples were not more egalitarian than other couples in their allocation of time to household labor. Wives performed about 79 percent of all the housework.

An analysis of data from 1,618 husbands and wives was conducted by Rexroat and Shehan (1987). Wives spent about 28 hours per week in housework compared to 5 hours for husbands. Women's housework time increased dramatically when they became mothers and increased somewhat until their oldest child entered school. Their hours were relatively stable until the children left home. Men's housework time increased modestly when they became fathers and then gradually declined over the life cycle.

Kamo (1988) explored factors that are associated with a husband's participation in domestic work using data from 3,649 couples from the American Couples Survey. The husbands did about 36 percent of the total domestic work. When the wife was employed full time the husband did an average of 41 percent of work, and this increased to 43 percent when the husband and wife earned the same amount of money. The amount of time husbands spent in domestic labor was positively associated with their education and egalitarian sex role orientations and negatively associated with their income. Also, the wife's level of earnings and egalitarian sex role orientation were positively associated with the husband's hours in housework.

Coverman and Sheley (1986) used data from two national surveys to examine change from 1965 to 1975 in men's housework and child care time. The final samples included 451 men in the 1965 survey and 371 men in the 1975 survey. For comparative purposes, they included data from 700 women from the 1965 survey and 441 women from the 1975 survey. Over the decade 1965–1975, there was no change in men's time in housework or child care, while they had a decrease in paid work time and an increase in leisure time. For the women there was a significant decrease in housework time and in paid work time, no change in child care time, and a significant increase in leisure time. Overall, men performed about one-fourth of all housework and child care in 1975. The total time in housework, child care, and paid work was somewhat higher for men than women. However, men's time in domestic work was not significantly different for men whose wives were employed than for men whose wives were not employed.

Condran and Bode (1982) interviewed 316 married adults in Middletown to determine domestic division of labor. Women were not usually responsible for household repairs or for disciplining children, while they were primarily responsible for other types of domestic work. Overall, men did not participate a great deal in tasks defined as domestic labor. There was a discrepancy between the perceptions of husbands and wives; husbands believed that they helped more than wives thought husbands helped.

Rosenthal (1985) extended our knowledge of domestic labor by examining kinkeeping among 458 adults in Canada. A kinkeeper is someone who works at keeping family members in touch with each other. Rosenthal found that kinkeeping was primarily a female activity that persists over time. Being a kinkeeper was frequently passed from mother to daughter.

Finley (1989) examined gender differences in caring for elderly parents. Data were obtained from a telephone survey of 325 adults who had living mothers over age 70. Caregiving of elderly parents was an activity that was dominated by women, even after other variables were controlled. Women were more involved in caregiving even after time demands were taken into account. Men who felt responsible to care for their elderly parents did not fulfill that responsibility to the extent that comparable women did. In every task, women did more than men. Neither time availability, attitudes toward obligation, nor external resources accounted for gender differences in caregiving.

Similar findings on division of labor have been found in a number of other subcultures and cultures. Broman (1988) found that black women were almost twice as likely as black men to feel overworked by household chores. Lupri and Symons (1982) examined data from eleven nations and reported that in both capitalist and socialist countries, employed wives do more housework than employed husbands. According to Dahlstrom and Liljestrom (1982) and Haas (1981), the egalitarian gender role ideology of Sweden seemed to have little influence on domestic division of labor. They found a continuing pattern in which men perform less housework and child care than women. In the Soviet Union, women's employment was not accompanied by changes in domestic work patterns (Junusbajev, 1985; Lapidus, 1988). Finally, in India employed women continued to do most of the housework and child care (Sethi, 1989).

The studies reviewed to this point suggest that the wife's employment has relatively little effect on the involvement of the husband in domestic work. In this section we review some of the research on characteristics associated with greater involvement of men in household labor. Using data from 244 couples, Seccombe (1986) found that gender role attitudes affected division of labor. The more spouses subscribed to nontraditional values regarding gender roles, the more likely they were to share housekeeping chores.

In an analysis of a national sample of 1,360 husbands and wives, Ross (1987) found that husbands with less traditional gender role beliefs and who were well educated were more involved in housework than husbands with less education or more traditional beliefs. In addition, the smaller the gap was between the husband's and wife's earnings, the greater was the husband's involvement in housework.

Barnett and Baruch (1987) found that predictor of the father's involvement in household work varied according to the mother's work status. In dual-earner families, the number of hours the wife worked per week was the strongest predictor of father's involvement in domestic work. Among these families, gender role attitudes were also important predictors of the father's household involvement. Among single-earner families, the father's attitude toward fathering was a consistent predictor of his involvement.

Bird, Bird, and Scruggs (1984) studied division of labor among 166 couples. The higher the income and job status of the wife, the more likely was the husband to be involved in housekeeping and child care. For men, having an egalitarian gender role orientation had an important influence on their involvement. In addition, having an employed wife was associated with more sharing of child care.

Marital Power. During the 1980s, there continued to be tests of resource theories of marital power. Rank (1982) studied influence on employment decision making among 375 couples with young children. They found that differences in conjugal resources were not related to influence. The greater were the wife's resources, the greater was her influence over her employment decision making. The greater were the husband's resources, the less was his influence over the wife's employment decision making. The data supported an exchange theory of marital decision making.

Shukla (1987) studied family decision making among 100 families in India. The husbands in single-career families had greater power than the husbands in dual-career families. Wives in dual-career families had greater power than wives in single-career families. Dual-career families were more egalitarian than single-career families. The findings were supportive of resource theory.

Brown (1983) examined decision-making patterns in thirty-three dual-career couples, forty-eight dual-worker couples in which both spouses were workers, thirty-two dual-worker couples in which the wives worked and the husbands were engaged in a career, and eighty-four couples in which the husband was employed and the wife was a homemaker. Compared to the other couples, dual-career couples shared more in decision making, were less sex typed in their decision making, and made more "very important decisions" together. Husbands in dual-career couples won fewer conflicts than their wives or a comparison group of husbands.

Sexton and Perlman (1989) used questionnaires as well as an observational task to study gender roles and marital power. Their sample contained fifty dual-career couples and fifty single-career couples. Although dual-career partners made more attempts to influence than single-career partners, the two types of couples did not differ in their perceived power or in self-reported strategies for influencing spouses. Gender role orientation did not predict marital power, and both types of couples demonstrated an ideology of gender equality. Perceived equity did not predict marital power differences.

Cooney and associates (1982) tested the theory of resources in cultural context among 100 intergenerationally linked families from Puerto Rico. In the parent generation, husbands with higher economic achievements had less power than husbands with lower economic achievements. This may be explained by the fact that higher achievers were socialized to more modern values. In the child generation, husbands with higher economic achievements had more power than husbands with lower economic achievements. This was explained by greater power resources obtained by high achievers among the child generation

Giles-Sims and Crosbie-Burnett (1989) examined the power of adolescents in eighty-seven stepfather families. They tested the normative-resource theory of power. Mothers had more power in major and daily decisions than did adolescents or stepfathers. There was greater adolescent power when the adolescent had alternatives to living with and receiving support from the stepparent. Ongoing financial support and contact with the noncustodial parent were resources that served as power bases. Stepfathers gained power by supporting the adolescent financially.

Marital Quality. One of the important issues is how gender role attitudes and behavior are associated with marital quality. Li and Caldwell (1987) examined this question among seventy-three couples. They divided their couples into four groups: (1) traditional husband–traditional wife, (2) traditional husband–egalitarian wife, (3) egalitarian husband–traditional wife, and (4) egalitarian husband–egalitarian wife. The couples with the highest marital satisfaction were the egalitarian husband–traditional wife, followed by the traditional husband–traditional wife. The lowest marital quality occurred when the husband was traditional and the wife egalitarian.

Two similar studies were conducted by Bowen and Orthner (1983) and Bowen (1989). In the first study, Bowen and Orthner examined gender role congruency and marital satisfaction among a sample of 331 couples in the U.S. Air Force. They found only partial support for the hypothesis that couples with congruent gender role attitudes would have higher marital quality than couples with incongruent gender role attitudes. The lowest marital quality occurred among couples in which the husband was traditional and the wife egalitarian.

In the second study Bowen (1989) found that the more egalitarian the husband was relative to his wife, the greater was the husband's marital quality. However, gender role attitudes were not predictive of the wife's marital quality and not strongly predictive of the husband's marital quality. Research by Linn (1983) and Bueche (1981) was consistent with these findings in that couples that were more egalitarian and shared decision making tended to be happier.

Lueptow, Guss, and Hyden (1989) reported, however, that a modern gender role ideology was negatively correlated with the marital success of women. Using data from the General Social Survey from 1974 to 1986, nontraditional women were less happy and more likely to be separated or divorced than traditional women.

Nicola (1980) tested Scanzoni's role interchangeability theory among sixty-nine couples. The data did not support the theory that role interchangeability would increase marital satisfaction. Wives with high career commitment were less satisfied than other wives, and role overload appeared to be one reason for the dissatisfaction.

These data suggest that two related factors may affect marital quality: the degree to which the gender role attitudes of husbands and wives are similar and the degree to which the gender role attitudes are egalitarian. The research indicates that, other things being equal, egalitarian attitudes tend to be positively associated with marital quality, and congruency of gender role attitudes is associated with marital quality. Some of the conflicting data appear to be the result of *other things not being equal.* That is, couples may be congruent in their attitudes but may face strain because of norms and structural factors that do not support egalitarian attitudes. And if one spouse is egalitarian and one is traditional, this will tend to reduce happiness.

Other research indicates that imbalances in power and household work tend to hurt marital satisfaction. Mirowsky (1985) interviewed a random sample of 680 married couples and found that each spouse is least depressed if marital power is shared. Yogev and Brett (1985) reported that marital satisfaction was higher when marital division of labor was shared. Using data from 148 couples, Benin and Agostinelli (1988) found that an equitable division of labor and the husband's sharing of traditional household chores were associated positively with marital satisfaction. Broman (1988) observed that married, employed persons who do most of the housework are less satisfied than employed persons who have a spouse who shares in household work. Other research has shown that being in a dependent, powerless role tends to produce stress (Horwitz, 1982), while androgynous gender role orientation tends to be associated with more coping strategies (Patterson and McCubbin, 1984).

Work and Family Roles. Bielby and Bielby (1989) examined how men and women form and balance work and family identities. Time out of the labor force eroded family identities for men but not for women, while having an employed spouse increased family identity for women and decreased work identity for men. Married working women gave precedence to family in balancing work and family, while married men had the discretion to build identification with work and family roles without trading off one against the other. Nevertheless, married men who took on the family responsibilities of the typical working wife formed family identities that were not much different from their female counterparts. The overall process of commitment to family and work roles appeared similar for both men and women. Bielby and Bielby concluded that gender differences in commitment to family and work are due to inequality in the household division of labor and to segregation at the workplace. As work and family roles become more equal, they predicted, women's work identity and men's family identity are likely to increase.

Although men are much less involved in household work than women, Pleck (1985) observed that the majority of men are more psychologically involved in their families than in their jobs. This contradicts that common belief that the essential role for men is their job. Cohen (1987) interviewed thirty Boston men to examine the assumption that the male role centers on work. He found that becoming a husband and father had a significant effect on most men and that they tended to have greater attachments to marriage and fatherhood than is usually assumed.

Gerson (1986) conducted in-depth interviews with sixty-three women to study how men influence the work and family choices of women. She identified two basic types of women: domestic and nondomestic. More than 60 percent of the domestic women had entered adulthood with career aspirations but had become traditional over time. Four factors influenced their choice of domesticity. First, most were in committed heterosexual relationships, which meant commitment to the male career, even among those who were employed. Second, they did not experience severe economic problems. Third, about 90 percent encountered blocked mobility at work and turned to domestic pursuits for fulfillment. Fourth, they experienced pressure to bear children, and this provided an escape from the labor force and an alternative source of fulfillment.

The nondomestic women were faced with very different social constraints. First, almost two-thirds experienced unstable, dissatisfying heterosexual relationships. The recognition that a man would not always be there to depend on prompted the development of increased self-reliance and the postponement or rejection of marriage and motherhood. Second, many moved away from domesticity when men's earnings failed to meet family needs. In short, most nondomestic women did not receive male economic and social support for domesticity. Some of the nondomestic women chose childlessness because they felt it was difficult to get men involved in parenting. The nondomestic women who chose parenthood tended to have male partners who wanted children, would help with parenting, and supported their partner's career.

Class and Status. In the research already reviewed, employment was explored as it relates to division of labor and power. In this section, we review some of the research that deals directly with occupational achievement and its relationship to family roles.

Coltrane (1988) studied how father involvement with his children is related to the status of women. Using data from the *Ethnographic Atlas,* he found that father involvement with children had a positive association with female status in a society. When fathers were more affectionate and involved in routine child care, females were more involved in community decision making and had more positions of authority.

One important status issue is the gender gap in earnings. Shelton and Firestone (1988) analyzed how household labor time was related to the male-female wage gap using data from 996 respondents from the Study of Time Use. The found that time spent in household labor was associated with the gender gap in earnings; that is, one reason that women earn less than men is that they spend more time in domestic labor. Although this factor was more important than any other single characteristic they examined, it accounted for only a small part of the gender wage gap.

England and co-workers (1988) also examined the issue of sex segregation and wages using data from the young women's and young men's cohorts of the National Longitudinal Survey (N = 10,000). They found evidence of pay discrimination against both men and women who were employed in predominantly female occupations.

Class identification has received some attention in recent years. Beeghley and Cochran (1988) explored how gender role attitudes affected class identification among employed married women. They found that employed married women with traditional gender attitudes used only their husband's characteristics in their class identification. Employed married women with egalitarian attitudes used both their own and their husband's characteristics in determining their class position.

Stevens (1986) explored how gender influences intergenerational occupational mobility. Using data from the Canadian National Mobility Study (N = 9,624), he found that the influence of fathers' occupations was greater than the influence of mothers' occupations. There was a tendency for sons and daughters to enter the occupation of their same-sex parent, and this was more pronounced for sons. Even with these differences, the influence of mothers' and fathers' occupations on their children was similar.

Atkinson and Boles (1984) examined couples in which the wife was occupationally superior to her husband. They interviewed forty-six individuals from thirty-one different marriages they labeled "wives as senior partners" (WASP). Three conditions existed among the WASP marriages: wives had traditionally male jobs, the husbands had flexible jobs, and there was an absence of children. Although the WASP marriages were costly to the couples because they were perceived as deviant, there were also some unique benefits. Wives received household and emotional support from their husbands and the opportunity to achieve. Husbands obtained freedom from responsibility to provide and were able to engage in risky, less remunerative occupational pursuits.

Socialization. Lueptow (1980) explored parental influence on gender role socialization of 5,600 seniors. Most often the adolescents were influenced by both parents, but when they perceived influence by only one, it was most often the same-sex parent. Both males and females tended to perceive the higher-status parent as influential. There was no evidence that patterns of gender role socialization had changed from 1964 to 1975.

Stephan and Corder (1985) studied how dual-career families affected the gender role attitudes of 327 high school students. Adolescents from dual-career families held more egalitarian gender role attitudes than adolescents from traditional families. This included having more favorable attitudes toward women working—the females from dual-career families desired to work, and the boys aspired to have wives who would work.

In a study of seventy-four pairs of mothers and daughters, Smith and Self (1980) found that the mother's attitudes were more important predictors of daughters' attitudes than the mother's occupational status. Similarly, Baruch and Barnett (1986) observed that the mother's attitude was the strongest predictor of gender stereotyping among 160 children. The involvement of the father in family work was only weakly related to gender role attitudes.

Kiecolt and Acock (1988) used the General Social Survey to study how family structure was related to gender role attitudes. Adults from intact and nonintact families held similar views concerning gender roles. Women whose mothers had been employed had more eglitarian attitudes than women whose mothers had not been employed. Among the men, their mother's employment status was not associated with their gender role attitudes.

Fertility and Contraception. During the 1980s there were only a couple of studies on gender roles and fertility. MacCorquodale (1984) obtained data from 1,367 single persons in a midwestern city and found a positive association between eglitarian attitudes and the belief that contraception use and responsibility should be shared. This relationship was stronger among men than women. Among women there was a positive association between egalitarian attitudes and the frequency of contraceptive use. Men with egalitarian attidues reported more frequent and more effective contraceptive use than traditionally oriented men.

Shea (1983) explored the relationship between voluntary childlessness and involvement in the women's movement. Questionnaires were obtained from 257 women who had graduated from an eastern state university. Women with pro-feminist attitudes were less likely to have had a child and less likely to desire a child in the future. However, the relationship was not strong, and a majority of the women expected to have at least one child regardless of their involvement in the women's movement.

The Decade in Review

Theory and Methodology. About one-third of the studies used some type of explicit theoretical framework to guide the research. The most common theory was some form of exchange theory, although resource theory and role theory were also commonly used theoretical frameworks. (See table 10–6.)

A large majority of the scholars used questionnaires or interviews to collect their data. There were only a few observational studies or experiments. One of the important trends during this decade was the use of large, national data sets such as the General Social Survey, the National Longitudinal Survey, and the Panel Study of Income Dynamics. Fifteen of the studies had samples larger than 10,000 and twenty-six had samples greater than 1,000.

Almost all of the studies used some type of statistical significance test to compare groups. The use of analysis of variance, multiple regression, and LISREL was common.

The most popular topic of the decade was division of labor; one-third of the studies explored some aspect of this topic. Other topics were trends in gender role attitudes and behavior, the effect of gender roles on marital quality, and marital power.

A number of noteworthy studies were conducted during the decade. Thornton (1989) documented a significant trend toward more egalitarian gender role attitudes between 1960 and 1985. There were relatively small changes in the amount of household work by men, although they did more in the 1980s than in previous years (Pleck, 1985). Estimates of total amount of housework performed by men varied between 15 and 36 percent (Berardo et al., 1987; Kamo, 1988; Li and Caldwell, 1987; Rexroat and Shehan, 1987). When men in two-and one-earner families were compared, there was virtually no difference between them in time spent in household work. When the total time in domestic and employed work was combined, there was little difference between married men and married women (Coverman and Sheley, 1986). Two significant differences between dual-earner and single-earner families were that women in dual-earner families spent significantly less time in housework and in leisure (Geerken and Gove, 1983). Two characteristics that were associated with male involvement in household work were education and egalitarian attitudes.

Marital satisfaction tended to be higher when attitudes were egalitarian and when the attitudes of husband and wife were congruent. The lowest level of marital satisfaction was among traditional men married to egalitarian women (Li and Caldwell, 1987).

Children who came from dual-career families tended to have more egalitarian attitudes than children from single-career families (Stephan and Corder, 1985). Gender role attitudes were shaped significantly by the happiness and stability of heterosexual relationships and the economic status of those relationships (Gerson, 1986).

Married women who were employed tended to give precedence to the family in balancing work and family demands, while married men were not required to trade one off against the other in building work and family identities. Nevertheless, the process of gaining work and family identities was similar for men and women; men who took on family responsibilities were not much different from their female counterparts who were employed and had family responsibilities (Bielby and Bielby, 1989).

Guttentag and Secord (1985) demonstrated an association between an undersupply of men and egalitarian attitudes, divorce, and unwed births. South (1988) extended their theory by showing that female economic power counteracted the tendency for high sex ratios to preserve women's traditional roles.

Four studies during the decade appear particularly significant. Thornton (1989) documented changes in gender role attitudes. Geerken and Gove (1983)

Table10–6
Overview of Research on Gender Roles in the Family, 1980–1989

Year	*Author*	*Topic*	*Theory*	*Method*	*Sample*	*Strengths*[a]
1989	Thornton	Trends	None	Questionnaire	9,000	S,M,St,I
1987	Weeks and Botkin	Trends	None	Questionnaire	326	
1984	Dambrot, Papp, and Whitmore	Trends	None	Questionnaire	129	
1987	Long	Trends	Life course	Census/surveys	N.A.	
1987	Yao	Trends	None	Questionnaire	341	S
1984	McBroom	Trends	None	Questionnaire	800	
1984	Tavecchio et al.	Trends	None	Questionnaire	183	
1988	Counihan	Trends	None	Life history	15	
1986	Tallichet and Willits	Trends	None	Questionnaire	294	
1981	Jackson	Division of labor	None	Questionnaire	208	
1983	Chai	Division of labor	None	Interview	26	
1988	Antill and Catton	Division of labor	None	Questionnaire	108	
1985	Pleck	Division of labor	Role	Interview	3,921	S,M,T,I
1983	Geerken and Gove	Division of labor	Exchange	Interview	1,225	S,M,T,I
1987	Berardo et al.	Division of labor	None	Interview	1,565	S
1987	Rexroat and Shehan	Division of labor	Development	Interview	1,618	S
1988	Kamo	Division of labor	Exchange	Interview	3,649	S,M,St,I
1986	Coverman and Sheley	Division of labor	None	Interview	2,053	S,M
1982	Condran and Bode	Division of labor	Role	Interview	316	M,St,I
1988	Benin and Agostinelli	Division of labor	Exchange	Questionnaire	320	
1990	Grant et al.	Division of labor	None	Interview	204	
1982	Lupri and Symons	Division of labor	None	Census	N.A.	
1982	Dahlstrom and Liljestrom	Division of labor	None	Questionnaire	N.A.	
1981	Haas	Division of labor	None	Questionnaire	300	
1989	Sethi	Division of labor	Culture	Survey	N.A.	
1985	Junusbajev	Division of labor	None	Interview	500	
1988	Lapidus	Division of labor	None	Census	N.A.	
1988	Bromen	Division of labor	None	Interview	876	
1986	Seccombe	Division of labor	Resource	Questionnaire	488	

1987	Ross	Division of labor	None	Interview	1,360	
1987	Barnett, and Baruch	Division of labor	None	Interview	160	
1984	Bird, Bird, and Scruggs	Division of labor	None	Interview	332	
1986	Shamir	Division of labor	None	Questionnaire	285	
1988	Coltrane	Division of labor	None	Ethnography	N.A.	
1982	Condran and Bode	Division of labor	None	Questionnaire	316	
1984	Maret and Finley	Division of labor	None	Questionnaire	1,223	
1983	Linder	Division of labor	None	Questionnaire	170	
1984	Tavecchio et al.	Division of labor	None	Questionnaire	166	
1985	Denmark, Shaw, and Ciali	Division of labor	None	Questionnaire	20	
1986	Daley	Division of labor	None	Interview	20	
1988	Cowan and Cowan	Division of labor	None	Interview	94	
1987	Moen and Dempster-McClain	Division of labor	Role	Interview	224	
1983	Chai	Division of labor	None	Interview	26	
1986	Krausz	Division of labor	None	Questionnaire	130	
1985	Koopman-Boyden and Abbott	Division of labor	None	Questionnaire	137	
1988	Simpson, Wilson, and Young	Division of labor	None	Questionnaire	695	
1985	Stamp	Division of labor	None	Interview	32	
1988	Hill	Division of labor	None	Interview	150	
1980	Aneshensel and Rosen	Division of labor	None	Questionnaire	1,041	
1988	Haddad and Lam	Division of labor	None	Questionnaire	117	
1989	Voydanoff and Donnelly	Division of labor	Role	Interview	630	
1980	Hawkes, Nicola, and Fish	Division of labor	None	Interview	69	
1980	Lopata	Division of labor	Interaction	Interview	996	
1987	Ramu	Division of labor	None	Interview	980	S
1982	Rank	Power	Exchange	Questionnaire	375	T
1987	Shukla	Power	Resource	Questionnaire	101	
1983	Brown	Power	Exchange	Questionnaire	197	S
1989	Sexton and Perlman	Power	Exchange	Observation	100	M,I
1989	Williams	Power	None	Interview	520	
1982	Cooney et al.	Power	Resource	Interview	400	S,M,T,I
1989	Giles-Sims and Crosbie-Burnett	Power	Resource	Questionnaire	261	S,M,T,I
1989	Godwin and Scanzoni	Power	Exchange	Interview	376	T,I
1980	Austin and Porter	Power	None	Questionnaire	233	
1981	Yogev	Power	None	Questionnaire	106	

Table 10–6 continued

Year	*Author*	*Topic*	*Theory*	*Method*	*Sample*	*Strengths*[a]
1985	Hollus and Leis	Power	None	Obseration	40	
1989	Tashakori and Thompson	Power	None	Questionnaire	732	
1989	Kingsbury and Scanzoni	Power	Resource	Interview	51	
1987	Bokemeier and Maurer	Marital quality	None	Questionnaire	777	S
1987	Terry and Scott	Marital quality	Role	Questionnaire	89	
1982	Little	Marital quallity	None	Interview	75	
1988	Broman	Marital quallity	None	Interview	876	S
1988	Benin and Agostinelli	Marital quality	Exchange	Questionnaire	296	
1985	Yogev and Brett	Marital quality	Exchange	Questionnaire	478	
1980	Nicola	Marital quallity	Role	Interview	138	
1989	Lueptow, Guss, and Hyden	Marital quallity	None	Interview	2,761	S,I
1983	Linn	Marital quality	None	Questionnaire	181	
1981	Bueche	Marital quality	None	Questionnaire	196	
1989	Bowen	Marital quallity	None	Interview	1,856	S
1983	Bowen and Orthner	Marital quallity	None	Interview	662	S
1987	Li and Caldwell	Marital quality	None	Questionnaire	134	
1988	Kiecolt and Acock	Socialization	Role	Interview	10,056	S,I
1986	Baruch and Barnett	Socialization	None	Interview	160	
1980	Smith and Self	Socialization	None	Questionnaire	148	
1980	Lueptow	Socialization	Learning	Questionnaire	5,600	S,I
1985	Stephan and Corder	Socialization	Role	Questionnaire	948	I
1984	Weintraub et al.	Socialization	None	Observation	142	
1987	Oliveri and Reiss	Socialization	None	Questionnaire	228	
1985	Brody and Steelman	Socialization	None	Questionnaire	3,925	S
1982	Powell and Steelman	Socialization	Role	Interview	1,500	
1984	Tomeh	Socialization	Reference group	Questionnaire	659	
1988	Shelton and Firestone	Class and status	Human capital	Questionnaire	996	
1988	England et al.	Class and status	Human capital	Interview	14,000	S,M,St,I
1988	Beeghley and Cochran	Class and status	Class	Interview	1,610	

1986	Stevens	Class and status	Class	Interview	9,624	S,M,St,I
1984	Atkinson and Boles	Class and status	Exchange	Interview	46	I
1984	Corder and Stephan	Class and status	None	Questionnaire	948	
1976a	Scanzoni	Fertility	Role	Interview	754	
1976b	Scanzoni	Fertility	Role	Interview	154	
1978	Wicks and Workman	Fertility	None	Questionnaire	194	
1983	Shea	Fertility	None	Questionnaire	257	
1984	MacCorquodale	Fertility	None	Interview	1,376	S
1982	Davis and van den Oever	Sex ratios	None	Census	N.A.	
1983	Guttentag and Secord	Sex ratios	Exchange	Demographic	N.A.	S,M,T,I
1988	South	Sex ratios	Exchange	Demographic	111	S,T,I
1988	South and Trent	Sex ratios	Exchange	Demographic	117	S,T,i
1987	Maines and Hardesty	Work and family	Interaction	Interview	101	
1986	Gerson	Work and family	Role	Interview	63	T,I
1988	Beeghley and Cochran	Work and family	None	Questionnaire	1,500	
1988	Plutzer	Work and family	None	Questionnaire	1,500	S,I
1985	Kaufman	Religion	None	Interview	50	
1987	Morgan	Religion	None	Questionnaire	318	
1983	Hartman and Hartman	Religion	None	Questionnaire	458	
1986	Amatea et al.	Role expectations	None	Questionnaire	626	
1981	Christie	Role sharing	Conflict	Questionnaire	76	
1985	Rosenthal	Kinkeeping	Role	Interview	458	
1989	Finley	Caregiving	Role	Interview	325	
1984	Bassoff and McCubbin	Adjustment	None	Questionnaire	195	
1984	Patterson and McCubbin	Coping	None	Interview	84	
1985	Mirowsky	Depression	Equity	Interview	680	
1986	Goldsheider and Waite	Marriage	Exchange	Interview	10,000	S,M,St

[a] S = sample; M = measurement; St = statistics; T = use of theory; I = importance.

and Pleck (1985) conducted the most thorough examinations of division of labor in the family and were grounded in a theoretical perspective. Guttentag and Secord (1985) developed a creative theory of how sex ratios influence gender role attitudes and behavior.

Conclusions

Theoretical and Methodological Trends

During the 1930s and 1940s, there was almost no research on gender roles in the family. Only 9 studies were discovered from 1930 to 1950. From 1950 to 1970, a modest amount of interest was shown in this area; 41 studies were identified. During the 1970s and 1980s, a large amount of research was conducted on gender roles in the family. We have identified 61 empirical studies in the 1970s and 128 in the 1980s. Although we have tried to be comprehensive in our search, there undoubtedly are empirical studies we did not discover, and we limited our search to research on gender roles in the family. There is a vast literature on gender differences that makes no direct reference to the family.

Much of the research has described gender roles in the family or compared two groups (men versus women, dual earner versus single earner, previous time period versus later time period) without any explicit theoretical base. However, during the 1970s and 1980s, most studies had explicit hypotheses and at least an implicit theoretical framework. An increasing number of studies were based on an explicit theory—exchange theory most commonly. The resource theory of family power received considerable attention and refinement. Some version of symbolic interaction theory was fairly common. Other theories that occasionally appeared in the literature were conflict, equity, human capital, development, and social learning.

The methodological sophistication improved considerably over the sixty-year period from 1930 to 1989. Sample sizes became larger and more representative. During the 1980s, a number of studies used large, national probability samples. Several scholars used panel data over a considerable period of time. A large majority of the scholars used questionnaires or interviews to collect their data. Multivariate statistical techniques were often used to control for confounding variables and test theoretical models.

The major topic of study was division of labor in the family. Other important topics were trends in gender role attitudes and behavior, employment of women, marital power, quality of marriages, and gender role socialization.

Major Findings

1. From 1930 to 1990, there was a trend toward more egalitarian attitudes. Changes were striking between 1960 and 1980, with some moderating of changes during the 1980s.

2. From 1930 to 1990, family roles have become more egalitarian, with more wives working outside the home and more husbands helping in domestic work. However, behavior changes have been much less than attitudinal changes, and women continue to do most domestic labor.
3. Attitudes toward women's involvement in education, politics, and the labor force are more egalitarian than attitudes toward women's domestic role (care of house and children).
4. Behavior tends to be much less egalitarian than attitudes.
5. Women have more egalitarian attitudes than men.
6. The young have more egalitarian attitudes than the old.
7. Compared to husbands of nonemployed women, husbands of employed women perform somewhat more housework and child care; however, the difference is relatively small.
8. Husbands perceive that they do more housework than wives perceive that husbands do.
9. Regardless of their employment status, women in most countries tend to do a large majority of the housework.
10. Domestic chores tend to be segregated by gender. Women tend to do inside work such as cleaning, laundry, and child care, while men tend to do the outside work such as care of lawn and automobiles.
11. Women tend to do much more kinkeeping and care of elderly relatives than men, even after controlling for time constraints and felt responsibility.
12. Married women who are employed tend to spend less time in housework and in leisure activities than married women who are not employed.
13. Egalitarian gender role attitudes are positively associated with an egalitarian division of labor in the home.
14. When hours spent in employment and housework are combined, the total hours are about the same for married women and men.
15. Women tend to modify their employment (type of work, hours) because of family constraints. Men usually do not have to balance work against family constraints.
16. There is a negative relationship between amount of time in domestic labor and wages; the more time women or men spend in domestic labor, the lower are their overall wages.
17. Women tend to face role conflict between the feminine roles of being nurturant, supportive, passive, and domestic versus the expectation to achieve and be egalitarian.
18. A majority of men are more psychologically involved in their families than their careers.
19. Some of the characteristics of women that are positively associated with

egalitarian attitudes are education, employment, income, being divorced, having had an employed mother, being childless, and being never married.

20. Husbands who have egalitarian attitudes tend to be more involved in domestic work than husbands with traditional attitudes. Husbands with more education tend to have more egalitarian attitudes.
21. Couples in which the wife earns more than the husband tend to have the following characteristics: The wife tends to have a traditionally male job, the husband has a job with flexible hours, and they tend to be childless.
22. The more husband and wife gender role attitudes are congruent, the higher is their marital satisfaction. The least satisfying marriages are a traditional man married to an egalitarian woman.
23. The more egalitarian are the gender role attitudes of husband and wife, the higher is their marital satisfaction.
24. A low amount of husband involvement in domestic chores tends to be associated with low marital satisfaction for the wife.
25. A majority of couples in the United States perceive their marriages as egalitarian.
26. Compared to whites, blacks in the United States tend to be more egalitarian in behavior but less egalitarian in attitudes.
27. The status of women tends to be higher in societies in which the father is involved in child care than in societies where the father tends not to be involved in child care.
28. A low sex ratio (undersupply of men) tends to be associated with egalitarian gender role attitudes, low rates of marriage and fertility, and high rates of divorce, single-parent families, and abortion.
29. The comparative resources of husband and wife influence marital power, although this relationship is influenced by the norms of the society.
30. Egalitarian ideals, education and the joint resources of the couples are more predictive of marital power than the comparative resources of husband and wife.
31. Gender role attitudes are influenced by interpersonal and economic experiences in adulthood.
32. Domestic women tend to have had a committed, stable heterosexual relationship, no serious economic problems, and blocked career opportunities. Nondomestic women tend to have had unsatisfying heterosexual relationships and severe economic problems.
33. The gender role attitudes of adolescents are influenced more by the attitudes than the occupational status of their parents.
34. The mother's attitudes are more important for the gender role socialization of her children than her employment status.
35. Adolescents whose mothers are employed tend to have more egalitarian gender role attitudes than adolescents whose mothers are not employed.

36. Individuals with egalitarian attitudes tend to desire fewer children than individuals with traditional attitudes.
37. Egalitarian attitudes are associated with more frequent and effective use of contraception.

Future Research

From 1970 to 1990, there was an impressive growth in the quantity and quality of research on gender roles in the family. There are several areas where future research would be profitable. First, there needs to be continuing work on the conceptualization and measurement of gender role attitudes. It has often been assumed that gender role attitudes vary on a single dimension from traditional to egalitarian. There is some evidence that there is more than one dimension of gender role attitudes (Mason and Bumpass, 1975). Explorations into those dimensions and their correlations are needed.

Second, the relationship of gender role attitudes and marital quality needs additional study. The data indicate that egalitarian marriages tend to be more satisfying than relationships where one partner dominates, but there have been some contradictory data. For example, a couple of scholars have observed that egalitarian marriages may be less satisfying than traditional relationships. This is a complex phenomenon that requires an examination of the attitudes and behaviors of husband and wife, as well as the social context of their relationship.

Third, examination of attitudes and behaviors is needed. The data indicate that attitudes are more egalitarian than behaviors. Why is this so, and how does this influence family relationships? Despite rather large changes in attitudes, some scholars have observed that husband and wife behaviors have not been converging (Coverman and Sheley, 1986). Why not? What implications does this have for marriages?

Fourth, there have been relatively few examinations of how social structures influence gender roles in the family. One of the few recent studies in this area was Guttentag and Secord's (1983) analysis of how the sex ratio influences gender role attitudes and behaviors. There is a great need to expand and refine their work, as well as conduct other macro studies. Perhaps one reason for the dearth of research of this type is that micro theories have tended to dominate studies in marriage and the family, such as exchange and symbolic interaction theories. Gettentag and Secord (1983) bridged the gap between micro and macro theories, and more theorizing of that type seems worthwhile.

References

Albrecht, Stan L.; Bahr, Howard M.; and Chadwick, Bruce A. 1979 Changing family and sex roles: An assessment of age differences. *Journal of Marriage and the Family* 41:41–50.

Amatea, Ellen S.; Cross, E. Call; Clark, Jack E.; and Bobby, Carol L. 1986. Assessing the work and family role expectations of career-oriented men and women: The life role salience scales. *Journal of Marriage and the Family* 48:831–838.

Anderson, W.A. 1943. Family-member roles in social participation. *American Sociological Review* 8:718–720.

Aneshensel, Carol S., and Rosen, Bernard C. 1980. Domestic roles and sex differences in occupational expectations. *Journal of Marriage and the Family* 42:121–131.

Angrist, S.S. 1966. Role conception as a predictor of adult female roles. *Sociology and Social Research* 50:448–459.

Antill, John K., and Catton, Sandra. 1988. Factors affecting the division of labor in households. *Sex Roles* 18:531–553.

Araji, Sharon K. 1977. Husbands' and wives' attitude-behavior congruence on family roles. *Journal of Marriage and the Family* 39:309–320.

Aronoff, J., and Crano, W.A. 1975. A re-examination of the cross-cultural principles of task segregation and sex role differentiation in the family. *American Sociological Review* 40:12–20.

Arnott, Catherine Cameron. 1971. Commitment and congruency in the role preference of married women: an interpersonal approach. Ph.D. dissertation, University of Southern California.

Atkinson, Jean. 1987. Gender roles in marriage and the family: A critique and some proposals. *Journal of Family Issues* 8:5–41.

Atkinson, Maxine P., and Boles, Jacqueline. 1984. WASP (Wives as Senior Partners). *Journal of Marriage and the Family* 46:861–869.

Austin, Roy L., and Porter, Elaine. 1980. Adolescent perception of parental power in three Caribbean islands. *Social and Economic Studies* 29:247–263.

Axelson, L.J. 1963. The marital adjustment and marital role definitions of husbands of working and nonworking wives. *Marriage and Family Living* 25:189–195.

Bahr, Rosemary Frances Smith. 1977. The marital power structure and attitudes toward women's liberation and marital equality. Ph.D. dissertation, Washington State University.

Balkwell, Carolyn; Balswick, Jack; and Balkwell, James W. 1978. On black and white family patterns in America: Their impact on the expressive aspect of sex-role socialization. *Journal of Marriage and the Family* 40:743–747.

Balswick, Jack, and Avertt, Christine Proctor. 1977. Differences in expressiveness: Gender, interpersonal orientation, and perceived parental expressiveness as contributing factors. *Journal of Marriage and the Family* 39:121–127.

Barnett, Rosalind C., and Baruch, Grace K. 1987. Determinants of fathers' participation in family work. *Journal of Marriage and the Family* 49:29–40.

Baruch, Grace K., and Barnett, Rosalind C. 1986. Father's participation in family work and children's sex-role attitudes. *Children Development* 57:1210–1223.

Bassoff, Evelyn Silten. 1984. Relationships of sex-role characteristics and psychological adjustment in new mothers. *Journal of Marriage and the Family* 46:449–454.

Beeghley, Leonard, and Cochran, John. 1988. Class identification and gender role norms among employed married women. *Journal of Marriage and the Family* 50:719–729.

Benin, Mary Halland, and Agostinelli, Joan. 1988. Husbands' and wives' satisfaction with the division of labor. *Journal of Marriage and the Family* 50:349–361.

Berardo, Donna Hodgkins; Shehan, Constance L.; and Leslie, Gerald R. 1987. A residue of tradition: Jobs, careers, and spouses' time in housework. *Journal of Marriage and the Family* 49:381–390.

Berk, Richard A., and Berk, Sarah Fenstermaker. 1979. *Labor and Leisure at Home: Content and Organization of the Household Day.* Beverly Hills: Sage.

Bielby, William T., and Bielby, Denise D. 1989. Family ties: Balancing commitments to work and family in dual earner householders. *American Sociological Review* 54:776–789.

Bird, Gloria W.; Bird, Gerald A.; and Scruggs, Marguerite. 1984. Determinants of family task sharing: A study of husbands and wives. *Journal of Marriage and the Family* 46:345–355.

Blood, R.O. Jr., and Wolfe, D.M. 1960. *Husbands and Wives.* New York: Free Press.

Bokemeier, Janet, and Maurer, Richard. 1987. Marital quality and conjugal labor involvement of rural couples. *Family Relations* 36:417–424.

Boserup, E. 1970. *Women's Role in Economic Development.* New York: St. Martin's Press.

Bowen, Gary L. 1989. Sex-role congruency and marital quality revisited. *Journal of Social Behavior and Personality* 4:61–72.

Bowen, Gary Lee, and Orthner, Dennis K. 1983. Sex-role congruency and marital quality. *Journal of Marriage and the Family* 45:223–230.

Bridges, Judith S. 1987. College females' perceptions of adult roles and occupational fields for women. *Sex Roles* 16:591–604.

Brody, Charles J., and Steelman, Lala Carr. 1985. Sibling structure and parental sex-typing of children's household tasks. *Journal of Marriage and the Family* 47:265–273.

Broman, Clifford L. 1988. Household work and family life satisfaction of blacks. *Journal of Marriage and the Family* 50:743–748.

Brown, Prudence; Perry, Lorraine; and Harburg, Ernest. 1977. Sex role attitudes and psychological outcomes for black and white women experiencing marital dissolution. *Journal of Marriage and the Family* 39:549–561.

Brown, Sandra Zoe. 1983. The distribution of marital power in dual-career couples as measured by decision-making patterns. Ph.D. dissertation, University of North Carolina at Greensboro.

Brown, Stephen Ernest. 1970. Husbands' attitude toward and consequences of wife-mother employment. Ph.D. dissertation, Florida State University.

Bueche, Nancy Ann. 1981. Relationship of family employment status to husband and wife marital satisfaction and sex role preferences. Ph.D. dissertation, University of North Carolina.

Buerkle, J.V.; Anderson, T.R.; and Badgley, R.F. 1961. Altruism, role conflict, and marital adjustment: A factor analysis of marital interaction. *Marriage and Family Living* 23:20–26.

Buerkle, J.V., and Badgley, R.F. 1959. Couple role-taking: The Yale marital interaction battery. *Marriage and Family Living* 21:53–58.

Burchinal, L.G., and Bauder, W.W. 1965. Decision-making and role patterns among Iowa farm and nonfarm families. *Journal of Marriage and the Family* 27:525–530.

Burke, Ronald J., and Weir, Tamara. 1976. Some personality differences between members of one-career and two-career families. *Journal of Marriage and the Family* 38:453–459.

Campbell, Frederick L. 1970. Family growth and variation in family role structure. *Journal of Marriage and the Family* 32:45–53.

Carter, T.M. 1941. Comparison of the attitudes of college men with the attitudes of college women in regard to fellowship behavior. *Journal of Social Psychology* 14:145–158.

Cavan, R.S., and Cavan, J.T. 1929. Education and the business girl. *Journal of Educational Sociology* 3:83–93.

Caycedo, J.C. 1988. Employment status and life satisfaction of women in nine Western European countries. Ph.D. dissertation, Brigham Young University.

Chai, Alice Yun. 1983. Sexual division of labor in the contexts of nuclear family and cultural ideology among Korean student couples in Hawaii. *Journal of Social Relations* 10:153–174.

Christenson, Robert A. 1970. The effects of reward and expert power on the distribution of influence in Mormon couples. Ph.D. dissertation, Brigham Young University.

Christie, Leo Anthony. 1981. Antecedents and consequences of role sharing: A study of sex role preferences and marital interaction from a conflict theory perspective. Ph.D. dissertation, Florida State University.

Cohen, Theodore F. 1987. Remaking men: Men's experiences becoming and being husbands and fathers and their implications for reconceptualizing men's lives. *Journal of Family Issues* 8:57–77.

Coltrane, Scott. 1988. Father-child relationships and the status of women: A cross-cultural study. *American Journal of Sociology* 93:1060–1095.

Condran, John G., and Bode, Jerry G. 1982. Rashomon, working wives, and family division of labor: Middletown, 1980. *Journal of Marriage and the Family* 44:421–426.

Cooney, Rosemary Santana; Rogler, Lloyd H.; Rurrell, Rosemarie; and Ortiz, Vilma. 1982. Decision making in intergenerational Puerto Rican families. *Journal of Marriage and the Family* 44:621–631.

Corder, Judy, and Stephan, Cookie White. 1984. Females' combination of work and family roles: Adolescents' aspirations. *Journal of Marriage and the Family* 46:391–402.

Counihan, Carole M. 1988. Female identity, food, and power in contemporary Florence. *Anthropological Quarterly* 61:51–62.

Coverman, Shelley, and Sheley, Joseph F. 1986. Change in men's housework and child-care time, 1965–1975. *Journal of Marriage and the Family* 48:413–422.

Cowan, Carolyn Pape, and Cowan, Philip A. 1988. Who does what when partners become parents: Implications for men, women, and marriage. *Marriage and Family Review* 12:105–131.

Cromwell, Vicky L., and Cromwell, Ronald E. 1978. Perceived dominance in decision-making and conflict resolution among Anglo, black and Chicano couples. *Journal of Marriage and the Family* 40:749–759.

Cronkite, Ruth C. 1977. The determinants of spouses' normative preferences for family roles. *Journal of Marriage and the Family* 39:575–585.

Dahlstrom, Edmund, and Liljestrom, Rita. 1982. Gender and human reproduction. *Polish Sociological Bulletin* 1–4:199–215.

Daley, Nelda Knelson. 1986. Economic change, value shifts, and the definition of women's labor: A comparison of the coal counties of central Appalachia and the beef county of Ontario, Canada. *Western Sociological Review* 15:33–52.

Dambrot, Faye H.; Papp, Mary E.; and Whitmore, Cheryl. 1984. The sex-role attitudes of three generations of women. *Personality and Social Psychology Bulletin* 10:469–473.

Davis, Kingsley, and van den Oever, Pietronella. 1982. Demographic foundations of new sex roles. *Population and Development Review* 8:594–611.

Davis, R.J. 1931. Are women taking men's jobs? *Political Quarterly* 2:126–130.

Denmark, Florence L.; Shaw, Jeffrey S.; and Ciali, Samuel D. 1985. The relationship among sex roles, living arrangements, and the division of household responsibilities. *Sex Roles* 12:617–626.

Dietrich, Katheryn Thomas. 1975. A reexamination of the myth of black matriarchy. *Journal of Marriage and the Family* 37:367–374.

Duberman, Lucile, and Azumi, Koya. 1975. Sexism in Nepal. *Journal of Marriage and the Family* 37:1013–1021.

England, Paula; Kilbourne, Barbara Stanek; Farkas, George; and Dou, Thomas. 1988. Explaining occupational sex segregation and wages: Findings from a model with fixed effects. *American Sociological Review* 53:544–558.

Epstein, Gilda F., and Bronzaft, Arline L. 1972. Female freshmen view their roles as women. *Journal of Marriage and the Family* 34:671–672.

Ericksen, Julia A.; Yancey, William L.; and Ericksen, Eugene P. 1979. The division of family roles. *Journal of Marriage and the Family* 41:301–313.

Fernberger, S.W. 1948. Persistence of stereotypes concerning sex differences. *Journal of Abnormal and Social Psychology* 43:97–101.

Fine-Davis, Margret. 1979. Social-psychological predictors of employment status of married women in Ireland. *Journal of Marriage and the Family* 41:145–158.

Finley, Nancy J. 1989. Theories of family labor as applied to gender differences in caregiving for elderly parents. *Journal of Marriage and the Family* 51:79–86.

Fogarty, Michael P.; Rapoport, Rhona; and Rapoport, Robert N. 1971. *Sex, Career, and Family.* Beverly Hills: Sage.

Fox, Greer Litton. 1973. Another look at the comparative resources model: Assessing the balance of power in Turkish marriages. *Journal of Marriage and the Family* 35:718–730.

Geerken, Michael, and Gove, Walter R. 1983. *At Home and at Work: The Family's Allocation of Labor.* Beverly Hills: Sage.

Gerson, Kathleen. 1986. What do women want from men? *American Behavioral Scientist* 29:619–634.

Gianopulos, A., and Mitchell, H.E. 1957. Marital disagreement in working wife marriages as a function of husband's attitude toward wife's employment. *Marriage and Family Living* 19:373–378.

Giles-Sims, Jean, and Crosbie-Burnett, Margaret. 1989. Adolescent power in stepfather families: A test of normative-resource theory. *Journal of Marriage and the Family* 51:1065–1078.

Gillespie, Dair L. 1971. Who has the power? The marital struggle. *Journal of Marriage and the Family* 33:445–458.

Godwin, Deborah D., and Scanzoni, John. 1989. Couple consensus during marital joint decision-making: A context, process, outcome model. *Journal of Marriage and the Family* 51:943–956.

Goldscheider, Frances Kobrin, and Waite, Linda J. 1986. Sex differences in the entry into marriage. *American Journal of Sociology* 92:91–109.

Guttentag, Marcia, and Secord, Paul F. 1983. *Too Many Women: The Sex Ratio Question.* Beverly Hills: Sage.

Haas, Linda. 1981. Domestic role sharing in Sweden. *Journal of Marriage and the Family* 43:957–967.

Haavio-Mannila, E. 1967. Sex differentiation in role expectations and performance. *Journal of Marriage and the Family* 29:568–578.

Haddad, Tony, and Lam, Lawrence. 1988. Canadian families—men's involvement in family work. A case study of immigrant men in Toronto. *International Journal of Comparative Sociology* 28–29:269–281.

Harrell-Bond, B.E. 1969. Conjugal role behavior. *Human Relations* 22:77–91.

Hartley, R.E., and Klein, A. 1959. Sex-role concepts among elementary-school-age girls. *Marriage and Family Living* 21:59–64.

Hartman, Moshe, and Hartman, Harriet. 1983. Sex-role attitudes of Mormons vs. Non-Mormons in Utah. *Journal of Marriage and the Family* 45:897–902.

Hawkes, Glenn R.; Nicola, JoAnn; and Fish, Margaret. 1980. Young marrieds: Wives' employment and family role structure. In F. Pepitone-Rockwell (ed.), *Dual-Career Couples,* pp. 75–89.

Hawkes, Glenn R., and Taylor, Minna. 1975. Power structure in Mexican and Mexican-American farm labor families. *Journal of Marriage and the Family* 37:807–811.

Heath, D.B. 1958. Sexual division of labour and cross-cultural research. *Social Forces* 37:77–79.

Hill, Malcolm D. 1988. Class, kinship density, and conjugal role segregation. *Journal of Marriage and the Family* 50:731–741.

Hobart, C.W., and Klausner, W.J. 1959. Some social interactional correlates of marital role disagreement, and marital adjustment. *Marriage and Family Living* 21:256–263.

Hochschild, Arlie Russell. 1973. A review of sex role research. *American Journal of Sociology* 78:1011–1029.

Hollos, Marida, and Leis, Philip E. 1985. "The hand that rocks the cradle rules the world": Family interaction and decision making in a Portuguese rural community. *Ethos* 13:340–357.

Holmstrom, Engin Inel. 1973. Changing sex roles in a developing country. *Journal of Marriage and the Family* 35:546–553.

Holmstrom, Lynda Lytle. 1972. *The Two-Career Family.* Cambridge, Mass.: Schenckman Publishing.

Horwitz, Allan V. 1982. Sex-role expectations, power, and psychological distress. *Sex Roles* 8:607–623.

Hurvitz, N. 1961. The components of marital roles. *Sociology and Social Research* 45:301–309.

Ichilov, Orit, and Rubineck, Bracha. 1977. The relationship between girls' attitudes concerning the family and their perception of the patterns existing in the family of origin. *Journal of Marriage and the Family* 39:417–422.

Jackson, Dixie Porter. 1981. The determinants of household time allocations for husbands and wives. Ph.D. dissertation, Cornell University.

Jacobson, A.H. 1952. Conflict of attitudes toward the roles of the husband and wife in marriage. *American Sociological Review* 17:146–150.

Johnson, M.M. 1963. Sex role learning in the nuclear family. *Child Development* 34:319–333.

Joseph, J. 1961. A research note on attitudes to work and marriage of six hundred adolescent girls. *British Journal of Sociology* 12:176–183.

Junusbajev, Mutan Dzunusbaevich. 1985. Household division in the Kazakh family [according to a survey in the Chemkent Region]; Raspredelenie domashnego truda v kazakhskoy sem'e (po materiyalam doprosa v Chemkentskoy oblasti). *Sotsiologicheskie Issledovaniya* 12:106–109.

Kammeyer, K. 1964. The feminine role: An analysis of attitude consistency. *Journal of Marriage and the Family* 26:295–305.

———. 1966. Birth order and the feminine sex role among college women. *American Sociological Review* 31:508–515.

———. 1967. Sibling position and the feminine role. *Journal of Marriage and the Family* 29:494–499.

Kamo, Yoshinori. 1988. Determinants of household division of labor. *Journal of Family Issues* 9:177–200.

Kando, Thomas M. 1972. Role strain: A comparison of males, females, and transsexuals. *Journal of Marriage and the Family* 34:459–464.

Kaufman, Debra Renee. 1985. Women who return to orthodox Judaism: A feminist analysis. *Journal of Marriage and the Family* 47:543–551.

Kenkel, W.F., and Hoffman, D.K. 1956. Real and conceived roles in family decision making. *Marriage and Family Living* 18:311–316.

Kiecolt, K. Jill, and Acock, Alan C. 1988. The long-term effects of family structure on gender-role attitudes. *Journal of Marriage and the Family* 50:709–717.

Kingsbury, Nancy M., and Scanzoni, John. 1989. Process power and decision outcomes among dual-career couples. *Journal of Comparative Family Studies* 20:231–246.

Kirkpatrick, Clifford. 1936. A comparison of generations in regard to attitudes toward feminism. *Journal of Genetic Psychology* 49:343–361.

Knudsen, D.D. 1969. The declining status of women: Popular myths and the failure of functionalist thought. *Social Forces* 48:183–193.

Komarovsky, M. 1946. Cultural contradictions and sex roles. *American Journal of Sociology* 52:184–189.

———. 1950. Functional analysis of sex roles. *American Sociological Review* 15:508–517.

Koopman-Boyden, Peggy G., and Abbott, Max. 1985. Expectations for household task allocation and actual task allocation: A New Zealand study. *Journal of Marriage and the Family* 47:211–219.

Kosa, J., and Koker, Jr., R.E. 1965. The female physician in public health conflict and reconciliation of the sex and professional roles. *Sociology and Social Research* 49:294–305.

Kotlar, S.L. 1965. Middle-class marital role perceptions and marital adjustment. *Sociology and Social Research* 49:283–293.

Krausz, Susan Lavinsky. 1986. Sex roles within marriage. *Social Work* 31:457–464.

Lapidus, Gail Warshofsky. 1988. The interaction of women's work and family roles in the U.S.S.R. *Women and Work* 3:87–121.

Larson, Lyle E. 1974. System and subsystem perception of family roles. *Journal of Marriage and the Family* 36:123–138.

Lewis, Helen Matthews. 1970. Occupational roles and family roles: A study of coal mining families in the southern Appalachians. Ph.D. dissertation, University of Kentucky.

Li, Jason T., and Caldwell, Robert A. 1987. Magnitude and directional effects of marital sex-role incongruence on marital adjustment. *Journal of Family Issues* 8:97–110.

Linder, Joan Hammes. 1983. Work-family linkages: Career commitment, performance of and preferences for the performance of family activities among dual-professional couples. Ed.D. dissertation, University of Cincinnati.

Linn, James Gary. 1983. Task performance and decision-making as related to marital satisfaction in Wisconsin farm families. Ph.D. dissertation, University of Wisconsin.

Little, Bernadette Gray. 1982. Marital quality and power processes among black couples. *Journal of Marriage and the Family* 44:633–646.

Long, Susan Orpett. 1987. *Family Change and the Life Course in Japan.* Ithaca, N.Y.: China-Japan Program, Cornell University.

Lopata, Helena Z. 1971. *Occupation: Housewife.* London: Oxford University Press.

———. 1980. Spouses' contributions to each other's roles. In F. Pepitone-Rockwell (ed.), *Dual-Career Couples,* pp. 111–141. Beverly Hills: Sage.

Losh-Hesselbart, S. 1987. Development of gender roles. In M.B. Sussman and S.K. Steinmetz (eds.), *Handbook of Marriage and the Family,* pp. 535–563.

Lu, Y.C. 1952. Marital roles and marital adjustment. *Sociology and Social Research* 36:364–368.

Lueptow, Lloyd B. 1980. Social structure, social change and parental influence in adolescent sex-role socialization: 1964–1975. *Journal of Marriage and the Family* 42:93–103.

Lueptow, Lloyd B.; Guss, Margaret B.; and Hyden, Colleen. 1989. Sex role ideology, marital status, and happiness. *Journal of Family Issues* 10:383–400.

Lupri, Eugen, and Symons, Gladys. 1982. The emerging symmetrical family: Fact or fiction? *International Journal of Comparative Sociology* 23:166–189.

Lynn, D.B. 1963. Learning masculine and feminine roles. *Marriage and Family Living* 25:103–105.

McBroom, William H. 1984. Changes in sex-role orientations: A five-year longitudinal comparison. *Sex Roles* 11:583–592.

MacCorquodale, Patricia L. 1984. Gender roles and premarital contraception. *Journal of Marriage and the Family* 46:57–63.

McCurdy, Paula Carol Kresser. 1978. Sex role, decision making practices, marital satisfaction and family problems with economically disadvantaged Anglo, black, and Chicano couples. Ph.D. dissertation, University of Missouri.

McKee, J.P., and Sherriffs, A.C. 1959. Men's beliefs, ideals, and self-concepts. *American Journal of Sociology* 64:356–363.

Maines, David R., and Hardesty, Monica J. 1987. Temporality and gender: Young adults' career and family plans. *Social Forces* 66:102–120.

Maret, Elizabeth, and Finlay, Barbara. 1984. The distribution of household labor among women in dual-earner families. *Journal of Marriage and the Family* 46:357–364.

Mason, Karen Oppenheim, and Bumpass, Larry L. 1975. U.S. women's sex-role ideology, 1970. *American Journal of Sociology* 80:1212–1219.

Meier, Harold C. 1972. Mother-centeredness and college youths' attitudes toward social equality for women: Some empirical findings. *Journal of Marriage and the Family* 34:115–121.

Miller, Joanne, and Garrison Howard H. 1982. Sex roles: The division of labor at home and in the workplace. *Annual Review of Sociology* 8:237–262.

Mirowsky, John. 1985. Depression and marital power: An equity model. *American Journal of Sociology* 91:557–592.

Mirowsky, John, and Ross, Catherine E. 1987. Belief in innate sex roles: Sex stratification versus interpersonal influence in marriage. *Journal of Marriage and the Family* 49:527–540.

Moen, Phyllis, and Dempster-McClain, Donna I. 1987. Employed parents: Role strain, work time, and preferences for working less. *Journal of Marriage and the Family* 49:579–590.

Morgan, Carolyn Stout, and Walker, Alexis J. 1983. Predicting sex role attitudes. *Social Psychology Quarterly* 46:148–151.

Morgan, Mary Y. 1987. The impact of religion on gender-role attitudes. *Psychology of Women Quarterly* 11:301–310.

Motz, A.B. 1961. The roles of the married woman in science. *Marriage and Family Living* 23:374–376.

Mowrer, E.R. 1969. The differentiation of husband and wife roles. *Journal of Marriage and the Family* 31:534–540.

Mueller, Charles W. 1979. The effect of marital-dyad status inconsistency on women's support for equal rights. *Journal of Marriage and the Family* 41:779–791.

National Center for Health Statistics. 1986. Advance report of final divorce statistics, 1984. Monthly Vital Statistics Report Vol. 35, No. 6, Supplement, DHHS Pub. (PHS 86-112). Public Health Service, Hyattsville, Md., September 25.

Nicola, Jo-Ann Scull. 1980. Career and family roles of dual-career couples: Women in academia and their husbands. Ph.D. dissertation, University of California.

Nye, F. Ivan. 1976. *Role Structure and Analysis of the Family.* Beverly Hills: Sage.

Oliveri, Mary Ellen, and Reiss, David. 1987. Social networks of family members: Distinctive roles of mothers and fathers. *Sex Roles* 17:719–736.

O'Neill, W. 1967. Marital stability in America, past, present, and future. In G. Levinger and O.C. Moles (eds.), *Divorce in the Progressive Era.* New Haven: Yale University Press.

Osako, Masako Murakami. 1978. Dilemmas of Japanese professional women. *Special Problems* 26:15–25.

Osmond, Marie Withers, and Martin, Patricia Yancey. 1975. Sex and sexism: A comparison of male and female sex-role attitudes. *Journal of Marriage and the Family* 37–744–758.

Ort, R.S. 1950. A study of role-conflicts as related to happiness in marriage. *Journal of Abnormal and Social Psychology* 45:691–699.

Papanek, M.L. 1969. Authority and sex roles in family. *Journal of Marriage and the Family* 31:88–96.

Parelius, Ann P. 1975. Emerging sex-role attitudes, expectations, and strains among college women. *Journal of Marriage and the Family* 37:146–153.

Parker, S., and Kleiner, R.J. 1969. Social and psychological dimensions of the family role performance of the Negro male. *Journal of Marriage and the Family* 31:500–506.

Parsons, T., and Bales, R.F. 1955. *Family, Socialization, and Interaction Process.* Glencoe, Ill.: Free Press.

Patrick, C. 1946. Relation between government and the status of women. *Journal of Social Psychology* 23:163–174.

Patterson, Joan M., and McCubbin, Hamilton, I. 1984. Gender roles and coping. *Journal of Marriage and the Family* 46:95–104.

Peterson, E. 1964. The status of women in the United States. *International Labour Review* 89:447–460.

Pfeil, E. 1968. Role expectations when entering into marriage. *Journal of Marriage and the Family* 30:161–165.

Pleck, Joseph H. 1979. Men's family work: Three perspectives and some new data. *Family Coordinator* 28:481–488.

———. 1985. *Working Wives/Working Husbands.* Beverly Hills: Sage.

Plutzer, Eric. 1988. Worklife, family life, and women's support of feminism. *American Sociological Review* 53:640–649.

Poloma, Margaret Mary. 1970. The married professional women: An empirical examination of three myths. Ph.D. dissertation, Case Western Reserve University.

Popenoe, P. 1933. Can the family have two heads? *Sociology and Social Research* 18:12–17.

Powell, Brian, and Steelman, Lala Carr. 1982. Testing an undertested comparison: Maternal effects on sons' and daughters' attitudes toward women in the labor force. *Journal of Marriage and the Family* 44:349–355.

Quarm, Dasy. 1983. The effect of gender on sex-role attitudes. *Sociological Focus* 16:285–303.

Ramu, G.N. 1987. Indian husbands: Their role perceptions and performance in single- and dual-earner families. *Journal of Marriage and the Family* 49:903–915.

Rank, Mark R. 1982. Determinants of conjugal influence in wives' employment decision making. *Journal of Marriage and the Family* 44:591–564.

Raschke, H.J. 1987. Divorce. In Marvin B. Sussman and Suzanne K. Steinmetz (eds.), *Handbook of Marriage and the Family,* pp. 597–624. New York: Plenum Press.

Rexroat, Cynthia, and Shehan, Constance. 1987. The family life cycle and spouses' time in housework *Journal of Marriage and the Family* 49:737–750.

Rice, Rachel Winslow. 1973. Sex role definition—Attitudes toward marriage and careers of teacher trainees as compared to married couples. Ph.D. dissertation, Indiana University.

Richmond, Marie LaLiberte. 1976. Beyond resource theory: Another look at factors enabling women to affect family interaction. *Journal of Marriage and the Family* 38:257–266.

Roos, P.A. 1985. *Gender and Work: A Comparative Analysis of Industrial Societies.* New York: State University of New York Press.

Roper, Brent S., and Labeff, Emily. 1977. Sex roles and feminism revisited: An intergenerational attitude comparison. *Journal of Marriage and the Family* 39:113–119.

Rose, A.M. 1951. The adequacy of women's expectations for adult roles. *Social Forces* 30:69–77.

Rosen, Bernard C., and Aneshensel, Carol S. 1976. The Chemelson Syndrome: A social psychological dimension of the female sex role. *Journal of Marriage and the Family* 38:605–617.

Rosenthal, Carolyn J. 1985. Kinkeeping in the familial division of labor. *Journal of Marriage and the Family* 47:965–974.

Ross, Catherine E. 1987. The division of labor at home. *Social Forces* 65:816–833.

Russell, Joyce E.A., and Rush, Michael C. 1987. The effects of sex and marital/parental status on performance evaluations and attributions. *Sex Roles* 17:221–236.

Safilios-Rothschild, Constantina. 1970. The influence of the wife's degree of work commitment upon some aspects of family organization and dynamics. *Journal of Marriage and the Family* 32:681–691.

Scanzoni, John. 1975. Sex roles, economic factors, and marital solidarity in black and white marriages. *Journal of Marriage and the Family* 37:130–144.

———. 1976a. Sex role change and influences on birth intentions. *Journal of Marriage and the Family* 38:43–58.

———. 1979b. Gender roles and the process of fertility control. *Journal of Marriage and the Family* 38:677-691.

———. 1979. Sex-role influences on married women's status attainments. *Journal of Marriage and the Family* 41:793-800.

Schlesinger, Yaffa. 1977. Sex roles and social change in the kibbutz. *Journal of Marriage and the Family* 39:771–779.

Schmitt, D.R. 1965. An attitudinal correlate of the status congruency of married women. *Social Forces* 44:190–195.

Seccombe, Karen. 1986. The effects of occupational conditions upon the division of household labor: An application of Kohn's theory. *Journal of Marriage and the Family* 48:839–848.

Sethi, Raj Mohini. 1989. Status and power of working women within the family: A test of Marxian perspective. *Journal of Sociological Studies* 8:97–108.

Seward, G.H. 1945. Cultural conflict and the feminine role: An experimental study to investigate women's attitudes toward their role in the postwar period. *Journal of Social Psychology* 22:177–194.

Sexton, Christine S., and Perlman, Daniel S. 1989. Couples' career orientation, gender role orientation, and perceived equity as determinants of marital power. *Journal of Marriage and the Family* 51:933–941.

Shamir, Boas. 1986. Unemployment and household division of labor. *Journal of Marriage and the Family* 48:195–206.

Shea, Gail Anne. 1983. Voluntary childlessness and the women's liberation movement. *Population and Environment* 6:17–26.

Shelton, Beth Anne, and Firestone, Juanita. 1988. An examination of household labor time as a factor in composition and treatment effects on the male-female wage gap. *Sociological Focus* 21:265–278.

Shukla, Archana. 1987. Decision making in single- and dual-career families in India. *Journal of Marriage and the Family* 49:621–629.

Simpson, Ida Harper; Wilson, John; and Young, Kristina. 1988. The sexual division of farm household labor: A replication and extension. *Rural Sociology* 53:145–165.

Siperstein, Judith Wendy. 1978. An assessment of communications and role perceptions of career and non-career wives with their husband. Ph.D. dissertation, State University of New Jersey.

Smith, M. Dwayne, and Self, George D. 1980. The congruence between mothers' and daughters' sex-role attitudes: A research note. *Journal of Marriage and the Family* 42:105–109.

South, Scott J. 1988. Sex ratios, economic power, and women's roles: A theoretical extension and empirical test. *Journal of Marriage and the Family* 50:19–31.

South, Scott J., and Trent, Katherine. 1988. Sex ratios and women's roles: A cross-national analysis. *American Journal of Sociology* 93:1096–1115.

Spitze, Glenna D. 1978. Role experiences of young women: A longitudinal test of the role hiatus hypothesis. *Journal of Marriage and the Family* 40:471–479.

Stafford, Rebecca; Backman, Elaine; and Dibona, Pamela. 1976. The division of labor among cohabiting and married couples. *Journal of Marriage and the Family* 39:43–57.

Stamp, Peggy. 1985. Research note: Balance of financial power in marriage: An exploratory study of breadwinning wives. *Sociological Review* 33:546–557.

Stephan, Cookie White, and Corder, Judy. 1985. The effects of dual-career families on adolescents' sex-role attitudes, work and family plans, and choices of important others. *Journal of Marriage and the Family* 47:921-929.

Stephens, W.N. 1963. *The Family in Cross Cultural Perspective.* New York: Holt, Rinehart, & Winston.

Stevens, Gillian. 1986. Sex-differentiated patterns of intergenerational occupational mobility. *Journal of Marriage and the Family* 48:153–163.

Strodtbeck, F.L., and Creelan, P.G. 1968. The interaction linkage between family size, intelligence, and sex-role identity. *Journal of Marriage and the Family* 30:301-307.

Szinovacz, Maximiliane E. 1977. Role allocation, family structure and female employment. *Journal of Marriage and the Family* 39:781–791.

———. 1978. Another look at normative resource theory: Contributions from Austrian data—a research note. *Journal of Marriage and the Family* 40:413–421.

Tallichet, Suzanne E., and Willits, Fern K. 1986. Gender-role attitude change of young women: Influential factors from a panel study. *Social Psychology Quarterly* 49:219–227.

Tashakkori, Abbas, and Thompson, Vaida D. 1989. Sex and SES differences in reports of parental involvement in different interaction areas with Iranian adolescents. *Journal of Comparative Family Studies* 20:197–213.

Tavecchio, Louis W.; van Ijzenoorn, Marinus H.; Goossens, Frits A.; and Vergeer, Marie M. 1984. The division of labor in Dutch families with preschool children. *Journal of Marriage and the Family* 46:231-242.

Terry, Deborah J., and Scott, William A. 1987. Gender differences in correlates of marital satisfaction. *Australian Journal of Psychology* 39:207–221.

Tharp, R.G.; Meadow, A.; Lennhoff, S.G.; and Satterfield, D. 1968. Changes in marriage roles accompanying the acculturation the Mexican-American wife. *Journal of Marriage and the Family* 30:404–412.

Thompson, Linda, and Walker, Alexis J. 1989. Gender in families: Women and men in marriage, work, and parenthood. *Journal of Marriage and the Family* 51:845–871.

Thornton, Arland. 1989. Changing attitudes toward family issues in the United States. *Journal of Marriage and the Family* 51:873–893.

Thrall, Charles A. 1978. Who does what: Role stereotypy, children's work, and continuity between generations in the household division of labor. *Human Relations* 31:249–265.

Tomeh, Aida K. 1978. Sex-role orientation: An analysis of structural and attitudinal predictors. *Journal of Marriage and the Family* 40:341–354.

———. 1984. Parents, friends, and familial sex role attitudes. *Sociological Inquiry* 54:72–88.

Tomeh, Aida K., and Gallant, Clifford J. 1983. The structure of sex-role attitudes in a French student population: A factorial analysis. *Journal of Marriage and the Family* 45:975–983.

Touba, Jacquiline Rudolph. 1975. Sex role differentiation in Iranian families living in urban and rural areas of a region undergoing planned industrialization in Iran (Arak Shahrestan). *Journal of Marriage and the Family* 37:437–445.

Turner, R.H. 1964. Some aspects of women's ambition. *American Journal of Sociology* 70 (3):271–285.

United Nations. 1973. *Demographic Yearbook*. New York: United Nations, Department of Economic and Social Affairs.

Vanfossen, Beth Ensminger. 1977. Sexual stratification and sex-role socialization. *Journal of Marriage and the Family* 39:563–574.

Voydanoff, Patricia, and Donnelly, Brenda W. 1989. Work and family roles and psychological distress. *Journal of Marriage and the Family* 51:923–932.

Wallin, P. 1950. Cultural contradictions and sex roles: A repeat study. *American Sociological Review* 15:288–293.

Weinraub, Marsha; Clemens, Lynda Pritchard; Sockloff, Alan; Ethridge, Teresa; Gracely, Edward; and Myers, Barbara. 1984. The development of sex role stereotypes in the third year: Relationships to gender labelling, gender identity, sex-typed toy preference, and family characteristics. *Child Development* 55:1493–1505.

Weeks, M. O'Neal, and Botkin, Darla R. 1987. A longitudinal study of the marriage role expectations of college women: 1961–1984. *Sex Roles* 17:49–58.

Weiss, R.S., and Samelson, N.M. 1958. Social roles of American women: Their contribution to a sense of usefulness and importance. *Marriage and Family Living* 20:358–366.

Wicks, Jerry W., and Workman, Randy L. 1978. Sex-role attitudes and the anticipated timing of the initial stages of family formation among Catholic university students. *Journal of Marriage and the Family* 40:505–516.

Williams, Linda B. 1989. Postnuptial migration and the status of women in Indonesia. *Journal of Marriage and the Family* 51:895–903.

Winslow, M.N. 1923. Married women in industry. *Journal of Social Hygiene* 9:385–395.

Wise, G.M., and Carter, D.C. 1965. A definition of the role of homemaker by two generations of women. *Journal of Marriage and the Family* 27:531–532.

Yao, Esther Lee. 1987. Variables for household division of labour as revealed by Chinese women in Taiwan. *International Journal of Sociology of the Family* 17:67–86.

Yogev, Sara. 1981. Do professional women have egalitarian marital relationships. *Journal of Marriage and the Family* 43:865–871.

Yogev, Sara, and Brett, Jeanne. 1985. Perceptions of the division of housework and child care and marital satisfaction. *Journal of Marriage and the Family* 47:609–618.

Index

About the Contributors

Dean M. Busby is currently an assistant professor in the marriage and family therapy program of the Department of Child and Family Studies at Syracuse University. He received his Ph.D. in marriage and family therapy from Brigham Young University. Research interests include the prevalence and consequences of premarital violence, the effectiveness of marital and family therapy, and the reliability and validity of the Preparation for Marriage Instrument.

Julio C. Caycedo is an assistant professor of sociology at the University of Guam. He received his Ph.D. from Brigham Young University and previously was a Romance languages librarian at Brigham Young University. His research interests include family, gender roles, deviance, criminology, race and ethnic relations, information sciences, and Romance languages.

Cynthia R. Christopherson recently completed her M.S. degree and is a doctoral student in family and human development at Utah State University. She has taught courses in marriage and the family, developed curriculum in sex education, and worked on adolescent pregnancy prevention. Her interests include adolescent sexual behavior, sex education, parent-child relations, and adolescent pregnancy.

Patricia H. Dyk is an assistant professor in the Department of Sociology at the University of Kentucky. She received her Ph.D. in family and human development from Utah State University. Her research interests include adolescent development in the family context, adolescent sexuality, gender-role development, and work and family issues.

James M. Harper is a professor of marriage and family therapy in the Department of Family Sciences at Brigham Young University. He received his Ph.D. in counseling psychology from the University of Minnesota. Research and teaching interests include family systems, family-communication interaction, and observational research of family processes.

Steven R. Hawks received his doctor of education degree from the Department of Health Sciences at Brigham Young University. He is currently an assistant professor of health education at North Carolina State University. He taught previously at East Carolina University. His research interests include stress management, the role of the family in the prevention of alcohol and drug abuse, and emergency health care.

I-Chiao Huang is currently a doctoral candidate in sociology at Brigham Young University. She has previously worked for the Church of Jesus Christ of Latter-Day Saints on studies of family violence, the impact of religion on the family, and adolescent socialization. Recently she published a chapter on remarriage among the elderly, and her forthcoming Ph.D. dissertation is a study of remarriage.

Craig L. Israelsen is currently an assistant professor in the Department of Consumer and Family Economics at the University of Missouri at Columbia. He received his Ph.D. in family resource management from Brigham Young University. Research interests include the impact of debt upon family relationships, financial planning in low-to-middle income households, and children's involvement in family financial management.

Kip W. Jenkins is currently the director of the Institute of Religion of the Church of Jesus Christ of Latter-Day Saints, which is adjacent to the University of Idaho in Moscow, Idaho. He received his Ph.D. from Brigham Young University. He was previously the institute director of the Institute of Religion adjacent to Westminster College in Salt Lake City. His research interests include religious socialization in the family, communication within the family, and family culture.

Brent C. Miller is a professor in the Department of Family and Human Development at Utah State University. He received his Ph.D. from the University of Minnesota and has previously taught at the University of Tennessee. His research has focused on adolescent sexual behavior and pregnancy, especially as these relate to family contexts and processes.

Ann B. Parkinson is completing her M.S. degree at Utah State University in family and human development. She has interned for the Utah Extension Service and worked as a consultant for Headstart. Her major research and teaching interests are primary prevention and educating low-income families.

Gary L. Steggell received his Ph.D. in marriage and family therapy from Brigham Young University. He is currently a clinician in Colton, California and is an adjunct faculty member at California State University at San Bernardino. Current research and teaching interests include family interaction, human sexuality, and counseling skills.

Gabe Wang is a Ph.D. student in the sociology department at Brigham Young University. He graduated from Yunnan University in China majoring in English and literature; after graduation he taught English there for several years. He received undergraduate training in sociology at Whitman College and earned his M.S. in Sociology at Brigham Young University. His major research interests include population, organizational behavior, and social and economic development.

Jie Zhang is a Ph.D. candidate in sociology at Brigham Young University. He received his M.A. degree in linguistics from Brigham Young University and his B.A. degree in English and literature from Shandong University in China. His teaching and research interests include social psychology, criminology, ethnic relations, and cultural differences.

About the Editor

Stephen J. Bahr received his Ph.D. in sociology from Washington State University. He is a professor in the department of sociology and in the Center for Studies of the Family at Brigham Young University. Previously he worked at the University of Texas at Austin and the University of North Carolina at Chapel Hill. Current research and teaching interests include adolescent drug use, family policy, and criminology.